Caribbean Popular Music

Caribbean Popular Music

*An Encyclopedia of Reggae, Mento, Ska,
Rock Steady, and Dancehall*

DAVID V. MOSKOWITZ

GREENWOOD PRESS
Westport, Connecticut · London

Library of Congress Cataloging-in-Publication Data

Moskowitz, David Vlado.
  Caribbean popular music: an encyclopedia of reggae, mento, ska, rock steady, and dancehall / David V. Moskowitz.
    p. cm.
  Includes bibliographical references and index.
  ISBN 0-313-33158-8 (alk. paper)
  1. Popular music—Caribbean Area—Encyclopedias.   I. Title.
ML102.P66M67 2006
781.64'09729'03—dc22   2005018629

British Library Cataloguing in Publication Data is available.

This book is included in the *African American Experience* database from Greenwood Electronic Media. For more information, visit: www.africanamericanexperience.com.

Library of Congress Catalog Card Number: 2005018629
ISBN: 0-313-33158-8

First published in 2006

Greenwood Press, 88 Post Road West, Westport, CT 06881
An imprint of Greenwood Publishing Group, Inc.
www.greenwood.com

Printed in the United States of America

The paper used in this book complies with the Permanent Paper Standard issued by the National Information Standards Organization (Z39.48-1984).

10 9 8 7 6 5 4 3 2 1

Contents

Acknowledgments

Although this book appears under a single name, there is a wide variety of people who helped made it possible. Most specifically, thanks go to my wife, Jennifer, without whose help I could not have undertaken or completed this project. Further appreciation goes to our children, Heather, Lucas, and Katie, for their patience with me as I worked through research and writing. Special thanks also go to Althea, Arthur, and Danielle Moskowitz for all of their support throughout the process. Walter Clark, professor of musicology at the University of California–Riverside, also deserves praise because without his encouragement I would not have followed my heart into the type of research that I find most interesting.

Several others helped me collect research for the writing of the encyclopedia. Peter Carlson, Andrew Converse, Bryce Mayrose, Teresa Gonzalez, and the Student Musicians Council were instrumental in helping to accumulate background information and early research. Further, I thank the Carey's crew for all of their kind support along the way.

I would also like to thank UrbanImage for providing the wonderful images contained herein. The period photography provided by Adrian Boot, Rico D'Rozario, Jean Bernard Sohiez, David Katz, Wayne Tippetts, Tim Barrow, Ron Vester, Trax on Wax / Ossie Hamilton, and Brian Jahn goes far in helping to bring the history of Jamaican popular music alive. One Love.

Preface

This encyclopedia is in standard A-to-Z format. However, there are a few specific features of which the user should be aware. The Jamaican popular music scene has been rather insular, and as such, there is a degree of overlap among related entries. To better serve the reader, the first time a word that is defined elsewhere in the book is used, it appears in boldfaced type. These concordances are meant to allow the reader the easiest use of the volume. There are several different types of entries contained in this encyclopedia. The most common are entries concerning an individual singer, songwriter, producer, engineer, studio owner, or label executive. In addition, there are larger entries that tie these individuals together. These larger entries discuss musical styles, bands, labels, studios, and organizations.

Another feature of use to the reader is the indexing. The front of the book contains a list of entries, and the index at the end of the encyclopedia provides a ready guide for locating subjects. The index also includes items that do not have their own headings in the A-to-Z list. Thus, the index is a valuable tool for identifying points of correspondence between individual essays and peripheral items. For the most complete coverage of any person or concept contained herein, it is recommended that one follow all of the highlighted points of correspondence from one essay to the next.

One aspect that can be difficult to navigate is the language. The official language of Jamaica is English; however, the actual spoken language is a patois that combines English with idiomatic African phrases and a wide variety of slang. Thus, spelling can be difficult with such words in song and album titles. This book uses phonetic spelling for consistency. Every effort was made to use the most popular spelling of artists' names and nicknames and to then maintain consistency once a specific spelling was chosen.

The significance of Jamaican popular music to the Caribbean, the United States, the UK, and, by extension, the rest of the world is manifold. While early Jamaican popular music was affected by popular music in the United States, the Caribbean, and the UK, once it manifested and matured it, in turn, had direct influence on these countries. An example is a recent global resurgence in the rock steady style. The Jamaican popular styles of ska, rock steady, reggae, and dancehall have each had tremendous impact on the western popular music scene. For the past thirty years there have been revivals of these styles in several prominent music centers throughout the United States and the UK. Further, the most globally recognized and copied type of Caribbean popular music is reggae. In the new millennium, each of these styles continues to be explored on the contemporary global music landscape.

Introduction

The Jamaican popular music scene is rich with a long and storied history. However, because much of the island's history was maintained orally, it is often difficult to ascertain details of many of its principal figures' early lives. One helpful aspect of the island's music history, for example, is that one cannot discuss the history of Jamaican popular music without quickly encountering the producer and label owner Clement "Coxsone" Dodd. Dodd is one of the lynchpins who helped to codify the island's music from the mid-1950s to the turn of the century. This volume points out other key figures who have shaped and are a part of the Jamaican popular music scene.

Popular music did not find prominence in Jamaica until the 1950s for a variety of reasons—principal among them, there was no recording studio on the island until that time. This was remedied by Ken Khouri when he opened the Federal Records studios in Kingston in 1954. Once Khouri succeeded at recording mento and calypso singles, other Jamaicans clambered onto the scene. By the mid-1960s, Khouri was vying with several other Jamaican producers, such as Clement "Coxsone" Dodd, Leslie Kong, Sonia Pottinger, Lee "Scratch" Perry, Bunny "Striker" Lee, and several others. It was during the 1960s that the Jamaican popular music scene exploded, first on the island and then around the world.

It is a common misconception that Jamaica's only type of popular music is reggae. The fact is that there has been a long line of other types that illustrate some of the origins of reggae. In the first half of the twentieth century, Jamaican musicians were interested in the American popular styles that they heard coming over the radio waves from the Mississippi delta. This meant that they were part of the jazz explosion that took place in the United States in the 1920s and 1930s. Jamaican dance bands heard and reproduced these sounds to entertain audiences in Kingston clubs and along the north shore of the island. Alongside this American musical influence was indigenous Jamaican music that ran the gamut from the traditional mento to the more popular calypso. During the 1940s and 1950s, the Jamaican popular music scene was filled with the sounds of American jazz music played with a Caribbean flavor. Additionally, American rhythm and blues was making an increasing impact on the island. The music coming out of the southeastern American cities, especially New Orleans, influenced Jamaican popular music and drove the style forward. Artists such as Fats Domino with his triplet-rhythm approach to keyboard playing, the jump band style of Louis Jordan, and the pioneering production spirit of Alan Toussaint factored heavily into Jamaican popular style. By the mid-1950s, many Jamaican bands were making a living covering American rhythm and blues standards. Further, this American style directly influenced the formation of the earliest Jamaican popular style, ska. Ska became the most important music in Jamaica in 1961–1962. It replaced the island tendency to remake American rhythm and blues standards and injected Jamaican music with its own spirit. The birth of the ska movement coincided directly with the island's 1962 independence and was fostered by an intense interest in asserting Jamaican national identity and pride.

The general ska band lineup was a core of singer, guitar, bass, and drums, with the addition of a horn line of varying size. At barest minimum, the horn line included a saxophone, trumpet, and trombone, much like the jump bands. The style itself was a mixture of influences including Jamaican mento, American rhythm and blues, jazz, jump bands, calypso, and others. It took over the island and invaded radio, dancehalls, and clubs. The ska beat was fast, appropriate for dancing, and emphasized offbeat accents that propelled the music forward. The style held sway on the island for the next five years before succumbing in 1966–1967 to the slower rock steady beat.

Important ska performers included Desmond Dekker, the Ethiopians, Jackie Mittoo, the Skatalites, Roland Alphonso, Alton Ellis, Tommy McCook, Rico Rodriguez, Byron Lee, Derrick Morgan, and others. Although ska was no longer the dominant popular style on the island, it remained active in the background, always ripe for revival. This trend in popular music happened in American jazz and was also the case in Jamaican popular music. In the late 1970s and early 1980s, ska returned to prominence in the United Kingdom with the two-tone movement, also called the second wave of ska. More recently, ska revived again with the third wave in the late 1980s and early 1990s. This most recent revival mostly took place in the United States and involved bands such as No Doubt and the Mighty Mighty Bosstones.

In 1966, rock steady replaced ska. It was a sub-style of Jamaican popular music. The beat of rock steady music was roughly half the speed of the standard ska beat, and the texture of the instrumentation was much less dense. Also, in rock steady the reggae accent patterns started to emerge. The guitar was played on the second and fourth beats of the four-beat measure, while the bass guitar emphasized the first and third beats. The role of the drums was absorbed by the percussive playing of the guitar and bass, so the drummer's role was diminished. Additionally, the use of the keyboard player in rock steady largely replaced the ska horn section.

Many rock steady groups emphasized the lyrics over the instruments, and they delivered the lyrical content in tight vocal harmonies reminiscent of American rhythm and blues. The lyrics discussed issues of cultural awareness and social uplift. Many of the reggae groups that came to prominence in the early 1970s got their starts in the rock steady era; among them was Bob Marley and the Wailers. Examples of rock steady groups and singers included Desmond Dekker, the Ethiopians, the Heptones, Jackie Mittoo, Alton Ellis, Dave and Ansel Collins, the Gladiators, the Melodians, the Paragons, and others. As was the case with ska, when the rock steady era ended in the late 1960s, many artists continued to work in the style, and it remained popular.

Next, the era of the most popular style of Jamaican music dawned: reggae. The term *reggae* came into common use in the late 1960s. The style developed from a combination of island and international influences. Reggae surfaced in 1968 and adapted elements of ska and rock steady and mixed them with American rhythm and blues and African drumming. Traditional reggae often employed the horns of the ska style, the slowed-down beat of rock steady, the shuffle beat of New Orleans rhythm and blues, and African burru drum rhythms filled with syncopation. The guitar was played on the second and fourth beats of the four-beat measure while the bass guitar emphasized the first and third beats. The drum rhythm in the reggae style did take on a very specific character called the one-drop rhythm (with only the third beat of a four-beat measure accented).

The term *reggae* went on to encompass a wide variety of styles. It became an umbrella term describing the music that preceded it and the styles that came after, such as dancehall and ragga. This overarching use was mirrored in the American use of the term *rock and roll* to mean a great variety of styles that fit under one general umbrella. As a result, a great many artists described themselves as reggae musicians when they actually had widely divergent styles. The most internationally renowned style of reggae is the roots variety that was popularized by Bob Marley and the Wailers in the 1970s.

The roots variety of reggae used a rock band lineup and lyrics that focused on issues related to Rastafari, the Marcus Garvey-inspired belief that Ethiopian King Haile Selassie (Ras Tafari) was the biblical savior brought forth to deliver the oppressed from tyranny. This arrangement was affected by the influences listed above, but was performed by a band comprising a lead singer, lead guitar, rhythm guitar, bass, drums, percussion, keyboard, and background vocal harmony. This brand of reggae became enormously popular in the late 1970s and early 1980s and remains so today. The style is featured in the ongoing internationally touring Reggae Sunsplash concerts that are staged annually. An aspect of reggae music often overlooked is that not all reggae groups are or were Rastafarians. Many of the most visible singers were, but Rasta had its own brand of music called nyabinghi, which also affected reggae's development. An interesting feature of reggae music was that, like American jazz, as new styles emerged the older styles remained popular with their core audiences. Artists who fit under the reggae music umbrella include Black Uhuru, Burning Spear, Jimmy Cliff, Desmond Dekker, Inner Circle, Gregory Isaacs, Peter Tosh, Bunny Wailer, Freddie McGregor, Augustus Pablo, and many, many others.

While standard roots reggae emphasized the one-drop rhythm (with only the third beat of a four-beat measure accented), the rockers rhythms accented all four beats of the four-beat measure, loosely analogous to American disco. The bass drum was struck on each of the four beats of the measure in rockers songs and propelled the music forward. The style was pioneered by Sly Dunbar for Joseph "Joe Joe" Hookim at his Channel One studio, in Kingston, Jamaica, and was most often accompanied by lyrics on social consciousness topics. The double drumming style gave the music a military sound, and this caught on with the other producers. From 1975 to 1978, most of the producers in Jamaica ventured into production of rockers material, and the advent of the sound stratified reggae output with roots on one side and rockers on the other.

Also during the reggae era, there was a major change in the manner in which Jamaican popular music was sold. From the beginning of the island's era of recorded music in the mid-1950s until the early 1970s, Jamaican popular music was marketed almost exclusively as singles. Thus, the singer/songwriter had to combine a series of successful singles in order to have enough material to even consider releasing an album. When Bob Marley signed the Wailers to Chris Blackwell's Island Records label, this all changed. From their 1983 release *Burnin'*, the format in Jamaican popular music changed from the single to the full-length album.

Dancehall is a style of Jamaican popular music that developed in the 1980s. The style involves a DJ singing or toasting over a repetitive beat, the result of which is a relatively thin texture. Dancehall takes its name from the venues in which it developed. The lyrics of many dancehall songs involve sexual situations, drug use, or criminal activity ("slackness"). The style has roots in its predecessor reggae, often using existing reggae rhythms that are reproduced on a drum machine at a much greater speed.

A hybrid of dancehall is the raggamuffin style, which is essentially the same, but uses only digital or electronic music for the beats. The style increased in popularity in the 1990s and began to cross over into the American popular music market, with many "gangsta" rappers using dancehall rhythms for their songs. This crossover was made more complete when contemporary hip hop artists began involving dancehall stars in their songs. In the most recent past, dancehall DJs have become increasingly active in American hip hop. Artists such as Beenie Man, Capleton, and Yellowman commonly record with U.S. hip hop artists and appear on their albums. The union of dancehall and hip hop has brought Jamaican popular music to the forefront of the American music scene to an extent that it never previously enjoyed. Significant dancehall DJs include Buju Banton, Dennis Brown, Capleton, Cocoa Tea, Dillinger, Beres Hammond, Yellowman, Shabba Ranks, Maxi Priest, Shinehead, Eek-A-Mouse, and many others. Dancehall continues to be the prevalent style in Jamaican popular music today.

Ragga was a sub-genre of reggae that emerged in the mid-1980s. It was categorized as a dancehall toasting over computer-generated rhythms. Thus, the product is all digital, except for the vocals. The term itself is short for *raggamuffin*, and the style of music is very closely allied with dancehall. The only real difference is the sound source of the instrumental accompaniment: acoustic is dancehall, and digital is ragga. Ragga became wildly popular with producers, as it was significantly less expensive to make than was traditional dancehall.

The use of digital rhythmic elements also enlivened the style, as producers could work with new sound sources instead of continuing to build from rhythms created in the ska and rock steady eras. Ragga has the same lyrical distinctions as dancehall in that the topics of the lyrics vary widely. Discussions of slack elements, such as womanizing and gun culture, are found alongside discussions of cultural uplift and Rastafarian doctrine. The first ragga single was "Under Me Sleng Teng," recorded by Wayne Smith in 1985. The rhythm for the song was generated with a Casio keyboard that had just been brought into the studio. Examples of ragga artists include Ini Kamoze, Mad Cobra, Beenie Man, Dennis Brown, Shaggy, and Pato Banton, among many others. As a reggae music sub-style, ragga is still being written in the new millennium.

As was the case with American jazz and rock and roll music, when a new style developed in Jamaica, it did not replace the existing style. Instead, the new style and the existing style ran concurrently as the new style gradually absorbed part of the existing style's audience. This allowed bands such as the Skatalites to be popular playing in the same style for over forty years.

List of Entries

A

A&M RECORDS

Co-founded by Herb Alpert and Jerry Moss in 1962, A&M was originally located in Los Angeles, California. The co-founders' last initials were used as the name of the label.

Alpert was born in Los Angeles in 1935 and became interested in music at age eight. He was trained on the trumpet, and he was encouraged by a teacher at an early age to become a classical musician. As a teenager, Alpert formed the Colonial Trio with a drummer and pianist. The band was good enough that they procured paying jobs on the weekends.

After high school, Alpert spent a year at the University of Southern California as a music major. The following year he enlisted in the U.S. Army and was sent to Fort Ord in Monterey, California. While in the military, Alpert married his high school sweetheart and gained an affinity for jazz music.

After being discharged from the army in 1956, Alpert returned to Los Angeles, became an active bandleader, and started writing songs. Next, he formed a songwriting team with Lou Adler. Their first published song was "Circle Rock," recorded on Keen Records. Alpert and Adler were subsequently hired by Keen Records as staff songwriters. This brought them into contact with artists such as Sam Cooke. Upon leaving Keen Records, Alpert and Adler became independent producers. They worked with Jan and Dean for Dore Records, but soon the production team split to find individual opportunities.

In 1961, Alpert met Jerry Moss. Moss had been a record promoter on the East Coast before moving to California to promote and produce music. Together Alpert and Moss formed Carnival Records. Their 1962 release "Tell It to the Birds" brought them the attention of Dot Records. Dot purchased their master for $750 and re-released the song. On a break in 1962, Alpert visited Tijuana, Mexico, and was inspired to infuse his songwriting with Mariachi band flavor. He achieved this with the song "The Lonely Bull" when he overdubbed an additional trumpet line that was slightly out of synch with the original. The song was released by Herb Alpert and the Tijuana Brass in August 1962. It should have been under the Carnival name; however, Alpert and Moss had learned that this name was already taken. They decided to change the name of their label to A&M. Six months after being released, "The Lonely Bull" had sold over 700,000 copies and was on the Top 10 charts.

This success was repeated with the album *Herb Alpert's Tijuana Brass, Volume 2*. With this release, the label location moved from Alpert's garage to 8255 Sunset Boulevard in Hollywood. The label continued to succeed, and Alpert was able to stop overdubbing himself and hire professional musicians from the real Tijuana Brass. The next two releases were "The Mexican Shuffle" and "A Taste of Honey," both of which charted simultaneously in 1965. The following year, Herb Alpert and the Tijuana Brass sold 13 million records, assuring the financial basis for A&M Records.

Alpert and Moss next turned to recruiting new talent to the label, and by the mid-

'60s, the Baja Marimba Band, Sergio Mendes & Brazil '66, Chris Montez, Claudine Longet, the Sandpipers, and We Five were on their label. Due to the success of these acts, A&M outgrew its existing location and, in 1966, moved to the Charlie Chaplin movie studio on La Brea and Sunset Boulevards. Despite its success, A&M was described as a "middle of the road" label. Hence, to diversify their offerings, Moss went to England and signed Procol Harum and Joe Cocker. He also obtained U.S. release licensing from **Christopher Blackwell** of **Island Records** for Spooky Tooth, Fairport Convention, Free, **Jimmy Cliff**, and Cat Stevens.

In the 1970s, A&M was releasing singer/songwriters in rhythm and blues, comedy, rock, and **reggae**. Other significant acts included Peter Frampton, Styx, Supertramp, the Carpenters, Cat Stevens, Quincy Jones, Bryan Adams, the Police, Sting, Amy Grant, Janet Jackson, Captain Beefheart, the Tubes, Joe Jackson, Suzanne Vega, John Hiatt, and the Neville Brothers. A&M existed for twenty-seven years as an independent company. However, in 1989 the label was sold to Polygram Corporation for $500 million. In 1998, Polygram merged with Universal Music Group.

ABC RECORDS

Formed in New York City in 1955, ABC was originally named ABC-Paramount and was the record label of the Am-Par Record Corporation, a subsidiary of American Broadcasting-Paramount Theaters, Inc. The label released primarily pop, jazz, rhythm and blues, and spoken word material. In 1959, ABC-Paramount bought the following labels: Audition, Command Performance, Colortone, Grant Award, and Waldorf Music Hall. In 1966, ABC-Paramount bought the Dunhill label and, in 1973, the Duke/Peacock labels. At this time, ABC-Paramount also had distribution deals with Anchor, Blue Thumb, Chancellor, Colonial, Deb, Fargo, Hunt, LHI, Royal, Shelter, Sire, Tangerine, Topsy, and Wren.

ABC-Paramount formed early in the rock and roll era and had a keen sense of marketing to the American teen. This is reflected in the 1957 signing of Paul Anka, whose presence on the label was quite profitable, as he not only recorded sixteen chart hits and ten albums for ABC-Paramount but also wrote for artists such as Frank Sinatra ("My Way") and Tom Jones ("She's a Lady"). Other important ABC-Paramount artists in the late 1950s and early 1960s included the Poni-Tails, Lloyd Price, Ray Charles, Cliff Richard, **Fats Domino**, and B. B. King. In 1966, ABC-Paramount formed the blues subsidiary Bluesways and signed Jimmy Reed, Johnny Lee Hooker, Otis Spann, Joe Turner, Eddie "Cleanhead" Vinson, T-Bone Walker, Jimmy Rushing, Jimmy Witherspoon, Charles Brown, Roy Brown, Brownie McGhee, and Sonny Terry. Also on the Bluesway label was the James Gang, a power trio that featured Joe Walsh, who would go on to replace Bernie Leadon in the Eagles.

In 1966, *Paramount* was removed from the label name, leaving ABC Records. In the 1970s, ABC experienced continued success with acts such as Steely Dan. However, in 1979, ABC was sold to the Music Corporation of America (MCA) and soon ceased to exist as a label. MCA then offered re-releases of several of the more successful ABC artists. In 1998, MCA was subsumed into Geffen Records by Universal Music Group.

ABENG

By one definition, *abeng* is the West African Twi word for "conch shell," which was a horn blown for communication by slaves in the sugarcane fields of the West Indies. The abeng was also used as an instrument by the **Maroon** armies to pass messages up and down the hills of Jamaica. Abeng also refers to a Jamaican side-blown instrument made from a cow's horn.

Abeng is also the name of a New York-based reggae group that was active in the 1980s. In 1989, they released the album *Unconquerebel* on the Strata Records label. Their style was socially conscious, modern roots reggae in the vein of **Burning Spear**, **Israel Vibration**, and the **Meditations**.

ABYSSINIANS

Formed in 1969, the Abyssinians are the vocal trio **Bernard Collins**, Donald Manning, and Linford Manning. Throughout its career, the group specialized in close harmonies, Rastafarian themes, and lyrics of social uplift. Recorded in 1969 at **Clement "Cox-sone" Dodd's Studio One**, their first single, "Satta Massagana," went against the early reggae grain—it was dark and spiritual instead of upbeat. The song title is Amharic for "give thanks and praises." Dodd did not think that the single would be successful. However, in 1971, the song was re-released on the Abyssinians' own Clinch label and became an instant classic. That same year the Abyssinians released three more singles, all of which did well in the Jamaican market.

Through the 1970s, the group continued to release successful singles, both on their Clinch label and with other producers. In 1976, the group recorded its first full-length album, *Forward to Zion*. This collection of older hits and new material garnered the group international fame. Their sophomore release, 1978's *Arise*, was not as strong as *Forward to Zion*. Although it had the backing of **Robert Marley's Tuff Gong** label, the album had only one hit single, "Hey You." There followed a period of little productivity.

After the recording of the second album, Collins quit the band and was replaced by Carlton Manning. The Manning family lineup performed at **Reggae Sunsplash** in 1979. In 1980, their third album, *Forward*, was released with some notoriety. In the late 1980s, Bernard Collins launched his own version of the Abyssinians and again activated the

The Abyssinians. © *UrbanImage.tv*.

Clinch label. The Manning family lineup competed with Collins's version of the group. **Heartbeat Records** released a "best of" album in 1993 that was followed by a similar release on France's MusicDisc label. In the wake of this renewed interest in the band, the original members of the group re-formed in 1998. They promptly released *Reunion*, but the original roster did not last long. In 1999, Collins again left the group and released material as Collins and the Abyssinians.

ACCOMPONG
(1) Accompong is the brother of the **Maroon** army commander Colonel Cudjoe. Accompong was active in the Maroon wars and helped make Jamaican Maroons the first group of free blacks on the island.
(2) Accompong is the name of a town in the northern part of St. Elizabeth, Jamaica. The town takes its name from its founder, a brother of the Maroon warriors Quao, Cuffy, and Cudjoe. The town was founded in 1739 as part of Maroon's peace treaty with the British.
(3) Accompong is also the name of the supreme deity in the **Ashanti** religion, known as Nyame or Nyankopong.

ACE, CHARLIE (1945-)
Born Valdern Dixon on December 27, 1945, Charlie Ace's reputation has a twofold basis. First, Ace was a noted record-shop owner in downtown Kingston, Jamaica. Second, he was a background vocalist on albums by **Big Youth**, **Bob Marley and the Wailers**, **Lee "Scratch" Perry** and the **Upsetters**, and **Peter Tosh**.

ACE, JOHNNY (1929-1954)
Born on June 9, 1929, Johnny Ace began life as John Alexander. His music career started as a blues vocalist and pianist on the Sun Records label. In the early 1950s, Ace had a string of successful singles on both Sun and Don Robey's Duke Records in Houston, Texas. On December 24, 1954, Ace was backstage at the city auditorium in Houston while on a promotional tour. He played a game of Russian roulette and shot himself. He died Christmas day, and his 1955 single "Anymore" went on to become one of the major hits of that year.

ACES
Aces was **Desmond Dekker's** backing group during the 1960s and 1970s. The group was made up of singers Wilson James and Easton Barrington Howard. Together, Dekker and the Aces were active in the **rock steady** and **ska** styles. The group had a string of twenty, number one hits in Jamaica in the mid to late 1960s and went on to enjoy success in the United States. In the early 1970s, Dekker and the Aces became an international success that was second only to that of **Bob Marley and the Wailers**. Important singles include the James Bond-inspired "007," "Unity," and "It Mek."

ADAMS, AUBREY
A keyboardist, piano player, and bandleader, Aubrey Adams was active in both the jazz and **ska** styles. For a time, Adams directed a band at the Courtleigh Manor Hotel that included tenor saxophone player **Tommy McCook**. His keyboard credits include work with Cluett Johnson (Clue J) and his band the Blues Blasters, who recorded for **Coxsone Dodd**. Additionally, Adams recorded with **Roland Alphonso**, **Clancy Eccles**, **Pat Kelly**, the Soul Defenders, and others. His piano and organ playing were influential as

Jamaican tastes turned from big band jazz to ska. Adams was also influencial with his own band the Dewdroppers, who scored a hit with the single "Marjie," recorded on Clement "Coxsone" Dodd's Whirdisc label.

ADAMS, GLEN

Born Glenroy Philip Adams, Glen Adams was a noted keyboardist and singer for the **Heptones**, the Hippy Boys, and the **Upsetters**. Additionally, Adams has worked with **Johnny Clarke**, **Harry J**, the Insteps, the **Jamaicans**, **Junior Byles**, **Pat Kelly**, Macha Dub, the Pioneers, the Reggae Boys, **Max Romeo**, the Soulmates, and the **Wailers**. His career began in the late 1960s and spanned several decades. Adams worked as a session organist for **Lee "Scratch" Perry** and was a bandleader and sideman. A few of his classics include "Mr. Brown," "Live Injection," "Clint Eastwood Rides Again," and "For a Few Dollars More."

ADEBAMBO, JEAN

Active in the 1980s, Adebambo worked with Jamaican producer **Leonard Chin** after he relocated to London in 1975. She helped to define the **lovers rock** genre with her Chin-produced single "Paradise," released on his Santic label.

ADMIRAL BAILEY

Born Glendon Bailey in Kingston, Jamaica, Admiral Bailey was among the most successful DJs active with **King Jammy**. A few highlights of Bailey's work are found on his album *Undisputed.* The singles "Big Belly Man" and "Kill Them with It" brought Bailey success, and this album serves as an unofficial greatest hits collection. In addition to King Jammy, Bailey also had success with producer **Bobby "Digital" Dixon**. Bailey was most active in the 1980s and 1990s and espoused the **dancehall** style. His albums appear on the VP, **Dynamic Studio**, and Peter Pan labels, and his singles are on a wide variety of compilations.

ADMIRAL TIBET (1960–)

Born in Freehill, Jamaica, in 1960, he abandoned his original name, Kenneth Allen, when he became active as a **dancehall** artist in his teens. Tibet differs from his **ragga** and dancehall peers in his spirituality. A member of the Twelve Tribes of Israel, Tibet avoids any slackness or discussion of guns, drugs, and sex in his lyrics. Also known as "Mr. Reality," Tibet is regarded as the first cultural singer of the **DJ** era. His career has spanned the last three decades and includes hits such as "Babylon War," "Serious Time," and "Leave People Business." Tibet is a crooning singer, as opposed to the **toasting** style of many other dancehall DJs. His material from the 1980s appeared on Sherman Clacher's Arabic Records.

In the 1990s, Sherman recorded with Maurice Johnson, also known as **Black Scorpio**. More recent hits include "Unity," "Innocent Life," and "Cannot Hold Me." Tibet continues to separate himself from his peers by singing about roots and culture versus slackness. In addition to solo albums, Tibet has appeared on records with **Gussie Clarke**, **Jah Screw**, **Shabba Ranks**, and others.

AFRICAN BROTHERS

Formed in 1969, the African Brothers consisted of **Lincoln "Sugar" Minott**, Winston "Tony Tuff" Morris, and Derrick "Bubbles" Howard. The three met as teenagers and were influenced by the close harmonies of the **Abyssinians**, the **Gaylads**, and the

Heptones. The trio took their name from their consciousness of their African roots and camaraderie. Initially, Morris was the principal songwriter, as he had the most music experience. However, Minott and Howard were fast learners and began to contribute harmonies. In 1970, the group began to attract local attention with their roots reggae sound, and soon they were in the studio with **Rupie Edwards**. Their first single was "Mystery of Nature." This led to subsequent recordings with **Clement "Coxsone" Dodd**, Winston "Merritone" Blake, and Micron Music. In addition to top producers, the three were also working with the best musicians in Kingston. Session players included **Aston** and **Carlton Barrett**, **Sly and Robbie**, and **Soul Syndicate**. Hits such as "Party Night" and "Hold Tight" soon followed.

The next step for the three was to do their own producing. This allowed them greater freedom, and the results were the 1970s singles "Torturing," "Want Some Freedom," and "Practice What You Preach."

At the end of the decade, the three decided to move in different directions. Minott and Morris continued as singers, while Howard became a full-time producer working with acts such as **Cocoa Tea**, **Gregory Isaacs**, and **Sanchez**. The studio **Easy Star Records**, based in New York City, has helped to spur a comeback for the African Brothers. In 2001, they released the album *Want Some Freedom*, which contained mid-1970s hits.

AFRICAN REFORM CHURCH

Jamaican Rasta leader Claudius Henry formed the African Reform Church in the late 1950s. He called himself the "Repairer of the Breach." In 1959–1960, this Jamaican minister organized a false repatriation movement. He sold hundreds of fake passports to be used for passage to Africa on October 5, 1959. Thought to be planning a military takeover, Henry was imprisoned for six years.

AFRICAN STAR

Based in Jamaica, the African Star label has released several prominent artists in the past decade. Artists available on the label include **Capleton**, Michael Rose, **Yami Bolo**, Terry Ganzie, and Jah Cure.

AGGROVATORS, THE

The Aggrovators is the name used by any of the session musicians working under **Bunny "Striker" Lee** from the mid-1970s to the mid-1980s. The most repeated lineup included Lennox Brown, **Tony Chin**, **Ansell Collins**, **Carlton "Santa" Davis**, **Bobby Ellis**, **Vin Gordon**, **Bernard "Touter" Harvey**, **Tommy McCook**, **Robbie Shakespeare**, and **Earl "Chinna" Smith**. Together, this collection of studio musicians enjoyed great success in the roots reggae and **rock steady** styles. The labels on which these tracks appear include Attack, Culture Press, and **RAS Records**. A sampling of the artists whom the group backed ranges from **Dennis Brown** and **Johnny Clarke** to **Dillinger**, **I-Roy**, and **Prince Jazzbo**.

AITKEN, LAUREL (1927–)

Born Lorenzo Aitken in 1927, Aitken is known as the godfather of **ska**. During his nearly fifty-year career, Aitken worked in the ska, **lovers rock**, roots reggae, calypso, and **mento** styles. He was a pioneer of Jamaican popular music, being the first real recording star, the first artist ever to release a ska record, the first to promote his music in the United Kingdom, and among the first Jamaicans to record on the famed **Island Records** label.

Aitken was born in Cuba but relocated to his father's homeland of Jamaica in 1938. As a teenager he distinguished himself as a talented singer and was part of a calypso group. Illustrating Jamaican popular music's roots in music from the southern United States, Aitken was heavily influenced by the jump band music of Louis Jordan, New Orleans rhythm and blues, and Jamaican **mento**. In 1957, Aitken entered the Jamaican recording industry with his single "Roll Jordan Roll." In 1958, he began recording for **Chris Blackwell's Island Records** and is credited as releasing the first single on the label, "Little Sheila"/"Boogie in My Bones." The release was a hit in Jamaica and was the first Jamaican popular music record to be released in the United Kingdom. "Judgment Day" followed in 1959 with the assistance of producer **"Duke" Reid**. Significantly, Aitken worked with several major Jamaican producers in the late 1950s: **Ken Khouri**, **Leslie Kong**, **Prince Buster**, and Reid.

On the heels of his Jamaican success, Aitken moved to Brixton, England. The area was heavily populated with West Indian immigrants, who spurred his success. In England, Aitken recorded on the Blue Beat label and released fifteen singles before returning to Jamaica in 1963. There he recorded tracks with "Duke" Reid that were backed by the **Skatalites**, including "Zion" and "Weary Wanderer." Back in the United Kingdom, Aitken switched in 1966 to the **Pama** family of labels, for which he recorded a series of hits. It is with this series of recordings, such as "Fire in Mi Wire" and "Landlord and Tenants," that he garnered a wider audience, including white listeners. The 1970s saw a decrease in Aitken's productivity; however, he achieved his first UK charting single in 1981 with "Rudy Got Married."

In 2004, Aitken released *Live at Club Ska*, which is a testament to his staying power. The music of Laurel Aitken charts the progression of style in Jamaican popular music. He began approximating American rhythm and blues, was crucial in the development of Jamaican **ska**, and carried the style through to the dawning of the **reggae** era.

AITKEN, MARCIA

Marsha Aitken worked with producers **Joe Gibbs** and **Errol Thompson**, known as the Mighty Two, in the late 1970s. Her songs were well crafted and romantic in nature, and included such works as "I'm Still in Love with You Boy," based on an **Alton Ellis** hit. Aitken also performed tunes by Ansel Cribland of the **Meditations**. Her music is still available on several compilation albums dedicated to women in **reggae**.

AKETE (AKETTE OR REPEATER)

An akete is one of the three drums used in **nyabinghi** playing. It is accompanied by the **funde** and the bass drum. All three are double-membrane drums, with the bass being the largest and the funde and repeater being smaller and similar in size. The principal difference between the repeater and the funde is that the repeater's head is tight, making it the treble drum, while the funde's is slack. Each of the three drums has a prescribed role in performance. The bass drum is sounded on beats one and four in a four-beat measure. The funde plays an eighth-note, syncopated cross rhythm that is layered in on top of the bass. To this is added improvisational melody by the repeater.

The use of nyabinghi drums in **reggae** music is traced back to traditional African drumming. **Burru** drumming was documented in Kingston as early as 1930 and manifested in **Kumina** and Revival dancing. In turn, popular musicians in the west Kingston ghettos adopted the drumming style. The repeater is used in some reggae music.

ALCAPONE, DENNIS (1946–)

Born Dennis Smith on August 6, 1946, Dennis Alcapone hails from Clarendon, Jamaica. He rose to popularity as one of the three earliest **toasting DJs**, or toasters. Along with **Big Youth** and U-Roy, Alcapone ruled Jamaica in the 1970s. After a move to Kingston, Alcapone set up the El Paso sound system, which was among the most popular on the island. In February 1970, he took to the studio with producer **Keith Hudson** and recorded his first single. He went on to work with **Coxsone Dodd** of **Studio One**, who was reeling from losing U-Roy to a rival label and was determined to push Alcapone up the charts. This was achieved by releasing versions of classics with Alcapone's infectious singing and catch phrases over recognizable beats. Versions of songs by **Alton Ellis**, the **Heptones**, **John Holt**, **Delroy Wilson**, and others were released.

In addition to **Hudson** and **Dodd**, Alcapone began working with other producers. In 1971, he began recording with **Bunny Lee**. This collaboration produced hits such as "Ripe Cherry," a version of "Cherry Oh Baby." Another Lee single introduced gun talk into the DJ vocabulary. Based on Eric Donaldson's "Love of the Common People," Alcapone's "Guns Don't Argue" was not only a hit single but also the name of his 1971 album. Alcapone next migrated to **Duke Reid's Treasure Isle** label; his 1973 *Soul to Soul* album garnered the DJ additional notoriety and an ever-increasing fan base. Alcapone was also popular in the United Kingdom, attested to by his successful 1972 tour, followed by another UK tour that was even more successful than the first. Between 1970 and 1973, Alcapone released over 130 singles and worked with all of the big-name producers in Jamaica.

In 1974, he moved to London and his popularity began to slide. The four albums released between 1974 and 1977, *Belch It Off*, *King of the Track*, *Dread Capone*, and *Investigator Rock*, failed to return the DJ to his lost heights. The **RAS** label released *Universal Rockers* (1977), which was a greatest hits collection. Alcapone then seemed to leave the music industry entirely. However, he made a triumphant return in 1988 and continues to release new material. His latest work is not on par with the early 1970s material, but he remains musically active.

ALEXANDER, JOHN. *See* ACE, JOHNNY

ALEXANDER, MONTY (1944–)

Born Montgomery Bernard on June 6, 1944, in Kingston, Jamaica, Monty Alexander has spent the past five decades infusing American jazz with Jamaican roots. Early on, he listed Oscar Peterson, Gene Harris, and Nat "King" Cole as his early influences. His early musical training was on piano and began at age six. In his teenage years, he entered the Jamaican club scene playing piano and then as the leader of Monty and the Cyclones in the late 1960s. With the Cyclones, Alexander had several songs on the Jamaican charts.

In 1961, Alexander moved to the United States and had a long career as a sideman for a variety of famous figures, including Frank Sinatra, Natalie Cole, Ray Brown, Milt Jackson, Dizzy Gillespie, Ray Brown, and **Ernest Ranglin**. His prodigious American career began in Las Vegas with the Art Mooney Orchestra. He then moved to New York to work for Jilly Rizzo in his club. Next, Alexander met Milt Jackson and his bassist Ray Brown, with whom Alexander would perform and record extensively. These early entries into the American popular music scene helped him make increasingly more connections with top-flight artists. Alexander has been an annual contributor at the Montreux Jazz Festival since 1976. In addition to jazz and American popular music,

Alexander formed an all-Jamaican **reggae** group that has recorded on the **Island** label imprint Jamaica Jazz. Their 1996 release, *Yard Movement*, returned Alexander to his Jamaican musical roots.

A prolific recording artist, Alexander had almost sixty albums to his credit by the mid-1990s. In 1999, he teamed with the Telarc label, and another round of recording ensued. Also in 1999, he issued *Stir It Up*, a collection of **Bob Marley** songs, which was followed in 2000 by *Monty Meets Sly and Robbie*. The latter was a joint venture with the seminal reggae rhythm section **Sly Dunbar** and **Robbie Shakespeare**. Next, backed by a six-piece band of Jamaica's finest instrumentalists, Alexander released *Goin' Yard* in 2001. He revisited his jazz roots on the 2002 release *My America*. This return to jazz continued with *Impressions in Blue* (2003), a collection of songs that again teamed Alexander with his jazz trio. Exhibiting his musical versatility, Alexander planned to release the Jamaican-flavored album *Rocksteady* in 2004. This collection of songs was the product of a collaboration with Jamaican guitarist **Ernest Ranglin**. Through a great diversity of styles, including jazz, soul, reggae, and **rock steady**, Alexander continues to release musically and culturally relevant material after nearly fifty years in the business.

ALLIGATOR RECORDS

Started in 1971 by Bruce Iglauer, who had been working for Delmark Records (Chicago) but needed a vehicle to record the band Hound Dog Taylor and the Houserockers, the Alligator label has been active for the past thirty-three years and is home to many of the top names in blues and roots rock. In the spring of 1971, the album *Hound Dog Taylor and the Houserockers* was recorded in two nights. One thousand copies were pressed, and Iglauer set about promoting the album by visiting radio stations and small local distributors. Iglauer ran all facets of Alligator from booking to promotions. In the early 1970s, progress for the label was slow, and there was only one release a year. However, what was released was received favorably. Additional artists were added to the roster, including Big Walter Horton, Son Seals, and Fenton Robinson. In 1975, Koko Taylor joined the ranks at Alligator and quickly garnered the label its first Grammy nomination, for *I Got What It Takes*. Also in 1975, Iglauer was able to hire his first employee and move to the north side of Chicago.

The late 1970s and early 1980s saw the artist roster and list of accolades continue to grow. This progress continues to the present. Alligator is nationally recognized as the leader in independent blues labels in the world. Its artists have won thirty-two Grammy Awards and include Luther Allison, Albert Collins, Professor Longhair, Buddy Guy, Johnny Winter, Lonnie Mack, Clarence "Gatemouth" Brown, Otis Rush, Charlie Musselwhite, and many others. The Alligator legacy of over thirty years of quality blues music continues to impact the American popular music scene.

ALPHA AND OMEGA

The duo of Christine Woodbridge (bass) and John Sprosen (keyboards) has been active since the 1980s. Alpha and Omega espouse a **dub** style with particular British flavor. Woodbridge is one of the few female instrumentalists in the style. Both she and Sprosen have worked in other **reggae** bands. They list Jamaican influences including **King Tubby**, **Augustus Pablo**, and **Lee "Scratch" Perry**. Their sound is characterized as having thunderous bass, driving drum tracks, and digital instrument flourishes. In 1990, Alpha and Omega released its first album, *Daniel in the Lion's Den*, on its own A&O imprint. Greensleeves signed the pair in 1992, and they continue to release new music. They also appear as backup artists with other reggae luminaries such as **Jah Shaka**. Their album catalog continues to grow in the new millennium with *Mystical Things* (2000), *Dub Philosophy* (2001), and *Spirit of the Ancients* (2003).

ALPHA BOYS CATHOLIC SCHOOL

Founded in the 1880s in central Kingston, Jamaica, the Alpha Boys Catholic School was established as a home for wayward boys and was meant to provide disadvantaged youths with education and practical training. In 1893, the school established the Alpha Boys' Band. Although begun as a drum and fife group, the school soon acquired some brass instruments, and a larger ensemble was formed. During the 1940s and 1950s, the music program at the school gained a reputation for turning out advanced instrumentalists. Alpha school-trained musicians went on to influence the foundation of the Jamaican **ska** style. **Donald Drummond**, John "Dizzy" Moore, Lester Sterling, and **Tommy McCook**, four founding members of the **Skatalites**, attended the school. After the ska era, Alpha school graduates were prominent players in the **reggae** and **rock steady** styles.

ALPHONSO, ROLAND (1931–1998)

Born in Havana, Cuba, on January 12, 1931, tenor saxophonist Alphonso was a founding member of the seminal Jamaican group the **Skatalites** and is remembered as one of the island's most important and celebrated musicians. His fifty-year career began with jazz playing in Eric Dean's Orchestra, progressed to calypso and **mento** recordings with Stanley Motta, and ushered in the new **ska** sound by playing on the first such recording—**Theophilus Beckford's** "Easy Snappin.'" Alphonso's accomplishments were also recognized by the Jamaican government with the award of the Order of Distinction in 1977.

Alphonso's musical roots trace back to his work in Kingston hotel orchestras. He left these groups to play calypso with artists such as Lord Kitchener and Lord Flea. Next, he became a session player for **Coxsone Dodd** at **Studio One**. At Studio One, Alphonso was given the task of voicing arrangements for the session players, which allowed him to alter the lightweight sound that he had inherited, turning it into the heavier ska sound. It was through his association with Studio One that, in 1963, he became a member of the Skatalites. The band broke up in August 1965, but not before Alphonso had put his mark on numerous recordings. The group released its own material as well as serving as a backup band for artists such as **Bob Marley and the Wailers**.

After the Skatalites' split, Alphonso and **Jackie Mittoo** formed the **Soul Brothers** who, in 1967, became the **Soul Vendors**. Through all of these outfit changes, he maintained currency with the prevailing Jamaican styles. Alphonso's recordings run the stylistic gamut. He played alto sax, tenor sax, baritone sax, soprano sax, and flute. Alphonso stayed musically active from the late 1960s through the 1970s and was part of the reformed Skatalites in the 1980s and 1990s. In November 1998, Alphonso suffered a brain aneurism that resulted in his death a few weeks later on November 20, 1998.

ALTHEA AND DONNA

Singing duo Althea Forrest and Donna Reid had a hit with their single "Uptown Top Ranking." The song went to the top of the Jamaican and British charts in 1978 and was subsequently covered by a wide variety of other artists. The song was written in response to **Trinity's** hit "Three Piece Suit." Althea and Donna recorded their chart

Althea and Donna. © *UrbanImage.tv.*

topper for **Joe Gibbs**, which resulted in the duo receiving a recording contract with Front Line Records. This contract resulted in their only album, also titled *Uptown Top Ranking* (1978). On the album, the duo is backed by the **Revolutionaries**. The album was not as well received as the single because the relatively inexperienced singers could not match the strength of the veteran backing band. A total of five singles were released in 1977 and 1978, but Althea and Donna were unable to recapture their original single's popularity.

ALTON AND EDDIE
Alton and Eddie formed their singing duo in 1959. Their first single, "Muriel," was released by **Coxsone Dodd** and became a substantial hit in Jamaica. A month later they recorded the single "My Heaven." The duo's existence was cut short when Perkins won a singing contest and moved to the United States.

ALTON, ROY (1943–)
Born in Dominica in 1943, Roy Alton relocated to England in 1961 and formed the Entertainers. This group was a five-piece calypso outfit that recorded its first record in 1971. Their first single, "Carnival Night," was followed in 1973 with "Kung Fu International." Neither track received much attention, so Alton abandoned the Entertainers name for Roy and the Challengers.

AMHARIC
The official language of Ethiopia, a country in east Africa, Amharic continues to be studied in the West Indies by some **Rastafarians** as a means of sustaining their African identity.

ANDERSON, ALBERT "AL" (1950–)

Born Albert Anderson in New York, his early music experience included playing trombone during high school. As a young adult, Anderson enrolled at the Berklee School of Music where he took up the bass and continued to hone his skills. At this time he joined the Centurions. Anderson came to the attention of Christopher Wood of the rock band Traffic; through Wood, Anderson became affiliated with **Island Records** (Traffic was signed to **Chris Blackwell's** label). While in the **Island** stable, Anderson was brought in to play lead guitar with **Bob Marley and the Wailers** on the *Natty Dread* (1974) sessions. Anderson went on to appear on "Crazy Baldheads" and the *Live* (1975) album. In 1976, Anderson left the Wailers and began playing with **Word, Sound, and Power**, the backup band for **Peter Tosh**. Alongside **Sly and Robbie**, Anderson recorded Tosh's *Legalize It* (1976) and *Equal Rights* (1977) albums. He returned to work with Marley in 1979 and remained with the Wailers alongside new lead guitarist **Junior Marvin**.

In the wake of Marley's death in 1981, Anderson continued playing with the Wailers. Even without Marley, the Wailers performed in Europe and the United States. Next, Anderson returned to New York to work as a session guitarist. In the 1990s, he recorded with luminaries such as Nile Rogers and the Jamaican Papa Curvin.

ANDERSON, GLADSTONE "GLADDY" (1934–)

Anderson was active as a pianist and keyboard player from the 1960s into the 1990s. Working in the **reggae** and **rock steady** styles, he recorded as both a session player and an independent artist. The nephew of **Aubrey Adams**, he worked with **Duke Reid** at his **Treasure Isle** imprint and went on to work for producer Harry Mudie as the leader of Gladdy's All Stars. Next, with Strange Cole, Anderson had several successful singles, including "Just Like a River" (1967), "Over Again" (1968), and "Pretty Cottage" (1969). In 1972, he released the best-selling album *It May Sound Silly* on the Moodisc label and went on to release several other solo works through the 1970s and 1980s. He also appeared on the albums *Harry Mudie Meets King Tubby in Dub Conference, Volumes 2 and 3* (1977–1978). Anderson's keyboard playing defined the **ska** sound, and he was instrumental in cultivating the slower rock steady beat.

ANDERSON, LYNFORD. See CAPP, ANDY

ANDERSON, RITA. See MARLEY, RITA

ANDY, BOB (1944–)

Born Keith Anderson in Jamaica, Andy rose to prominence in the mid-1960s as the lead singer of the **Paragons**. Later that decade, he went solo and had several successful singles for **Coxsone Dodd's Studio One**. Andy has worked in several Jamaican popular styles including **reggae**, **rock steady**, and **ska**. He had a string of hits in the late 1960s. Several of his songs have become reggae standards, including "Unchained," "Going Home," "Feeling Soul," "My Time," "Sun Shines for Me," and "Feel the Feeling." More recently, Andy scored with his 1992 hit "Fire Burning." Many of his most popular songs were released in 1988 on a compilation album called *The Bob Andy Songbook*. Andy's fame grew in the 1970s when he teamed with **Marcia Griffiths**, a member of **Bob Marley's** female backup singing trio **I-Threes**. Under the name **Bob and Marcia**, the duo had a couple of hits such as "Pied Piper" and "Young, Gifted, and Black." In the early 1990s Andy was not active in music, but in 1997 he re-emerged. That year, an album of new material called *Hangin' Tough* was released, and his 1988 album *Freely* was re-released.

ANDY, HORACE (1951–)

Horace Andy was born Horace Hinds in Kingston, Jamaica, in 1951. He spent the last thirty-five years writing and recording a series of the most important **reggae** albums under the name Horace Andy (a name given to him by producer **Coxsone Dodd**). Hinds's first recording came in 1966, and he spent the rest of the 1960s perfecting his delivery of his tenor voice. He also worked to become an accomplished guitarist to complement his voice and to aid in songwriting.

In 1972, he re-emerged with a series of hits on the **Studio One** label that culminated in the album *Skylarking*. Hit singles from this album included "Just Say Who" and "See a Man's Face." There followed a period during which Hinds recorded with a series of different producers on a variety of labels including Crystal, **Channel One**, and Jackpot. He released two albums during this period titled *You Are My Angel* and *Horace Andy Sings for You and I*. Next Hinds relocated to Connecticut and launched his own label called Rhythm. He released several modestly successful singles of his own. By 1980, he was again in Jamaica. This time he worked with producer **Tappa Zukie** and had his biggest success yet with the song "Natty Dread a Weh She Want." This project grew into an album of the same name.

His productivity continued into the 1990s, and in 1997 he teamed with producer **Mad Professor** for the hit "Roots and Branches." This led to the release of another album of this same name. This was quickly followed by another album, 1999's *Living in the Flood*. An aspect of this release is that the title track was co-written with punk music legend and Clash member Joe Strummer. The new millennium has been especially productive for Hinds. Also in the 1990s, Hinds was recruited by the UK-based group Massive Attack. Hinds and the Attack worked together, and Hinds appeared on all of their recordings from that decade. He released *Moonlight Lover* and *Roots and Classics* in 2001, and followed that with a series of four albums in 2002. In 2003, Hinds put out the album *Mek It Bun* and continued to write and release new material progressively.

ANDY, PATRICK (c. 1960–)

Born in Clarendon, Jamaica, Andy's earliest musical activities were on recordings with **Yabby You**. Early hit singles included "Woman, Woman, Woman" with Ranking Barnabus and a solo hit titled "My Angel." Andy next recorded with **Joseph Hookim** at **Channel One** in the early 1980s. In 1984, his most famous song, "Get Up, Stand Up," was produced by the team of Myrie Lewis and **Errol Marshall**. He also released a version of **Brigadier Jerry's** hit "Jamaica Jamaica" with "Cowhorn Chalice" on the Ujama label. Andy's popularity allowed him to release several "clash" albums with the likes of **Horace Andy**, **Half Pint**, Frankie Jones, and **Wayne Smith**.

ANTHONY B (c. 1970s–)

Born Keith Anthony Blair in Clarks Town, Jamaica, Anthony B's reputation was made in the 1990s and continues in the present decade as a DJ of some skill. His ability to mix DJing with chanting meaningful lyrics, together with a strong stage sense, increases his allure.

Anthony B began his music experience by singing in church and school groups. He then came out on the Shaggy Hi-Power sound system. After moving to Portmore and recruiting young disc jockeys Determine, **Mega Banton**, and Ricky General, he made the move from the street to the studio. Anthony B's debut single, "Life Is Hard," debuted in 1993. It was followed by a series of successful singles including "Rumour," "Fire pon Rome," "Repentance Time," and "Raid di Barn." In the late 1990s, he issued several albums starting with *So Many Things* (1996) and followed by *Universal Struggle* (1998). His work continued with the albums *Seven Seals* (1999) and *More Love* (2001).

ANTHONY, MIKE (c. 1960–)

Mike Anthony is one of the artists to emerge from the UK Saxon sound system from Lewisham, London. In the late 1980s, Anthony began releasing strong **lovers rock** singles and scored a charting hit with "Crash Crash." He followed this success with several other singles that exhibited his smooth vocal styling. Anthony again found success with his Gussie Prento-produced single "Still Your Number One." This was followed in 1991 with his version of David Ruffin's (the Temptations) "Walk Away from Love." Anthony continued to succeed throughout the 1990s with several other UK reggae Top 10 singles. His two albums are *Short of Nothing* (1992) and *Back for More* (1996).

APACHE INDIAN (1967–)

Born Steve Kapur on May 11, 1967, in Birmingham, England, Apache Indian grew up in Handsworth. Although of Asian descent, Apache Indian most closely associated himself with the early-1980s UK reggae explosion that was ushered in by **Steel Pulse**. His early reputation was made locally as a **dancehall** rapper. He injected his music with a mixture of **ragga** and Asian bhangra, and his appeal soared. The single "Movie over India" was a crossover success and resulted in him being picked up by the world's largest **reggae** music distributor, Jet Star. He followed this early success with two more singles, "Don Raja" and "Chok There," which led to a record contract with the **Island** label.

In 1993, Apache Indian released *No Reservations*, which was recorded in Jamaica with the help of **Bobby "Digital" Dixon**, **Sly Dunbar**, and Robert Livingstone. This release was more mainstream and cast him in the role of social commentator. Further, it secured his standing and artfully illustrated his ability to make a mark in reggae music. The album yielded several crossover hits, such as "Boom Shack a Lack" and "Arranged Marriage." This material spent time on the charts, and he won several prominent awards. In 1993, he released *Make Way for the Indian*, which continued his success. However, by the mid-1990s his fan base had weakened. His 1993 release *Real People* came out shortly after he was dropped from **Island** and failed to garner large-scale support.

ARAWAK

The Arawak were peoples native to Jamaica prior to European colonization. Spanish colonialists had eradicated the island's inhabitants by the time of the 1655 British invasion. Their language was preserved in more remote territories in the Andes Mountains in Peru and Bolivia as well as across the Amazon basin. Sometimes referred to as Taíno, the language was also spoken in Cuba, Hispaniola, Puerto Rico, and in the Bahamas.

ARCHIE AND LYNN

Archie and Lynn enjoyed limited success with their **dancehall** cut "Rat in the Corner." The basis of the song is traceable back to the **Soul Vendors' rock steady** instrumental "Real Rock." The "Real Rock" rhythm has been used as the basis of many other singles as well. (Papa) **Michigan and** (General) **Smiley** used it in their tune "Nice Up the Dance," as did Willie Williams in his "Armageddon Time." The Archie and Lynn version was released on the High Note imprint and told the story of a community hall that was infested by rodents. According to the story, the only remedy to the situation was found in the form of producer **Sonia Pottinger's** cat.

ARISTA RECORDS

Though not a **reggae** label, Arista Records did periodically sign Jamaican artists. One example is the signing of **Danny Ray** in 1982. The label picked up Ray on the heels of his success with the single "Why Don't You Spend the Night," a duet with Shirley James. Upon signing Ray, Arista re-released the single. The current Arista roster does not include Jamaican artists, but they were still important to the distribution of Ray's material. The Arista imprint is now a division of BMG/Bertelsmann. The current Arista roster is filled with hip hop and neo-soul acts such as Usher and Outkast.

ARIWA SOUNDS

Ariwa Sounds is Britain's most successful label of UK-produced reggae. Its output spans twenty years, and it has over 160 albums and a multitude of singles in its catalog. Specializing in **dub**, **lovers rock**, and roots reggae, Ariwa started out as an eight-track studio with the legendary **Mad Professor** at the controls. It grew to include several thirty-two, twenty-four, and sixteen-track digital boards along with a twenty-four-track analog studio to provide the vintage 1970s sound. The list of successful artists who have worked at Ariwa includes **Pato Banton**, **Johnny Clarke**, **Macka B**, Mad Professor, John McLean, Black Steel, **Tippa Irie**, and Phillip "Papa" Levi.

The studio's success continued through the 1980s and into the 1990s with acts such as **Yabby You**, Ranking Joe, Susan Cadogan, and **J. C. Lodge**. The studio is home to Mad Professor, who has recorded over twenty albums there, in addition to doing a large quantity of versions of other artists' works. Interestingly, Professor does not limit himself to Jamaican or UK-based artists. Instead he has remade an eclectic group of songs by artists who include Massive Attack, the Orb, **UB40**, Sade, Jamiroquai, Rancid, and the Beastie Boys. Ariwa continues to move forward and plans to expand its international reputation with the exposure of new talent.

ASHANTI

The Ashanti are a group of West African people in Ghana. The Ashanti Empire flourished for almost 200 years before the British overcame it at the end of the nineteenth century. In the early days of the empire, the Ashanti traded slaves to the British and Dutch in exchange for guns. With the power of its firearms, the Ashanti Empire expanded and developed to its fullest in the latter half of the eighteenth century. In 1807, the British abolished slavery, and this marked the beginning of the end for the Ashanti. The nineteenth century was filled with warfare between the Ashanti and the British. The once-strong empire declined until 1901, when it was annexed by the Gold Coast Colony. The Ashanti speak the Akan language, which is the root of the **Maroon** names **Accompong** and Anansesem (or Anancy spider).

ASHER, TONY (c. 1955–)

Tony Asher was involved with the beginning of the use of computerized drumbeats in Jamaica. Although the first use is shrouded in controversy, the first song to employ a digital drum track generated on a computerized keyboard was **Wayne Smith's** "Under Me Sleng Teng" in 1984. Smith recorded for **King Jammy**, and together with Tony

Asher he found the beat on Smith's Casio keyboard. The beat was then slowed down and re-recorded by Asher for Jammy. This ushered in a new era of Jamaican popular music. The use of digital sound and rhythm generators was immediately accepted by Jamaican producers due to its reduced cost compared to that of studio musicians. "Under Me Sleng Teng" became the basis for several other singles in addition to becoming a heavily covered song.

ASWAD

Aswad (the Arabic word for "black") formed in 1975 in Notting Hill, West London. In the past thirty years they have become international successes by playing their breed of British **reggae**. The band's longevity owes to its ability to alter its style to fit the changing music scene. Originally a roots reggae band, their later material had greater pop crossover appeal. The original members of the group were **Brinsley Forde** (lead vocals, guitar), **Angus "Drummie Zeb" Gaye** (drums, vocals), **George Oban** (bass), and Donald "Benjamin" Griffiths (guitar). Oban was later replaced by Tony Gad. Other musicians associated with the band include Courtney Hemmings, **Vin Gordon**, Bongo Levi, Mike Rose, and Karl Pitterson. Aswad's breed of music mixes **Rastafarian** elements with issues specific to living in England. They were the first British reggae band to sign to a major label when in 1976 they joined the **Island Records** ranks. Their first and eponymous album was successful, but they did not reach their full roots reggae potential until *Hulet* (1978). In 1981 and 1982, they released two albums for Columbia Records, *New Chapter* and *Not Satisfied*, respectively. They then returned to the Island Records label for the rest of the decade and released *A New Chapter of Dub* (1992), *Live and Direct* (1983), and *Rebel Souls* (1984). With this quick succession of releases, Aswad began to appear on the UK charts.

Aswad. © *UrbanImage.tv.*

Their 1986 release, *To the Top*, found them at the peak of their composition and performing skills. The band's next move was in the direction of greater crossover appeal. They began to distill their standard sound with elements of funk and soul. This move garnered the band instant celebrity and notoriety on the charts. The 1988 album *Distant Thunder* illustrated that their change of style was complete. The album contained the UK number one single "Don't Turn Around." Aswad is considered among the most successful UK-based reggae bands. In the 1990s, Aswad continued to record and perform. They remain an important group and are highly sought after for live performances. To their credit, Aswad has a Grammy nomination and received the Outstanding Contribution to Black Music Award at the fifth annual MOBO Awards in the United Kingdom. In 2002, the band released the album *Summer Cool Reggae* on the Universal Records label. This compilation of songs includes covers of artists such as Sting, **Gregory Isaacs**, and Dianna King. Of the original members, only Angus "Drummie Zeb" Gaye and Tony Gad remain.

ATRA RECORDS

The British imprint Atra Records that was formed by Brent Clarke in the 1970s did not last long; however, it did yield many solid singles. Artists released on Atra seven-inch singles included the Righteous Flames, Freddie McKay, Prince Williams, **Big Joe**, **Leonard Chin**, **Johnny Clarke**, **Alton Ellis**, **Keith Hudson**, Donovan Drummond and the Cordils, **Soul Syndicate**, Leroy Moffatt, Winston Jarrett, and Locks Lee. Atra released recordings made by several important producers such as **Keith Hudson** and **Augustus Pablo**.

AUGUSTINE, DENNIS (c. 1965–)

Dennis Augustine was a rhythm guitarist for **Misty in Roots**, an important roots reggae band that formed in South Hall, London, in 1978. Their fan base was diverse, including both West Indians and whites. The band toured actively in the late 1970s and often supported UK punk bands, which led to a white following. There have been many membership changes, but the most stable lineup for the band has been, in addition to Augustine, Walford Tyson (lead vocals), Tyson's brother Delvin (vocals), Chesley Samson (lead guitar), Delbert McKay (guitar), and Tony Henry (bass).

B

BABYLON

(1) The name *Babylon* is derived from biblical language; many **Rastafarians** view western civilization as a Babylonian captor. Building from the ideas set forth in the Book of Revelations, any non-African location marked by excess or greed is called Babylon. The imagery of Babylon discussed by the Rastafarians came from the empire of Babylon as discussed in the Old Testament. Western authority figures such as police, military, and government are also viewed as Babylonian oppressors.

(2) Babylon is also any evil or oppressive force or school of thought that is in opposition to Rastafarian views.

BACK O' WALL

Back o' Wall is the nickname given by Kingston residents to the west Kingston ghetto that was created in the mid-1950s. In 1954, the Jamaican government raided and destroyed the **Leonard Howell**-led **Rastafari** commune called Pinnacle. The homeless Rastas moved to Kingston and established a shantytown that was again destroyed by police. On July 12, 1966, Back o' Wall was bulldozed, which left many followers of Rastafari again homeless. The Back o' Wall site was the location of the first island-wide grounation (a meeting where education and reason are discussed).

BACK TO AFRICA MOVEMENT

The Back to Africa movement was the popular reference for Marcus Garvey's Ethiopianist attempt at repatriation. Garvey's sentiments fostered black pride and spurred the development of **Rastafari**. The purpose of the movement was to inspire action in its constituents. It fostered belief in a black good, the regaining of dignity lost in the colonial period, and economic stimuli. Garvey organized a failed sea crossing in hopes of returning some movement members to Africa.

BAD BRAINS

Formed in Washington DC in 1979, Bad Brains mixes **reggae** and punk into its own distinctively American sound. With eleven albums to its credit, the band has had some lineup changes but maintains a strong cult following. The original band was formed around Dr. Know (Gary Miller), a jazz-fusion guitarist. Miller brought influences as diverse as the Sex Pistols and Bob Marley to the group. Miller's mission in Bad Brains was to create crossover between punk and reggae in the United States similar to the trend long in use in the United Kingdom. He was assisted in this pursuit by vocalist H. R. (Paul D. Hudson), bassist Darryl Aaron Jenifer, and drummer Earl Hudson. Bad Brains quickly acquired a large following on the East Coast, based largely on their live shows, but their recordings were difficult to find. Their early material was released in limited quantities and often only on cassette.

In 1983, the group released its first full-length album on the New York-based independent label Caroline. The album *Rock for Light* was produced by Ric Ocasek of the Cars. Bad Brains did not release another album for three years; during that time they toured sporadically. They brought out the album *I Against I* in 1986 on the SST label. The title of this album foreshadowed the band soon splitting in half. Miller and Jenifer wanted to move in a more hard rock direction while H. R. and Hudson were interested in sticking with their reggae roots. The Hudsons frequently left the band to pursue their reggae aspirations. In 1989, the two pairs split completely, and Israel Joseph-I (Dexter Pinto) and Mackie Jayson joined the band.

Riding the early 1990s alternative rock wave, Bad Brains got a major label contract with Epic, and 1993's album *Rise* followed. The release did poorly, and Epic dropped the band. In 1995, Maverick Records offered Bad Brains a record deal if the original four would reunite. They did, releasing *God of Love* that year. This release again sold poorly, and Maverick dropped the group. More recently, the band reunited in 1998 and is active under the name Soul Brains. In 2001, they released the live album *Live at Maritime Hall: San Francisco.*

BADAWAI (1973–)
Born in 1973 as Raz Mesinai, Badawai specializes in **dub** composing and programming. Badawai learned the dub craft by working with the collective Sub Dub. He gained his early music background in the Sinai Desert, where he learned Middle Eastern drumming. He mastered several drum types and brought his abilities to New York City. There he fell in with a group of underground **DJs** (including DJ Spooky). It was at this time that Mesinai took on the moniker Badawai, which means "desert dweller." His first album was the Reach Out International Records (ROIR) release *Sound Clash* (1996). This was followed by *Jerusalem under Fire* (1997), which solidified his status among the **reggae**/dub DJs in the late 1990s. Badawai released an album a year for the first four years of the new millennium, and each moved him further away from his dub roots.

BAILEY (BALEY), ELROY (c. 1955–)
Elroy Bailey, known as Ras Elroy, was the London-born bass player for the band **Black Slate**. Formed in 1974, Black Slate was a British **reggae** band that formed as the backup band for touring acts such as **Delroy Wilson**. Keith Drummond (vocals), Chris Hansen (lead guitar), Desmond Mahoney (drums), Cledwyn Rogers (rhythm guitar), Anthony Brightly (keyboards), and Bailey on bass made up the band. Although Bailey is from London, some members of the group hail from the Caribbean. Their late 1970s hits were a benchmark of the British reggae sound.

BAILEY, NOEL "SOWELL RADICS." *See* RADICS, SOWELL

BANTON, BUJU (1973–)
Buju Banton was born Mark Anthony Myrie in the Salt Lane slums of west Kingston, Jamaica, in 1973. Myrie's mother, who was descended from **Maroons**, was a street "higgler" or vendor who raised him along with his fourteen siblings. He earned his first nickname as a youth; he was dubbed Buju, which was the Maroon name for the Jamaican vegetable breadfruit. The second part of his name was taken from his greatest musical influence, Burro Banton. He entered the Jamaican music scene at the tender age of twelve under the nickname Lambada Man and quickly earned a strong reputation for his gruff-voiced **toasting** abilities on the area **sound systems**.

Banton plied his lyrical trade for a time and got his first big break when he met

Buju Banton. © *UrbanImage.tv.*

producer **Robert Ffrench** through the help of his friend Clement Irie. Ffrench and Banton recorded a series of singles including "The Ruler," "Boom Bye Bye," and "Stamina Daddy." In 1991, he met producer **Dave Kelly**, the engineer for the **Penthouse** imprint owned by **Donovan Germaine**. Kelly brought Banton into the studio and together they released a series of well-received singles, such as "Love Me Browning." The song sparked controversy, as it was an ode to light-skinned black women. This reference to skin color mixing was taboo on the island, and the situation was exacerbated by the song's adherence to the dancehall standard for its graphic depiction of sex. He quieted some of the conflict with his second single, "Love Black Woman."

In 1992, Banton issued his debut album on the Penthouse label, called *Mr. Mention.* The album was a smash hit and earned Banton the highest Jamaican sales records to date. Further, it even eclipsed **Bob Marley's** record for the most number one singles on the charts in the same year. These events all transpired while Banton was still a teenager. In 1993, at age twenty-one, Banton released his sophomore offering, *Voice of Jamaica*, on the Mercury imprint. What set Banton apart from many of his dancehall-style contemporaries was his increasing avoidance of the standard slack lyrics of gun culture and sex and his steadfast adherence to discussions of social matters and cultural uplift. The socially conscious tenor of the album was reached though songs such as "Willy Don't Be Silly" and "Deportee." Another important single from the album was "Murderer," which was written for his fallen comrades **Dirtsman** and **Pan Head**. This second release rocketed Banton to the upper echelon of the **dancehall** ranks. His popularity was not limited to his homeland.

In the early 1990s, Banton joined the **Rastafarian** faith, whose sentiment began appearing in his music. In 1995 he issued the album *Til Shiloh*, an instant classic with a blend of dancehall rhythms and roots sentiments. Next, Banton released *Inna Heights* (1997) and again had major success. The album went to number one on the strength of songs such as "Hills and Valleys" and "Destiny." His currency in the United States was growing, and his American live shows began to sell out. This crossover appeal was attested to by his teaming with U.S. band Rancid for a song on their 1999 release *Life Won't Wait* and further collaboration in the wake of this success. Throughout the 1990s, Banton continued his dominance of the Jamaican dancehall scene. He took further control of his creative output with the founding of his own Gargamel Productions and Aksum Recording Studio. In the new millennium, Banton issued *Unchained Spirit*, which was another well-received album. The release highlighted Banton's changed approach to songwriting with material on love instead of sex and greater importance placed on his faith, as shown in the single "23rd Psalm." The album also included a memorable collaboration with **Beres Hammond** on the single "Pull It Up." In 2003, Banton issued *Friends for Life*. This album reinvigorated his crossover appeal, as it was a blend of dancehall, hip hop, and rhythm and blues.

BANTON, MEGA (1973-)

Mega Banton was born Garth Williams in Kingston, Jamaica, in 1973. Like Buju Banton, Williams took his nickname from his predecessor Burro Banton. Banton broke onto the Jamaican popular music scene during the early 1990s. He was heralded as one of the new generation of **dancehall DJs**, **toasting** in a gravelly voice reminiscent of his namesake. Banton rocketed to success with his single "First Position." The track garnered enough success that it was released on a VP label album of the same name in 1994. In addition to this single, the album contained the stunning songs "Sound Boy Killing," "Decision," and "No Ninja, No Buju," which called out his rival DJs.

The following year Banton issued two full-length albums. The first, titled *New Year, New Style*, contained a variety of collaborations with other artists. The title track was made with the assistance of Ricky General backing up Banton on the lyrics. The song "She's Mine" included the assistance of **Barrington Levy**, and "Mr. Want All" enlisted **Leroy Smart**. Other guests who made an appearance on the album included Shirley McClean and Richie Scorpio, who was also the producer. The second offering from 1995 was the album *1,000,000 Watts*. This release by Relativity Records also featured the assistance of Ricky General. The standout songs on this release included "Good Ganja" and "Money First."

BANTON, PATO (c. 1960-)

Born Patrick Murray in Birmingham, England, Pato Banton took his nickname from the legendary **DJ** Burro Banton. He entered the music industry when the English Beat recruited him to guest on their 1982 album *Special Beat Service*. The young singer appeared next to **Ranking Roger** on the single "Pato and Roger A Go Talk." There followed a period during which the DJ issued a series of modestly successful singles on the Fashion Records label.

In 1985, Banton teamed with **Mad Professor** for his debut release *Mad Professor Captures Pato Banton*. The album featured the songs "Gwarn!" "My Opinion," and "King Step." Next, Banton issued the 1987 album *Never Give In*. This release was on the Greensleeves label and included the followup to his English Beat debut with "Pato and Roger Come Again." Also featured were "Don't Sniff Coke," "Absolute Perfection," and the title track. In 1989 he issued the pop **reggae** album *Visions of the World*, which was quickly followed by *Wize Up (No Compromize)* in 1990. The *Visions of the World* release was followed by a North American tour opening for **Ziggy Marley**. The *Wize Up* album featured a title track on which David Hinds of **Steel Pulse** guested. This material brought Banton success in the United Kingdom, but he struggled for recognition in the American market. There followed another effort with Mad Professor called *Mad Professor Recaptures Pato Banton* (1985) and a live album from a U.S. tour. The *Live and Kickin' All over America* (1991) album marked a period of increased popularity for the singer in the United States, and the tour was backed by Banton's Reggae Revolution band.

Next he issued the album *Universal Love* in 1992, but then seemed to enter a period of writer's block. In 1994, this was broken when Banton was persuaded to do a cover version of **Eddy Grant's** song "Baby Come Back." The release featured Robin and Ali Campbell of **UB40**. The song was an enormous success and finally allowed Banton to cross over and succeed in the United States. The song was released on the 1994 *Collections* album. The single's popularity led British musician Sting to invite Banton to join him on the single "Cowboy Song," and Banton's crossover audience continued to grow. Next came *Stay Positive* (1996) and the Grammy-nominated *Life Is a Miracle*

(2000). The latter album featured the songs "Legalize It" (not a **Peter Tosh** cover), "Mama Nature," and the title track. Next, Banton and the Reggae Revolution band issued *Tudo De Bom-Live In Brazil* in 2000.

In 2002, Banton opened a children's school for music technology in Birmingham, where children learned about the recording process. It was from here that he planned to issue an album collecting the material the children created.

BARNES, LLOYD "BULLWACKIE" (1944–)

Born in Jamaica in 1944, Lloyd Barnes entered the music business as an employee of **Duke Reid's Treasure Isle** imprint, where he worked as an engineer. In the early 1970s, Barnes moved to the Bronx, New York, and set up Wackie's House of Music record store. In the back room, Barnes soon built a studio that became the first major **reggae** recording studio in the United States. In 1974, Barnes began to record many of the best expatriate vocalists in the country. Barnes's style favored the roots reggae material, and he played to his strength working with artists such as **Horace Andy** on his *Dance Hall Style* album (1983), **Dennis Brown**, Wayne Jarrett, and **Junior Delahaye**. To support these singers, Barnes recruited a crack group of session musicians often referred to as the Chosen Brothers. Other significant singers who voiced songs for Barnes included Naggo Morris, **Stranger Cole**, **Tyrone Evans**, the **Meditations**, **Sugar Minott** for his *From the Heart* release (1985), **Jackie Mittoo**, **Johnny Osbourne**, **Michael Palmer**, the Love Joys, Jah Batta, and **Leroy Sibbles**. In addition to the studio, Barnes built a **sound system** to use to circulate the material being created at the label. The material from these artists was released on a collection of impromptu imprints until the Wackies label was formally established in 1983.

BARRETT, ASTON "FAMILY MAN" (1946–)

Aston "Family Man" Francis Barrett was born in Kingston, Jamaica, in 1946. Barrett was born into a musical family; both his father and grandfather were musicians. He earned his nickname while still a teenager for his many romantic relationships. The behavior that earned his nickname also resulted in him being sent to the Jamaican Youth Corporation camp for a time. While there he took up music and learned to play the bass. Upon release, he teamed with his younger brother **Carlton**, who was working to become a drummer; the pair began to play live. Ultimately, the brothers joined the Hippy Boys, with Carlton on drums and Aston on bass, and went into the studio with producer **Lloyd Charmers**. The Hippy Boys included the Barrett brothers, **Glen Adams** on keyboards, **Max Romeo** on vocals, and Alva "Reggie" Lewis on guitar. The session was a success and the two were soon in demand in studios around the island.

In 1968, the Hippy Boys began working with legendary producer **Lee "Scratch" Perry** and soon became part of his **Upsetters** studio collective. The Barrett brothers plus Adams and Lewis were responsible for the instrumental hit "Return of Django." The Barrett brothers participated in recording sessions with the **Bob Marley and the Wailers** vocal trio, appearing on "Black Progress," "Duppy Conqueror," "Soul Rebel," and "Small Axe."

From 1969 until the end of Marley's life, Aston and Carlton Barrett recorded with the **reggae** superstar and appeared on all of his tours. Along with working for the Wailers in 1970, Aston and Carlton began playing in a side project called the Youth Professionals with **Tyrone Downie**, who would go on to join the Wailers. As the Wailers vocal trio of Marley, **Peter Tosh**, and **Bunny Wailer** split up, the Barrett brothers continued to work with Marley. Not only did Aston and Carlton form the rhythm backbone of the new Wailers group, but Aston also began writing music with Marley and is credited as the co-author of "Rebel Music." In addition to being a reggae bass stalwart, Barrett was also becoming an accomplished recording engineer and producer. He received co-producer credits for all of the albums that Marley issued on the **Tuff Gong/Island** records collaboration.

In the wake of Marley's untimely death in 1981, Barrett took a short break before putting the band back together. The reconstituted Wailers released a series of albums with Aston at the helm as music director. Their releases were titled *I.D.* (1989), *Majestic Warriors* (1991), and *Jah Message* (1996). In the 1990s, in addition to his work with the Wailers band, Barrett also recorded with **Alpha Blondy**, **Burning Spear**, **Johnny Clarke**, **Joe Higgs**, **Israel Vibration**, **Junior Byles**, John Denver, the **Tennors**, and many others. He also continued to work as a producer and has served in this capacity for a variety of artists such as the Wailers, Jimmy Riley, Brimstone, Senya, and others.

In addition to his many other activities, Aston also owned his own label, called Fams, and issued his own material as well as the work of those he produced. Barrett's material was compiled and re-issued by the **Heartbeat** label under the titles *Cobra Style* (1999) and *Family in Dub* (1999). In the new millennium, Aston Barrett remains the benchmark of reggae bass players and continues to forward Bob Marley's musical legacy through his work in the Wailers.

BARRETT, CARLTON (1950–1987)

Carlton "Carly" Barrett was born in Kingston, Jamaica, in 1950 and was the younger brother of **Aston "Family Man" Barrett**. From an early age, Barrett took to playing the drums and was influenced by his musical grandfather, father, and brother. His earliest drum set was made of coffee cans and paint cans, and his early influence was Lloyd Nibbs of the **Skatalites**. With his brother he joined the Hippy Boys, with Carlton on drums and Aston on bass, and went into the studio with producer **Lloyd Charmers**. The Hippy Boys included the Barrett brothers, **Glen Adams** on keyboards, **Max Romeo** on vocals, and Alva "Reggie" Lewis on guitar. The session was a success, and the two were soon in demand in studios around the island.

In 1968, the Hippy Boys began working with legendary producer **Lee "Scratch" Perry** and soon became part of his **Upsetters** studio collective. The Barrett brothers plus Adams and Lewis were responsible for the instrumental hit "Return of Django." The Barrett brothers participated in recording sessions with the **Wailers** vocal trio, appearing on "Black Progress," "Duppy Conqueror," "Soul Rebel," and "Small Axe." From 1969 until the end of Marley's life, Carlton and Aston Barrett recorded with the reggae superstar and appeared on all of his tours. Along with working for the Wailers in 1970, Carlton and Aston began playing in a side project called the Youth Professionals with **Tyrone Downie**, who would on to join the Wailers. As the Wailers vocal trio of Marley, **Peter Tosh**, and **Bunny Wailer** split up, the Barrett brothers continued to work with Marley. Not only did Aston and Carlton form the rhythm backbone of the new Wailers group, but Barrett also began writing music with Marley, and he is credited as the co-author of "Talkin' Blues."

In addition to being a reggae drum stalwart, Barrett was also credited with developing the signature reggae drumming style called the **one drop**. This drumming style used only one heavy or accented beat per measure, which came on the third beat of a four-beat measure. The rhythm differs from that of western music, which typically accents beats one and three in a four-beat measure, and the rock and roll backbeat accent pattern of heavy second and fourth beats. The style is what gave roots reggae music its walking tempo feel; it was so popular that Marley went on to write a song about the rhythm's feel called "One Drop." Due to the walking tempo of the one-drop rhythm, the songs that employed it had a militant feel that Barrett played up. This resulted in him nicknaming himself "Field Marshal."

In the wake of Marley's untimely death in 1981, Barrett took a short break before putting the band back together. The reconstituted Wailers released a series of albums with Aston at the helm as music director. Their releases were titled *I.D.* (1989), *Majestic Warriors* (1991), and *Jah Message* (1996). Carlton Barrett was killed at his home on April 17, 1987. The master of the one-drop drumming style is remembered in myriad recordings and by all those who emulate his style.

BARRETT, PATRICK. *See* REBEL, TONY

BECKFORD, EWART. *See* U-ROY

BECKFORD, THEOPHILUS (1935–2001)

Theophilus Beckford began his musical training in piano in the 1940s while attending Boys Town School in Kingston, Jamaica. By the mid-1950s, Beckford had purchased his own piano, and by 1955 he was playing professionally. As a professional musician he is credited with helping to define the sound of Jamaican **ska**. His first recording, for **Coxsone Dodd**, came in 1956 and was titled "Easy Snappin.'" However, it was not released until 1959 when Dodd made the song available on his Worldisc label. The single went on to become a hit and was covered by several other groups. The style of playing on "Easy Snappin'" signaled a change in Jamaican popular music. The new beat was slower, and the accents were on the offbeats. The song was such a success that it was subsequently re-released on England's Blue Beat Records. Next, Beckford turned his attention to the creation of his own label, called King Pioneer. It was also in the late 1950s and early 1960s that he joined the studio group Clue J and His Blues Blasters. This collection of studio musicians included **Roland Alphonso**, Cluett Johnson, **Ernest Ranglin**, and **Rico Rodriguez**. This collection of performers released the single "Shuffling Jug," regarded by many as the first ska record. Beckford also played in other studio bands and recorded sessions for **Beverley's Records**, **Prince Buster**, **Duke Reid**, and Duke Eccles.

Through the 1970s, Beckford was active in studio bands in the above-listed studios along with recording for **Lee "Scratch" Perry**. Beckford then began to fade from the Jamaican music picture. However, in 1991 he re-emerged as a participant in **Studio One's** *The Beat Goes on: 35 Years in the Music Business* concerts that took place in Kingston's National Stadium. This led to the use of "Easy Snappin'" in a television advertisement that further revived Beckford's career. Throughout a lengthy career, Beckford was one of the key musicians who established the Jamaican ska style and helped to separate it from Jamaican rhythm and blues. On February 19, 2001, Theophilus Beckford went to settle a dispute in the Callaloo Mews section of Kingston and was murdered with a hatchet.

BEENIE MAN (1973–)

Born Anthony Moses Davis on August 22, 1973, in Kingston, Jamaica, Beenie Man began his music career early when he started **toasting** at age five. His entry into the music business came through his uncle, Sydney Wolf, who was a drummer for **Jimmy**

Cliff. With Wolf's encouragement, Beenie Man entered a **DJ** contest and won the Teeny Talent show at just eight years of age. This led to introductions to **King Jammy** and other **sound system** operators, though whom his notoriety increased. **Bunny Lee** then took Beenie Man into the studio and recorded his *Ten Year Old DJ Wonder* album, released in 1981. Based on the popularity of the album, successive singles were released through the 1980s.

In 1992, Beenie released his second album, *Gold Charm*. With this release his popularity increased to the level where battles with other well-known Jamaican DJs were arranged. The battle with **Bounty Killer** took place in 1993 and resulted in the release of *Guns Out* on the Greensleeves label. Beenie then toured, and in the United Kingdom he featured a cameo appearance by **Shabba Ranks**. A subsequent single with **Barrington Levy** entered the UK charts and was followed by other successful singles. By 1995, it was speculated that Beenie Man had taken the top Jamaican DJ spot from **Buju Banton**. His 1995 VP Records release with **Dennis Brown**

Beenie Man. © *UrbanImage.tv.*

and **Triston Palma** was titled *Three against War.* It was followed in the same year by *Mad Cobra Meets Lt. Stitchie and Beenie Man*, which was also released by VP. In 1996, Greensleeves released *Maestro*, followed by a highly acclaimed tour with the Shocking Vibes Crew. Also in 1996, Beenie called a truce with Bounty Killer, which was brokered by the Jamaican radio disc jockey Richard Burgess. The 1996 release party for Beenie Man's *Maestro* album drew thousands of New York fans. Next Beenie released the single "Dancehall Queen" for the feature film of the same name. He also starred in the movie, playing a character who was quite like him.

Beenie's first Grammy nomination came in 1997 for his album *Many Moods of Moses.* This exposure was further enhanced by his appearance on Vibe TV, MTV, and VH1. The most popular single on *Many Moods of Moses* was "Who Am I," which was popular on both the UK and many American radio stations. This single topped the UK charts in 1998 without the benefit of major label support and topped out at number six on Billboard's Hot Rap Singles chart. In Beenie Man's capable hands, the Jamaican **dancehall** style has crossed over to the American urban market. "Who Am I" was re-released as a single with the Neptunes-produced B-side "Girls Dem Sugar." This two-song combination remained popular for over two years.

In 2000, all of Beenie Man's work paid off when he was awarded a five-album deal on Virgin Records. The first of these releases was 2000's *Art and Life*, which featured a series of cameo appearances from American rock and roll, jazz, and hip hop acts. His

2002 release, *Tropical Storm*, also featured several cameos including **Lady Saw** and Sean Paul. In July 2004, Beenie released his third Virgin Records album, *Back to Basics*. The record is powered by the singles "King of the Dancehall" and "Dude." These singles continue to further his career and heighten his reputation as dancehall's best DJ. Throughout his career, Beenie Man has attempted to do for dancehall music what **Bob Marley** did for roots reggae, which was to bring it to international attention while maintaining a strong base of support in Jamaica.

BELL, RICHARD (c. 1960–)

Richard "Bello" Bell was a producer/songwriter and owner of the Startrail studio and a record label in Miami. Bell had success recording Jamaican acts in the early 1990s, such as **Cutty Ranks** and **Beres Hammond**, so he moved the label to Kingston and began a recording project with **Anthony B**. The result was Bell's involvement with Anthony B's *So Many Things* album (1996), which produced his most popular single, "Fire Pon Rome."

BELLTONES, THE

The Belltones began with Kenny Hart. In 1966, Hart and his steel drum band migrated from Trinidad and Tobago to Jamaica. They procured playing jobs and began making money until it was pointed out to Jamaican authorities that they did not have work permits. According to reliable sources, this point was made by **Byron Lee**, who made the Jamaican Music Union aware of the lack of proper paperwork. Hart managed to pay the required fees and stayed on the island for the next twelve years. He made his living as both an entertainer and steel pan instructor. In the mid-1970s, Hart formed the Belltones with Geoffrey Bell. This five-member group included a dancer and singer. The Belltones played for four years in Boston and had a successful United States tour. In 1976, Bell and his brother Kelvin organized the Harlem All Stars. This is a steel drum band that plays at most predominately black parades in New York City.

BENNETT, HEADLEY "DEADLY HEADLEY" (c. 1930–)

Headley Bennett received his earliest musical training at the **Alpha Boys Catholic School** in Kingston. He attended the school until age fifteen, during which time he learned to play the saxophone. After leaving the school, he had a semi-professional performing career in Canada; he has been a professional saxophone session player in Jamaica since then. Bennett earned a living in several important studios and groups around the island. He was active in the 1970s in **Coxsone Dodd's Studio One** group alongside **Roland Alphonso**, **Cedric Brooks**, **Jackie Mittoo**, **Leroy Sibbles**, and Bunny Williams. He was also part of the horn line for the **Revolutionaries** with ex-**Skatalite** members **Vin Gordon** and **Tommy McCook**. His other session credits included backing up the **Abyssinians**, **Culture**, **Alton Ellis**, **John Holt**, **Gregory Isaacs**, **Barrington Levy**, **Bob Marley**, and many others. In 1999, Bennett released a solo record called *35 Years from Alpha*. The album's title refers to his time spent at the Alpha Boys Catholic School. It was his only solo effort and received little recognition. The album was recorded by **Adrian Sherwood** for On-U Sound. The album's style alludes to Bennett's jazz influences in addition to his **reggae** roots.

BENNETT, JOSEPH "JO JO"

Like many other Jamaican instrumentalists, Joseph "Jo Jo" Bennett began his musical training at the **Alpha Boys Catholic School** in Kingston, Jamaica. There he studied the jazz and classical styles, focusing on drum performance. He became proficient in music theory and soon voluntarily switched from drumming to the trumpet. Bennett joined the Jamaica Military Band after graduation and was much sought after by popular music groups. After leaving the military band, Bennett moved to Jamaica's north coast. Ultimately, he joined **Byron Lee and the Dragonaires**, which was among the island's leading groups. He stayed with Lee until 1967, when he relocated to Canada after the Dragonaires played at the '67 Expo. Having settled in Toronto, he began performing with a group called the Fugitives. Bennett split the majority of his professional time between Canada and Jamaica. While visiting Jamaica in 1970, Bennett recorded his first and only solo album, *Groovey Joe*. He stayed on the island until 1979 and enjoyed a series of well-received singles.

By 1980, Bennett was back in Canada, where he helped establish the first black-controlled music school in the region. Called the Sattalite Music School, it allows anyone to receive music instruction on a "pay what you can" basis. He spent the 1980s performing and exploring a variety of Canadian musical endeavors. In 1982, Bennett and Fergus Hambleton formed the band Sattalite, which remains active. It consists of graduates from the music school as well as veterans such as Bennett. The band has achieved critical acclaim through its six-album catalog and has won two Juno Awards.

BENNETT, LORNA (1954–)

Born in Kingston, Jamaica, Lorna Bennett began her musical career singing in nightclubs. Early success was marked by producer **Geoffrey Chung's** personal involvement in her development. Together Chung and Bennett recorded a version of "Morning Has Broken," but the single did not succeed commercially. However, in 1972 it did catch the attention of producer **Harry J**, who asked Chung to record Bennett's version of "Breakfast in Bed." This single was a huge success throughout the West Indies and left its mark on both the UK and U.S. markets. The single's success was spurred by its appearance on the **Island Records** affiliate Blue Mountain. Bennett's success with this single ended a five-year stretch during which no female singer topped the Jamaican charts. Her second number one hit soon followed with her version of the Dixie Cups' tune "Chapel of Love." This led Harry J in 1976 to release rights for the singles "Run Johnny" and "Reverend Lee." Neither song had the charting power of the first two singles, and Bennett subsequently left the music business. In the interim, she earned her juris doctorate and has become a successful lawyer. Bennett's legacy lived on when **UB40** and Chrissie Hynde released their own version of "Breakfast in Bed" in 1988. Through this recording, the single again charted in the Top 10.

BENNETT, LOUISE (1919–)

Louise "Miss Lou" Bennett was born in Kingston, Jamaica, to a widowed dressmaker. She has spent her life collecting, researching, and interpreting Jamaica's vast supply of folk stories. The sources of these stories are as diverse as **Maroon** enclaves, religious ceremonies, and legends. All of this material is combined in Bennett's writing and works for the stage. Her output has been recognized and honored by the Jamaican populace. One such award is the Order of Jamaica, bestowed on Bennett in 1974.

Her decades-long career started in the 1970s when she began preserving the folk history of Jamaican culture. Bennett was raised by her mother and grandmother and educated at St. Simon's College and Excelsior College. She then moved to England to study at the Royal Academy of Dramatic Art. Bennett's writing style involves the use of dialect. This is not a practice that was approved of at the time; however, she persevered and raised this style of writing to an art form. Bennett's work in Jamaican culture and folklore studies has been instrumental in promoting the culture of the island abroad in the United Kingdom and United States.

BENNETT, MICHAEL "HOME T" (1962–)

"Home T" Bennett entered the Jamaican music scene in the early 1980s. He emerged as a **dancehall** presence with the help of **Cocoa Tea**, with whom he worked on several projects. He has also worked with **Shabba Ranks** and Cocoa T, having appeared on numerous recordings with each. His work with Shabba Ranks has crossed over into the new millennium with *Super Best* and *Greatest Hits*. In 2003, **Home T** appeared on *Rhythm King*, produced by King Jammy.

BENNETT, MIKEY (1962–)

Active on the Jamaican music scene since the 1980s, Mikey Bennett has served as a singer, producer, songwriter, and vocal arranger for a variety of artists and labels. Bennett began his music career as a member of the vocal quartet Home T4 in 1977, when he was recruited by the group. They had success in 1980 with the single "Irons in the Fire." In the late 1980s, **Cocoa Tea**, **Home T**, and **Shabba Ranks** formed a supergroup. They worked with producers **King Jammy** and **Gussie Clarke** to create their 1989 album *Hold On*. The release was a smash hit and yielded two successful singles, "Pirate's Anthem" and "Who She Love." Since this highly successful debut, Home T has gone on to release three more albums, *Hot Body* (1990), *Red Hot* (1991), and *Another One for the Road* (1992). Despite his success, Bennett relocated to Philadelphia to start his own label.

In the early 1990s, Bennett and Patrick Lindsay started the Two Friends label. They continued to record in the Music Works Studios, working on hits for **Dennis Brown**, Cocoa Tea, **Cutty Ranks**, and Shabba Ranks. Bennett and Lindsey produced the single "No More Walls" for Dennis Brown, and the tune became a big hit. Other Two Friends-produced hits include "Loverman," "Ram Dance," and "Show Them the Way." In 1992, Bennett again moved on, this time to producing with **Clifton "Specialist" Dillon** as Twin City Productions. This collective had international hits with **Chevelle Franklin** and Shabba Ranks's "Mr. Loverman," and **Maxi Priest** and Shabba's single "Housecall." Bennett received co-author credit for these two singles, which charted in the American Top 40. Twin City Productions went on to enjoy success with several other releases.

BENNETT, VAL (d. 1991)

Lovall Bennett was a tenor saxophonist of high reputation who began his career in the 1950s. He worked with two of Jamaica's most prominent producers, **Clancy Eccles** and **Lee "Scratch" Perry**. In the late 1940s, Bennett was the head of his own dance band called the Val Bennett Orchestra, whose members included a young **Ernest Ranglin**. Due to his strong studio connections, Bennett appears on many recordings from the mid-1960s to contemporary re-releases. He appears on recordings by artists such as **Theophilus Beckford**, **Pat Kelly**, **Barrington Levy**, **Delroy Wilson**, and many others. As a session player, Bennett sang vocals and performed on the saxophone, horn, and trombone.

BEVERLEY'S RECORDS

Beverley's Records was originally a record store located at 135 Orange Street, Kingston, Jamaica. Leslie Kong, one of three Chinese-Jamaican brothers working in Kingston, ran the store. In the early 1960s, **Jimmy Cliff** persuaded Kong to enter the recording industry. Cliff convinced Kong to produce his single "Hurricane Hattie" with the B-side "Dearest Beverley." Although the two were inexperienced in the recording industry, Kong's financial backing allowed them to hire veteran personnel. The first single was a success and was followed by a large number of others. Throughout the 1960s, the artist roster at Beverley's continued to increase both in size and popularity. In 1962, Kong recorded **Bob Marley's** first single at **Federal Records**. The single comprised two **ska** tunes, "Judge Not" and "One Cup of Coffee." Marley and Kong also recorded the song "Terror" during this session.

Kong's next step into the recording business came with the 1963 **Desmond Dekker** partnership. This resulted in the recording of the Dekker hit "Honour Your Mother and Father." Kong expanded his label by signing a licensing agreement with the UK Black Swan label. That lasted from 1963 to 1965. During this two-year period, Kong recorded several prolific Jamaican artists including **Laurel Aiken** and **Stranger Cole**. Next, Kong signed a new licensing agreement with the UK-based Pyramid label. A product of this business relationship was Desmond Dekker's UK hit "The Israelites." It was also in the latter half of the 1960s that Bob Marley returned to Beverley's Records. This time he brought the more mature Wailers lineup that included **Peter Tosh** and **Bunny Wailer**. The group recorded the tracks "Cheer Up," "Soul Shakedown Party," "Caution," "Stop the Train," and "Soon Come." The late 1970s were a productive and hit-filled period for Kong. He recorded **Ken Boothe**, the **Gaylads**, **Derrick Morgan**, **Bruce Ruffin**, and **Delroy Wilson**.

The success of the label seemed certain to continue into the 1970s; however, in 1971 Kong suffered a fatal heart attack. With Kong dead at age thirty-eight, Beverley's Label soon faded into obscurity. Subsequent compilations were released in the 1980s, such as *The King Kong Compilation*, issued by **Island** in 1981.

BIG JOE (1955–)

Born Joseph Spalding in west Kingston, Jamaica, in 1955, Joe began recording in the early 1970s with producer Harry Mudie, for whom he cut the tracks "Black Stick Rock," "Run Girl," and "Woodcutter Skank." He then moved on to work with producer Winston Edwards. Together this pair recorded "Selassie Skank" and "Weed Specialist." "Selassie Skank" went on to be a significant hit with the assistance of Dennis Harris's UK-based DIP label. The song uses the "Try Me" rhythm from Roman Stewart. Joe's next move was to **Studio One** where he recorded several other hits. He also set up his own **sound system**, Small Axe Hi Fi, and a record label. Big Joe continued to record into the 1980s and is found on a wide variety of compilations from the 1990s. After the turn of the century Joe became a successful hip hop producer. He is credited as the producer of LL Cool J's 2002 release *10*. Additionally, he worked as a programmer and mixer for the 2002 AZ release *Aziatic*. Most recently, Joe is credited as an engineer on the David Hollister release *Things in the Game Done Changed* (2003).

BIG MOUNTAIN

Big Mountain surfaced as a California-based **reggae** band in the mid-1990s. They achieved early success in 1994 with a version of Peter Frampton's "Baby, I Love Your Way." The band plays a diluted from of reggae. However, they do have some solid credentials in a pair of band members. Jamaican-born lead/rhythm guitarist **Tony Chin** and drummer **Santa Davis** both worked with **Peter Tosh** and were members of the **Soul Syndicate**. Big Mountain formed in San Diego in the mid-1990s under the name the Rainbow Warriors. The lineup included Chin, Davis, Quino (vocals, born James

McWhinney), Billy Stoll (keyboard), and Lynn Copland (bass). The original lineup did not include Davis, but rather drummers Gregory Blackney and Lance Rhodes. Additionally, the original rhythm guitarist was Jerome Cruz and the first keyboard player was Manfred Reinke. This early lineup released *Wake Up* (1992) on the Quality Record label, yielding the charting single "Touch My Light." The band supported this album with two years of touring that culminated in an appearance at the 1993 Reggae on the River Festival.

The following year, the band membership began to change. The most solid lineup, Chin, Quino, Copland, Davis, and Stoll, scored success with the Frampton cover for the movie *Reality Bites*. The single also appeared on the 1994 release *Unity*. This crossover appeal of the track, along with its extended exposure, led to it becoming a worldwide hit. Early success was spurred by concert exposure with **Black Uhuru**, **Steel Pulse**, and Peter Tosh. Regardless of mainstream success, the band has always had a solid Jamaican following, substantiated by being the headline act for two consecutive **Reggae Sunsplash** concerts (1994 and 1995). The band released *Resistance* in 1995 and *Free Up* in 1997. These two albums were recorded with the assistance of some of the premier members of the reggae elite, including **Sly and Robbie**. The *Free Up* album featured co-writing credits by singer/songwriter Sheryl Crow; however, it failed to reach the level of success that the early efforts had achieved.

BIG THREE

Big Three is the nickname given to **Coxsone Dodd**, **Vincent "King" Edwards**, and **Duke Reid**. Together these three men ran the Jamaican music scene though most of the 1950s. This was achieved in part by having the best **sound system** in central Kingston. The "Beat Street" area was where many sound system operators worked throughout the early 1950s. The path to sound system superiority involved having the best and latest American R&B records, a powerful system to play them on, and often some enforcers to sabotage the other systems. It was through these means that the Three stayed on top of Kingston's sound system wars through the 1950s. In the early 1960s, the Big Three went on to rule the Jamaican recording industry by starting their own labels. Each became a prolific producer; all three are responsible for recording much of the seminal early reggae material.

BIG YOUTH (1955–)

Born Manley Augustus Buchanan in February 1955 in Kingston, Jamaica, Big Youth earned his nickname before he entered the music business. His father was a policeman and his mother a preacher. Youth left school at age fourteen and found work as a cab driver. His next job was as a mechanic at two Kingston-area hotels. He was branded Big Youth as a lanky teenager working in the Kingston Sheraton Hotel.

Big Youth's musical reputation began when he first started **toasting** at area parties. He gained confidence, and by the late 1960s he had a small fan base. His big break came in the early 1970s when he began **DJing** for Lord Tipperton's **sound system**. Youth quickly became the most popular DJ on the sound system, and he decided to put his skills on vinyl. His first single, "Movie Man," on **Gregory Isaacs** and Errol Dunkley's African Museum label, did not do well. However, subsequent singles began to build his recording reputation. His recording career changed when he teamed with **Gussie Clarke** on the single "Killer," which was recorded over an **Augustus Pablo** recording. Together the two also released the hit "Tippertone Rocking." Youth next teamed with producer **Keith Hudson**, who helped him record "S.90 Skank." The song about the popular Honda motorcycle rocketed Big Youth up the charts. The single was followed by an equally successful effort with "Can You Keep a Secret."

In a move that foreshadowed the hip hop trend, Youth had red, green, and gold jewels inserted in his top front teeth to give him a distinct appearance. Next, he released a set of four singles for **Prince Buster** that further solidified his position on the Jamaican charts. The next step was to release a full-length album, which Big Youth did in 1973 with *Screaming Target*. The album was so well received that it lasted on the Jamaican charts for an entire year. At this point, only **Bob Marley** rivaled Youth's reputation as the biggest artist on the island. Youth then teamed with **Sonia Pottinger** for the hit single "Facts of Life." His style had matured, and he had innovated a more relaxed approach to toasting than did his rivals **Dennis Alcapone** and **U-Roy**.

In 1974, Youth launched his own record label called Negusa Nagast, Amharic for "King of Kings." He also opened the label Augustus Buchanan in the same

Big Youth. © *UrbanImage.tv.*

year. These labels released successful material, but Youth still periodically worked with producers such as **Joe Gibbs**, **Lee "Scratch" Perry**, and **Prince Buster**. The outcome of working with Perry was a version of the **Wailers** song "Keep on Moving." His list of singles from the 1970s is extensive and makes Big Youth a premier Jamaican artist. In 1977, Youth and **Dennis Brown** staged a tour of England that was immediately successful.

From the late 1970s to the present, Big Youth has continued his release of quality material with a series of albums including *Dreadlocks Dread* (1978), *Isaiah First Prophet of Old* (1978), *Progress* (1979), *Reggae Gi Dem Dub* (1979), *The Dancing Dread Inna Fine Style* (1983), *Manifestation* (1988), *Jamming in the House of Dread—Live* (1991), *Higher Ground* (1997), and *DJ Originators* (2001).

BIGGA RANKS (1965–)

Bigga Ranks has spent time in Jamaica, New York, and Massachusetts, and derives his name from his two favorite styles of music, **reggae** and hip hop. Bigga has been active on My Show Called Life Records, releasing the D-Tension produced single "Clubbin." The single will appear on an as-yet-untitled album on the My Show Called Life Records label.

BINGY BUNNY (1956–1994)

Guitarist Eric "Bingy Bunny" Lamont was born in 1956. He began his career in Jamaican popular music in the early 1970s as half of the duo Bongo Herman and Bingy

Bunny. Together this pair released the 1971 hit "Know Far-I." His partnership with Herman did not last, and by the mid-1970s he departed to join the **Morwells**. With the Morwells, Bunny sang and played lead guitar until he left to join the newly forming **Roots Radics**. The Radics included **Errol "Flabba" Holt** (who had also been in the Morwells), **Lincoln "Style" Scott**, Earl Fitzsimons, and Bunny. The group was backed by some of the most important artists in **reggae** during the 1980s. They were considered **Gregory Isaacs's** backup band and did session work with artists such as **Israel Vibration**, **Sugar Minott**, **Prince Far I**, and many others. Bunny played rhythm guitar for the group during the period when it was considered by many to be the best reggae backing band in Jamaica.

Also during this period, the Roots Radics worked on their own material. An example of this was the **Henry "Junjo" Lawes** single "Bounty Hunter." As the style of popular music changed from reggae to **dancehall** at the end of the 1970s, the Roots Radics helped to push the new sound forward. Throughout his work with session or touring bands, Bunny continued to pursue solo work. He released a series of solo albums as a singer and guitarist as he worked for others.

In 1994, Bunny died of prostate cancer and the Roots Radics disbanded. The group did re-form in 1996 to issue an album commemorating Bunny's achievements. Released on the **RAS** imprint, the album *Kingston 12 Toughie: A Tribute to Bingy Bunny* revels in the achievements of one of reggae music's most important and innovative guitarists.

BINNS, SONNY (c. 1955–)
Sonny Binns is the founding member and keyboard player for the UK **reggae** band the **Cimarons**. Together with **Franklyn Dunn**, Locksley Gichie (guitar), and Winston Reid (vocals), Binns helped form the band in 1967. Jah "Bunny" Donaldson (drums), formerly of **Matumbi**, joined the group later. The group released five albums that spanned the 1970s and 1980s. All of the band members are native Jamaicans who migrated to Britain in the mid-1960s. Before moving to Britain, the group members were employed primarily as session musicians who worked with acts such as **Jimmy Cliff**.

BLACK ARK STUDIOS
Lee "Scratch" Perry opened Black Ark Studios in the late 1970s. Working as a producer and engineer, Perry recorded many **reggae** legends in his studio. One of his earliest triumphs was recording **Bob Marley** on a series of early hits. Perry backed Marley with his studio musicians the **Upsetters**, which included **Aston "Family Man" Barrett** (bass) and **Carlton "Carlie" Barrett** (drums). This pair of brothers would end up as the longstanding rhythm section for Bob Marley's **Wailers** band. Two standout songs produced during these sessions were "Duppy Conqueror" and "Small Axe." Island Records then lured Marley and the Wailers away from Black Ark. The late 1970s and 1980s were filled with active recording at the studio. However, Perry began to believe that he was losing control of the studio and set fire to it. In 1997, **Island Records** released a three-disc compilation of the Black Ark material titled *Arkology.*

BLACK SCORPIO
Along with Jack Scorpio were other aliases used by Maurice Johnson. Johnson is a famed producer of roots reggae music whose reputation grew in the early 1980s and who continues to be a force in reggae music to the present. He got his start in the music business when he launched his own Black Scorpio sound system in the mid-

1980s. His sound was popular, and he quickly parlayed his success with the opening of the Black Scorpio Studios in Kingston, Jamaica. Johnson cultivated a strong stable of talent, and his products were highly sought after.

From the mid-1980s to the present, the Black Scorpio label has issued material by Determine, **Admiral Tibet**, **Buju Banton**, **Beenie Man**, **Everton Blender**, **Dennis Brown**, **General Trees**, **Gregory Isaacs**, **Barrington Levy**, **Echo Minott**, **Frankie Paul**, **Tony Rebel**, **Sanchez**, **Garnet Silk**, and many others. Most material was issued on the seven-inch format, but Johnson did release several full-length albums. Most notable were **Anthony B's** *Wiseman Chant*, **Capleton's** *Praises to the King*, **Johnny Clarke's** *Come with Me*, and **Frankie Paul's** *Blessed Be*. The Black Scorpio studio, with Maurice Johnson at the controls, gained a reputation as one of the best studios in Kingston and remains a strong and influential outlet of reggae and **dancehall** music.

BLACK SLATE

Black Slate was formed in London in 1974 through the efforts of musicians from several countries. The two London-born members were **Elroy Bailey** (bass) and George Brightly. Vocalist Keith Drummond, Chris Hanson (guitarist), and Desmond Mahoney (drums) hailed from Jamaica, and Cledwyn Rogers (rhythm guitar) was from Anguilla. Early on, the group worked backup for Jamaican touring acts like **Delroy Wilson**. Their most productive period was from the late 1970s to the early 1990s. The group scored a UK hit with "Sticks Man" in 1976. In 1980, they had two charting singles with "Boom Boom" and "Amigo." There followed a decade of success during which five albums were released, with the last two on the **Alligator** label. The early 1980s were their most successful period; during this time, their sound was characteristic of UK **reggae**.

BLACK UHURU

A legendary **reggae** group formed in 1974, Black Uhuru took its name from the Swahili word for "freedom"; its members included **Derrick "Duckie" Simpson**, Euvin "Don Carlos" Spencer, and Rudolph "Garth" Dennis, all of whom were from the Waterhouse district of Kingston, Jamaica. After a few years, Spencer and Dennis left the group; Simpson was left at the helm. He recruited Michael Rose and Errol Wilson to make the group again a trio. The three went into the studio and recorded the album *Love Crisis* (1977) with **Prince (King) Jammy** at the

Black Uhuru. © *UrbanImage.tv.*

controls. The standout single from the album was "I Love King Selassie," which became a classic over the next thirty years.

Next, the group added another new member, female singer **Sandra "Puma" Jones**. Puma's voice rounded out the harmonies and gave them a high end that had been lacking. The newly fortified group teamed with **Sly and Robbie** in the early 1980s and released a series of successful albums including *Sinsemilla* (1980); *Black Sounds of Freedom*, *Black Uhuru*, and *Guess Who's Coming to Dinner* (all in 1981); *Chill Out* and *Tear It Up—Live* (1983); and *Anthem* (1984). In 1985, the group won the Grammy Award for Best Reggae Album in the first year the category was offered.

In 1986, Michael Rose departed the group to pursue a solo career and was replaced by **Junior Reid**. The late 1980s saw the albums keep coming. In 1986, *Brutal* was issued, in 1987 *Positive*, and in 1988 there was another live album. In 1990, Puma died of cancer at roughly the same time the original three members re-formed. With Spencer and Davis back in the fold, Simpson and Black Uhuru moved forward into the early 1990s. They stayed together into the mid-1990s with the addition of Andrew Bees. Albums from the period included *Iron Storm* (1981), *Mystical Truth* (1993), *Strongg* (1994), *Black Sounds of Freedom Remix* (1999), and *Dynasty* (2001). The band continued to issue material into the new millennium.

BLACKA DREAD RECORDS

An affiliate of Greensleeves Records, the Blacka Dread imprint has released several seven-inch singles. The artists appearing on the label include **Anthony B**, **Beenie Man**, **Eek-A-Mouse**, Fred Locks, **Luciano** and the **Firehouse Crew**, **Mikey General**, **Frankie Paul**, and **Sizzla**. The Blacka Dread imprint has released a variety of singles and two full-length albums by these artists. They have issued Frankie Paul's album *Fire Deh A Mus Mus Tail* and Nitty Gritty's full length *Jah in the Family*.

BLACKWELL, CHRISTOPHER (1937–)

Christopher "Chris" Blackwell was born in London, England, in 1937. His parents were both affiliated with Jamaica: his father was a major in the Jamaican Regiment, and his mother's family had financial ties to the island's sugar and Appleton rum industries. Blackwell was educated at several of England's prestigious schools until he stopped attending at age eighteen. During his late teens and early twenties, Blackwell split his time between London and Kingston. While in Jamaica he worked a variety of jobs including assistant aide-de-camp to the British high commissioner.

During this phase of his early life, Blackwell made his first foray into the record industry when he opened R&B Records to record a north-shore jazz band from Bermuda. Another facet of his fledgling record enterprise in the mid-1950s was the importation of the latest American records from New York. He scratched out the original labels and sold the records to the sound system operators for use in the dance. In the late 1950s, Blackwell scored his first hit with the song "Boogie in My Bones" by **Laurel Aiken**, which was recorded at **Federal Records**. In the 1960s, Blackwell's record enterprise grew, and in 1962 he launched the **Island Records** label. It began in Jamaica but moved to England after the island declared independence. This move to the United Kingdom allowed Blackwell to compete with other Jamaican labels and make money from them as their European distributor.

The year 1964 saw the first major hit for the label with the release of **Millie Small's** single "My Boy Lollipop." The song was a smash hit in the United Kingdom and the United States and gave Blackwell enough capital to expand his label. This expansion was into the rock and roll style, and he signed the Spencer Davis Group with a young Steve Winwood on keyboards. By 1962, Blackwell had already issued twenty-six singles on the Island imprint. Though the rest of the 1960s, Blackwell and Island continued to have success but gradually moved away from the reggae market. By 1968, his only reggae acts were **Jimmy Cliff** and **Jackie Edwards**, while the label's rock roster continued to grow with the addition of Jethro Tull; Free; Fairport Convention; and Emerson, Lake, and Palmer.

In the early 1970s, Blackwell's success with rock acts continued to grow, but his own remained on the fringe of the reggae scene. This involvement with reggae was heightened when in 1972 Jimmy Cliff was rocketed to notoriety by the movie *The Harder They Come*. Cliff then promptly left Island, but a short time later **Bob Marley** sought out Blackwell after the Wailers had been stranded in London. Marley asked Blackwell to finance a single, and Blackwell agreed to put up the money for a full album, which was quite uncommon in the reggae market at the time. The product was the album *Catch a Fire* (1973), which Marley and the Wailers wrote and recorded and Blackwell remixed and overdubbed with rock guitar, organ, and clavinet lines. The album was released in its original Zippo lighter packaging in 1973, but initially sold poorly. The second Marley release through Blackwell was *Burnin'* (1973), which left the reggae spirit more intact. Eric Clapton noticed the song "I Shot the Sheriff," and his own version of the song topped the charts.

In 1975, Blackwell and the Wailers scored their first chart success with the single "No Woman, No Cry." This was followed by the release of *Natty Dread*, which was the first album after the exit of **Peter Tosh** and **Bunny Wailer**. The album was a runaway hit and drew Blackwell back into the reggae business. He went on to sign several major bands on the Jamaican horizon including **Aswad**, **Burning Spear**, and **Toots Hibbert**.

The end of the 1970s was filled with success for Blackwell. He gave Marley the house at 56 Hope Road; it subsequently became the headquarters and studio for the Wailers. Further, with Blackwell's distribution system in place, Jamaican reggae was exported to the United Kingdom as fast as it was being made. In 1977, he opened Compass Point Studios in Nassau, and the reggae and rock elite flocked to record in the state-of-the-art facility. In 1980, Blackwell again made a sound business decision when he signed the "Riddim Twins" **Sly and Robbie** as a production team for the label. The following year Marley died at age thirty-five, resulting in a contract dispute between the remaining Wailers and Blackwell. Through the mid-1980s, Blackwell continued to sign top talent from both the reggae and the rock arenas. Next, Blackwell began to diversify his businesses. He opened the film company Island Alive and a Canadian branch of his record label, but began cutting back their Jamaican roster.

Through the rest of the 1980s, Blackwell continued to favor his rock artists. In 1989, he began a deal to sell his Island Records label to A&M/PolyGram. With this move the label was no longer independent, but Blackwell stayed with the Island until 1997. Next, he opened Island Outpost to develop hotels in the Caribbean and south Florida. After formally severing his ties with Island, Blackwell turned his energy toward his new Palm Company, which was a record label (RykoPalm Records) and film production company (Palm Pictures).

The year 2001 saw Blackwell inducted into the Rock and Roll Hall of Fame. Two years later he opened the Goldeneye Film Festival, which creates an enormous draw for the island. In addition, Blackwell launched a songwriter's camp, to be followed by a scriptwriter's workshop to foster creativity in these areas. Further, he branched out into producing plays in Jamaica, sponsoring the performance of several single-actor productions. In 2004, Blackwell was awarded one of Jamaica's highest honors, the Order of Jamaica, for his impact on and contributions to the island.

BLAKE, KEITH. *See* PRINCE ALLAH

BLAKE, PAUL. *See* PAUL, FRANKIE

BLENDER, EVERTON (c. 1960–)

Born Everton Dennis Williams in Clarendon, Jamaica, Blender grew up in the west Kingston ghetto, where he held a variety of menial jobs. He soon realized that this work was keeping him from his true calling of singing and returned to Clarendon. Blender went into the studio and recorded a variety of singles, but none of them made an impression on the Jamaican listening audience until 1991's "Create a Sound." His early work included the singles "Where Is the Love" and the 1985 Danny Barclay production "Baba Black Sheep." The song was the singer's description of his life and **Rastafarian** faith, and it was a major success. Next, Blender worked on the Destiny sound system where he met and befriended **Garnet Silk**.

In 1994, Blender issued his debut full-length record, called *Lift Up Your Head*, on the Star Trail imprint. Blender had forged his connection with Star Trail when his friend Silk introduced him to label owner Richard Bell. The album featured songs such as "Bring Di Kutchie," "My Father's Home," "Gwaan Natty," and the title track. There followed a series of successful singles such as "Bob Marley," "Piece of the Blender," and

Everton Blender. © *UrbanImage.tv.*

"Blend Dem." Blender's style was a mixture of roots reggae sentiment and **dancehall** beats. This work was compiled on 1996's release *Piece of the Bender: The Singles* on the **Heartbeat** imprint.

Next, Blender opened his own label, Blend Dem Productions, to retain greater control over his creativity. Blender's relationship with Heartbeat grew; in 1999 his Blend Dem Productions issued *Rootsman Credential* on Heartbeat. The album included several standout songs such as "Ghetto People Song" and "These Hands" and sparked a tour of the United States, United Kingdom, and the Caribbean. The tour resulted in a live album also on Heartbeat, called *Live at the White River Reggae Bash* (2000). Next, Blender issued a collection of his up-and-coming acts over rhythms that he had crafted on Heartbeat's *Dance Hall Liberation* album. The release included material by **Anthony B**, **Tony Rebel**, Richie Spice, and others. This album exhibited Blender's skills as a producer, and he continued his work with a variety of new artists. Blender issued another album of his own material in 2001, *Visionary*, again on the Heartbeat label. This album adhered to the mold he had cast and included guest appearances by **Beenie Man**, **Marcia Griffiths**, Anthony B, and Tony Rebel.

More recently, Blender issued another Heartbeat release called *King Man* in 2003. This was again created through Blend Dem Productions and featured the songs "Hail the King," "Gone a Country," and the title track. Everton Blender continues to be a major force in reggae music both in his writing and his production work.

BLONDY, ALPHA (1953–)

Born Seydou Kone into the Jula tribe in Dimbokoro, Ivory Coast, in 1953, Kone was raised by his grandmother, who called him Blondy. To his nickname the young singer added the Greek *Alpha*. Together these words meant "first bandit." Early in his life he was sent to study at Hunter College in New York and then to Columbia University in adherence to his parent's wishes that he become an English teacher. Instead Blondy wanted to become a musician, and he played in a variety of bands in New York. He also discovered the music of **Bob Marley** and began singing it in a variety of languages.

Blondy's break came when a friend got him into an area talent show. He was a sensation. He gained success in his homeland as a bandleader whose songs were based on the rhythms, instrumentation, and militant spirit of roots reggae. His period of early success spanned the mid-1980s, during which he built his fan base both in West Africa and around the world. His music transcended geographic boundaries, and Blondy gradually became known worldwide. He facilitated a world audience through his ability to sing in the French, English, Hebrew, Arabic, and Dioula languages. Among his early recordings was *Cocody Rock* (1984). There followed an incendiary album, *Apartheid Is Nazism* (1987), which was a hit despite its controversial material. Next, Blondy traveled to Jamaica and recorded his followup album *Jerusalem* (1986), with the **Wailers** as his backing band. He played live with a twelve-piece band called the Solar System, and the product was reggae music with an African flavor and militant **Rastafarian** lyrics. *Revolution* was the next album, issued in 1987. With this, Blondy made his reputation on the international scale.

In 1992, Blondy issued *Masada*, which was made available around the world and led to the 1998 release of *Yitzhak Rabin*. In 2001, Blondy was riding the popularity of several international successes and issued *Paris Percy*, which was followed by *Elohim* (2005). Alpha Blondy remains at the top of the international reggae music scene, and his music continues to be issued on new releases, live albums, and compilations.

Alpha Blondy. © *UrbanImage.tv.*

BOB AND MARCIA

Bob Andy and **Marcia Griffiths** emerged in the late 1960s. They teamed in the wake of Andy's exit from the **Paragons**. Andy formed the Paragons in the mid-1960s and had hits such as "Love at Last," but he left the group to work as a solo artist. At **Clement "Coxsone" Dodd's Studio One**, Andy recorded several successful singles, including the 1966 hits "Going Home," "Feeling Soul," and "Too Experienced." He then teamed with Griffiths to recommend producer **Harry "Harry J" Johnson**. The pair scored a major hit with the **reggae** version of the Nina Simone song "Young, Gifted, and Black." The song charted in Jamaica and the United Kingdom in 1970 and won the duo significant popularity. The single sold over half a million copies in the United Kingdom and Europe, and Bob and Marcia appeared on the television show *Top of the Pops*. Next, the pair issued a reggae version of "Pied Piper," by Crispian St. Peters. Interest in the duo subsequently faded, and they split to pursue solo careers. Andy went back to releasing periodic solo works, and Griffiths joined **Rita Marley** and **Judy Mowatt** to form **Bob Marley's** backup trio the **I-Threes**.

BOB MARLEY AND THE WAILERS. *See* **MARLEY, ROBERT NESTA**

BONGO HERMAN. *See* **HERMAN, BONGO**

BONNER, JOSEPH. *See* **SPANNER BANNER**

BOOKER, CEDELLA. *See* **MARLEY, CEDELLA BOOKER**

BOOM SHAKA
The legendary Boom Shaka is a roots reggae group founded by Trevy Felix in 1986. The band released its first single, "Dig a Dis, Dig a Dat" with the B-side "Ponderous," and realized that they needed to fill out their sound. They added two new members and released their first album, *Creation*, in 1987 on their own label, Baga Style. Celluloid Records picked up the release and re-issued it in 1988 with the addition of several new songs. *Creation* climbed to number twenty-seven on the Cash Box World Music charts and was followed in 1991 with the album *Freedom Now* from Sling Shot Records. Subsequent albums include 1992's *Best Defense* on Liberty Records, *Freedom Now* on Stone Mountain Records in 1996, *Rebel Lion* in 1998 on **Shanachie** Records, and 2000's re-release of *Creation* on Baga Style Records. The group released its latest album, *Fertile Ground*, in the summer of 2004.

The collective called Boom Shaka has had a stable lineup since 1990. This has allowed the group to cultivate a signature sound that has popular appeal, yet is conscious in sentiment. The Boom Shaka sound has the roots elements of **Steel Pulse** and the mass appeal of **Third World**. The group consists of Trevy Felix (vocals) and Ray "Bass-I" Felix, who are brothers from Dominica. The lead guitarist is veteran Lester "Lesterfari" Johnson from the United States. Antigua-born Binghi-I Cornwell is the keyboard player, and Wadi Gad is the Trinidadian drummer. This international lineup has had great success throughout the 1990s and 2000s. Since 1996, the band has staged multiple tours and list more than 100 live shows. Their most recent accomplishments include the latest album and an international tour that included dates in Ethiopia.

BOOTHE, KEN (1948–)
Ken Boothe was born in the west Kingston ghetto called Denham Town, Jamaica, in 1948. His earliest exposure to music came when he began singing in school. In the early 1960s, he entered the music business, and by age eighteen he had a hit with his single "The Train." His earliest recordings were made with producer **Wilburn "Stranger"**

Cole and included the songs "Artibella," "Thick in Your Love," and "World's Fair." Boothe sang in the **rock steady** style, but his influences were as diverse as Mahalia Jackson, the Temptations, and Wilson Pickett. Boothe never moved too far from his American soul roots, as he often covered soul standards for singles and on albums. In 1966, he recorded the single "The Train Is Coming," which was rerecorded with **Shaggy** in 1995 for the *Boombastic* album. The original recording of the single contained backing work by the **Wailers**. The song's success led to its use in the film *Money Train* and several subsequent cover versions, including one by **UB40**.

Boothe recorded his first album in 1968 under the production of **Clement "Coxsone" Dodd**. The record was titled *Mr. Rock Steady* and contained a number of standout singles such as "Home, Home" and "When I Fall in Love." This was followed by a series of other well-received singles. In 1974, Boothe recorded "Everything I Own," which was generally credited with bringing **reggae** music fever to the United Kingdom. It was the first Jamaican single to earn an English gold record and spawned the growth of the fledgling market. He followed this international hit with the acclaimed single "Crying over You." From the late 1960s into the 1970s, Boothe's style changed in accordance with the dominant popular music style on the island. He made the move from rock steady to reggae and remained a potent force. Also, like his many Jamaican recording artists, Boothe began moving from one producer to the next and worked with **Keith Hudson**, **Sonia Pottinger**, and **Phil Pratt**.

Boothe continued to release material through the late 1970s to the 1980s, but it was not until the mid-1990s that he again had an international hit, this time with the **Leslie Kong** production "Freedom Street." He followed this up with further **Beverley's** singles such as "Why Baby Why" and "Now I Know." Again the singer made the rounds of Jamaican producers and worked with **Lloyd Charmers**, **Winston "Niney" Holness**, and **Tappa Zukie**. The singer's smooth, deep, and emotive voice made him a perennial favorite, and with twenty albums in his catalog, Boothe continued to make an impact into the new millennium.

BOUNTY KILLER (1972–)

Bounty Killer was born Rodney Basil Price in Kingston, Jamaica, in 1972. His mother soon relocated him and his eight siblings to the Riverton City area, once known as the Dungle. Price began learning about music from his father, who was a **sound system** owner who played in and around Kingston. This was when Price got his start, and he soon was grooming his **toasting** skills. At age fourteen, Price was shot by a stray bullet in a flurry of gunfire between warring political factions. While he convalesced in the hospital, Price hatched a plan for revenge on those who shot him. He took on the Bounty Killer name and became a voice for the underprivileged and desolate in the ghetto. Killer began to achieve this goal by plying his lyrical trade at an increasing number of dances in an ever-broadening region.

As Killer's profile grew, he went to the Waterhouse district of the Kingston ghetto to look up producer **King Jammy** for a recording session. Jammy took Killer into the studio based on the popularity the young **DJ** had acquired working the sound systems with songs such as "Dub Fi Dub." Killer recorded "Coppershot," but Jammy was not keen on releasing it, as it had gun culture posturing in its lyrics. Jammy's brother Uncle T disagreed and released the single. The song became a hardcore hit in Jamaica and went on to be an underground hit in New York. There followed a string of hardcore singles with lyrics of gun culture and violence.

With his initial success, Killer was on his way to becoming a force in Jamaican pop-

Bounty Killer. © *UrbanImage.tv.*

ular music. In 1995, he increased his creative control when he left Jammy and launched Scare Dem Productions and Priceless Records. Killer continued to build his reputation and often battled with other DJs. His hardcore style was first unleashed on **Beenie Man**, and many other DJs also fell into the battle of words that ensued. In the mid-1990s, Beenie and Killer realized the negative effect their feud was having on the industry and decided to sign a peace treaty.

Killer's songs are divided by lyric content. He has issued songs that deal with issues of love, pain, revolution, and political upheaval. His material is further divided pre and post-treaty. Also in the mid-1990s, Killer began to issue full-length recordings. The first two were *Roots, Reality and Culture* and *Face to Face*, released on VP Records in 1994. Killer followed this early success with *Down in the Ghetto* in 1995. In 1996, he issued *No Argument* and *My Xperience*. The latter was a huge success. *My Xperience* was issued as a double disc and spent six months at number one on the **reggae** Billboard charts. Further, the album had tremendous hip hop crossover appeal, as Killer had Busta Rhymes, Wu-Tang Clan, and the Fugees as guests on the release. His followup album *Ghetto Gramma* maintained his popularity. *Next Millennium* in 1998 was another huge crossover success with guest appearances by Coco Brovas, Mobb Deep, and Wyclef Jean. Killer's next album was titled *The 5th Element*.

The new millennium saw a renewed interest in **dancehall** and Bounty Killer's music. In 2001, Killer joined with the American band No Doubt for their song "Hey Baby" on their *Rocksteady* album. The album went three times platinum, and the single was a fixture on the charts. The single's popularity led to an appearance as part of the 2002 Super Bowl halftime show as well as constant rotation on MTV. Also in 2002, Killer released two albums, *Ghetto Dictionary Volume I: Art of War* and *Ghetto Dictionary Volume II: Mystery*. The pair of releases was successful, and the *Mystery* album went on to garner Killer a reggae Grammy nomination and critical acclaim. Bounty Killer remains in the upper echelon of contemporary dancehall favorites.

BOVELL, DENNIS (1953–)

Dennis Bovell was born in St. Peter, Barbados, in 1953. He immigrated to London as a youth and spent his formative years there. Early on, Bovell was entranced by **reggae** and **dub music**, and he built his own Jah Sufferer sound system in north London. He went on to co-found the UK reggae band **Matumbi** and produced and recorded a variety of other acts. Matumbi is widely credited as one of the best reggae bands formed in the United Kingdom. In addition to production work, Bovell was an accomplished guitarist and often went by the nickname Blackbeard. Along with his other work, Bovell also issued solo work and dub albums. In 1978, he issued *Strictly Dubwise*, which garnered him additional attention. He went on to produce punk material for the Pop

Group and the Slits. His next dub album, *I Wah Dub*, appeared in 1980. He followed this in 1981 with *Brain Damage*, which had a marked rock sensibility. In the 1980s, Bovell was a highly sought-after producer who worked with a variety of artists including **Alpha Blondy**, **Trevor Hartley**, **Linton Kwesi Johnson**, and **Janet Kay**. Bovell also formed a group called the Dub Band to back up Johnson's **dub poetry** in the studio and for live performances. With the Dub Band, Bovell issued *Audio Active* in 1986.

BRAMMER, ROBERT. *See* EASTWOOD, CLINT

BREVETT, LLOYD (c. 1955–)
Lloyd Brevett entered the Jamaican popular music scene when he was recruited to join the legendary **Skatalites** band. Brevett signed on as the group's bass player. The group formed in June 1964 and lasted until the end of 1965. Although they did not have a lasting physical presence, their musical impact was staggering. They defined the **ska** sound during its heyday and backed the majority of important ska singers in the middle of the decade. The band came together as the result of **Clement "Coxsone" Dodd's** need for an in-house group for his **Studio One** facility. Dodd had hired **Tommy McCook** to form a band and lead it; in turn, McCook recruited his old friends from the Alpha School. He hired **Roland Alphonso**, **Lloyd Brevett**, Lloyd Knibb, Lester Sterling, **Donald Drummond**, Jerry Haynes, Johnny Moore, Jackie Opel, Donna Schaffer, and **Jackie Mittoo**. For the next fourteen months the Skatalites worked for all of the major producers in Jamaica and played the backing music for virtually every important ska vocalist.

The band broke up as the result of trombonist **Donald Drummond's** arrest, and McCook went on to form the Supersonics. The Supersonics then became the studio band for **Duke Reid's Treasure Isle** studio. While the Skatalites were instrumental in the birth of ska, the Supersonics helped usher in the **rock steady** era. In the late 1970s and early 1980s, ska was reborn through the UK two-tone craze, and McCook reassembled the Skatalites. The group played in Kingston in 1983–1984 and ultimately landed another recording contract.

In the late 1980s and early 1990s, ska's third wave was in effect, and the Skatalites launched an international tour. They released a series of new recordings and were nominated for several Grammys. The lineup has changed significantly since the early days and now includes Lloyd Brevett, Lloyd Knibb, Doreen Shaffer, Lester Sterling, Karl Bryan, **Vin Gordon**, Devon James, Ken Stewart, and Kevin Batchelor. Lloyd Brevett continues to play bass in the reconstituted Skatalites band on record and on the road.

BRIGADIER JERRY (1957–)
Brigadier Jerry was born Robert Russell in Kingston, Jamaica, in 1957. He came on the scene as a **dancehall DJ** and began **toasting** on the Stur-Gav Hi Fi **sound system** and others. He went on to release a series of singles including "Every Man Me Brethren" and "Dance in a Montreal." Both releases were made on **Clement "Coxsone" Dodd's Studio One** imprint. Another standout single from this early period was titled "Pain," which Jerry voiced over a Studio One rhythm. In 1985, Jerry made his full-length recording debut with the release of *Jamaica, Jamaica*. This album was released on the **RAS Records** label and featured singles such as "Jah Jah Move," "Jah Love Music," and the title track. With this release, Jerry ushered in a new era of dancehall performance as he half sang and half chanted his lyrics, a style that has come to be called

"sing-jay." To support the album, Jerry toured the United States; his fan base grew exponentially.

Another stylistic element that set Jerry apart from the gun culture DJs was his emphasis on **Rastafarian** doctrine and his consciousness lyrics. Jerry's next album was *On the Road*, issued in 1990. Another product of Jerry's work on RAS, the album featured the singles "Lyrics of Mine," "Born to Love Jah," and the title track. After a period of silence from Brigadier, he released *Freedom Street* in 1995. This album was issued by VP Records with important selections including "Freedom Street," "One Man Ranch," and "Roots Man Skank." In the late 1990s, **U-Roy** re-launched his legendary Stur-Gav Hi Fi sound system, and Jerry returned to work as a touring DJ for the sound.

BROOKS, CEDRIC "IM" (1943–)

Born in Kingston, Jamaica, Brooks got involved in music while he attended the **Alpha Boys Catholic School** in Kingston. At the school, Brooks trained in performance on the saxophone and became proficient on all of the saxophone varieties, the clarinet, and the drums. Once Brooks finished school, he pursued a career as a professional musician. He worked to create a fusion of **reggae**, jazz, and a variety of other Afro-Caribbean and Latin American styles.

In the 1960s, Brooks went into **Clement "Coxsone" Dodd's Studio One** to record with David Madden. The producer noticed Brooks's abilities, and soon he was playing in the Dodd house band. This got him exposure to some of the island's heavyweights, such as **Roland Alphonso**, **Vin Gordon**, **Jackie Mittoo**, and **Ernest Ranglin**, a collection of performers that was an unofficial band working in Dodd's studio providing backing tracks for a long list of recordings.

In the mid-1970s, Brooks released a pair of solo albums. The first was 1977's *Im Fast Forward*, followed in 1978 with *United Africa*. Also in 1977, Brooks began an association that took him into the world of **Rastafarian** and **nyabinghi** drumming. In 1977, Brooks joined **Count Ossie** and his Mystic Revelation of Rastafari to record a pair of albums, *Grounation* and *Tales of Mozambique*. The albums are an expert melding of jazz saxophone playing with traditional African drumming. Also in the mid-1970s, Brooks started his own band, the Light of Saba, which accompanied him on the 1978 release *United Africa*. The album was an interesting stylistic combination of free jazz and Jamaican popular music.

More recently, Brooks continued his performing career in various locales around Jamaica. He played a series of **reggae** standards redone to conform to his jazz-centric approach. For these outings, Brooks was joined by Maurice Gordon on guitar, Marjorie Whylie on keyboards, Desi Jones on drums, and Billy Lawrence on percussion. The group played a variety of styles including kumina, **mento**, reggae, and **ska**.

BROWN, DENNIS (1957–1999)

Dennis Emmanuel Brown was born in Kingston, Jamaica, in 1957 and had such an impact on the **reggae** world that he was referred to as the "Crown Prince of Reggae." At age eleven Brown began making inroads into the reggae music scene. He was noticed by **Clement "Coxsone" Dodd**, and together they worked at **Studio One** and issued long lists of singles. In 1968, the pair teamed on the single "No Man Is an Island," a reggae version of the Impressions' song. The song was an instant hit and led to the release of an album with the same title in 1970. Next, Brown issued *If I Follow My Heart* (1971), which was again a Studio One product. This album brought the young singer greater acclaim, but he needed to demonstrate long-lasting appeal.

In the early 1970s, Brown began working with various producers around the island. He cut a series of successful singles with **Lloyd Daley's** Matador imprint and then moved on to Vincent "Randy" Chin's **Randy's** label. His Randy's material included "Cheater" and "Meet Me at the Corner." In 1973, Brown worked with producer **Derrick Harriott** for a collection of hit singles that culminated in the album *Super Reggae & Soul Hits.* With this, Brown began to emerge as singer/songwriter and not just a cover artist. Also at this time, Brown worked with **Joe Gibbs** and **Lee "Scratch" Perry** on a series of singles.

Next, Brown moved on to producer **Winston "Niney" Holness**, and together the pair released scorching reggae songs that made them the envy of the rest of the island's musicians. From

Dennis Brown. © *UrbanImage.tv.*

1974–1976, the pair issued singles such as "Yagga Yagga," "Wolf & Leopards," "Westbound Train," and many others. The collection was compiled on *Just Dennis*, released in 1977. With this, Brown was an enormous success. He rivaled **Bob Marley** as the most popular singer in the roots reggae style and was gaining an international reputation.

In 1976, Brown again worked with Joe Gibbs and his production partner **Errol Thompson**. The trio issued a vast quantity of material, including a series of albums such as *Visions* in 1976; *Joseph's Coat of Many Colors* in 1978; *Words of Wisdom* in 1979; *Spellbound* in 1980; *Yesterday, Today, and Tomorrow* in 1982; and *Love's Gotta Hold on Me* in 1984. With this body of work, Brown had significant success in the United Kingdom, and by the end of the 1970s he began to spend increasing time in London. As an extension of his work in London, he opened the DEB label and began issuing **lovers rock** material. He produced a variety of solid work for **Junior Delgado** and the female trio 15-16-17. This work marked Brown's gradual movement out of the Jamaican popular music scene. He curtailed his recording in Jamaica and decreased his level of productivity in general.

Brown issued only a few albums in the 1980s, including *The Exit*, which was produced by **ragga** master **King Jammy**. Other material from the late 1980s included *Inseparable* in 1988 and *Good Vibrations* in 1989. These records were classic Brown, but not as strong as his early material had been. This all changed when Brown went into the Music World Studio with **Gussie Clarke** in 1989. Their first smash was "Big All Around," recorded with Brown dueting with **Gregory Isaacs**. The unprecedented success of this single led to the release of *No Contest* (1989), which was an album of duets. With this, Brown returned to full strength and followed the duet effort up with the solo album *Unchallenged*.

Brown then entered the 1990s at the top of his form. He issued *Light My Fire* in 1994, and the hit-filled release garnered the reggae veteran a Grammy nomination. In 1995 he recorded the *Three against War* album with hitmakers **Beenie Man** and **Triston Palma**. Ultimately, Brown's health began to fail as the result of longstanding respiratory problems that culminated in pneumonia. These health complications led to the singer's death in 1999 at age forty-two. At his passing, his catalog included over sixty albums. His funeral was led by Jamaican Prime Minister Percival James Patterson, and he was the first entertainer to be buried in Jamaica's National Heroes Cemetery.

BROWN, ERROL (1950–)

Errol Brown emerged on the **reggae** music scene as a youth. He immersed himself in the inner workings of the **Treasure Isle** label in the late 1960s, as his uncle was producer **Arthur "Duke" Reid**. With this famous connection, Brown began working as an engineer for the label when he was about twenty years old. He apprenticed under Byron Smith and went on to replace Smith once he had the required skills. Brown did not want to replace his mentor, so he left the label for a time and worked for Jamaica Telephone.

When Smith left Treasure Isle, Reid again came looking for Brown. In his early career, Brown worked a two-track board, but as the label grew they expanded to an eight-track setup. For the next decade, Brown engineered hits for groups such as **Culture**, **Alton Ellis**, **Marcia Griffiths**, and the **Techniques**. From Treasure Isle, Brown moved over to the engineering job at **Bob Marley's Tuff Gong Studios**. Marley's studio was comparatively state-of-the-art and had twenty-four tracks. There he began working for Marley and the **Wailers** as of the 1978 release *Survival*. Brown went on to record **Rita Marley's** "Who Feels It Knows It" and Bob's *Uprising* and *Confrontation* albums.

In addition to his work for Bob Marley, Brown was also charged with the recording duties of **Ziggy Marley and the Melody Makers**. For this group of Marley's children, Brown helped craft a series of albums that garnered four Grammy Awards for Best Reggae Album. Brown stayed at Tuff Gong until the late 1990s and worked with an extended list of up-and-coming reggae talent. Throughout the course of a thirty-five-year career in recording, Brown helped to craft the sound of the reggae landscape. Although formally separated from Tuff Gong, he continues work in the studio on specific projects. In 2003, Brown was awarded the Member of the British Empire (MBE) by the Queen of England for his service to popular music. In 2004, he received the Ivor Novello Award for outstanding contribution to British music, and in 2005 he embarked on a UK tour.

BROWN, HOPETON. *See* SCIENTIST

BULLOCKS, LESTER. *See* DILLINGER

BUNNY RUGS (c. 1955–)

Born William Clark, Bunny Rugs has been active in the **reggae** scene since the mid-1970s, when he began performing as the lead singer and guitarist for **Third World**. Rugs was born in east Kingston and found early musical inspiration in American rhythm and blues singers Aretha Franklin and Nat "King" Cole. Rugs's earliest musical performances came when he was invited to audition for the Kittymat Club, where he became a member of Charlie Hackett and the Souvenirs. Next, Rugs moved to New York and joined Hugh Hendricks and the Buccaneers.

In 1971, he formed his own band called the Wild Bunch. He returned to Jamaica in 1973 to join **Inner Circle** as the replacement for **Jacob Miller** after Miller's untimely death. While in Jamaica, Rugs played with several musicians who would become Third World. Rugs has been caught between being the frontman for a band and being a solo artist through most of his career. As Third World was forming, Rugs moved back to the United States to try going solo, but in the late 1970s, Third World came to New York to implore Rugs to join the group and replace original singer Milton "Prilly" Hamilton. With Rugs in the band, Third World released their seminal album *96 Degrees in the Shade* (1990). Further, he helped the group establish themselves as one of the premier **reggae** bands in the world.

In addition to working with Third World, Rugs continued to explore his solo career. In 1995, he released his solo debut on the **Black Scorpio** label, *Talking to You*. He also teamed with his Third World band mate **Cat Coore** to sing backup vocals for artists such as **Capleton**, **Marcia Griffiths**, and **Beres Hammond**.

BUNNY WAILER. *See* WAILER, BUNNY

BURNETT, WATTY (c. 1950–)

Watty Burnett was born in Port Antonio, Jamaica. As a teenager, his began his music career with work for producer **Lee "Scratch" Perry**; however, he experienced his first success after leaving Perry's roster. He released several singles including the **Trojan** side "Rainy Night in Portland." He then became a member of the legendary **reggae** band the **Congos**. This collective included **Roydel "Ashanti" Johnson**, **Cedric Myton**, and Burnett. Together, the group went on to become one of the best roots reggae outfits of the 1970s. The group recorded at **Black Ark Studios** for Lee Perry. The outcome was the album *Heart of the Congos*, which became a 1970s roots reggae staple.

However, due to initial marketing deficiencies, the album sold poorly. The band eventually split, but Myton re-formed the group, and they released new material in the 1990s on the **RAS Records** label. Burnett also released additional solo material, most notably his album on the Wajesskor Music label titled *To Hell and Back* (2002). Throughout his career, Burnett also spent time as a producer. He was the producer of note for the **Shanachie** release *King Tubby Meets Lee Perry: Megawatt Dub* (1997). Burnett singles also appear on several compilation recordings released by Black Ark Studios.

BURNING SPEAR (1948–)

Born Winston Rodney in St. Ann, Jamaica, Burning Spear entered the music scene in 1969 when he went into the studio and recorded the single "Door Peep" at **Studio One**. With the release of this single, Rodney took the name Burning Spear, which he used as a reference to Jomo Kenyatta, a political freedom fighter in Kenya. After his initial recording success, Spear went back into Studio One and cut the tracks for a pair of albums with legendary producer **Clement "Coxsone" Dodd**. With Dodd at the controls, Spear recorded *Studio One Presents Burning Spear* (1973) with the featured tracks "Down by the Riverside" and "Door Peep Shall Not Enter."

In the following year Spear and Dodd released *Rocking Time* (1974), which

Burning Spear. © *UrbanImage.tv.*

featured "Weeping and Wailing," "Bad to Worst," and "What a Happy Day." With these releases, Burning Spear's career was off to a powerful start. As was the norm, Spear then changed studios and producers for his next series of releases. The next set came from the **Island** imprint, for which Spear cut six albums in a row. In rapid succession, he released *Marcus Garvey* (1975); *Garvey's Ghost* (1976); *Man in the Hills* (1976); *Dry and Heavy* and *Live* (1977); and *Marcus' Children*, aka *Social Living* (1978). With these releases, Spear established himself as a major force in **reggae** music and a viable international star. Next, he released *Hail H.I.M.* on EMI in 1980.

Spear continued his dominance of the reggae market throughout the decade with albums including *Farover* and *Fittest of the Fittest* (both in 1982), *Resistance* and *People of the World* (both in 1986), *100th Anniversary* (1987), and *Mistress Music* (1988.) Also during the 1980s, Spear launched his own record label, Burning Music Productions. Parts of his catalog were issued on his label, but he continued to release music on EMI and Island. Next, Spear released *Mek We Dweet* (1990), *Jah Kingdom* (1991), *The Original* (1992), *The World Should Know* (1993), *Love and Peace: Burning Spear Live* (1994), *Rasta Business* (1995), and several others.

In 1997, he released the classic *Appointment with His Majesty* and continued issuing music for the rest of the decade. His 1999 release *Calling Rastafari* was a massive hit and earned the seasoned reggae veteran a Grammy Award. In the new millennium, Spear issued a large series of compilation albums. He also released the new album *Free Man* in 2003 and toured extensively. Burning Spear remains at the height of reggae music success. He is a potent force and continues to write, record, and tour.

BURRELL, PHILIP "FATIS" (c. 1960–)

Philip "Fatis" Burrell's career began in 1979. He has been a producer of **reggae** hits for over thirty years. In that time, he has worked with artists including Fred Locks, **Gregory Isaacs**, **Luciano**, **Sizzla**, and **Sly and Robbie**. Further, he has had a long run of successful releases on his Jamaica-based record label Exterminator.

BURRU

Burru is a type of drumming that first appeared in Jamaica in the parish of Clarendon. It was then taken up in west Kingston. The burru tradition was carried into popular music on the hands of **Count Ossie** as early as the 1950s. Ossie introduced burru drumming style to the west Kingston Rastas, and it became part of the signature **reggae** sound. The burru drumming style makes use of African rhythms on the three **akete** drums.

The burru tradition of drumming dates back to the days of colonial Jamaica. During the colonial period, burru was allowed to survive because it was used in the field to encourage the slaves to work harder and to lift their spirits. After Count Ossie used the burru drumming style to reconnect his music with the African continent, it was taken up by several roots reggae artists, most notably **Bob Marley**. Lloyd Knibb also references the burru tradition in his recordings for the **Skatalites**.

BUSH CHEMIST

Bush Chemist is the name of Dougie Wardrop's side project from the band Centry. The group formed in 1993 and has consistently released albums and singles since 1996. Stylistically they fit into the UK roots and **dub** scene with releases such as *Dub Outernational* (1996), *Money Run Tings* (1996), *Dubs from Zion Valley* (1997), *In Dub: Light Up the Chalise* (1999), and *Dub Free Blazing* (2001). Bush Chemist's sound mixes roots reggae elements with the more updated qualities of dub music, forming a bridge between the earlier and more modern sounds.

BUSHAY, CLEMENT (c. 1955–)

A UK-based **reggae** producer with numerous albums and singles to his credit, Bushay's earliest work was for the Trojan label with artists such as **Owen Gray** and Louisa Marks. Active in the **lovers rock** style, Bushay began an association with the Burning Sound label. His run of successful singles began in the mid-1970s. He worked with **Tappa Zukie**, the Soul Rebels, Louisa Marks and the In Crowd, Locks Lee, Trinity, **Dillinger**, and Ranking Jah Son, producing releases that appeared on several imprints, including Burning Sounds and Dip Records. In the late 1970s, Bushay established his own label when the Burning Sounds label went out of business. Further, he established the Bushranger label, which released Owen Gray's *The Greatest Love of All.* Most recently, he worked with the legendary Owen Gray on the 2004 release *Shook, Shimmy, and Shake: The Anthology.* Bushay's label continues to release new music with recent material from **Gregory Isaacs**, **Barrington Levy**, **Prince Jazzbo**, and **Tony Tuff**.

BYLES, KERRIE "JUNIOR" (1948–)

Byles's earliest music experiences came in 1967, when he formed the group the **Versatiles** with Earl Dudley and Louis Davis. The threesome went into the studio with **Joe Gibbs** and recorded several singles in the late 1960s. The most notable of these is "Just Can't Win." Byles then went solo and began working with producer **Lee "Scratch" Perry**. In 1972, Byles won the Jamaican Song Festival competition with his Perry-recorded single "Da Da." He continued working with Perry through the early to mid-1970s and released a series of interesting **lovers rock** and roots reggae songs. This collaboration also released several militant and politics-laced tracks in late 1971 and early 1972.

The early 1970s saw Byles release several popular singles and his first album, 1973's *Beat Down Babylon*, on **Trojan Records**. It caught Byles and Perry at their peak and became an instant success. This was followed in 1974 by one of Byles's most recognizable songs, "Curley Locks," which also built the singer's reputation in England. In 1975, he began working with producer **Joseph "Joe Joe" Hookim** at **Channel One** and had a hit with the single "Fade Away."

He again changed studios in 1976 when he worked with Dudley Swaby and Leroy Hollett for the Ja-Man label. Unfortunately, Byles began to suffer bouts of depression and was committed to Bellevue Hospital in 1976. He returned to music in 1978 and began recording songs for Joe Gibbs. In the 1980s, he worked with **Maurice "Blacka Morwell" Wellington** and released 1982's *Rasta No Pickpocket.* Then Byles again fell into obscurity. In the early 1990s, he teamed with **Winston "Niney" Holness** for a series of singles that again brought the singer to prominence. In 1997, Byles teamed with **Earl "Chinna" Smith** for several Jamaican shows that were met with a warm reception.

In the interim, Byles again disappeared from the Jamaican music scene. However, his music has been rescued through the contemporary practice of reissue and compilation. He has appeared on at least two Trojan collections issued in the late 1980s. Further, his singles are present on at least fifteen compilation albums from the 1990s and 2000s. Byles's poignant, bittersweet, and often plaintive lyrics and singing style continue to bring him acclaim in these contemporary releases.

BYRON LEE AND THE DRAGONAIRES. *See* LEE, BYRON

CABLES, THE

The Cables were a short-lived **rock steady** group who worked with **Coxsone Dodd** at **Studio One**. The group was a vocal trio led by Keble Drummond. Backing Drummond were Albert Stewart and Vince Stoddard. The group released only one album, *What Kind of World* (1970), which contained several hits. Included on this release were "Be a Man," "Love Is a Pleasure," "What Kind of World Is This," "No New Lover," and "Baby Why." Stylistically, the group mixed Jamaican rock steady with American rhythm and blues. Unfortunately, after this release the group disbanded and never again recorded together. In 2001, **Heartbeat Records** reissued the seminal *What Kind of World*, allowing it to be appreciated by a second audience.

CAMPBELL, AL (1954–)

Born in Kingston, Jamaica, in 1954, Al Campbell became active in music when he began singing in the post-reggae **dancehall** style. However, he was not comfortable working in only one style. His tastes and compositions range from roots reggae to **lovers rock**. His recorded output includes at least eight albums from 1974 to the late 1980s. He continues to record and has several relatively new singles that are forthcoming on the Hi Power label, among others. These singles span 1974 to the present time.

CAMPBELL, ALI (c. 1960–)

Ali Campbell is the lead singer for the successful British pop-reggae band **UB40**. By the 1990s, his fame spread worldwide both in the band and as a solo artist. The band UB40 got their start in 1978. They took their name from a British unemployment form in order to reflect a working class and multiracial image. Campbell and his brother Robin formed the band, which also included Earl Falconer (bass), Mickey Virtue (keyboards), Brian Travers (saxophone), Jim Brown (drums), Norman Hassan (percussion), and Terence "Astro" Wilson (vocals/**toasting**). The group had several successful singles, including their well-known version of Neil Diamond's "Red Red Wine." They had several successful albums that bridged the gap between popular music and **reggae**. However, they found their principal success in covering already-successful singles.

CAMPBELL, CECIL. *See* PRINCE BUSTER

CAMPBELL, CORNELL (1948–)

Born in Jamaica in 1948, as a youth Cornell Campbell had the opportunity to record at **Studio One** for **Bunny Lee**, recording a series of **ska**-style singles as a soloist and as half of a duo with Alan Martin. Their association lasted until 1964, when Campbell seemingly disappeared from the music scene. He reappeared as part of the **rock steady** trio the **Uniques,** but this was a short-lived collective. Campbell next appears as the leader of the **Eternals**. His high falsetto voice was an excellent frontpiece for the band, which scored a few hits, such as "Queen of the Minstrels" and "Stars."

Campbell returned to his solo career in 1971 when he again began working with Bunny Lee. Together, they rerecorded several of his Eternals hits, which received a warm audience reception. In 1973, he released a solo album on the **Trojan** label that was met with critical acclaim. Nevertheless, he was dissatisfied and decided to change his style from **lovers rock** to the more edgy **Rastafarian**-based conscious lyric style. This produced singles such as "Natty Dread in a Greenwich Farm" and "Natural Fact." His change in approach garnered him the largest fan base that he had experienced yet. Next, Campbell and Lee released *The Gorgon* (1976) on Attack Records. The album was a huge success and had several popular singles.

Inexplicably, Campbell returned to the lovers rock style on his followup album, *Turn Back the Hands of Time*

Cornell Campbell. © *UrbanImage.tv.*

(1977). There followed a period of declining popularity, and in 1980 Campbell and Lee ended their alliance. He then worked with a variety of producers including **Winston "Niney the Observer" Holness** and **Winston Riley**. These new sessions did not succeed, and in the mid-1980s Campbell retired from the music business. Campbell's album credits include at least fourteen records, the most notable of which are *The Gorgon* and *Boxing.*

CAMPBELL, DENNIS (c. 1970–)

A **lovers rock** singer who has been active for the past fifteen years, Dennis Campbell has produced three albums in that time: 1994's *Album* and 2003's *Any Day Now* were both released on VP Records. Between these two recordings Campbell released *Rise Up* in 2001 on the Artists Only label. Campbell was born in England to black Jamaican parents. His prodigious talents, including a charming voice; the ability to write songs and program drums; and the talent to play rhythm guitar, keyboards, and bass allowed him to enter the music business as a relative youth. Thus, Campbell is in demand, having already worked for **Dennis Brown**, **Freddie McGregor**, **Maxi Priest**, and many others.

Campbell's first single was a collaboration with Trevor T at Juggling Records. "See It in Your Eyes" was wildly popular and stayed in the top spot on the Jamaican charts for eleven weeks. The followup single was "Lovers Do," which enjoyed substantial radio play and public popularity. Campbell's musical talents have garnered him wide acclaim, and he has been a featured artist at the British Reggae Industry Awards, where in 1993 he won six prizes, as well as being heralded as the most popular new UK **reggae** artist. Campbell has also been a successful collaborator with **DJ** and producer

General Saint. Together they have released a host of versions of famous songs including Neil Sedaka's "Oh Carol," Al Green's "Tired of Being Alone," and Bob Marley's "Redemption Song." This material has been compiled into the 1995 Copasetic Records release *Time on the Move*.

CAMPBELL, LLOYD (c. 1950–)

Known predominantly as a producer, Lloyd Campbell has also received vocal credits on a variety of offerings. As a producer, Campbell got his start in the early 1970s and has remained active since. He was the producer of name on the Fiona album *Forever* (2004). Further, he has been credited with supporting vocals on material by a wide variety of artists. His production credits include work with Claudette Clarke, Glen Washington, the Blues Busters, Barry Biggs, the **Itals**, **Sanchez**, and many others. Campbell's production credits include work in the **lovers rock**, **reggae**, and **ska** styles.

CAMPBELL, MICHAEL. *See* MIKEY DREAD

CAPITAL LETTERS

The Capital Letters were a **reggae** band active in the late 1970s and the early 1980s. They released two albums, *Headline News* in 1979 on Greensleeves, and *Vinyard* in 1982 on the Gulp imprint. The two albums yielded several popular singles including "Daddy Was No Murderer," "Fire," "Run Run Run," and "Smoking My Ganja."

CAPLETON (1967–)

Clifton George Bailey III was born on April 13, 1967, in the town of Islington, Jamaica. At an early age Bailey acquired his nickname Capleton when he intervened in an ongoing conversation and began making several important points, causing a comparison to be made between the boy and a prominent local lawyer, Capleton. The youth soon lived up to his name by exhibiting verbal prowess and a mind for logic. Additionally, Capleton had a keen ear for music, and he cited **Bob Marley and the Wailers** and **DJ Papa San** as early influences. His love of music drove him to seek out **sound system** parties around the island, and at eighteen he moved to Kingston to enter the music business. He made appearances with several area systems, but his break came when he began working with Stewart Brown's **African Star**, a sound system associated with a record label located in both Jamaica and Canada.

Capleton's big break came when he shared a Toronto stage with the already-popular **Ninjaman** in 1989. Discussion of the performance made it back to Jamaica, and upon his return Capleton was offered a chance to record with producer **Philip "Fatis" Burrell**. His first single sent him straight to the

Capleton. © *UrbanImage.tv*.

top of the list of active **dancehall** singers. "Bumbo Red" was banned from radio due to explicit lyrics but was still hugely popular around the island. This garnered the young up-and-coming star a spot on 1990's Reggae Sunsplash Festival. Capleton subsequently released a series of successful singles including "We No Lotion Man" and "Number One Pon." He went on to release his first album, 1991's *Capleton Gold*, on the Charm label.

As is often the case in the dancehall style, Capleton went on to release several split albums. The first was with **General Levy** in 1992; titled *Double Trouble*, this release was put out on the Gussie P. imprint. Next, he teamed with **Cutty Ranks** and Reggie Stepper for the *Three the Hard Way* (1991) album. Capleton's lyrical content then began to take on a greater cultural consciousness. This is apparent in the 1993 **Exterminator** Records release *Almshouse*. This album marked a turning point for Capleton, and he garnered huge success for singles such as "Matie a Dread," "Make Hay," and "Unnu No Hear."

In 1994, Capleton released the *Good So* album, which produced another collection of hit singles and cemented his reputation. The *Good So* release marked the completion of the artist's conversion to **Rastafarianism**, and his new convictions are apparent in the rest of his output. His rising success also resulted in attention from the American record labels, and in 1995 he signed with Def Jam Records. The association with a new label led to 1995's *Prophesy* album as well as *I-Testament* in 1997. Capleton's signing with Def Jam created the environment by which he was able to appeal to a wider audience. He received high praise for the two Def Jam offerings, which afforded Capleton a degree of crossover appeal. Subsequent hip hop versions of songs from these two albums appeared, most notably Method Man's (of the Wu-Tang Clan) version of "Wings in the Morning." Having conquered the American market, Capleton turned his attention back to Jamaica. His work from the late 1990s exhibits a rootsie style that is mixed with a degree of American rhythm and blues. Products of this approach include 1999's *One Mission* album, released on the J&D imprint.

Capleton continued to release popular material into the new millennium. In 2000, he produced the album titled *More Fire*. This was followed by 2002's *Still Blazin'* and *Reign of Fire* in 2004. The three most recent releases were all on VP Records. Most recently, Capleton has begun a loose collective of dancehall favorites that he calls the David House Crew. The Crew contains **Sizzla**, Determine, Jah Mason, Jah Thunder, Military Man, Jah Fiery, and several others. Together they created the single "Hail the King," and additional new material from the Crew is expected. Capleton has also considered other avenues in the music business with an expected start of his own record label, Reuben Records. The Reuben imprint will be based in St. Mary's Parish, Jamaica, which is where the artist was born.

CAPP, ANDY (1941–)

Lynford Anderson was born in Clarendon, Jamaica. His early studio experience began in 1959 while working for the RJR radio station. Anderson's next move was to West Indies Records Limited, where he gained experience on a two-track mixer. As an engineer, he recorded many hits for **Leslie Kong**, in addition to having several of his own compositions in the charts. When he began his engineer/producer career, Anderson heavily utilized **Rupie Edwards's** 1969 coined term *version*, which describes alternate recordings of existing songs. Anderson was among the first engineer/producers in Jamaica to use the Ampex two-track studio mixing board in the recording process. Also known as **Andy Capp**, Anderson employed the two-track machine to create versions of existing hits and to mix multiple musical sources into new songs. His songs

"Fat Man," "Pop a Top," and "Pop a Top (Ver. 2)" were successes and helped to illustrate the potential of the mixer.

CAPTAIN SINBAD (c. 1955–)

Born Carl Dwyer in Kingston, Jamaica, Captain Sinbad began his music career in the mid-1970s when he teamed up with Sugar Minott on the Sound of Silence **sound system**. Together they recorded and released the single "Pressure Rock." Minott recognized Sinbad's talent and convinced him to record at **Studio One**. The pair of singles they produced was not released. However, Sinbad stayed active in the business, and in the late 1970s he resurfaced as a producer. His production debut came on Little John's album A1 Sound (1980). Sinbad then worked with Dillinger's Oak Sound label in the early 1980s.

In 1983, he moved to England and launched his own label, Rockfort Records. With this imprint, Sinbad recorded John McLean's "If I Give My Heart to You." By the end of the 1980s he returned to Jamaica and launched another label. The new label debuted with a series of singles including Capleton's "Two Minute Man," Cobra's "Merciless Bad Boy," and material from Daddy Woody, General T. K., and Frankie Paul's "Heart Attack." Also in the 1980s, Sinbad released two of his own albums, *The Seven Voyages of Captain Sinbad* (1982) and *Sinbad and the Metric System* (1983).

In the early 1990s, Sinbad made his entrance into American hip hop style with a series of remixes. The outcome was a pair of albums titled *Sin Badda Than Them* and *Gangster*. At the same time his label roster continued to grow with the inclusion of Anthony Red Rose, Milton "Prilly" Hamilton, Sugar Flack, and Fragga Ranks. Starting in 1993, Sinbad began releasing his Romantic Raga series, which produced a series of hits throughout the mid-1990s.

CARIBBEANS, THE

The Caribbeans are a steel drum band whose members all hail from the Caribbean island of St. Kitts. Begun as a hobby, the band soon perfected their sound and began taking paying jobs, including the Working Men's Club and parties. They gained greater exposure on the program *Opportunity Knocks*, which was sponsored by Vere Johns on Radio Jamaica Rediffusion. They then went on a European tour that included playing for American troops in Germany and the Middle East and entertaining the Queen of England while in Great Britain. The group is still active and performs in the calypso, **reggae**, soul, Latin, and rock and roll styles. They have performed with a variety of talent, including Van Morrison, the Drifters, the Fortunes, and Alan Price.

CARLTON AND HIS SHOES

Carlton Manning is the leader of the collective referred to as "His Shoes." He is the brother of founding **Abyssinians** member Donald Manning and sings in the high falsetto range. Carlton, Donald, and Lynford Manning came together in the mid-1960s to form this vocal trio, whose style is described as a harmonious blend of soft rock and **reggae**. The trio's first release, with **Sonia Pottinger**, was not successful, but in 1968 they began to work with **Clement "Coxsone" Dodd** and produced successful work for his Supreme label. "Love Me Forever" with "Happy Land" was their first Dodd single and was an early reggae hit. "Love Me Forever" was a substantial **rock steady** hit and now appears in many versions. The B-side, "Happy Land," was later transformed into the **Abyssinians'** hit "Satta Massagana" and has also been massively remade.

Carlton and His Shoes worked together on several music projects, such as the early

1970s session with **Lee "Scratch" Perry** as the Carltons. Further, when **Bernard Collins**, one of the original members of the Abyssinians, left the group, Carlton Manning filled his position.

CARRINGTON, VERNON

Vernon Carrington is best known in **Rastafarian** circles as the Prophet Gad. Gad took his name from the Biblical figure who was one of the twelve sons of Jacob by Zilpah, his wife's handmaid. Gad was the founder, in 1968, of the Rastafarian sect called the Twelve Tribes of Israel. He is also known as the Doctor. The Twelve Tribes now have headquarters all over the world, including Los Angeles, New York, Trinidad, Africa, Canada, Sweden, and New Zealand. Further, many of **reggae's** most popular stars have been members of the Twelve Tribes, including **Dennis Brown**, **Israel Vibration**, and **Bob Marley**. Gad's message is for everyone to read the Bible, one chapter a day, from Genesis 1 to Revelations 22. He believes that those who do this will more clearly understand the beliefs of the Rastas and the Twelve Tribes.

CHAKA DEMUS AND PLIERS (1963–)

John Taylor was born in Kingston, Jamaica, in 1963. He is the rough-voiced **DJ** who uses the moniker Chaka Demus. Demus is backed by the smooth vocals of Everton Bonner, who goes by the name Pliers. Bonner was born in Rockhall Hills, Jamaica, in 1963. Together they have formed one of the most successful **dancehall** duos in Jamaican music. The duo formed after each artist had established a successful independent career. Demus had achieved a level of success with the Roots Majestic **sound system**, which was followed by the hit single "Increase Your Knowledge," recorded by **King Jammy**. Next he hit big in 1986 with the single "One Scotch" as a duo with **Admiral Bailey**. Following that, he teamed up with **Yellowman** for the single "Everyone Loves Chaka" and had several subsequent solo hits.

Pliers came out with early hits working with producers such as **Black Scorpio**, **Clement "Coxsone" Dodd**, **King Jammy**, **King Tubby**, and **Winston Riley**. His hip hop remake of a **Toots and the Maytals** tune garnered him early success. Demus heard Pliers sing and went on record as saying that he believed that they could sing well together. The collaboration resulted in the breakout hit "Murder She Wrote," produced by **Sly and Robbie**. "Tease Me" was their next single, and it stayed in the British top ten for three months. Other popular songs included a remake of the Curtis Mayfield song "She Don't Let Nobody" and the Beatles hit "Twist and Shout." Both of these songs also charted in the British top five. Following the success of their singles, Demus and Pliers released their debut album, *Tease Me*, in January 1994. Their second album came out in 1995 and was titled for their Mayfield cover *She Don't Let Nobody*. VP Records released the followup album *For Every Kinda People* in 1997.

CHALICE

Chalice formed in 1980 as a Jamaican-based **reggae** group. The word *chalice* is Jamaican slang for a style of pipe used for smoking marijuana. It was an appropriate term, as many of the group's songs were about this act. The group consisted of Alla on vocals, Desi Jones on drums, Mikey Wallace on drums, Trevor Roper on guitar and vocals, Keith Frances on bass, and Wayne Armand on guitar and vocals. The group remained together into the 1990s and recorded on labels such as **RAS Records**, CSA, and Sunsplash. Chalice relied heavily on synthesizers to produce their sound. The group was primarily known for its live shows, which always drew a crowd, exemplified when they were invited to perform on Reggae SuperJam and Reggae Sunsplash in 1982. The Sunsplash appearance was repeated for three additional years and brought the group international exposure and acclaim. This exposure led to international touring and a record deal with Ariola Records.

The band's material addresses several themes from smoking ganja to rootsie and Afrocentric messages. Several singles include conscious messages, such as "Good Be There" and "Stand Up." Additional tracks include a remake of Terence Trent D'Arby's "Let's Go Forward," "Handle Me Rough," and "Jamaican Anthem." The group consistently released albums from the early 1980s into the 1990s, including *Blasted* in 1982, *Live at Sunsplash* in 1994, and *Catch It* in 1990. In 1991, the group released the album *Si Mi Ya* on VP Records.

CHAMBERS, JAMES. *See* CLIFF, JIMMY

CHANNEL ONE STUDIOS

Joseph "Joe Joe" Hookim and his brother Ernest started Channel One Studios in 1970–1971. They had been involved in business before as the controllers of jukeboxes and slot machines. However, in 1970, the Jamaican government outlawed gambling, and the brothers thus had to find a new career. They opened the studio in the middle of the Kingston ghetto on Maxfield Avenue. At first, Joe hired Sid Bucknor as the studio's engineer, but soon Ernest was able to replace him and keep the business a family affair. The next step for the two brothers was to set up their own record-pressing plant and label-printing facility, which they did. The pair established the studio's reputation by recording already-established singers such as **Horace Andy** and **Junior Byles**. They took a profitable turn when they began working with the **Mighty Diamonds**. With the release of the Diamonds' album *Right Time* in 1976, the studio came into its own. The brothers were able to establish a stronger reputation with the use of their studio band, the **Revolutionaries**.

The Diamonds continued to release hot-selling material, and the studio's roster grew with the additions of **Dillinger** and **Trinity** and up-and-coming **DJs**. A controversy erupted when Joe Joe was criticized for using rhythms made popular by other studios, such as **Studio One**; however, he always readily admitted copying **Coxsone Dodd's** rhythms.

For the next fifteen years, Channel One Studios overflowed with talented musicians and producers. By the end of the 1970s, the recording equipment had been upgraded to a sixteen-track recorder, which only increased the quality and possibilities. The brothers not only introduced new technology in recording, they also carried this innovative attitude into the pressing plant. They are credited with being the first recording outfit in Jamaica to use the new twelve-inch, 45 RPM format. The format was first used with the Jayes release "Truly," a version of a **Marcia Griffiths** song. Another format innovation for the Hookim brothers was the seven-inch that played at 33⅓ RPM. Unfortunately, this format lacked quality fidelity and was soon discontinued. The brothers then began to branch out, opening a satellite studio in New York in the early 1980s. In the New York studio, they recorded a number of clash albums with a different artist on either side of the disk.

For unknown reasons, the late 1980s were a dark period for the label; both the New York and Kingston studios shut down. The sheer number of recordings is staggering, with the label producing over two hundred releases in fewer than twenty years. The artists who recorded on the label included a large sampling of the most important

reggae acts of the 1970s and 1980s. A sample of talent comes from the list of releases from 1980. Artists recorded on the Channel One imprint that year include **Horace Andy**, **Black Uhuru**, **Dillinger**, **Don Carlos**, **Clint Eastwood**, **Alton Ellis**, **John Holt**, **Barrington Levy**, **Freddie McGregor**, **Mikey Dread**, **Sugar Minott**, **Judy Mowatt**, **Augustus Pablo**, Ranking Joe, the **Revolutionaries**, the **Roots Radics**, **Leroy Sibbles**, **Soul Syndicate**, and **Yabby You**.

CHAPLIN, CHARLIE (c. 1960–)

Born Richard Bennett and nicknamed as a youth for the silent movie star, Charlie Chaplin gained his entrance into music in the early 1980s along with **Josey Wales** through the Stur-Gav **sound system**. As a **DJ** toasting on the sound system, he became an early pioneer in the post-**reggae dancehall** style. His reputation increased through an association with **U-Roy** (at the time, U-Roy was operating this sound system), and ultimately his reputation was on par with even **Yellowman**. This was attested to at the 1994 **Reggae Sunsplash** festival, where he almost dethroned the reigning king. Chaplin's association with Yellowman led to the release of the album *Slackness vs Pure Culture* on Arrival Records in 1984.

Even though Chaplin came onto the scene during the dancehall days with its slack (talk of guns, sex, and drugs) and ribald lyrics, he chose to deal with culturally conscious lyrics. Chaplin cut his first album for **Roy Cousins**, who had left the Royals and become a producer. The resulting products included *Presenting Charlie Chaplin* (1982), which included the singles "Mother in Law," "Chaplin's Chant," and "Jamaican Collie." Chaplin then moved on to work with the producer **George Phang**. Together this pairing produced the album *Que Dem* on the Powerhouse label in 1985. This album garnered Chaplin wide popularity and acclaim. The popularity of the album was due in no small part to the use of several **Studio One** samples.

Through the 1980s, Chaplin continued to released well-received singles. He worked with other producers including **Henry "Junjo" Lawes**, **Sly and Robbie**, and Bunny Roots. In the 1990s, he signed a multi-record deal with **RAS Records**; the records were solid but did not achieve the acclaim of the Chaplin/Phang material. Records from the RAS days include *The Two Sides of Charlie Chaplin* (1987), *Take Two* (1990), and *Cry Blood* (1991). On Ras Records, the studio band **Roots Radics** backed Chaplin. Chaplin then moved on to record with VP Records in the mid-1990s. In 1994, he released an album that again teamed with Josey Wales called *King of Dancehall*. He followed this release with the albums *Too Hot to Handle* (1994) and *Ras Portraits* (1997). Next, Chaplin began serving as his own producer in addition to working with **Doctor Dread**. After the turn of the century, Chaplin faded from the musical landscape; however, most of his groundbreaking material appears on several compilations.

CHARLIE CHAPLIN. *See* CHAPLIN, CHARLIE

CHARMERS, LLOYD (c. 1935–)

Lloyd Charmers was born Lloyd Tyrell and came of age during an especially productive time in Jamaican music history. In the mid-1950s he teamed with Roy Willis to form the singing duo the **Charmers** and scored several hits. He and Willis then began working with **Clement "Coxsone" Dodd** on a variety of his labels including All Stars, World Disc, Coxsone, and **Studio One**. The result was a degree of success and notoriety, especially for the single "Jeannie Girl."

In the mid-1960s, Charmers was inspired by **Alton Ellis** to learn the piano. He gained sufficient proficiency on the keyboards to start his own band, the Hippy Boys. The group included Charmers on piano, Reggie "Alva" Lewis on guitar, **Aston "Family Man" Barrett** on bass, and his brother **Carlton "Carly" Barrett** on drums. The Hippy Boys soon began working with producer **Bunny "Striker" Lee**, taking on the name Bunny Lee's All Stars. As Lee's studio band, the collective became an important backup band for acts such as Lester Sterling, Ken Parker, **John Holt**, **Pat Kelly**, **Max Romeo**, and Slim Smith. The Hippy Boys cultivated the reputation as one of the island's strongest session bands and soon were in demand by other producers, including **Lloyd Daley**, **Harry J**, and **Sonia Pottinger**. They also did some session work for producer **Lee "Scratch" Perry**, who called them his **Upsetters** for his sessions.

In 1969–1970, the group released several albums of their own material under the titles *Reggae Charm*, *House in Session*, and *Reggae Is Tight*. These recording were released on the **Trojan** imprint. Charmers was now a veteran session musician and skilled studio hand due to his experiences. Thus, he launched his own label, Splash Records, in the early 1970s. He went on to record several successful artists including **Ken Boothe**, the **Gaylads**, and **Lloyd Parks**. It was with Boothe that Charmers had the most success, with singles such as "Crying over You," "Have I Sinned," and "Black, Green, and Gold." All the while, Charmers continued to write and record his own music, evidenced by his early 1970s hits "Rasta Never Fails" and "Oh Me Oh My." In his own studio, Charmers had a session band that he called the **Now Generation**, which was led by guitarist **Mikey Chung**. In the early 1980s, Charmers's version of Phil Collins's "If Leaving Me Is Easy" was quite popular. His activities for the past twenty years are not known.

CHARMERS, THE

The Charmers were a singing duo founded by **Lloyd Charmers** and Roy Willis. They broke onto the Kingston music scene in the late 1950s and subsequently released a series of hits. Their success caught the attention of **Clement "Coxsone" Dodd**, who recorded them on several of his labels, including All Stars, World Disc, and Coxsone. Dodd was responsible for producing the duo's biggest hit, "Jeannie Girl." From 1962 to 1967, Charmers and Willis continued their association with Dodd on his newly established **Studio One** imprint. By the end of the 1960s, Lloyd Charmers had moved on to become a session keyboard player and the leader of his own band.

CHEMIST (c. 1960–)

Donovan "Peter Chemist" Thompson (P. Chemist or Chemist) has been active in the Jamaican popular music scene since the mid-1980s. His credits appear as producer, engineer, or both. His early material appears on Kingdom Records with two releases in 1984. Chemist is credited with production on both the *Dub Mixture* album and *Dub Prescription*. In 1995, Chemist again surfaced as the producer of **Tenor Saw's** album *Fever*. Professor Nuts enlisted Chemist's engineering assistance for his 1991 album *Mite It Again*. In 1996, Chemist was credited as the producer on the **RAS**-produced album *Ragga Mania, Volume 4*. More recently, Chemist was the engineer on Ghost's album *Love You*, released in 2000 on the Music Ambassador label.

CHIN, CLIVE (c. 1955–)

Clive Chin made his entry into Jamaican music through his family's business, **Randy's** Record Store, and the upstairs studio Randy's Studio 17, located on North Parade, Kingston, Jamaica. Randy's record shop and studio were opened by Chin's father Vincent "Gauntlet" Chin, the head of this Chinese-Jamaican family.

Clive was involved with several of the most important bands and recording sessions in the **reggae** heydays of the 1970s. The studio opened in 1969 and immediately became one of the most popular places to record in Jamaica. Chin began working in the studio as a teenager when he functioned as a bass player, drummer, and fledgling producer. The studio musician's playing style led to a trademark Randy's sound that was highly sought after by recording artists and producers such as **Black Uhuru**, **Alton Ellis**, **Gregory Isaacs**, **Tommy McCook**, **Lee "Scratch" Perry**, the **Wailers**, and many others.

Chin's breakout recording session came when he teamed with **Augustus Pablo** for the instrumental album *Java* in 1971. This record eventually brought both men international acclaim and led

Clive Chin. © *UrbanImage.tv.*

to further albums, such as *This Is Augustus Pablo* and *Java Java Dub*. Another artist to hit big with Chin at Randy's was Carl Malcolm with his British chart topper "Fatty Bum Bum."

The Chin family closed their Randy's Studio in 1978 and moved the entire operation to New York, where they launched the VP distribution company. To date, VP is the largest distributor of reggae music in North America. However, Chin drifted away from the music business and became involved in another family venture, the restaurant business. He was active in the family's Bronx-based eatery J&C Kitchen, which served Jamaican food. Twenty years later, in 1998, Chin reentered the music business by recording again and allowing the reissue of many of his seminal recordings. These reissues feature the Impact All Stars, which included **Aston "Family Man" Barrett** on bass and **Sly Dunbar** on drums. Further reissues and compilations are planned and will assist in preserving the legacy of this legendary Jamaican producer.

CHIN, JUNIOR (c. 1960–)

Junior "Chico" Chin has been a trumpet, horn, or saxophone player for many of **reggae's** greatest performers. He began appearing on record in 1979 and continues to the present. A few of his efforts include working with **Black Uhuru** on the *Anthem* album in 1984 and the *Nub Carbon* album in 1996. He has also worked with **Peter Tosh** on the 1983 release *Momma Africa*. Additionally, he has worked with **Ziggy Marley and the Melody Makers**. However, his most significant contributions come from playing with the **Mighty Diamonds**. He appeared on six of their releases from the late 1970s until the mid-1980s. A few such albums include *Deeper Roots*, *Reggae Street*, *The Roots Is There*, *Backstage*, *Kouchie Vibes*, and *Pass the Kouchie*. Chin also did session work with **Burning Spear** and **Israel Vibration**.

CHIN, LEONARD (c. 1955–)

Leonard Chin is part of the legendary Chin family that ran **Randy's** record shop and studios. He was intermittently associated with the studio and produced several hits for the label. The artists that Chin worked for include **Horace Andy**, **Jah Woosh**, and **Augustus Pablo**. For Pablo, Chin produced the hit single "Lover's Mood" and for Woosh he produced "Chalice Blaze." His teaming with Andy yielded the 1973 hit "Don't Let Problems Get You Down."

CHIN, TONY (c. 1950–)

Born Albert Valentine Chin in Kingston, Jamaica, Tony Chin got his start in the music business as a drummer. He found his niche in **reggae** music when he switched to the guitar and teamed with bassist **George "Fully" Fullerton** to form the Riddim Raiders. This duo worked in the **rock steady** style in the late 1960s and evolved into the 1970s reggae players the **Soul Syndicate**. The Soul Syndicate also included **Carlton "Santa" Davis**, **Earl "Chinna" Smith**, and Keith Sterling. The Syndicate's resume includes support on albums by **Big Youth**, **Ken Boothe**, **Dennis Brown**, **Burning Spear**, **Johnny Clarke**, **Don Carlos**, **Gregory Isaacs**, **Bob Marley**, **Freddie McGregor**, the **Mighty Diamonds**, and many others. They also worked for a variety of producers such as **Winston "Niney" Holness**, **Keith Hudson**, and **Bunny "Striker" Lee**.

While Chin was working for Lee, he was part of a session group that the producer called the **Aggrovators**. Additionally, Chin was credited with pioneering a new guitar style that became known as the "flyers" rhythm guitar style. This manner of playing was widely popular and appears on songs such as **Dennis Brown's** "Cassandra" and **Johnny Clarke's** "Move out of Babylon." During the 1970s, Chin supported major acts such as Big Youth, the Mighty Diamonds, and **U-Roy**, and on international tours. He also worked with **Peter Tosh** in the second incarnation of Tosh's **Word, Sound, and Power** band.

In 1981, Chin relocated to California and joined forces with Jack Miller and the International Reggae All Stars. He also played in the band that supported Peter Tosh's son **Andrew Tosh**. In the early 1990s, Chin joined the multiracial band **Big Mountain** and was part of the session that produced the international hit "Baby I Love Your Way." In this band, Chin played guitar and sang and was involved in songwriting. In 1996, Chin again joined forces with George Fullwood and helped form the California-based **reggae** band the Fully Fullwood Band. Five years later, Chin released his first solo album, *Music and Me*. More music is still to come from this reggae music veteran.

CHOSEN FEW, THE

The Chosen Few got their start in the late 1960s when Franklin "A. J. Franklin" Spence and David "Scotty" Scott teamed up as a Jamaican club band. Throughout the 1970s the pair had a string of hits that led to touring in America, Canada, and England. Rounding out the band with Spence and Scott, who had been in a band called the Federals, were Noel "Bunny" Brown and Richard "Richie" MacDonald. The group got its first break when Derrick Harriott, who knew Spence and Scott from the Federals, brought them into the studio. Scott soon left the group to pursue solo work as a **DJ** and to form a new band called the Crystalites. Buster Brown, who was exiting the recently disbanded Messengers outfit, replaced him. MacDonald also left the group and was replaced by **Errol Brown**, who had such an impact on the vocal styling of the band that they were occasionally billed as Errol Brown and the Chosen Few. Brown had been actively recording in New York and brought with him a strong sense of American soul music.

The Chosen Few, with its original lineup, often performed **reggae** versions of American rhythm and blues standards. They had a degree of success with covers such as "Everybody Plays the Fool" and "You're a Big Girl Now." Their first album, 1973's *Hit after Hit*, contained a series of such covers. Later work featured a move toward mainstream soul and involved the assistance of the **ska** singer King Sporty. The Sporty association produced the band's second album, 1975's *Night and Day* (also known as *The Chosen Few in Miami*). Both of the band's recordings from the 1970s were released on the **Trojan Records** label.

The Chosen Few maintained a lively recording and performance schedule into the 1980s. They added a new member with the inclusion of Michael Deslandes and launched their own label, Kufe.

CHUNG, GEOFFREY (1950–)

Geoffrey Chung spent most of his life active in the Jamaican music business. He was born in Kingston, Jamaica, and got his start in the business as an instrumentalist. He was partly responsible for forming the **Now Generation** session band with his brother **Michael Chung**; Now Generation also included Val Douglas, **Earl "Wya" Lindo**, **Mikey "Boo" Richards**, and Robert Lynn. This collective was among the most reputable in Jamaica and in high demand around the island. Chung had the ability to play the guitar and keyboards as well as to produce and engineer recording sessions.

Next, he fell in with the **reggae** singer Sharon Forrester, and together they created her debut album *Sharon*, on which Chung had a major impact. The album was a success, and it encouraged Chung to open his own production company, Edge Production. Important Edge artists included **Marcia Griffiths** and the **Heptones**. Chung branched back out from his production projects to work with the **burru** drumming group **Ras Michael** and the **Sons of Negus**. The result, 1975's *Rastafari Dub* album, was a big hit in both Jamaica and the United Kingdom. Other reggae luminaries who appeared on the album were **Carlton "Santa" Davis**, **Tommy McCook**, **Robbie Shakespeare**, **Earl "Chinna" Smith**, and **Peter Tosh**. On the release, Chung is credited with playing the synthesizer, organ, and piano.

After his association with the Sons of Negus, Chung teamed with singer Pablo Moses, for whom he played keyboards and did production work. Chung appears on Moses's 1975 album *Revolutionary Dream*, released on the **Shanachie** label. He went on to work on subsequent albums with Moses, such as *A Song* and *Pave the Way*, both on the **Island** imprint. More recently, Chung was credited as the producer/engineer for **Maxi Priest's** 1991 album *Best of Me*. In 2003, Chung worked with Ijahman on his Melodie Records release *Roots of Love*. On this recording he is credited with playing rhythm guitar, brass, and organ, and arranging the instrumental parts. Also in 2003, Chung was involved with **Everton Blender's** album *King Man* on the Rounder imprint.

CHUNG, MICHAEL (1954–)

Michael "Mikey" Chung was born in 1954 in Kingston, Jamaica. The Chinese-West Indian was the guitarist for **Lloyd Charmers's Now Generation**, as a backing band for artists such as **Bob Marley**. He then went on to play with **Jacob Miller** and Ian and Roger Lewis.

In 1978, Chung joined **Peter Tosh's** backup band **Word, Sound, and Power**, whose core was **Sly Dunbar** and **Robbie Shakespeare**. Tosh's third album, *Bush Doctor*, became a Chung family affair as Michael played guitar and keyboard and his brother Geoffrey took charge of engineering and production. Michael Chung's association with Sly and Robbie has endured. In 1979, the three recorded "Oriental Taxi" and followed it up with the sessions that would yield *Mystic Man.* The three then returned to work with Peter Tosh for the *Wanted Dread and Alive* (1981) sessions. Chung, Sly, and Robbie then worked with **Black Uhuru** on the session for the albums *Red* (1981) and *Chill Out* (1982).

Chung's guitar, keyboard, and arranger credits in the 1980s, 1990s, and 2000s are too numerous to list. A few high points in the 1980s include keyboard work on **Shinehead's** *Unity* album, guitar on **Rita Marley's** *Who Feels It Knows It* (1981) release, and electric piano on **Toots Hibbert's** *Toots in Memphis* (1988) album. In the 1990s Chung sessioned with a wide range of **reggae** and American music notables. He appeared on several releases by Joe Cocker and Grace Slick. Further, he stuck to his roots playing guitar on sessions for Pablo Moses. In the first few years of 2000, Chung has worked with **Buju Banton**, **Beenie Man**, **Inner Circle**, **Luciano**, **Ernest Ranglin**, and many others. Clearly, the session work of this legendary reggae guitarist will continue.

CIMARONS, THE

The Cimarons formed in 1967 with the lineup of **Franklyn Dunn** (bass), Sonny Binns (keyboards), Locksley Ginchie (guitar), Maurice Ellis (drums), and Winston Reid (vocals). The group has a couple of interesting distinctions: first, they are widely credited as the first UK-based **reggae** band; second, the band is still active, having played together for over thirty-five years. They got their start rehearsing at a north London Methodist youth club and made an early living supporting touring Jamaica-based bands. The band built a respectable reputation in these early days and was invited on a tour of Africa in the early 1970s. Back in the United Kingdom, the band went into the studio and recorded their first single, "Mammy Blue," on Downtown Records. Followed was a pair of albums, *In Time* and *On the Rock*, both surfacing in 1977. In the late 1970s, the band put out the *Maka* album, which contained the successful single "Ethiopian Rhapsody." The next release was the 1982 Halmark Records offering *Reggaebility*, which featured a series of Beatles tunes redone in reggae versions. Though the band's membership has changed over the years, with the drummer changing from Maurice Ellis to Jah "Bunny" Donaldson, the group has remained active and continues to perform live shows.

CLARENDONIANS, THE

The Clarendonians formed in 1965 when youths from Clarendon, Jamaica teamed together. The original duo was Ernest Wilson and Peter Austin, who had early success in area talent competitions. Their regional notoriety brought them the attention of **Clement "Coxsone" Dodd**, who signed them to a recording contract with his **Studio One** imprint. Dodd also suggested that they add a third member to their group, seven-year-old **Freddie McGregor**. Now a trio, the three went into the studio and recorded successful singles such as "You Can't Keep a Cool Man Down," "You Can't Be Happy," and "Rudie Gone a Jail." Their most well-known song was the single "Rudie Bam Bam."

The Dodd-enhanced collective worked together for only four years. Ernest Wilson split from the group to pursue a solo career that garnered him some notoriety. In fact, he continues to surface intermittently on the Jamaican music scene. Peter Austin faded from the musical picture shortly after the Clarendonians broke up. The most successful of the three was McGregor, who went on to enjoy considerable popularity as a solo artist.

CLARK, CLAUDETTE (c. 1970–)

Claudette Clark's soprano voice is part of one of the fastest-growing styles of Jamaican popular music. This style is called reggae gospel and is a mixture of Christian gospel music and the **reggae** performing style. Clark has been most active in the late 1990s, during which she released three albums. The first album was 1998's *Reggae Song of Praise.* Her second album, appearing in the same year, was titled *God Is a Mountain.* The album *The Prayer* was released in 1999 and garnered the singer a degree of success. Other reggae musicians who have recently turned to the reggae gospel style include Clive Tennors, **Hopeton Lewis**, **Judy Mowatt**, **Papa San**, and **Sanchez**.

CLARKE, AUGUSTINE "GUSSIE" (c. 1950–)

Augustine Clarke was born in Kingston, Jamaica, in the early 1950s. His music career began in the early 1970s, during which he quickly rose to prominence as a producer of **dancehall** and **reggae** hits. His first success came from producing U-**Roy's** hit single "The Higher the Mountain." In 1973, he blasted onto the dancehall scene as the producer of **Big Youth's** debut album *Screaming Target.* He quickly followed this success with another hit production by **I-Roy**. He approached recordmaking as a craft and handled his studio musicians as craftsman. He called the group of performers in the studio Simplicity People.

Clarke's popularity was most profound in Jamaica and Great Britain due in large part to **Trojan Records** releasing his material. During the early 1970s, Clarke worked with legends such as **Augustus Pablo** on his Gussie and the Puppy imprint. In the mid-1970s, Clarke raised his profile, producing **Dennis Brown's** "To the Fountain" and **Gregory Isaacs's** "Private Beach Party." **Heartbeat Records** employed Clarke in the early 1980s to produce their two-album compilation *Dee-Jay Explosion.*

Clarke's next big move took place in 1988; he opened his own studio called Music Works. The first single to emerge from Clarke's new studio was **Gregory Isaacs's** "Rumours." The studio quickly gained the reputation as the most important place to record, which served to further Clarke's reputation as a producer. In the 1990s, he continued to be active in his studio, working with many of Jamaica's most important artists. Throughout his career, Clarke produced many of Jamaica's finest artists, including **Aswad**, **Cocoa Tea**, **Eek-A-Mouse**, **J. C. Lodge**, **Papa San**, **Shabba Ranks**, and **Sly and Robbie**. In 1990, Clarke did release a record on which he was the featured artist. Titled *Ram Dancehall,* Clarke is credited both as producer and pianist.

CLARKE, ERIC "FISH" (1960–)

Eric "Fish" Clarke entered the Jamaican music scene as a drummer alongside his older brother **Johnny Clarke**. During the late 1970s and into the early 1980s, the younger Clarke was engaged as the drummer for the late **Prince Far I**. He was active on Far-I's 1978 album *Message from the King,* as well as playing on 1981's *Voice of Thunder.* At this time, Far-I's backup band was called the Arabs and included Clarke (drums), **Errol Holt** (bass), **Earl "Chinna" Smith** (lead guitar), and Winston "Bo Peep" Bowen on keyboards. Also during the late 1970s, Clarke appeared on **Keith Hudson's** album *Rasta Communication.*

Clarke left the Arabs and played with several other groups throughout the 1980s and 1990s. He sat in with the **Roots Radics** when needed, and also worked with **Maurice "Blacka Morwell" Wellington**. In 1986, he was active with **Mikey Dread** on the recording of "African Anthem." In the early 1990s, Clarke surfaced on releases by the **Ethiopians** and Ras Sam Brown. In the new millennium, Clarke's drumming contributions have been released on three compilation albums, as a sideman for Prince Far I as well as with the Ja-Man All Stars.

CLARKE, GEORGE (c. 1960–)

British keyboard player George Clarke was first active with a band called the Regulars, who were recorded on CBS in 1978. The sole album that they released was *Victim.* The group disbanded shortly after the release and Clarke fell into musical obscurity.

CLARKE, JOHNNY (1955–)

Born in Whitfield Town, Jamaica, in 1955, Johnny Clarke entered the music business by entering a talent contest staged in Bull Bay. In 1971, he won the contest at Tony Macks, which led to a meeting with producer **Clancy Eccles**. Clarke's first single, "God Made the Sea and Sun," did not garner the singer any attention. However, Clarke changed producers to **Rupie Edwards** for his next three singles, "Everyday Wandering," "Julie," and "Irie Feeling," and came away with a series of hits. Next, Clarke worked with several different producers including Glen Brown and **Bunny "Striker" Lee**. With Brown, Clarke released "Jump Back Baby" to modest returns. However, with Lee, Clarke reached his full vocal potential. With the assistance of Lee's "flying cymbal" production, the two released a series of hit singles. The first of these major hits was "None Shall Escape the Judgment."

Stylistically, Clarke was a chameleon. He wavered between roots reggae and softer **lovers rock** tracks. His prolific production of singles includes "Move out of Babylon, Rastaman," "Rock with Me Baby," "Enter into His Gates with Praise," and "Too Much War." In addition to his own material, Clarke released several covers of other important Jamaican singers' material. His first two albums include mostly his own work; however, some covers are also present.

In 1974, Clarke released the album *None Shall Escape the Judgment.* A year later his followup release, *Moving Out,* came out. Both were huge successes and resulted in Clarke being awarded Artist of the Year honors in both 1975 and 1976. Lee was at the controls through all of this success, and their relationship continued when in 1976 Clarke was signed to Virgin record's subsidiary Front Line. The union produced the *Authorized Version* (1976) album, which contained the hit single "Roots Natty Roots Natty Congo." Clarke next released the album *Rockers Time Now* (1976). This album is generally considered the apex of his career. Lee's flying cymbal rhythm is in effect and his studio band, the **Aggrovators**, are as tight and potent as ever. Again, the album contained many original tunes with a series of covers interspersed. Cover tunes on this release were from the likes of the **Abyssinians** and the **Mighty Diamonds**.

Johnny Clarke. © *UrbanImage.tv.*

Regardless of acclaim, Virgin did not choose to keep Clarke on its roster; he was dropped at the end of the year. The following year Clarke rebounded with two more albums, *Up Park Camp* and *Girl I Love You.* These albums did not sell as well as *Rockers Time Now*, but did produce several lasting hits such as "Judgment Day" and "Blood Dunza." Through the late 1970s, Clarke kept releasing full-length material including 1978's *Sweet Conversation*; *Lovers Rock*; and *Lovers Rock, Vol. 2*; along with a series of hit singles in collaboration with **dancehall** sensation **Dillinger.** In the early 1980s, Clarke switched producers again and released *Down in a Babylon* (1980). He returned to work with Lee on the album *I Man Come Again*, which returned him to his past glory days musically.

In 1993, Clarke released a split album with **Cornell Campbell** on the Vista Sounds imprint. Even with Clarke's deep catalog of recordings, record sales, and popularity, he somehow continued to be omitted from Jamaica's premier annual concert **Reggae Sunsplash.** In disgust over this longstanding oversight, Clarke left Jamaica for London in 1983. He immediately teamed with **Neil "Mad Professor" Fraser** to release 1983's *Yard Style*. The new record contained hits such as "Nuclear Weapon" and "Mount Zion." In 1985, the duo again hit big with *Give Thanks*. Also in 1985, Clarke teamed with **Sly and Robbie** and produced the *Sly and Robbie Present the Best of Johnny Clarke* album. Through the late 1980s and into the 1990s, Clarke continued to release solid material. Further, he was gratified in 1995 by being invited to play Reggae Sunsplash. To this day, Johnny Clarke continues to record and tour, and his material is ever-present on Jamaican compilation albums.

CLARKE, LLOYD (c. 1945–)

A noted **ska** style vocalist who was active in the *early* 1960s, Lloyd Clarke's early hits include the singles "Fool's Day," "You're a Cheat," and "Love You the Most." Subsequently, his voice has appeared on a variety of compilation albums, which feature his more popular singles such as "Girl Rush," "Japanese Girl," "and "Parapinto Boogie." Clarke's material appears on the compilation album *Scandal Ska* (1989). This was followed in 1994 with an appearance on *Ska Boogie: Jamaican Rhythm and Blues, the Dawn of Ska.*

CLARKE, WILLIAM "BUNNY RUGS." *See* BUNNY RUGS

CLIFF, JIMMY (1948–)

Born on April 1, 1948, in St. Catherine, Jamaica, Jimmy Cliff exhibited early musical talent as a youth and began making public appearances at local events. At age fourteen, Cliff moved to Kingston intending to become a recording artist. He cut two singles that did not result in any notoriety. However, they did get him noticed by **Derrick Morgan**, who took him to see producer **Leslie Kong**. For Kong, Cliff wrote and recorded the single "Hurricane Hattie" about the actual storm that had just terrorized the Caribbean. The song was an instant hit and resulted in a solid relationship between the two that lasted until Kong's death. Together, the duo released a series of hits that helped solidify the fledgling **ska** style.

They also had success in Great Britain, where Cliff's songs were simultaneously being released on **Island Records**. Hit singles of particular note include "Pride and Passion," "One Eyed Jacks," "King of Kings," and "Miss Jamaica." Cliff had risen to such a high level of popularity that in 1964 Jamaica sent him to represent the country at the World's Fair. From the World's Fair, Cliff spent time in Paris, where he performed to

Jimmy Cliff. © *UrbanImage.tv.*

some acclaim. He then met with Island Records head **Chris Blackwell**, who was in the process of changing his label's focus from Caribbean music to progressive rock and roll. Cliff was convinced to move to Great Britain and subsequently began to alter his style to conform to the label's new leaning.

In 1968, Cliff's debut album, *The Hard Road to Travel*, was released. This album was of such quality that its hit single, "Waterfall," won the International Song Festival. The single was not popular in Great Britain, but it was a smash in South America, which caused Cliff to relocate there for a time to parlay his success. This also gave him greater time to write new material, the result of which was "Wonderful World, Beautiful People." This single brought Cliff international acclaim. It reached number six on the British charts and cracked the top twenty-five in the United States. Cliff followed this with a song titled "Vietnam" that dealt with anti-war sentiment. Cliff then released his album *Wonderful World*, which was another hit and even made inroads on the radio.

In 1971, Cliff's career sustained a serious setback when producer Leslie Kong unexpectedly died of a heart attack. Kong had been supportive of Cliff through his entire career and now Cliff was on his own. Cliff was able to bounce back, though, and released his *Another Cycle* album in the same year. He then embarked on both the filming and recording of the soundtrack for *The Harder They Come*. The soundtrack for the film was the last project that Kong had worked on, and the film featured Cliff in the lead role. The soundtrack became an instant classic and featured several of Cliff's songs, including the title track. The film received critical acclaim, if not commercial success, and has become a cult favorite. Jimmy Cliff was experiencing the most profound success of his career. Unfortunately, it was at this same time that his record label shifted its attention away from Cliff and toward **Bob Marley**. Due to the lack of support, Cliff left Island and signed with Reprise in the United States and EMI in the United Kingdom. Unfortunately, Cliff's 1974 release *Struggling Man* and 1975's *Brave Warrior* did not fare as well as his early records had.

During this time, Cliff also made a change in his personal life. He converted to Islam and made a visit to Africa. The changes were reflected in his music and in his next record, *Follow My Mind*. The album did well in the United States, and its popularity led Reprise to call for a greatest hits album. This was to be achieved through record-ings of Cliff in live performance while on tour. The resulting album, *Live—In Concert*, is a searing set of Cliff's most popular songs. On the heels of this album, Cliff contin-ued to record and release material for Reprise until 1981's *Give the People What They Want*. He then switched labels again to Columbia, formed a backing band that he called Oneness, and launched a U.S. tour with **Peter Tosh**. Cliff went on to record a series of three albums for Columbia, each of which was a success. The Columbia releases culminated in 1989's *Hang Fire* release.

For the next fifteen years, Cliff continued to record for labels such as **Trojan**, Island, and Musidisc. He released several albums in the late 1980s and through the 1990s. Of particular note is the 1993 U.S. chart success "I Can See Clearly Now." Although a cover of an already-successful song, Cliff's take on the single made it on the soundtrack for the movie *Cool Runnings* (1993). He had already appeared in another movie, co-starring in *Club Paradise* (1986). Cliff continues to record and perform and has been making increasingly more frequent appearances on compilation albums.

CLINT EASTWOOD. *See* EASTWOOD, CLINT

COBRA. *See* MAD COBRA

COCOA TEA (1959–)

Calvin Scott was born in Rocky Point in Jamaica's Clarendon parish on September 3, 1959. He entered the Jamaican music scene by singing in school and church choirs. He recorded his first song, titled "Searching in the Hills," in 1974 for producer Willie Fran-cis. The single was a failure and led Scott to spend the next five years working as a racehorse jockey and fisherman. He reentered the music business as a **DJ**, **toasting** in the **dancehall** style on several **sound systems**. It is at this time that he gained the nickname Cocoa Tea, so named for his favorite hot beverage, which in Jamaica is equivalent to hot chocolate.

In 1983, Tea moved to Kingston to pursue his singing aspirations. In the island's capital he joined forces with producer **Henry "Junjo" Lawes** and cut three singles, "Rocking Dolly," "Informer," and "I Lost My Sonia." In 1985, he released his debut album on Volcano Records, *Wha Them Ago Do, Can't Stop Cocoa Tea*. Through the sec-ond half of the 1980s, Tea released a fast succession of successful albums on a variety of imprints, the lyrical content of which was of the conscious nature and many of which were produced by **King Jammy**. The series includes the follow-ing releases: *Sweet Sweet Cocoa Tea* (1986); *The Marshalls* (1986); *Cocoa Tea* (1986); *Cocoa Tea with Tenor Saw*, a clash album (1987); *Come Again* (1987); and *Cocoa Tea with Shabba Ranks*

Cocoa Tea. © *UrbanImage.tv.*

and Home T, another clash release (1989). Tea, Ranks, and Home also released another album called *Holding On,* which was a significant Jamaican hit.

In the 1990s, Tea's career continued to grow with the success of 1991's Greensleeves release *Riker's Island.* This album's singles included "No Blood for Oil" and "Oil Ting," both of which were banned in Jamaica during the Gulf War. He then joined **Cutty Ranks** and **Home T** for the clash release *Another One for the Road.* In 1992, Tea again teamed with King Jammy and released the album *I Am the Toughest.*

In the later 1990s, Tea worked with a series of producers who assisted him in his continued hit production. He released the single "Holy Mount Zion" with the producer Digital B in 1995 and the hit "I'm Not a King" with the production assistance of the **Exterminator.** Tea was able to imitate his idol **Bob Marley** when he covered the hit "Waiting in Vain" with DJ **Cutty Ranks.** Tea then launched his own label called Roaring Lion, on which he released his own singles as well as those by several others. Additionally, Motown Records released a compilation of Tea's 1990s hits titled *Holy Mount Zion.* Cocoa Tea continues to be active in the Jamaican popular music scene with his combination of hard-hitting conscious lyrics and sweet love songs.

COLE, COURTNEY (c. 1970–)

Courtney Cole is an active producer and arranger of **reggae** music who has been active in the industry since the beginning of the 1990s. Cole has produced material for several heavy hitters in the reggae, **dancehall,** hip hop, and **ragga** styles. In addition to solo album credits, Cole has produced a series of compilation releases. The producer has worked with **Capleton,** Jigsy King, Tony Curtis, Snagga, **Cutty Ranks, Half Pint,** and **Garnet Silk.** In 2000, Cole produced the album *Three Wise Men: Love Peace and Consciousness,* a major release for **Anthony B, Luciano,** and **Sizzla.** Regarding compilations, Cole has the production credits for 1993's *Reggae Hits, Vol. 10; Strictly the Best, Vol. 9 and 10; Mash Up the Place: the Best of Reggae Dancehall,* and many others. Cole's production work has extended into the new millennium; the producer continues to work on new music.

COLE, WILBURN "STRANGER" (1945–)

Born in Kingston, Jamaica, in 1945, Wilburn Cole quickly acquired the nickname "Stranger" because he did not look like anyone else in his family. He entered the Jamaican popular music scene in the 1960s with the release of the single "Rough and Tough," a **ska** song that was well received. Producer **Duke Reid** worked on this single with Cole, and the two stayed together through the ska era. In 1965, Cole referenced American jump band saxophonist and band leader Louis Jordan when he reprised "Run Joe."

Cole was a strong singer; however, it is speculated that an apparent shyness in the studio led him to do considerable duet work. His duet partners include Patsy Todd, **Gladstone "Gladdy" Anderson,** and **Ken Boothe.** Other Reid-produced singles that brought the singer notoriety included "Stranger at the Door" and "We Are Rolling." After leaving Reid, Cole worked with several important Jamaican producers such as **Clement "Coxsone" Dodd, Bunny "Striker" Lee, Lee "Scratch" Perry,** and **Sonia Pottinger.** In 1971, he moved to England and toured before again relocating in 1973, this time to Canada. In Toronto, he released three albums, one of which was a retrospective on his singing career. The three releases all appeared on Cole's own label and included *The First Ten Years of Stranger Cole* (1978), *Captive Land* (1980), and *The Patriot* (1982).

In 1986, Cole's first album to be released in the United States, titled *No More Fussing and Fighting,* came out. **Trojan Records** also released a collection of Cole's hits with 2003's *Bangarang: The Best of Stranger Cole 1962–1972*. Cole's son "Squiddly" is also active in the **reggae** music scene as a drummer for **Ziggy Marley**, **Mutabaruka**, and many others.

COLLINS, ANSEL (1949–)

Ansel Collins was born in Jamaica in 1949 and entered the Jamaican popular music scene in the 1960s. He began his career as a singer but subsequently switched to drums, then keyboards. Early in his career he teamed with his brother Dave; together they recorded for the **Trojan Records** label. In 1971, the duo released "Double Barrel." Widely credited as one of the earliest international reggae hits, the song was popular in both England and the United States. It charted in both countries and is characterized by heavy reverb and a solid **rock steady** groove. Unfortunately, the pair could not capitalize on this popularity. They never charted another single in the United States and only had one other notable song in Britain, "Monkey Spanner." The duo parted and Ansel Collins had success with producer **Winston Riley**.

In 1973, Riley and Collins released the song "Stalag 17," which became a major seller in Jamaica and has lived on in many subsequent versions. For the rest of the 1970s, Collins worked as a studio keyboard player with a couple of the most high-profile Jamaican session bands. He regularly played with the **Aggrovators** and the **Revolutionaries**, in addition to **Sly and Robbie** at **Channel One**. Through this session experience, Collins was able to work with many of the prominent Jamaican producers and recording artists. His work from the 1980s and 1990s with Sly and Robbie was compiled into the 2002 recording *Jamaica Gold*, and he appeared on albums from **reggae** luminaries such as **Jimmy Cliff**, **Israel Vibration**, and **U-Roy**. Collins also released a pair of solo albums along the way. In 1978, **Heartbeat Records** released his album *So Long* and in 1987 *Ansel Collins*.

COLLINS, BERNARD (1948–)

Born in 1948 in Kingston, Jamaica, Bernard Collins did not plan to make a career in the music business; however, he ended up as one third of the legendary roots reggae trio the **Abyssinians**. The Abyssinians consisted of Collins and a pair of brothers, Donald and Linford Manning. The group got their start in 1968 when they wrote the seminal reggae hit "Satta Massaganna," which is **Amharic** for "give thanks and praises." The song became an unofficial hymn of the **Rastafarian** movement as it was popularized in post-colonial Jamaica. The Abyssinians went on to release a series of significant records that were immensely popular in Jamaica, the United States, and Europe (primarily England). In 1983, the group broke up. They have attempted a pair of subsequent revivals, but no lasting truce resulted. Most recently, Collins released a solo album in September 1998. The recording is titled *Last Days* and includes the singles "Last Days" and "African Princess." These two songs were produced during the original Abyssinians' final recording session in 1988. In addition, the record contains new original material by Collins.

COLLINS, CLANCY (c. 1970–)

Clancy Collins is a producer of **reggae** material who has worked for a variety of artists. His period of greatest activity spans the 1990s, and he has continued to be productive into the new millennium. Artists for whom Collins has done production work include Donald Drummond Jr. (the son of the great **ska** trombone player **Donald Drummond**), Vincent McLeod, and **Owen Gray**. Collins's material has been released on several labels, such as Rico's and the **Trojan** imprints. He is credited as the producer of Trojan's 1992 release *Tighten Up* and the 1997 *Trojan Jungle, Vol. 2* release. Further, he worked on *Trojan Box Set: Reggae Sisters*. Recently, Collin has worked on several compilations, such as the 2003 releases *Dancehall '69: 40 Skinhead Reggae Rarities* and *Trojan Box Set: British Reggae*. In 2004, he was the producer credited with Owen Gray's *Shook, Shimmy, and Shake: The Anthology*.

COMMON GROUND

Common Ground is composed of six musicians from the Nashville, Tennessee, area. The group began as a cover band but quickly evolved into writing all their own songs that bridged stylistic gaps among **reggae**, funk, hip hop, rock and improvisation. The group formed around guitarist/songwriter Rocky Brown. Brown is surrounded by a solid lineup that includes singer Jason Schneider, drummer Jim Merrit, bassist Jeff Perratta, turntablist Chris Sellers, and guitarist Phil Hebert.

CONGOS, THE

The Congos are the vocal pair **Cedric Myton** and **Roydel "Ashanti" Johnson**. The pair joined forces after a chance meeting and began working with producer **Lee "Scratch" Perry**. Myton and Johnson increased their sound by adding baritone **Watty Burnett**. The group's first album was recorded at Perry's **Black Ark Studio** in the mid-1970s. The resulting record was *Heart of the Congos* and included the singles "Fisherman," "Congoman," and "La Bam-Bam." Although it was the Congos' debut, many considered this recording to be on par with the work of **reggae** superstars such as **Burning Spear**, **Bob Marley**, and the **Mighty Diamonds**. Of particular note on the

The Congos. © *UrbanImage.tv.*

album is the juxtaposition of Johnson's tenor voice, Myton's high falsetto, and Burnett's baritone. The style of the music is representative mid-1970s roots reggae.

Unfortunately, the group split shortly after the release of their debut album. However, material under the Congos name continued to surface, as both Myton and Johnson used it to identify themselves or their new bands. Myton went on to record with other singers as the Congos, and Johnson went solo as Congo Ashanti Roy. The next release under the Congos name was 1979's *Congo*, on the CBS label.

There followed a long hiatus during which it seemed that there would no longer be songs released under the Congos name. However, in the mid-1990s, Myton re-formed the Congos with Burnett and Lindburgh Lewis. In 1994, new material was cut for the VP Records release *Congos Ashanti*. This was followed by 1997's *Natty Dread Rise Again* on **RAS Records**. In 1999, the reconstituted Congos released *Revival* on the VP Records imprint. Following it was a 2000 live album titled *Live at Maritime Hall: San Francisco*. In 2003, the *Congo Ashanti* album was re-released with bonus tracks added. In addition to new material, the work of the Congos has recently been added to a series of compilations that further immortalize this pair.

COOKE, FABIAN (c. 1970–)

Fabian Cooke has been an active producer and engineer in **reggae** music over the past two decades. As such, he has worked with many acts including **Big Mountain**, **Boom Shaka**, **Ken Boothe**, **John Holt**, **Ini Kamoze**, **Bob Marley**, Michael Rose, **Steel Pulse**, Caribbean Pulse, Mark Tyson and BNX, **Third World**, and many others. Cooke is also credited on the Walt Disney movie soundtrack of *The Lion King* as the producer of the international hit "Hakuna Matata." He continues to be active in the reggae music scene and oversees production of compilation albums such as *Unleaded Reggae Diamonds*.

COOPER, MICHAEL (c. 1955–)

Michael "Ibo" Cooper has had a long and storied career in Jamaican popular music. He was the keyboard player in two of the most prolific and beloved **reggae** bands of the past forty years, **Inner Circle** and **Third World**. Cooper and **Stephen "Cat" Coore** were both formally trained in music and had been playing semi-professional gigs around Kingston, Jamaica, when they joined the **Inner Circle** lineup in 1968. In 1973, they left to form their own band and took with them Inner Circle bass player **Richard Daley**. In this group, Cooper became part of the reggae mainstream with over twenty albums to the band's credits. They have stayed together for over thirty years, and the resulting discography is massive, including studio, live, and anthology recordings. In addition to his work with the band, Cooper has also become a skilled engineer and producer and plies these trades with many other artists. He also guests on recordings, including as the keyboard player of record on Walt Disney's *Little Mermaid Soundtrack: Sebastian's Song* (1990).

In the studio, Cooper has produced, arranged, or engineered recordings for artists such as the **Abyssinians**, **Aswad**, **Buju Banton**, **Beres Hammond**, **Maxi Priest**, **Super Cat**, and many others. He also maintains a busy schedule as a guest artist on other musicians' recordings. Examples of this include keyboard work for **Burning Spear**, **Cat Coore**, Lenny Kravitz, and others.

COORE, STEPHEN "CAT" (c. 1960–)

Stephen "Cat" Coore shares much of his early history with **Michael "Ibo" Cooper**. He was formally trained in music from an early age. At his mother's prompting, Coore took up the study of the cello at age six. He gained additional music training in school at Priory High School. It was in high school that Coore changed his musical tastes and gravitated toward popular music. He took up the guitar and at age thirteen began playing with the band **Inner Circle**. Through Inner Circle, Coore became a full-time musician and learned about the business of music as well as how to build a song.

At age sixteen, Coore fell under the influence of **Bob Marley** and directed his energy into writing songs. Next, Coore had the idea of creating his own band in the mold of the three-piece group that was popular at the time. He split from Inner Circle, beginning a new band with Carl Barovier and Colin Leslie. Cooper, who had also been in Inner Circle, immediately joined Coore's new band. Several other members then came on board, and the product was a new band, **Third World**. Producer **Clancy Eccles** originally gave the name as Suns of the Third World, but the beginning of the name was soon dropped.

In a career that has lasted over forty years, Coore has worked with a large number of important reggae artists. He has intermittently guested on numerous albums by artists such as **Black Uhuru**, **Dennis Brown**, the **Congos**, **Bob Marley**, **Judy Mowatt**, and **Sly and Robbie**. He also cut one solo album, 1998's *Uptown Rebel*. Coore continues to be active in the Jamaican popular music scene. Indeed, he has recently gone on record as saying that Third World still has more music to come.

COUNT BOYSIE (c. 1940–)

Jeremiah "Count" Boysie, also known as the Monarch, spent years running a Kingston **sound system**. From this early experience, he went on to work as a producer. Much of the material that he produced came out on the **Trojan** label, and his skills became quite popular. An early example of his work was **Jimmy Cliff's** single "Daisy Got Me Crazy." This marked Cliff's first break in the studio and the beginning of his career. Boysie went on to produce numerous successful releases over several years.

COUNT LASHER (c. 1940–)

Count Lasher was born Terence Perkins; he would become one of Jamaica's most successful **mento** singers. He released at least fifty singles, yet has no full-length albums or even anthologies of his work. Lasher helped to establish the difference between rural and urban mento styles, recording in both styles. An early example is his "Mango Time" release with the B-side "Breadfruit Season." Lasher and Calypso Quintet went on to release "Sam Fi Man," which warns of the activities of a "con" man and uses a banjo playing in a proto-**reggae** style.

The list of singles by Count Lasher is long, and each song is quintessential Jamaican mento. The lyrics are a breed of rural Jamaican storytelling that helped to secure Lasher a place in Jamaican history. Late Count Lasher recordings tended to be more urban in approach. An example is "Calypso Cha Cha Cha," which **Bob Marley and the Wailers** would go on to cover. Lasher's output spans the period from the late 1950s to the mid-1970s, and he continues to be explored as an artist who set the stage for the birth of reggae.

COUNT MATCHUKI (c. 1940–)

Count Matchuki was born Winston Cooper in Kingston, Jamaica. His career in music began as a sound system **DJ** for **Duke Reid**. It was as a Reid DJ that Matchuki made his first mark. He is credited as being the first DJ to begin talking to the crowd while spinning records. This practice, now called **toasting**, became popular, and Matchuki's toasting evolved into telling jokes or stories over the beat of the cueing record. He moved from jokes to lyrics, which resulted in the earliest rap over an existing beat. Some also credit Matchuki with pioneering what became known as beatboxing, an activity he called making "peps," the outcome of which was still making instrumental sounds with one's voice and mouth over a recorded beat. Matchuki, however, was not well recorded. Only a few examples of his work still exist, and they are hard to find. However, Matchuki's legacy is enormous and led to the practice of Jamaican toasting, with DJs such as **U-Roy**, American hip hop, and contemporary reggae rappers such as **Bounty Killer**, **Capleton**, and **Elephant Man**.

COUNT STICKY (1935–)

Count Sticky hit the Jamaican **mento** recording scene during the style's heyday in the 1950s. He is different from many of his contemporaries insofar as he did not stay in the mento style; instead, his style evolved into **reggae** in the 1970s. Sticky was not a prolific recording artist, but he still produced several excellent mento tracks in traditional and other mento styles. There is no anthology recording of his output, but glimpses of his material are still circulating on the original seven-inch recordings. Early efforts by Sticky include singles such as the Caribou Records release "Tempting Powder" with the B-side "Sticky Mento." Sticky put out a variety of mento sides that included "Calypso Ten," "Chico Chico," "Bam Cielena," and "Dry Acid."

In the early to mid-1970s, Sticky worked with producer **Lee "Scratch" Perry** to release about twenty tracks in the burgeoning reggae style. The reggae material was fast and left the vestiges of mento behind. A later reggae single by Sticky is the 1974 release "What Do You So." However, Sticky was not a typical reggae singer; rather, he was a **DJ** in the style of **Big Youth** and U-Roy.

COUSINS, ROY (c. 1945–)

Born in Kingston, Jamaica, Roy Cousins's music career began in the early 1960s when he worked to get other acts recorded. Acts he was involved with included the **Congos**, Nicky Thomas, and Tina Stewart. In 1963, he formed the Royals, a **reggae** group that garnered critical acclaim. The group was in the studio by 1966 and recorded hits such as "Ghetto Man," "Blacker Black," and "When You Are Wrong." Unfortunately, Cousins did not look like a typical reggae star; he wore his hair cropped and did not quit his day job at the Kingston Post Office. As a result, international fame eluded him. However, Cousins's tenacity paid off. By 1972 he had the money to start his own record label and launched the Tamoki Records imprint. This was followed two years later with his Wambesi label. Through these outfits, Cousins was able to release a series of records by the Royals in the late 1970s and early 1980s that included *Israel Be Wise*, *Moving On*, and *Royals Collection*. Cousins is still active in the music business today, producing tracks for himself and as part of **Heartbeat Records**.

COWAN, TOMMY (c. 1945–)

Tommy Cowan has been in the middle of the Jamaican **reggae** scene for several decades as a singer, producer, manager, concert promoter, and longstanding emcee of the **Reggae Sunsplash** music festival. Cowan got his start in the music business in 1964 when he joined a group called the Mericoles, who went on to call themselves the **Jamaicans**. The group had a major hit in 1967 with "Ba-Ba Boom," which won the Festival Song Competition that year. The Jamaicans then launched a tour of the United States and Canada, and Cowan found himself on the road with other reggae greats

Tommy Cowan. © *UrbanImage.tv.*

such as **Byron Lee and the Drago-naires**. As a result of the tour, Cowan left the Jamaicans in the early 1970s to work with Lee at **Dynamic Studio**. Cowan was hired to work in market-ing; he quickly learned the business of Jamaican popular music.

With Lee's help and guidance, Cowan was soon working with major American and UK labels, promoting Lee's products. Further, he was pro-moting island concert appearances by major American stars such as Aretha Franklin, Percy Sledge, the Drifters, and the Temptations. At the time, Cowan was assisting Lee in the man-agement of several outstanding Jamai-can recording artists. With his newly acquired business acumen, Cowan opted to move out on his own. Fortunately, Lee put his full backing behind Cowan's fledgling Talent Corporation. Artists flocked to Cowan's roster, and soon he was managing the likes of **Inner Circle**, **Israel Vibration**, **Ras Michael** and the **Sons of Negus**, and **Zap Pow**.

Another set of musicians who were active around Cowan were **Bob Mar-ley**, **Peter Tosh**, and **Bunny Wailer**. Cowan's Talent Corporation was located at 1C Oxford Road in Kingston, and this loca-tion became a hotbed for reggae luminaries. Cowan and Marley became close, since they were working in the same neighborhood. In fact, from Marley's 56 Hope Road location, Cowan promoted the 1978 One Love Peace Concert. Cowan also toured with Marley and was instrumental in arranging the **Wailers** trip to Zimbabwe. After Marley's death in 1981, Cowan teamed with the **Reggae Sunsplash** organization and became the emcee for the event, traveling with its international tour as emcee. More recently Cowan converted from **Rastafarianism** to Christianity, and his wife, **Car-lene Davis**, has become the driving force behind the organization Glory Music, which promotes gospel music.

COXSONE, LLOYD (c. 1955–)

Lloyd Coxsone was born Lloyd Blackwood in Morant Bay, Jamaica. As a youth, he left his island home, relocating to the United Kingdom in 1962. He settled in southwest London, in Wandsworth, and entered the music scene by setting up a **sound system** called Lloyd the Matador. Before establishing his sound system, Blackwood spent six months working on the British rail system. He did not succeed with his initial effort, so he went to work with the UK-based **Duke Reid** sound until 1969.

When Blackwood left the Reid system he took some of its personnel; they worked under the name of Reid's biggest competitor on the island, **Clement "Coxsone"**

Dodd, establishing the Sir Coxsone Sound System. The Coxsone sound caught on and soon was active at the UK nightclub Roaring Twenties. This led Coxsone to greater heights, during which his system was considered the best through the 1970s. He was able to maintain his standing by keeping current with what was happening back in Jamaica and playing the most recent records. Further, he had a crew of young **DJs** who kept the music coming, and he had solid equipment that allowed for echo, reverb, and equalizing during the dance.

Coxsone Sound's premier selector was a DJ called Festus who mixed up the styles of music that he played so that the output appealed to everyone in the audience. Coxsone then moved into more of the music business and became the premier **lovers rock** producer. His first success came with Louisa Marks's hit "Caught You in a Lie." Coxsone also began issuing his own material and had a hit with the album *King of the Dub Rock*, which contained his own material along with that of **Gussie Clarke**.

In 1982, a second volume in this series was released on the Regal label. The imprints that Coxsone used for recordings throughout the late 1970s and early 1980s were Tribesman and Lloyd Coxsone Outernational. Artists whom Coxsone recorded included Faybiene Miranda, Fred Locks, and the Creation Steppers. Many of these early recordings were again made available on the compilation *12 the Hard Way*. Another significant selector that worked for Coxsone in the mid-1980s was Blacka Dread, who went on to become a reputable producer in his own right. Late in the 1980s, Coxsone went into semi-retirement but has emerged again to regain control of the UK sound. Coxsone's sound has been the subject of several recordings, most notably **I-Roy's** singles "Coxsone Time" and "Lloyd Coxsone Time."

CREARY, DENNIS (c. 1960–)

A singer and songwriter active in the reggae scene for the past twenty years, Dennis Creary released several singles in the mid-1980s and went on to have his material included on the 1988 compilation album *Telephone Track*. His material also appears on releases by several other **reggae** luminaries such as **Cocoa T**, **Freddie McGregor**, and **Shabba Ranks**.

CREATION REBEL

Creation Rebel was a band formed to back up the late **Prince Far I**, consisting of **Eric "Fish" Clarke**, **Lincoln "Style" Scott**, Clinton Jack, Bigga Morrison, and Crucial Tony. From 1977 to 1980, this collective teamed with **Adrian Sherwood** to create a series of **dub** hits that rivaled the material produced by **Lee "Scratch" Perry**. At the time, the group and Sherwood were located in England and released some of the best dub **reggae** of the decade. The group went on to record a set of five albums, beginning with 1980's *Starship Africa*, on 4D Rhythms. This was followed by a pair of albums in 1981, *Psychotic Junkanoo* and *Threat to Creation*. In 1982, the group put out *Lows and Highs* on the Cherry Red imprint. More recently, On-U Sound released material from the first two Creation Rebel Records, *Dub from Creation* and *Rebel* Vibrations, in 1994. In 1995, Lagoon Records released *Creation Rebel*, another collection of the group's material.

CROOKS, SYDNEY (1945–)

Born Sydney Roy Crooks on February 24, 1945, Crooks entered the music scene upon joining the singing group the **Pioneers**, which also contained **Glen Adams** and Sydney's brother Derrick. The trio had a series of hit singles from 1968 to 1970 and even charted in the United Kingdom with 1969's "Longshot Kick De Bucket" and "Let Your Yeah Be Yeah" in 1971. In 1969 they released their debut album, *Longshot*, on **Trojan Records**. A series of other releases followed, including 1970's *Battle of the Giants*; *Yeah* in 1971; *Freedom Feeling* and *I Believe in Love* in 1973; and *I'm Gonna Knock on the Door*, *Roll On Muddy River*, and *Pusher Man* in 1974. The group worked with a series of important producers, such as **Jimmy Cliff**, **Joe Gibbs**, and **Leslie Kong**. After the group split up, Crooks went on to become a producer in demand by some of reggae's big names, including **Dennis Brown** and **Gregory Isaacs**. In 2002, Trojan Records employed Crooks to produce its release *Trojan Skinhead Reggae Box Set*.

CROSS, SANDRA (1965–)

Born in South London in 1965 and making her singing debut in a Pentecostal church choir, Sandra Cross led the choir at age nine. A few years later she became half of the singing duo Love and Unity. Together the pair recorded the single "I Adore You," which won first prize at a local talent show. As part of their prize, the song was released on Studio 76 Records and went to the top of the British **reggae** charts for a month in 1979. Three hit singles followed, including "I Just Don't Care," "I Can't Let You Go," and "Put It On."

Shortly thereafter, the duo split up and Cross began working with the **Ariwa** Records head **Mad Professor**. Under the Professor's tutelage, Cross joined the all-girl group the **Wild Bunch**, which went on to Top 20 success in 1984. Subsequently, the band toured Europe but broke up within the year. Cross then went solo and released a version of the Stylistics single "Country Livin.'" The single stayed in the British Top 10 for ten weeks in 1985. Cross parlayed this success with a second single, "You're Lying," and again had chart success. Professor's Ariwa sounds then released Cross's debut album in 1986. This led to critical acclaim, and she was presented with a British Reggae Award for Best Female Singer for six consecutive years. She went on to receive numerous other awards, including the 1990 Chicago Radio Award for Highest-Selling Record.

Throughout her storied career, Cross stayed on the Ariwa label; she now boasts a catalog of six albums. Stylistically, she branched out in the 1990s. She now sings in a reggae hybrid style that evidences jazz elements. In 1996, she released the album *Just a Dream*, her first foray into the new style. Most recently, Cross's recordings are coming out on her own SCM Records (Sandra Cross Music) label. In addition to her own recording projects, Cross has made guest appearances and lent her songs to many artists across the stylistic spectrum.

CULTURE

The vocal trio Culture has existed for forty years. Their success, roots reggae style, and longevity are due in large part to **Joseph Hill**. Hill is the group's singer and songwriter and is responsible for the spiritual elements that stay central in their music. The group formed in 1976; their debut album, *Two Sevens Clash*, was released the following year and became an instant classic. In addition to Hill, the band includes Albert Walker and Roy "Kenneth" Dayes, both cousins of Hill's.

In the early 1970s, Hill was involved in several bands around his hometown of Linstead, Jamaica, the most notable being the Soul Defenders. However, these early bands did not garner any success. With Culture, Hill formed a vocal trio that had unlimited potential. Originally calling themselves African Disciples, early on the group worked with producer **Joe Gibbs** in Kingston. With Gibbs's tutelage and with the assistance of

Culture. © *UrbanImage.tv.*

Errol Thompson, the group changed their name to Culture and released the single "This Time." The song came out on Gibbs's Belmont label and led to a string of breakthrough singles, including "When Two Sevens Clash" and "See Them a Come."

In 1977, the group released its debut album, which featured the songs "Natty Dread Take Over" and "Ger Ready to Tide the Lion to Zion." Because the album was rife with **Rastafarian** images, it served as a spiritual guide for its listeners and enjoyed enormous popularity in both Jamaica and the United Kingdom. Unfortunately, the success of the album was not financially transferred to the band through their producer Gibbs, so after the album Culture severed ties with him. They moved on to work with **Duke Reid**, but this too was an unhappy alliance. The product of the brief Reid dealings was the album *Africa Stand Alone*, released in 1978. Gibbs still had control over the earliest Culture material, and he went on to release two more albums of work that had not been included on the *Two Sevens Clash* release. These two releases were made available as *Baldhead Bridge* and *More Culture*.

Culture's next producer was **Sonia Pottinger** and her High Note imprint. For Pottinger, the group recorded a series of three albums that came out in 1978 and 1979. *Harder Than the Rest*, *Cumbolo*, and *International Herb* were released in quick succession. The next major step for the band was the 1978 performance at the One Love Peace Concert, which then kicked off a major UK tour. On tour, the singing trio were backed by the **Revolutionaries**, who included **Sly and Robbie**. In 1982, however, the trio split; it seemed that as a band, Culture was a thing of the past. Hill went on to record *Lion Rock*, a solo album released under the Culture name. Fortunately, the trio reunited in 1986 and went back in the studio to produce *Culture at Work* and *Culture in Culture*. There followed subsequent albums in the late 1980s and throughout the 1990s. Overall, the group has released at least thirty albums of substantial roots reggae material. Some notable recent work includes *Payday* (2000) and *Live in Africa* (2002).

CUTTY RANKS (1965–)

Born Philip Thomas in Kingston, Jamaica, in 1965, Cutty Ranks honed his **DJ** music skills on several **sound systems**. Ranks got his start at fourteen on the Gemini sound system. He then moved on to the **Tony Rebel** and Papa Roots outfits. His big break came when he joined the Killamanjaro system and worked with **Early B**, **Super Cat**, Puddy Roots, and Little Twitch. From there, Ranks moved on to the Sturmars system, where he worked with **Josey Wales**, **Nicodemus**, Super Cat, **U-Brown**, and **Yami Bolo**. Reputedly the best system, Sturmars dominated **dancehall** in the late 1980s.

Ranks next moved onto a new system called Arrows, working with Professor Nuts, Conrad Crystal, Chicken Chest, and others. A strong reputation established, Ranks went into the studio and cut a single for **Winston Riley's** Techniques imprint called "Gunman Lyrics." The song was a dancehall hit and led to a string of singles for Ranks. In the early 1990s, Ranks had his first international hit with the single "The Bomber." This was followed by "Pon Mi Nozzle," "Liberty," and "Lambada." Ranks had become popular enough to warrant an album; thus, the Penthouse label released a collection of his most popular singles. Ranks's next single, "The Stopper," was a major hit in the United Kingdom and even garnered a hip hop remix.

The 1990s were filled with successful material from the dancehall phenomenon. Toward the late 1990s, Ranks slowed down, confident that his legacy was well assured. He continued to release singles periodically, such as "Guiltiness," but the hits were less frequent. Cutty Ranks continues to be active in the dancehall scene. In the early part of the new millennium he was in the United Kingdom working on new material at Third Eye Studio, preparing a new record.

D

DA COSTA, GLEN (c. 1955–)

Glen Da Costa is one of the many superb Jamaican musicians trained at the **Alpha Boys Catholic School**. While at the school, Da Costa was exposed to the same kind of training that yielded the likes of the **Skatalites**. After leaving the school, he became a session saxophone player and has performing credits on a long list of classic Jamaican **ska** and **reggae** albums. Possibly Da Costa's greatest claim to fame is his work with **Bob Marley**. Da Costa played with the horn section that accompanied the **Wailers** on many of their groundbreaking releases. Alongside **Vin Gordon** on trombone, Da Costa was a studio and live performance mainstay through much of the late 1960, 1970s, and 1980s.

More recently, Da Costa again teamed with Gordon and helped to form the Coyabalites, who released 1997's *Unhinged* on the **Shanachie** imprint and later 2001's *Coyaba Ska*. The records are collections of ska and reggae classics. The band also contains **Dean Fraser** (saxophone), **Ernest Ranglin** (guitar), David Madden (trumpet), and Harold Butler (keyboards). While the two Coyabalite albums to date are criticized as a distilled form of ska that is meant for a broader audience, they still maintain the proper flavor of the originals. The group is rounded out by the tenor vocals of legendary Jamaican singer **Justin Hinds**. The band continues to play ska versions of Jamaican classics by artists such as **Donald Drummond**, **Toots Hibbert**, **Jackie Mittoo**, Bob Marley, and many others.

DACOSTA, TONY (c. 1955–)

A **ska** singer active in the mid-to-late 1960s, Tony DaCosta's principal appearances came at the hands of the **Skatalites**, the legendary ska instrumental group. The group included **Roland Alphonso** (tenor sax), Lester "Ska" Sterling (alto sax), **Lloyd Brevett** (bass), **Donald Drummond** (trombone), **Tommy McCook** (tenor sax), John Moore (trumpet), and Lloyd Knibb (drums). To this core of instrumentalists were often added various sidemen and singers. DaCosta performed with the Skatalites as a singer on some recordings and also for live performances.

DADDY COLONEL (c. 1965–)

Daddy Colonel got his start in music and earned his reputation working for the Saxon Studio International sound system, started in 1976. By the early 1980s it was the premier UK system and had many of the best **DJs**. The crop of talent included Papa Levi, **Tippa Irie**, Daddy Rusty, and Daddy Colonel. Along with DJing for the system, Colonel released several singles. Some of these singles are solos; others are group efforts for which Colonel enlisted the participation of Tippa Irie. An example of a solo effort is the Colonel single "Take a Tip from Me," released on the UK Bubblers label. The single features Colonel on vocals with the **Regulars** backing him up. Another Bubblers single is "Colonel." Additionally, a few of Colonel's singles are now available on compilation albums such as *Saxon Studio International: Coughing Up Fire*.

DADDY SCREW (1968–)

Born Michael Alexander Johnson on March 29, 1968, in Kingston, Jamaica, Screw was raised in a religious household and matriculated from Vauxhall Comprehensive High School. While in school he exhibited musical talent; indeed, he had already honed some **DJ** skills while in school, and in 1984 he released his first single, "Dimbo Bucket." Once finished with school, Screw became a full-time DJ and went to work for Black Stone sound system. It was with this system that Screw realized that his method of **toasting** over the instrumental version of a song made the audience come alive. Screw then went into the studio to record a single on the **Tuff Gong** label titled "Madda Mampie." Through Tuff Gong producer Tony Kelly, Screw met Kelly's brother **Dave Kelly**, who advised Screw to alter his salacious lyrics in order to garner radio play. With the help of Kelly, Screw began to record at Penthouse Studios and teamed with the DJ **Terror Fabulous**. Next, Terror Fabulous and Kelly formed the Madhouse label, releasing a string of hits by a variety of DJs including Daddy Screw.

Throughout the 1990s, Screw has continued to release solid, hard-edge material. In 1993 he released the album *Loverman* on VP, and in 1996 he put out *Multiple Choice*. He has also been active in collaborations and guest appearances working with stars such as **Sharon Forrester**, **Barrington Levy**, Terror Fabulous, and others. Screw continues to be active in the hardcore DJ style.

DALEY, GEORGE (c. 1945–)

Involved in the Jamaican popular music scene in the 1960s and early 1970s, Daley is a cousin to one of the **Clarendonians** and had the opportunity to sing backup vocals on several of their songs. He released solo material under the moniker Prince George; an example of his early work is the 1976 single "Babylon Kingdom Fall." Daley continues to be active as a singer. He resides in Brooklyn, New York, and has teamed with Barry Llewellyn from the **Heptones**.

DALEY, LLOYD (1939–)

Lloyd Daley was born in Kingston, Jamaica, in 1939. After graduating from Kingston Technical College with a degree in electronics, he became an electrician and ran his own shop. This experience helped him set up a **sound system** in the late 1950s, which was his entrance into music. He chose the name Lloyd the Matador for his system, and from there it was not a large step into the production booth. He was entering some pretty serious company with his competitors being **Clement "Coxsone" Dodd**, **Duke Reid**, and **Prince Buster**. Because he had difficulty acquiring the same records as his competitors, Daley went into **Ken Khouri's Federal Records** and cut some of his own material with many of the most famous names in Jamaican studio performance. Daley went on to launch his own label, first called Matador and then Mystic, and set about recording many of **ska's** most popular artists.

In the late 1960s, Daley hit with Scorcher's song "Ugly Man," which was followed by several others. He recorded for the **Heptones**, the **Viceroys**, and the **Ethiopians**, among others. At the height of his recording career he was working with the **Abyssinians**, **Dennis Brown**, and **Alton Ellis**. By the early 1970s, with the encroaching popularity of **reggae**, Daley's run was coming to an end. However, he did release two essential albums, *Scandal* and *Back When*, and much of his material exists on a compilation released by **Heartbeat** in 1992, titled *Lloyd Daley's Matador Productions 1968-1972*. While Daley's output is not prolific, it is of great substance and marks many of the sides that he produced that have become ska standards.

DALEY, RICHARD (c. 1960–)

Part of two of the most significant **reggae** bands of the last thirty-plus years, Richard Daley plays both bass and rhythm guitar and is often credited as a multi-instrumentalist on recordings. His first major appearance was as a member of the seminal **Inner Circle** band. However, when **Michael "Ibo" Cooper** and **Stephen "Cat" Coore** left Inner Circle to form **Third World**, Daley went with them. With Third World, Daley has been active on the Jamaican reggae scene and continues to perform and record. The group's most well-known song is the hit "Bad Boy," which has been featured as the theme song on the television show *Cops*.

DANCEHALL

Dancehall is a style of Jamaican popular music that developed in the 1980s. The style involves a **DJ** singing or **toasting** over a repetitive beat, the result of which is a relatively thin texture. Dancehall takes its name from the venues in which it developed. The lyrics of many dancehall songs involve sexual situations, drug use, or criminal activity ("slackness"). The style has roots in its predecessor **reggae**, often using existing reggae rhythms that are reproduced on a drum machine at a much greater speed. A hybrid of dancehall is the **raggamuffin** style, which is essentially the same, but only uses digital or electronic music for the beats.

The style's popularity increased in the 1990s and began to cross over into the American popular music market, with many gangsta rappers using dancehall rhythms for their songs. This crossover was made more complete when contemporary hip hop artists began involving dancehall stars in their songs. In the most recent past, dancehall DJs have become increasingly active in American hip hop. Artists such as **Beenie Man**, **Capleton**, and **Yellowman** commonly record with U.S. hip hop artists and appear on their albums. The union has brought Jamaican popular music to the forefront of the American music scene to an extent that it never previously enjoyed. Significant dancehall DJs include **Buju Banton**, **Dennis Brown**, Capleton, **Cocoa Tea**, **Dillinger**, **Eek-A-Mouse**, **Beres Hammond**, **Maxi Priest**, **Shabba Ranks**, **Shinehead**, and Yellowman. Dancehall continues to be the prevalent style in Jamaican popular music today.

DASILVA, EVERTON (c. 1950–)

Everton DaSilva has been active as a **reggae** percussionist since the late 1970s. His first appearance was on **Augustus Pablo's** *East of the River Nile* album in 1979. Through the course of his career, he has played with a series of important reggae artists, including **Horace Andy**, **Aston "Family Man" Barrett**, **Carlton "Carly" Barrett**, **Tommy McCook**, **Robbie Shakespeare**, and **Earl "Chinna" Smith**. More recently, DeSilva has appeared on Pablo's 2000 release *Dub, Reggae and Roots*, and the Dubmaster's 1999 release *X-Ray Music*. He also has turned to producing and has worked on several compilations as both producer and arranger.

DAVIS, CARLENE (c. 1970–)

An active **reggae** vocalist for the past fifteen years, Davis is noted for her smooth voice and her religious convictions. Her early material, such as *No Bias* (1991), *Jesus Is Only a Prayer Away* (1992), *Carlene Davis* (1992), *Songs from Bob Marley* (1994), and *Echoes of Love* (1995), are in a more straight-ahead reggae style. However, in the mid-1990s she converted to Christianity, and her music reflects this change in her private life. Her 1998 album *Vessel* is in a new style now commonly referred to as reggae gospel. The year 2000's *Redeemed* is an affirmation of her new life and speaks of her experiences. Her single "This Island Needs Jesus" was a number one hit in the Caribbean and popular around the world.

Also in 2000, Davis was named minister of music for the Family Church on the Rock in Kingston, Jamaica. She has subsequently released a series of albums with 2004's *Author and Finisher* and others. During her career, Davis has also appeared on several other artists' albums, including work with the **Heptones**, **Gregory Isaacs**, David Keane, and **Byron Lee**. Davis has been assisted in her career by her husband/manager **Tommy Cowan**, who was formerly **Bob Marley and the Wailers'** tour manager, known internationally as the longstanding emcee for the **Reggae Sunsplash** annual concert.

DAVIS, CARLTON "SANTA" (c. 1950–)
A **reggae** drummer active on the Jamaican popular music scene since the late 1970s, Davis has played and recorded with a series of major recording artists. He has the percussion/drum credits for recording with artists such as the **Abyssinians**, **Big Youth**, Peter Broggs, Dave and **Ansell Collins**, **Dillinger**, **Doctor Alimantado**, I-Roy, **Gregory Isaacs**, and **Mikey Dread**. He also released a single solo album in 1997, *Adrenalina*, on the Sarzo Music imprint. In addition to his recording credits, Davis has played with top artists such as **George Fullwood**, **Tommy McCook**, and **Leroy "Horsemouth" Wallace**.

DAVIS, JANET LEE (c. 1970–)
Janet Lee Davis was born in London and moved to Jamaica at age three. She grew up in Old Harbor Bay, St. Catherine. Active in the church choir as a youth, Davis spent the time inside and outside of church learning songs in a variety of styles. At fifteen, she joined the sound system Ghetto and began **DJing** and **toasting**. She also began singing at staged events during her late teen years. At age twenty-one she returned to London; in 1987 she caught her big break when she went into the recording studio with Vego Wales. Through Wales she met popular DJ Joseph Cotton and was asked to guest on his album *No Touch the Style*. The single became a major hit; based on its success she was able to cut her debut album *Never Gonna Let You Go*.

In 1989, Davis again entered the studio, releasing the single "Two Timing Lover" on the Fashion label. The song was a huge success and spent time on the charts. She released several subsequent singles and assured her reputation as a charting vocalist. Her success caught the attention of **Island Records**, and she signed a four-album deal in the early 1990s. Unfortunately, no albums materialized. However, the Island sessions did produce several more successful singles, including "Spoiled by Your Love," "Pleasure Seekers," "Love Is Alive," "Never Say Never," and "Just the Lonely Talking Again." Davis then worked with Jamaican producer **Augustine "Gussie" Clarke**, and he put her backing vocals on **Cocoa Tea's** album *Authorized* (1992).

In 1992, Davis returned to the Fashion imprint and has since maintained her dominance of the UK **lovers rock** style. She released a series of hits that includes singles such as "Ooh Baby Baby," "Big Mistake," and "Ready to Learn." The Fashion label connection led to Davis's first album, *Missing You* (1994), which contains many of her successful singles in addition to a few new songs. Davis has enjoyed years of success as a female lovers rock vocalist. She is critically acclaimed and has won numerous awards such as the Bob Marley Award for Best Female Artist in 1995. Davis continues to be active, with ongoing performances and studio work, and she continues to dominate the UK lovers rock scene.

DAVIS, RONNIE (1950–)

Ronnie Davis was born in 1950 in Savanne La Mar, Jamaica. His music career began when he joined the **Tennors** at age seventeen. When Davis joined the Tennors, they already had a reputation in the business for their work with Maurice Johnson and George "Clive" Murphy. Once Davis joined the group, he was groomed into the lead singer position; soon they entered the studio. They recorded **rock steady** hits for labels such as **Dynamic**, **Prince Buster**, and **Treasure Isle** and worked with a series of talented producers. However, in the early 1970s, the **reggae** style was progressively taking over from rock steady, and the Tennors split. Davis went solo and produced a large quantity of material in the burgeoning reggae style. He was living in Kingston and was part of the explosion of the new Jamaican popular music style.

Between 1971 and 1975, Davis recorded in excess of 100 tracks. At first he only worked with **Bunny "Striker" Lee**, but soon he branched out to record with several other producers. His collaboration with **Lloyd Campbell** produced the single "Won't You Come Home," which was a number one hit. Additionally, Campbell introduced Davis to Keith Porter, and the two recorded together under the name the **Itals**. Their song "Inna Dis a Time" became a major hit in 1977.

In the 1980s, **Nighthawk Records** courted the Itals; the result was the group's debut album *Brutal out Deh*. Although the album did not sell well at first, a year after its release it caught on and soon the demand for the album was too great for the relatively small label to keep up with. In 1983 the Itals went on tour with the **Roots Radics** backing them up. The next step for the band was their sophomore release. This came in the form of 1987's *Rasta Philosophy*, which was nominated for a Grammy Award.

Despite the Itals' success, Davis felt it was time to go solo and left the band in 1995. His solo debut came out the following year with his new group, Idren, which consisted of Roy Smith and Robert Doctor singing backup for Davis. The group released another album in 1997 titled *Come Straight*. Although Davis left the Itals, he and Idren continue to record for the Nighthawk imprint. Davis continues to release solid roots reggae even after almost thirty years in the business.

DEADLY HEADLEY. *See* BENNETT, HEADLEY

DEKKER, DESMOND (1941–)

Born Desmond Dacres in Kingston, Jamaica in 1941, Dekker lost both of his parents during his teenage years and was forced to survive on his own. He earned a living as a welder; it was in the welding shop that his coworkers recognized his vocal talents. In 1961, Dekker auditioned for **Duke Reid** at **Treasure Isle** and **Clement "Coxsone" Dodd** at **Studio One**. He was rebuffed by both studios, but tried out for **Leslie Kong** and his **Beverley's** label. At Beverley's, Dekker sang for **Derrick Morgan**; his talent was validated. Kong promised Dekker a session, but first the aspiring singer had to write a song to record. This took two

Desmond Dekker. © *UrbanImage.tv.*

years. However, the product was 1963's "Honor Your Father and Mother," which Kong recorded and released as a single. The song reached the top of the Jamaican charts and was the beginning of Dekker's recording career. The singer then recorded a series of other singles, the most notorious being "King of Ska." This track was backed by the **Maytals** and quickly went on to be a **ska** classic.

Once Dekker had established a reputation he formed his own band, the **Aces**. The group was a collection of four brothers, Barry, Carl, Clive, and Patrick Howard. With them, Dekker scored a series of hits including "Parents," "Mount Zion," and "This Woman." Dekker made the transition from ska to **rock steady** with his single "007," a Jamaican hit that entered the top fifteen in the United Kingdom. Dekker parlayed his UK success by making a trip to England. Upon returning to Jamaica, he went back into the studio and recorded a series of rude boy anthems in the rock steady style. Rude boy songs included titles such as "Rudie Got Soul" and "Rude Boy Train."

Also in the mid-1960s, Dekker released one of the earliest songs that dealt with the theme of African repatriation, "Pretty Africa." This theme would go on to pervade countless roots reggae hits. Dekker had another hit in 1967 with "It Pays"; this assured his superstar status in Jamaica. A year later he released "The Israelites," which again stunned Jamaica and charted in the United Kingdom. It also charted in the United States and opened up the singer's music to a whole new audience. With so many hit singles, Beverley's released Dekker's first album, a compilation of hits titled *Action* (1968). The year 1969 was an especially good year for Dekker. He charted several singles and released the song "It Mek," which again stormed Jamaica and charted in the United Kingdom. Beverley's released another compilation, this time of Dekker's hits from 1969, titled *The Israelites*.

In the 1970s, Dekker's career path changed. He spent less time in the studio and more time touring, and he moved to England. The recordings that he did make were with the Aces backing him up on vocals and Beverley's All Stars playing the instruments. Dekker's next hit was his version of **Jimmy Cliff's** tune "You Can Get It If You Really Want." It was shortly after the release of this single that Kong unexpectedly died of a heart attack in 1971. Like Cliff, Dekker had only worked for Kong, and both singers took the loss of the label head hard. But by the mid-1970s, Dekker had regained his footing and released a series of solid and successful singles. Dekker turned to the production team of Tony Cousins and Bruce White, releasing "Everybody Join Hands" and "Sing a Little Song."

The end of the 1970s found Dekker releasing few singles and lacking chart success in the United Kingdom. This changed, however, when the **two-tone** movement dawned in the United Kingdom at the end of the 1970s. Dekker signed with Stiff Records and released the *Black & Dekker* album. Dekker then charted with his single "Please Don't Bend" and his version of Cliff's "Many Rivers to Cross." The early 1980s found Dekker working with a series of different producers and lackluster albums. By 1984, Dekker had to declare bankruptcy. He disappeared from the popular music scene for the rest of the 1980s, only to re-emerge in 1990. Dekker teamed with the Specials and released *King of Kings*, which revitalized his legacy. In 1996, Dekker released *Moving On* on the **Trojan** imprint. Dekker continues to enjoy success, primarily from his early catalog, which has remained available on the Trojan label and in re-release.

DELAHEYE, NOEL "JUNIOR" (c. 1960–)

Junior Delaheye was a roots reggae and **lovers rock** singer in the 1980s and early 1990s. He released three full-length albums and scored several local hits. His output commenced with 1981's *Movie Show*, which came out on the Wackies imprint. This was followed by 1982's *Showcase*, which featured the singles "All I Need Is Jah" and "Love." These releases offer a glimpse into Delaheye's singing style. He has a sweet tenor voice that effortlessly crosses over into the falsetto range. His most recent release was 1983's *Working for the Rent Man*. All of his material was released on the Wackies label and is currently available on re-release.

DELGADO, JUNIOR (1958–2005)

Junior Delgado was born Oscar Hibbert in Kingston, Jamaica, in 1958. He began his singing career in the early 1970s under the name Junior Hibbert as part of a singing group called Time Unlimited. **Lee "Scratch" Perry** eventually took the group into production and assisted in their stardom. Under Perry, Time Unlimited did have modest success with the single "Reaction." With this success, the group began working with other producers such as **Tommy Cowan**, **Rupie Edwards**, and **Bunny "Striker" Lee**. However, they could not recapture their early success, and in 1975 the group split.

Hibbert began a solo career and changed his name to Junior Delgado. He had a difficult start, recording for **Winston "Niney" Holness** with little success. He briefly changed his name again to "Jooks" (pronounced Jux), but this change did not yield any hits. Delgado's success finally came when he started working with **Earl "Chinna" Smith** at the DEB Studios. With a new producer in a new studio, Delgado finally had the right setup and recorded a string of hits that led to his first album, 1978's *Taste of the Young Heart*. The album was successful and allowed Delgado to start his own label, the Incredible Jux imprint, on which he released his second album, *Effort*.

Throughout the early 1980s, Delgado worked with a series of producers and cut several hit singles. He also spent time touring and was popular in both Jamaica and the United Kingdom. In 1981, Delgado released two new albums. *More She Love It* and *Disco Style Showcase* exemplify the singer's move with the musical trend from roots reggae to more of a **dancehall** style. As Delgado's stock continued to rise, he wrote in both the roots and dancehall style. He reunited with Perry for the "Sons of Slaves" single and worked with **Sly and Robbie** on "Fort Augustus." Both singles were big successes and led to his self-produced "Rich Man Poor Man," an instant classic. In 1982, Delgado released *Bushman Revolution* on his own Incredible Jux label. Following that was an eighteen-month stint in prison during which Delgado continued to write songs.

Throughout the latter half of the 1980s, Delgado released at least one album per year, each of which was successful. In the 1990s, Delgado's productivity slowed, but he still released five albums during the decade. He worked with **Augustus Pablo**, the Specials, Maxi Jazz, Smith and Mighty, and the Jungle Brothers. Delgado's 1999 release, *Reasons*, was produced by **Adrian Sherwood** and released on the On-U imprint; it showed that the singer could still write hits. Currently, Delgado continues to play and record his music. He had European and South American tour dates in 2004; he also spent time in his studio, Junior Delgado's Incredible Music Studios, where he recorded with his band. The band lineup included guitarist Steven Wright, bassist Caswell Swaby, Dennis Hutchinson on keyboards, and the drummer known as Tan. Until Delgado's death on April 14, 2005, he and his band recorded in his Bickerseth Road, London, studios.

DELLIMORE, OSSIE (c. 1970–)

Born on the Caribbean island of St. Vincent, Ossie Dellimore moved to Brooklyn, New York, in 1981, and began making a name for himself as a roots reggae singer. In addition to being a singer, Dellimore is also an accomplished guitar, bass, keyboard, harmonica, and bamboo flute player. In 1990 he won the Caribbean Amateur Night at the Apollo Theater, but continued to toil away without a record deal. He spent most of the 1990s playing live shows around New York City, making a name for himself and fine-tuning his playing and songwriting skills.

Dellimore's luck changed when he was invited into the studio in the late 1990s with the **Easy Star Records** All-Stars. The results of this session were Dellimore's debut CD *Freedom's Journal* and its associated single "Time Has Come." Dellimore continues to perform live, and subsequent recordings will be forthcoming.

DEMUS, JUNIOR (c. 1970–)

Junior Demus is an expert **DJ** who patterned himself after first-generation **dancehall** DJ **Nicodemus**, his namesake. He released his first single, "When Me Come," in 1991; it was followed by his 1994 debut album on Luke Records, *Bad Fowl.* The album was greeted with a degree of success and yielded memorable singles such as "Come Quick," "Son of a Gun," and "Hold Me Down." There followed a series of singles, the most popular of which was "Cabin Stabbin." This track was cut with **Super Cat** and Nicodemus; it has enjoyed a long period of popularity. The trio also worked together on the Sony Music release *The Good, the Bad, the Ugly, and the Crazy* in 1994. Demus has worked in the dancehall and **ragga** styles and has worked with major recording artists such as **Sugar Minott**, **Sluggy Ranks**, Foxy Brown, and the Frisco Kid. More recently, Demus has signed on to work with the **Easy Star** record label in New York with the expectation of future recordings.

DENNIS, RUDOLPH "GARTH" (c. 1960–)

One of the founding members of the legendary **reggae** band **Black Uhuru** (*uhuru* is Swahili for "freedom"), Rudolph Dennis helped form the band in the early 1970s with **Don Carlos** and **Derrick "Duckie" Simpson**. The trio of singers recorded a version of Curtis Mayfield's "Romancing to the Folk Song" on the **Dynamic** imprint but failed to have initial success. This caused Dennis to leave the group and join the **Wailing Souls**. Dennis was one of several performers who came and went in the Wailing Souls lineup. Others who were in the group include Buddy Haye and **Joe Higgs**. While Dennis was in the Wailing Souls, the group enjoyed their highest level of popularity. They released a series of popular albums in the late 1970s and throughout the 1980s. These works include 1979's *Wild Suspense*, 1980's *Firehouse Rock*, *Lay It on the Line* in 1986, and *Kingston 14* in 1987; all garnered the group success and cemented their legacy.

In the 1990s, the original Black Uhuru reformed and have subsequently toured and recorded. Their first reunion release was the 1990 album *Now.* Black Uhuru remains a seminal reggae band that has a Grammy Award to its credits. The band continues touring and recording.

DILLINGER (1953–)

Dillinger was born Lester Bullocks on June 25, 1953. He was part of the second generation of great Jamaican **toasters** and got his nickname from the living legend **Lee "Scratch" Perry**. Dillinger got his start in the music business in the early 1970s by following several **sound systems**. He first helped out with the El Paso system, home to **Dennis Alcapone**. It was from this association that he got his first nickname, Dennis Alcapone Jr., because the first-generation **DJ** occasionally passed the mix to his protégé.

Dillinger moved from the El Paso system to Prince Jackie's system and there had his first professional job in the music business. Soon Dennis Alcapone left the El Paso system and Dillinger returned to fill his position.

By 1973, Dillinger had made a reputation for himself, and Perry took him into the **Black Ark Studios** to make some recordings. The first outcome was the single "Dub Organizer"; it, along with several others, failed to make any impact. Next, Dillinger moved on to work with producer **Yabby You**, and together the two produced several hit singles. Dillinger then set about recording his debut album. From this he sought the help of **Clement "Coxsone" Dodd** at **Studio One**. The product was the 1975 release *Ready Natty Dreadie*, which contained Studio One beats with Dillinger DJing over them. The big break, however, came in 1976 with the release of *CB 200*, named for Dillinger's motorcycle and containing several hit singles, including "Plantation Heights," "Cocaine in My Brain," and "CB 200." "Cocaine" became a major hit both in Jamaica and in the United Kingdom.

Next, Dillinger recorded a clash album with fellow DJ **Trinity**, which contained the

Dillinger. © *UrbanImage.tv.*

hit single "Rizla Skank." It was followed by *Bionic Dread* in 1976, which did not yield a hit single. There followed a series of albums in the late 1970s that cemented the DJ's reputation in Jamaica, but went unnoticed off the island. Dillinger did not again achieve international success until 1979's *Marijuana in My Brain*. This album stormed Jamaica and was successful in the United Kingdom and United States. Based on its U.S. success, **A&M Records** offered Dillinger an American recording deal. In 1980, Dillinger and A&M released *Badder Than Them*. The album was meant to have new wave crossover potential; however, no one was ready for this from Dillinger, and the album did poorly. Dillinger was subsequently dropped from the label. Undeterred, the DJ toured the United Kingdom and released two live albums that highlighted his showmanship.

Through the rest of the 1980s and the entire 1990s, Dillinger continued to write, record, and tour. However, it seemed that his best work was already behind him. Since 2000, the DJ has continued to release new material and has regained some of his earlier glory. He has put out five albums in the past four years and maintains a solid standing among dancehall fans.

DILLON, CLIFTON "SPECIALIST" (c. 1970–)

Clifton "Specialist" Dillon has been an active **reggae** and **dancehall** producer for the past twenty years. He earned his nickname producing music for a variety of artists who include **Patra**, **Maxi Priest**, and **Shabba Ranks**. In 1993, Dillon realized that it was time for him to take greater control of his output, so he launched the Sheng

Records label. He established offices in Kingston, Jamaica and New York City and immediately began making a name for his new label through the introduction of an international marketing strategy that proved successful for his artists. This early roster included **Mad Cobra**, Richie Stephens, Shabba Ranks, and Petra.

Dillon's business acumen resulted in the interest of several major American labels becoming interested in his stable of talent. His success was not limited to marketing. Dillon-produced tracks from the mid-1990s garnered two Grammy Awards; furthermore, he produced four gold and two platinum singles. Dillon then consolidated his two branch offices under one roof in Miami Beach, Florida. New talent then entered the roster, with the most high profile acquisition being **Bob Marley's** son **Ky-Mani**. Dillon has also diversified his offerings by entering the movie soundtrack arena. He put songs on the soundtracks of *Addams Family Values*, *Money Talks*, and *Senseless*. Further, Dillon and Sheng, which now has offices in Jamaica, Paris, Canada, and London, plan to open a state of the art recording studio called Backstage Recording Studios.

DILLON, LEONARD "JACK SPARROW" (1942–)

Born on December 9, 1942, in Port Antonio, Jamaica, Leonard Dillon moved to Kingston in 1963, where he became friends with **Peter Tosh**. Tosh introduced him to **Clement "Coxsone" Dodd**, who gave the young singer/songwriter some time in the studio. Tosh, Dillon, and Dodd produced four songs, one of which was the hit "Ice Water." The song came out in 1965 under the artist name Jack Sparrow.

Dillon next formed the seminal **reggae** singing group the **Ethiopians**, composed of Dillon, Stephen Taylor, and Aston Morris. The Ethiopians went on to become one of the premier **rock steady** groups; they enjoyed a series of successful albums. Unfortunately, their successful run came to an end with bandmember Steven Taylor's death in 1975, during a time of financial difficulties as the result of withheld royalties. Taylor had gone to work in a gas station and was crossing the street to make change when he was struck by a passing vehicle. The loss of Taylor sent Dillon back to Port Antonio for a two-year period.

In the late 1970s, Dillon resurfaced and re-formed the Ethiopians for another recording session. This time the group worked with producer **Winston "Niney the Observer" Holness**, and the outcome was the 1977 release *Slave Call*. After completing this record, Dillon turned to solo work and has released two albums. *On the Road Again* and *One Step Forward* both came out in the 1990s and illustrated Dillon's mastery of the style.

DILLON, PHYLLIS (1948–2004)

Born in 1948 in Linstead, St. Catherine, Jamaica, Phyllis Dillon got her start in Jamaican popular music when she began to sing in the **rock steady** style in the mid-1960s. Her earliest musical experience came from singing in church and school. She also joined a singing group called the Vulcans. Initially, her talents went unnoticed until she released the 1966–1967 singles "Perfidia" and "Don't Stay Away." These songs came out with backing material provided by **Tommy McCook** and his band the Supersonics. The recordings were made at **Treasure Isle** studios and produced by **Duke Reid**. Her reputation grew, and soon she was justly crowned the "Queen of Rock Steady."

In 1967, she moved to New York but continued to make trips to Jamaica to record and stay current. While in New York, Dillon had a longstanding job at a bank. When the rock steady sound began to evolve into **reggae**, Dillon was able to evolve with it and thus maintain her fan base and currency. Dillon's work with Reid yielded several major singles in the early 1970s, which included "One Life to Live, One Love to Give," "The Love That a Woman Should Give a Man," "I Can't Forget about You Baby," and "Close to You." Through these recordings, Dillon became the most successful female vocalist to record for Reid. This series of hits charted in Jamaica and with their licensing to **Trojan** also became popular in the United Kingdom. By the mid-1970s, Dillon had moved away from the music business, but she did re-emerge in the mid-1990s for a relatively successful comeback. Unfortunately, Dillon was diagnosed with cancer in the early part of the new millennium and died in April 2004.

DIRTSMAN (1966–1993)

Dirtsman was born Patrick Thompson in Spanish Town, Jamaica, in 1966. He burst onto the scene displaying high potential as a **dancehall DJ**. Dirtsman came from a musical family that included his father, the owner of the Black Universal **Sound System**, and his brother, DJ **Papa San**. Dirtsman had been active in the music business from the mid-1980s and had scored some successful singles with "Thank You" and "Hot This Year."

Like other contemporary DJs, Dirtsman showed himself to have crossover potential to America's hip hop market, which resulted in a recording contract with the BMG imprint. His 1992 debut album, *Acid*, was a success and featured a song by **Bobby "Digital" Dixon**, "Bubble and Wine." Unfortunately, just as Dirtsman was about to enter the mature phase of his career, he was gunned down at only twenty-seven years old. His legacy has been immortalized in his solo release and several compilations. His songs appear on a variety of releases from the past ten years. Examples of his compilation appearances include *Strictly Dancehall* (1993), *Essential Dancehall: 20 Boom Sounds '89–'93* (1999), and *Reggae Mix* (2001).

DISCIPLES

Formed in the 1990s, the Disciples are the UK-born pair Russ D and his older brother Lol. The two emerged as a formidable roots and **dub** reggae collective. In the late 1980s, they got their start experimenting with the recreation of the beats of their favorite **reggae** songs. Eventually they purchased a drum machine and four-track recorder and began making dub plates (versions of the rhythm and beats of popular reggae songs without the vocals). The two honed their skills until they had a viable product. They took their plates to **Jah Shaka**, and the **DJ** was immediately impressed. Shaka, running one of the premier UK sound systems, took what the Disciples had brought him and asked for more.

Over time, Lol faded from the picture and Russ learned to play the guitar. Subsequently, Russ created the dub plates himself with the aid of the proper electronic equipment. As time passed, Russ upgraded his equipment to an all-digital setup and was able to create a wide range of beats. Next, Russ launched Boomshacka Lacka **sound system** and again enlisted his brother's assistance. Boomshacka Lacka records released several of the most powerful UK dub recordings of the era.

Eventually, Russ and Lol felt that their system was getting stagnant and that the scene did not accommodate the type of sound they wanted to push, so they closed their system. They have, however, continued to make music constructing dub plates of reggae beats. Further, Russ hopes to make a trip to Jamaica to incorporate the island's sound and vibe. Examples of their material include *Prowling Lion* and *Dub Revolution*. The pinnacle of their production came with *Resonations*, which exemplifies their love of Jamaican roots music. They have also launched a second label called Back-yard Movements, on which they release their own singles as well as singles by other Jamaican artists.

DIXON, BOBBY "DIGITAL" (c. 1965–)

Bobby Dixon got his start in the music field as a repair technician working on radios and audio components. This early experience with the inner workings of electronics led the young Dixon to start up his own small sound system, Heatwave. This in turn introduced him to **King Jammy**, who allowed Dixon to learn from his engineer. By age nineteen, Dixon was becoming skilled in the recording-booth side of making records. Jammy took him on as an engineer and let Dixon work on the dub machine. Dixon began working for Jammy in 1984 and stayed with him until 1989.

From engineering, Dixon began working on production and learned the art of craft-ing a record, all while working for Jammy. While with Jammy, Dixon was involved in the recording of the first **reggae** song with a digital drumbeat. The song was "Under Mi Sleng Teng" and used a Casio keyboard to generate the beat. The Casio beat was recorded, then slowed down, and used as the background to the vocals. This was a watershed moment in reggae recording and marked the dawn of the digital age, as well as giving Bobby Dixon his nickname.

In 1989, Dixon left Jammy and began to build his own studio. He ultimately fash-ioned a sixteen-track recording studio and immediately went into production of new music. He had artists such as **Shabba Ranks** in to record; Ranks's hit "Wicked in Bed" helped build the reputation of the new studio. Over time, Dixon produced material for **Anthony B**, **Buju Banton**, **Beenie Man**, Prezident Brown, **Capleton**, **Cocoa Tea**, Louie Culture, **Chaka Demus and Pliers**, and many others. Along with the vocalists whom Dixon recorded, there was a series of important studio musicians he employed, including **Firehouse Crew**, **Steely and Clevie**, and others. In the new millennium, Dixon has continued to produce hit music that is primarily in the **dancehall** style. Since 2000, Dixon has worked with **Shaggy**, **Lady Saw**, **Luciano**, **Ninjaman**, Prince Malachi, and **Sizzla**.

DIXON, TEXAS (1948–)

Born in 1948 in Kingston, Jamaica, Texas Dixon became half of the singing duo Keith and Tex with Keith Rowe. In the late 1960s the pair went into the studio with **Derrick Harriott** and produced a series of powerful singles, several of which were covered by popular artists in the mature **reggae** style. Keith and Tex sang in the **rock steady** style that was most prevalent in late-1960s Jamaica. Singles by the pair include "Don't Look Back" from 1968, "Let Me Be the One" from 1968, and "Lonely Man" from the same year. "Don't Look Back" was the original recording of the song popularized by **Peter Tosh**. In its original form, recorded February 11, 1968, Keith and Tex were backed up by **Lynn Taitt** and the Crystalites.

The year 1967 saw the release of the single "Stop That Train" and "Tonight." The pair released "This Is My Song" in 1968, and Rowe left for the United States as Dixon moved to Canada. The pair has reunited more recently for several revival shows. They also issued a comeback album in 1997, which was recorded at Rowe's New Jersey-based studio.

DJ MUSIC

In the early 1970s, Jamaican singers created a niche by toasting (or rapping) over dub tracks. **Dub** plates, or tracks, are popular songs with the words omitted so that the recording is just the beat and the instruments. Over this are performed words that are usually delivered half spoken and half sung (**toasted** or rapped), rather than sung lyrically. The one who selects the records and does the toasting is the **DJ**. The DJ style began during the heyday of the **sound system** era. At this time, DJs chanted over dub plates and rallied the crowd to their shows. However, with artists such as **U-Roy**, DJing turned into a marketable art form with commercial viability. With U-Roy's success, other producers and sound system owners rushed to add performers to the style.

Through the 1970s, roots reggae was still king in Jamaica. However, DJs such as **Big Youth** were making inroads and enjoying success. As roots reggae waned in the early 1980s, the DJs stepped in to fill the gap. The most popular Jamaican style in the late 1980s into the 1990s was **dancehall**, and DJing was a big part of the new style. The new popularity of the DJ was intensified by newly formed connections to American rap and later hip hop. Contemporary DJs include **Beenie Man**, **Bounty Killer**, **Yellowman**, and a female DJ named **Lady Saw**. Dancehall continues to be the most prevalent style of Jamaican popular music, and as long as dancehall is the style, then the DJ will be king.

DOBSON, HIGHLAND "DOBBY" (DOBBIE) (1942–)
Dobby Dobson was born in Kingston, Jamaica, in 1942. He got his start singing in a vocal group called the Deltas. Dobson wrote the first song that the group recorded: "Cry a Little Cry." The song was successful, but the group did not last. Dobson stayed with the single's producer **Sonia Pottinger** and continued to record as a solo artist singing in the **lovers rock** style. As was the Jamaican fashion, Dobson also worked with producers **Clement "Coxsone" Dodd** and **Duke Reid**. For Reid he penned the infamous "Loving Pauper," which gave him his nickname and became the song most associated with him. Dobson recorded the song several more times; it has also been covered by several other artists.

Dobson parlayed his early success into further recording sessions with **Rupie Edwards**, and together they produced the single "That Wonderful Sound." The single sold well and was followed by a string of other popular releases. The single "Endlessly" marked Dobson's entrance into the UK market and charts. Three full-length albums were recorded that compiled Dobson's work from the 1950s and 1960, but these failed to sell well and Dobson turned to producing. He has had a successful run as a producer and has worked with several of the major names in **reggae** music, such as the **Meditations**, **Steely and Clevie**, and many others. In 1979, Dobson relocated to New York and moved out of the music business. However, he continues to make occasional performances, both in the studio and on the stage.

DOCTOR ALIMANTADO. *See* THOMPSON, WINSTON JAMES

DOCTOR DREAD. *See* HIMELFARB, GARY

DOCTOR PABLO (c. 1955–)
Doctor Pablo was a member of the **Dub Syndicate**, which first came onto the UK popular music scene as the backup band for **Prince Far I**. Born Pete Stroud, Pablo is credited with performing the melodica and keyboard parts for the Syndicate and was also a credited member of **Creation Rebel**. Creation Rebel, begun in 1978, replaced Dub Syndicate as Creation Rebel's members gradually moved to the Syndicate and the former band faded into obscurity. Doctor Pablo entered the mix in 1984 and is first

credited as part of Dub Syndicate on the release *North of the River Thames* (1984). The release marks the beginning of Pablo's long career. Doctor Pablo continues to perform as part of the On-U Sounds Dub Syndicate collective. They were credited with providing overdubs with the producer of the record, **Adrian Sherwood**.

DODD, CLEMENT "COXSONE" (1932–2004)

Clement Seymour "Coxsone" Dodd was at the forefront of all of the major styles of Jamaican popular music. His earliest foray into the music business was through his **sound system** Sir Coxsone's Down Beat, started in the 1950s. His system was marked by having the most progressive American rhythm and blues records and the most powerful amplifiers to transmit sound. Coxsone, who gained his nickname from a famous 1950s cricket player, spent time in the early 1950s working in the sugarcane fields in the southern United States. This allowed him to collect the records that he subsequently used for his sound system. He is also noted as having made periodic trips back to the United States to collect further recordings. Dodd's signature song was Willis "Gator" Jackson's "Later for Gator," a danceable jump band tune. Under Dodd it was renamed the "Coxsone Hop" and was played at all of his system performances.

With the dawning of the American rock and roll era in the 1950s, Dodd's rhythm and blues recordings dried up, so he began recording Jamaican artists for use on his system. Many of these records became so popular that Dodd had them pressed for sale, which led him into the recording industry; in 1959 he opened his World Disc label. Through World Disc, Dodd released what is considered the first Jamaican **ska** record, **Theophilus Beckford's** "Easy Snappin." There followed a period during which many major recording artists in Jamaica worked with Dodd. Clue J and His Blues Blasters, **Roland Alphonso**, **Donald Drummond**, **Alton Ellis**, **Derrick Harriott**, the **Maytals**, the earliest incarnation of the **Wailers**, and others were among the extensive list of artists produced by Dodd. With these recordings, Dodd was at the helm of the Jamaican style change from rhythm and blues to ska.

With an active studio, Dodd needed a studio band; thus he helped form the **Skatalites**, who went on to become one of the premier groups on the island. In the early

Clement "Coxsone" Dodd. © *UrbanImage.tv.*

1960s, Dodd opened the first black-owned recording studio in Jamaica, the Jamaican Recording and Publishing Studio, known throughout the music business as **Studio One**. With the opening of the studio, Dodd hired several of the island's best producers; the studio's output was a compendium of influential 1960s and 1970s Jamaican popular musicians. Artists who recorded with Dodd during that time included **Horace Andy**, **Ken Boothe**, **Dennis Brown**, **Burning Spear**, **Alton Ellis**, the **Ethiopians**, **Marcia Griffiths**, the **Heptones**, and **Jackie Mittoo**.

Dodd still had a keen sense of popular music style, and he moved with the taste from ska to **rock steady** to **reggae**. He also diversified his music business by opening a branch office and recording studio in New York City. Still, Dodd continued to make periodic trips to the island to oversee the latest recordings. In 1991, two concerts were staged to celebrate Dodd's thirty-five years in the industry. Many of his longstanding recording artists turned out for the celebration. In homage to the achievements of the legendary label owner, the street on which the original Studio One was located was renamed Studio One Boulevard, changed from Brentford Road. Dodd continued to collect accolades in the wake of a long and successful career. He suffered a heart attack and died May 5, 2004, just prior to one such engagement.

DON CARLOS (c. 1970–)

Born Euvin Spencer in Kingston, Jamaica, Carlos's initial claim to music fame was as the singer for the **reggae** trio **Black Uhuru**. He formed this group in 1974 with his friends **Rudolph Dennis** and **Derrick "Duckie" Simpson**. However, Carlos recorded only briefly with them; they recorded "Folk Song" for **Dynamic Studio** and "Time Is on Our Side" for **Randy's**. Carlos then went solo and worked with his own group, Don Carlos and Gold. With Gold, Carlos released three albums, *Raving Tonight* (1983), *Ease Up* (1994), and *They Know Natty Dread Have Him Credential* (1995). The first two of these releases was on **RAS Records**, and the third came out on **Channel One**.

In 1990, Carlos rejoined the original members of Black Uhuru and together they released the album *Now*. This release helped to reassert the band's reputation and bring them back to their early glory. In the mid-1990s, the three released the album *Iron Storm*, after which Carlos again left to pursue solo work. In 1997, he released *Seven Days a Week*, which was his most successful solo album. Carlos's solo work comprises at least sixteen albums' worth of material that appears on a wide variety of labels. His most recent offering is *Hebron Gates*, released on Young Tree records in 2003.

DONALDSON, ERIC (1947–)

Eric Donaldson was born June 11, 1947, in St. Catherine, Jamaica. He began his music career in 1964 by recording at **Studio One**, but these early sides remain unreleased. He went on to form the singing group the West Indians with Leslie Burk and Hector Brooks; in 1968, the group had a hit with the J. J. Johnson-produced single "Right on Time." This led them to work with producer **Lee "Scratch" Perry**, during which time they changed their name to the Killowatts. The new producer and name failed to stimulate interest in the group even with a series of singles released. The group split and Donaldson went solo.

In 1971, he submitted a song to the Festival Song Competition. The song that he submitted was "Cherry Oh Baby"; it won first prize and began a string of seven song contest wins for Donaldson. "Cherry Oh Baby" has become a longstanding hit, with versions by **UB40** and the Rolling Stones. The single's success led to Donaldson's invitation to **Dynamic Studio**, where he recorded his 1971 self-titled release. In the wake of the first album, Donaldson went on to release six more solo recordings, the most recent of which was 2004's *Mr. Pirate*. In the interim, he has moved to Kent Village, Jamaica, where he runs the Cherry Oh Baby Go-Go-Bar. He continues to enjoy musical popularity and a wide fan base.

DONALDSON, LLOYD (c. 1970–)

Active for the last thirty years as a **reggae**-style drummer for a variety of artists, Donaldson has drumming credits on albums for **Dennis Bovell**, **I-Roy**, **Matumbi**, Poet and the Roots, and others. In the mid-1990s he turned his attention to producing and has subsequently produced two compilation albums, *Dancehall Queens: What a Bam Bam* (1996) and *Disco Kandi* (2000).

DONEGAN, PATRICK (c. 1960–)

Patrick Donegan is a multitalented instrumentalist and producer. He got his start in **reggae** music as a guitarist and keyboard player. However, he soon crossed over to production and launched his own studio, Progressive Sound. The Progressive Sound studio, with Donegan at the controls, produced solid records for a variety of artists including **Jah Shaka**, **Mad Professor**, **Tippa Irie**, and Don Ricardo.

DOWE, BRENTON (c. 1945–)

Brenton Dowe began his musical career as the tenor-range singer in the **Melodians**. As such, he was instrumental in assisting the establishment of the **rock steady** style that directly preceded **reggae**. Dowe met the other members of the group in the 1960s, and together they had a series of successful recordings. Like many Jamaican recording artists, the group worked with several different producers, including **Clement "Coxsone" Dodd**, **Sonia Pottinger**, and **Duke Reid**. They achieved their greatest success while working with the producer **Leslie Kong** in the late 1960s. Kong released their single "Rivers of Babylon" on his **Beverley's** label, and the song became successful in Jamaica and the United Kingdom. The success of the song was further assured with its appearance on the soundtrack for the movie *The Harder They Come* (1972). The group disbanded in the mid-1970s; however, they have reunited several times over the past twenty years for public performances. During the initial breakup, Dowe released a solo album title *Build Me Up*.

DOWNIE, TYRONE (c. 1950–)

Tyrone Downie has had a long career in **reggae** music. His most significant claim to fame is as the longstanding keyboard player for **Bob Marley and the Wailers**. However, he has also played and recorded with many other reggae notables, such as the **Abyssinians**, **Buju Banton**, **Aston Barrett** (on solo projects), **Beenie Man**, and **Black Uhuru**. Before joining the Wailers, several members of the band worked for Vincent "Randy" Chin as studio musicians. The collective was called the Impact All-Stars and included **Aston "Family Man" Barrett**, **Carlton "Carly" Barrett**, **Sly Dunbar**, **Earl "Wya" Lindo**, **Tommy McCook**, and **Augustus Pablo**. These musicians formed the core of Chin's studio band from 1968 to 1977.

However, the Barrett brothers and Downie left Chin and joined Marley's band. Downie appears on most of Marley's legendary recordings, including *Catch a Fire*, *Live*, *Exodus*, *Survival*, and *Conformation*; he is primarily credited for supplying the keyboard part but is also mentioned as providing backing vocals and percussion. In the wake of Marley's 1981 death, Downie continued to be active in the reggae music scene. He released a solo album in 2001 called *Orgon-D*, which again illustrates his command of the reggae keyboard style.

DREAD AND FRED (c. 1960–)

Dread and Fred were active in the UK **dub** scene throughout the 1980s and 1990s. Their innovative approach to constructing rhythm tracks revitalized the style, and they left a major impact. Their first big hit was the song "Warrior Stance," which used electronic sounds to produce syncopated drum parts, heavy bass, and blazing horns. Their music was popularized by UK **DJ Jah Shaka**, who would use the pair's songs to work the crowd into a frenzy. The pair released three albums in the course of their career. The year 1988 saw the release of *Iron Works, Vol. 1 & 2* and *Iron Works, Vol. 3*; after an interim of almost ten years, they released *Powerhouse* in 1996. Their most notable songs include "Iron Works," "Steady Rock," "African Seashore," "African Dawn," and "Zulu Skank."

DRUM AND BASS

The drum and bass movement has been almost exclusively based in England. It is built from layers of polyrhythmic lines played at a rapid tempo. The true drum and bass material does not employ vocals; rather, it consists almost entirely of fast drum machine-generated beats and booming bass lines. A sub-movement of drum and bass is jungle, which involves influences from **dub** and **reggae** music. The principal difference between jungle and reggae or **dancehall** music is that the jungle tempo is too fast to develop a groove. Jungle recordings almost all surface as singles; one particularly popular jungle artist is Goldie.

DRUMMOND, DONALD (1943-1969)

At the forefront of the **ska** movement when it hit Jamaica in the 1960s, Donald Drummond was one of the founding members of the **Skatalites** and wrote over 300 songs in the ska style. Drummond got his musical start at the **Alpha Boys Catholic School** in Kingston, Jamaica. There he learned to play the trombone and honed his skills as a jazz player. He ultimately became so adept that the school hired him as one of its teachers. As such, he had the opportunity to work with several up-and-coming talents as they came through the school, such as **Vincent Gordon**, **Tommy McCook**, and **Rico Rodriguez**.

At the peak of his performing ability, an opportunity opened up in Jamaica. It was at this time that sound system operators on the island began recording local musicians to fill the gap left when American music tastes changed from rhythm and blues to rock and roll. Drummond was among the musicians asked to record in these sessions. Drummond and the Skatalites were the most important band during this period and recorded countless singles for the **sound systems** and record stores. Sadly, the genius of Drummond's musical talent was matched by his fragile mental condition. On New Year's Day 1965, Drummond was arrested for the murder of his common-law wife, exotic dancer Marquerita Mahfood. Drummond was found not guilty of her death by reason of insanity and was subsequently committed to Bellevue Mental Hospital.

With Drummond incapacitated, the Skatalites broke up within the year. Tragically, Drummond died on May 6, 1969, while institutionalized. His death was officially ruled a suicide; however, a variety of rumors are associated with his passing. Drummond's material exists in period recordings and compilation reissues. His work with the Skatalites was the best in the style and has left a permanent mark on Jamaican popular music.

DUB MUSIC

The practice of creating dub music stems from making instrumental versions of popular singles to put on the B-sides of 45 RPM recordings. The style is achieved by taking a completed song and stripping away the majority of the melody material in a new mix of the song. Thus there are no vocals or lead instrumental parts. The remaining material is the **drum and bass**, often called a dub plate.

The practice began in 1967 when it was discovered that the crowds at sound system dances enjoyed singing the lyrics themselves. Another attribute of the dub version was that it allowed the **DJ** of the **sound system** to **toast** (or rap) over the playing drum and bass line. This started in the late 1960s as DJs progressively toasted over the instrumentals. With the invention of toasting over dub plates, **dancehall** DJs' abilities began to be measured by how well they improvised their own lyrics on a dub. This led to artists such as **U-Roy** surfacing as the first generation of dub toasters. U-Roy was working on **King Tubby's** sound system, credited with some of the earliest dub plates. The practice became so popular that by 1973 the first full-length dub albums began to appear. Significant dub figures were **Bunny "Striker" Lee**, who worked with melodica player **Augustus Pablo** and **Lee "Scratch" Perry**. Many dub artists flourished, such as **Big Youth**, the **Congos**, **Dub Syndicate**, **I-Roy**, **Scientist**, and others. By the mid-1970s, dub was the second most important Jamaican popular music style behind roots reggae. Dub artists enjoyed substantial notoriety on the island and were popularized in the United Kingdom through the **Island Records** label and the work of British producer **Adrian Sherwood**. The dub era of toasters paved the way for the next significant style change in Jamaica, the move away from roots reggae toward dancehall DJing.

DUB POETRY

As a current offshoot of the **dub music** phenomenon, dub poets take their cues from early dub music artists such as **Big Youth** and U-Roy. The most notable dub poet is **Linton Kwesi Johnson**, who began writing in the dub style after failed attempts in traditional language. Johnson writes his poetry in the patois of the Jamaican people and then sets it to music. The musical element makes dub poetry a sub-style of contemporary Jamaican popular music, but the musical element is very sparse to avoid obscuring the words. Johnson launched a trend in writing that has been followed by several others, including **Mutabaruka**, Michael Smith, Benjamin Zephaniah, and others.

DUB SYNDICATE

Dub Syndicate first appeared as additional musicians on **Prince Far I's** album *Tuff Dub Encounter Chapter 3* (1979). They have been associated with **Adrian Sherwood** and On-U Sounds from its inception. Dub Syndicate includes **Headley Bennett** (saxophone), **Doctor Pablo** (melodica), **Lincoln Valentine "Style" Scott** (drums), and Bim Sherwood (vocals). The group was most popular during the late 1970s and early 1980s, during which time they worked with producers such as Sherwood, **Lee "Scratch" Perry**, Skip McDonald, and **U-Roy**. In 1982, the collective released their debut album *Pounding System*, which was met with a degree of praise. However, they went on to substantial acclaim with subsequent releases such as *One Way System* (1983), *Tunes from the Missing Channel* (1985), and *Strike the Balance* (1990).

More recently, Dub Syndicate released two albums in 1996, a disc of new material titled *Ital Breakfast*, and a remix album called *Research and Development*. In 2001, they released *Acres of Space*, which was recorded in Jamaica in collaboration with Adrian Smith. Along the way, the band recorded two albums' worth of material for Lee "Scratch" Perry; however, difficulties with ownership caused a slow release. One such record was *Time Boom X De Devil Dead* (1987). The Dub Syndicate's reputation has grown to the point that their recent guest artists include stars such as **Capleton**, **Gregory Isaacs**, **Luciano**, and **Cedric Myton**.

DUBE, LUCKY (1964–)

Philip Dube was born in 1964, and his mother nicknamed him Lucky for her good fortune. He hails from a small town named Ermelo that is west of Johannesburg, South Africa. As a youth, Dube procured a job as a groundskeeper in order to help support his family. He ultimately enrolled in school, and it was there that he discovered music. He sang in the choir and also learned about instrumental music. Dube began pursuing his passion for music in earnest at age eighteen. He joined a band started by his cousin Richard Siluma called the Love Brothers. The band played all the shows that they could possibly book. Over time, Dube's cousin rose in the ranks of Teal Music to eventually become a producer. In that position he signed Dube, who has stayed with the label for over twenty years. Dube went into the studio with his cousin and recorded his first album, which did not contain any of his own songs. His second recording, which held some of his own material, met with regional success. The third release was even more commercially viable and gave Dube the money to purchase several instruments. Further, he took the time to learn English, which allowed him to converse with people from the record industry. With his fourth release, Dube had enough financial success to feel a degree of security.

All of the early albums were in the African Mbaqanga style, but **reggae** songs were gradually creeping into his output. Songs such as "Reggae Man" and "City Life" began to pique the audience's attention. It was at this time that Dube teamed with engineer Dave Segal, who helped to guide his career and steer him in the reggae direction. Dube went into the studio and cut a four-track release of all reggae songs. The release was not successful but did get him started on the second phase of his career.

Eventually, Dube associated more and more with the reggae style, and it began taking over his live shows. His second reggae record was titled *Think about the Children*, and it was a breakthrough hit. Dube continued to record, releasing an album a year throughout the 1990s. He has more additional records such as *The Other Side* and *Captured Live*, both from 2004. Lucky Dube is considered South Africa's biggest star.

DUNBAR, LOWELL CHARLES "SLY" (1952–)

Lowell Dunbar is one half of the most well-known and respected rhythm section in **reggae** music, the Riddim Twins. He would eventually earn the name "Sly" for his love of Sly and the Family Stone. Dunbar developed his interest in drumming at an early age. His earliest inspiration was Lloyd Knibbs of the **Skatalites**. At fifteen he began playing in his first band, the Yardbrooms. Next Dunbar teamed with Dave and **Ansell Collins** for their 1969 release *Double Barrel*. He then worked with the **Mighty Diamonds** and **I-Roy**, which led him to work with **Bunny "Striker" Lee**. During this time he met and teamed with **Robbie Shakespeare** and the two immediately recognized their connection. They joined forces in 1974 and launched their own label, Taxi Records. The pair marketed themselves as a rhythm section and production team, attracting the attention of stars such as **Burning Spear**, **Jimmy Cliff**, and **Bob Marley**.

The two broke into major stardom when they recorded with **Peter Tosh** on his *Legalize It* album in 1976. With all of the publicity gained from playing with Tosh, the pair had instant credibility and were involved in a series of important recordings. In the late 1970s, Sly not only worked with Robbie, he also released two solo albums titled *Simply Sly Man* in 1976 and *Sly, Wicked and Slick* (1977). These two records were followed by a third solo release titled *Sly-Go-Ville* in 1982. Together, Sly and Robbie released *Sly and Robbie Present Taxi* in 1981. This touched off a series of releases by the two men that spanned the end of the 1980s into the 1990s. These albums reflect a shift in their style from roots reggae to the more popular **dub** style.

In addition to their own releases, Sly and Robbie continued working for other artists, such as **Black Uhuru**, **Maxi Priest**, Grace Jones, Mick Jagger, Bob Dylan, Cindy Lauper, Herbie Hancock, Carly Simon, and KRS-ONE. In the 1990s, the pair continued to work together but again altered their style. This time they moved from the dub style into **dancehall**. Sly and Robbie continue to be productive and forward the Riddim Twins name.

DUNN, FRANKLYN (c. 1950–)

Franklyn Dunn was born in Jamaica and began to realize his musical dreams when he joined the band the **Cimarons**. The band, including Dunn as its bass player, moved to England in 1967. In England, the band enjoyed a long string of successes as session musicians. They worked with **Jimmy Cliff** and many others. They also recorded their own material, beginning with 1974's **Trojan** release *In Time*. The band continued to work and record together through the 1970s. Their material was again made available on compilations released at the end of the 1990s.

DYCE, BILLY (c. 1950–)

Born Ransford White, Billy Dyce recorded several popular singles released on the **Trojan** label. Along with his band the Untouchables, Dyce released singles such as "Fari Time," "Unity Is Love," and "Take Warning." The latter of these three singles was used by **U-Roy** as the basis for his song "Way Down South." Dyce and the Untouchables material continue to surface as they appear on compilation releases. They are present on *Musik City: The Story of Trojan* and *Trojan's 35th Anniversary*, both from 2003.

DYNAMIC STUDIO

Dynamic Studio was one of the major recording venues in Kingston, Jamaica, from the 1960s to the 1980s. The studio was run by **Byron Lee** and ultimately became a subsidiary of the **Trojan** label. Lee's Dynamic Studio was located at 15 Bell Road in Kingston, Jamaica. In the late 1960s, as the **rock steady** style was turning to **reggae**, Lee entered the picture with his new studio and helped to further the burgeoning sound. By the end of 1969, reggae had overtaken Jamaica with Lee at the forefront. Along with his studio band the Dragonaires, Lee released some of the earliest reggae singles such as "Reggay [sic] Eyes." At the time, **Lee "Scratch" Perry"** was working A&R (finding and recruiting new talent) for Lee; in this position he assisted in defining the sound. Over the years, Lee's Dynamic Studio has been the home to many reggae greats such as **Admiral Bailey**, **Count Ossie**, **Eric Donaldson**, **Groundation**, **John Holt**, and **Ras Michael** and the **Sons of Negus**. As the reggae style transformed into **dancehall**, Lee followed the trend and released many of the new style's greats, such as **Sanchez**, **Yellowman**, and Mad Lion.

DYNAMITES, THE

The Dynamites gained notoriety in the late 1960s as the studio band for producer **Clancy Eccles**. Working for Eccles, the band backed numerous **rock steady** recordings released on Eccles's Clan Disc imprint. They recorded with Cynthia Richards, **King Stitt**, and Eccles himself. Like many studio bands of the era, their lineup was not constant; however, the core of **Gladstone "Gladdy" Anderson** (piano), **Hux Brown** (guitar), **Winston Wright** (keyboards), Jackie Jackson (bass), and Paul Douglas (drums) was the most popular combination. With King Stitt, the group recorded *Fire Corner* (1969), and with Eccles they released *Herbsman Reggae* (1970). Additionally, material from the band appears on numerous compilations released in the 1990s and into the new millennium, such as *From the Dynamite Treasury* (1996), *Clancy Eccles Presents His Reggae* (1990), and *Fatty Fatty* (1998).

E

EARL SIXTEEN (1958–)

Born Earl Daley, Earl Sixteen began his singing career at the age of fifteen. At this tender age he won a singing contest that involved some severe competition. As is often the case, Daley did not go on to immediately experience success. He formed a group called the Flaming Phonics, but they only recorded one song. It was complete coincidence that he again entered the studio. This time he went to **Joe Gibbs's** studio to help out a friend, Winston McAnuff, who had a session scheduled. Gibbs's engineer **Errol Thompson** heard Daley's voice and recorded him instead. The result was a single that brought Daley moderate success in the mid-1970s.

Next, Daley joined a traveling band run by Boris Gardiner and honed his skills in a professional group. He ended up being fired for his **Rastafarian** associations, but then teamed up with **Hugh Mundell** and **Lee "Scratch" Perry** at **Black Ark Studios**. The collective recorded and released two singles, "Cheating" and "Freedom." In addition to solo work, Perry employed Daley as a studio singer, which led him to appear on tracks by **Augustus Pablo** and **Yabby You**. Daley's song "Freedom" had been getting regular spins by Kingston radio **DJ Mikey Dread**, and the two ended up working together. The pair ended up at **King Tubby's** studio with the **Roots Radics** supplying backup. These sessions caused **Clement "Coxsone" Dodd** to hear of Daley's talents; together they recorded "Love Is a Feeling," which became a significant hit. The song was among the earliest **dancehall** releases in the early 1980s. In light of their success, Dodd and Daley again teamed for a **Studio One** release. This time they brought out a version of Simply Red's song "Holding Back the Years." Daley delivered the song in his characteristic falsetto and it was his biggest hit. More recently, Daley had some success in collaboration with **Mad Professor** and continues to release material.

EARL ZERO

Born Earl Anthony Johnson in Greenwich Town, Jamaica, Zero developed a love of **reggae** music alongside his childhood friend **Earl "Chinna" Smith** and became an accomplished singer and songwriter. Along the way, he established two record labels, Don Mais' Roots Tradition and Freedom Sounds. Zero relocated to the United States in 1979, where he settled in northern California. In his new locale he established himself as a voice of true roots reggae. Also in 1979, Zero released his debut album on **Epiphany Records**, titled *Visions of Love*. This was followed two years later by *Only Jah Can Ease the Pressure*, on his own Freedom Sounds. Zero went on to enjoy an active recording and performing career throughout the 1980s and 1990s. Examples of Zero's material include singles such as "Shackles and Chains" and "None Shall Escape the Judgment."

EARLY B (d. 1997)

Early B was a **dancehall** artist at the forefront of the style as it was first forming. In the late 1970s, dancehall was just gaining a foothold in Jamaican popular music. Early B entered the scene and made his mark by **toasting** in a unique manner, having a characteristic delivery, and relating his experiences to the audience. He was an important early artist as dancehall evolved in the 1980s. His work with **Josey Wales** and his solo material both garnered recognition; in fact, the Josey Wales material was successful enough that it entered the charts in 1986. He released a single solo album titled *Send in the Patient*, which contained singles such as "Girls Dem Sexy" and "Call the Doctor for Me." Unfortunately, Early B was shot and killed in 1997.

EARTH AND STONE

Earth and Stone, the duo of Albert Bailey and Clifton Howell, came onto the Jamaican popular music scene in 1972. Different from many of their contemporary bands insofar as they are a duo rather than a trio, they began recording at **Studio One** right away. They then moved to **Channel One** the following year and began working with the Hoo Kim brothers. Their style is a mixture of roots reggae and **lovers rock**, but the pair is equally proficient in either style. As the decade progressed, they tended to work more in the roots style and cut singles with **Rastafarian** messages. Their debut album, *Kool Roots*, was released in 1978 and contained many of their earlier successes.

The group's successful sound is due to its delivery style, whereby both singers take turns as lead vocalist. *Kool Roots* contains both roots songs and love songs; "Jail House Set You Free" exemplifies roots style, and "Once Bitten Twice Shy" demonstrates lovers rock style. Although the pair did not have a prolific output, their material continues to appear on compilations such as *Channel One—Hit Bound: The Revolutionary Sound* (1989) and *Reggae's Greatest Hits, Vol. 4* (1995).

EASTWOOD, CLINT (c. 1950–)

Born Robert Brammer, **dancehall toaster** Clint Eastwood has had a significant career with several hit albums. He entered the music scene in the late 1970s and became popular in Jamaica, but he found his real success in the United Kingdom. Eastwood got his start working with **DJ** General Saint and parlayed his early success into a longstanding recording career. The style that Eastwood espouses is hardcore dancehall with some roots crossover appeal. As was common in the dancehall, Eastwood chose his name from that of a popular Hollywood actor. He is the younger brother of DJ **Trinity** and has long been friends with **Dillinger**. Eastwood's material was primarily produced by **Bunny "Striker" Lee**; he was backed in the late 1970s by the **Aggrovators**.

Eastwood's catalog includes at least eleven solo releases that begin in the late 1970s and continue through the 1990s.

Clint Eastwood. © *UrbanImage.tv.*

Examples of Eastwood's output include the 1978 album *African Youth*, released on the Third World imprint, and *Death in the Arena* and *Love and Happiness* in 1979. Later material surfaced on Greensleeves, such as 1980's *Sex Education*, 1981's *Two Bad DJ* (which was a big hit), and 1983's *Stop That Train*. More recently, Eastwood released *Live in London* in 1987; *BBC Radio 1 in Concert*, another live album, in 1993; and 1999's *Real Clint Eastwood*. Although Eastwood has harder dancehall material, he is still able to change his style to accommodate more roots-oriented material.

EASY STAR RECORDS

The Easy Star imprint was launched in New York City in 1996. Easy Star was founded by four friends: Eric Smith, Lem Oppenheimer, Michael Galdwasser, and Remy Gerstein; together these men have produced one of the premier labels in the U.S. today. They realized that there was a significant American market for roots reggae that was not being filled and that there was a whole host of young fans who wanted access to this music. Hence, the label sponsors recordings, hosts a weekly **reggae** party in Manhattan, and works to recapture the original strains of reggae's heyday.

The Easy Star roster is filled with hitmakers from the height of the reggae style. Artists on the label include the **Meditations**, **Sugar Minott**, **Sister Carol**, and Ranking Joe. To this have been added the **African Brothers**, **Ossie Dellimore**, **Junior Demus**, **Triston Palma**, **Sluggy Ranks**, **Rob Symeonn**, Patrick Junior, Gary "Nesta" Pine, and others. Though less than a decade old, Easy Star has already garnered a stellar reputation for releasing reggae classics backed by their house band the Easy Star All Stars, composed of Michael Goldwasser and Victor Axelrod. The group specializes in roots and contemporary **reggae**. Together these two worked on Rob Symeonn's "Anything for Jah" and have backed label releases from the **Meditations**, **Sugar Minott**, and **Sister Carol**. More recently they worked on Easy Star's release of *Dub Side of the Moon*, a remake of the Pink Floyd favorite.

EBONY SISTERS, THE

Active in the late 1960s and early 1970s, the Ebony Sisters recorded on the Moodisc label and put out several well-received singles. At Moodisc, they worked with producer Harry Mudie on their more well-known releases. Examples of their more popular work were the singles "Let Me Tell You Boy" from 1969 and "Take Warning." Also popular was "I Must Be dreaming," released on the Soul Beat label. The Ebony Sisters worked with several notable **reggae** artists such as Ralph Haughton and **I-Roy**. In 1996, they reappeared on the compilation album *Reggae Songbirds: Seventeen Great Tracks from the High Note Label*, a record dedicated to re-releasing material by the often-overlooked women of reggae music.

ECCLES, CLANCY (1940–2005)

Clancy Eccles was born in Jamaica on December 19, 1940. He became a well-known and respected producer, although not of the magnitude of **Duke Reid** or **Clement "Coxsone" Dodd**. Eccles was not only a producer, but also a singer of solid reputation. He was most active in the late 1960s and early 1970s and was active in the **rock steady** and **reggae** styles. His production work most often appeared on his own Clandisc label, on which he made many releases. Eccles got his start in music working with Dodd as a singer and went on to work with several other notable Jamaican producers.

Ultimately he put aside singing to work in production and mastered tracks for several stars, including **Alton Ellis**, **Beres Hammond**, **Joe Higgs**, **Lord Creator**, and **Lee "Scratch" Perry**. Eccles was active in the heyday of rock steady and the dawn of the reggae movement. He achieved the stylistic transition, and this furthered his reputation. Recordings by Eccles include *Fattie, Fattie*, on which he sings, and the production credits on *Fire Corner, Herbsman Reggae, Freedom* and several others. His work also continues to surface on compilation albums that have been coming out since the mid-1990s. Many of Eccles's recordings were cut with the backing band the **Dynamites**, who appear both credited and uncredited.

Outside of music, Eccles was also involved in politics. A staunch supporter of socialist politics in Jamaica, his endorsement of Michael Manley directly illustrated his political leanings.

Clancy Eccles. © *UrbanImage.tv.*

Eccles died on June 30, 2005, in Spanish Town, Jamaica, of complications following a stroke.

ECHO MINOTT. *See* MINOTT, ECHO

EDWARDS, RUPIE (1945–)

Rupie Edwards was born in Jamaica in 1945. After becoming interested in music as a youth he moved to Kingston and started a band. In the early 1960s Edwards began to release singles and had modest success. By the end of the decade, Edwards was a member of the Virtues and began to do his own production work. His first self-produced single was "Burning Love." His production skills soon outpaced his desire to sing, and he dedicated himself to working on recordings for many **reggae** luminaries. Although he had gotten his start in the **ska** style, in the early 1970s he made the transition to reggae and recorded acts such as the **African Brothers**, **Bob Andy**, **Johnny Clarke**, **Bobby Dobson**, and **Gregory Isaacs**.

Also in the 1970s, Edwards began producing recordings of the first generation of **DJs** emerging from the **dancehalls**. Although he had become an accomplished and respected engineer, Edwards still returned to singing intermittently. He released an album of new material in 1975 on the **Trojan** imprint titled *Irie Feelings: Chapter and*

Verse. The single of the same name went on to chart in the United Kingdom, and Edwards moved there to parlay his success. Throughout the late 1970s and 1980s, Edwards continued to record and produce his in-demand products. In 1990, he released a **dub** album on the Trojan label titled *Let There Be Version* and continued producing for artists such as **Bobby Dobson**.

Later in the 1990s, Edwards provided background vocals for popular music legend David Bowie on his 1995 release *Outside*. More recently, he has been active producing a series of compilation albums in addition to performing vocals on several releases himself.

EDWARDS, VINCENT "KING" (c. 1940–)

Vincent "King Edwards the Giant" Edwards entered the Jamaican popular music scene at the height of the sound system days. In the mid-1950s, Edwards started a system in competition with the other two major systems, those of **Clement "Coxsone" Dodd** and **Duke Reid**. Edwards was able to compete with the two existing legends due to the constant influx of rare American rhythm and blues records. He followed his time's popular practice of obtaining obscure recordings, scratching out all their identifying markings, and then using them in clashes with other system owners. The competition was fierce and often extended beyond wars of words to actual physical clashes between members of rival systems. After a decade of vying for the crowd's attention at the **sound system** dances, Edwards turned his attention to politics and in the mid-1960s was elected a member of Parliament for the People's National Party of Jamaica.

EDWARDS, WILFORD "JACKIE" (1938–1992)

Active in the early **reggae** and late **rock steady** styles, Wilford Edwards gained international recognition for his smooth vocals. Edwards was born in Jamaica and first made a mark on the Jamaican musical landscape with singles such as "Whenever There's Moonlight" and other hits from the late 1950s. In 1962, Edwards moved to the United Kingdom, where his audience increased dramatically. With the assistance of a recently opened **Island Records**, and with the help of label owner **Chris Blackwell**, he burst onto the popular music scene with his song "Keep on Running," which was popularized by the Spencer Davis Group. His success with the Spencer Davis Group and other Island Records artists continued through much of the 1960s. His material with the Spencer Davis Group also involved a young Steve Winwood, with whom he co-wrote "When I Come Home."

Through the 1960s, Edwards released a series of Island recordings such as *Most of Wilfred Jackie Edwards* (1964), *Stand Up for Jesus* (1964), *Come on Home* (1966), *By Demand* (1967), *Pledge My Love* (1969), and *Premature Golden Sands* (1967). In the early 1970s, Edwards returned to Jamaica and continued his recording career. Through the 1970s, Edwards continued to release solid material, but did not regain his early international success. He recorded the albums *Let It Be Me* (1970), *I Do Love You* (1973), *Do You Believe in Love* (1976), and *The Original Cool Ruler* (1983). Edwards continued to record in to the 1990s when he put out *Dearest* (1995), *In Paradise* (1995), and *Escape* (1995). After the turn of the century, Edwards's material began to appear on re-release on the Rhino label.

EEK-A-MOUSE (1957–)

Eek-A-Mouse was born Ripton Joseph Hilton in Kingston, Jamaica, on November 19, 1957. Mouse got his nickname from a racehorse that he often lost money on. He entered the Jamaican popular music scene in the mid-1970s and had limited success with two early singles titled "My Father's Land" and "Creation." Next, Mouse worked on several Kingston-area **sound systems**, including Black Ark, Gemini, and Virgo. Mouse's big break came when he began working with producer **Joe Gibbs** in the 1980s. Mouse's 1980s single "Wah Do Dem" gained the young singer considerable acclaim and allowed him to release an album. Next, Mouse worked with producer **Henry "Junjo" Lawes** and had success with the singles "Once and Virgin" and "Virgin Girl." With Lawes' help, Mouse also worked with remix master **Scientist** and had a hit with the remake of "Virgin Girl." Scientist also reworked "Wah Do Dem" and, with this, Mouse was a huge success. In addition to his singing, Mouse also has a larger-than-life stage presence that fed his popularity.

He was a hit at the 1981 **Reggae Sunsplash** and continued his success throughout the next several months. The following year, Mouse had success with several singles and released his most popular album, titled *Wah Do Dem*. Mouse appeared at Sunsplash again in 1984, and this performance was released as a live album called *Skidip*. The 1980s was a busy and profitable decade for Mouse with the release of a series of popular releases, including *The Mouse and the Man* (1983), *The Assassinator* (1983), *Mouseketeer* (1984), *King and I* (1985), *Mouse-A-Mania* (1987), and *Eek-A-Nomics* (1988). In 1991, Mouse signed with **Island Records,** which yielded the *U-Neek* album. Truly making the album unique, Mouse included a remake of the Led Zepplin hit "D'Yer Maker." Mouse maintained his popularity, but not his relationship, with Island. In 1996, he released his next album, titled *Black Cowboy*, on the Sunset Blvd. Label. During the late 1990s, Mouse toured constantly and released a greatest hits album called *Ras Portaits* (1997).

In the new millennium, Mouse popularity has thrived with touring and new releases. Recent albums include *Eeksperience* (2001), *The Very Best: Volume 2* (2003), *Mouse Gone Wild* (2004), and *Eek-A-Speeka* (2004). Eek-A-Mouse continues to produce his unique brand of **reggae** music and, in the fall of 2005, will tour western Europe.

ELLIS, ALTON (1944–)

Born in 1944 in Kingston, Jamaica, into a musically inclined family, Ellis learned to sing and play piano as a youth. At times in his career he sang with his brother, Leslie,

Alton Ellis. © *UrbanImage.tv.*

and his sister, Hortense. He left an indelible mark on the Jamaican musical landscape with a long string of hits that began in the late 1950s. Ellis teamed with Eddie Perkins to form the singing duo **Alton and Eddie**; the pair had early success. In 1959, they released the single "Muriel" for **Clement "Coxsone" Dodd** and scored an immediate Jamaican hit. They followed this with the single "My Heaven," also a success on Dodd's **Studio One** label. Perkins then moved to the United States and Ellis went on to a highly acclaimed solo career. His earliest songs were in the **ska** style, but he would make his mark in the two subsequent styles.

Many credit Ellis as being on the cutting edge of the style's evolution. He released several of the earliest **rock steady** singles, the most successful including "Girl I've Got a Date" and "Cry Tough." He often sang with his sister under the duo name Alton and Hortense; he also recorded with a backing group called the Flames. Ellis did many of his recordings in the late 1960s and early 1970s, during the transitional period between the ska and rock steady styles. During the mid-1960s, Ellis made a series of memorable rock steady recordings for **Duke Reid's Treasure Isle** imprint. With Reid he scored several hits such as "Dance Crasher" and "Get Ready—Rock Steady." Ellis was unique in that he was able to record for both Reid and Dodd, notorious rivals, at the same time. He released the record *Sunday Coming* in 1970, recorded at Studio One and filled with solid material.

In addition to Dodd and Reid, Ellis worked with several other producers at this point in his career, including **Lloyd Daley** and **Keith Hudson**. Disenchanted by his lack of major success, Ellis moved to Canada for a period, during which time he made a living as a soul singer. In 1973 he moved to England, which has become his permanent residence. In England, he launched his own label, Alltone Records, on which he released his new material and compilations of his earlier work. In the mid-1980s, he made two successful Jamaican appearances in the **Reggae Sunsplash** festival and returned to Dodd's studio to cut a new single in the early 1990s.

Continuing to perform today, Ellis's career spans forty years. Several releases of Ellis's material came out in the late 1990s and beyond, including *Reggae Valley of Decision* (1996), *Still in Love* (1996), *Change My Mind* (2000), *More Alton Ellis* (2001), and *Many Moods of Alton Ellis* (2001).

ELLIS, BOBBY (c. 1932–)

Born in west Kingston, Jamaica, Ellis began playing the trumpet in 1941 at the **Alpha Boys Catholic School**. Once he left school he continued playing for a living and found work in various nightclubs. In the early 1960s, Ellis recorded several of his original compositions at **Studio One**. After this he began doing session work and recorded trumpet parts on several hit records, including "Lonesome Feeling" by **Bob Marley and the Wailers**, "I've Got to Go Back Home" by **Bob Andy**, and "There's a Reward" by **Joe Higgs**. Next, Ellis joined **Lynn Taitt's** band the Jets and continued to do session work with this band. Also in Taitt's band were **Gladstone Anderson** (keyboards), **Headley Bennett** (saxophone), Carlton Samuels (saxophone), Joe Isaacs (drums), and Brian Atkinson (bass). Ellis played through the changing styles of Jamaican popular music: he worked in the **rock steady** style and made the transition to **reggae**. In the early 1970s, when Ellis's trumpet playing was in demand, he worked on a pair of **Burning Spear** albums. Ellis toured and recorded with Burning Spear for ten years and appears on several of the most important Spear recordings. During a long and storied career, Ellis worked with several of the top performers such as Bob Marley, **Toots and the Maytals**, and Burning Spear. As the reggae style evolved and **dancehall** took over, there was increasingly less demand for live horn players. However, Ellis has stayed active in the music scene working with the **Abyssinians, Horace Andy, Aston Barrett, Mighty Diamonds,** and **Bunny Wailer**. He also continues to record, having gone into **Tuff Gong's** studios in 2003.

EMOTIONS, THE

Composed of **Robbie Shakespeare's** brother Lloyd, Kenneth Knight, and **Max Romeo**, the Emotions enjoyed limited popularity in the late 1960s and early 1970s and recorded with **Lee "Scratch" Perry** at his **Black Ark Studios**. The group released a pair of albums in the 1960s, titled *Rude Boy Confession* (1966) and *Love You Most of All* (1968).

ENGLISH, JUNIOR (1951–)

Junior English was born Lindel Beresford in Kingston, Jamaica, in 1951. He began his music career as a teenager with some initial success, prompting him to move to England where he continued his career in addition to finishing his education. By the early 1960s he had already been in the studio recording "My Queen," a duet with Errol Dunkley recorded by **Prince Buster**. He won a talent contest at Club 31 in London, which was run by the **Pama** label; unfortunately he was underappreciated due to his predilection for the Jamaican sound.

In the early 1970s, English released a series of singles under the production of **Clement Bushay**, which were received favorably. This success allowed him to record a pair of late-1970s albums that further cemented his reputation. The 1980s were an especially productive decade for English as he released *Jack the Ripper* (1981), *In Loving You* (1988), *Lover's Key* (1988), and *Mr. Man* (1990). English remained active in the 1990s and appeared on a series of compilation albums such as *Just My Imagination, Vol. 2* in 1991 (covering "Candle in the Wind"), *Burning Reggae, Vol. 3*, and *Reggae Celebrates the Detroit Sound* in 1999. English continues to perform with appearances that include his performance at the Lovers Rock Gala of 2002.

EPIPHANY RECORDS

Epiphany is a record company run by owner/producer Warren Smith, who has logged thirty-five-plus years in the record business. In the 1990s, his northern California-based label reissued several recordings that ranged in scope, but were all of the highest quality. The albums include artists such as **Earl Zero, Soul Syndicate**, Dub Nation, Flo and Eddie, and others.

Early examples of products bearing the Epiphany name included 1998's reissue of Zero's *Visions of Love*, originally released in 1979. Also in 1998, they released Max Edwards's *Rockers Arena* from 1982; Dub Nation's *Let The Truth be Known*; and *Was, Is, Always*. In 1999, Epiphany released Flo and Eddie's *Rock Steady*, which boasts some significant talent such as **Aston "Family Man" Barrett, Dean Fraser, Augustus Pablo**, and **Earl "Chinna" Smith**. Next came Dub Nation's *One Great World*; Soul Syndicate's *Harvest Uptown, Famine Downtown*; and *Friends and Family*. Smith and the Epiphany label continue to produce quality releases that keep the music of past eras alive.

ETERNALS, THE

Formed in the late 1960s as the backing group for singer **Cornell Campbell**, the Eternals worked at **Studio One**, and with Campbell released a series of hits such as

"Queen of the Minstrels" and "Stars." In 1971, Campbell moved on to work with producer **Bunny "Striker" Lee** and rerecorded his Eternals hits as a solo act. Although the Eternals and Campbell did not work together for long, they did release a series of strong singles on the Moodisc imprint. Examples of Campbell and the Eternals sound are "Let's Start Again" (1970), "Reach Out Darling" (1972), and "You're No Good" (1973). The music of the Eternals can be found in various compilation recordings such as 2001's *Studio One Soul.*

ETHIOPIANS, THE

A vocal trio begun in 1966, the Ethiopians consisted of **Leonard "Jack Sparrow" Dillon**, Steve Taylor, and Aston "Charlie" Morris. Founding member Dillon had already scored several **mento** and **ska** songs and had a hit with the single "Ice Water," produced by **Lee "Scratch" Perry** for **Clement "Coxsone" Dodd**. The three performed together for a year, after which Morris decided to leave the group. However, these early sessions produced singles such as "Live Good," recorded at **Studio One**.

The Ethiopians originally sang in the **ska** style but seamlessly made the transition to **rock steady**. Their song lyrics often speak of social injustice and racism, but there are also occasional love songs interspersed. In 1968, they recruited Melvin "Mellow" Reid and again performed as a threesome. With the new member, the Ethiopians went back into the studio; the result was *Train to Skaville*, which went on to become a major hit and entered the UK Top 40. Included on this record are songs such as "The Whip," which is often discussed as the first **reggae** tune driven by percussion.

In 1968, Dillon and Taylor released a followup to *Skaville* titled *Engine 54*. In the early 1970s, the group recorded with producer Carl "J. J." Johnson; it was this combination that yielded their best output. After the Johnson material, the group went on to work with several other producers, including Harry Robinson, **Lloyd Daley**, and **Derrick Harriott**.

Sadly, Taylor died in 1975 after being struck by a van while crossing a street, and the Ethiopians disbanded. However, after a two-year break the remaining members reformed and continued to issue records through the rest of the 1970s. This incarnation of the group was produced by **Winston "Niney the Observer" Holness** and yielded the album *Slave Call* (1977). After this release, Dillon again went solo and continues to work in the business. He intermittently uses the Ethiopians' name and formed a new incarnation of the group in the late 1990s with female singers Jennifer Lara and Merlene Webber. Together this group released 1999's *Tougher Than Stone.* The Ethiopians' catalog is ten albums deep, and their musical legacy as a style-setting group continues.

EVANS, TYRONE (d. 2000)

One of the founding members of the singing group the **Paragons**, Evans went on to be active in the **Techniques**. In the Paragons he sang with **Bob Andy** and Howard Barrett, and together they recorded with **Clement "Coxsone" Dodd** and **Duke Reid**. The group experienced their greatest fame with the release "On the Beach" for Reid's **Treasure Isle** label. Their stock grew with songs such as "The Tide Is High" (Blondie covered this song, and it was a significant hit for the band), "Only a Smile," and "Happy Go Lucky Girl." Several of their more popular songs appeared on the 1968 album *Riding High with the Paragons.*

In addition to working with the Paragons, Evans also released a single with Andy and Dodd titled "I Don't Care." As was customary in Jamaican recording practices, Evans also did some work with producer **Leslie Kong's Beverley's** label. In the late

1970s, Evans returned to **Studio One**, and with Dodd released the hit "How Sweet It Is." The Paragons went on to release a successful album on **Chris Blackwell's Island Records** imprint and another for **Bunny "Striker" Lee**. These albums failed to bring the success of the earlier material and Evans relocated to New York, where he began working with **Lloyd Barnes** at the Wackies label. For Barnes, Evans cut the album *Tyrone Evans Sings Bullwachies Style*, which is a collection of successful love songs and roots reggae cuts. The album contains songs such as "History," "Sparkles of My Eyes," and "I Gave You Love."

In 1983, Evans was in Jamaica again and working with **Winston Riley** in a group called the Techniques. While working for the Techniques, Evans occasionally went by the name Tyrone Don. Evans returned to New York and continued to work with Barnes at Wackies where he recorded a body of material that to this time is unreleased. Still in New York, Evans succumbed to cancer in 2000.

EXTERMINATOR

Exterminator is a Jamaican popular music label run by owner/producer **Philip "Fatis" Burrell**. On many of the Exterminator releases, Burrell backs his singers with studio musicians known as the Exterminator Crew. So popular are the songs cut with the crew that when label artists tour, they often take the Crew out with them for backup. The list of **dancehall** and **reggae** favorites released on the Exterminator imprint is substantial. Artists such as **Luciano** got their start on the label and have had a degree of loyalty to Burrell.

Burrell launched the label in the early 1990s after having worked as a producer for several years. The Exterminator imprint has a long list of releases that often feature the names of the most popular artists. The label has also released many compilations that have kept both old and new music in vogue. Artists who appear on the Exterminator imprint include **Admiral Tibet**, **Buju Banton**, **Capleton**, Turbulence, Prince Malacki, **Beres Hammond**, **Ini Kamoze**, **Gregory Isaacs**, **Lady G**, **Luciano**, **Mikey General**, Tenor, the Herbalist, **Ninjaman**, **Sizzla**, and many others. Burrell and his Exterminator crew continue to release cutting-edge reggae and dancehall music.

F

FAGAN, BEVIN (c. 1960–)

Bevin "Bagga" Fagan has been active in the music business since the late 1970s. His principal claim to fame is his lead vocal singing in the band **Matumbi**. Also in the band was lead guitarist Dennis Blovell, who later became a successful producer and creator of **dub** records. The group formed in 1972 in London when the prevailing sound was still **lovers rock**. With the help of Matumbi, the English taste was guided toward the new roots reggae style.

The height of Matumbi's output came in the latter half of the 1970s. During this period, the group released four albums that each had the characteristic **reggae**/soul sound. The group released *Seven Seals* in 1978, *Point of View* in 1979, *Matumbi* in 1981, and *Testify* in 1982. These four albums form a solid representation of the group's output. In 2001, EMI Records released the Matumbi compilation *The Best Of Empire Road: 1978-1981*, which compiled this material and brought the best tracks forward. Examples of several of the songs available on this release include "Bluebeat and Ska," "Music in the Air," and "Guide Us Jah." The album also contains several straight-ahead, conscious reggae songs such as "Blackman" and "War."

Beyond his work with Matumbi, Fagan also played bass and percussion for **I-Roy** on his *Whap'n Bap'n* release from 1980 and has the production credits on the compilation *Ranking Miss P Presents: Sweet Harmony* from 2003. Also more recently, Fagan has teamed with German guitar virtuoso Frank Schittenhelm to create an album called *Fire and Water.*

FAITH, GEORGE (1946–2003)

Earl George Turner (also known as Earl George and George Faith) was born in Jamaica in 1946. Faith got an early start in music by singing in church and at community events. Like many Jamaican-born singers of his generation, Faith was influenced by American rhythm and blues singers such as Sam Cooke. As a teenager, he joined the singing group the Enchanters but did not work well in the group dynamic. He went solo at age sixteen and released his first single, "Little Miss." The single was released under the name George Faith and garnered enough attention to allow him into **Black Ark Studios** with producer **Lee "Scratch" Perry**. The result of the session was the single "(To Be a Lover) Have a Little Mercy." The single was then packaged with other songs and cover versions on the 1977 **Island Records** release of the same name.

The following year, Faith recorded with producer Alvin "G. G." Ranglin at **Channel One Studios**. Under Ranglin, Faith recorded as Earl George and achieved some modest success with the release of *One and Only* (1978) on the Burning Sounds imprint. Also in 1978, Faith released *Loving Something* and *Working on a Guideline* (with Perry), both of which were well received. In 1982, again under the name George Faith, the singer released *Since I Met You Baby*; it did not have the same level of success as his previous releases. For the rest of the 1980s, Faith continued to release albums and play live. His principal venues came from the hotel circuit on the north coast of the island. In the early 1990s, he also gave live performances in Toronto, Canada, and toured with **Gregory Isaacs**. In 1992, he recorded another album at **Studio One** titled *Just the Blues*, but the producer on this work was Doris Darlington (the mother of **Clement "Coxsone" Dodd**).

Faith remained active in the music business until his death on April 16, 2003. After the release of his last studio album, subsequent releases have surfaced that compile his early work. In 1995, Jamaica Gold released *Loving Something*; in 1996, House of Reggae released *Soulful*; in 1998, *Rock for Lovers* came out; and in 1999, the Charly imprint released *Reggae Got Soul*.

FAME, GEORGE (1943–)

George Fame was born Clive Powell in Lancashire, England, in 1943. Early in his career, Powell adopted George Fame and launched his band the Blue Flames. For several years the group worked at the Flamingo Club playing their breed of English rhythm and blues and **ska**. In 1964, they released their debut album, *Rhythm and Blues at the Flamingo*. This was followed by the release of the single "Yeh, Yeh," which achieved the top spot on the UK charts. The song became a classic and was followed by a dozen other major singles, two of which also charted.

Next, Fame changed his style and studio, moving more toward the pop sound and from the Columbia Records label to CBS. In his new style, Fame released a series of recordings that were less substantial than his early material. In addition to pop music, Fame also played jazz and found work playing in this style on the club circuit. He is also an accomplished keyboard player and has worked as part Van Morrison's backup band.

In the early 1990s, Fame released a new album, *Cool Cat Blues*. It featured guest appearances by rock luminaries such as Steve Gadd and Boz Scaggs. On this release is a version of "Yeh, Yeh" reworked as a **reggae** song. Fame has continued to issue new material, and two of his sons play with him as members of the Flames. More recently, Fame has returned to playing in the jazz style and released albums such as *Poet in New York*, *Walking Wounded: Live at Ronnie Scott's*, and *Relationships*.

FASHION RECORDS

The Fashion Records label was formed by Luke James, John Mulligan, and Dick Davis in the late 1970s in Birmingham, England. The founders were members of a band of the same name who originally released their own material. The group released three singles of their own on the label and then opened it up to other artists. Eventually, the Fashion label imprint became known for releasing the highest-quality British **dub** and **dancehall** music. The label distributed its products through the Dub Vendor Record store in Clapham, southwest London. In addition to the material brought out by the band Fashion, other artists soon began appearing on the label, such as Clifton Morrison, Clevie, Joseph Cotton, King Kong, Daddy Freddy, Barry Boom, Professor Nuts, **Aswad**, **Pato Banton**, **Junior Delgado**, **Sly Dunbar**, **Macka B**, and **Frankie Paul**. The heyday of the label was the 1980s, and compilations of its material are now surfacing through other labels. IRS Records was launched in the early 1990s as the American equivalent of Fashion Records and has subsequently taken over Fashion's back catalog.

FATHEAD (c. 1960–)

Vernon Rainford was born in Kingston, Jamaica, and made a mark on the **reggae** scene through his collaborations with **Yellowman** in the early 1980s. Rainford performed under the name Fathead and was part of the climax of Yellowman's career, a time sometimes referred to as "Yellow Fever" that lasted from 1980 to 1982. Yellowman and Fathead were both solo **DJs** with solid reputations; however, they paired and created a whirlwind that began while the duo was singing on the club scene. The club that they were most known for performing in was called Aces; there they cut a live album with the assistance of producer **Lloyd Campbell**. On the record, Fathead performs solo songs such as "Gi Me the Music" and duets with Yellowman where he punctuates the albino DJ's line. The success of the early release led to two subsequent albums, the most important being 1982's *Bad Boy Skank*. Yellowman and Fathead's pairing then ended and Fathead went on to work with others.

In 1983 he scored a hit with Lloyd Campbell on the single "It's Me." Additionally, he performed next to **Beenie Man**, **Early B**, Johnny Ringo, and **Ranking Toyan**. Throughout these recordings, Fathead maintained a strong reputation and continued to find success. In the late 1980s, Fathead faded from the popular music picture. However, in the mid-1990s, he re-emerged as an engineer and worked with artists such as **Culture** and **Morgan Heritage**.

FATHER SWEETS (1971–)
Father Sweets was born in Kingston, Jamaica, but moved to New York City in 1983. His early exposure to music came from singing in church and hearing the diverse musical styles of the city. In New York, Sweets teamed up with **Easy Star Records**, which released his debut single "Sight of an Eagle" in 1997. His music shows the influence of **dancehall**, hip hop, jazz, and rhythm and blues; being a **DJ** himself, he is further exposed to a wide range of styles. Sweets's writing includes both love songs and serious roots messages about racism, poverty, and Afrocentrism. His dancehall style is infused with lyrics about the struggles of growing up in Kingston and in Brooklyn, resulting in a hybrid of roots and culture dancehall. Sweets aspires to become a producer later in his career.

FEARON, CLINTON (1951–)
Clinton "Basie" Fearon was born in St. Catherine, Jamaica, in 1951. During the early years of his life he moved frequently, ultimately ending up in Kingston in 1967. His first attempt at starting a band was not successful. However, in 1970s he teamed with Errol Grandison and Albert Griffiths and formed the **Gladiators**. Grandison did not stay in the group and soon was replaced by Gallimore Sutherland. The group began working at **Studio One**, where they recorded original material as well as serving as the studio's house band for a time. As the studio band, they played sessions for several major Jamaican recording artists, including **Burning Spear** and **Stranger Cole**. Fearon primarily played bass and sang but was able to cover the guitar parts when necessary.

As was the custom in Jamaica, the band moved to a different label after a time: in 1974 they went to work at **Black Ark Studios** for producer **Lee "Scratch" Perry**. For Perry, the Gladiators continued to record original material and serve as a studio band. The Gladiators released a series of albums beginning in 1976. Over their twenty-year career, they released ten albums that chronicled contemporary Jamaican style, and they toured the United States and western Europe.

In the late 1980s, Fearon left Jamaica and the Gladiators to move to Seattle, Washington. He formed a short-lived band called the Defenders, and then in 1993 he formed his current band, the Boogie Brown Band. The Boogie Brown Band has already released four albums: *Disturb the Devil* (1994), *Mystic Whisper* (1997), *What a System* (1999), and *Soon Come* (2002). The band's style is straight-ahead roots reggae with special emphasis on the drum and bass lines. Its members are Fearon on lead vocals, guitar, and percussion; harmony provided by Barbara Kennedy and Soo Jin Yi; Heff DeMelle on bass; Sergio Cuevas on drums; and Izaak Mills on tenor saxophone. The Boogie Brown band continues to write new music, record, and tour.

FEDERAL RECORDS

Federal Records has the auspicious distinction of being the first record label established in Jamaica. In 1954, **Ken Khouri** launched Federal Records to release locally licensed, American-made material. The label was housed on Kingston's Bell Road and originally released 78 RPM recordings. Soon, Khouri began releasing local records and the business thrived. He established his own pressing plant and was able to manufacture sizable runs of new recordings and reissues.

By the end of the 1950s, Khouri had some competition when **Clement "Coxsone" Dodd** and **Duke Reid** got into the recording business. However, Federal Records's studio kept them ahead of the competition, because of the popularity of its sixteen-track recording board compared to the four-track equipment used by Dodd and Reid. Many of Federal Records's releases were by the hitmakers of the day, including **Roland Alphonso**, **Jimmy Cliff**, **John Holt**, and **Johnny Nash**. As the style of Jamaican popular music evolved, many of the **sound system DJs** came to Khouri's studio to record their original material.

By the mid-1970s, Federal Records was a Jamaican recording institution. Seminal recordings by bands such as the **Meditations** were made there, including hit albums such as *Message from the Meditations* and *Wake Up*. Like many recording outfits, Federal Records had its own house band that backed vocalists in the studio, and many of the most famous Jamaican-born instrumentalists worked for Khouri (a notable example is legendary guitarist **Ernest Ranglin**). Federal Records holds a place of respect and reverence in the Jamaican recording industry.

FERGUSON, LLOYD "JUDGE" (c. 1950–)

Ferguson is one third of the singing trio the **Mighty Diamonds**. The group formed in 1969 when Kingston natives Ferguson (vocal harmonies and some lead vocals), Donald "Tabby" Shaw (lead vocals), and Fitzroy "Bunny" Simpson (vocal harmonies) joined forces. They began their singing careers emulating the Motown sound. In the mid-1970s, the trio went into the studio at **Channel One** with producer **Joseph "Joe Joe" Hookim** and began a string of hit singles that started with "Country Living" and "Hey Girl." Their first album, *Right Time*, was issued on the Virgin imprint in 1976; this early work has gone on to become classic **reggae**, and their single of the same name is a perennial favorite. Another of their hit songs was "Pass the Kouchie," which became an international hit when covered by the group Musical Youth (as "Pass the Dutchie").

Throughout the remainder of the 1970s, Ferguson and the Mighty Diamonds released an album per year, all of which were enthusiastically received. The group continues to perform today with the original three singers still intact. Over the course of their career they have released over forty albums and have toured the world. Their continued popularity is attested to by their continued appearances at the **Reggae Sunsplash** festival.

FFRENCH, ROBERT (c. 1950–)

Robert Ffrench has been active on the Jamaican **reggae** scene since early 1979. His entrance into the music business came with the recording of two singles, "Car Girl" and "Set Me Free." He is known as both singer and producer; and as such, he has worked with a series of the style's best artists. Through the course of the last twenty years, Ffrench has released a variety of singles. His most well known is the 1989 hit "Modern Girl," which features Courtney Melody. He has also worked with **Anthony B**, Senya, and the Pietasters. Further, in 2001 he released a solo album titled *Yesterday and Today*. Ffrench singles appear on a variety of compilation albums, including 1983's *Rising Stars* and 1998's *Platinum Reggae.*

In addition to his work as a performer, Ffrench has long been a producer of note. He has worked with artists such as **Buju Banton**, **Dennis Brown**, **Beres Hammond**, **Sizzla**, and George Nooks. Ffrench has also branched out into hip hop production, working with singers such as Foxy Brown and Heavy D. To work with these noted hip hop stars, Ffrench temporarily relocated to New York City. Since returning to Jamaica, Ffrench has been working on a new album, and his latest single is titled "Little Daughter." Other artists featured on the single include **Luciano**, **Mikey General**, and Turbulence. Beyond singing and producing, Ffrench also runs the Ffrench label and Ffrench distribution; both are located in Kingston, Jamaica.

FIREHOUSE CREW

The Firehouse Crew is a group of **rock steady** instrumentalists who have backed many of the most important singers in **reggae** music since the 1970s. The group remains active and continues to record and tour to this day. Led by the legendary saxophonist **Dean Fraser**, the group consists of ex-**Third World** guitarist **Stephen "Cat" Coore**, multi-instrumentalist Donald "Danny" Dennis, keyboardist Robert Lynn, and drummer **Sly Dunbar**. Together these musicians have performed in the roots reggae, **dancehall**, and **dub** styles and have backed a series of recording artists. The group has backed reggae luminaries such as **Admiral Bailey**, **Anthony B**, **Buju Banton**, **Beenie Man**, **Big Youth**, **Black Uhuru**, **Everton Blender**, **Capleton**, **Mikey General**, **Sizzla**, Michael Rose, and Fred Locks. As a band, the group has released several albums of their own, such as *Firehouse Platinum Series, Vol. 1* and *Tribute to King Tubby*. Recent recordings by the Crew include backing up Junior Kelly, LMS, Ras Shiloh, and Jah Cure.

FITZROY, EDI (1955–)

Edi Fitzroy was born in Clarendon, Jamaica, in 1955. Fitzroy's father was a sound operator, and others in his family were musically active. After finishing school he took a clerking job with the Jamaican Broadcasting Corporation, which allowed him to use the station's equipment to practice his singing. In the mid-1970s, then-radio **DJ Mikey Dread** heard one of Fitzroy's recordings and mentored the young singer. With Dread's assistance, Fitzroy scored a charting single with "Miss Molly Colly." The next single, "Country Man," was just the second in a long string of successful releases by Fitzroy with the help of Dread. The culmination of his 1970s success was a 1978 UK tour backing the punk group the Clash.

Once he returned to the island, he began the traditional movement from one producer to another. In 1981, he released the album *Check for You Once*, which went to number one in Jamaica for four weeks. He scored hits of varying degree through the early 1980s and was asked to perform in the 1984 installment of the **Reggae Sunsplash** Festival. Also in 1984, Fitzroy received the Rocker's Award for the Most Conscious Performer for his single "Princess Black." In addition, he released the album *Coming Up Strong* with songs such as "Sow Your Corn," "Easy Ride," and "Love the

People Want." Fitzroy's musical reputation was solid. Furthermore, Fitzroy had a long-standing commitment to equal rights, not just for blacks but also for women. The second half of the 1980s was on par with the first. Fitzroy continued to release successful material and receive acclaim for his efforts.

In the 1990s, he continued on the same path, in 1993 releasing *Deep in Mi Culture*, which further cemented his conscious vibe. Following this album, Fitzroy launched a tour of the United States with his backing band Massawa. He also began releasing material on his own label, Confidence. In the mid-1990s, Fitzroy recorded with several other important reggae artists, for example "Guiltiness" with **Cutty Ranks**. The year 1998 saw another U.S. tour, and Fitzroy continued to issue successful singles.

In 2000, Fitzroy performed in Gambia, West Africa, and released the album *We a Lion*, which continued the conscious vibe that he had had for the past decade. More recently, Fitzroy released *First Class Citizen* in 2001. It is a collection of his earlier hits that have been re-mastered. By all indications, the singer will continue to perform indefinitely.

FLOURGON (c. 1970–)

Flourgon was born Michael May in Kinston, Jamaica. Like many of the youths on the island, he got his first exposure to music through the sound systems and eventually began to **DJ** for them. He worked with the Stone Love, Small Axe, and Rambo Mango systems before starting his own Sweet Love system. Flourgon often paired with his brother, Red Dragon, also a DJ. Utilizing his popular brand of rough vocal **dancehall** performance style, Flourgon had a string of successful singles throughout the 1990s. In addition to pairing with his brother, Flourgon has also released successful singles with other artists, including **Sanchez**, Daddy Lizard, **Ninjaman**, Thriller U, and Clement Irie. His success has continued to a degree in the new millennium with singles such as "Million and More" and "Zig It Up," although his output has begun to wane. He is now regarded as a dancehall legend who makes periodic guest appearances. Examples of this are his vocal credits on albums by **Beres Hammond**, **Ninjaman**, and Sanchez, all from the past few years.

FLYERS (FLYING CYMBALS)

The Flying Cymbal drumming technique was popularized by producer **Bunny "Striker" Lee**. It was used repeatedly on the recordings he produced; termed "flyers," the technique became part of his signature sound. With his studio band the **Aggrovators**, Lee pioneered the different approach to drum playing. In a one-drop rhythm, where only beat three of a four-beat measure is accented (the standard **reggae** drumbeat), the hi-hat cymbal is played—open rather than closed—on the second and fourth beat of each measure. **Sly Dunbar** is an example of a drummer who has mastered the flying cymbal style of playing.

FOLKES BROTHERS

The Folkes Brothers were a **mento** group formed in 1960 by three brothers: John, Michael, and Eric ("Junior") Folkes. The group existed only for a year, but during that time they released a classic **reggae** recording. Together with drummer **Count Ossie** and pianist **Owen Gray**, the trio went into **Prince Buster's** studio and recorded the seminal single "Oh Carolina." After cutting this record, the group disappeared from the scene. In 1994, **dancehall** sensation **Shaggy** remade the song and scored an international hit. However, in a subsequent court battle, it was ruled that the Folkes still owned the copyright. The song has appeared in its original version on several compilation recordings in both the 1990s and the new millennium.

FORDE, BRINSLEY (c. 1955-)

Brinsley was one of the founding members of the UK-based **reggae** group **Aswad**. The group formed in 1975 and comprised Forde (lead vocals and guitar), **Angus "Drummie Zeb" Gaye** (drums), **George "Ras Levi" Oban** (bass), Donald "Benjamin" Griffiths (guitar), and Courtney Hemmings (keyboard). From its inception, the band combined soul, jazz, and funk with roots reggae, **dub**, and **lovers rock**. The band had the distinction of being the first reggae outfit to sign with **Chris Blackwell's Island Records**; they went on to become a driving force in the UK reggae scene.

Forde, a native of Guyana, had experienced the limelight as a child actor on the BBC. As the lead singer of Aswad, Forde helped develop the band's distinctive style. He returned to acting in 1980 when he appeared in the film *Babylon*, whose soundtrack contained the Aswad song "Warrior Charge." He stayed with the band until 2000, playing a crucial role in creating many of their many albums, including *Showcase* (1981), *Live and Direct* (1983), *Rebel Souls* (1984), *Distant Thunder* (1988), and *Rise and Shine* (1994). In 2000, he left the band to pursue other interests. Since leaving Aswad, Forde has begun a weekly radio show on BBC Radio 6. Each week he hosts a mixture of **dancehall**, **dub**, **rock steady**, **ska**, and reggae.

FORRESTER, SHARON (1956-)

Sharon Forrester was born in Kingston, Jamaica, in 1956 and began singing in church at an early age. As a professional singer, she enjoyed periods of prosperity during both the 1970s and the 1990s. In the mid-1970s, she scored a hit with the Gregory Chung-produced single "Silly Wasn't I"; the song became an international sensation. In 1974, she released the album *Sharon* on the **Ashanti** label. Following her self-titled album, Forrester lapsed into a twenty-year hiatus from the Jamaican recording scene. In 1995, she re-emerged with the album *This Time* on the VP imprint. On the album are songs such as "Goodbye"; "Remember the Love"; "This Time"; "Money Isn't Everything," featuring **Daddy Screw**; and the **reggae** version of "That's the Way Love Goes," by Janet Jackson. With her career revitalized, Forrester has guested or provided backing vocals for other artists such as **Alpha Blondy**, **Burning Spear**, **Jimmy Cliff**, the **Heptones**, **Spanner Banner**, and **Yami Bolo**.

FOSTER, WINSTON. *See* YELLOWMAN

FOUNDATION

Foundation was a **dancehall** collective that brought out four albums in the late 1980s and the 1990s. The group consisted of Errol "Keith" Douglas, Jack "L. Lino" Ruby, Emillo "Father" Smiley, and Euston "Ipal" Thomas. Their first two releases were on the Mango imprint, titled *Flames* (1988) and *Heart Feel It* (1989). Their style is dancehall with consciousness lyrics and an attempt at crossover appeal. Early on they enlisted the assistance of **Stephen "Cat" Coore**, formerly of **Third World**, to help with their crossover potential. However, they have not been successful in bridging the gap between the dancehall and popular music audiences. In the 1990s, the group released *One Shirt* on the Island Jamaica label in 1995 and *Smell the Poonany* in 1996. Although the material that Foundation released is solid island fare, they remain a little-known band.

FRANCIS, ERROL (c. 1965–)

Errol Francis performed under the name Errol Anthony Starr and has been active in the music business of the last three decades. A Jamaican native, Francis mixed **reggae** and rhythm and blues to form his sound. He spent time living in London and, more recently, Canada; he works as a singer, songwriter, producer, and engineer. Over the course of his career, Francis has released several albums, including 1985's *Temple of Love*, 1994's *From the Inside Out*, 1997's *I'll Learn to Fly*, and *Attune Your Spirit* in 1998. His albums have yielded a series of successful singles that brought Francis critical acclaim. In addition to his own work, Francis has appeared on recordings by Bushman, **Sly Dunbar**, the Regulars, and others. In the early 1990s, Francis launched his own studio and productions company in Ottawa Valley, Ontario. The outfit is called Asoma Music Production and services the audio needs of radio, television commercials, video projects, and film.

FRANCIS, PATRICK. *See* JAH LION

FRANKLIN, CHEVELLE (c. 1975–)

Chevelle Franklin was born in Spanish Town, St. Catherine, Jamaica. She dropped out of school at age fourteen to find work on the north coast. She got a job singing on the club circuit and moved again after a year. This time she went to Kingston in search of a record contract. At first Franklin struggled to find anyone willing to put the money up to record her. However, she eventually teamed with **Mikey Bennett** and began cutting singles. With Bennett, she recorded songs such as "Shy" and "Pushover" and was encouraged to duet with **dancehall** favorites. This led to her singing "Loverman" with **Shabba Ranks** and "Dancehall Queen" with **Beenie Man**. "Dancehall Queen" was released in 1997 and was a huge success, propelling Franklin's career forward. Her greatest period of productivity was the second half of the 1990s, during which she released her 1996 album *Serious Girl*. The album contained the singles "Nice and Naughty," "Dead or Alive," and "Pushover." This release brought her critical acclaim and popularity, which she parlayed into a world tour. In addition to releasing her own material, Franklin frequently appears as a backup vocalist for artists such as **Dennis Brown**, **Chaka Demus and Pliers**, **Beres Hammond**, **Gregory Isaacs**, and **Spanner Banner**. More recently, Franklin has used her voice to sing about spiritual matters, and her first gospel recording, *Joy*, has already been released.

FRASER, DEAN IVANHOE (1955–)

Dean Fraser has been an integral part of the Jamaican music scene for thirty years. His performance credits appear on over 1,000 recordings, and he is equally comfortable in the **dancehall**, **reggae**, and jazz styles. Fraser was born in Kingston, Jamaica, in 1955, and began performing at an early age. His first experience came as a clarinet player with his community club in 1967.

In 1970, Fraser took up the saxophone and soon was proficient enough to start his own band. His band, the Sonny Bradshaw 7, played at the Sheraton, where **Jacob Miller** sometimes sat in with them. Miller subsequently took Fraser into the studio, and his string of recording successes began. Soon he had earned the reputation as the island's best saxophone player, which led to countless hours in the studio backing famous singers and bands.

By 1983, he had established himself as a serious artist with his **Reggae Sunsplash** performance of **Bob Marley's** classic "Redemption Song." Next, Fraser worked with

Dean Fraser. © *UrbanImage.tv.*

Philip "Fatis" Burrell and his **Exterminator** crew. He was also associated for a time with the **Firehouse Crew**. Over the course of his career, Fraser has released at least ten of his own albums, including *Call on Dean* (1989), *Taking Chances* (1992), *Big Up* (1998), and a series of extremely popular recordings, *Dean Plays Bob* and *Dean Plays Bob, Vol. II.* (1990), which resulted from Fraser covering Bob Marley.

FRASER, NEIL.
See MAD PROFESSOR

FRATER, ERIC (c. 1950–)
Eric "Rickenbacker" Frater is a legendary reggae guitarist who often used a twelve-string guitar, which gave his guitar parts a denser quality. Frater has been active on the scene since 1968, when he went into **Studio One** and began recording with **Jackie Mittoo** (keyboard). Early singles on which he recorded include "Fat Girl," "Hello Carol," and "Ram Jam." Before working with Mittoo, Frater worked with the Mighty Vikings and the Virtues. With Mittoo, Frater played in the **Soul Vendors** with **Roland Alphonso**. After leaving the Soul Vendors, Frater worked with the group Sound Dimension. More recently, Frater has played guitar with the **Abyssinians, Aston "Family Man" Barrett, Ken Boothe**, the **Heptones**, and many others.

FREE-I (c. 1950–)
Free-I was born Jeff Dixon and entered the music arena as a disc jockey for the Jamaican Broadcasting Company. Dixon left that job to move to the United States and had success as a producer. He returned to Jamaica with a new name, Free-I, and a new perspective, which involved staunch **Rastafarianism**. He went on to enjoy a solid recording career that involved the release of several successful singles, such as "Super Bad," "Tickle Me," and "The Rock." Additionally, he recorded with **Marcia Griffiths** in 1968. The **Clement "Coxsone" Dodd**-produced track was titled "Words" and was successful for both Dixon and Griffiths. Unfortunately, Dixon was killed on September 11, 1987, in the same robbery that took the life of **Peter Tosh**. Free-I and his wife were at Tosh's house when three gunmen attempted to rob the Tosh home. They opened fire and killed both Free-I and Tosh. Now, Free-I's music lives on through his son, who calls himself Kulcha Knox.

FRISCO KID (c. 1970–)
The Frisco Kid was born Stephen Wray in Kingston, Jamaica, in the early 1970s. He started **DJing** while still a teenager attending Kingston Secondary School. His rise to

prominence as a **dancehall** star was slow; along the way he considered leaving the music business to become a horseracing jockey. However, he stayed in the business and worked small **sound system** gatherings to hone his skills. While working a subsistence job in Kingston, he met and began to work with Father Romey, the owner of the Exodus Nuclear sound system. With success on Exodus under the name Parro Kid, Wray gained the confidence to go into **King Jammy's** studio under the moniker Frisco Kid. He cut some sides based on his Exodus work; the singles helped launch his career. By the mid-1990s, Frisco had established a solid reputation and was appearing on a variety of recordings. Through the end of the decade he recorded over thirty original singles and in 1998 released his debut album, *Finally*. His singles continued to gain popularity and included titles such as "Calico," "Rubbers," "Tink We Nice," "Want a Spiderman," and many others. He also began appearing with other artists, most notably on **Barrington Levy's** *Duets* album of 1995. Frisco Kid's reputation as a dancehall star is solid, and he continues to release singles, appear on compilations, and perform in the new millennium.

FULLWOOD, GEORGE "FULLY" (c. 1950–)

George Fullwood has been an essential part of the Jamaican roots reggae scene since the 1970s. Often referred to as "Fully," Fullwood has worked with and recorded for virtually every major Jamaican recording artist over the past thirty years, such as Michael Rose, **Black Uhuru**, **Dennis Brown**, **Joe Higgs**, **Gregory Isaacs**, **Bob Marley**, **Mighty Diamonds**, **Mikey Dread**, **Peter Tosh**, and many others. Fullwood is a legendary bass player whose credits include being a founding member of **Soul Syndicate** and part of Peter Tosh's backing band **Word, Sound, and Power**. Through the course of his storied career, Fullwood played on Tosh's *No Nuclear War* album in addition to backing up artists such as the **Abyssinians**, **Johnny Clark**, **Doctor Alimantado**, and Dennis Morgan. More recently, Fullwood has been working with **Beenie Man**, **Big Youth**, and Peter Tosh's son **Andrew Tosh**. He now lives in Orange County, California, and is the mentor for bands such as Rascalin & the Roots Rockers and Kyng Arthur. In addition, Fullwood runs his own band, the Fully Fullwood Band, which includes **reggae** legends **Tony Chin** on guitar and **Carlton "Santa" Davis** on drums.

FUNDE

The funde drum is one of the three **akete** drums used in the **Rastafarian** style of **nyabinghi** drumming. It has only one head and is played with the fingers and hands with the instrument secured between the player's legs. It is accompanied by the **repeater** and the bass drum. All three are double membrane drums; the bass is the largest, and the funde and repeater are smaller and similar in size. The principal difference between the repeater and the funde is that the repeater's head is tight, making it the treble drum, while the funde's is slack. Each of the three drums has a prescribed role in performance. The bass drum is sounded on beats one and four in a four-beat measure. The funde plays an eighth-note syncopated cross-rhythm that is layered in on top of the bass. To this is added improvisational melody by the repeater.

The use of **nyabinghi** drums in **reggae** music is traced back to traditional African drumming. **Burru** drumming was documented in Kingston as early as 1930, and used in **kumina** and revival dancing. In turn, the drumming style was adopted by popular musicians in the west Kingston ghettos.

GABBIDON, BASIL (1955–)

Born in Buff Bay, Jamaica, on October 29, 1955, Gabbidon came from a musical family whose patriarch was an entertainer and comedian. The family moved to Kingston during Gabbidon's youth, and Gabbidon spent his time in nearby St. Mary's parish. Ultimately, the family relocated to England just as Gabbidon was entering his teenage years, settling in a Caribbean community in Birmingham. There Gabbidon attended Handsworth Wood Boys School, where he was classmates with David Hind. While in school, he began playing the trombone; this was the start of his life in music. From trombone he quickly moved to guitar and soon caught on to **reggae** music after hearing **Bob Marley's** classic album *Catch a Fire*.

After matriculation from primary school, Gabbidon and Hinds attended Bournville College of Art. While at college, Hinds and Gabbidon worked on their music together in their spare time; Gabbidon, Hinds, and Gabbidon's younger brother on make-shift drums rehearsed in the family kitchen. Soon they added their friend Ronnie McQueen on bass and formed their first band. They next added a keyboard player, Selwyn Brown, and a backing vocalist, Michael Riley. At this early stage, the group played cover versions of songs by Marley and the **Abyssinians**, **Burning Spear**, and **Peter Tosh**, but they soon began to work on their own, original material and to perform as **Steel Pulse**, named for a favorite racehorse. Steel Pulse became immensely popular, touring and recording several albums.

Just before the group's fourth album, Gabbidon quit the band, feeling that Steel Pulse had lost its edge. After leaving the band, he disappeared from the music scene for a time. But in 1987, he re-emerged with a new band called Bass Dance. In 1990 the band released the album *Loud*, followed in 1995 by their second album *Louder*. Although the band experienced some success, they did not survive the 1990s. Since the second band's breakup, Gabbidon has continued to play as a solo artist.

GAD, PABLO (c. 1960–)

A UK-based roots reggae singer, Gad has been active in the music business since the late 1970s. Even in the roots style, the content of Gad's lyrics was militant and conscious, and this brought the singer acclaim. His early singles were compiled by the artist himself on *Best of Pablo Gad (1977–1980)*. He also released a series of albums of mature work such as 1978's *Blood Suckers*, *Don't Push Jah*, and *Life without Death*; and 1980's *Trafalgar Square*. More recently, Gad has worked with the Conscious Sounds label and plans to bring out new material. Other important artists on Conscious Sounds include **Bush Chemist** and Kenny Knotts.

GARRICK, NEVILLE (c. 1950–)

An artist who has been part of the roots reggae scene in Jamaica, Garrick has produced album covers for **Bob Marley's** releases *Survival* and *Rastaman Vibrations* on the **Tuff Gong** label, among many others. Another Garrick creation of note is **Peter Tosh's** *No Nuclear War.* In addition to creating album art, Garrick was a longstanding confidant of Marley's and remains active in the scene as both an artist and periodic live performance emcee.

GAYE, ANGUS "DRUMMIE ZEB" (c. 1960–)

Gaye is one of the founding members of the UK-based **reggae** group **Aswad** and remains in the group today. Over the course of twenty years of releases, Gaye played on all fifteen of Aswad's albums. He was also involved in the creation of the band's latest release, 2002's *Cool Reggae Summer.* Additionally, Gaye and Aswad bassist Tony Gad have formed a production team and have worked on releases for artists such as **Janet Kay**, Sweetie Irie, Joe, and Trevor Hartley. Gaye continues to record and perform.

GAYLADS, THE

The Gaylads formed as a singing group in 1963, during the **ska** era. The singing trio consisted of Maurice Roberts, Winston Delano Stewart, and Harris "B. B." Seaton. Stewart and Seaton were originally a singing duo called Winston and Bibby. They had worked with **Clement "Coxsone" Dodd** in their earlier incarnation, so once the trio was formed, the three went to Dodd to record. At **Studio One**, they recorded a series of singles including "There'll Come a Day" and "What Is Wrong with Me," which received local acclaim.

As the prominent Jamaican style shifted from ska to the slower **rock steady**, the Gaylads made the change and hit with a series of well-received singles. These singles were ultimately compiled into the group's debut album, *The Soul Beat.* After the success of the first album, the Gaylads returned to the studio to cut their sophomore release, *Sunshine Is Golden.* This record was also successful; subsequent to its release the Gaylads began the producer and studio-moving that are common in Jamaica. They next worked with producer **Sonia Pottinger** and recorded several hit singles such as "Over the Rainbow's End" and others.

In 1968, at the height of the group's success, Stewart left to pursue a solo career, and the remaining two members continued working as a duo under the Gaylads name, leaving Pottinger to work with producer **Lee "Scratch" Perry**. Under Perry's direction and with his production skills, the Gaylads again had a series of hit singles. The group's next hit single was "There's a Fire," which was released under yet another producer, **Leslie Kong**. With Kong, the Gaylads enjoyed a period of renewed success, even recording a version of James Taylor's "Fire and Rain."

The Kong union was short-lived, as Kong died of a heart attack in the summer of 1971. The group then moved to producer **Rupie Edwards** and scored another series of hits. Through the early 1970s, Seaton was gradually getting involved in a variety of recording projects outside the Gaylads, and soon he left the group. Roberts attempted to continue the group name with two new members but was not successful in regaining the group's early magic. He ultimately changed the group name to the Psalms, and the new lineup worked as backing vocalists for **Bunny Wailer**. In 1991, Seaton and Stewart reunited for a concert celebrating Studio One, and in 1993 Roberts rejoined them for a **rock steady** reunion show. In posterity, several compilations of the group's material have been released, including *After Studio 1* (1992), *Over the Rainbow's End: The Best of the Gaylads* (1995), and *Fire and Rain* (1996).

GENERAL DEGREE (c. 1970–)

Born Cardiff Butt, General Degree (or Degree) got his musical start as a **DJ** in the late 1980s. Degree DJs in the **dancehall** style and often writes sexually explicit lyrics. His first single was 1989's "Mother Rude Pickney," and from there he released a series of successful songs, having continued success through the course of the 1990s. Examples of his style are evident on his albums *Bush Baby, Degree, Granny,* and *Smash Hits.* Hit singles by Degree include "Granny," "When I Hold You Tonight," and "Inna Body." In addition to his recording work, Degree has also launched his own label, which he calls Size 8.

GENERAL ECHO (d. 1980)

Born Errol Robinson, General Echo (also known as Ranking Slackness) came onto the early **DJ** scene in the late 1970s. Echo worked with producer **Winston Riley**, and together they recorded the album *The Slackness LP* (1980), half of which was produced by Riley, the other half by **Henry "Junjo" Lawes**. The lyrical content of the album was entirely focused on rude and slack topics (risqué or ribald language and talk of guns, sex, and drugs); the album was ultimately a major influence on the generation of DJs who surfaced in the 1980s. In addition to recording music, Echo also ran his own **sound system** called Echo Tone Hi Fi sound system. Material from the system was recorded and released in 1980 as the album *12 Inches of Pleasure;* tragically, Echo and two of his system workers were shot and killed by police in 1980.

GENERAL LEVY (c. 1970–)

Paul Levy, better known as General Levy, is a UK-based **DJ** who bridges **dancehall**, **ragga**, and **reggae** styles. Levy debuted in the early 1990s and had instant success with the **Sly and Robbie**-produced single "Heat," from 1993. His delivery is raw and his voice is dark and gravelly, while his lyrics tend toward slackness (risqué or ribald language; talk of guns, sex, and drugs). In the mid-1990s, Levy began to work jungle rhythms into his DJ sets, allowing him to cross over and be accepted into the jungle style. Levy released two albums in the 1990s, *Mad Dem* in 1995 and *New Breed* in 1999. He continues to work and has received critical acclaim and several awards from the UK record industry.

GENERAL TREES (c. 1960–)

General Trees was born Anthony Edwards and fast became one of the most popular **DJs** on the **dancehall** scene in the 1980s. He got his start in music through the **sound systems**, where he DJ-ed dances and honed his style. Trees toasts his lyrics in a dancehall style that is a mixture of slackness (ribald talk of sex, guns, and drugs) and consciousness elements. He recorded his first single on the **Black Scorpio** label and soon began the typical Jamaican practice of switching from one producer to another. Ultimately, he returned to Scorpio and released his album *Heart, Soul, and Mind.* He went on to release *Nuff Respect* in 1987; *Ragga, Ragga Ragamuffin* in 1988; and a clash album with **Yellowman** called *A Reggae Calypso Encounter* in 1987. Important singles from General Trees include "Fire in Rome," "Deportee," and "Top End." In addition to his own releases, Tree's material has begun to appear on dancehall compilations.

GERMAINE, DONOVAN (c. 1960–)

Donovan Germaine is an important producer in **reggae** and **dancehall** and has been active since the early 1980s. He has worked with many Jamaican recording stars and continues to do so. Early recordings on which Germaine worked include Cultural Roots's self-titled debut in 1980, their followup in 1982, and albums by the **Mighty Diamonds**. Additionally, Germaine has produced work for **Buju Banton**, **Beenie Man**, **Cutty Ranks**, **Dean Fraser**, **Marcia Griffiths**, **Maxi Priest**, **Sanchez**, and others. He has also produced a few compilation albums.

GIBBONS, LEROY (c. 1960–)
Leroy Gibbons is a veteran Jamaican singer who has been on the scene for years. His list of hit singles is long and includes "Magic Moment," "Chant Down Babylon," "You and I," "Missing You," and "Build Up the Vibes." An example of his album material is 1992's release *Four Season Lover*, which appeared on the **Dynamic Studio** imprint. The day following the terrorist attack in New York City on September 11, 2001, Gibbons went into the studio and recorded "Love Light Shine." The song was a significant hit, serving to calm people in the wake of the tragedy.

GIBBS, JOE (1945–)
Born Joel Gibson in Montego Bay, Jamaica, in 1945, Joe Gibbs became one of the most important musicians in the formation of the roots reggae style. Gibbs entered the Jamaican popular music scene in the early 1980s and immediately made his mark as a producer; however, he is also a proficient vocalist. Some early bands that Gibbs produced material for include **Dennis Brown**, **Culture**, the **Heptones**, and the **Pioneers**. Once Gibbs began producing hits, his run lasted for twenty years.

After spending time in the United States, Gibbs returned to Jamaica and set up a television repair shop in Kingston. Soon he was also selling records out of his shop to supplement his income. He gained early production experience as an assistant to Ken Lack and soon began producing on his own. His studio was in the back of his repair shop and the equipment was rudimentary; however, Gibbs was immediately successful and even launched his own label in 1967, the Amalgamated imprint. In his small two-track studio he recorded the single "Hold Them" by Roy Shirley; the song is now regarded by many to be the first **rock steady** example. In the late 1960s, Gibbs was among the most active producers on the island, with dozens of singles and talent that included the **Slickers**, **Peter Tosh**, and the **Versatiles**.

Gibbs was open-minded about the music that he produced, which allowed him to cross styles, even recording early **DJ** material. Gibbs's studio band, which included many of the best players on the inland, was **Lynn Taitt** and the Jets. Often, he also had the Hippy Boys doing backup work at the studio. The Jets featured a solid lineup and a horn section that included trombonist **Vin Gordon**, while the Hippy Boys featured the drum and bass playing of the Barrett Brothers.

In the early 1970s, Gibbs stayed current as the popular music style on the island changed from **rock steady** to **reggae**. He also launched a new set of imprints, opened a Kingston-based record store, and set up a new studio. Yet another studio was set up in 1972, and at this location Gibbs recorded **Dennis Brown's** "Money in My Pocket." This recording was an instant success and an early example of the work of Gibbs teamed with engineer **Errol Thompson**; the pair would go on to be known as the Mighty Two.

Thompson and Gibbs released scores of recordings over the next several years, many of which reached the top of the charts. Over the course of the 1970s, Gibbs continued to enhance his recording facilities; he built a record-pressing plant and continued to record the highest-quality musicians on the island. An example of his work during this period is **Culture's** album *Two Sevens Clash*. This album was enormously popular, both in Jamaica and in England, and gave the UK-based punk band the Clash their name. Gibbs's studio band through this period was the Professionals, which included **Sly and Robbie** along with guitarist **Earl "Chinna" Smith**. Despite Gibbs's numerous successes in the music business, he ended up in a lengthy legal struggle over the licensing of **J. C. Lodge's** hit "Somebody Loves You." The song, written by Charley Pride, caused a battle over ownership that eventually drove Gibbs out of the business.

In the early 1990s, Gibbs re-emerged with a modernized studio and reconnected with his Mighty Two partner Thompson. The Joe Gibbs legacy continues; he is currently releasing solid material, and the **Trojan** label is beginning to mine the vaults of his early recordings for reissue.

GLADIATORS, THE

The Gladiators were a legendary Jamaican vocal trio group that formed in 1967. Lead singer and rhythm guitarist Albert Griffiths, David Webber, and Errol Grandison formed the group. Early on, they went into the studio and recorded "The Train Is Coming Back," which was a minor hit on Edward Seaga's West Indian Records Limited (WIRL) label. The group then released a series of singles that were produced at various studios around the island. Their first big hit, "Dear Carol," came with producer **Clement "Coxsone" Dodd**. Two years into the band's existence, Webber departed and was replaced by **Clinton Fearon**; the group continued to release solid singles. Their early work culminated in the release of their debut album *Presenting the Gladiators*.

However, by 1973, Grandison had also left the group and was replaced by Dallimore Sutherland. The group then linked with producer Tony Robinson and produced a series of albums that included *Trench Town Mix Up* and *Proverbial Reggae*. This work

The Gladiators. © *UrbanImage.tv.*

came out on the Groovemaster label in Jamaica and the Virgin imprint in the United Kingdom. Throughout the 1980s, the group recorded with various labels, including **Heartbeat Records** and **Nighthawk**. On Nighthawk, the Gladiators released the albums *Symbol of Reality, Serious Thing*, and *Full Time*, which cemented their place at the top of the **reggae** elite. Through Heartbeat, the group released five more albums and continued to have success. The Gladiators released a pair of impressive albums in the 1990s.

Unfortunately, Fearon left the group during this period; however, Griffiths retained and used the Gladiators name. After the turn of the century, the Gladiators released the album *Something a Gwaan* on the **RAS** label. The Gladiators have been a foundational group in the history of Jamaican popular music and remain active.

GLAMMA KID (1978-)

Glamma Kid was born in 1978 and has quickly risen to the top of the UK-based **ragga** scene. Before his twenty-first birthday he already had three singles, which were released on the WEA imprint. Kid's sound was cultivated listening to the UK **sound system DJs**, from whom he picked up themes such as sex, politics, and current events. To these stock themes Kid added an element of humor and took a more popular music approach. Unfortunately, this stylistic blend only served to dilute his appeal, and Kid had difficulty scoring hits.

Glamma Kid's biggest success was 1999's cover of Sade's hit "Sweetest Taboo," recorded with UK soul singer Shola Ama. The song was a success and created buzz for the young emcee. He has subsequently scored another notable success with the single "Bills 2 Pay," which comes from his 2000 release and debut album *Kidology*. Also featured on this release is a collaboration with **Beenie Man**: the single "Bling, Bling, Bling." To further enhance his credibility, Kid teamed with Nerious Joseph, **Peter Hunnigale**, and **Mafia and Fluxy** to form the short-lived supergroup Passion. The group released the hit single "Share Your Love." Glamma Kid's interest has turned to parlaying his early success into a long career blending **reggae** and popular music.

GLASGOW, DEBORAHE (1965–1994)

Deborahe Glasgow was born in England in 1965. She began her recording career as a child, recording the single "Falling in Love" for **Mad Professor** at his **Ariwa** studios. During her teenage years, Glasgow worked with the London area **sound systems** to hone her singing skills, which resulted in a record deal with **Patrick Donegan** and the UK Bubblers imprint. In 1989, Glasgow released her only album, *Deborahe Glasgow*, which has become a UK-**reggae** classic. The album contains a cameo by **Shabba Ranks**, the renowned **toaster** of **dancehall**. Glasgow's career was cut short when she left the music business to raise a family. Diagnosed with cancer in the early 1990s, Glasgow died in 1994.

GORDON, MICHAEL (c. 1955-)

Michael Gordon got his start on the UK **reggae** scene as a member of the band the Private I's. The group scored several minor hits but gained recognition through singles such as a cover of **Black Uhuru's** "Folk Song." In 1975, Gordon joined the Investigators, which also included Lorenzo Hall, Ian Austin, Reg Graham, and Martin Christie. This **lovers rock** collective continued the success that the Private I's had found on the **Fashion** label. The Investigators released a series of solid singles and gained critical acclaim. In 1981 they toured the United Kingdom and the United States opening for Black Uhuru, and in 1985 they were on the UK bill for the **Reggae Sunsplash** concert.

They released their debut album, *First Case*, in 1982 and continued their success with subsequent singles. Their 1984 song "Woman I Need Your Loving" was a hit, but the group did not last. Gordon went on to a solo career that included the album *Changing Circles*, which was released on MCS Records. The label is home to several other UK reggae luminaries such as **Daddy Colonel**, Papa Levi, and **Tippa Irie**.

GORDON, VIN (c. 1945–)

Vin Gordon has been Jamaica's most sought-after trombone player since the late 1960s. Gordon began recording as a session trombonist and found early work at **Randy's** Studio 17, which was owned and operated by Vincent "Randy" Chin. Gordon's trombone skills were in high demand during the **ska** era and into the early days of the **reggae** style. Gordon was part of the Impact All-Stars and supplied trombone lines alongside artists including **Aston "Family Man" Barrett**, **Carlton "Carly" Barrett**, **Sly Dunbar**, **Tyrone Downie**, **Earl "Wya" Lindo**, **Augustus Pablo**, and **Tommy McCook**. The group backed many performers working at Chin's studio and even cut a few singles of their own. After leaving Chin's studio, Gordon and various other members of the studio band went on to record with many of reggae music's most important stars. Gordon's credits appear on albums by **Alpha Blondy**, **Dennis Brown**, **Jimmy Cliff**, the **Maytals**, the **Mighty Diamonds**, **Bunny Wailer**, and many others.

Of special note, Gordon was part of the backing band for **Culture's** seminal album *Two Sevens Clash*. He also played in the other studios around Jamaica. In the 1970s, he was intermittently part of **Lee "Scratch" Perry's Upsetters**, Perry's studio band. Gordon recorded for **Clement "Coxsone" Dodd** on his **Studio One** imprint, and by the mid-1970s was recognized as the best reggae trombone player on the island. This reputation led to Gordon's association with **Bob Marley and the Wailers**, which encompassed the early part of Marley's career. Gordon supplied the trombone lines on Marley's albums *Kaya*, *Exodus*, *Freedom Time*, and the Dodd compilation *The Wailers Greatest Hits at Studio One*. After leaving Marley, Gordon recorded with **Aswad**, **Pato Banton**, **I-Roy**, **Mikey Dread**, **Tippa Irie**, and others.

More recently, Gordon has been in the supergroup the Coyabalites, which includes **Glen Da Costa**, **Dean Fraser**, **Justin Hinds**, **Ernest Ranglin**, David Madden, and Harold Butler. The group has had several successful singles and released its debut album, *Coyaba Ska*, in 2001. Gordon continues to be active and further lengthens his list of performing credits.

GRAHAM, ANTHONY (c. 1960–)

Anthony Graham began working in the Jamaican **reggae** business in the late 1970s. He has gone by a variety of names, including his given name, Crucial Bunny, Bunny Graham, and Bunny Tom Tom. Under any name, he has long been in demand as an engineer, mixer, and producer. Early on, Graham began working with **King Tubby's Channel One Studio**; through this association he was able to work with a series of the major figures in reggae music. Beginning in the late 1970s, Graham mixed albums for **Big Youth**, **Black Uhuru**, the Blackstones, **Al Campbell**, **Early Zero**, the **Heptones**, **Freddie McGregor**, **Roots Radics**, **U-Brown**, and many others. As an engineer, Graham's list of credits is equally lengthy and includes **Dub Syndicate**, **Earl Sixteen**, the **Ethiopians**, **General Echo**, **Beres Hammond**, **Prince Far I**, and many others. His career spanned the late 1970s to the late 1980s. He has production credits on albums by **Mikey General** and others. Along the way, Graham also worked on a list of compilation recordings that encompassed the output of all the aforementioned artists.

GRANT, BOYSIE (c. 1945–)

Boysie Grant was among the earliest recording artists whom the island of Jamaica produced. He was active in the early 1960s and performed in the **mento** style. Several of his popular singles were released on seven-inch recordings, including "Noisy Spring," which was recorded with the Reynolds Calypso Band. Another important release was "Solas Market," recorded with Eddie Brown and the Reynolds Calypso Band. Over the ensuing forty years, Grant's material has largely fallen into obscurity. However, the 2004 V2 label recording *Mento Madness* seeks to bring this early material back to life. On the album, Grant has three singles, all of which beautifully illustrate his brand of mento.

GRANT, EDDY (1948–)

Edmond "Eddy" Grant was born in Guyana, spent his formative years in London, and ultimately settled on Barbados. He got his start in music as one of the founding members of the UK-based multiracial pop band the Equals, formed in 1965. With the Equals, Grant scored a number one hit in 1968, the single "Baby Come Back." By 1970, Grant had gone solo and established his own record label called Torpedo. Grant had not completely abandoned the Equals yet, though, and in early 1971 the group hit with another chart-topping single, "Black Skinned Blue Eyed Boys."

In the wake of this hit, Grant's health gave out. He suffered a heart attack and collapsed lung at age twenty-three. This led him to quit the Equals permanently. In 1972, Grant also sold his label and used the proceeds to open a recording studio that he called Coach House. To this was added another label, Ice, and Grant produced and recorded artists for release on his new imprint. Grant again felt the pull to perform and in 1977 wrote, sang, played all the instruments on, and produced his first album, *Message Man*, released on his Ice label. He followed this in 1979 with *Walking on Sunshine*, which cemented his reputation as a force in Caribbean popular music. Grant parlayed his success into a third album, *Love in Exile*, which did not chart. However, his fourth release, *Can't Get Enough* (1981), again made Grant's music popular and broke the Top 40.

Along the way Grant continued to produce, scoring a hit with the **Gladiators'** eponymous 1980 album. With success at hand, Grant released a series of five albums in four years. Notable singles include "Electric Avenue" from 1984's *Going for Broke*. Also in the mid-1980s, Grant relocated his studio to Barbados. There he was able both to mentor rising talent and to work on perfecting the new sound that he had a hand in creating, soca. The use of the word *soca* created a substantial conflict between Grant and Lord Shorty, who also claimed to have invented this new style. Grant's Barbados-based Blue Wave studio has produced hits for many important artists, in the **reggae** style as well as in the popular music styles. Artists who have recorded there include Sting, Elvis Costello, and many fledgling Caribbean groups.

In 1988, Grant turned out some new music of his own on the album titled *File under Rock*. Although the material from the late 1980s did not chart, Grant continued to issue new material intermittently throughout the 1990s and into the new millennium. Most recently, Grant has been involved with the evolution of a new type of music that he has named *ringbang*. Having learned his lesson from the soca controversy, Grant patented the word *ringbang* and thus maintains control over its use.

Grant continues to be active in the Caribbean popular music scene and mentors young artists through his Blue Wave studio.

GRAY, OWEN (1939–)

Born in Kingston, Jamaica, in 1939, Gray made an early entrance into the popular music business. At age nine he was already singing in public, having gained training at the **Alpha Boys Catholic School**. In 1960, he released the single "Please Let Me Go," which went to number one on the Jamaican charts. His next important single was "On the Beach," which was followed by a series of other hit singles. Gray's early hits were compiled into the album *Owen Gray Sings*, released by **Clement "Coxsone" Dodd**. Gray had excellent support for his 1960s material, working with either the **Skatalites** or the Caribs for each session. He performed in a number of styles ranging from gospel to **ska**. Gray was not only a talented singer, but also a multi-instrumentalist, exemplified by his piano appearance on the **Folkes Brothers** tune "Oh Carolina." In 1962, Gray moved to England, where he continued to sing and record. He did, however, return to Jamaica intermittently to keep current with the changing island styles. Gray's success continued through the 1970s, culminating in his being chosen by **Sly and Robbie** for their **dub** album *Sly and Robbie Present Owen Gray*. In the 1980s, Gray worked for a series of labels and the hits continued. Currently, Gray is in retirement in Miami, Florida.

GRIFFITHS, MARCIA (1954–)

Linneth Marcia Griffiths was born in Kingston, Jamaica, in 1954. Her earliest vocal experience was in church and school choirs. She established herself as a reputable singer in the mid-1960s, working with producers **Clement "Coxsone" Dodd** and **Byron Lee**. Her music career began in earnest when she teamed with **Bob Andy** of the **Paragons** fame and formed the duo Bob and Marcia. The two sang together from 1970 to 1974 and had a series of international hit singles. In 1974, Griffiths joined **Rita Marley** and **Judy Mowatt** in the **I-Threes**, the female vocal trio that backed **Bob Marley**. As part of the I-Threes, Griffiths recorded and toured with Marley from 1974 to 1980. After Marley's death in 1981, Griffiths went solo and enjoyed a substantial individual singing career. Griffiths is now revered as one of the most important female singers in **reggae** music.

GROUNDATION

Formed in 1998 by Sonoma State University (California) students Harrison Stanford and Ryan Newman, the band Groundation takes its name from the **Rastafarian** word *grounation*, the term for a meeting where education and reason are discussed. The band is a ten-piece collective that plays roots reggae with some modern flair. The style that the band plays involves roots influences with the addition of jazz and **dub** flavoring. Harrison (known as the Professor or Prof) provides vocals and guitar, and Ryan "Iron" Newman plays both electric and acoustic bass. To this has been added Marcus Urani on keyboards and melodica, David "King" Chachere on trumpet, Kelsey Howard on trombone, and Jason Robinson on saxophone and flute. To date, Groundation has released four albums: 1999's *Young Tree*, followed by *Each One Teach One* in 2001, *Hebron Gates* in 2002, and *We Free Again* in 2004. Groundation continues to write, perform, and record. During their five-year career, the group has performed onstage with **Pato Banton**, the **Congos**, **Gregory Isaacs**, **Israel Vibration**, **Morgan Heritage**, and others.

HALF PINT (1962–)

Born Lindon Andrew Roberts in Kingston, Jamaica, Half Pint grew up in the
Rose Lane community, which also produced **Dennis Brown**, **Toots Hibbert**, **Lee "Scratch" Perry**, and others.
He got his start in music singing in the
school choir. After graduation, Pint
immediately moved into the popular
music scene. He made the rounds on
the **sound system** circuit and **toasted**
for **Black Scorpio**, Jammys, Gemini,
and Killimanjaro. On the systems he
honed his talents and soon was ready
to go into the studio. He went to work
with **King Jammy** and released singles
including "Money Man Skank" and
"One in a Million." Pint went on to
work with many of the major producers on the island, spending time in the
studio with **Bobby "Digital" Dixon**,
George Phang, King Jammy, **Sly and
Robbie**, and many others.

In the early 1980s, Pint began working in the studio in earnest. He released
"Sally" and "Winsome," and both of the
singles were fast hits. These were
quickly followed by "Substitute Lover,"
"Level the Vibes," and "Victory." Half
Pint broke through in 1985 with his
song "Greetings." This led to an album

Half Pint. © *UrbanImage.tv.*

of the same title produced by **George Phang**. By the mid-1980s, Pint had moved from
singles to albums, and he released *Victory* (1986). Pint's stock increased dramatically
when the Rolling Stones covered his song "Winsome" under the title "Too Rude."

In the late 1980s, Pint crossed over into film work and appeared in *Substitute 2* and
Mookie. In the 1990s, he released a host of albums: *Pick Your Choice* (1993), *Classics
in Dub* (1995), *Joint Favorites* (1997), and *Legal We Legal* (1998). In 1998, Pint
signed to the BMG Music company and remained at the top of the reggae spectrum. In
the new millennium, Pint has continued his success with the release of *Closer to You*
(2000).

HALL, LANCELOT (c. 1955–)

Hall was a member of the reconstituted **Inner Circle**, which was originally formed in Kingston, Jamaica, in 1979. The reconstituted Inner Circle have released twelve albums over the past twenty years and remain a force in **reggae** music. Through the course of these twelve releases, Hall has provided all of the drum and percussion parts. Further, he has worked as a producer for the band, most notably on the 1994 album *Bad Boys*, which contains their most well-known song, "Bad Boy," the theme for the popular television show *Cops*. The album won a Grammy for Best Reggae Album and went on to sell over seven million copies internationally. Inner Circle and Hall continue to record and perform to this time. Their most recent release was 2000's *Big Tings*.

HAMMOND, BERES (1955–)

Hugh Beresford Hammond was born in Annotto Bay, Jamaica, in 1955. Hammond has enjoyed an enormously successful thirty-year career as a **reggae** singer with a powerful, soulful voice. His career began in the early 1970s when he came out as a soul-style singer performing in area talent competitions. His early success led to the lead singer role in the 1970s group **Zap Pow**. In the late 1970s, Hammond went solo and began to release his own material. In 1976, he recorded his debut album *Soul Reggae* and has had a string of successful releases since. His second release was 1980's *Just a Man*, which was produced by **Joe Gibbs**. The following year he teamed with **Willie Lindo** for his third release, *Comin' at You*.

Throughout the 1980s, Hammond released reggae material with soul undertones. His relatively low productivity was a result of dedicating much of his energy to his newly formed studio, Harmony House, opened in 1985. His 1988 album *Have a Nice Weekend* encapsulated his style and melodic gift. The following decade saw a marked increase in Hammond's productivity; he released seven albums through the course of the 1990s. His music from the late 1980s and the 1990s exhibits an evolution of style from reggae to **dancehall**. In the late 1980s, Hammond spent time in New York, but by 1990 he was back in Jamaica. Hit singles from the decade include "Tempted by Touch" and "Who Say," with **Buju Banton**.

Beres Hammond. © *UrbanImage.tv.*

Although Hammond recorded extensively in the dancehall style in the 1990s, he was also able to pen **lovers rock** hits, as his 1996 album *Love from a Distance* attests. Further, in 1990 Hammond collaborated with **Maxi Priest** on the single "How Can We Ease the Pain." The 1990s proved to be his busiest decade, producing a multitude of albums including *In Control*, *Putting Up Resistance*, and *Getting Stronger*. Hammond continued to record into the new millennium, releasing two albums, both compilations, in 2000, and two more in 2001, one compilation and one album of new material. His 2001 album *Music Is Life* presented a range of styles from straight-ahead reggae to dancehall material. Hammond was joined on the album by guitarist **Earl "Chinna" Smith** on "Honey, Wine and a Love Song"; **Flourgon** on "I Love Jah"; and Wyclef Jean on "Dance 4 Me." Hammond continues to write, record, and enjoy his well-deserved status as a reggae legend.

HARARE DREAD (c. 1960–)

Harare Dread was born Pax Nindi in Zimbabwe, Africa. In the 1970s he moved to Malawi, returning to his homeland seven years later. Dread pursued a recording contract but, due to controversial and anti-government lyrics, was passed over. In 1985, he again relocated, this time to England. Skilled on the bass guitar, bongos, lead guitar, mbira, and keyboards, and also as a vocalist, Dread gained critical acclaim in the United Kingdom and soon found that his skills as a multi-instrumentalist and roots reggae vocalist were in demand. An added feature of Dread's performance is his use of the Shona, Chewa, and English languages. As a result, Dread began recording and subsequently released four albums, titled *Afritek*, *Afrikan Dubmaster*, *Dzidzo* (1996), and *Pax Nindi* (2004). He has also been in demand on the reggae circuit, having performed at festivals such as Reggae on the River. Dread's blend of roots reggae and African consciousness has made him an emerging international talent and the recognized leader of the African **reggae** movement.

HARDER THEY COME, THE

The Harder They Come was a film released in 1973 that has become an international cult classic. The film's director, Perry Herzell, enlisted **reggae** artist **Jimmy Cliff** for the lead role of Ivan Martin. The film's main character, Martin, comes from the country to settle in Kingston and runs afoul of the law. He gains fame as an outlaw and Robin Hood figure who represents the oppressed Jamaican underclass. Not only was the film successful, but the soundtrack for the movie went on to gain significant fame and is currently available in a deluxe, remastered version.

The album contains hit songs by many of reggae's most popular artists, including Cliff. The songs on the soundtrack are "007 (Shanty Town)" by **Desmond Dekker**, "You Can Get It If You Really Want" by Cliff, "Draw Your Breaks" by Scotty (David Scott), "Sweet and Dandy" by the **Maytals**, "Rivers of Babylon" by the **Melodians**, "Many Rivers to Cross" by Cliff, "The Harder They Come" by Cliff, "Johnny Your Too Bad" by the Slickers, "Pressure Drop" by the Maytals, and "Sitting in Limbo" by Cliff. The release and subsequent success of the movie and album helped to bring reggae music to the American audience. Further, due to its countercultural themes, the movie caught the spirit of the time.

HARRIOTT, DERRICK (1942–)

Derrick Harriott was born in Kingston, Jamaica, in 1942. Harriott was active in the **reggae** music scene from the 1950s into the 1990s. He got his start at age sixteen as a member of the singing group the Jiving Juniors. He stayed with the group for four years, after which he moved on to a solo career. As a solo singer whose style ranged from **ska** to **rock steady** to reggae, Harriott distinguished himself as a successful, influential, and significant force on the island. As a solo artist he made reggae versions of several Motown-label American rhythm and blues hits, wrote original material, and achieved fame as a producer. His most famous single was the original song "The Loser." As a recording artist, he recorded for the **Trojan** and Jamaican Gold labels. For these two labels he released over ten albums from 1970 to 1996. His earliest release was *The*

Derrick Harriott. © *UrbanImage.tv.*

Undertaker (1970), with *Acid Rock* (1982) and *Step Softly* (1988) along the way, culminating in *Derrick Harriott and the Giants* (1996). He was also among the first artists to use **King Tubby's** new studio.

In the late 1990s, Harriott moved over to the Pressure Sounds label and has subsequently released two albums for them. As a producer, Harriott worked with artists such as the **Ethiopians**, Keith, and Tex. A measure of Harriott's success is his Scotty (David Scott) version of "Draw Your Brakes" on the soundtrack for the movie *The Harder They Come.*

HARRY J. *See* JOHNSON, HARRY "HARRY J"

HARRY J'S STUDIO

This is the name of the studio where Harry Johnson repeatedly made Jamaican popular music history. **Harry "Harry J" Johnson** made many of the seminal **reggae** recordings in this space and recorded countless reggae luminaries there. The studio enjoyed an extended run as one of the best in Jamaica; however, it fell into disuse during the 1990s. In the wake of his Grammy Award-winning album *Calling Rastafari*, Winston **"Burning Spear"** Rodney reopened Harry J's studio for what may be Spear's final album. For Spear, the use of the studio was a homecoming, as he recorded his album *Dry and Heavy* for Harry J there. He also cut the singles "Swell Headed" and "Creation Rebel" at the studio. Burning Spear finished his *Free Man* album at Harry J's, and it was released in 2003. The future of Harry J's studio remains unknown.

HARTLEY, TREVOR (c. 1960–)

Trevor Hartley was born in Morant Bay, Jamaica. Hartley was interested in singing as a young man and was spurred on by the island music that he heard on local radio. Working with legendary producer **Joe Gibbs**, he recorded a pair of singles for the Pele label; but this early entry into the music business was cut short when he moved to the United Kingdom. In London, he teamed with **Dennis Bovell** and in 1978 released the single "Selassie I" with "Skip Way" on the B-side. Both of these songs sold well and brought the young singer success.

Hartley then moved onto the Burning Sounds imprint and producer **Phil Pratt**. The result was his 1979 debut *Innocent Lover.* Unfortunately, the Burning Sounds label soon closed, which resulted in little distribution of the album. In the 1980s, Hartley worked with **Sugar Minott** through his Youth Promotions and Black Roots label. Next he moved to the **Arawak** label where he recorded the singles "Hanging Around" and "Closer Together," a **reggae** version of the Curtis Mayfield hit. After Arawak, Hartley moved to the Top Ranking label, but again he did not last long on the imprint, and this further hampered the advancement of his career. Next, Hartley got picked up by the Massive label, where he worked with Erskine Thompson. With Thompson's help, Hartley worked with the legendary UK reggae producers **Angus "Drummie Zeb" Gaye** and Tony Gad of **Aswad** fame. Also as a result of his association with Thompson, Hartley was invited to sing on the "Let's Make Africa Green Again" recording, which brought him international fame. Hartley parlayed his newfound fame into a brief recording project with the London Records imprint. During this period he had a series of successful singles and he stayed with London longer than he had with any previous label.

After his association with London, Hartley again changed labels and landed on Peter's Street Vibes. There he recorded with **Peter Hunnigale** and **Tippa Irie**. On Peter's, he released a series of successful singles, several of which were picked up for inclusion on compilation recordings. He also released his second album, *Hartical*, which has received modest success. Hartley continues to tour and make music. Sadly, he also continues his quest for a home label, having recorded with Rock and Groove and Fu Manchu in the late 1990s. His success continues in the United Kingdom, and he still hopes to break the international market.

HARVEY, BERNARD "TOUTER" (1956–)

Born in Jamaica in 1956, Harvey began to study the keyboard as a youth and soon was in demand as a **reggae** keyboardist, both in the studio and for live sessions. Over his thirty-plus-year career he has played with a wide variety of reggae luminaries. Harvey experienced extreme fame at an early age when he was invited to join **Bob Marley's Wailers** band in 1974. Harvey was only seventeen years old when Marley enlisted his keyboard talents for the recording of the *Natty Dread* album. On this release, Harvey supplied the keyboard parts for the legendary song "No Woman, No Cry." Harvey went on to tour with Marley, and he also appears on the 1975 release *Live!*

After leaving the Wailers, Harvey went on to work with **Burning Spear**, appearing on most of Spear's releases from the mid-1970s to the present. While working with Spear, Harvey was also able to do session work, playing piano, organ, and other keyboard instruments for **Althea and Donna**, **Johnny Clarke**, **Sly Dunbar**, Martha Velez, **Justin Hinds**, Rico, Ranking Trevor, **Jacob Miller**, **Bunny Wailer**, and many others. Harvey's productivity continued with Burning Spear, but in 1986 he also joined the reconstituted **Inner Circle** band. With Inner Circle, Harvey worked on a series of successful albums and also appeared on their greatest hits compilations. In the new millennium, Harvey has continued to work for many recording artists in addition to Burning Spear and Inner Circle. Most recently, he has supplied the keyboard parts for artists such as Rick Wakeman, **Cornell Campbell**, **Sugar Minott**, and **Prince Far I**. Harvey continues to be a heavily in-demand keyboard player on the reggae scene.

HEARTBEAT RECORDS

Founded in 1981 by Duncan Browne and Bill Nowlin in Cambridge, Massachusetts, the label is the largest nationally distributed imprint for its parent company, Rounder Records. In the past twenty-three years, Heartbeat has built a strong reputation for releasing **ska**, **rock steady**, **reggae**, **dancehall**, and **dub** material of the highest quality.

The label got started with releases by **Big Youth**, **Linton Kwesi Johnson**, and **Mikey Dread**, and from its modest beginnings has grown to international prominence. Its roster of talent currently includes over fifty artists, and its list of titles numbers over 250 releases. Heartbeat simultaneously releases both vintage and contemporary material, forming unique alliances with several of the original Jamaican labels in order to release new compilations and remastered versions of artists such as **Bob Marley and the Wailers**. The label has also re-released a large quantity of material from producers such as **Clancy Eccles**, **Joe Gibbs**, and **Lee "Scratch" Perry**. The label also releases new material from veteran performers, including **Culture**, **Gregory Isaacs**, and **Michael Rose**.

On the contemporary side, Heartbeat works with many of the most popular Jamaican dancehall artists, such as **Buju Banton**, Sean Paul, **Beenie Man**, and **Sizzla**. Additionally, Heartbeat fosters up-and-coming artists such as **Everton Blender** and **Spanner Banner**. In addition to its single artist releases, in 1989 the label launched the Original Reggae Masters series, a group of compilations that now spans ten volumes.

HENZELL, PERRY (c. 1950–)

Perry Henzell is most known in the **reggae** music community as the director of the 1972 cult classic film *The Harder They Come*. Henzell cast a young **Jimmy Cliff** in the lead role of Ivan. Since its release, the film has garnered critical acclaim and has continued to enjoy a considerable amount of attention. The soundtrack for the film is filled with what have become reggae standards; it features material by Cliff, **Desmond Dekker**, the **Maytals**, the **Melodians**, and others. Henzell continues to live in Jamaica, making his home in Runaway Bay on the north coast, working on the south coast at the family-owned business, Jake's Place, in Treasure Beach. At Jake's Place, Henzell continues to pursue literary and film projects and hosts an annual literary festival.

HEPTONES, THE

Formed in Kingston, Jamaica, in 1965, the vocal trio of the Heptones consisted of **Leroy Sibbles**, Barry Llewellyn, and Earl Morgan. The group originally formed in the early 1960s under the name the Hep Ones, but their audience changed the name. All three men hailed from Kingston, Jamaica, and were born in the mid-1940s. The group

The Heptones. © *UrbanImage.tv.*

got its start singing at the end of the **ska** era and the start of the **rock steady** style. They recorded a series of popular sides for **Clement "Coxsone" Dodd** at his **Studio One** in the latter half of the 1960s. Their first hit came in 1966 with the release of the single "Fatty Fatty." Additionally, the Heptones were instrumental in the change of style from ska to rock steady.

Still with Dodd in the early 1970s, the trio released another hit single with "Pretty Looks Isn't All." For Dodd, the group released their debut album, 1970's *On Top*. Sibbles and Dodd began to have difficulty in their working relationship, which resulted in the typical Jamaican recording artist activity of moving from one studio to another. The group moved on to work with producer **Joe Gibbs** and then moved again to work with **Rupie Edwards**. In the mid-1970s, they settled with **Lee "Scratch" Perry** and continued their success. With Perry at the controls, the group was able to update its sound while maintaining its original roots appeal.

In 1977, they released the album *Party Time*, which garnered them international notoriety. However, in 1978, Sibbles went solo and the group replaced him with singer Naggo Morris. Without Sibbles's singing and songwriting skills, the group has not regained its original sound and popularity. They did continue to produce material, though, and in 1979 released a new album called *Good Life*. This album and most of their material from the 1980s pales in comparison to their earlier work. However, in 1995, the original trio re-formed and released a new album, *Pressure*, produced by **Tappa Zukie**. The Heptones have cultivated a deep catalog of hits in their illustrious career, and their music continues to appear on numerous compilation albums. Of note is the 1997 compilation of Heptones tunes, *Sea of Love*, released on Rounders Records, and the most recent Rounders compilation, 2004's *Deep in the Roots*.

HERMAN, BONGO (c. 1950–)

Born Herman Davis, Bongo Herman began his recording career in 1969. He came onto the Jamaican popular music scene as a talented percussionist and has remained a fixture in the studio for the past thirty-five years. During his illustrious career, Herman has played with virtually all of the important recording artists on the island. Beginning in the early 1970s, Herman played with the **Abyssinians**, **Jimmy Cliff**, **Don Carlos**, the **Heptones**, Pablo Moses, and **Prince Far I**, and he worked with the **Revolutionaries**.

In the late 1970s, Herman played percussion for the **Congos**, **Culture**, the **Gladiators**, and Ranking Joe. Throughout the 1980s, he worked with a series of other recording artists, including the Abyssinians, **Doctor Alimantado**, and **Mikey Dread**. Additionally, Herman served as the longtime percussionist for the **Itals**, appearing on their *Give Me Power*, *Brutal out Deh*, and *Easy to Catch* releases. The list of artists whom Herman recorded for is significant and runs the gamut of **reggae** and **rock steady** artists.

In the 1990s, he made the transition to the **dancehall** style and worked with **Beenie Man**, **Lady Saw**, **Sizzla**, and **U-Roy**. Herman continues to be active, having recently recorded with **dub poet Mutabaruka** and continuing his relationship with the Itals. Since the beginning of the new millennium, Herman has appeared on a variety of recordings, including a series of releases entitled *Reggae for Kids*, as well as on releases for Barry Briggs, the African Brothers, and the Abyssinians.

HIBBERT, FREDERICK "TOOTS" (c. 1946–)

Frederick Nathaniel "Toots" Hibbert was born in Clarendon, Jamaica, on December 10, 1946. He got his start in music by singing in church but was also exposed to American

Toots Hibbert. © *UrbanImage.tv.*

rhythm and blues at an early age, hearing the sounds of Otis Redding, the Temptations, and Ray Charles over a transistor radio. Hibbert combined his two earliest exposures to music and created a Jamaican gospel and soul hybrid that made him famous first around the island and then around the world. In pursuit of his singing goals, Hibbert moved to Kingston and took a job to support himself while pitching his singing skills to anyone who would listen.

In 1962, he formed a vocal trio with his friends Raleigh Gordon and Jerry Mathias; the vocal trio called themselves the Maytals. In 1963, as the Jamaican popular music style moved from imported American songs to indigenous **ska**, the Maytals went to **Studio One** to try to impress **Clement "Coxsone" Dodd** and get recorded. Dodd liked what he heard, and the group was offered recording time. Out of these sessions came **Toots and the Maytals'** first album, which included hits such as "Six and Seven Books" and "Hallelujah."

Although the trio had a record and achieved success, they were not financially rewarded by Dodd, which caused them to leave the Studio One imprint. The Maytals went to record with **Cecil "Prince Buster" Campbell** and cut several successful singles in 1964. During the same year, they moved again and worked with producer **Bunny "Striker" Lee** and his fledgling BMN label. With Lee they recorded their second album and perfected their brand of **ska** vocal harmony. In 1966, during the shift in Jamaican popular music away from ska toward **rock steady**, Hibbert was incarcerated for six months for possession of marijuana. Upon his release, Hibbert immediately immersed himself in the new style with the hit "54-46, That's My Number" (his inmate number).

In 1968, the style again began to change and Hibbert was a forerunner in the move from rock steady to **reggae**. He is credited with one of the earliest reggae style releases, the single "Do the Reggae." By this time the Maytals were on **Leslie Kong's Beverley's** record label; with Beverley's they released their third album, *Sweet and Dandy*. In addition to being at the leading edge of the evolving Jamaican popular music style, Hibbert was also among the first singers to mention Ethiopia's King Haile Selassie by name on a recording.

Throughout the 1970s, despite the sudden death of Kong from a heart attack in 1971, Toots and the Maytals continued their dominance of the reggae market. Their popularity began to catch on with the UK audience, and an international reputation built up. This international fervor was further extended when the Maytals launched a successful international tour in the mid-1970s. Toots and the Maytals continued their success into the 1980s. The group released *Knock Out* on the **Island** label and then spent much of the decade touring relentlessly. In 1986, Toots revisited his American popular music roots with *Toots in Memphis*, a collection of soul and rhythm and blues standards.

Toots was again on the road in the early 1990s. However, he did stop touring long enough to open his own studio in the late 1990s. His first release on the Alla Sons label is titled *Recoup*, for all of the money he has lost to other label heads over the years. Hibbert remains a massive presence on the international reggae scene. He continues to write, record, and tour. In 2004, Hibbert released his twenty-sixth album, *True Love*. The release, a collection of Hibbert's classic hits, finds the legendary singer in a duet with another popular talent for each song. Examples of these pairings include Hibbert and Bonnie Raitt on "True Love Is Hard to Find"; Hibbert and Eric Clapton on "Pressure Drop"; and Hibbert, **Ken Boothe**, and **Marcia Griffiths** on "Reggae Got Soul."

HIBBERT, LEEBA (c. 1970–)

Leeba Hibbert is the daughter of **Frederick "Toots" Hibbert**. Through her musical upbringing, Hibbert grew into an accomplished vocalist; her background vocal credits have increased rapidly over the last ten years. She began recording as a background singer with Kotch in 1993. This was followed by an appearance on **Luciano's** 1995 album *Where There Is Life*. During the latter half of the 1990s, Hibbert appeared on recordings by **Cocoa Tea**, **Dean Fraser**, **Beres Hammond**, **Ernest Ranglin**, Claudelle Clarke, and Joanna Marie.

In 2000, she continued her steady recording appearances with Queen Yemisi for both the *I Have Feelings Too* and *Lovefire* releases. Since then, Hibbert has continued to record with many of **reggae** music's stars. She has appeared on another recording with Luciano and broadened her output, working with **Anthony B**, Stevie Face, Chrisinti, Fat Eyes, **Sanchez**, and Junior Kelly. In 2004, she provided background vocals on the Bob Dylan tribute album *Is It Rolling Bob? A Reggae Tribute to Bob Dylan*, and she remains active in the studio.

HIBBERT, OSCAR. *See* DELGADO, JUNIOR

HIBBERT, OSWALD "OSSIE" (c. 1950–)

Ossie Hibbert has had a presence on the Jamaican popular music scene since the mid-1970s. His contributions range from keyboard player to producer to owner of his own production company. Additionally, Hibbert spent many years as a foundation of the studio band known as the Professionals, a continually evolving collection of musicians employed by the legendary producer **Joe Gibbs**. For Gibbs and his engineer **Errol Thompson,** who were together known as the Mighty Two, Hibbert recorded with many of the most significant Jamaican recording artists in the 1970s and 1980s. Musicians who were part of the Professionals include **Gladdy Anderson**, **Sly Dunbar**, **Bobby Ellis**, **George Fullwood**, **Vin Gordon**, **Tommy McCook**, **Lloyd Parks**, **Robbie Shakespeare**, **Earl "Chinna" Smith**, and Ruddy Thomas. During his recording career, Hibbert supplied keyboard for artists such as **Johnny Clark**, **Dillinger**, **Justin Hinds**, **Ijahman**, the **Mighty Diamonds**, and **Derrick Morgan**.

Further, with the experience Hibbert gained in the studio, he began working as a producer and engineer in the early 1980s. He opened Ossie Hibbert Productions and worked with artists such as **Carlene Davis**, **Gregory Isaacs**, and **Pat Kelly**, producing many compilation albums. In the new millennium, Hibbert's legacy has continued with production credits for **Chaka Demus and Pliers**, **Gregory Isaacs**, Errol Dunkley, Lloyd Brown and **Peter Hunnigale**, the **Wailing Souls**, and many others. Hibbert continues to be active in **reggae** music and makes his presence known as a producer of the highest quality.

HIGGS, JOE (1940–1999)

Joe Higgs first appeared on the Jamaican popular music scene in the late 1950s. He had several successful singles as half of the singing duo Higgs and Wilson (Roy Wilson), with their most significant release being 1960's "Oh Manny Oh." Regardless of his early success, he went solo and worked with Edward Seaga, who became the prime minister of Jamaica in the 1980s. With Seaga, Gibbs recorded his first single and gained exposure through live performances. He parlayed his success into studio time with **Clement "Coxsone" Dodd**; in 1964, on Dodd's **Studio One** imprint, he released his hit single "There's a Reward for Me."

Higgs went on to become one of the true legends in Jamaican popular music. He helped drive the changes in style from **ska** to **rock steady** and then to **reggae**. Further, he was highly influential in the generation of reggae performers who emerged in the late 1960s and early 1970s, such as **Derrick Harriott**, **Bob Marley**, **Peter Tosh**, and **Bunny Wailer**. These aspiring artists spent time with Higgs and from him learned the craft of song composition, vocal technique, and aspects of the music business. It was Higgs who honed the **Wailers'** raw vocal harmonies into the product that would attract attention from Dodd. All the while, Higgs continued to write and record music himself.

After the split with Wilson, Higgs worked with the **Soul Brothers** and **Lynn Taitt**. Higgs maintained his involvement with the young Wailers singing trio and provided vocals for the trio when Bunny quit the group just prior to a North American tour. Another rising star Higgs worked with in Kingston was **Jimmy Cliff**. Higgs coached Cliff just as the young singer was rocketing to popularity in the wake of the movie and

Joe Higgs. © *UrbanImage.tv.*

soundtrack for *The Harder They Come.* Higgs also performed with Cliff in live shows, which brought him exposure to a much wider audience.

In 1975, Higgs finally released his debut solo album, *Life of Contradiction.* The record was successful and further cemented his position in the upper echelon of Jamaican popular music. In the late 1970s, Higgs released the controversial single "So It Go," which was not well received by the Jamaican government, as the song scolded it for not addressing the hardships of the Jamaican underclass. The backlash from the project led to Higgs's relocation to Los Angeles to avoid harassment on the island.

Higgs spent the 1980s and 1990s continuing his efforts to mentor upcoming reggae talents, touring, and forwarding the reggae sound. He began to work with author Roger Steffens on an official biography, but Joe Higgs died on December 18, 1999, during the project.

HILL, JOSEPH (c. 1955–)

Joseph Hill is the lead singer of the longstanding roots reggae band **Culture**. Hill is the singer and songwriter for the group and is responsible for the spiritual elements that stay central in their music. The group formed in 1976, and their debut album, *Two Sevens Clash*, which was released the following year, was an instant classic. In addition to Hill, the group includes Albert Walker and Roy "Kenneth" Dayes, both of whom are Hill's cousins. In the early 1970s, Hill was involved in several bands around his hometown of Linstead, Jamaica, the most notable being the Soul Defenders. However, these early bands did not garner any success.

With Culture, Hill formed a vocal trio that had unlimited potential. Originally calling themselves African Disciples, the group worked initially with producer **Joe Gibbs** in Kingston. Under Gibbs's tutelage and with the assistance of **Errol Thompson** (known as the Mighty Two), the group changed its name to Culture and released the single "This Time." The song came out on Gibbs's Belmont label and led to a string of breakthrough singles. These early hits included "When Two Sevens Clash" and "See Them a Come." In 1977, the group released its debut album, which featured the songs "Natty Dread Take Over" and "Get Ready to Ride the Lion to Zion." Because the album was rife with **Rastafarian** images, it served as a spiritual guide for its listeners and enjoyed enormous popularity in both Jamaica and the United Kingdom. Unfortunately, through Gibbs, the album's success was not financially transferred to the band, so after the album Culture severed ties with him.

They moved on to work with **Duke Reid**, but this too was an unhappy alliance. The product of the brief Reid dealings was the album *Africa Stand Alone*, released in 1978. Gibbs still had control over the earliest Culture material and went on to release two more albums of work that had not been included on the *Two Sevens Clash* release. These two releases were made available as *Baldhead Bridge* and *More Culture*. Culture's next producer was **Sonia Pottinger** and her High Note imprint. For Pottinger, the group recorded a series of three albums released in quick succession in 1978 and 1979; the first was *Harder Than the Rest*, the second was *Cumbolo*, and the third was *International Herb*.

The next major step for the band was the 1978 performance at the **One Love Peace Concert** to kick off a major UK tour. On tour, the singing trio was backed by the **Revolutionaries**, who included **Sly and Robbie**. In 1982, the trio split, and it seemed that Culture was a thing of the past. Hill went on to record *Lion Rock*, which was a solo album but was released under the Culture name. Fortunately, the trio reunited in 1986 and went back into the studio to produce *Culture at Work* and *Culture in Culture*, both in 1986. There followed subsequent albums throughout the late 1980s and throughout the 1990s. Overall, the group has released at least thirty albums of substantial roots reggae material. Some notable recent work includes the 2000 release of the album *Payday* and the 2002 release of *Live in Africa*. Joseph Hill and Culture continue to be active, and Hill's steadfast Rastafarian sentiment of elevating the oppressed over the oppressor remains strong.

HILTON, RIPTON. *See* EEK-A-MOUSE

HIMELFARB, GARY "DOCTOR DREAD" (c. 1950–)

Gary "Doctor Dread" Himelfarb founded **RAS Records** in 1979. RAS stands for "Real Authentic Sound," and Himelfarb has spent the last twenty-five years recording authentic Jamaican popular music on his label. Himelfarb got started in the music business through his associations with several Jamaican artists. He set out to bring Jamaican culture and music and the message of **Rastafari** to the world. He began the label in his own home, but it was soon moved to formal offices in Washington DC as it grew. The RAS Records list grew throughout the 1980s and soon was home to acts such as **Black Uhuru**, **Don Carlos**, **Inner Circle**, **Freddie McGregor**, and **Junior Reid**.

Through Himelfarb's work, the link between Jamaican roots reggae artists and the American market has grown significantly. In pursuit of his goals, Himelfarb has established links to countries as far-reaching as South Africa, parts of South America, Holland, and Japan. The current artist roster for RAS includes almost one hundred of the finest acts in Jamaican popular music. The label's roster now lists **Dennis Brown**, **Culture**, **Gregory Isaacs**, **Israel Vibration**, **Barrington Levy**, **Luciano**, **Augustus Pablo**, Junior Reid, **Sizzla**, **Sly and Robbie**, **Yami Bolo**, and many others. Additionally, Himelfarb is credited as the producer and author of the liner notes for the material released on the label. In addition to these significant releases, Himelfarb has also launched a series of releases made specifically for kids, called *Reggae for Kids*. Another aspect of the label is the release of compilation albums. The RAS catalog currently includes thirty-eight compilation recordings that feature a series of reggae stars.

Furthermore, in 2004, RAS released a compilation of songs by American artist Bob Dylan with all songs redone in reggae versions. The album, titled *Is It Rolling Bob: A Reggae Tribute to Bob Dylan*, includes Apple Gabriel of Israel Vibration, **Angus "Drummie Zeb" Gaye**, **Beres Hammond**, **Toots Hibbert**, **J. C. Lodge**, the **Mighty Diamonds**, Billy Mystic of the Mystic Revealers, Luciano, Michael Rose of Black Uhuru, Sizzla, and Gregory Isaacs. In the past two years, RAS has enjoyed a period of high productivity with new releases by **Horace Andy**, Dennis Brown, **Eek-A-Mouse**, **Mad Professor**, **Steel Pulse**, Nasio, Gregory Isaacs, Sizzla, Israel Vibration, Turbulence, and Sly and Robbie.

HINDS, HORACE. *See* ANDY, HORACE

HINDS, JUSTIN (1942–2005)

Hinds was born in Steertown, Ocho Rios, Jamaica, in 1942. Like most of the Jamaican youth of the time, his musical taste favored American rhythm and blues greats such as Louis Jordan's jump band style and the New Orleans style of Fats Domino. Hinds got his start in the music business as a singer in the Ocho Rios tourist industry. However, in the late 1950s, he dedicated himself to a career as a recording artist; his music reflected an ever-increasing interest in **Rastafari**. In 1963, Hinds and his singing partners Junior Dixon and Dennis Sinclair (known as the Dominos) went into **Duke Reid's Treasure Isle** studio and cut a series of hits including the seminal "Carry Go Bring Come."

Hinds and the Dominos stayed with Reid until 1966, producing a series of successful singles. In 1966, Hinds followed the evolving style in Jamaican popular music, shifting from **ska** to **rock steady**. His transition was seamless, and he continued to release hits. Hinds and Reid stayed together until 1972 and during their partnership released hit singles such as "Here I Stand," "Save a Bread," "No Good Rudie," "Nebuchadnezzar," and "Mighty Redeemer." Reid had nurtured Hinds as the young singer grew; consequently, Hinds was at a loss when Reid died in 1974. In 1976, Hinds began working with producer Jack Ruby, and together they produced a series of hits. These works were compiled on the 1976 album *Jezebel*.

As the decade wore on, Hinds's productivity continued to decrease. His next work did not appear until the mid-1980s with the album *Travel with Love*, recorded at **Tuff Gong** records in Kingston. In the late 1980s, Hinds formed his own band that included his son on drums. The band was dubbed the Revivers and included **reggae** luminaries such as **Headley Bennett** and **Vin Gordon**. The group mounted a U.S. and European tour in the early 1990s, and in 1992 released the album *Know Jah Better.* Hinds continued to write, record, and tour through the 1990s. During this time, he also joined a reggae

Justin Hinds. © *UrbanImage.tv.*

supergroup called the Coyabalites, which includes an all-star cast of long-time reggae hit-makers. In the new millennium, Hinds has overseen the release of two live albums, *Let's Rock Live* and *Live at the Grassroots*, both in 2002. Of note is the backing band on the Grassroots album, which is one of America's finest reggae bands, John Brown's Body.

Justin Hinds died of lung cancer in March 2005, ending his forty-year singing career.

HINDS, NEVILLE (c. 1950–)

Neville "Iron" Hinds has been active on the Jamaican popular music scene since the early 1970s. His credits include work as a keyboard player, arranger, and producer. His earliest appearances were as a session organist for artists such as **Hopeton Lewis**, Garland Jeffreys, and **Toots and the Maytals**. In 1972, he was recruited by American Paul Simon (of Simon and Garfunkel fame) to play organ on one of the earliest non-Jamaican reggae songs. The song, "Mother and Child Reunion," appeared on Simon's self-titled 1972 release.

By the 1980s, Hinds had moved into the role of producer and worked with artists such as Eric Donaldson, Brand New Second Hand, Cynthia Schloss, Arrow, and others. He also continued to supply organ parts for recordings by **reggae** luminaries such as the **Clarendonians**, **I-Roy**, the **Jamaicans**, and **Sly and Robbie**. More recently, Hinds has continued to produce, arrange, and play the organ on numerous recordings. Since the beginning of the new millennium, Hinds has appeared with **Byron Lee and the Dragonaires**, **Carlene Davis**, and on many compilations. In 2004, Hinds lent his keyboard expertise to the tribute album *Tribute to Reggae's Keyboard King Jackie Mittoo.* He continues to be active on the Jamaican popular music scene.

HOLNESS, WINSTON "NINEY THE OBSERVER" (1951–)

Producer Winston "Niney the Observer" Holness was instrumental in the construction of the classic roots **reggae** sound in the early 1970s. Holness was born in Montego Bay,

Winston "Niney the Observer" Holness.
© *UrbanImage.tv.*

Jamaica, in 1951. He gained entry into the music business in the late 1960s working with producers **Bunny "Striker" Lee** and **Lee "Scratch" Perry**. Called "Niney" due to the loss of a thumb at an early age, Holness's first hit came in 1970 with **Dennis Alcapone's** single "Mr. Brown." With an ever-growing reputation as a solid roots producer, Holness embarked on an independent career, forming the Observer label. His success continued through the 1970s and into the 1980s. During this period, he produced hits for reggae standouts such as **Dennis Brown**, **Gregory Isaacs**, and **Freddie McGregor**. In the early 1970s, Holness teamed with Dennis Brown to record a series of seminal reggae tracks. He seamlessly made the transition to **dancehall** and produced hits for acts such as **Beenie Man**, **Big Youth**, and **I-Roy**.

Inexplicably, Holness disappeared from the music scene in the late 1970s. He re-emerged in 1982 and briefly worked at **Channel One Studios** reunited with Scratch Perry. However, by the end of the 1980s, he was again on his own, producing material for the next generation of rising stars. In addition, Holness intermittently released compilations of material, an example of which was his 1992 release *Freaks*. Here Holness displays his skills on songs from artists such as Michael Rose, Gregory Isaacs, Dennis Brown, and several others. During the 1970s and early 1980s, Holness and his Observer label had virtually every important reggae act in the studio. In the new millennium, Holness continues his production work, appearing on multitudes of compilations and with artists such as **Anthony B**, **Dillinger**, the **Heptones**, and **Rita Marley**.

HOLT, ERROL "FLABBA" (c. 1959–)

Errol "Flabba" Holt was born in Kingston, Jamaica, in the late 1950s. He made his entry into the Jamaican popular music scene in the early 1970s when he provided the bass lines for singles by **Don Carlos**, Ja Man, **Winston "Niney the Observer" Holness**, and **Prince Far I**. Early on, Holt also had several hits of his own with the singles "A You Lick Me First," "Gimme Gimme," and "Who Have Eyes to See." He went on to provide session bass work for a wide variety of musicians throughout the 1970s and 1980s. Holt appears on recordings by **Junior Delgado**, **Clint Eastwood**, **Gregory Isaacs**, the **Itals**, **Barrington Levy**, **Augustus Pablo**, Ranking Joe, Peter Broggs, and many others.

In 1976, he was recruited into the **Morwells** and stayed with the band until the early 1980s. He then went on to form the **Roots Radics** with **Eric "Bingy Bunny" Lamont**, and together they had a series of hits with producer **Henry "Junjo" Lawes**.

Even as part of the Morwells or the Roots Radics, Holt continued to perform session bass lines for a wide range of other artists. This session work continued into the 1990s when he appeared on recordings by significant artists such as **Israel Vibration**, **Mikey Dread**, **Sugar Minott**, **Mutabaruka**, **Bunny Wailer**, and **Yami Bolo**.

Also in the 1990s, Holt turned to producing records in addition to supplying the bass lines for them. In this capacity, he offered his production talents to artists such as **Dennis Brown**, Gregory Isaacs, and Israel Vibration. In 2004, Holt remained active with appearances for **Cocoa Tea**, the **Maytones**, **Ninjaman**, and others.

HOLT, JOHN (1947–)

Born in Kingston, Jamaica, in 1947, Holt grew up in Greenwich Fall and entered the music business at a very early age. At twelve, he entered a talent contest, the Vere Johns Opportunity Hour, at the urging of his friends. The show did not go well, but his friends continued to urge him to pursue a career in music. His second appearance was more successful and launched his career in the music industry. He continued to sing in public and in 1962 was noticed by **Leslie Kong** from the **Beverley's** label. Kong took Holt into the studio and cut the single "Together I'll Stay." As was the fashion, Holt also began working with other producers and recorded at a wide variety of studios. Holt experienced a degree of success as a solo artist, but in 1964 he joined the **Paragons** and his career advanced quickly. The other members of the vocal group were **Bob Andy**, Howard Barrett, and **Tyrone Evans**. Together the four made a single recording for **Clement "Coxsone" Dodd** before Andy decided to go his separate way, causing the group's dissolution.

At the end of the 1960s, Holt cultivated a solo career that involved touring the United Kingdom. In 1970, he released his debut album, *Love I Can Feel*, and his success skyrocketed. After playing a show at Wembley Stadium, he remained in England and released a series of hit records: *Still in Chains* in 1973, *Holt* in the same year, *Time Is the Master* and *The Further You Look* in 1974, and *1000 Volts of Holt* in 1974. He continued to fill the second half of the 1970s and all of the 1980s with hits. He released at least one album per year, including several live recordings and a Christmas album. More recently, Holt has released several albums in the past five years. In 2001, he released *John Holt*, *Kiss and Say Goodbye*, and *John Holt in Symphony*. Holt continues to be among the most popular and in-demand singers from Jamaica. In 2004, he was presented with Jamaica's most prestigious award, the governmental Order of Distinction.

John Holt. © *UrbanImage.tv.*

HOME T. *See* **BENNETT, MICHAEL "HOME T"**

HOOKIM, JOSEPH "JOE JOE" (c. 1955–)
Joseph "Joe Joe" Hookim and his brother Ernest opened **Channel One Studios** in 1970–1971. Hookim was born in Jamaica to Chinese parents. His family ran several small businesses, and he and his three brothers got started in business themselves. They began their entrepreneurial enterprises running slot machines in the gambling industry. When the government outlawed gambling, Hookim and his brother Ernest launched the Channel One label. The studio went into use in 1972 and the Hookims hired producer Syd Bucknor to run the equipment. They opened the studio in the middle of the Kingston ghetto on Maxfield Avenue. The brothers were able to establish a stronger reputation with the use of their studio band, the **Revolutionaries**. At times this band contained **Ansel Collins**, **Sly and Robbie**, and several other veteran players.

The house band and the ever-growing artist roster made the Hookims' label especially popular in the second half of the 1970s. Controversy erupted when Joe Joe was criticized for using rhythms made popular by other studios, such as **Studio One**; however, he always readily admitted copying **Coxsone Dodd's** rhythms. For the next fifteen years, Channel One Studios overflowed with talented musicians and producers. By the end of the 1970s, the recording equipment had been upgraded to a sixteen-track recorder, which only increased the quality and possibilities.

By the late 1970s, the artist roster at Hookim's Channel One imprint had included **Horace Andy**, **Junior Byles**, the **Mighty Diamonds**, and many others. Unfortunately, in 1977, Hookim's brother, Paul, was shot and killed during a robbery, which resulted in Joe Joe leaving the island to escape the violence. The brothers then branched out and opened a satellite studio in New York in the early 1980s. In the New York studio, they recorded a number of clash albums with a different artist on either side of the disk. Without cause, the late 1980s were a dark period for the label, and both the New York and Kingston studios shut down. However, the sheer number of recordings produced by Hookim is staggering: over two hundred releases in a span of less than twenty years.

HOPE, ALLAN. *See* **MUTABARUKA**

HOWELL, LEONARD P. "GUNGURU" (c. 1900–1981)
Leonard Percival Howell is revered as the first Rastafarian. In the 1920s, he described in detail the importance of Haile Selassie's rise to the Ethiopian throne and was a key figure in the founding of the syncretic religion **Rastafari**. The details of Howell's life have long lingered in obscurity, as his legacy was maintained largely through oral history and suppressed by the government. Howell was Jamaican, born in the lineage of African slaves. He was the son of a farm worker and immigrated to New York to escape island oppression and to be part of the early 1900s Harlem Renaissance.

Upon his return to Jamaica, he met Marcus Garvey, and the two shared their ideas on African repatriation. Howell delved deeply into the formative period of Rastafarianism and founded the first Rasta enclave, Pinnacle. The obscure location in the Jamaican hills was chosen to avoid scrutiny and persecution. Soon, Pinnacle was home to thousands (although now it is largely abandoned and in ruins) who followed the tenets of Rastafarianism, including daily participation in the Rastafarian sacrament of smoking marijuana. Their subversive and anti-government behavior, along with their drug use, made them easy targets for the police and government.

In 1954, the government raided Pinnacle under the auspices of stopping drug traf-
ficking. In the wake of the raid on Pinnacle, Howell disappeared into obscurity until
his death in 1981. In the wake of the raid, many of the displaced Rastafarians moved
out of the mountains into the west Kingston ghetto, Trenchtown. It was in this place,
with these people, that **reggae** music came to fruition.

In the 1960s, the believers in Howell's doctrine of Rastafari suffered in Trenchtown.
Lacking any real leadership, in 1968 a faction of the Rastas formed the Twelve Tribes of
Israel, a move that divided the faithful into twelve sects. Throughout this twisted
unraveling, some of the most steadfast and vocal advocates of Rastafari have been
the **dancehall**, **reggae**, **rock steady**, and **ska** musicians in Jamaica and the United
Kingdom.

HUDSON, KEITH (1946–1984)

Keith Hudson was a **reggae** multi-instrumentalist, arranger, writer, singer, and producer who sang and played drums and guitar, in addition to owning his own label.
Hudson grew up in a musical family in Kingston, Jamaica, where he was born in 1946.
His grandfather had been a musician with several noteworthy Cuban bands. As a youth,
he worked for the **Skatalites** and learned as much from them as this association
would allow.

At age twenty-one, he cast off his formal training as a dental technician and founded
his own label, Imbidimts (a word coined by Hudson meaning "known sound"). His
first success came with the 1968 single "Old Fashioned Way," sung by **Ken Boothe**.
Early success fast earned him a high reputation, and his artist roster included **Dennis
Alcapone**, **Big Youth**, **Alton Ellis**, **John Holt**, and **U-Roy**. Hudson had the foresight
to sense the change of style to **DJing** and was responsible for cutting U-Roy's first
single, "Dynamic Fashion Way." Hudson also worked on his own material and in 1974
released his debut album, *Entering the Dragon*, followed by one release of original
material per year for the next three years.

In 1976, Hudson and his label moved to New York. The hits kept coming, both for
him and for his roster. In 1976, he released *Too Expensive*; in 1978, *Rasta Communication*; *Brand* was released in 1979; and *Steaming Jungle* and *Black Morphologist of
Reggae* both came out in 1983. Additionally, he continued to produce hits for his label
with artists such as Eddie Campbell, Jah Wobble, **I-Roy**, and Shirley King. Hudson died
of lung cancer in 1984 at age thirty-eight.

HUNNIGALE, PETER (c. 1960–)

Peter Hunnigale, "Mr. Honey Vibes," was born in London, England, in the early 1960s,
of Jamaican parentage. He quickly rose to the top of the UK **lovers rock** ranks, and in
the 1990s scored a series of hits. Over the past fifteen years, he has cultivated a large
and faithful following in the United Kingdom. Hunnigale writes, produces, and is a
multi-instrumentalist. The vast majority of his works were produced by UK producers,
but he did record several sessions with Jamaican producer **Gussie Clarke**.

He released his first album, *In This Time*, in 1987 on the Level Vibes imprint. In
1991, his **Tippa Irie**-produced sophomore release, *The New Decade*, appeared. *Mr.
Vibes* was released in 1992 on the Street Vibes label and was followed in the same year
by another release with Tippa Irie titled *Done Cook and Currie*. Hunnigale continued
his success with the 1994 release *Mr. Government*. Hunnigale's popularity earned him
the honor of a spot in the 1996 **Reggae Sunsplash** concert. In addition to being a
noteworthy singer, he was also active as a producer, having worked with other **reggae**

music heavies such as **Maxi Priest** and Papa Levi. His *Reggae Max* release of 1996 was recorded at Cave Studios for Jet Star records. Hunnigale continues to be highly sought after as a singer and producer. Additionally, he remains active as a live performer. Along with his own recordings, he has appeared on several compilations as a singer, bass player, drummer, producer, and vocalist.

HUNT, CLIVE (c. 1955–)

Clive Hunt was born in St. Catherine, Jamaica, in the mid-1950s. As a young man he trained as a trumpet player and joined the Jamaica Military Band. After leaving the service he was recruited by **Byron Lee** and became a member of the Dragonaires. He toured with the group and upon returning to Jamaica became an in-demand studio instrumentalist. Hunt grew from playing the trumpet to being an outstanding multi-instrumentalist, playing bass, flute, horn, keyboards, trumpet, saxophone, and arranging and producing.

Known by the nicknames "Lizzard" and "Azul," Hunt's earliest recorded appearances are with Pablo Moses on his *Revolutionary Dream* (1975) album. From there, Hunt appeared on the seminal **Abyssinians** recording *Satta Massagana* (1976). For the rest of the 1970s and into the 1980s, he worked with a variety of artists including **Dennis Brown**, **Culture**, **Gregory Isaacs**, **Max Romeo**, the **Skatalites**, and **Peter Tosh**. In the 1990s, Hunt continued his successful studio work, adding recordings with **J. C. Lodge**, the **Mighty Diamonds**, **Sugar Minott**, **Judy Mowatt**, **Ninjaman**, and others. In the new millennium, Hunt remains active, producing records for Dennis Brown, **Horace Andy**, Culture, and **Chaka Demus and Pliers**. Additionally, he has continued his session work as a multi-instrumentalist. In 2004, Hunt played organ on **Luciano's** *Lessons in Life*, supplied vocals for the compilation *Riddim Driven: Doctor's Darling*, and provided the trumpet lines on **Sly and Robbie's** *Unmetered Taxi*.

I

IDENTITY

A group formed in the 1980s, Identity enjoyed modest success through the 1980s and into the 1990s. The group featured Deighton Charlemagne on vocals, Virginia Hunt and Gabriel Mondesir on keyboards, Greg Copening on bass, Nigel Lacher on percussion and background vocals, Scott Kochak on trumpet and background vocals, Marius Felix on saxophone, and Matthew Watson on drums. Together the group released a series of three albums on the Mango imprint, the first of which was 1988's *All in One*. The release was a blend of roots reggae rhythms and **dancehall**-flavored club-friendly songs. One of the more successful singles from the album was "Too Hot on the Beach." This was followed by their self-titled album in 1989. In 1990, the group released its third and final release, *Ska Scandal*. Through the course of their three releases, Identity moved progressively toward a pure dancehall sound. In the more recent past, popular singles from the band have continued to appear on various compilation albums, such as *Reggae on Mango*, *Million Dollar Album*, and *Spread Yo Hustle*.

IJAHMAN LEVY (c. 1946–)

Trevor Sutherland was born in Manchester, Jamaica, and grew up in the west Kingston ghettos. Like most of his friends, he aspired to rise out of his poor situation though music. In his early teens, he went to an audition held by **Island Records** head **Christopher Blackwell** and conducted by **Jackie Edwards**. Sutherland sang well enough to get past Edwards, but Blackwell sent him away for further practice. In 1963, Sutherland left Jamaica and immigrated to England with his parents. Before Sutherland left Jamaica, he recorded a single for **Duke Reid** called "Red Eyes People." The single was never released. In the United Kingdom, Sutherland formed a group called the Vibrations, but in the late 1960s his singing partner left for the United States, leaving Sutherland a solo act. Undaunted, he continued to sing and mixed Jamaican material with American soul and rhythm and blues.

During the early 1970s, Sutherland spent time in prison on a variety of charges. While incarcerated, he read the Bible and upon release changed his name from Trevor Sutherland to Ijahman. He returned to Jamaica and continued reading the Bible, coming to believe that the Bible described him as a Levite; hence the name Ijahman Levy. Upon his return to England he cut a series of deep roots reggae singles such as "Jah Heavy Load." Blackwell heard the single, and twelve years after their first meeting the pair was reunited. The Island label boss brought Ijahman into the studio, and the product was *Rastafari: Hail I Hymn* (1978). The followup was *Are We a Warrior* (1979); after its release the pair separated due to disagreements about money.

In 1982, Ijahman released his first independent album, *Tell It to the Children*. To release the album, Levy had to launch his own label, Jahmani. The venture was a success, and he went on to issue fifteen more albums through his imprint. Over the course of his career he worked with a series of legendary studio musicians such as

Lloyd Parks, Sly and Robbie, Earl "Chinna" Smith, and many others. In the mid-1990s, Levy toured the United States for the first time and has subsequently gone on to continue his busy schedule of recording and live performances.

I-KONG (c. 1950–)

I-Kong was a roots reggae singer active in the 1970s. Born **Richard Storme**, I-Kong formed a band, Jamaica, and released two albums. The first was 1976's *Africa Is Calling*, which featured the singles "Down, Down, Babylon Walls" and "Life's Road." Kong and Jamaica's second release was titled *The Way It Is*. This album came out in 1979 on the Top Ranking label and basically contained the same songs as the first album with the addition of "Sinner Man" and "Set Black People Free."

Under his given name, Kong was credited as a background vocalist for **Max Romeo's** *Reconstruction* (1978) album. Kong and Jamaica have also appeared on several compilations released in the 1990s and the new millennium. In 1995, Kong and Jamaica's song "Babylon Walls" appeared on the Lagoon label release *Reggae Babylon*, a collection of songs that all have the word *Babylon* in their titles. In 2000, their song "Life Road" appeared on the Culture Press release *Zion Land*; and in 2001, "Babylon Walls" was included on the compilation *Reggae Collection, Volume 3*.

IN CROWD, THE

A band formed by Phil Callender in the mid-1970s, the In Crowd was long active as a session guitarist on the Jamaican roots reggae scene. Callender spent time working for **Clement "Coxsone" Dodd** on the **Studio One** label and was often part of the sessions that involved the legendary keyboardist **Jackie Mittoo**. Callender had a sweet singing voice that he put to use when he formed the In Crowd. The band became one of the most popular Jamaican bands on the island in the late 1970s. They released a series of hit singles that included "We Play Reggae," "His Majesty Is Coming," and "Back a Yard." The band also included Errol Walker on vocals, Clevie Brown on drums, Freddie Butler on keyboards, Tony Lewis on bass, and Wigmore Frances on guitar. In addition, the group had a three-member horn line to round out its sound. It released its debut album, 1978's *His Majesty Is Coming*, followed by *Man from New Guinea* in 1979. After the second album, the group split and Callender pursued a solo career. Another notable member of the group was Clevie Brown, who later became half of the dominant **dancehall** rhythm section **Steely and Clevie**.

INI KAMOZE (c. 1960–)

Born Cecil Campbell, Ini Kamoze went on to become a successful **reggae** singer and popular crossover artist in the United States. Kamoze made his appearance on the reggae music scene in the early 1980s. He entered the music business with the assistance of **Jimmy Cliff**, who delivered Kamoze to legendary rhythm section and production team **Sly and Robbie**. Kamoze debuted in 1983 with the release of the hit single "Trouble You a Trouble Me." The single was so successful that he was put on the Taxi Connection International Tour with **Half Pint** and **Yellowman**. He parlayed this early success into the release of his first full-length album, 1984's *Pirates*. Although *Pirates* was not as enthusiastically received as his earlier material, he forged ahead and had a series of hit singles on his own Slekta label. His next release, "Shocking Out," led to the album of the same title in 1988.

In the 1990s, Kamoze reasserted himself with a more aggressive image and hit with a series of popular releases. His 1995 release *Here Comes the HotStepper* was an international success and even appeared on the soundtrack of the film *Pret-A-Porter.* This unprecedented success resulted in Kamoze being signed by Electra Records. For Electra he released another album in the same year, *Lyrical Gangsta.* The Electra release found Kamoze recasting himself in a more militant stance, which has continued until the present.

INNER CIRCLE

Inner Circle was a band that emerged in the late 1960s with the lineup of brothers Ian and Roger Lewis, **Michael "Ibo" Cooper**, **Stephen "Cat" Coore**, and **Richard Daley**. Initially, the group played the Jamaican club scene and had modest success. However, in 1973 they split when Coore, Cooper, and Daley went on to form **Third World**. At this time the Lewis brothers added **Bernard "Touter" Harvey**, Charles Farquharson, and Rasheed McKenzie to create a reconstituted Inner Circle. The band played its own breed of pop-oriented **reggae** that had crossover appeal.

In 1976, **Jacob Miller** joined the group and immediately gave them serious legitimacy. Miller had been a longstanding **Rastafarian** and solo artist of high repute. With Miller in the band, the next several releases were more serious in tone. The Miller association also led to a record deal with Capital Records in the United States and the release of *Reggae Thing* (1976) and *Ready for the World* (1977). In 1978, Inner Circle performed at the **One Love Peace Concert**, which was a monumental showcase that drew such heavies as **Bob Marley and the Wailers**. The band suffered a terrific blow when Miller was killed in a car accident in 1980. This sent the remaining members scattering, and there was no new music from Inner Circle for several years.

In 1986, Inner Circle made a comeback with the Lewis brothers and Harvey, plus new drummer **Lancelot Hall** and a new lead singer named Carlton Coffee. Their comeback release was done by **RAS Records** in 1986 and was titled *Black Roses*. The following year the band found success with the followup album *One Way*, which contained the original version of their now-seminal hit "Bad Boys." In 1989, the television show

Inner Circle. © *UrbanImage.tv.*

Cops premiered with Inner Circle's song "Bad Boys" as its theme song. The song was an international number one hit. This was followed by the equally popular song "Sweet (La la la la Long)." This acclaim propelled the band to new heights, and they parlayed this success into a new set of recordings in the early 1990s. Throughout this decade the group continued to release solid albums, including *Identified* (1989), *Burnin' Reggae* (1992), and *Reggae Profile* (1994). In 1994, they released the album *Reggae Dancer*, which featured the single "Summer Jammin.'" This single was picked up for use on the soundtrack for the Eddie Murphy film *Beverly Hills Cop III.*

In 1997, Coffie was sidelined with a serious illness and was replaced by the band's current singer, Kris Bentley. The first album that appeared with Bentley singing was 1997's *Da Bomb.* In the new millennium, Inner Circle continues to be a successful reggae band. Their album *Barefoot in Negril*, released in 2001, featured the singles "Boardwalk" and "Jump Right in It." More recently, RAS has issued a collection of Inner Circle hits as part of its *This Is Crucial Reggae* series. The Inner Circle band continues to work in the studio and on the stage.

IPSO FACTO

Hailing from Minneapolis, Minnesota, Ipso Facto is a combination of three brothers. The trio, Wain, Juju, and Greg McFarlane, sons of a Jamaican father and an African American mother, have been a **reggae** mainstay in the Twin Cities for over a decade. They have released several albums, the first two on the Atomic Theory label. *Carry On* (1992) and *More Communication* (1993) exemplify the band's sound, which is a mixture of roots reggae and American funk. *Carry On* contains the funk/reggae tracks "Guilty" and "Need Your Love."

In 1995, the band switched to the Mouthpiece label and released their third album, *Welcome to Jamerica.* After only three albums, Ipso Facto released their *Best of* album in 1998. Here the band illustrated its mixture of reggae, funk, and even rap leanings. The collection includes their most solid material, with tracks produced by **Geoffrey Chung**, **Steely and Clevie**, and other notables. The band subsequently toured with artists such as **UB40** and Tracy Chapman. More recently, the trio that was Ipso Facto has gone separate ways. Wain McFarlane continues to be active in the music business with his new pop-rock band Zydeco Blue.

IRIE, TIPPA. *See* TIPPA IRIE

I-ROY (1949–1999)

Roy "I-Roy" Samuel Reid was born in 1949 in St. Thomas, Jamaica. He entered the Jamaican popular music scene as a teenager and began **toasting** on area **sound systems**. Reid followed in the footsteps of his predecessors and influenced **U-Roy** and **Dennis Alcapone**. In the late 1960s and early 1970s, I-Roy honed his toasting skills while maintaining his civil service job. In 1972, Reid entered the studio and had a series of successful singles with a variety of Jamaican producers. He ultimately worked with every big-name producer on the island, including Prince Tony, **Gussie Clarke**, Harry Mudie, and others. In the early 1970s, I-Roy recorded a pair of popular albums, *Presenting I-Roy* and *Hell and Sorrow*, which were successful both in Jamaica and the United Kingdom. These early albums featured material such as "The Drifter," "Black Man Time," and "Welding." They were followed by *I-Roy* (1974) and *Truth and Rights* (1975).

In 1976, he caught his big break and signed with the Virgin Records label. With Virgin, I-Roy released the 1976 album *Musical Shark Attack.* He also took a job in the

Channel One Studios as the resident producer. While working at the studio, I-Roy continued to record. He issued *Can't Conquer Rasta* (1977), *Dreadlocks in Jamaica* (1978), *Godfather* (1978), and *Heart of a Lion* (1978). Also in 1978, he released *Ten Commandments*, which was a collection of ten **Bob Marley and the Wailers** songs redone in I-Roy's toasting style. This was followed in 1979 by *Cancer* and in 1980 with *Whap'n Bap'n*. In the 1980s, I-Roy's recording career continued to be fruitful. He released *Doctor Fish* and *Many Moods* in 1981, and *Outer Limits* in 1983.

The second half of the 1980s marked a sharp decline in the dancehall hero's career. In the early 1990s, I-Roy was rendered destitute by a series of health problems. He had nowhere to turn and at times was forced to live on the streets. In 1999, I-Roy died at age fifty.

ISAACS, GREGORY "COOL RULER" (1951–)

Gregory "Cool Ruler" Isaacs was born in Kingston, Jamaica. He rose from modest beginnings to become one of the most well-respected Jamaican popular musicians of the past fifty years. In his early professional life, he was an electrician and cabinetmaker; during this time he cultivated a taste for American soul music and island favorites such as **Ken Boothe** and **Alton Ellis**. Isaacs changed careers in the late 1960s when he recorded the single "Another Heartache" for producer Winston Sinclair. The single did not fare well, but the experience gave Isaacs the confidence to form his own band, the Concords, in 1969. The vocal trio released a series of singles for **Rupie Edwards's** Success label. The group did not gain popularity with the island audience, and in 1970 Isaacs went solo. He teamed with producer **Prince Buster** and released several sides, but again was displeased with the reception.

In 1973, Isaacs paired with Errol Dunkley and launched his own label, African Museum. With newfound creative control, he was able to begin issuing the type of material that made him a **reggae** legend. In the mid-1970s, Isaacs released a series of successful singles that culminated in his 1975 debut album *In Person*. In the studio, Isaacs worked with a variety of producers while maintaining his own imprint. There followed a period of great creative output with late 1970s and early 1980s albums such as *Cool Ruler* (1978), *Extra Classic* (1977), *Lonely Lover* (1980), *Mr. Isaacs* (1977), *Night Nurse* (1982), and many others. During this period, Isaacs worked with several major labels, including Virgin, Charisma, and the legendary reggae imprint **Island**.

Unfortunately, Isaacs had a run of legal problems culminating in a mid-1980s arrest for drug possession that landed him in jail for a short stint. When he was released, he reasserted himself in the popular music business and again released a collection of solid albums. The latter half of the 1980s saw Isaacs again rise to the pinnacle of reggae stardom. He worked with all of the significant producers on the island and enjoyed nonstop productivity, leading to another series of albums.

In the early 1990s, Isaacs's recording output continued unabated. He released *On the Dance Floor* (1989) with producer **Winston "Niney" Holness** and the following year teamed with **Philip "Fatis" Burrell** for the album *Call Me Collect*. While Isaacs's productivity in the 1990s was not as great as it had been before that, he still released a new album almost every year. Isaacs continues to be active. Over the course of a career that spans thirty-plus years, Isaacs has been a prolific writer and perennial stage favorite, attested to by numerous appearances in the **Reggae Sunsplash** concerts. He maintains an ongoing music career that includes writing, recording, and live performances. Much of Isaacs's back catalog remains available thanks to the efforts of both **Heartbeat** and **RAS Records**.

ISLAND RECORDS

Island Records is a label that has been instrumental in bringing **reggae** music to the world. The label was started in Jamaica in 1962 by **Christopher Blackwell**. Blackwell already had an established reputation in the UK record industry, and he used his connections in his plan to distribute reggae music internationally. In its infancy, Island issued only reggae music, but it soon began broadening its offerings and ultimately was one of the most important international labels in the 1980s.

Blackwell's most notable reggae act was **Bob Marley and the Wailers**. He was responsible for bringing the group to a wider audience and was instrumental in finessing their sound to make it more marketable. Blackwell is credited with producing the Wailers albums *Burnin'* (1973), *Catch a Fire* (1973), *Natty Dread* (1974), and *Live!* (1975). He is also responsible for producing several releases by **Third World** and **Toots and the Maytals**. Blackwell is further credited with mixing several albums for the Wailers, Toots and the Maytals, and **Ijahman**. As Island Records grew, Blackwell expanded the roster to include other Jamaican acts such as **Jimmy Cliff**. Additionally, he signed rock and roll acts including U2, Traffic, Roxy Music, Jethro Tull, Grace Jones, Melissa Etheridge, and many others. At the height of its run, Island Records included the subsidiary labels Pyramid, Trojan, Mango, Antilles, and Sue.

In 1989, Blackwell sold Island to Polygram Records, and in 1998 Polygram merged with Def Jam and has become part of the Universal Music Group. Blackwell remains active in the music business and has again expanded his horizons by entering the resort hotel business, with his Island Outpost chain.

ISRAEL VIBRATION

The vocal trio Israel Vibration met at a home for polio sufferers in the early 1970s. The trio included Albert "Apple Gabriel" Craig, Cecil "Skeleton" Spence, and Lascelle "Wiss" Bulgin. The group spent several years singing on the streets of Kingston to hone their skills. In 1975, the trio entered the studio with Ernest Hookim and cut a single. However, the song was never released and the group had to start over. All three men were **Rastafarians**, and as such prevailed on the Twelve Tribes of Israel to support their next entry into the studio. This attempt was successful and was followed by greater success in subsequent singles. Their first album, 1977's *The Same Song*, was well received, even garnering international acclaim, and spurred the trio forward.

In 1979, the group released its second album, *Unconquering People*, and established itself as a roots reggae force. The trio appeared on the **Reggae Sunsplash** concert, and their singles "Crisis" and "We a de Rasta" were instant island classics. The group's material is a mixture of conscious and militant sentiments couched in Rastafarian imagery. In the early 1980s, Israel Vibration's support began to wane, and they moved to the United States, settling in New York in 1983. The move to the United States was not successful for the group, however, and they soon fell into obscurity; this led to their breakup, after which each of the three pursued solo projects.

The group reunited in 1987, and with the assistance of **Doctor Dread's RAS** label again entered a successful time in their careers. With Dread, and backed by the **Roots Radics**, the trio released *Strength of My Life* (1988), *Praises* (1980), *Israel Dub* (1980), and *Forever* (1991). Helped by the popular reception of the albums, by the early 1990s Israel Vibration was again a solid **reggae** force. The group went on to release a series of successful albums throughout the middle and late 1990s. However, in 1997 Craig left the group to again pursue a solo career. Undaunted, the remaining two members forged ahead and released *Pay the Piper* (1999) and *Jericho* (2000). In the new millennium, Israel Vibration has remained active and has released four new albums on RAS. The group continues to write, record, and perform live.

ITALS, THE

The Itals formed in 1976 when Ronnie Davis and Keith Porter came together as a vocal duo. The pair was originally from Jamaica's Westmoreland district and never made Kingston their permanent residence. The word *ital* is pidgin English (a Caribbean patois) for something that is pure, natural, and from the earth. The group came to prominence during the heyday of the roots reggae style; its approach matched the current movement in Jamaican popular music. The Itals worked with **Lloyd Campbell**, for whom they recorded their most memorable material. Their first success, achieved on Campbell's Spiderman imprint, was the 1976 single "In a Dis a Time." The single was a hit and climbed the charts to the top position. The group added a third singer when Lloyd Ricketts joined the group. As a trio, they released "Don't Wake the Lion" and "Brutal." These songs were popular in both Jamaica and the United States.

In 1981, the trio played the **Reggae Sunsplash** concert, which further cemented their reputation. In 1982, they began working with the **Nighthawk** imprint and made their first album, *Brutal Out Deh*. The trio then launched a North American tour on which they were backed by the **Roots Radics**. Subsequent albums were also successful, such as their 1984 *Give Me Power* and 1987's *Rasta Philosophy*, which earned a Grammy nomination. This success was followed by *Cool and Dread* in 1989 and a collection of their early hits called *Early Recordings*. However, it was at this time that Ricketts was imprisoned and lost his visa, making him unable to reenter the United States. He was then replaced by David Isaacs. The new trio released *Easy to Catch* in 1991 on the Rhythm Safari label and subsequently spent much of the decade touring.

During the 1990s, the group's lineup changed when Davis departed and was replaced by Porter's daughter Kada. The reconstituted trio continues to be active and performs its time-honored hits as well as new material.

I-THREES

The I-Threes were a female vocal trio of **Rita Marley** (Bob Marley's wife), **Judy Mowatt**, and **Marcia Griffiths**. The group was formed in an effort to give greater vocal presence to **Bob Marley and the Wailers** once **Peter Tosh** and **Bunny Wailer** left the band in 1974. The three women began performing, recording, and touring with Marley in 1974 and stayed with the **reggae** legend until his death in 1981.

Each of the women had enjoyed a singing career before forming the I-Threes; however, only Griffiths had attained any national exposure. Griffiths had been in a singing duo with **Bob Andy** called **Bob and Marcia**. Together they had scored the **Studio One** hit "Young, Gifted and Black." The first song that the I-Threes performed with Marley was the 1974 single "Jah Live." This song was especially poignant as it was Marley's response to the death of Haile Selassie. They appeared on all subsequent Marley albums and tours. In the wake of Marley's death, the three women continued to sing together for several years. However, in 1985 the trio split to again work as solo acts.

J

JACKSON, VIVIAN. *See* **YABBY YOU**

JAD RECORDS

JAD Records was a foundational Jamaican label in the development of the roots reggae style. The label was started by Danny Sims, and through a meeting with **Bob Marley** and American singer **Johnny Nash**, Simms signed Marley in 1967. Marley and the Wailers had already been active recording artists for **Clement "Coxsone" Dodd**, but had become disillusioned by the lack of artistic control and financial gain. At the time that Simms signed Marley, he was working with a business partner named Arthur Jenkins; the pair offered the Wailers a deal that provided them with the support they needed. For JAD, the Wailers recorded over two hundred songs, from remakes of their earlier material to a host of new tracks. Although the JAD tracks contained precious early material, little of it was released until the series of complete Wailers box sets began to be issued in 1996 (as of 2005, three volumes are extant).

The relationship that the Wailers had with JAD allowed them to record both for Nash and Perkins and for other producers at the same time. These other producers included **Leslie Kong**, **Bunny Lee**, and **Lee "Scratch" Perry**. The result was an enormously productive period for the band and the creation of many of the Wailers' most prized recordings. Although the Wailers had a strong relationship with JAD, the partnership ended in 1972 and most of their JAD material fell into obscurity. Through the efforts of Simms and others, such as reggae archivist Roger Steffens, this material is now available again. The *Complete Bob Marley and the Wailers* box sets came out in three volumes. All three span the period 1967–1972 and represent an excellent accounting of the material that the Wailers cut for JAD.

In addition to the three box sets, Simms signed a deal in January 2004 to re-release more of the Wailers' early work through Universal Music International. This ten-year deal will bring more of the recordings from the JAD period to light and promises additional rarities and previously unreleased tracks. With this deal, Universal now holds licensing for Bob Marley and the Wailers' material from 1967–1972 and from 1972–1980, the latter work acquired through the Island-Polygram merger when Universal absorbed Polygram.

JAFFE, LEE (c. 1955–)

Lee Jaffe entered the **reggae** music scene after enjoying a successful career as an international art filmmaker. He made the transition from filmmaker to musician with the assistance of **Chris Blackwell** and the **Island Records** label. Jaffe was working as a representative for Island when he met **Bob Marley**; he went on to spend the next three years working with **Bob Marley and the Wailers**. He became the Wailers' harmonica player and Marley's constant companion, both on tour and in Kingston. Examples of his work are the harmonica parts in "I Shot the Sheriff" and "Rebel Music."

Further, he served as producer for many important reggae albums from the late 1970s, 1980s, and 1990s. Jaffe is credited as the producer for several albums by **Peter Tosh**, **Joe Higgs**, **Bob Marley**, **Barrington Levy**, and **Bounty Killer**. He has also produced albums for Lenny Kravitz.

In 2003, Jaffe released the book *One Love: Life with Bob Marley and the Wailers*, which contains an accounting of Marley's life through first-hand reports and vivid photography. In 2004, Jaffe appeared on four tracks of *Is It Rolling Bob?*, a compilation album of reggae versions of Bob Dylan songs.

JAH JERRY (1921–)

Jah Jerry was born Jerome Haynes and went on to enjoy a long and storied career in the Jamaican popular music business. Haynes was one of the founding members of the legendary **Skatalites**, for whom he played guitar. He gained his early training on the guitar from **Ernest Ranglin** in the late 1940s. Ranglin and Haynes would go on to work together as members of producer **Prince Buster's** studio band. In the early 1950s he began playing in regional bands and eventually put in session time with every important **reggae** producer on the island. He worked in the studio for producers such as **Count Boysie**, **Clement "Coxsone" Dodd**, **Duke Reid**, Prince Buster, and many others.

In 1964, the original Skatalites formed and Haynes was the third official member. Through the influence of his teacher, Haynes added jazz chords to the group's material. From the **ska** to **rock steady** to reggae styles, Haynes continually pushed styles of Jamaican popular music forward. In addition to his work with the Skatalites, Haynes also recorded with reggae luminaries such as **Jimmy Cliff**, **Desmond Dekker**, **Bob Marley and the Wailers**, and others. Material by guitarist Jerry "Jah Jerry" Haynes remains popular, and many of the recordings that he appeared on are considered essential listening to reggae fans internationally.

JAH LION (d. 1999)

Patrick Francis's career in the music business had two sides: one as a singer and another as a label owner. As a singer, Francis recorded under the name **Jah Lloyd** or **Jah Lion** and released a series of albums in the late 1970s. In 1978 he released *The Humble One* and in 1979 *Black Moses*, both of which came out on the Frontline imprint. Also in 1979, he released *Reggae Stick*. These three albums yielded several popular singles, including "Honour Me" and "Green Bay Massacre." As a singer, Francis's talents ranged from **DJing** and **toasting** to more lyrical singing. The other half of his life in music began when he and longtime friend Mike Brooks established the Teem Records label in 1969. Brooks got his start with **Channel One** and learned the craft of production through his work with their house band, the **Revolutionaries**. Together, Brooks and Francis ran the label together and released a host of singles. Francis reportedly died in July 1999.

JAH LLOYD. *See* JAH LION

JAH SCREW (c. 1960–)

Jah Screw was born Paul Love and got his start in Jamaican popular music as a **sound system** operator for **U-Roy's** Stur-Gav and the Symbolic sound system. After leaving the systems, Screw moved on to production work and teamed with Ranking Joe for a time. Ultimately, he went out on his own and had a huge hit with **Barrington Levy's**

"Under Mi Sensi." The song was an instant classic and stayed on the charts several months. Levy and Screw hit again with their 1985 single "Here I Come," which was another massive success, this time on an international scale. The Levy/Screw collaboration culminated in the album *Broader Than Broadway*, released on the Profile label.

Levy then went on to work with **Black Scorpio**; but in 1992 he again paired with Screw and the magic returned on "Turning Point," released on the Greensleeves imprint. In 1993, the pair released the *Duets* album, which cast Levy together with a series of **dancehall** luminaries including **Beenie Man** and **Lady Saw**. In addition to his work with Levy, Screw also produced albums for Barry Brown, Earl Cunningham, and Tony Tuff.

As a singer, Screw backed releases for **Admiral Tibet**, **Dennis Brown**, Barrington Levy, and many others. Jah Screw's influence continues to be felt around the Jamaican popular music community and through the music of Barrington Levy.

JAH SHAKA (c. 1950–)

Jah Shaka was a UK-based roots and **dub sound system** operator who was among the elite in the style. He got his start in the 1970s working as an operator on Freddie Cloudburst's system. Shaka has been a longstanding **Rastafarian** and a true believer in the power of the sound system. He used it as a means of entertaining the dancers, educating them, and lifting their spirits.

Shaka took his name from the famous African king and Zulu warrior Shaka Zulu, and he has used it throughout his ascent to the throne of UK **dancehall**. He went out on his own in the early 1970s and cultivated an impressive reputation throughout the 1970s, 1980s, and 1990s. During the 1980s he was a mainstay at several popular London-area clubs such as the Club Noreik, Studio 200, Cubies, and Phoebes. In addition to working the sound systems, Shaka also released a series of albums beginning with *Revelation Songs* (1983), which was followed by a host of dub versions that started with *Jah Shaka Meets Mad Professor at Ariwa Sounds* (1984).

Through the rest of the 1980s and the 1990s, Shaka continued to make and release dub albums that included the *Commandments of Dub* and the *Dub Solute* series. Additionally, he launched the Jah Shaka Foundation, which offered assistance to underprivileged children in Jamaica, Ethiopia, and Ghana. The Foundation provided medical supplies, wheelchairs, books, tools, and many other necessities. Jah Shaka's work continues in both music and humanitarian endeavors.

Jah Shaka. © *UrbanImage.tv.*

JAH STITCH (c. 1955–)

Born Melbourne James, Jah Stitch got his start in the Jamaica popular music industry through the **sound systems**. He worked for the Tippertone and Black Harmony systems and honed his skills. Stitch's lyrics tended toward the conscious side; he dealt with cultural issues in the same manner as **Big Youth**. In the mid-1970s, Stitch released a series of singles that allowed him greater exposure. The singles were produced by **Vivian "Yabby You" Jackson** and **Bunny "Striker" Lee**; through their popularity Stitch's reputation was made.

In 1978, he released his first album, *My Precious Locks*, which was followed by *Watch Your Step Youth Man* (1979). These early albums further cemented Stitch as a conscious **dancehall** force. Then Stitch's studio productivity slowed. However, the Blood and Fire label released a collection of his early material titled *Original Raggamuffin: 1975–1977*, which kept Stitch in the limelight. In 2000, Blood and Fire also released *The Killer*, another collection of Stitch's work that immortalized one of his more popular singles. In addition to his own albums, Stitch has appeared on a host of compilations.

JAH THOMAS (1955–)

Nkrumah Manley Thomas was born in Kingston, Jamaica, and made his entry into the Jamaican popular music scene in the mid-1970s, quickly rising to the upper echelon of young **DJs**. His ascension began at **Channel One**, where he cut sides for the **Hookim** brothers. Thomas's first hit came in 1976 with producer G. G. Ranglin (**Ernest Ranglin's** brother). The single was titled "Midnight Rock" and became Thomas's signature song. During this time he took the stage name Jah Thomas.

In 1978, Thomas worked a deal with the UK-based Greensleeves imprint and released his debut album *Stop Yu Loafin.'* As did many Jamaican artists, Thomas moved from studio to studio and worked with a series of producers. His next two releases, *Dance on the Corner* (1979) and *Dancehall Connection* (1982), came from two different producers. By the mid-1980s, he had diversified his offerings to the music business and moved into the studio as a producer. In this capacity, Thomas worked on material for **dancehall** figures such as **Early B**, **Anthony Johnson**, **Sugar Minott**, **Triston Palma**, **Ranking Toyan**, and Little John.

Throughout this time Thomas continued to record his own material. In addition, he launched his own label, Midnight Rock, and released his own material on this imprint. The label was strengthened through the use of the **Roots Radics** as the backing band for many sessions. At this time, the Radics included **Gladstone Anderson**, **Bobby Ellis**, **Bongo Herman**, **Errol "Flabba" Holt**, **Eric "Bingy Bunny" Lamont**, and **Lincoln "Style" Scott**. Many of Thomas's tracks were picked up by legendary producer **King Tubby** and made into rhythms for some of the hottest dub tracks of the decade. In addition to working with Tubby, Thomas also cut dub tracks with **Hopeton "Scientist" Brown**. This pairing produced the album *Jah Thomas Meets Scientist in Dub Conference* (1996).

As the 1990s dawned, Thomas stepped out of the spotlight. He continued to appear on occasional sessions, but his output diminished. Much of Thomas's material has re-emerged in the interim on compilation albums.

JAH WOOSH (c. 1955–)

Born Neville Beckford, Jah Woosh entered the music scene in the mid-1970s. He was most active in the United Kingdom and established a sizable fan base there, **toasting** in the **dancehall** vein established by **Big Youth**. In 1974, he released his debut self-titled album, which kicked off a period of serious productivity. There followed a series of releases including 1976's *Dreadlock Affair* and *Jah Jah Dey Dey*. In 1977, Woosh released one of his most well-respected albums, *Lick Him with the Dustbin*, which was followed in 1978 by *Gathering Israel* and *Religious Dread*. Other important albums by Woosh include *Sing and Chant*, *Some Sign*, and *Marijuana World Tour*. In addition to toasting on records, Woosh launched his own label, Original Music, which reissued all of his best material. By the mid-1980s, Jah Woosh had faded from the UK dancehall scene.

JAMAICA RECORDING AND PUBLISHING COMPANY

Clement "Coxsone" Dodd began recording Jamaican popular music in 1955, and as his reputation grew he opened his now legendary **Studio One** facility. The studio opened in 1960 at 13 Brentford Road, Kingston, Jamaica. Along with Studio One, Dodd also opened the Jamaica Recording and Publishing Company Limited. Through these business endeavors, Dodd was able to stay on the leading edge of Jamaican popular music styles from **ska** to early **dancehall**. His recording and pressing facilities were used by many of the most important artists of the time, including **Roland Alphonso**, **Bob Andy**, **Bob Marley and the Wailers**, **Donald Drummond**, **Alton Ellis**, **Marcia Griffiths**, the **Heptones**, **John Holt**, **Tommy McCook**, **Jackie Mittoo**, **Toots and the Maytals**, and the **Skatalites**. In deference to Dodd's impact, Brentford Road was renamed Studio One Boulevard.

JAMAICAN RECORDINGS

The Jamaican Recordings label was established to release Jamaican **reggae** and **dub** material from the 1970s. The imprint deals directly with producers, artists, and studios to recover lost or forgotten material from the decade that saw the vast majority of reggae and dub material emerge. Re-releases of seminal albums are achieved through working directly with the original master tapes. To supplement each release, the label also includes copious sleeve notes. Artist who are currently available on Jamaican Recordings reissues include the **Aggrovators**, **King Tubby**, **Augustus Pablo**, **Lee "Scratch" Perry**, the **Revolutionaries**, **Sly and Robbie**, **Linval Thompson**, and **Tappa Zukie**.

JAMAICANS, THE

The Jamaicans formed in the mid-1960s and entered the Jamaican popular music scene in 1967. The vocal trio comprised **Tommy Cowan**, Norris Weir, and Martin Williams. They sang in a **rock steady** style and had early success with the single "Ba Ba Boom." For the rest of the 1960s and into the 1970s the group continued to release modestly successful material. They worked for the producer **Duke Reid** and released their material on his **Treasure Isle** imprint. In addition to their original rock steady material, the group also made cover versions of soul material such as Curtis Mayfield's "Dedicate My Song to You." The group was at the height of its popularity as the style of Jamaican popular music changed from rock steady to **reggae**; the trio's style followed the change. Although the group enjoyed a level of success for a five-year period, it disbanded in 1972. Of note, Cowen went on to be a successful talent scout, producer, and longstanding emcee of the **Reggae Sunsplash** concert. In 1996, the group's most popular material was re-released on a Jamaica Gold imprint compilation titled *Ba Ba Boom Time*.

JAMES, HUGH (c. 1960–)

Reggae producer Hugh "Redman" James has been active in the music business since the mid-1980s. His work appeared on many labels; however, he was most prolific on the Greensleeves imprint from the late 1980s to the present. James has produced material for artists such as **Cutty Ranks, Flourgon, Sugar Minott, Papa San, Pinchers, Sanchez**, Carl Meeks, Cultural Roots, Clement Irie, and many others. His work was most often featured on compilation releases such as *Greensleeves Sampler, Vol. 3*; *Greensleeves Sampler, Vol. 4*; *Reggae Hits, Vol. 30*; and *Rough and Ready*.

JAMES, MELBORNE. *See* JAH STITCH

JARRETT, CLIVE (c. 1965–)

Clive Jarrett was an active producer of **reggae** music in the early 1980s. He often worked with singer/producer Beswick "Bebo" Phillips; the pair is credited on a host of releases. Additionally, Jarrett launched his own label, Dynamite Records. Artists with whom Jarrett worked include **Al Campbell** on the CSA imprint release *Bad Boy*, Carlton Livingston on the *Rumors* album, Peter Metro, the **Lone Ranger** on the Greensleeves release *Hi Ho Silver Away*, Welton Irie, and many others. Jarrett's heyday was the period from 1980 to 1985; since then, he has fallen into obscurity.

JARRETT, IRVINE "CARROT" (c. 1955–)

Irvine "Carrot" Jarrett has had a long career in the **reggae** music business, a career that began in the mid-1970s. Jarrett made his entrance onto the Jamaican popular music scene when he joined **Third World** as the band's percussionist. He had already gained considerable experience and was recognized as a veteran percussionist, in addition to having worked in television production. Jarrett's first album credit for Third World was its self-titled 1976 release. On this album, Jarrett is credited with percussion, conga, and **akete**. He remained part of the Third World band until 1989 when he departed to work with other acts. Since that time, Jarrett has branched out and become involved in engineering recordings as well as playing on them. In the 1990s and the new millennium, he is credited as the engineer for recordings by **Culture**, Morgan Heritage, **Shaggy**, Bobby Womack, and others. He also continues to perform on percussion and worked in this capacity with Peter Broggs, **Joe Higgs**, Sister Breeze, Social Distortion, the **Wailers**, and others. Jarrett remains active as both an engineer and performer.

JEWELS, THE

The Jewels formed in the summer of 1994 in Canada as a **reggae** vocal group. The group was led by singer Kay Morris, who voiced spiritual lyrics over reggae grooves that mixed the Jamaican sound with soca and the blues. Morris was born in Jamaica and raised on both the reggae style and the spirituality of the Pentecostal church. In addition to Morris, the group included Ray Fraser, Marsha Walker, Marcia Walters-Rodriguez, and Janice Hudson.

The Jewels have released a series of successful singles and several albums. Their first was 1995's *Live Again*, which earned them the Canadian Reggae Music Award for Top Female Newcomer. Their second album, 1999's *Armageddon*, was also released to favorable reviews and garnered the Jewels additional awards. On this release, the group again mixes styles including reggae, gospel, **ska**, and calypso. Album standouts include "He's Coming Again," presented in the ska style, and "Armageddon," delivered in a roots reggae style. "Satin Time Expire" is a calypso tune that evokes the island spirit through its steel drum work. The group gained national prominence in Canada in the late 1990s and continue their popularity in the new millennium. They have toured internationally and continue to work on new material.

JIVING JUNIORS

A vocal pairing of **Derrick Harriott** and Claude Sang Junior in the mid-1950s, the two won the Vere John's Talent Hour and soon recruited Neville "G-Bobs" Esson and Roy Robinson into their ranks. The new group was called the Hurricanes, but this arrangement did not last long. In 1958, Harriott and Sang again emerged as a vocal group with the additions of Valmont Burke and Winston Service; this time they called themselves the Jiving Juniors and had immediate success with the single "Lollipop Girl." The song was popular in the **sound systems** and was released in 1959 under the production of **Duke Reid**. The quartet followed this success with a series of singles including "Dearest Darling," "I Love You," and "I Wanna Love You."

The group sang in the Jamaican rhythm and blues style that copied the American radio offerings and recorded material popular in the southeastern United States. The Juniors then moved over to **Clement "Coxsone" Dodd's Studio One** label in 1960 and 1961, in addition to recording with Edward Seaga and others. For Dodd, the group hit with several singles, among them "Hip Rub," "Over the River," and "Sugar Dandy." These Dodd-produced singles brought the Jiving Juniors international attention, and several of their singles were popular in the United Kingdom. Of note, the single "Over the River" was in the doo-wop style, but employed a heavy guitar backbeat that made it an immediate precursor to the **ska** sound.

In 1962, Derrick Harriott left the group for a solo career and Sang recruited a new lineup that included Maurice Winter, Eugene Dwyer, and Jimmy Muldahaye. This split came at the transition of Jamaican popular music style from rhythm and blues to ska, and without Harriott's leadership the band did not survive the style change. Although the reconstituted Jiving Juniors remained a popular live act, they were unable to recapture their earlier fame in the studio.

JOHNNY P (c. 1960–)

Born Orville Morgan, he entered the **dancehall** music scene in the early 1980s. He experienced early success with several popular singles, which culminated in the release of his 1990s album *P Is for Perfect*, produced by **Gussie Clarke**. He parlayed this success into several more popular releases in the 1990s, including the hit singles "False Preacher," "Look Good," and "Bad Inna Dancehall." The single "False Preacher" appeared on his 1991 Peter Pan label release of the same title, and "Look Good" was also the title track of his 1993 album on Metal Blade. With the release of *Look Good* (1993), Johnny P shot to the top of the dancehall ranks and charted both in Jamaica and the United States. Due to this success, he was offered a production deal with Relativity Records.

In 1998, Johnny P released another album, *The Next*. By this time his popularity had grown to the point that this album came out on the Virgin label imprint. Along the way, P's material also appeared on a wide variety of compilation recordings such as the 2004 Centron Music release *It's All about the Music*. On this release, Johnny P is featured with two singles. The first is "Pum Pum Cream" in the hard dancehall style and the softer and more soulful "Money and No Love." Also in 2004, Johnny P lent his voice to the Kung Fu Vampire release *Blood Bath Beyond*, as well as guest appearances with artists such as **Ninjaman**.

JOHNSON, ANTHONY (c. 1960–)

Born in Kingston, Jamaica, Johnson first appeared on the Jamaican popular music scene as part of the vocal trio Mystic Eyes. Mystic Eyes reached the height of their popularity with the single "Perilous Times," which was released in the United Kingdom by Greensleeves records in the later 1970s. Johnson then embarked on a solo career that teamed him with several of the most popular producers of the day, including **Jah Thomas**, Prince Jammy (later **King Jammy**), and **Linval Thompson**. Johnson's sound was bolstered by the **Roots Radics**, who were his usual backing band.

In 1982, Johnson released his debut album *Gunshot*, which was produced by Jah Thomas and released on Greensleeves. The song has enjoyed an extended life as the **dub** plate "Soundclash" found in the crates of all the good **sound systems**. Throughout the 1980s, Johnson continued to release popular material, such as the Jammy-produced single "A Yah We Deh," which resulted in an album of the same name. In 1982, Johnson released the album *Reggae Feelings*, which was followed in 1983 by the *I'm Ready* release. In 1984 Johnson brought out *We Want More Lovin.'*

In the late 1980s, Johnson moved to London and began teaming with producers such as Jah Warrior, Rootsman, and Mike Brooks. The London recordings included some new material, but more importantly, they included a series of reworkings of his biggest hits. Recently, Johnson continues to perform live throughout western Europe and maintains an active recording schedule.

JOHNSON, HARRY "HARRY J" (c. 1945–)

Johnson has been a Jamaican record producer and label head beginning in the mid-1960s. He got his start releasing records by the end of the decade and was integral to the evolution from **rock steady** to **reggae**. In fact, Johnson contended that he was the originator of the new reggae style of 1969. Johnson makes this claim based on the single "The Liquidator." On this Harry J All Stars tune, the **Winston Wright** organ line is syncopated, the guitar and the bass lines are percussive, and the horn parts punctuate the chord changes. The production of the first reggae style song remains under dispute; many believe that Johnson's song is still in the rock steady style and that **Clement "Coxsone" Dodd** actually began the style with the assistance of an echo pedal hooked up to the guitar. Regardless of this controversy, Johnson was still a key figure in the evolution of the style and released numerous reggae albums including material by **Dennis Brown**, **Burning Spear**, the **Heptones**, Leslie Butler, **I-Roy**, the **Melodians**, **Zap Pow**, and others. He went on to become one of the most important producers and studio heads of the reggae era.

Johnson stayed active and continued to release successful material through the 1970s, 1980s, and 1990s. Artists whom he worked with through this period included the **Abyssinians**, **Cedric Brooks**, **Cocoa Tea**, **Gregory Isaacs**, **Hugh Mundell**, and countless others who appeared on compilation recordings.

JOHNSON, LINTON KWESI "LKJ" (1952–)

Known as LKJ, Johnson was born in Clarendon, Jamaica. In 1963, his family relocated to London, and Johnson attended secondary school and university there. While still in school, Johnson became interested in the UK black radical movement. He also joined the Black Panthers and began to express his social, cultural, and political sentiments through poetry.

In the mid-1970s, Johnson worked with **Dennis Bovell** and the Dub Band, who supported Johnson's words with drumbeats. At this same time, Johnson's poetry was also being published. Early on, he was recognized as the first **dub poet**. Dub poetry is in the vein of the **DJ toasting** of artists such as **U-Roy**. However, the vocal delivery is quite different. As opposed to the fast, braggart-like delivery of the **DJ**, the dub poet's cadence is slow, stylized, and streetwise. His first collection was 1974's *Voices of the Living and the Dead.* His second collection, *Dread Beat an' Blood*, was published the following year. Next, Johnson joined Rasta Love, which was a group of like-minded poets and drummers, and with Bovell released a series of critically acclaimed recordings. Two early standout albums were *Forces of Victory* (1979) and *Bass Culture* (1980). Johnson also published one of his many books of poetry, *Inglan Is a Bitch*, in 1980.

Throughout the early 1980s, Johnson remained active as a dub poet and released seven albums, including several live ones. He launched his own record label in 1981, using his LKJ imprint to release dub poetry of his own, as well as that of others such as Michael Smith and Jean Binta Breeze. In the latter half of the 1980s, Johnson produced a ten-part radio show titled *From Mento to Lovers Rock* and worked for UK television Channel 4. In 1991, he released his *Tings an' Times* album along with a collection of selected poems. Johnson followed this in 1996 with the album *LKJ Presents*, which features the dub poetry of various authors including Johnson himself. Throughout the 1990s, Johnson remained productive, and his work garnered a series of awards. In addition, Johnson toured around the world, and his poetry has been translated into a variety of languages.

JOHNSON, MICHAEL ALEXANDER. *See* DADDY SCREW

JOHNSON, ROYDEL "CONGO ASHANTI ROY" (1947–)

Born in Hanover, Jamaica, in 1977, Johnson helped form the vocal duo the **Congos** with **Cedric Myton**. Johnson got his start in the Jamaican popular music scene working with **Ras Michael** and the **Sons of Negus** and had attended school with the producer **Lee Perry**. Johnson and Myton's group, the Congos, rose to prominence at the end of the **reggae** era; their most important album, *Heart of the Congos*, has been held in the same regard as seminal recordings by **Bob Marley and the Wailers**, **Burning Spear**, and the **Mighty Diamonds**. The album was produced in 1977 by **Lee "Scratch" Perry** for his **Black Ark Studios** in Kingston, Jamaica. The album includes the singles "Fisherman," "Congoman," and "La Bam-Bam"; it utilized the talents of legendary instrumentalists such as **Sly Dunbar**, **Ernest Ranglin**, and **Uziah "Sticky" Thompson**.

Shortly after the *Heart of the Congos* album was released, Johnson and Myton split to pursue solo projects. In the wake of the breakup, Johnson began calling himself Congo Ashanti Roy and worked with legendary UK producer **Adrian Sherwood** on several of his projects.

In the new millennium, Congo Ashanti Roy has appeared on several new projects. One such album was the *Slackers and Friends* release of 2002. Also on this album are several other reggae luminaries including **Glen Adams**, **Cornell Campbell**, Doreen Shaffer, Ari-Up, Ranking Joe, and others. Projects such as these have kept Roy active on the international stage in the wake of the Congos.

JONES, SANDRA "PUMA" (1953–1990)

Born in the United States, Jones earned her master's degree in social work from prestigious Columbia University. She then traveled to Jamaica to work in her field in underprivileged areas of Kingston. While there, Jones was overheard singing in her apartment by a group of aspiring **reggae** musicians who asked her to join with them to form a group. The group that formed was **Black Uhuru** (*uhuru* is Swahili for "freedom"). Jones assumed the name Puma and began working as a backup singer for the band. With Puma Jones in their ranks, Black Uhuru went on to be the first reggae band to win a Grammy Award. By 1986, Jones's health had begun to fail and she left the band. On January 28, 1990, she died from cancer.

JONES, VIVIAN (1957–)

Born in Trewlaney, Jamaica, Vivian Jones's family relocated to England when he was ten. At twenty-one, Jones joined the group the Spartans and began to hone his songwriting skills. He then passed through a series of bands on his way to a solo career by 1980. In that same year he released the chart-topping single "Good Morning." In the wake of this success, Jones formed a backing band called the Pieces but was discouraged by the contemporary practice of withholding artists' royalty checks. As a result, Jones returned to Jamaica where he worked with **sound system** legend **Jah Shaka**.

In 1988, Jones again scored a number one hit with the single "Sugar Love." The single was followed by a series of successful releases that found Jones in the charts for extended periods of time throughout the late 1980s. Jones again returned to the United Kingdom for a period but was back in Jamaica by 1993 for more recording sessions. In 1993, he teamed with producers **Bobby "Digital" Dixon** and **Junior Reid**. He again crossed the Atlantic to record the singles "Ethiopian Eyes" and "African Love." Next, Jones turned his attention to recording the *Love Is for Lovers* album, which was released in 1994. The album was a success and solidified Jones's position as a serious **reggae** artist.

The following year, Jones released a duet with Sylia Tella on his own Imperial House label, as well as a series of other singles on a variety of labels. The following year, Jones and his Imperial House backing band released a four-song EP that mixed roots reggae, rude boy, and love song styles. In 1997, Jones released the single "Moments of Magic" and scored another chart success.

In the new millennium, Jones continues to write, record, and produce. He pursues crossover appeal, having conquered the Jamaican and UK markets. A collection of his greatest hits is now available as part of the Reggae Max series.

JOSEY WALES. *See* WALES, JOSEY

JUDGE DREAD (1945–1998)

Born Alex Hughes in Kent, England, this artist worked in a series of clubs in the late 1960s and learned about music while on the job. Hughes entered the UK music scene around 1970 when he took the name Judge Dread from a **Prince Buster** character and recorded the single "Big Six" in the **DJ** style. The single went to the charts, where it resided for almost six months. It was, however, not radio friendly due to its ribald lyrics, sung over a nursery rhyme tune. Dread followed this single with "Big Seven" and "Big Eight," which were two more novelty tracks in the **reggae** style. The Judge then released his debut album *Dreadmania* (1973). The album did not do well, but subsequent singles continued to keep Dread on the charts.

In the midst of his success from salacious lyrics, Dread attempted to release legitimate material under the names DJ Alex and Jason Sinclair, but all of his material was banned by radio regardless of the name under which it was recorded. In 1974, Dread

released his second album, *Working Class 'Ero*, but the album's lack of popularity signaled the end of Dread's run. His next two singles were also disappointing. Dread
regained some currency with his "Big Ten" single and the album *Bedtime Stories*
(1975). Dread released another album the following year titled *Last of the Skinheads*,
which was his statement on the change in UK taste from reggae to punk music.
Throughout the rest of the 1970s, Dread flirted with the charts but did not regain his
early acclaim.

By 1980 his run of great success was over. Dread continued to perform live in small
venues for stalwart fans through the 1980s and into the 1990s. On March 15, 1998, as
Judge Dread walked off stage from an evening's performance, he suffered a fatal heart
attack and was pronounced dead upon his arrival at the hospital.

JUNIOR BYLES. *See* **BYLES, KERRIE**

K

KAY, JANET (1958–)

Born Janet Kay Bogle in London, England, of Jamaican parents, she originally pursued training and work in secretarial studies; however, she was drawn into the recording industry by the members of **Aswad**, who recommended her to **Alton Ellis**. With Ellis as producer, Kay sang on the single "Loving You," which was a cover version of the Minnie Riperton original and went to the top of the charts, launching her career as a **lovers rock** vocalist. Kay went on to release a series of singles including "I Do Love You" and "That's What Friends Are For." In 1979, she released her debut album, *Capricorn Woman*, on the Solid Groove imprint. Her **Dennis Bovell**-produced single "Silly Games" was her most successful release and resulted in her second album of the same title in 1980. The single came out on the

Janet Kay. © *UrbanImage.tv.*

Arawak imprint in 1979 and brought her to the height of her popularity.

In the 1980s and 1990s, Kay has continued work in the lovers rock style. Additionally, she became part of the Black Theatre Cooperative (now called Nitro) and has had several acting roles on television, most notably on the show *No Problem*, for Channel 4. Kay has continued to record and release material including subsequent albums such as *Loving You* (1988), *Sweet Surrender* (1989), and *Dub Dem Silly* (1994). Kay also performed on the **Reggae Sunsplash** concert during the 1993 tour.

More recently, Kay released the 1996 album *In Paradise* with the production crew of Tony Gad and **Angus "Drummie Zeb" Gaye** of Aswad fame. This was followed by the 1998 album *Making History*. In the new millennium, Kay continues to be popular in the United Kingdom, and even more so in Japan, and she has launched the successful series Queens of Lovers Rock. The Queens show is produced by Write Thing Limited and Tee Productions and features Kay and Carroll Thompson and others. Additionally, throughout her career, Kay intermittently lent her voice to Aswad as a background vocalist for several of their releases.

KEITH AND ENID

Keith Stewart and Enid Cumberland formed a vocal duo in 1960 and released a series of influential **ska** singles in the early part of the decade. In 1961, they released several successful singles on the Starlite imprint, including "It's Only a Pity," "Never Leave My Throne," "What Have I Done," and "Your Gonna Break My Heart." These were followed by "Worried over You" and "When It Is Spring," which were also popular. By the mid-1960s, the pair had moved out of approximating the U.S. rhythm and blues style and into the new Jamaican **ska** style.

In 1965, Cumberland and Stewart split and Stewart was replaced by Roy Richards. With Richards, Cumberland again had success working for **Clement "Coxsone" Dodd** at his **Studio One** facilities. Several of Keith and Enid's and Cumberland and Richards's singles remain popular through appearances on compilation albums.

KELLY, DAVID "RUDE BOY" (c. 1960–)

Kelly began working in the music business in the late 1980s and quickly became renowned as a multi-instrumentalist, engineer, and producer. His early work included engineering sessions for the likes of **Chaka Demus and Pliers**, **Marcia Griffiths**, Little Kirk, **Little Lenny**, **Steely and Clevie**, Rula Brown, and others. In addition to his engineering work, Kelly often performed on one or more instruments for the sessions. He played drums, keyboards, and bass, and provided backing vocals on many recordings.

In the 1990s, Kelly gradually became one of the most sought-after **dancehall** producers. During the decade he worked with various artists including **Buju Banton**, **Beenie Man**, **Bounty Killer**, **Elephant Man**, **General Degree**, **General Trees**, **Lady Saw**, **Tony Rebel**, **Sanchez**, **Shaggy**, **Shinehead**, **Spragga Benz**, **Terror Fabulous**, and Vicious. At the same time, he continued producing material for honored members of the roots reggae elite such as **Beres Hammond** and Marcia Griffiths. Also in the 1990s, Kelly began working as a hip hop producer running sessions for En Vogue, Foxy Brown, and DJ Hardware.

Notably, it was during this decade that many of the **dancehall DJs** were crossing over into the American hip hop mainstream. Kelly assisted in this crossover, producing for Beenie Man, Elephant Man, Shaggy, and Bounty Killer. Along with all of his named artist production efforts, Kelly has produced a long list of compilation albums for various labels.

In the new millennium, Kelly's reputation as an innovative producer has continued to grow. He is now universally regarded as a trendsetter who has influenced the production work of hip hop stalwarts such as Timbaland and Swizz Beats. Through Kelly's continued production work, he is bringing dancehall further into the mainstream and keeping it a vital style of Jamaican popular music almost twenty years after its creation.

KELLY, PAT (1949–)

Born in Kingston, Jamaica, Pat Kelly got his start in the popular music business in the mid-1960s. In 1967, he replaced **Slim Smith** as the lead singer of the **Techniques**. Kelly, whose voice sounded much like Curtis Mayfield's, was a good match for the Techniques as they had their greatest successes covering American rhythm and blues standards by acts such as the Impressions.

Although the Techniques had a series of hits in their catalog, Kelly left the group in 1968 to pursue a solo career. His debut single was a **rock steady** version of Curtis Mayfield's "Little Boy Blue," produced by **Bunny "Striker" Lee**. For Lee, Kelly released a series of Mayfield songs on which he was backed by the band the **Uniques** or Bobby Aitkin and the Carib-Beats. This collective released versions of "Daddy's Home," "You Are Not Mine," and several other Mayfield tunes (often crediting them to Kelly rather than Mayfield). Kelly then returned to the Techniques for several new singles that continued the use of their original formula of making rock steady versions of rhythm and blues standards.

At the end of the 1960s, he again left the group, adopted the new **reggae** style, and released material for both Bunny Lee and **Lee "Scratch" Perry**. At this time, Kelly's popularity was on the rise and he was selling records in the Caribbean and the United Kingdom. He made a trip to London in the late 1960s; the trip resulted in a record deal with **Pama Records**. The result of this union was the release of his debut album *Pat Kelly Sings* (1969). Subsequent singles were released on Pama subsidiary Gas Records and Kelly continued to make versions of U.S. standards. Kelly went on to release *Talk about Love* (1975), *Lonely Man* (1978), *One Man Stands* (1979), and *Wish It Would Be Rain* (1980). Kelly continued to record and release music until the mid-1980s, when he took a job as a recording engineer for **Channel One Studios**.

KELSO, BEVERLY (1945–)

Beverly Kelso is one of the two surviving members of the original **Wailers** group. The group was formed by sixteen-year-old **Bob Marley** in 1962 and included **Marley**, **Peter Tosh**, **Bunny Wailer**, Junior Braithwaite, and Kelso; Cherry Smith made occasional contributions. The only members still alive are Wailer and Kelso. Kelso's job was to provide high harmony to round out the men's vocals. In 1963, the Wailers won the approval of **Clement "Coxsone" Dodd** and recorded their first hit single, "Simmer Down." The following year, the Wailers, with the backing of the **Skatalites**, recorded a series of singles including "Maga Dog," "Amen," "Habits," and "Wings of a Dove."

At the end of 1964, Braithwaite left the group and moved to the United States. In 1965, Kelso quit the Wailers due to Marley's constant criticism for imperfect singing in rehearsals, and the Wailers' core of Marley, Tosh, and Wailer was established. Although Kelso left the group, her voice still appeared on a wide variety of compilation recordings from the group's early period.

KERR, JUNIOR MARVIN (c. 1950–)

Junior Marvin was born Donald Hanson Marvin Kerr Richards Junior in Kingston, Jamaica. His family relocated to England, and he began working in the music business as a guitarist in the late 1960s. His first band was called the Blue Ace Unit, which he soon left; he subsequently moved through several other groups. He settled in the Keef Hartley Band in the 1970s and was at that time calling himself Junior Kerr. For Hartley, Marvin played lead guitar and sang on several albums.

In 1971, Hartley broke up the band so he could join John Mayall's group, and Marvin moved on to the band Salt and Pepper. In 1973, Marvin (under the name Junior Hanson) started his own band, Hanson. The group released one album, titled *Now Hear This*, before going through a significant lineup change. The year 1974 was spent touring and releasing a second album.

In 1977, Marvin joined **Bob Marley and the Wailers** as lead guitarist under the name Junior Marvin. He played lead guitar for Marley from 1977 to 1981 when Bob died of cancer. However, prior to his death, Marley asked Marvin to keep the band together and continue recording. Marvin had been a part of the Wailers' two-guitar lineup, along with **Al Anderson**, through the band's most powerful recordings, including

Survival and *Uprising*. Marvin managed to keep the band operative for a time, with the lineup being himself on guitar and vocals, Andrew McIntyre on guitar, **Aston "Family Man" Barrett** on bass, **Irvine "Carrot" Jarrett** on percussion, **Earl "Wya" Lindo** on keyboards, and Michael "Boo" Richards on drums. Together the Wailers released the 1989 album *ID*, followed in 1991 by *Mystic Warriors*.

The year 1994 brought the *Jah Message* release, which was produced by Marvin and Barrett. In 1997, the group released a live album on the Melting Pot label titled *My Friends*. Marvin was successful in his efforts to hold the Wailers together until 1997, when he left the group to pursue his own projects. Of particular difficulty during this period was the Wailers' lack of a record contract, having split with **Chris Blackwell**. Marvin next surfaced as the leader of the Brazilian band Junior Marvin and Batuka; the band has released at least one album. Without Marvin, the Wailers continued on, releasing an album in 1998 with Don Elan as the singer, covering many classic early hits.

The year 2000 brought another live album with Barrett as the producer and Gary "Nesta" Pine as the singer. In April 2003, the Wailers' *Live* album was released by Image Entertainment and was produced by Famsmuzik. More recently, Marvin has been trying to launch a Wailers spinoff band, which includes original member **Alvin "Seeco" Patterson** on percussion and Earl Fitzsimmons on keyboards.

KHOURI, KEN (1917–2003)

Born Kenneth Lloyd Khouri in St. Catherine, Khouri was responsible for opening the first record studio on the island of Jamaica. His facility, **Federal Records**, opened in 1954 and located itself at 220 Marcus Garvey Drive (the facility now houses **Tuff Gong International**). In addition to opening the first studio on the island, Khouri also opened a record-pressing plant at 129 King Street in the mid-1950s. Because Khouri's studio was the first, it was used by all of the early recording artists and producers. **Clement "Coxsone" Dodd** used the facility before opening his own studio.

Early recordings by Khouri included several of Jamaica's first **mento** and calypso recordings by important acts such as Lord Flea and Lord Fly. Khouri was universally recognized as the founder of the Jamaican popular music scene. He received many honors, including several from the Institute for Jamaica, and was respected by artists and producers throughout his career. In the early 1980s, Khouri retired and spent the rest of his life outside the music business after a thirty-year career.

KING JAMMY (c. 1960–)

King Jammy (formerly Prince Jammy) was born Lloyd James in Kingston, Jamaica, and rose to prominence in the Jamaican popular music scene in the 1980s when he helped to pioneer the birth of the **ragga** style, or digital reggae music. The digital style involves use of computer-generated beats and bass lines instead of acoustic instruments and live performers to support the vocals. With Jammy's progressive approach, he formed the bridge between the roots reggae of the 1970s and the frantic **dancehall** rhythms of the late 1980s. He got his start working with the **sound systems** for which he built amplifiers and repaired damaged equipment.

Once Jammy learned the workings of the sound systems, he launched his own, called Super Power, using equipment that he had built himself. At this time, Jammy formed a relationship of mutual respect with the legendary **King Tubby**; together the two producers worked to push change in the **reggae** style. Jammy left Jamaica for Canada in the early 1970s and upon arrival was greeted with an enthusiastic reception

King Jammy. © *UrbanImage.tv.*

at live shows. He performed live and worked at several studios; however, he soon returned to Jamaica and opened a studio. At this time, Tubby's lead engineer departed for New York, and Jammy stepped in to fill his spot. Together, Jammy and Tubby worked in the studio with producers such as **Bunny "Striker" Lee** and **Yabby You**. They expanded their studio and by the end of the 1970s had begun producing music themselves, working on **Black Uhuru's** debut release.

It was also at this time that the pair was increasingly surrounded by **dancehall** artists such as **Half Pint**, **Echo Minott**, and others. Jammy's biggest break came in 1985 when he recorded the young singer **Wayne Smith** for the single "Under Me Sleng Teng." The beat for the song, generated by a Casio "Music Box" keyboard, was then slowed down by Jammy in the studio. The result was the first digitally backed example of Jamaican popular music. With the popularity of the single, many producers shifted to using digital beats instead of live musicians.

Jammy remained on the top for the rest of the 1980s and throughout the 1990s. He hired **Bobby "Digital" Dixon** to work as his producer along with the rhythm section **Steely and Clevie**. With these personnel in place, Jammy's setup rivaled any in Jamaica. He had the best of the young talent clamoring to record in his studio and the veterans coming around to see how Jammy could revamp their sounds.

KING SOUNDS (c. 1945–)

Born in St. Elizabeth, Jamaica, King Sounds entered the popular music scene by dancing at **ska** concerts and talent shows. In 1974, he moved to the United Kingdom and landed a job as the emcee of a show with the help of his friend **Alton Ellis**. He displayed an ease at running the crowd, and this led to further work warming up audiences before the headlining bands took the stage. His debut recording came in 1975 with the single "Rock and Roll Lullaby." The song was a modest success and spurred Sounds on to form the Grove Music collective with **Michael Campbell**. Together the pair emceed shows for **Aswad**, **Delroy Washington**, and others. They went on to produce songs with **Yabby You** under the name the Prophets. Sounds often opened for Aswad live; his reputation and number of appearances increased through the late 1970s and through the 1980s.

His debut album, *Come Zion Side*, was released in 1979 on his own Grove imprint. His second album was released on **Island Records** in 1981 and was titled *Forward to Africa*. This record was successful in the United Kingdom and features the singles "Batman" and "Patches." With this newfound popularity, Sounds appeared on the British installment of the **Reggae Sunsplash** tour. Next, Sounds launched another label called King and I. On this new imprint he released his next four albums *Moving Forward*, *There Is a Reward*, *Strength to Strength*, and *I Shall Sing*. This output spanned into the early 1990s and assured his place as a UK **reggae** legend. Through the latter half of the 1990s, Sounds continued to tour, taking advantage of the success he had enjoyed in the 1980s.

KING STITT (1940–)

Born Winston Cooper, Stitt was nicknamed the Ugly because his facial features were disfigured. He called himself the Ugly after the American western film *The Good, the Bad, and the Ugly*. Stitt entered the music business as a **DJ** for **Clement "Coxsone" Dodd's sound system** in 1956. He became popular among **dancehall** revelers for his shouted style that ratcheted up the atmosphere of the dance. He was the third of Dodd's big three DJs along with **Count Matchuki** and Red Hopeton. His early DJing was of American rhythm and blues material—especially the jump band sound of Louis Jordan—and he made the transition smoothly into the **ska** era.

At the height of his DJ popularity, Stitt even relegated legendary DJ **U-Roy** to the number two position. He soon caught the attention of producer **Clancy Eccles**, with whom he went into the studio. Together the pair recorded tracks such as "The Ugly One," "Fire Corner," and "Dance Beat." Eccles collected these singles on the album *Reggae Fire Beat*. To back up Stitt, Eccles used the **Dynamites**, who contained **Winston Wright** and **Hux Brown**. He also released a single titled "Van Cleef," which was named for Lee Van Cleef, the actor who played the part of the "ugly" in the western film from which Stitt took his nickname. In the mid-1990s, **Studio One** released *Dancehall '63*, which was essentially a live album of Stitt **toasting** over tracks from **Roland Alphonso**, **Donald Drummond**, **Joe Higgs**, the **Maytals**, and others. King Stitt remains a Jamaican DJ and dancehall legend.

KING TUBBY (1941–1989)

Born Osbourne Ruddock in Kingston, Jamaica, Tubby rose to the pinnacle of success as a producer and label owner. In the mid-1960s, Tubby studied electronics and began building speaker boxes and amplifiers. By the late 1960s, he had constructed one of the largest **sound systems** on the island, called Home Town Hi Fi. Rivalry between the sounds was vicious, and Tubby rose to each occasion with a series of the hottest **DJs** on the island, including **U-Roy**. Part of the game of staying on top in the sound systems was to have access to the newest and most popular songs.

In the early 1970s, Tubby realized the most effective way to get access to this music was to record it himself. To that end, he bought a two-track recorder and began making homemade mixes of new songs. For this purpose he hired producers **Bunny "Striker" Lee** and **Lee "Scratch" Perry** to work on the new mixes. He also worked with producers such as **Augustus Pablo**, **Winston Riley**, **Jah Thomas**, and others. Through his association with Bunny Lee, he made an inroad at **Byron Lee's Dynamic** studios. There Tubby purchased a four-track mixer, which he used to enhance the quality of his recordings. With his new cache of equipment and his electronics background, Tubby constructed a means by which he could cut two songs together and add effects without the problem of "punched in" or overdubbing sounds.

In 1974, Tubby was hard at work developing the new **dub** style, and Bunny Lee was feeding him new rhythms to work with. The setup was an enormous success and resulted in numerous "dub version" hits for the likes of **Cornell Campbell** and **Johnny Clarke**. The premise of dub was to take an existing song (often with the original lyrics removed) and create new material from it through the use of added effects. Tubby was a master with echo and reverb effects, and he was able to electronically create sounds like thunder, sirens, and gunshots. Dub style took off almost immediately, and the dub plates were used in the **dancehalls** and on the sound systems for the DJs to **toast** over.

As the demand for dub increased, Tubby trained new producers to work with the style, including Prince Philip Smart and **Prince (King) Jammy**. In the late 1970s, Tubby took in another new producer who proved to be of the highest quality: **Hopeton "Scientist" Brown**. In 1985, Tubby opened a new studio and was poised again to hit the Jamaican popular music scene with the backing of his studio band the **Firehouse Crew**. However, in 1989 he was gunned down in front of his house, and his creative output was silenced. Over the course of his expansive career, Tubby worked with a variety of performers such as **Alpha and Omega**, **Michael Campbell**, **Chaka Demus and Pliers**, **Earl Sixteen**, **Prince Far I**, **Ranking Dread**, **Red Dragon**, and many others.

KINGSTONIANS, THE

The Kingstonians formed in 1966 and included Jackie Bernard, his brother Footy, and Lloyd Kerr. They went into the studio with producer J. J. Johnson, with little success. In the late 1960s, the group stood at the end of the **rock steady** style just before the transition to **reggae** and achieved the height of their popularity with material produced by **Derrick Harriott**. The results were the singles "Sufferer" and "Winey Winey," which climbed the Jamaican charts. These singles and other original material were compiled into the group's 1970s debut album *Sufferer.* The group did not outlast the transition of styles and broke up after working with a couple of other producers. Material by the Kingstonians has appeared on several compilation albums from the late 1980s to the present. Examples of such releases include *Tighten Up, Vol. 1-2* and *Vol. 3-4*, *Reggae's Greatest Hits, Vol. 5*, and others.

KINSEY, DONALD (1953–)

Before Kinsey was born in Gary, Indiana, into a musically talented family, his father, Lester "Big Daddy" Kinsey, was an internationally renowned blues guitarist and harmonica player in the style of Muddy Waters. Big Daddy had three sons: Donald, Ralph, and Kenneth; once the boys were skilled enough to become their father's sidemen, Big Daddy Kinsey and His Fabulous Sons was formed. Donald began playing guitar at age five, Kenneth played bass, and Ralph was the drummer for this delta blues-style collective.

In 1972, the group disbanded when Ralph joined the U.S. Air Force and Donald joined Albert King's band as the rhythm guitarist. He appeared on two King albums before forming a new band in 1975 with his brother Ralph (back from the service), Felix Pappalardi, and Busta "Cherry" Jones. The band was called White Lightning, and it played in the heavy metal style. They toured with major acts such as Aerosmith, Yes, Jethro Tull, and others. During this time, Donald met **Bob Marley** and **Peter Tosh** while the three were in New York. Tosh brought Kinsey into the studio and liked what he heard. As a result, Kinsey appeared on Tosh's *Legalize It* (1976) album and subsequent tour.

The following year, Marley enlisted Kinsey for the *Rastaman Vibration* (1976) sessions. After releasing the album, the band embarked on the tour that was documented on the *Babylon by Bus* (1978) live album. Kinsey's association with Marley led to his life being endangered when in 1976 several would-be assassins burst into Marley's Hope Road kitchen. Marley, Don Taylor, and Kinsey were all shot in the ensuing melee, and though they all survived, Kinsey left the group and returned to the United States. Kinsey briefly returned to work with Tosh and appeared on his *Bush Doctor* (1978) album. He played on several dates of the following tour, during which Tosh was opening for the Rolling Stones. In California, Kinsey left the tour and went back to work with his brother. Through several different bands, Donald Kinsey continued to play with his brothers and together they have been working in the contemporary blues style since.

KONG, LESLIE (1933–1971)

Born of Chinese/Jamaican descent in Kinston, Jamaica, Kong entered the Jamaican music business with his three brothers as the owners/operators of **Beverley's** record shop. In 1961, Kong noticed a young **Jimmy Cliff** singing outside his store, and the two struck a deal whereby Kong recorded Cliff singing the single "Dearest Beverley." This move launched Kong's production career and Cliff's career as a recording artist. This made Kong one of the earliest producers on the island and a major figure in Jamaica's fledgling music business. The following year, Kong recorded **Bob Marley** on the singles "Judge Not" and "One Cup of Coffee." Kong was a savvy businessman who quickly entered into a partnership with the UK-based **Island Records** imprint for the European distribution of his label's material.

Throughout the 1960s, Kong produced music for a series of **rock steady** and **reggae** luminaries including Cliff, Marley, **Stranger Cole**, **Desmond Dekker**, **John Holt**, the **Maytals**, **Derrick Morgan**, and many others. In 1967, Dekker had an international hit with "007" with Kong at the controls. Marley returned to Beverley's studio in the late 1960s, accompanied by the **Wailers**, and cut another series of sides. Kong had cultivated a reputation for being a ruthless businessman through the course of his career, attested to by his release of 1970's *The Best of Bob Marley and the Wailers*, over the furious outcry of the group. The group was understandably upset, as the release was a collection of subpar singles made by a young band and was released without their permission. Bunny Wailer protested, and he and Kong had an altercation during which it was pointed out that this material could not be the best of the Wailers as their best was yet to come.

Regardless of the conniving, by the end of the decade Kong had a large stable of recording artists and was considered among the three most important producers on the island. Additionally, he had already banked a considerable income from his relatively brief career in the industry. This all came to an end in August 1971 when Kong suffered a fatal heart attack and died at thirty-eight.

KOOL DJ HERC (1955–)

Born Clive Campbell in Kingston, Jamaica, Campbell spent his first twelve years living in Jamaica during the heyday of **ska**, the dawning of **reggae**, and the first mobile sound systems. In 1967, he moved to the Bronx, New York, and began carving out his musical legacy. He earned his nickname Hercules by his weight-lifting achievements while still in high school. He is widely revered as the first hip hop **DJ**; it is through him that the progression from Jamaican **toasting** to rap and hip hop can be traced. By

1969, Herc was DJing New York block parties using the **sound system** techniques that he had learned as a Jamaican youth. He was notorious for having a massive sound system that compelled people to dance. Next, he took the Jamaican idea of toasting a step further. Instead of playing an entire single (without the words) and improvising new words over it, he began crafting new material from existing rhythms and the most danceable sections of records. These sections were called breaks, and combining a series of them into a song resulted in creating new break beats, the essence of hip hop. This idea caught on immediately and influenced other early figures in American hip hop, such as Grandmaster Flash and Afrika Bambaataa.

While Herc was a strong DJ, he was not a master at vocal presentation. For this he employed a young emcee called Coke La Rock. While Herc is credited with creating the catalyst for hip hop, he eventually drifted away from the scene as the result of being stabbed at one of his own parties. More recently, Herc has re-emerged as a part of the hip hop community. He is respected by all as the elder statesman of hip hop.

KUMINA

The Pocamania religion came to Jamaica from Ghana on the slave ships of the colonial era. The musical element of this religion was called kumina, and it was practiced by the **Burru** people. The kumina drumming style existed in Jamaica for many years in the rural parishes, such as Clarendon. However, with mid-twentieth-century urban migration, kumina moved to Kingston. In the kumina drumming style, there are only two drums, unlike the three in the Burru tradition. The drums are called the kbandu and the cast, and each has a single membrane and large body. The kbandu is larger than the cast and serves as the lifeline or rhythmic basis. The open end of the kbandu could also be played by another performer using sticks. The cast is the smaller of the two drums and presents syncopated rhythms over the foundational line of the kbandu. In the 1950s, the **Rastafarians** adopted elements of kumina drumming while they lived at their enclave, Pinnacle. In the rhythms of Rasta drumming, one can hear aspects of both the kumina and the burru drumming traditions.

L

LADY G (1974–)

Born Janice Fyffe in Kingston, Jamaica, Lady G was one of the few female **DJs** active on the 1990s **dancehall** scene. She began her career working for the **Black Scorpio sound system** in the mid-1980s and soon made a name for herself as the leader of the dances. In 1988, she went into the studio with **Gussie Clarke** and cut the single "Nuff Respect," which was a success and contained lyrics that empowered women in the male-dominated dancehall world. This was followed by the **Papa San** duets "Round Table Talk," "Man Have a Right," and several other popular songs.

In the early 1990s, Lady G went on hiatus to raise her children, but in 1994 she returned to the stage. The mid-1990s found her working with **Chevelle Franklin** on several recordings including the hit song "Thank You." The following year, Lady G released her debut album *God Daughter* with the production assistance of **Philip "Fatis" Burrell**. On this album, the singer exhibited several styles of Jamaican popular music including roots, **lovers rock**, and dancehall. Along the way, she has worked with several important artists such as **Barrington Levy**, **Luciano**, and **Shabba Ranks**.

Recently, Lady G has taken to the studio as both a DJ and a producer. In 2004, VP records released *Riddim Driven Flava*, which she produced. Her song "Enough" also appears on the album next to work by **Capleton**, **Sizzla**, **Spragga Benz**, and many others.

LADY SAW (1972–)

Lady Saw was born Marion Hall in St. Mary's, Jamaica. In her relatively brief career, she has become universally recognized as the "First Lady of **Dancehall**" by other artists and fans alike. She gained entrance into the Jamaican popular music scene by working for several regional **sound systems**. Saw burst onto the Jamaican popular music scene in 1994 with the release of *Lover Girl*. This early album came out on the VP imprint, and Saw has remained loyal to this label for all of her releases.

The dancehall scene in the 1990s was dominated by men, and Saw had to show she was capable of competing with them. She achieved this with her

Lady Saw. © *UrbanImage.tv.*

Shabba Ranks duet "Want It Tonight." Her second album was *Give Me the Reason* (1996). The following year Saw released her third album, *Passion*, which featured cameos from **Beenie Man** and **Shaggy**. With this work, whose lyrics invariably contain sexually explicit material, Lady Saw established herself as the leading female slack DJ.

Throughout the early 1990s, her reputation as a dancehall DJ of the highest order continued to grow. In 1998, she released *99 Ways*, which was followed by a set of *Best of* releases. In 2004, Lady Saw stormed back onto the dancehall scene with her September release *Striptease*. With this album, she put herself in a position to be compared with the first ladies of contemporary hip hop, such as Missy Elliott, Lil' Kim, and Foxy Brown. In addition to promoting her recent release, Lady Saw is also trying her hand at production and has created a series of popular beats.

LADY SHABBA (c. 1975–)

Born Sharon Peterkin in Kingston, Jamaica, Lady Shabba sang as a youth for a series of producers including **Prince Jammy**, **Sly and Robbie**, and **Steely and Clevie**. These early works yielded a degree of success with the release of singles such as "Ram Ram" and "Stick to Yuh Man." This work appeared in the early to mid-1990s, but by the end of the decade Lady Shabba was appearing less frequently. However, in 2000 she re-emerged under the new name Ruffi-Ann. Along with the name change, Ruffi-Ann also diversified her musical offerings by moving into the production arena and opening her own label called Sugar Pan Production. On this new imprint, she has released two singles of her own music, "You Are" and "Sex, Sex, Sex."

In 2004, Ruffi-Ann continued to release new material with singles such as "Mi Put-tus." With the new name and the renewed desire to succeed, Ruffi-Ann remains a force in Jamaican popular music. Additionally, much of Lady Shabba's early work is appearing on compilation releases such as *Buyaka: The Ultimate Dancehall Collection*.

LAING, CLEVELAND. *See* LIEUTENANT STITCHIE

LAMONT, ERIC. *See* BINGY BUNNY

LAWES, HENRY "JUNJO" (c. 1920–1999)

Born in the late 1940s in the ghetto of west Kingston, Jamaica, Lawes began his career in the music business as a singer, but soon turned to production. As a producer, Lawes had early success working with a young **Barrington Levy** on his debut singles and first album *Bounty Hunter*. It was at this early stage that Lawes cast the mold for his success. He employed the **Roots Radics** as his backing band and later used them in virtually all of his early sessions. He also enlisted the engineering assistance of a very young **Scientist** for the session. He used the **Hookim**-owned **Channel One Studios**, as he did not have his own, and released material on his fledgling Volcano imprint. Lawes made these early Levy recordings at the end of the 1970s.

By the end of the decade, Lawes was already regarded as one of the top producers on the island and was credited with launching the **dancehall** style in 1979. He had a series of hits in the early 1980s with artists such as Levy, **Clint Eastwood**, **Eek-A-Mouse**, **Michigan and Smiley**, **Hugh Mundell**, and **Yellowman**. At this time, Lawes also worked with veterans such as **Johnny Osbourne** and **Tony Tuff**. Additionally, he did production for up-and-coming dancehall **DJs** like **Frankie Paul**. Although Lawes was successful with a wide variety of artists throughout this period, one of his greatest triumphs was his work with the **Wailing Souls**. With Lawes, the Souls

Henry "Junjo" Lawes. © *UrbanImage.tv.*

released much of their highest-quality material, such as their album *Fire House Rock* (1980). The cultural and roots concerns of the group were counter to Lawes's dancehall aspirations; however, the Wailing Souls experienced their greatest success with Lawes.

Through the late 1980s, Lawes's stable of talent increased exponentially. During this period, he worked with **Black Uhuru, Ken Boothe, Alton Ellis, John Holt, Nicodemus, Augustus Pablo, Ranking Toyan, Josey Wales,** and many others. It was also at this time that he began using the skills of a different studio band, the High Times Band featuring **Earl "Chinna" Smith.** By 1985, Lawes had proven he was a master of the dancehall sound while remaining a respected roots producer. In that year, he left Jamaica and relocated to New York. While in the United States, Lawes was incarcerated and spent much of the late 1980s in jail. As a result, he missed the dawning of the **ragga** or digital reggae style of the decade's second half.

In the early 1990s, Lawes re-emerged as a force in Jamaican popular music with new material from **Cocoa Tea,** Yellowman, and Josey Wales. Lawes reestablished a strong reputation, but it was never as good as it had been in the early 1980s. In June 1999, Henry "Junjo" Lawes was fatally shot in Harlesden, London.

LEE, BYRON (1935–)

Born in Jamaica, Lee emerged in 1956 as a singer with the backing band the Dragonaires. The group opened for U.S. headlining acts when they toured through Jamaica. The group's first exposure came from the James Bond film *Dr. No,* in which they appeared as the house band at a club. As a result, the band's music was featured on the sound track. The Dragonaires were a loose collection of fourteen instrumentalists with a revolving door of members. With Lee at the helm, they are credited as one of the island's first **ska** bands.

Lee and the Dragonaires toured the Western Hemisphere in the late 1960s to popularize the ska sound and released a series of successful recordings. As their popularity grew, he bought his own studio and went into the production business under the **Dynamic Studio** imprint. By this time, Lee was considered by many to be the most well-known Jamaican musical product around the world. As the 1960s wore on, Lee changed his style to conform to the current sounds. In the mid-1960s he moved from ska to **rock steady,** and by the early 1970s he had adopted the **reggae** sound. All the while, he was releasing much of the best Jamaican popular music through his Dynamic studio. The studio was also host to several popular rock and roll acts: the Rolling Stones, Paul Simon, and Eric Clapton recorded there.

In the 1980s and 1990s, Lee and the Dragonaires changed styles again and this time settled on the soca sound. In the past twenty-five years, they have released a significant series of soca albums that have kept the group active and in the public eye. Through his musical performances, recordings, and production work, he gained a reputation as one of the most influential figures in Jamaican popular music. Byron Lee and the Dragonaires remain active.

LEE, EDWARD O'SULLIVAN "BUNNY" OR "STRIKER" (1941–)

Born in Jamaica, Lee entered the music business in 1962 through his brother-in-law **Derrick Morgan**. Morgan got Lee a job with **Duke Reid** as a record plugger for Reid's **Treasure Isle** label. Lee next paired with Caltone label owner Ken Lack. Under Lack, Lee did his first production work in 1967. The success of this early work pushed Lee to open his own label called Lee's. Early products from the Lee's label included work by Derrick Morgan, Slim Smith, Lester Sterling, **Stranger Cole**, and others. By the end of the 1960s, Lee had established himself as the producer of some of the most marketable music on the island.

The first four years of the 1970s were especially profitable for the young label owner. An example of his output from the period was Eric Donaldson's song "Cherry Oh Baby," which became a hit for **UB40**. By the mid-1970s, Lee's understanding of the commercial record market allowed him to help break the stranglehold that the big producers had on the industry. Lee also had the foresight to employ several of the most important engineers on the island, such as **King Tubby**, **King Jammy**, and Philip Smart. With the help of King Tubby, Lee released an astonishing quantity of material that embraced the **dub** approach to recording. Lee and Tubby pioneered this recording technique, which removed the vocal track from a song and altered the mix on the other instruments, invariably making the bass line louder.

Lee's most productive period came at the end of the 1960s and through most of the 1970s while he was working with Tubby and his house band the **Aggrovators**. He released thousands of tracks in all of the active styles. Artists on his roster from this period included **Dennis Alcapone**, **Ken Boothe**, **Johnny Clarke**, **Doctor Alimantado**, **Alton Ellis**, **I-Roy**, **Linval Thompson**, David Isaacs, **U-Roy**, and many others.

In the early 1980s, Lee's production slowed because he did not own a studio. He remedied this in the latter part of the decade when he purchased the studio that **Joe Gibbs** was vacating. In the mid-1980s, Lee changed to the digital **ragga** style and continued to release material while gradually moving into retirement.

LEVY, BARRINGTON (1964–)

Born in Kingston, Jamaica, Levy began his music career in the late 1970s. In 1977, he released the single "My Black Girl" under the name Mighty Multitude,

Bunny Lee. © *UrbanImage.tv.*

Barrington Levy. © *UrbanImage.tv.*

but his real claim to fame did not manifest until the dawning of the **dancehall** style in 1979. His early material did not garner him any success, so in 1980 he entered the dancehalls and began **DJing**. His crystal-clear voice and ability to carry the dance gained him notoriety quickly.

With the success of his early dancehall style material, Levy released his debut album, 1979's *Bounty Hunter.* The album was a modest success and led to subsequent recordings such as *Shine Eye Gal* (1979), *Englishman* (1980), and *Robin Hood* (1980). Levy catapulted to the head of the dancehall style with these releases, and he parlayed that fame into a continued run of successful albums through the rest of the decade. In 1981, Levy was noticed by **Henry "Junjo" Lawes**, who was at the height of his own popularity. Lawes and Levy teamed in the early 1980s and released a series of groundbreaking singles including the hit "Collie Weed."

By the mid-1980s, Levy ruled Jamaican dancehall and set out to conquer the United Kingdom. He had a successful tour in 1984 that resulted in him teaming with **Jah Screw** for the infamous single "Under Mi Sensi." This was followed with "Here I Come," and both songs were huge hits in the United Kingdom and the Caribbean. In the wake of this success, Levy and Screw attempted unsuccessfully to cross over into the rock market. This failed effort, along with constant travel among Jamaica, the United States, and the United Kingdom caused Levy to lose productivity. However, by the end of the decade he had recaptured his early stride and released four albums between 1988 and 1990.

In the early 1990s, Levy continued his success with several new releases and again attempted to cross over into the U.S. market with the release of *Barrington* (1993). Although this record contained much of his best material, Levy continued to suffer at the hands of the American listening audience. This was not true in the United Kingdom or the Caribbean, though. The latter half of the 1990s found Levy's material highly prized. By the end of the decade, Levy did succeed in the United States with his 1998 release *Living Dangerously.* For this record, Levy succeeded by teaming with artists such as the hip hop icon Snoop Doggy Dog, **Bounty Killer**, **Lady G**, and others. He scored a hit that spurred him on into the new millennium. Levy's most recent project is a new album featuring Jamaican hip hop artist CeCile titled *It's About Time.* On the new record, Levy and CeCile are paired on the single "Want You to Know."

LEWIS, HOPETON (1947–)

Born in Kingston, Jamaica, Lewis began his music career in the mid-1960s. His first significant single was the song "Take It Easy," produced by Winston Blake. With this release, Lewis laid claim to being the father of the **rock steady** sound. The **ska** era was fast waning, and with Lewis's single, the beat was slowed down considerably. The track is now legendary, and for it alone Lewis would remain part of the **reggae** pantheon. In 1970, Lewis won the fifth annual Jamaican Festival contest and continued his rise to fame. Through the rest of the 1960s and the early 1970s, Lewis continued to release successful material, which culminated in the 1971 album *Groovin Out on Life*. On the record, Lewis was backed by the Dragonaires, of whom he had intermittently been a member as a vocalist. The material on the album was well received and led to further recordings such as 1974's *Dynamic Hopeton Lewis*.

More recently, Lewis's musical path has shifted from rock steady to gospel reggae. In the past several years, Lewis has released twelve gospel albums, such as 2000's *Reaching Out to Jesus*. He remains active as a gospel singer, recording artist, and businessman.

LIEUTENANT STITCHIE (c. 1965–)

Born Cleveland Laing, Lieutenant Stitchie hailed from Spanish Town, Jamaica. In the mid-1980s, Laing left his profession of schoolteacher to work in the music business. He joined the Django sound system and took a series of nicknames. The height of his work on the systems came when he landed a **DJ** job for Stereo One under the name Stitchie. His first single was "If I Don't Care," which he released as Ranking Citrus. Next, he released "Two Is Better Than too Many" and earned the name Stitchie through a misprinted label.

In 1986, Stitchie teamed with producer **King Jammy** and cut the single "Wear Your Size." In 1987, he released his debut album *Great Ambition*. The success of this early record led to a major-label record deal, and Stitchie signed with Atlantic Records in 1990. In the same year he released his Atlantic debut *The Governor*. This was followed by a series of albums including *Wild Jamaican Romances, Rude Boy* (1993), and *Gansta* (1995). Important singles from this period include "Don't Cheat on Your Lover" and "Sugar Cane Song."

In 1997, on his way to perform at Reggae Sumfest, Stitchie was nearly killed in a car accident. In the wake of this experience, Stitchie left behind his **dancehall** roots (and the *Lieutenant* portion of his name) and began writing gospel **reggae**. He released *To God Be*

Lieutenant Stitchie. © *UrbanImage.tv.*

the Glory (1999), which marked his entry into this new market. His 2000 album, *Real Power*, was his most successful album to date. More recently, Stitchie has been active with touring and in April 2004 released his most recent album. Titled *King Ambassador*, this release illustrates Stitchie at his most powerful through a series of gospel songs, several of with include guest Dr. Myles Munroe and all of which are produced by the legendary **Bobby "Digital" Dixon**.

LINDO, EARL "WYA" OR "WIRE" (c. 1950–)

Lindo is best known for his work with **Bob Marley**, for whom he played keyboards. However, prior to working with Marley, Lindo had an active career first as a member of the **Now Generation** band and then as part of **Taj Mahal's** group. Further, Lindo was a songwriter in addition to being an organ, piano, clavinet, and synthesizer player. Lindo had joined the **Wailers** in the early 1970s and was part of the group in time for their international launch in 1972. He appeared on Marley releases including *Burnin'* (1973), *Natty Dread* (1974), *Babylon by Bus* (1978), *Survival* (1979), *Uprising* (1981), and *Confrontation* (released posthumously in 1983).

However, he also played for a great number of other artists along the way. As early as 1975, he recorded with **Sharon Forrester**; in 1976 he worked with Taj Mahal; in the same year he recorded with **Beres Hammond** and **Toots and the Maytals**. In 1977 he recorded keyboard parts for **Burning Spear**, appeared on **Peter Tosh's** *Equal Rights* release, and sat in with **U-Roy**. Through the rest of the 1970s, Lindo recorded with a long list of **reggae** luminaries including **Big Youth**, **Culture**, **Ijahman**, **I-Roy**, **Max Romeo**, and **U-Brown**.

In the 1980s, his hectic schedule continued, as he was one of the most sought-after reggae keyboard players. During this decade he recorded with **Alpha Blondy**, Burning Spear, **Gregory Isaacs**, **Israel Vibration**, Pablo Moses, **Mikey Dread**, the **Wailers**, and **Ziggy Marley and the Melody Makers**. In the 1990s, Lindo recorded with **Culture**, **Cedella Booker Marley**, the **Meditations**, **Bunny Wailer**, **Wailing Souls**, Burning Spear, Bad Yard Club, U-Roy, Barbara Jones, **Delroy Wilson**, and others. Lindo has remained active in the new millennium. Since 1999, he has recorded with **Beenie Man**, **Garnet Silk**, **Soul Syndicate**, Big Youth, Israel Vibration, Trinity, and **Yabby You**; and has appeared on countless compilation releases. Earl "Wya" Lindo has played with many of the most important and influential reggae artists over the past thirty-five years and serves as a linchpin holding the style together.

LINDO, HOPETON (c. 1955–)

Hopeton Lindo entered the Jamaican popular music business in the mid-1970s and began associating himself with several already-established artists. One such teaming was with the producer **Mikey Dread** for the single "Black History." After this relatively successful first release, Lindo worked for the Blackstar sound system, where he was in close contact with **DJs** such as **Brigadier Jerry** and others. Lindo's next break came in 1980 when he paired with producer **Gussie Clarke** and released the single "Sidewalk Traveler." Clarke ran the Music Works studio and Lindo continued to work for him as a songwriter. At Music Works, Lindo also worked with **Home T** to create the single "Telephone Lover," along with several other important sides. This work gained Lindo a strong reputation as a songwriter, and he ultimately teamed with a series of artists including **Aswad** and **Gregory Isaacs**.

In the early 1990s, Lindo collaborated with the Two Friends crew and released his debut album *Word* (1991). The record was in the **dancehall** style and featured the popular singles "Gun Ting," "Oppressor No," and the title track. Lindo followed his debut with a second album, *Whatever Reason* (1992), released on the **RAS** imprint. The album featured the singles "Gi Mi More," "For Whatever the Reason," and "Your Song." Since its release, this album has fallen into obscurity and now is quite difficult to find.

LINDO, WILLIE (c. 1955–)

Willie Lindo's career in **reggae** music has spanned the past thirty-five years, during which he was a multi-instrumentalist, songwriter, and producer. In the mid-1970s, Lindo teamed with **Beres Hammond**, and together they produced a large body of high-quality work. Their first release was the album *Soul Reggae* (1977), on which Lindo was credited for guitar parts, arranging, production, and remixing. Throughout the end of the 1970s, Lindo went on to work with a series of talented **reggae** artists. In 1977 he recorded with **Dennis Brown**, **Burning Spear**, **Culture**, the **Heptones**, **Ijahman**, **Delroy Washington**, and several others. For these sessions, Lindo typically supplied the guitar work and also often served as the engineer.

In the 1980s, Lindo went on to work with an ever-growing list of artists such as **Big Youth**, **Black Uhuru**, Dennis Brown, Manu Dibbing, **Fathead** and **Yellowman**, **Derrick Harriott**, **J. C. Lodge**, the **Meditations**, the **Mighty Diamonds**, **Lee "Scratch" Perry**, and **Toots and the Maytals**. During this period, Lindo primarily supplied guitar and production work.

The 1990s brought more of the same as Lindo split his duties between guitar and production work for an increasingly long list of artists such as **Carlene Davis**, **Maxi Priest**, Beres Hammond, Don Perez, Cynthia Schloss, Leroy Smart, the Heptones, **U-Brown**, and others. Also in the 1990s, Lindo's work began appearing on various compilation releases. In the new millennium, Lindo has continued at a brisk pace. He produced or supplied guitar work for Larry Marshall, **Ky-Mani Marley**, **Freddie McGregor**, **Jacob Miller**, Dennis Brown, Lee "Scratch" Perry, Barry Briggs, Prince Lincoln, **Sly and Robbie**, and others. Of special note is his involvement as guitarist, producer, and engineer for Kashief Lindo, his son. In 2002, Kashief emerged as a recording artist in his father's mold with his debut album *Love Knows the Way.* Willie Lindo remains active in the reggae music scene as both guitarist and producer, as well as a guiding force behind his son's fledgling career.

LITTLE LENNY (c. 1960–)

Born Nigel Grandison, Little Lenny began making his mark on Jamaican popular music in the late 1980s. Lenny **toasted** in the **dancehall** and **ragga** styles, and his lyrics exhibited the usual slackness (rudeness; X-rated language; and talk of guns, sex, and drugs). His debut album came in 1980 when **RAS Records** released *Gun in a Baggy.* This release included the singles "Diana," "Original," and "Teach Reality." Since then, Lenny has gone on to release a series of albums on the VP Records label such as *My Name*, *All the Girls*, *Still Coming*, and *Little Lenny Is My Name.* In addition to his solo material, Lenny has appeared on other artists' releases, putting in studio time as a backup vocalist for **Dennis Brown**. Lenny's material continues to appear on an increasing number of compilation releases.

LITTLE ROY (1953–)

Born Earl Lowe in Kingston, Jamaica, Little Roy began working in the music business in 1965 as a roots reggae singer. At age twelve, Lowe did his first recording at **Studio**

One with **Clement "Coxsone" Dodd**. This yielded little success, as did another session with **Prince Buster**, but Buster did give Lowe the nickname "Little Roy." Roy next teamed with **Lloyd Daley** on his Matador label and scored a number one single in 1969 with the track "Bongo Nyah," backed by the Hippy Boys (**Aston** and **Carlton Barrett**). Other important Matador singles followed, including "Righteous Man," "Hardest Fighter," and "Keep on Trying."

Next, Roy set up his own label to provide himself the opportunity to record any material that he desired. This matched up well with his conversion to the **Rastafarian** teachings and allowed Roy to infuse his lyrics with the sentiment that he desired. Thus, in the early 1970s, Roy established the Tafari and Earth labels with the assistance of Maurice Jackson. Now that Roy had an outlet for his Rasta-tinged tracks, he needed a studio where he could record his work. This was supplied by **Lee "Scratch" Perry**, and in 1974 Roy cut "Tribal War" and "Black Bird" at the **Black Ark Studio**. "Tribal War" was an instant hit and remains one of Roy's most significant contributions to the style. Since its release, many other artists have covered this single, including **John Holt**, **Freddie McGregor**, **Prince Far I**, and **Junior Reid**.

Next, Roy released a series of successful albums including *Free for All Dub* (1975), *Columbus Ship* (1981), *Prophesy* (1989), and *Live On* (1991). During this period he had continued success, which spurred him on to release *Tafari Earth Uprising* (1995), *Long Time* (1996), and *Packin' House* (1999). His most recent project was the late-1999 album *More from a Little*, which featured the title track.

LIVINGSTON, NEVILLE O'RILEY "BUNNY WAILER, JAH BUNNY, JAH B." *See* WAILER, BUNNY

LODGE, J. C. (c. 1960–)

Born June Carol Lodge to a Jamaican mother and British father, she moved with her family to Jamaica as a youth and grew up listening to the popular **reggae** music of the island. She began singing during high school, and with the encouragement of her boyfriend, Errol O'Meally, she sought the opinion of **Joe Gibbs**. Gibbs liked Lodge's voice; in 1980 he recorded her singing a version of "Someone Loves You, Honey." The single was a huge international success and sent Lodge's career as a singer off to a strong start.

Since the early 1980s, Lodge has continued her early success and has gone on to release ten more albums. Her style is a mixture of **reggae**, pop, country, and rhythm and blues. She also crossed over into the **dancehall** style when she released "Telephone Love" in 1988. The single was produced by **Gussie Clarke** at his Music Works studio and marked the beginning of Lodge's crossover career. "Telephone Love" impacted the U.S. rhythm and blues and hip hop markets and gave Lodge a record deal from Tommy Boy Records, an American hip hop label. In the wake of the Tommy Boy deal, Lodge released *Tropic of Love* in an attempt to speak to the hip hop, rhythm and blues, and reggae audiences.

In the mid-1990s, Lodge and husband O'Meally had a baby girl, which prompted the pair to turn their attention to educational children's material. The pair released two albums of material specifically geared toward children called "Sing n' Learn." Additionally, the pair was hired by the Jamaican national television station to produce a children's television series based on their albums. In 2001, Lodge relocated to the United Kingdom and continued to release material. In 2002, Jetstar Records released her album *Reggae Country*, a collection of reggae versions of country songs.

More recently, Lodge released a second album of reggae/country songs and in 2004 released a compilation of many of her greatest hits titled *This Is Crucial Reggae*. Jetstar has also issued a second album of country covers called *More Reggae Country*. In addition to her solo work, Lodge has long been a sought-after session singer. She has appeared on recordings for artists such as **Aswad**, **Eek-A-Mouse**, **Gregory Isaacs**, **Maxi Priest**, the **Mighty Diamonds**, Cocoa T, and **Shabba Ranks**.

LONE RANGER (c. 1950–)
Anthony Waldron was born in Kingston, Jamaica; moved to England; and then returned to Kingston in 1971 and adopted his TV series-inspired name when he entered the music scene as a **dancehall DJ**. Lone Ranger's claim to fame in the dancehall was his penchant for **toasting** on the beat and in a more

Lone Ranger. © *UrbanImage.tv.*

singsong style than many of his predecessors did. His best early material was a pair of albums recorded for **Clement "Coxsone" Dodd** on the **Studio One** imprint. These were collections of versions of earlier hits. At the same time as these early recordings, he was working the Virgo Hi-Fi **sound system** (among others) and his reputation was on the rise. His Alvin Ranglin-produced album *Barnabas Collins* (1980) solidified his reputation. This album was followed by a series of nine more successful releases throughout the 1980s and 1990s. Lone Ranger's best work came from time spent with Dodd, and he continues to record with him. In 2004, Ranger released *Dub Salvador, Volumes 1 and 2*; and he appeared on Grant Phabao's *KulchaKlash* release.

LORD CREATOR (c. 1940–)
Lord Creator was born Kendrick Patrick in Trinidad. He moved to Jamaica in 1962 in the wake of his popular song "Evening News," which made a mark throughout the Caribbean. Patrick's singing style was in the mold of the crooner in front of the large dance band. He focused on ballads and love songs performed over a **ska** or calypso background. Once in Jamaica, Patrick scored a timely hit with his 1962 single "Independence Jamaica." The single was issued on **Island Records** and was a hit in Jamaica and the United Kingdom. Next, Patrick issued the single "Don't Stay Out Late," which would eventually became one of his signature songs. It was released in 1963 and was a major hit in Jamaica.

Patrick rode his successful singles into the studio and recorded his debut album *Me Mama Never Taught Me* (1964). The album featured a host of popular singles including "Wreck a Pum Pum," "6 Million Frenchmen," and "The Lizard." In 1965, Patrick, who had been working under the name Lord Creator, was one of the brightest stars on the island. At the end of the 1960s, Creator teamed with producer **Clancy Eccles** and recorded one of his most popular songs. The 1970s Clan Disc single was called "Kingston Town" and became a smash hit in the United Kingdom. The single sold well and brought Creator increased notoriety.

However, in the early 1970s, the style of Jamaican popular music was changing and Lord Creator's soft ska crooning was losing popularity. He ended up on the streets; but through Eccles's generosity, enough money was raised to send him back to Trinidad, where his family could care for him. British **reggae** band **UB40** picked up Creator's single "Kingston Town" and recorded it on their 1989 Virgin Records album *Labour of Love*. In 1995, VP Records issued a compilation of Creator's greatest hits titled *Don't Stay Out Late*. The collection finds Creator in his best form with backing music by a young **Skatalites** band. Featured songs include "Man to Man" and "King and Queen." Although Lord Creator made a huge impact on the reggae scene, even appearing in the James Bond movie *Dr. No*, he never received his proper due during his career.

LORD TANAMO (1934–)

Born Joseph Gordon, Lord Tanamo entered the popular music scene as a **mento** singer and instrumentalist who mastered the mento essential rumba box. Tanamo's first hit was the single "Crinoline Incident" in 1955. This was followed by a series of successful singles that spanned the transition from the mento to **ska** style. In 1964, Tanamo was one of the founders of the legendary **Skatalites**, for whom he supplied lead vocals in 1964–1965.

In 1965, Tanamo released his debut album, which featured singles such as "Television." Tanamo was next employed as a traveling mento, ska, and **reggae** singer for the Jamaican Tourist Board. This led to extensive touring and great exposure. He subsequently settled in Canada and worked with his Tanamo Mento Group. Although living in Canada, Tanamo made frequent trips back to Jamaica and each time recorded successful singles. Additionally, Tanamo was on hand for any Skatalites reunion such as the group's 1989 concert in Japan. In 1994, Tanamo recorded and produced the album *Skamento Movement*, a compilation of his hits from fifteen years in the business.

In the new millennium, Tanamo continues to write and record new music. Further, he was active in the 2003 Skatalites tour of Europe and Japan. He is working on another album of new material and actively books public appearances.

LOVE, PAUL. *See* JAH SCREW

LOVERS ROCK

The lovers rock sub-genre of **reggae** emerged in the 1970s in the United Kingdom. Unlike the cultural sentiments of roots reggae, lovers rock was the first indigenous black British reggae style. The lovers rock style was marked by a reggae bass line, light production, Motown and Philadelphia soul crooning, and lyrics that dealt with affairs of the heart. Labels that were central to the style included **Arawak**, Santic, and Hawkeye. The style enjoyed a long period of vogue that spanned from the mid-1970s through the 1980s. The songs of this style were heard on the radio and at **sound system** dances, and several of the singles went to the UK charts.

The first official lovers rock single was Louisa Marks's 1975 song "Caught You in a Lie." Examples of artists in the style included **Janet Kay**, Carroll Thompson, Brown Sugar, and **Trevor Hartley**. Just as the American jazz style was the first indigenous type of music to reverse the pattern of influence back to western Europe, lovers rock reversed Jamaican influence on the United Kingdom. Several Jamaican artists were introduced to the style in the United Kingdom and took it back to Jamaica, where it also flourished. Artists of this sort included **Dennis Brown**, **John Holt**, **Gregory Isaacs**, and **Johnny Osbourne**.

LOWE, EARL. *See* LITTLE ROY

LUCIANO (1974–)

Born Jepther McClymont in Davy Town, Jamaica, Luciano got his musical start singing in church and soon took the moniker "Stepper John" and moved to Kingston. The young singer went into Aquarius Studios with Herman Chin-Loy and recorded his first single. He then moved on to work with several other producers before settling with Homer Harris at Blue Mountain Records and recording a body of work under the name Luciano.

He went on to work with other labels such as Big Ship, New Name Muszik, and Sky High, and scored his first hit single, "Give My Love a Try," which paved the way for further success. Luciano sings in the roots reggae style, but with a baritone-voiced balladeer's approach. In the United Kingdom, Luciano scored a string of hits with the production assistance of **Philip "Fatis" Burrell** in early 1993. This international

Luciano. © *UrbanImage.tv.*

success launched Luciano's career. Also in 1993, Luciano released his debut album *Moving Up.* The album was well received, and the singer's reputation was increasing in Jamaica and the United Kingdom.

A long series of other albums followed with *One Way Ticket* (1994), *Life* (1995), *Messenjah* (1997), and *Sweep over My Soul* (1999). Of particular note is 1995's hit "It's Me Again Jah," which exhibits the young singer's ability to step into the spiritual void left by **Bob Marley's** death.

Luciano's success continued in the new millennium. Since 2000, the singer has released a multitude of albums on the **RAS**, Charm, and VP labels. Luciano remains active and is producing new material.

MACKA B (c. 1960–)

Born Christopher MacFarlane in Wolverhampton, England, his interest in music manifested early; he studied the violin and sang in the choir while still in school. As a youth, B became interested in the **reggae** music of **dancehall** sensations **I-Roy**, **Prince Jazzbo**, and **U-Roy**. He made his formal entrance into the music industry when he joined the Exodus **sound system**. B **toasted** as often as he could and began building a reputation as an excellent **DJ**. In 1982, B visited Jamaica, where his inspiration was bolstered. Back in England he joined the group Pre-Wax and recorded a single that received local attention.

During the mid-1980s, B appeared on the radio and continued his sound system work. In the wake of the Exodus system closing, he worked for the Wassifa Hi-Fi and Skippy and Lippy systems. The tape of a clash between the Wassifa and Saxon systems resulted in B recording the single "Bible Reader" for Chris Lane and John MacGillivray's Fashion Records label. The single was well received and led to a second release titled "Gentleman with Manners." B's popularity had spread to the point that in 1985 he signed with the **Ariwa** imprint and released his debut album *Sign of the Times*. B's partnering with Ariwa resulted in a longstanding relationship with the label's premier producer **Mad Professor**. The release reached number one on the UK reggae charts and earned B a spot on the 1986 Sunsplash at Wembley concert. This was followed by a second album titled *We've Had Enough* (1987) and a successful European tour. The following year, B again visited Jamaica, after which he recorded his third album, *Looks Are Deceiving*, which was his most successful to that time. He quickly followed this with another album titled *Buppie Culture* (1989), which featured the single "Dread a Who She Love." The tour that followed this fourth Ariwa release spanned parts of western Europe, the Caribbean, and Africa.

In 1990, B released a tribute to African freedom fighter Nelson Mandela called "Proud of Mandela" on his album *Natural Suntan*. This marked a phase of B's career that was filled with lyrics of social commentary. Throughout the 1990s, B continued to release solid material on the Ariwa label. Additional albums include *Peace Cup*, *Jamaica, No Problem*, *Here Comes Trouble*, *Discrimination*, *Roots and Culture*, and *Live Again!* More recently, B released his *Global Messenger* album in 2000, which found the UK dancehall sensation in great form. Macka B continues to record, tour, and compose new music to this time. His mixture of dancehall toasting, roots reggae **one-drop** rhythms, and conscious lyrics makes him a perennial favorite.

MAD COBRA (1968–)

Born Ewart Everton Brown in Kingston, Jamaica, Cobra spent much of his youth in St. Mary's Parish, Jamaica, before returning to the capital city. He got caught up in the Jamaican popular music scene in the mid-1980s and honed his **toasting** skills in order to rule the **dancehall**. However, this was met with opposition from his parents, who wanted him to pursue a career in the trades. Brown could not be stopped and, taking the name Mad Cobra from the popular GI Joe cartoon series, in 1991 burst onto the dancehall scene with his debut album *Bad Boy Talk*. Cobra's emergence had been facilitated by his uncle **Delroy "Spiderman" Thompson**, who produced Cobra's first single, "Respect Woman," in 1989. This first single was popular locally, and Cobra increased his reputation by appearing on several area **sound systems**. Dancehall fans flocked to hear Cobra's early efforts, and his popularity grew. This increased attention allowed him to release a series of successful singles including "Gundelero," "Yush," and "Feeling Lonely."

In 1991 and 1992, Cobra released at least five number one singles and parlayed this success into albums in Jamaica and the United Kingdom. In 1992, *Step Aside* was released on the **RAS** label and *Flex* was released by Sony. Cobra's early style contained the typical dancehall slackness lyrics about sex. However, as he grew into his mature style, his lyrics focused more on romance and relationship situations. The success of the "Flex" single led to an album deal with the Columbia record label in the United States. The new label deal yielded the 1992 release *Hard to Wet, Easy to Dry*, which along with "Flex" gave Cobra a degree of crossover success. There followed a collection of singles that took Cobra back to his dancehall roots and culminated in the release of the *Venom* album.

Throughout the 1990s, Cobra's success continued through a string of albums including *Mr. Pleasure*, a clash album with **Beenie Man** titled *Beenie Man Meets Mad Cobra*, and *Milkman*. In the late 1990s, Cobra teamed with Mr. Vegas for the single "Guns High," which brought both men success and greater crossover appeal. Revered as one of the top dancehall DJs in the 1990s, Cobra continues to release material. In 2003–2004, Cobra was working on a new album titled *Mixed Personalities*, which featured the single "Betrayal."

MAD PROFESSOR (c. 1955–)

Neil (Neal) "Mad Professor" Fraser was born in Guyana, South America, in the mid-1950s. His entry into the music business came as a youth when he learned about electronics and constructed his own radio. Fraser relocated to London at age thirteen and by the end of his teenage years was working toward opening a recording studio. In 1979, his studio dream was realized when he opened the **Ariwa** studio in his living room. He began recording **lovers rock** artists and soon relocated the studio to Peckham, South London.

In addition to producing, Fraser is also a recording artist in his own right, his penchant for the **dub** style apparent in his recording style both for himself and others. He released his first album, *Dub Me Crazy*, in 1982. Fraser's second album, *Beyond the Realms of Dub*, came out the following year. The year 1984 saw the release of one of his most popular albums, *The African Connection*. The sale of these records allowed Fraser to move the studio to a more upscale location and continue his recording career. Settled in the new location, Fraser took on recording higher-profile artists, such as **Pato Banton**, **Sandra Cross**, and **Macka B**. Additionally, his own recordings continued unabated.

From 1982 to the present, Fraser has released at least one album of his own material per year. In the late 1980s, he joined forces with his principal early production idol, **Lee "Scratch" Perry**, the result of which was 1989's *Mystic Warrior*. In the 1990s, Fraser focused on production work and touring. He added **U-Roy** to his stable of recording artists and expanded the label's sound into the **dancehall** style. As the millennium drew to a close, Fraser began to work with artists outside the **reggae** style. He has done remixes and production work for Massive Attack, Sade, the Beastie Boys, Jamiroquai, Rancid, Depeche Mode, and Perry Farrell (of Jane's Addiction). Over the course of several decades, Fraser has recorded and worked in the dub, reggae, dancehall, and alternative music styles. His Ariwa imprint continues to be vital, and he performs and tours regularly.

MAFIA AND FLUXY

The legendary UK-based rhythm section Mafia and Fluxy comprises Leroy Heywood (b. 1962) on bass and David Heywood (b. 1963) on drums. The brothers pattern themselves after the seminal **reggae** rhythm section **Sly and Robbie** and have followed closely in the latters' footsteps. The duo surfaced on the UK reggae scene in the late 1980s and have subsequently worked with many of the biggest names in reggae music around the world. Further, they have also branched out into the production business and are now heavily sought after for either their instrumental backing music or their production skills.

The Heywood brothers grew up in Tottenham, London, and quickly rose to prominence by backing acts such as **Pato Banton**, **Chaka Demus and Pliers**, **Cutty Ranks**, and **Maxi Priest**. In the 1990s, Mafia and Fluxy experienced a flurry of activity that had them working with **Bounty Killer**, **Capleton**, **Cocoa Tea**, **Don Carlos**, **Beres Hammond**, **Lieutenant Stitchie**, **Pinchers**, **Garnet Silk**, **Yellowman**, and many others. Through this work, the pair established themselves as the premier rhythm section in the United Kingdom. Also in the 1990s, the pair showed with their album *Finders Keepers* (1992) that they could release their own material.

In the new millennium, the brothers began working as a production team and have subsequently produced material for Chukki Starr, **Beenie Man**, Chaka Demus and Pliers, and others. They have also moved into the American hip hop market with production work for Aaliyah, Soul II Soul, and Urban Species. Mafia and Fluxy remain active and currently write, record, and produce.

MAHAL, TAJ (1942–)

Born Henry St. Claire Fredericks in Harlem, New York, Mahal grew up in a musical household in Springfield, Massachusetts, under the guidance of his father, who was a jazz pianist, composer, and arranger from the Caribbean. His mother was a schoolteacher from South Carolina, as well as a gospel singer. As a youth, Mahal studied piano briefly, but quickly realized that he did not fit into the mold of standard western music. His desire to become a multi-instrumentalist manifested early as he also learned to sing and play the trombone, clarinet, and harmonica. As a teenager, he took up the guitar and began playing in the delta blues style.

Along with studying how to play music, Mahal also explored the origins of African American music. In the early 1960s, he enrolled in the University of Massachusetts–Amherst, where he linked up with a band on campus called the Elektras. Four years later, he departed the East Coast for Los Angeles to immerse himself in the West Coast blues experience. He formed a band called the Rising Sons that included a collection of solid players, such as Ry Cooder, and he began playing at the Whiskey A Go Go. It was at the Whiskey that Mahal met and played alongside blues legends such as Howlin' Wolf, Junior Wells, Muddy Waters, and Buddy Guy. These experiences led Mahal into the studio to record a series of albums—*Taj Mahal* (1967), *Natch'l Blues* (1968), and *Giant Step* (1969)—that have become landmarks of his early career.

In the 1970s, Mahal released another series of recordings on which he pushed his sound outside of the blues and infused it with elements from the Caribbean and Africa. During this decade he released *Happy to Be Just Like I Am* (1971), *Recycling the Blues* (1972), *Mo' Roots* (1974), *Music Fuh Ya'* (1977), and *Evolution* (1978). Of note, in 1976 one-time **Wailers** band member **Earl "Wya" Lindo** joined the Taj Mahal band for a brief period. During the 1980s, Mahal released fewer albums and instead spent his time touring. His output from this decade included 1987's *Taj* and several children's albums.

The 1990s brought a return to his more productive output and he wrote music for the play *Mule Bone* and the movie *Zebrahead*, and he released four more albums. Also in the 1990s, Mahal released the album *World Music*, on which his style further evolved. Mahal's move toward world music stuck, and in the new millennium he has continued to mix the blues with other styles from around the world. In 2000 he released *Shoutin' in Key* and in 2003 *The Hula Blues*.

During Mahal's long and storied career, he has reached the pinnacle of success. He has won two Grammy Awards and been nominated nine times. Further, his creative energy continues, and he is able to pursue his musical dreams through his own label, Kandu Records. Taj Mahal's dreams of an international world music style continue unabated.

MANDATORS, THE

The Mandators are a Nigerian **reggae** band who have brought their style to a large audience, often playing sold-out stadium shows in their homeland. The band plays a blend of roots reggae and world beat that has not been successful outside of Africa. The group's frontman, Victor Essiet, aspired for them to catch on in the same manner as their countryman **Lucky Dube**. As yet this has not happened, and their album *Crisis* has gone largely unnoticed in the United States. Rounder records (and their subsidiary Heartbeat Music) attempted to rectify this situation by releasing *Power of the People: Nigerian Reggae* (1992). The album contained samples of the group's music from the late 1980s including "Apartheid," "Injustice," and "Survival." As yet the Mandators have lacked crossover appeal in the United States, but through the support of projects such as the Heartbeat release and a few appearances on compilation albums, the group may yet find an audience in the United States.

MANGO RECORDS

Mango Records was a subsidiary of **Christopher Blackwell's** legendary **reggae** label **Island Records** imprint. The label was most active in the 1970s, but continued into the 1980s and 1990s. The list of artists who appeared on the label included many of the most popular reggae acts of the past three decades. The label released both seven- and twelve-inch offerings by artists such as **Aswad**, Baaba Maal, **Black Uhuru**, **Burning Spear**, **Chaka Demus and Pliers**, **Dillinger**, **Marcia Griffiths**, **Inner Circle**, **Gregory Isaacs**, **Lee "Scratch" Perry**, Teacher, Angelique Kidjo, **Steel Pulse**, the **Taxi Gang**, **Third World**, **Tippa Irie**, **Toots and the Maytals**, and King Sunny Ade.

MAPFUMO, THOMAS (1945–)

Born in Marondera, Rhodesia, Mapfumo spent his childhood years on a rural farm where he learned traditional songs accompanied by the ngoma drums and the music of the mbira. The family moved to the city Harare when Mapfumo was ten, and he was exposed to English and American popular music of the 1960s such as the Beatles and Otis Redding. Mapfumo took to music and began performing as a guitarist in a variety of different bands during his teenage years. As a young adult, he played in the Acid Band and then in 1978 formed Blacks Unlimited, where his confidence as a musician grew. He took up singing and used the Shona language and rhythms to create distinctly nationalist music. Mapfumo was a musical trailblazer, as he chose to write new music instead of abiding by the longstanding tradition of composing music based on traditional tunes.

By this time the Rhodesian civil war was brewing and Mapfumo's music became the sound of the birth of Zimbabwe. This resulted in some political problems for the singer; he was briefly detained by the outgoing Rhodesian army in 1977. Mapfumo sang in the style called chimurenga, which means "music of struggle." In the 1980s, Robert Mugabe rose to power, and Mapfumo and Blacks Unlimited played at the new nation's first celebration. **Bob Marley and the Wailers** also played at the celebration. Unfortunately, in the past twenty years Mugabe has changed his opinions on Mapfumo's music, and he is now banned and living in exile in the United States.

Throughout the course of his lengthy career, Mapfumo has gained acceptance worldwide, toured extensively, and released a series of albums that is eagerly awaited by his large and diverse fan base. Mapfumo has also received many honors during his career, including honorary degrees (among them a PhD in music from Ohio University), Zimbabwe's Person of the Century Award, and the 1999 Artist of the Year Award from the American World Music Awards. During the course of an often-tumultuous career, Mapfumo released over twenty albums and remains active today. His most recent album is the 2004 release *Choice Chimurenga*.

MARLEY, CEDELLA BOOKER (1926–)

Cedella Booker Marley was born in 1926 in St. Ann, Jamaica, and at age eighteen married Norval Sinclair Marley, a white British military man. However, shortly after their wedding, Norval Marley left St. Ann and subsequently had little to do with Booker. The couple did have children, the most famous of whom was **Robert Nesta Marley**, born February 6, 1945. Booker and Bob ultimately moved to the west Kingston ghetto called Trenchtown in hopes of building a better life in the city. This was not to be. Rather, their lives in Jamaica's capital city were harsh and poverty-stricken. In 1964, Booker moved to the United States and encouraged Bob to follow. During the late 1960s and the 1970s, both Booker and Marley returned to Jamaica; however, Booker maintains a house in Miami, Florida. In the wake of Bob's death in 1981, Booker has been the protector of his legacy. She still lives in the Florida home that Bob bought her, and she forwards his music and message. Booker has also served as a mother figure not just to her own children, but also to the children Bob fathered during his short life.

In the 1990s, Booker released two albums of her own music. In 1991, she released *Awake Zion* on the RIOR label with the production assistance of **Aston "Family Man" Barrett**. She followed this in 1992 with the release of *Smilin' Island Song*. Booker has also co-authored a book on Bob's life called *Bob Marley My Son: An Intimate Portrait by His Mother*. Booker has toured widely, speaking or performing in the United States, Europe, Africa, Mexico, and the Caribbean. Her most recent endeavor is the manufacturing of handcrafted dolls.

MARLEY, DAMIAN "JR. GONG" (1978–)

Damian was born to **Robert Nesta Marley** and his then mistress, 1977 Miss World Cindy Breakspeare, on July 21, 1978. He was only three years old when his father died, but early on he earned the nickname "Junior Gong" (his father was nick-named "Tuff Gong"). Damian formed his first band at age thirteen, called the Shepherds, which also included the son of guitarist **Cat Coore** from the legendary band **Third World**, and **Freddie McGregor** and **Judy Mowatt's** daughter. The group was successful and even earned an opening spot on the 1992 installment of **Reggae Sunsplash**, riding the success of the single "School Controversy." The Shepherds parted ways in the early 1990s and Damian went solo. With the help of his father's label, Tuff Gong, he released his debut album, *Mr. Marley*. His brother Stephen Marley, who functioned as producer and co-author, assisted Damian on this project. The album was a combination of roots reggae rhythms and hip hop vocal styling (called **toasting** in Jamaica and rapping in the United States).

Damian Marley. © *UrbanImage.tv.*

In 2001, Damian released his second album, *Halfway Tree*, after the location of the same name in Kingston where uptown meets downtown. The album was produced by Marley Boyz productions and released by Universal through a production and distribution deal between Motown Records and Ghetto Youths International. The 2001 Grammy Award-winning *Halfway Tree* included a host of cameo appearances from artists as diverse as **Bounty Killer**, **Capleton**, Dragon, Eve of the Ruff Ryders, Treach of Naughty by Nature, **Bunny Wailer** (the only living member of the original **Wailers** vocal trio), and many other luminaries of contemporary hip hop and reggae.

In 2003, Damian and Stephen Marley, together as Ghetto Youths, released *Educated Fools*. The album was produced by the Marley Boyz and includes another host of reggae music stalwarts such as **Buju Banton**, Capleton, Determine, **Ky-Mani Marley** (another Marley brother), **Spragga Benz**, and **Yami Bolo**. Together with his brothers, Damian Marley continues to write, record, and produce new music. Additionally, in the new millennium, Damian has appeared on several other artists' recordings, providing vocals or production for Eve, Cypress Hill, Krayzie Bone, Mr. Cheeks, and Queen Pen.

MARLEY, DAVID "ZIGGY" (1968–)

Born in 1968, the oldest son and second-oldest child of **Robert Nesta Marley** and **Rita Marley**, David earned his nickname from his love of David "Ziggy Stardust" Bowie. He got his start in the Jamaican popular music business at an early age. His father gave him guitar and drum lessons, and at age ten he was already singing backup with his father and the **Wailers**. Ziggy was the driving force in founding **Ziggy Marley and the Melody Makers**, which consisted of his sisters Cedella and Sharon and his brother Stephen.

The Marley children were not strangers to the business and had already recorded with their father in 1979 for the "Children Playing in the Streets" release. The group made their first musical impact singing at their father's funeral in 1981, and have gone

Ziggy Marley. © *UrbanImage.tv.*

on to critical acclaim since. In the mid-1980s, Ziggy and the Melody Makers released a pair of albums that sparked interest within the **reggae** community. The releases, 1985's *Play the Game Right* and 1986's *Hey World*, brought the young group greater notoriety and paved the way for subsequent releases. Ziggy's music picked up the torch that his father carried for two decades. His lyrics contain commentary on social, political, and cultural injustices, which makes them approachable to a wide range of listeners.

In 1989, the group released *Conscious Party*, which marked their arrival on the Atlantic Records label. The album was enormously successful and featured the single "Tomorrow People." The group quickly followed this success with the release of *One Bright Day.* This album was also greeted with enthusiasm and cemented Ziggy and the group's reputation as a force to be reckoned with in reggae music. The album won a 1989 Grammy Award and spent time on the charts. In 1991, Ziggy and the Melody Makers released *Jahmekya*, which was another album filled with consciousness lyrics. It was not as commercially successful as the previous two releases but did well enough to keep the group's momentum pushing forward. The remainder of the 1990s was filled with four more albums that resulted in two more Grammy Awards.

In the new millennium, Ziggy has branched out and formed his own record label called Ghetto Youth United. The label was conceived as an outlet for emerging new Jamaican talent. In 2003, Ziggy went solo and released the album *Dragonfly.* It was a more diverse musical offering but continued forwarding his father's legacy. On this album, Ziggy also departed from his standard recording process, the album having been written in Jamaica and recorded in the United States. In more recent releases, Ziggy and the Melody Makers have included diverse influences and styles in their music. The group mixed the sound of roots reggae, American rhythm and blues, hip hop, and blues to create their own musical hybrid. Throughout his career, Ziggy has pursued greater opportunities for underprivileged children. He was named the Goodwill Youth Ambassador to the United Nations and works steadfastly to lend support and encouragement to youth.

MARLEY, JULIAN (1975–)

Born to **Robert Nesta Marley** and Lucy Ponder in London, England, Julian began studying music at an early age and has become skilled on the guitar, bass, keyboards, and drums. Julian grew up in England but has since spent much of his time in Jamaica and Florida. In 1992, Julian moved to Jamaica and formed a band that quickly learned the songs that he had written. Julian's band then went on tour and traveled around the world. They played numerous Bob Marley Birthday Bashes and have appeared on

Reggae Sunsplash. In 1996, Damian released his debut single, "Loving Clear." The single was successful and resulted in the release of his first full-length album in the same year, *Lion in the Morning*. This early material established Julian's sound in the roots reggae vein with lyrics that contained messages of spirituality and uplift. In the late 1990s, Julian became part of the Marley Magic North American Tour along with his brother **Damian**.

Julian's mature style came to bear in his latest album, *A Time and a Place*. This 2003 release illustrated Julian's musical development, maturity, and consciousness of social issues. With the connections forged by his father, Julian has played with legendary **reggae** artists such as **Aston "Family Man" Barrett**, **Earl "Wya" Lindo**, and **Earl "Chinna" Smith**. Along the way he has also performed on a variety of other artists' releases, including appearances on albums by Lauryn Hill, Krayzie Bone, Damian Marley, **Ziggy Marley**, and several others. Julian continues to write, release, record, and perform live.

MARLEY, KY-MANI (1976–)

Ky-Mani (Kikuyu for "adventurous traveler") Marley was the penultimate child born to **Robert Nesta Marley**. His birth was a result of Bob's relationship with Jamaican table tennis champion Anita Belnavis. He was born in Jamaica and during his youth spent time with Bob and his wife **Rita** learning about the music business, **Rastafari**, and life. At age nine, Ky-Mani moved to Miami and learned to play the piano, guitar, and trumpet in school. However, his earliest love was for sports, which manifested in competitive soccer and football playing. This early experience in the United States gave Ky-Mani a mixed background of Jamaican and American musical styles.

After finishing school, Ky-Mani teamed with Miami-based producer **Clifton "Specialist" Dillon** and cut a few singles. The songs "Judge Not" and "Dear Dad" had deep significance to the young singer. "Judge Not" was one of the first songs that his father recorded, and "Dear Dad" is based on a letter he wrote to his deceased father. This early material established Ky-Mani as a musical force and got him attention on several musical horizons. His debut album was soon to follow. Called *Like Father, Like Son*, the release is a collection of covers of his father's music. He broke on a national level when he teamed with Praswell (from the Fugees) for a version of **Eddy Grant's** hit "Electric Avenue." The success of the single brought Ky-Mani a record contract from the New York-based, independent label Gee Street/Sheng Records. Ky-Mani then went into the studio to record his first album of original material, *The Journey*, which was released in 1998. The album featured "Dear Dad" and a duet with **Morgan Heritage** called "Country Journey." The release of the album was followed by a world tour and periodic appearances with his brothers **Damian**, Stephen, and **Ziggy**. His second release, titled *Many More Roads*, came in 2001 on the Artists Only label and further propelled his career forward. The release garnered him a Grammy nomination in 2002 in the Best Reggae Album category.

In addition to music, Ky-Mani has also found a home as an actor, illustrated by his appearance in the movie *Shottas* alongside **Spragga Benz**. Through all of this work, Ky-Mani Marley has cultivated a large and diverse fan base that anxiously awaits his next offering. Overall, his style is a mixture of roots reggae and American rhythm and blues. In 2003, Ky-Mani embarked on another acting adventure as the star of the film *One Love*. The movie was an adaptation of William Shakespeare's play *Romeo and Juliet*.

MARLEY, RITA (ANDERSON) (c. 1950–)

Born Alpharita Anderson in Cuba, Rita relocated to Jamaica at an early age and settled in the west Kingston ghetto called Trenchtown. Her entrance into the Jamaican popular music scene came when she joined a female **ska** group called the Soulettes. The trio began recording for producer **Clement "Coxsone" Dodd** in 1964 at his legendary **Studio One** facility. It was through Rita's business relationship with Dodd that she met **Bob Marley**. Dodd had employed Marley to coach young singers and help them work on tightening up their harmonies. Dodd instructed Marley to do this work with the Soulettes. In 1966, after a period of courtship Marley and Anderson got married.

Rita had a degree of success as a member of the Soulettes. Their single "Pied Piper" was a modest hit and brought the trio regional acclaim. However, teamed with Marley, Rita found her greatest musical heights. After **Peter Tosh** and **Bunny Wailer** left the **Wailers**, the **I-Threes**, which consisted of Rita Marley, **Judy Mowatt**, and **Marcia Griffiths**, stepped in to provide vocal harmony. The female backing trio went on to appear on all of Wailers albums from 1974 to 1981. In 1976, Rita was in the yard of the Marley house at 56 Hope Road on December 3 when gunfire broke out during an assassination attempt on her husband. She was wounded during the altercation when a bullet glanced off her head.

The period between 1976 and 1981 was filled with music making, touring, and child rearing in the Marley household. During this period, Rita was aware of Bob's many infidelities, but believed that it was her charge to hold the family together, mother the children, and support Bob in his musical endeavors. However, in 1981, Robert Nesta Marley succumbed to cancer and died on May 11. In the wake of Bob's death, Rita released a series of solo albums that began with *Who Feels It Knows It* (1981), followed by *Harambe* (1988), and *We Must Carry On* (1988). Her solo material is strong and illustrates a highly trained voice that benefits from years of practice. In the 1990s, Rita released another series of albums, this time on the **Shanachie** imprint.

In 2003, Rita issued *Sings Bob Marley and Friends*. Her style is roots reggae filled with a conscious message that often recalls Bob's lyrical content. Currently, Rita remains active in the music business largely through the activities of her many children. She is engaged in the furthering and protection of her husband's legacy and attends worldwide birthday celebrations held for Bob yearly. She also established a humanitarian organization called the Rita Marley Foundation that provides supplies and improvements to the infrastructure in underprivileged parts of Africa. The group funds water recourses for schools and villages, works with teachers to improve their curriculum, and helps provide basic necessities for children to give them a chance at a productive life.

MARLEY, ROBERT NESTA "BOB, GONG, TUFF GONG" (1945–1981)

Widely recognized as the first Third World superstar and the universal icon of **reggae** music, Bob Marley was born in St. Ann's Parish, Jamaica, on February 6, 1945. His father was Norval Sinclair Marley, a white British military man stationed in Jamaica, and his mother was a black teenager from the rural interior of the island. Bob spent the earliest part of his life in St. Ann on a farm owned by his paternal grandfather, Omariah Malcolm. Although his mother, **Cedella Booker Marley**, and his father were married, they quickly became estranged and Bob spent very little time with his father.

When Bob was fourteen, he left his rural roots and moved to Kingston to find work. He ended up in the west Kingston ghetto called Trenchtown, but this is where his musical journey began. Bob pursued his interest in music alongside his longtime friend **Neville "Bunny Wailer" Livingston**; together the pair began frequenting **Joe Higgs's** yard. Higgs was a known professional musician, **Rastafarian**, and teacher who held singing clinics at his home to help young and talented aspiring musicians. Under Higgs, Bob studied guitar and singing. Bob then set about the task of getting recorded. He spent many days trying to impress producer **Leslie Kong** with his vocal stylings but was unsuccessful. However, with the encouragement of **Jimmy Cliff** and **Desmond Dekker**, Bob returned to Kong's studio and was permitted to make a recording.

In 1962, Bob cut his first single with Kong, titled "Judge Not." He quickly severed ties with Kong over a monetary dispute, but he was at the dawning of his career with this early recording. The following year in Higgs's yard, Bob and Bunny met **Peter McIntosh (Tosh)**; the three teamed to form a vocal trio. In addition to singing, Tosh and Livingston performed on rudimentary homemade instruments. To the core of the three young men were added additional personnel including Junior Braithwaite, **Beverly Kelso**, and Cherry Smith. Another important member of their group was their percussionist, **Alvin "Seeco" Patterson**, who was slightly older, skilled in the art of **burru** drumming, and acquainted with legendary reggae producer **Clement "Coxsone" Dodd**. The group called themselves the Teenagers and began shopping themselves around for studio time. Over time the name of the group changed to the Wailing Rudeboys, then the Wailing Wailers. With Patterson's help, they ultimately struck a recording deal with Dodd and recorded a pair of singles.

Braithwaite and Smith then left the group, and the name changed to the **Wailers**. Also at this time, and through the urgings of Dodd, Bob emerged as the frontman for the group. In 1964, they released the single "Simmer Down," which was a call to area youth to avoid violence, as it most often led to jail time. The single was a success and led to a series of singles such as "Dancing Shoes," "Jerk in Time," and "Who Feels It Knows It." Also at this time, Bob took on additional responsibilities at **Studio One**. Along with recording his own material, he was charged with assisting in vocal rehearsals for other acts. Additionally, Dodd let Bob stay in an unused room in the back of the studio. During the mid-1960s, the Wailers recorded over fifty singles for Dodd before their arrangement came to an end.

It was also at this time that Bob met a female singer from a group called the Soulettes. The singer's name was **Rita Anderson**; she would soon become **Rita Marley**. On February 10, 1966, Bob and Rita were married, and much as his father had done, Bob immediately departed. He relocated to the United States for a time to work in a Newark, Delaware, auto factory to save money for recording. He lived with his mother, who had been in the United States since 1963.

Bob Marley, 1969. © *UrbanImage.tv.*

Eight months later Bob returned to Jamaica and rejoined Bunny and Peter. The reconstituted Wailers released "Bend Down Low" on their Wail 'N' Soul 'M imprint in 1967. The following year found all three members of the Wailers embracing the teachings of **Rastafari** and also entering one of the most productive phases of their career together. In 1968, the trio worked with producer Danny Sims on his **JAD Records** label and recorded several successful songs. The JAD imprint was co-owned by Danny Sims and Johnny Nash; Bob and the Wailers recorded over eighty songs for the pair. However, in 1969 the group teamed with producer **Lee "Scratch" Perry** and his studio band the **Upsetters** and had a string of hits. At this time, the Upsetters employed **Carlton "Carly" Barrett** (drums) and his brother **Aston "Family Man" Barrett** (bass) as their rhythm section. The pair would go on to become longtime members of the Wailers band.

In their earliest incarnation, the Wailers were a vocal trio singing in a Jamaican approximation of the American rhythm and blues sound. As they matured, their style evolved with the popular styles on the island, moving from **ska** to **rock steady** to **reggae**. In the early 1970s, the Wailers launched their own label, named **Tuff Gong** after one of Bob's nicknames. Later that same year, Bob went to Sweden to work on a movie project with Nash. Soon the rest of the Wailers joined him in Europe, but the project fell apart, and the group was stranded without money or the ability to work. Bob approached **Christopher Blackwell** about an advance for a record so that the band could get back to Jamaica. In 1972, they signed with Blackwell's **Island Label**. This led to a cooperative deal whereby most of the Wailers's best material was released jointly by Tuff Gong and Island. In 1973, the Wailers hit big with their debut Island release *Catch a Fire*. The album was a mixture of roots reggae supplied by Bob and the Wailers and rock production supplied by Blackwell.

Interestingly, this was not their first album. Several years earlier, Kong had released a *Best of the Wailers* album that collected their strongest early material. The group vehemently opposed the release but was powerless to block it. In the same year, they released their second album, titled *Burnin.'* Legendary English guitarist Eric Clapton covered "I Shot the Sheriff" from the *Burnin'* album; his version was enormously popular. The acclaim from the first two albums plus the attention garnered by Clapton's version sent the Wailers name around the Caribbean, the United States, and western Europe.

Just as the Wailers were about to become an international phenomenon, both Bunny and Peter quit the group. Undaunted, Bob enlisted his wife Rita, **Marcia Griffiths**, and **Judy Mowatt** as a female vocal backing trio that became known as the **I-Threes**. Along with the I-Threes, the Wailers now regularly contained the Barrett brothers for the rhythm section. In addition, the group employed **Bernard "Touter" Harvey** on organ and Lee Jaffe on harmonica. In 1975, the group recorded *Natty Dread* and launched an international tour. The album contained the single "No Woman, No Cry," which went on to be a chart topper. A tour in support of the album ensued and produced the *Live!* album, which was a recording of their show at the Lyceum Theater in London.

The following year, the group released the *Rastaman Vibration* album, marking their first crossover success in the United States. The album charted in the U.S. top ten and showed the group that they could make marketable music for an American audience. The lineup for this album exhibited further change in the group. **Earl "Chinna" Smith** played rhythm guitar and **Don Kinsey** replaced **Al Anderson** on lead guitar.

In December 1976, tragedy struck Bob Marley's home. Due to his popularity, Bob had begun to be perceived as a powerful political player; as such, various Jamaican political factions viewed him as a threat. This resulted in an armed assault on his 56

Hope Road house in Kingston. Two gunmen entered the property and opened fire, injuring Bob, his wife, Kinsey, and his manager Don Taylor. After the assassination attempt, Bob was treated and released from the hospital. The bullet that struck him bounced off his sternum as he wedged himself into a corner of the kitchen. The bullet then lodged in his left arm, where doctors were forced to leave it for fear of inflicting nerve damage in the removal, which would prevent Bob from playing the guitar.

After the shooting, Bob went into self-imposed exile and did not return to Jamaica for more than a year. Bob's next record again ratcheted up his fame. *Exodus* was released in 1977 and was an instant hit with featured singles such as "One Love," "Waiting

Bob Marley, 1977. © *UrbanImage.tv.*

in Vain," and "Jamming." For this album, Blackwell recruited yet another lead guitarist. In 1977, **Junior Marvin** (aka Junior Kerr) took over the lead guitar parts and stayed with the Wailers through the *Exodus* and *Kaya* period. *Kaya* followed *Exodus* in 1978. Also in 1978, Bob and the Wailers released a second live album recorded during the tour to support *Kaya*. The live recording was titled *Babylon by Bus*; it compiled several standout performances by then-veteran Marley.

In 1979, the *Survival* album was released and marked a new label agreement with Polygram, who bought Island from Blackwell. In 1980, Bob and the Wailers were enthralled when they were invited to perform at the Zimbabwe liberation celebration. They also announced an international tour in support of *Survival*. During the U.S. leg of the tour, Bob was jogging in New York's Central Park with his friend Alan "Skill" Cole when he collapsed and suffered a brief seizure. As the result of this event, Bob's health was screened and it was discovered that cancer was quickly spreading throughout his body. In the wake of Bob's diagnosis, the album *Uprising* was released. The album was one of the band's more sparse offerings and removed the horns in favor of a greater emphasis on African sounds.

On May 11, 1981, Robert Nesta Marley died at age thirty-six. In an odd twist, just prior to his death, Marley converted to the Ethiopian Orthodox Church and took the name Berhane Selassie. Marley's funeral was planned, and it was agreed that he would be entombed in a mausoleum at his childhood home in Nine Mile. On May 21, 1981, Robert Nesta Marley was laid to rest. The funeral procession began in Kingston and wound its way around the island to St. Ann. During the procession hundreds of thousands of people lined the streets. Even the prime minister of Jamaica attended. Two years later the last album that Bob worked on was posthumously released. The album was titled *Confrontation* and contained a mixture of roots reggae, traditional chanting, and upbeat dance numbers. This was followed in 1984 by a greatest hits collection called *Legend* that captured many of his most well-received songs in a single collection. Since the mid-1980s, there have been countless greatest hits collections of his music with the Wailers, some sanctioned by his estate and many unsanctioned. His children, his wife, his mother, and his band have continued to pursue careers in music, and they all endeavor to glorify Bob's legacy through music.

MARLEY, ZIGGY. *See* MARLEY, DAVID "ZIGGY"

MAROON

The Maroons of Jamaica came to existence as the result of fighting between the Spanish and the English. In 1655, an English fleet descended on Kingston to route the Spanish and take their supplies. When the English arrived, they outmatched the Spaniards but offered them surrender instead of overwhelming them with military might. While the English waited for the Spanish to consider the terms of the surrender, the Spanish fled to the north coast and eventually escaped to Cuba. In the process, they destroyed anything of use to the English and left them nothing. When the English marched into Spanish Town, they found it uninhabited and empty. Another move that the Spanish made as they departed was to free their slaves, who then ascended into the mountains in the center of the island. These slaves became the Maroons. They settled in St. Catherine and organized themselves into a loose fighting force.

The Maroon name was likely derived from the Spanish *cimaroon*, meaning "wild or untamed." The Maroon numbers continued to grow throughout the seventeenth century as more escaped slaves joined their enclave. In addition, they began making trouble for the English, who continued to occupy the island, as they raided the English plantations and caused difficulty with the English colonization efforts. The English attempted an unlikely peace with the Maroons when they offered a tract of land and freedom to those Maroons who surrendered. This offer was ignored, and the subsequent seventy-five years were filled with periodic wars between the English and the Maroons.

At the end of the seventeenth century, a large group of slaves in Clarendon revolted and escaped into the island's interior. This group was composed primarily of Coromantees, who were from Africa's Gold Coast and were notoriously strong warriors. The escapees joined with the existing Maroons and together assembled under a leader named Cudjoe. Cudjoe's two brothers, **Accompong** and Johnny, and two low-level chiefs, Quao and Cuffee, began the first Maroon war on Jamaica. The war started as intermittent attacks on the English occupiers that resulted in robbery and death. The newly reinforced Maroon warriors primarily attacked through ambush and were able to stay a step ahead of the English through messenger calls using the **abeng** horn. The English suffered significant losses and were unable to subdue the Maroon warriors.

In the early eighteenth century, the English Captain Stoddart attacked the Maroon enclave at Nanny Town and left it decimated. This forced the Maroons farther into the interior of the island into the Cockpit region of Trelawny, but they were still able to levy successful raids on the plantations. The constant threat of attack led the English to mount a heavily financed and well-orchestrated attack on the Maroons. The Maroon army was suffering and low on provisions, but the English were unaware of their desperate circumstances.

In 1738, the king of England demanded that Cudjoe be found and that a peace settlement be reached. The English Colonel Guthrie was charged with this task; upon his finding Cudjoe, the two men reached an agreement. The Maroons were granted 1,500 acres of land and their freedom and Cudjoe was named the chief commander of Trelawny Town. In exchange, the Maroons agreed to end all hostilities against the English, refuse any new runaway slaves, and become allies with the English in the event of foreign invasion. This treaty led to the end of the First Maroon War. In the wake of the first war, there were two more Maroon conflicts with the English, the Second and Third Wars; however, they were both minor, and the Maroon descendents continue to inhabit the Trelawny region. In the twentieth century, many of the Maroon descendents became active in the Jamaican popular music business and have become an integral part of the **reggae** community.

MARQUIS, HERMAN (c. 1945–)

Marquis got his start in the **reggae** music scene in the early 1970s as an alto saxophone player and has enjoyed a long and storied career in the Jamaican popular music business. Marquis began performing and recording early in the 1970s with the likes of the **Abyssinians**, **Althea and Donna**, **Dennis Brown**, **Burning Spear**, the **Heptones**, **Justin Hinds**, **Gregory Isaacs**, **Lee "Scratch" Perry**, **Sly and Robbie**, **Bunny Wailer**, and many others. By the mid-1970s, Marquis was the premier alto saxophone player on the island, which led to him spending a great deal of time in the studio. In the late 1970s and throughout the 1980s, Marquis recorded with **Culture**, Burning Spear, **Doctor Alimantado**, the **Mighty Diamonds**, Bunny Wailer, the **Revolutionaries**, Gregory Isaacs, and the Mighty Two—**Joe Gibbs** and **Errol Thompson**.

In the 1990s, Marquis continued his domination of the studio as the lead alto saxophone player on the scene. He recorded new material with Lee "Scratch" Perry, Burning Spear, Culture, **Aston "Family Man" Barrett**, Dave and **Ansell Collins**, Barry Brown, **Junior Byles**, the **Maytones**, **Max Romeo**, Trinity, the Abyssinians, and a wide variety of others. In addition, his horn parts have appeared on a host of compilation albums from the late 1980s to the present. Marquis continued his success and heavy studio time in the new millennium, again recording for a litany of reggae luminaries. Since 2000, Marquis has recorded with Burning Spear and **Ernest Ranglin** and has continued to appear on various artist collections. Herman Marquis became a legend in reggae alto saxophone playing, and his impact is felt through the extensive list of recordings on which he played over the past thirty years.

MARSHALL, ERROL (c. 1960–)

Errol Marshall was one of Jamaica's more popular **reggae** producers in the 1980s and 1990s. During the second half of the 1980s, he teamed with Myrie Lewis and produced several hits for the singer Tanto Irie. There followed a period of productivity with artists from Kingston's Waterhouse District. Together with Lewis, Marshall produced material for Pad Anthony, **General Trees**, King Everall, **Half Pint**, **Michael Palmer**, **Echo Minott**, **Sugar Minott**, Michael Rose, and **Junior Reid**. Much of this work has been compiled on a two-volume set titled *Waterhouse Revisited*, released by Hightone Records in 1995.

Apart from this collection, Marshall and Lewis worked extensively with Half Pint and Michael Palmer during the late 1980s and into the 1990s. Many listeners believe that Half Pint's best material was produced by Marshall. An example of this is the single "Winsome," which was a success for Half Pint and was covered by the Rolling Stones in 1987 as "Too Rude." During the late 1990s, Marshall also did production work for several compilation releases including *Reggae for the Arena*; *Greensleeves Sampler, Vol. 6*; and *Dancehall 101, Vol. 4*.

MARSHALL, LARRY (1941–)

Born Fitzroy Marshal in St. Anne, Jamaica, in 1941, Marshall had his first exposure to music through his mother, who often sang around the house and enchanted the young

Marshall with her voice. In school, Marshall was encouraged to sing by one of his teachers, and his talent blossomed. He moved to Kingston in the mid-1950s, and in 1960 he entered a singing contest at the Ward Theater. He won the contest, which resulted in Philip Yap of Top Deck records taking an interest in his singing abilities. He cut a single for Yap called "Too Young to Love" in 1962, based on the U.S. single "Stand by Me." The single was successful and led to a recording session at **Studio One** for the single "Please Stay." His next big success was with the 1965 single "Snake in the Grass," a version of an already-popular American single.

As was the custom in Jamaica, Marshall moved from studio to studio, next landing at **Clement "Coxsone" Dodd's Studio One**. Dodd attempted to enlist Marshall in a pre-existing group, the Checkmates, but Marshall was dissatisfied and in 1967 moved on to producer **Prince Buster**. Marshall recorded several singles for Buster; the most successful was "I've Got Another Girl." He also recorded as a background singer on a host of Buster releases from the mid-1960s. Marshall was disappointed with the amount of attention he was getting from Buster, so he again changed producers; this time he moved to **Clancy Eccles**.

In the late 1960s, as the style of Jamaican popular music was changing from **rock steady** to **reggae**, Marshall cut a series of successful singles with Eccles. His song "Nanny Goat" and "Throw Me Corn" exhibited qualities of the new style and put Marshall at the forefront of the evolving Jamaican popular music style. Marshall then returned to Studio One and moved into the recording booth as an engineer. As part of Dodd's production team, Marshall worked with **Horace Andy**, **Dennis Brown**, **Burning Spear**, and **Alton Ellis** as the new reggae style was solidifying.

In 1973, Dodd and Marshall parted company over monetary disagreements and Marshall moved to the Black and White imprint for the singles "Can't You Understand" and the classic "I Admire You." In 1975, disgusted with working for others, Marshall formed the Amanda imprint and released his solo debut album *I Admire You*. Since the 1970s, there have been several other Marshall releases including *Presenting Larry Marshall* (1973), *Come Let Us Reason* (1974), and *I Admire You* (1975).

Marshall had the skills, timing, and vision to be a much larger presence in reggae music. Unfortunately, he has been largely passed over in favor of other singers at the dawn of the reggae era. Since the 1970s, Marshall has remained active in the music business as a producer, engineer, and keyboard player for Joe Cocker, **Freddie McGregor**, and many others.

MARTIN, ALPHONSO NATHANIEL "PHONSO" (1956–)

Born in Birmingham, England, in 1956 to Blossom and Eric Martin, Martin was one of the founding members of **Steel Pulse**. His parents were Jamaican immigrants who arrived in England in the 1950s. Martin began his musical career as a roadie for childhood friend David Hinds. He joined the band that Hinds was forming in 1978 and became a founding member of Steel Pulse. Martin was originally recruited as a singer and later became a songwriter and percussionist for the group. In 1978, he played percussion for Steel Pulse's debut album *Handsworth Revolution*. Martin remained active with the band for over a decade and is credited as the songwriter for "Your House" from the *True Democracy* album. He was active through the band's first seven releases and even filled the lead singer roll on a U.S. tour with INXS in 1988. In 1991, in the wake of the *Victims* album release, Martin left Steel Pulse and appears to be out of the music business. He currently resides in Birmingham, England.

MARVIN, JUNIOR. *See* **KERR, JUNIOR MARVIN**

MATTHEWS, WINSTON "PIPE" (c. 1945–)

Winston Matthews began his career in **reggae** music as a founding member of the Renegades and the **Wailing Souls**. His nickname "Pipe" reportedly came from being a singer at an early age, thus having good "pipes." He had learned singing from Kingston legend **Joe Higgs**, and he formed a singing group in 1963 called the Schoolboys. The active style of the time was **ska**, and the Schoolboys released several ska singles for producer **Prince Buster**.

In 1965, Matthews moved from the Schoolboys to a new group called the Renegades, which included Lloyd "Bread" MacDonald and George "Buddy" Haye. Together the trio worked with artists such as **Ernest Ranglin** as background vocalists. They also recorded a series of singles with **Clement "Coxsone" Dodd** during this period. However, by 1968, the trio split and a reconstituted version of the group emerged. The new lineup was called Wailing Souls and included Matthews, MacDonald, Oswald Downer, and Norman Davis. The Wailing Souls had a degree of success in the late 1960s. They worked with Clement "Coxsone" Dodd at the legendary **Studio One**, where they recorded a pair of successful singles as Pipe and the Pipers in the early 1970s. Also in the early 1970s, the Wailing Souls moved to **Bob Marley's Tuff Gong** label. This early success kicked off a lengthy career that has included a large quantity of high-quality roots reggae.

In the mid-1970s, the lineup of the group again changed, as did its producer. They moved on to work with **Joseph "Joe Joe" Hookim** and recorded a series of hits for **Channel One**, with the **Revolutionaries** backing them. To gain greater control of its output, the group then launched its own label called Massive; its early offerings were well received. The first two singles on the new label were "Bredda Gravalicious" and "Feel the Spirit," both hugely successful.

In 1979, the group released its debut album *Wild Suspense* on **Chris Blackwell's Island Records** imprint. The group then jumped to **Sly and Robbie's** Taxi label and released a pair of albums in the early 1980s. *Fire House Rock*, the next release, was produced by **Henry "Junjo" Lawes**, and the group reached the peak of its output. In the 1980s, the Wailing Souls, with MacDonald and Matthews at the helm, continued their success. They even made a brief foray into the newer **dancehall** style with the help of **King Jammy**.

In the 1990s, the group continued its steadfast progress, which landed it a deal with Sony Records. In 1992, the Wailing Souls released their most adventurous album to date. *All over the World* saw the enlisting of a new vocalist, Maisha, and a host of guest artists including **U-Roy**. The album ran the stylistic gamut and earned the group a Grammy nomination. The Wailing Souls' second and final album for Sony was the live release *Live On*. A few of their more recent releases were 1997's *Tension*, 1998's *Psychedelic Souls*, and 2000's *Equality*. The *Equality* album featured the single "Don't Say." Its release spawned a U.S. tour. In addition, material from the Wailing Souls continues to appear on a variety of compilation albums such as *The Wailing Souls* and *Soul and Power*. The group remains a powerful musical force and is heavily sought after for live performances.

MATUMBI

A London-based **ska** and **reggae** group active during the 1970s and 1980s, the band Matumbi was formed in 1972; its central figure was **Dennis Bovell**. Bovell was a

Matumbi. © *UrbanImage.tv.*

known **sound system** operator with the Jah Sufferer sound and brought his dub sensibilities to Matumbi's sound. The band's biggest hit was the song "Man in Me," which was written by Bovell and recorded by Matumbi in 1976. They went on to release several full-length albums including *Seven Seals* (1978), *Point of View* (1979), *Oh Who She? Go Go Deh!* (1979), *Matumbi* (1981), and *Testify* (1982). Matumbi was one of the United Kingdom's earliest reggae bands and was highly influential on others that followed.

In the early 1980s, Bovell left Matumbi to pursue other musical outlets, and the band faded into obscurity. However, Bovell remained active in music as a singer, songwriter, producer, and engineer. He went on to work with **Alpha Blondy**, **Linton Kwesi Johnson**, the Pop Group, the Slits, Bananarama, the Thompson Twins, the Boomtown Rats, Marvin Gaye, and many others.

MAYTALS, THE. *See* HIBBERT, FREDERICK

MAYTONES, THE

Formed in Kingston, Jamaica, in the mid-1960s when Vernon Buckley and Gladstone "Son" Grant joined forces, the pair known as the Maytones were friends from youth, having both grown up in the May Pen district of Jamaica. Throughout the second half of the 1960s, the Maytones recorded and released singles. Their earliest singles were produced by Buckley and released on the VB label. At this time the duo came to the attention of Alvin "G. G." Ranglin, who went on to work as their producer and manager. Ranglin brought his GG's label out of dormancy and issued a series of Maytones singles on it. Their first break came when they released "Black and White" in the early

1970s. The single was successful and was followed by other successes, such as "Preaching Love," "Loving Reggae," and "Serious Love." The duo was most successful with love songs, but they also hit with songs on **Rastafarian** themes. Examples of singles of this type included "Cleanliness," "Bongo Man Rise," and "Little Boy Blue." Further, as the Maytones moved more in the Rastafarian faith, they gained a greater fan base. They had success with the mid-1970s singles "Babylon a Fall" and "Run Babylon."

Regardless of lyrical content, the pair never fit the typical Rasta image; for example, they did not wear their hair in dreadlocks. The group's debut album was recorded by Ranglin at **Channel One Studios** in 1976. The release was titled *Madness* and scored the Maytones significant success. It was followed by 1978's *Boat to Zion*, which was again a success. Unfortunately, the Maytones's success was largely regional, and they were passed over for recording contracts by major labels outside of Jamaica. The year 1979 saw the release of *One Way*, which was successful if only in the Caribbean.

By the end of the 1970s, the Maytones had disbanded, and in 1981 Buckley moved to Canada. Subsequent compilations have been issued, such as *The Maytones, Their Greatest Hits* and other *Best of* offerings. In the mid-1990s, Buckley and Grant reformed the Maytones for a brief period. They cut the album *Madness 2* (1998), after which Buckley again went solo.

MCCLYMONT, JEPTHER. *See* LUCIANO

MCCOOK, THOMAS "TOMMY" (1932–1998)

McCook grew up in the west Kingston ghettos of Jamaica. As a youth, he attended the **Alpha Catholic Boys School**, where he learned about music and how to play the tenor saxophone and flute. He also met a large number of likeminded young Jamaican musicians with whom he would go on to work throughout the course of his life. After leaving Alpha School at age fourteen, he toured with several dance bands.

In the late 1940s and early 1950s, McCook worked with the legendary **Rastafarian** hand drummer **Count Ossie**. In 1954, he moved to the Bahamas and played jazz for five years, mastering the style. Simultaneously, the popular music scene in Jamaica was transforming from **mento** to **ska**. McCook arrived back in Jamaica in 1962 just as the ska era was dawning. He was offered a job as part of **Clement "Coxsone" Dodd's** studio band, and after a time he conceded. McCook became the leader of the band, which he dubbed the **Skatalites**. The original band included McCook, **Roland Alphonso**, **Lloyd Brevett**, Lloyd Knibb, Lester Sterling, **Donald Drummond**, Jerry Haynes, Johnny Moore, Jackie Opel, Donna Schaffer, and **Jackie Mittoo**. For the next fourteen months, the Skatalites worked for all of the major producers in Jamaica and played the backing music for virtually every important ska vocalist.

The band broke up as the result of trombonist Donald Drummond's arrest, and McCook went on to form the Supersonics. The Supersonics then became the studio band for **Duke Reid's Treasure Isle** studio. While the Skatalites were instrumental in the birth of ska, the Supersonics helped usher in the **rock steady** era. Throughout the mid-1970s, McCook issued a series of solo albums for producer **Bunny "Striker" Lee**, including *Cook'in* (1974), *Brass Rockers* (1975), and *Hot Lava* (1977).

In the late 1970s and early 1980s, ska was reborn through the UK **two tone** craze, and McCook re-formed the Skatalites. The group played in Kingston in 1983–1984 and ultimately landed another recording contract. In the late 1980s and early 1990s, ska's third wave was in effect, and the Skatalites launched an international tour. They released a series of new recordings and were nominated for several Grammys. In the early 1990s, the Skatalites signed a new record deal with the **Island** label, and McCook retired from the band. McCook settled back into his Atlanta, Georgia, home with his family. Although he stopped touring, he still recorded, and his last material was captured on the album *Tommy McCook and Friends: The Authentic Sound of Tommy McCook.*

On May 4, 1998, Tommy McCook died at his home. Even in the wake of their founding member's demise, the Skatalites continue on. The lineup has changed significantly since the early days and now includes Lloyd Brevett, Lloyd Knibb, Doreen Shaffer, Lester Sterling, Karl Bryan, **Vin Gordon**, Devon James, Ken Stewart, and Kevin Batchelor.

MCGREGOR, FREDDIE (1956–)

Born in Clarendon, Jamaica, McGregor began his career in music at an early age when he began singing backup harmonies for the **ska** band the **Clarendonians** when he was only seven. Through his association with the Clarendonians, McGregor met **Clement "Coxsone" Dodd**, who was the group's producer at the time. While at Dodd's **Studio One**, McGregor was influenced by artists such as **Bob Andy**, **Ken Boothe**, **Alton Ellis**, and **Bob Marley**.

McGregor's first break came when the Clarendonians disbanded in the mid-1960s. He teamed with ex-Clarendonian Ernest "Fitzroy" Wilson, and together they became the singing due Freddie and Fitzroy. The duo recorded several singles, such as "Why Did You Do It" and "Do Good and Good Will Follow You," and Freddie gradually cultivated a larger audience. In the early 1970s, McGregor continued his association with Dodd and Studio One. He recorded for Dodd as the lead singer of Generation Gap and **Soul Syndicate**. Also at this time, he was increasingly influenced by the Philadelphia sound being made by Gamble and Huff and select Detroit-based groups.

McGregor changed his artistic direction when he became a **Rastafarian** in 1975 and began to espouse Rasta doctrine in his music. With help from **Earl "Chinna" Smith**, McGregor recorded the singles "Mark of the Beast," "Sgt. Brown," "I Am a Rasta," "Rasta Man Camp," "Collie Weed," and several others. These successful singles were followed by his debut album *Mr. McGregor* (1977), which was produced by **Winston "Niney" Holness**. The album was a major success and brought McGregor to the forefront of **reggae** music.

For the rest of the 1970s, McGregor continued to record for Studio One and branched out into production working with **Judy Mowatt**, **Johnny Osbourne**, and Jennifer Lara. In 1980, McGregor released his second album, *Bobby Babylon*. The album was his biggest success to date, and he quickly followed it with the major single "Big Ship." With this single, McGregor became one of the top three reggae singers in the wake of Bob Marley's death in 1981.

The 1980s were McGregor's biggest decade. He released a series of albums beginning with 1980's *Zion Chant* and

Freddie McGregor. © *UrbanImage.tv.*

including *Big Ship* (1982), *I Am Ready* (1982), *Come On Over* (1983), *Across the Border* (1984), *All in the Same Boat* (1986), and several others. During this decade, McGregor reached markets outside of the Caribbean. He appeared on the UK charts in the middle of the decade and continued to garner attention in Europe for several years. By the end of the 1980s, McGregor was the most successful and sought-after reggae artist in Jamaica. Next, McGregor launched his own label, Big Ship. His first release established the *Jamaica Classics* series that went through several volumes. Big Ship remains a presence on the reggae scene today and covers production, manufacturing, distribution, and promotion.

Through the 1990s, McGregor continued his success. His productivity waned, but this was due to touring and continued efforts to recruit and nurture new Jamaican reggae talent. In the 1990s, McGregor released another series of albums, of which *Push On* (1994) was the most significant.

In the new millennium, McGregor continues to produce new music. His 2000 album *Signature* illustrated a renewal of his career. He followed *Signature* with 2002's *Anything for You*, which received a Grammy nomination. McGregor remains active in the reggae music scene today, and his forty-plus-year career is a testament to his staying power and his talent.

MCINTOSH, WINSTON HUBERT. *See* TOSH, PETER

MCLEAN, BERTRAM "RANCHIE" (c. 1960–)

Active in the Jamaican popular music scene for over twenty-five years, McLean has long been revered as a high-quality multi-instrumentalist playing guitar, bass, and keyboards. McLean surfaced in the late 1970s with appearances on albums by Earth and Stone, **Culture**, and **Jimmy Cliff**. In the 1980s he appeared on the soundtrack for the movie *Club Paradise* and recorded with Sadao Watanabe, the **Clarendonians**, and others. The 1990s were an even more productive decade for McLean, as he recorded with **Burning Spear**, **I-Roy**, Culture, the **Meditations**, **Prince Far I**, the **Revolutionaries**, the Chantells, Larry Marshall, Jimmy Cliff, **Sly and Robbie**, and others. McLean has also appeared on a host of reissues and compilation releases such as the *Ultimate Collections* series releases for Burning Spear, Sly and Robbie, **Dennis Brown**, and **Gregory Isaacs**. McLean remains active, having worked on material for Sly and Robbie and others during 2004.

MEDITATIONS, THE

The Meditations were a singing trio formed in Kingston, Jamaica, in 1974. The group was composed of Ansel Cridland, Danny Clarke, and **Winston Watson**; together the three became one of the most significant singing outfits on the island. The group used close vocal harmonies inspired by American soul and bass heavy rhythms to deliver their brand of Marcus Garvey-influenced lyrics. Cridland had been in an earlier group called the Linkers and had scored a **rock steady** hit with the late 1960s single "Nyah Man Story."

In the early 1970s, Clarke and Watson began working for producer **Lee "Scratch" Perry** as a duo called the Flames. In addition to duo material, the Flames also backed **Alton Ellis**. The three joined forces in the mid-1970s and began recording for **Ken Khouri's Federal Records** imprint. In 1976, they released their debut album, *Message from the Meditations*, which was followed in 1977 by *Wake Up*. The *Message* release had been recorded with the assistance of **Bobby Dobson** and included singles such as "Woman Is like a Shadow," "Running from Jamaica," and "Changing of the Times." The *Wake Up* album was equally strong with the singles "Fly Natty Dread," "Turn Me Loose," and the re-release of "Nyah Man Story." These early albums gained the group notoriety throughout the Caribbean and the United States. The trio proceeded to tour these locations, and their popularity grew.

The group also came to the attention of **Bob Marley** and worked for him as studio backup harmonists. They parted with Dobson over unhappiness with their royalties and struck a deal with Perry. The Meditations provided backing vocals for Marley on the songs "Rastaman Live Up," "Blackman Redemption," and "Punky Reggae Party." Along with recording directly for Marley, the Meditations also recorded on Marley's **Tuff Gong** label while continuing their work with Perry's **Black Ark** imprint.

In the late 1970s, the group worked on a new album for **Island Records**. However, the deal with Island did not go through, and this material was not made available until its release on **Nighthawk Records** under the title *Reggae Crazy*. The album *Guidance* was released in 1980 as the group's third album and was another strong collection of classic songs. In 1983, the Meditations released *No More Friend* on Greensleeves.

By the end of 1984, the Meditations had decided to move in separate directions. Cridland went on as Ansel Meditations, and Clarke and Watson retained the Meditations group name. The Clarke/Watson version of the group continued to build a reputation in the United States and landed a record deal with **Heartbeat Records**. *For the Good of Man* was released in 1988 on the Heartbeat imprint. However, in 1990 the three singers again came together and released *Return of the Meditations*. In 1994, they released *Deeper Roots—The Best of the Meditations* on the Heartbeat imprint. The Meditations are now viewed as three of reggae music's elder statesmen, and their material is highly revered.

MEINAI, RAZ. *See* BADAWAI

MELODIANS

Tony Brevett, Brent Dowe, and Trevor McNaughton formed the Melodians in 1963 in Greenwich Town, Kingston, Jamaica. While the group was a functional vocal trio, they also had a fourth member named Renford Cogle who did not sing, instead preferring to write the songs. The trio went on to become one of the most popular early **rock steady** acts from Jamaica. Their earliest recordings were done for **Clement "Coxsone" Dodd's Studio One**, after they won a local singing contest. Of these early recordings, only the single "Lay It On" achieved any success.

However, like so many of their fellow Jamaican recording artists, they soon moved on to work with other producers, namely **Sonia Pottinger** and **Duke Reid**. For Reid's **Treasure Isle** imprint, the group had a rapid succession of hits. On Pottinger's High Note label, the group continued its success with singles such as "Little Nut Tree." The trio ultimately had their highest level of success recording for **Leslie Kong**. For Kong's **Beverley's** imprint, the group recorded several of its classic songs, such as "Rivers of Babylon" and "Sweet Sensation." In the wake of Kong's death in 1971, the group again made the rounds of all of the major studios in Jamaica.

The tides had turned in Jamaica by the early 1970s, and the Melodians' brand of rock steady was no match for the burgeoning **reggae** style. The group had some limited success, but then split in the mid-1970s. In the 1990s, the Melodians re-formed and continued to perform and record.

MELODY, COURTNEY (c. 1965–)

Born in St. Andrew, Jamaica, Melody became interested in singing while still in school. He got his earliest exposure to the music business through working with the Black Spider **sound system**, where he began to cultivate a reputation. He then moved on to the Stereo One system, where he worked with Daddy Freddy and **Lieutenant Stitchie**. While with Stereo One, Melody released the single "Screechy across the Border," which brought him international acclaim. Like so many other Jamaican recording artists, Melody worked for many different producers. He next worked for **Winston Riley's Techniques** imprint on the singles "Exploiter" and "How Long Will Your Love Last." By this point, Melody had gained a substantial reputation in the **dancehall**. However, he reached true international stardom with 1986's "Bad Boy." Sensing his time had come, Melody released a series of singles that all charted, including "Ninja Mi Ninja," "Tell Dem," "Modern Girl," "Downpressor," and several others that remain popular.

At the height of his success, Melody was involved in a motorcycle accident that took him out of the music business for a time. By the time he returned, his place as the leader of the dancehall had been filled by a score of up-and-coming **DJs**. This did not prevent him from issuing a series of albums including *Bad Boy Reggae* (1990), *Take a Look at Life* (1996), and *Nothing but Love* (1996). He did regain a degree of his past success with the single "In the Street." In 1999 Melody again became popular due to the use of his song "Ninja Mi Ninja" in the New York World Clash. Once the Mighty Crown sound system re-popularized Melody, the singer was quick to parlay the renewed interest into new music. In the new millennium, Melody worked with Third Eye Studio on the single "Rebel" and continues to issue new music.

MELODY MAKERS, THE. *See* ZIGGY MARLEY AND THE MELODY MAKERS

MENTO

Mento is one of the several important styles of Jamaican popular music that preceded **reggae**. In the early twentieth century, several indigenous musical styles led to reggae, and mento was the first: mento, **ska**, **rock steady**, then reggae. Mento was Jamaican folk music that combined sacred and secular elements. The styles mixed Pocamania church music, Junkanoo fife and drum sounds, the European quadrille, slave-era work songs, and even elements of American jazz. It was the first type of music recorded in Jamaica; like the early American jazz styles, it did not disappear when later styles emerged. Mento differs from other Jamaican popular music styles in that it was not a product of the urban landscape; instead it emerged from the rural island interior.

Roots of mento can be traced back into the nineteenth century; however, its earliest recorded history dates to the 1920s. The more refined mento style came from the 1950s, which is dubbed the golden age of mento. There are several varieties of mento to consider. The classic mento sound is generated on acoustic instruments and has an informal and folk quality. It is often referred to as country mento and is performed with the banjo, acoustic guitar, homemade reed instruments, and hand percussion such as the rumba box. The slicker, more urban, version of mento surfaced in the wake of the Caribbean jazz bands' emergence in the 1920s. Here the homemade rural instruments were replaced by professional instruments such as the saxophone, clarinet, bass, and piano. The more urban mento sound also contained elements of calypso and jazz.

Mento is meant to be danced to as well as sung. Mento lyrics run the gamut from rural themes of food preparation to more cosmopolitan images of relationship issues and even bawdy topics. As a style of Jamaican popular music, mento paved the way for ska, rock steady, reggae, and **dancehall**. It did so without subversion and continues to be a popular style today.

MESSENJAH

Messenjah was a **reggae** band formed in 1981 in Kitchener, Ontario, by Errol Blackwood, Rupert "Ojiji" Harvey, Eric Walsh, Hal Duggan, and Raymond Ruddock. They quickly established themselves as a rising force and were credited as one of Canada's first reggae bands. In 1982, the group released its debut album, *Rock You High*, independent of record label support. In the following year, the album was re-released on the WEA imprint. In 1984, Tony King was added to the group for additional support on percussion, and they released *Jam Session*, also on WEA (a Warner Brothers, Electra, and Atlantic corporation).

After issuing *Jam Session*, Blackwood left the group, and Harvey stepped into the leadership role. Next, the group released its third album, *Cool Operator* (1987). More lineup changes ensued before the 1990 release of *Rock and Sway*. Through the rest of the 1980s, Messenjah toured extensively in Canada and the United States, and they performed in Jamaica on the **Reggae Sunsplash** concert in 1985. The band's international reputation had been established, testified to with its appearance in the 1988 U.S. film *Cocktail*.

In the early 1990s, the band's success continued with appearances at large music festivals such as Reggae on the River. Messenjah continues to perform live.

MICHIGAN AND SMILEY

Papa Michigan and General Smiley were born Anthony Fairclough and Erroll Bennett and emerged on the Jamaican popular music scene as one of the earliest two **DJ** outfits. Michigan and Smiley went into the studio with **Clement "Coxsone" Dodd** and struck gold at **Studio One**. The pair formed in the late 1970s while still in school and scored early hits with "Rub a Dub Style" and "Nice Up the Dance."

Shortly after releasing the pair's singles, Dodd embarked for New York, and Michigan and Smiley moved over to **Tuff Gong Records**. They parlayed their early success into an appearance on the **Reggae Sunsplash** concert in 1980, and reappeared annually until 1985. They continued their success with early 1980s hits including "Diseases" and "One Love Jam Down." The song "Diseases" was recorded by **Henry "Junjo" Lawes** in 1982, and it was picked up and released in a version by **Fathead** and **Yellowman**. Also in 1982, the pair released its debut album *Step by Step*, which was recorded at **Channel One**.

The following year the pair was again in the charts with the single "Sugar Daddy," produced by **Doctor Dread** for his **RAS Records** imprint. There followed a series of successful albums including *Back in the Biz* (1983) and *Sugar Daddy* (1986). The pair did not outlast the 1980s, but they periodically re-form for specific occasions. Recently, General Smiley released his solo debut *O.G.S.* on Upfulone Records.

MIGHTY DIAMONDS

The Mighty Diamonds were formed in 1969 by Donald "Tabby" Shaw, Fitzroy "Bunny" Simpson, and Lloyd "Judge" Ferguson. The singing trio hailed from Trenchtown, Kingston, and has spent the past thirty-six years writing, recording, and performing live. The Diamonds sing in a harmonious roots reggae style that disguises their **Rastafarian** and often-militant messages. The group was heavily influenced by the Motown sound

Mighty Diamonds. © *UrbanImage.tv.*

and worked to perfect its close harmonies in the die cast by Berry Gordy. Their first single, 1973's "Shame and Pride," was on the **Dynamic Studio** imprint. The trio also had success early in their career with the singles "Hey Girl" and "Country Living," both released on the **Channel One** imprint. They then landed a deal with Virgin Records in 1975 and recorded their debut album *Right Time*. The album and its title track single went on to become classics.

Their next major hit was the international stunner "Pass the Kouchie" from the album *Changes* (1981). The song scored twice for the group, once in its original form and then again in a version by Musical Youth as "Pass the Dutchie." Through the course of its long and storied career, the group has recorded in excess of forty albums, such as *Deeper Roots* (1979), *The Roots Is Here* (1982), *Reggae Street* (1987), *Speak the Truth* (1994), and more recently *Revolutions* (2003). The trio has performed internationally and has appeared on the **Reggae Sunsplash** concert in Jamaica numerous times.

MIGHTY DREAD (c. 1955–)
Born Winston Watson, Dread was one of the founding members of the singing trio the **Meditations**. He supplied the high harmony parts, singing in a sweet falsetto voice. The group formed in Kingston, Jamaica, in 1974, when Watson joined with Ansel Cridland and Danny Clarke. Cridland had been in an earlier group called the Linkers and had scored a **rock steady** hit with the late 1960s single "Nyah Man Story." In the early 1970s, Clarke and Watson began working for producer **Lee "Scratch" Perry** as a duo called the Flames. In addition to duo material, the Flames also backed **Alton Ellis**. The three joined forces in the mid-1970s and began recording for **Ken Khouri's Federal Records** imprint.

In 1976, they released their debut album *Message from the Meditations*, which was followed in 1977 by *Wake Up*. The *Message* release had been recorded with the assistance of **Bobby Dobson** and included singles such as "Woman Is like a Shadow," "Running from Jamaica," and "Changing of the Times." The *Wake Up* album was equally strong with the singles "Fly Natty Dread," "Turn Me Loose," and the re-release of "Nyah Man Story." These early albums gained the group notoriety throughout the Caribbean and the United States. The trio proceeded to tour these locations, and their popularity grew.

The group also came to the attention of **Bob Marley** and worked for him as studio backup harmonists. They parted with Dobson over unhappiness with their royalties and struck a deal with Perry. The Meditations provided backing vocals for Marley on the songs "Rastaman Live Up," "Blackman Redemption," and "Punky Reggae Party." Along with recording directly for Marley, the Meditations also recorded on Marley's **Tuff Gong** label while continuing work with Perry's **Black Ark** imprint.

In the late 1970s, the group worked on a new album for the **Island Records** label. However, the deal with Island did not go through, and this material was not made available until its release on **Nighthawk Records** under the title *Reggae Crazy*. The album *Guidance* was released in 1980 as the group's third album and was another strong collection of classic songs. In 1983, the Meditations released *No More Friend* on Greensleeves.

By the end of 1984, the Meditations had decided to move in separate directions. Cridland went on as Ansel Meditations, and Clarke and Watson retained the Meditations group name. The Clarke/Watson version of the group continued to build a reputation in the United States and landed a record deal with **Heartbeat Records**. *For the Good of Man* was released in 1988 on the Heartbeat imprint. However, in 1990 the three singers again came together and released *Return of the Meditations*. In 1994, they released *Deeper Roots—The Best of the Meditations* on the Heartbeat imprint. The Meditations are now viewed as three of reggae music's elder statesmen, and their material is highly revered.

MIGHTY SPARROW (1935–)

Born Slinger Francisco in 1935 in Gran Roi Bay, Grenada, Mighty Sparrow got his start in the Caribbean popular music business in 1956 in Trinidad, where he began singing in the calypso style. Eventually, Sparrow ascended to the throne as King of Calypso on the strength of songs such as "Only a Fool," "Ah Fraid De Aids," "Invade South Africa," and "Coke Is Not It." Sparrow's career began in the 1950s when he left his native Grenada and immigrated to Trinidad. There he was selected to be part of the choir at St. Patrick's Catholic Church, where he honed his vocal skills. In addition to his early island singing influences, Sparrow was also weaned on the American rhythm and blues of singers such as Ella Fitzgerald and Sarah Vaughn. To this mixture of influences were added early calypso artists, such as Lord Kitchener, Lord Invader, and others.

In 1955, Sparrow hit with the single "Jean and Dinah" and went on to score at least one hit per year for the next several decades. In the late 1950s and repeatedly in the 1960s, Sparrow won the Calypso Road March Competition and positioned himself as an educator of the youth, not just a musician. In the 1970s, Sparrow began to release albums at a furious pace. He issued *Hot and Sweet* (1974) and *Peace and Love* (1979) as he laid claim to the title of most popular calypsonian of the time.

In the 1980s, he released at least seven full-length albums beginning with 1980's *Latin Black*. This was followed by *Vanessa* (1985), *King of the World* (1985), *A Touch of Class* (1986), *One Love One Heart* (1987), *Dr. Bird* (1988), and *The Party Classics, Volume 2* (1988). By the mid-1980s, Sparrow was an international sensation. He was awarded an honorary doctorate from the University of the West Indies; thus the *Dr. Bird* album. During the 1990s, Sparrow maintained his fevered pace, releasing another series of albums. His reputation was assured, but Sparrow continued to push his music forward. By the end of the decade he had won his eleventh Road March in addition to winning the Trinidad and Tobago Carnival Road March eight times.

In the new millennium, Mighty Sparrow continues to assert his supremacy. He has released at least six albums since 1999 and remains in the top position in Caribbean calypso and soca.

MIKEY DREAD (1948–)

Born in Port Antonio, Jamaica, in 1948, Dread's earliest claim to fame was gleaned as a radio personality in the 1970s for the Jamaican Broadcasting Company (JBC). It was for this show that Michael Campbell adopted the name **Mikey Dread**. He hosted a weekly four-hour program that he called Dread at the Controls, which made him a household name and won him substantial popularity. Dread made his debut during a period of relative stagnation on Jamaican radio. There were only two stations on the island, and imported American **DJs** ruled them both. Further, the stations largely ignored music created on the island, so a new format had to be cultivated to change this. The solution was found when larger Jamaican record companies began buying blocks of radio time and paying for it as advertising time. The result sounds like payola, but this was the only means by which local labels could receive any airtime.

The block time approach was less than successful, and Dread stepped in to alter the format. Dread's show featured local music; he benefited by spinning the most cur-rent and popular songs, all of which were informed by his vast knowledge of the roots of the music that he passed on to the listeners.

Dread's entrance into creating music came by recording radio jingles at **King Tubby's** studio. He employed anyone on hand to assist with these projects. However, he had the fortune of using **Althea** (Forrest) **and Donna** (Reid); soon the pair was making a name for themselves. Forrest and Reid's success spurred Dread on to further studio work. The result was his pairing with **Lee "Scratch" Perry**, titled "Dread at the Controls." He followed this with the singles "Schoolgirls" and "Homeguard," both of which garnered some level of popularity.

Dread's reputation was on the rise even as he was endangering his job. The conservative JBC owners, and even other DJs at the station, did not appreciate Dread's approach, so he left in the late 1970s. After a brief stint as an engineer for **Treasure Isle**, Dread formed a production team with Carlton Patterson. He then formed his own label, called Dread at the Controls, and quickly released his first album in 1979. *African Anthem*

Mikey Dread. © *UrbanImage.tv.*

and *At the Controls Dubwise* followed in the same year. Dread's reputation had grown on the island and in the United Kingdom to the point that he was approached for guest appearances by **UB40** and the Clash. He appears on the Clash single "Bank Robber."

Dread continues to write and record. Throughout the 1980s and 1990s, he released at least nine albums on his Dread at the Controls imprint, **Heartbeat Records**, and the **RAS Records** label. Dread now lives in the United States and continues to be active in the music business as a recording artist and live performer.

MIKEY GENERAL (1963–)

Born Michael Taylor in London, England, in 1963, when he was two his family immigrated to Jamaica, and since then he has split his time between the United States and the Caribbean. While still in school, Taylor gained the nickname General from his fellow St. George Catholic high school football players due to his large stature. As a singer, General delivers his lyrics in a high falsetto used to express his sentiments about Afrocentrism and **Rastafarianism**.

General's earliest musical experiences were with his church choir and area **sound systems**. Throughout his teenage years General continued to hone his vocal skills by appearing at any dance that he could to take a turn on the microphone. This brought him to a few of the more popular sounds, such as Killamanjaro and Virgo. At age sixteen, General recorded his first single, "Roots Mi Roots," and his career began in earnest. In the 1980s, General returned to England and worked for a series of sound systems including Saxon. He also took a job with the **Fashion Records** studios.

After having experienced a small degree of success in Jamaica, General found England not as kind to him so, in 1992, he returned to the Caribbean. Back in Jamaica, General teamed with **Luciano** and immersed himself in the **Rastafarian** teachings of the Rastas. With this religious element injected into his lyrics, General again ascended the ladder of success. His first album, *Rastaman Stronger*, was released in 1996 with production by **Philip "Fatis" Burrell**. Next, General toured with **Luciano** and the **Firehouse Crew**, and his reputation soared. More recently, General released *Spiritual Revolution* (2000) on the label that he and Luciano established, called Qabalah. The album contained a heavy dose of the General's views on Rasta and its teachings.

In the wake of the second album, General continued to tour with Luciano and became known worldwide. In the new millennium, Mikey General continues his work, and he procured a production deal with the Stone Tiger record label.

Mikey General. © *UrbanImage.tv.*

MILLER, JACOB "KILLER" (1955–1980)

Born in Mandeville, Jamaica, in 1955, the only child of Joan Ashman and Desmond Elliot, Miller was also a cousin to the UK-born singer **Maxi Priest**. At eight years old, Miller was sent from Mandeville to Kingston to live with his grandparents on Rousseau Road. There he attended Melrose High School and frequented area studios, befriending **Augustus Pablo**. Through Pablo, Miller met all of the major producers of the day and sang for them. In addition, Pablo gave Miller airtime on his Rockers **sound system**.

Miller's first single, "Love Is the Message," was recorded in 1968 for **Clement "Coxsone" Dodd**, and his musical reputation began to grow. Miller did not immediately get picked up by one of the major studios. However, he continued to rehearse, and when Pablo and his brother Garth Swaby launched the Rockers imprint, they brought Miller into the studio to record "Keep On Knocking." There followed a series of successful singles on the Rockers label, including "Each One Teach One" and "Baby I Love You So."

With a stronger reputation in place, Miller was approached by **Inner Circle** who, due to lineup changes, was looking for a new lead singer. In 1976, Inner Circle added **Bernard "Touter" Harvey** on keyboards and Jacob Miller as lead singer. There followed a series of Inner Circle records with Miller singing, such as *Blame It on the Sun* (1975), *Reggae Thing* (1976), *Ready for the World* (1977), and a solo offering from Miller called *Dread Dread* (1978). With Miller, Inner Circle played the **One Love Peace Concert**, and Miller continued to release material with the band and on his own. He followed *Dread Dread* with another album, *Jacob "Killer" Miller* (1978). In 1979, Miller again released a solo album, this one called *Wanted.*

With all of his work, both with and without Inner Circle, Miller was at the top of the **reggae** scene. With Inner Circle came the seminal album *Everything Is Great* (1979). Tragically, Jacob Miller died in a car accident in March 1980 when the car he was traveling in struck a pole on Hope Road.

MILLIE. *See* SMALL, MILLIE

MINOTT, ECHO (1963–)

Born Noel Phillips in the Maverley area of Kingston, Jamaica, Phillips got an early start in music and began singing as a youth for local talent competitions and with his school choir. In 1980 at age seventeen, Phillips caught his big break and recorded his debut album *Youthman Vibration* for **King Jammy**. The record was not released in Jamaica, but did achieve a degree of success in the United Kingdom. Next, Phillips worked with his cousin, producer **Errol Marshall**, and released the single "Ten Miles" in 1983. Success followed (along with a name change) with another UK release, "Man in Love," which appeared on the album *Echo Minott Meets Sly and Robbie* (1984).

Minott sang in a **dancehall toasters** style, but mixed his songs on slack topics (talk of guns, sex, and drugs) with more sincere love songs. In 1984, Minott scored his first Jamaican hit with the single "Love Problems," produced by **Joe Gibbs**. Several other successful singles followed. The next year, Minott's fame bloomed on an international level with the hit "Lazy Body." The song was so successful that it resulted in an entire album of versions of its rhythm. Minott next released the album *Rock and Calypso* (1985) for producer **Harry J**.

At the height of his career, Minott was influencing the dancehall scene with regular work on both the King Jammy and Black Scorpio **sound systems**. In 1986, he released "What the Hell," another huge hit in Jamaica. In the wake of the success of this single, King Jammy released the *What the Hell* (1986) album. Throughout the rest of the 1980s and into the 1990s, Minott continued to release hits such as "Follow Me," "Article Don," and "Mr. Ruddy." In 1992, Minott immigrated to New York and scored another international hit with "Murder Weapon." Back in Jamaica, in 1994, Minott's success continued with a series of releases including "I Am Back" and "Sensitive."

The rest of the 1990s were a dry period for Minott, during which he was not as active in the music scene. However, in September 1999, Minott faced arrest in Jamaica when he failed to appear in court on charges of robbery with aggravation and illegal possession of a firearm. In the new millennium, Minott returned to music and has joined forces with Rootsman and Third Eye studios. In 2002, he cut a series of singles including "Oh Jah" and "Sharp Shooter," and has been planning a new album on Third Eye.

MINOTT, LINCOLN "SUGAR" (1956–)

Born Lincoln Minott in Kingston, Jamaica, he got his start in the various singing contests held around the island. After high school, Minott launched the Black Roots **sound system**, later Youth Promotion, and honed his skills on the microphone. At the end of the 1960s, he joined forces with Derrick Howard and Winston **"Tony Tuff"** Morris to form the **African Brothers**. The trio sang in the traditional close harmony style and released several solid singles such as "Party Night," "Lead Us Father," and "Torturing." Though this work fell into obscurity, it was re-issued by **Easy Star Records** as the album *Want Some Freedom* (2001), which included many of the rare, early 1970s recordings from the group. By 1974, the group had disbanded, and each artist went his separate way.

Sugar Minott. © *UrbanImage.tv.*

As a solo artist, Minott worked with **Clement "Coxsone" Dodd**, and together they returned **Studio One** to the height of its glory. Songs that the two men created together include "Vanity," "Hang On Natty," and "Jah Jah Children." By the end of the decade, Minott's music was on the cutting edge of the evolution of **dancehall**, which was attested to when he launched his Black Roots label in 1979. Minott then embarked on a lengthy project of sponsoring up-and-coming talent. Through his Youth Promotion agency he furthered the careers of **Tristan Palmer**, Barry Brown, **Junior Reid**, **Garnet Silk**, **Tenor Saw**, **Tony Tuff**, Little John, Captain Sinbad, **Yami Bolo**, and many others.

Also in the 1980s, Minott's own musical career continued its ascent. He released a series of high-quality albums such as *Ghetto-ology* (1983), *Bitter Sweet* (1983), *Slice of the Cake* (1984), *Inna Reggae Dance Hall* (1987), and at least five others. Through the course of these albums, Minott showed that he could perform in a variety of styles from the smoothest **lovers rock** to the grittiest **dancehall**. In the 1990s, Minott's output stayed strong. He released another series of albums, including *Sugar and Spice* (1990), *With Lots of Extras* (1995), and *Musical Murder* (1997).

In the new millennium, Minott has continued his reign. He has worked extensively with the Third Eye imprint and has released four albums with Easy Star. Sugar Minott remains an active force in reggae music as he maintains an active writing, recording, and live performance career.

MISTY IN ROOTS

A roots reggae band that has been on the Jamaican popular music scene since the 1970s, Misty in Roots formed in London in 1975 when Delbert "Ngoni" Tyson teamed with his brother Wolford "Poko" Tyson and a third brother Delvin "Duxie" Tyson. The three were the Afrocentric backup band to Jamaican singer Nicky Thomas. With Thomas, the group released "Living in the Land of the Common People." In 1978, Thomas left the group, and they soldiered on and cultivated their own style. In 1979, the group released their debut album. Titled *Live at Counter Eurovision*, the album featured the vocal trio plus Joseph Brown, Vernon Hunt, Dennis Augustin, and Antony Henry. Featured tracks on the release included "Man Kind," "Ghetto of the City," and "How Long Jah." During this same period, Misty in Roots became a major force in the Rock against Racism campaign, active in the United Kingdom.

The group's second album was titled *Wise and Foolish* and was released in 1982. Featured songs on this release were "Wise and Foolish," "Live Up," and "Life Boat." This release further helped to establish Misty in Roots as a legitimate reggae force. In the wake of the second album, the band spent nine months in Africa living in Zimbabwe and Zambia. Upon their return to the United Kingdom, the group's next releases exhibited the effects of their African experience. Both *Earth* (1983) and *Musi-O-Tunya* (1985) were highly Afrocentric in spirit and message. The latter album title meant "the smoke that thunders" (a reference to the Victoria Waterfalls) and described the place where Zambia and Zimbabwe meet.

Next, the band released *Forward* (1989) on the Kaz Records imprint and illustrated that it was staying at the peak of its abilities. In the 1990s, the Misty in Roots members formed a relationship with legendary producer John Peel. A series of sessions took place before Peel's death and yielded the material for the albums *The John Peel Sessions* (1995) and *The John Peel Memories* (1996).

In the new millennium, Misty in Roots remains active. In 2002, they released their most recent album, *Roots Controller.* The album again illustrates the group at its most potent with featured songs such as "True Rasta," "Cover Up," and "Almighty." Misty in Roots continues to make new music and is a highly sought-after live act.

MITTOO, JACKIE (1948–1990)

Born Donat Roy Mittoo in Browns Town, Jamaica, Jackie's earliest musical training came from his grandmother, who taught him the piano beginning at age four. At age ten he made his first public performance and began branching out from his early classical music training to the popular styles he heard on the radio. During his teenage years he was exposed to American rhythm and blues and the boogie woogie piano style coming out of the Mississippi delta.

While at Kingston College, Mittoo began playing with **Tyrone Downie** and **Augus-**

tus Pablo. In 1963, he had the good fortune of catching the attention of **Clement "Coxsone" Dodd**, who was producing a session for which the keyboard player had not shown up. Dodd enlisted Mittoo's help and was impressed by what he heard. Dodd then had Mittoo run sessions at his **Studio One**. In 1964, his association with area artists at **Federal Records** paid off and he joined the **Skatalites**. Early on, the Skatalites played versions of American rhythm and blues and jazz standards and were on the cutting edge at the dawning of the **ska** era. Soon the band gained a strong reputation with the **sound system toasters**, and the Skatalites were asked into the studios of all of the island's major producers. Mittoo and Dodd worked together throughout the 1960s, and Mittoo appeared on countless Dodd sessions.

In the wake of the Skatalites' split, Dodd formed the **Soul Brothers**, for which Mittoo wrote the music and **Roland Alphonso** made the horn arrangements. With Mittoo at the helm, the Soul Brothers became the **Soul Vendors** and then Sound Dimension, all the while making rhythms for Dodd. The members of the various incarnations of Mittoo's bands are a who's who of **reggae** instrumentalists. At the end of the 1960s, Mittoo left Jamaica and settled in Canada. He still recorded with Dodd during intermittent trips to Jamaica throughout the next two decades. In addition to working with Dodd, Mittoo also recorded with **Bunny "Striker" Lee** and **Sugar Minott's** Youth Production. In 1990 Jackie Mittoo died of cancer in Toronto, Canada.

MORGAN, DERRICK (1940–)

Morgan Derrick grew up in Kingston, Jamaica, and began his career in music at an early age, putting him on the scene at the dawning of the Jamaican recording industry at the end of the 1950s. He won the Vere Johns Opportunity talent show at age seventeen, which began his career. Morgan entered the studio with **Duke Reid** immediately after the completion of its construction and began recording a series of successful singles such as "Lover Boy," "Fat Man," and "Forward March." He next worked with **Clement "Coxsone" Dodd** for a series of singles that continued his rise to fame.

Morgan recorded extensively in the **ska** and **rock steady** styles in the 1960s and 1970s. His early 1960s singles were highly successful with songs such as "Housewives' Choice," "Don't Call Me Daddy," and "Moon Hop." He worked with a variety of different studios and producers and began releasing full-length albums by the end of the 1960s. His early 1960s recordings put him at the forefront of first-wave ska, and he released his debut album in 1969, *Seven Letters*. Along the way he released the 1966 single "Tougher Than Tough," which is widely credited as the first rock steady song. In the 1970s, he released a series of successful albums including *Feels So Good* (1975), *People Decisions* (1977), and *Still in Love* (1977). In addition to singing, Morgan also became a successful producer and worked with **Jimmy Cliff**, **Bob Marley**, and **Garnet Silk**.

MORGAN HERITAGE

Morgan Heritage is a singing group formed in 1991 and consists of many of Denroy Morgan's children. The New York-based group was originally seven of Morgan's numerous children who got their start singing backup for their father. They began making inroads into the music industry in the early 1990s and released the single "Wonderful World," which led to *Growing Up* (1991). Next, the group managed an appearance on the 1992 installment of the **Reggae Sunsplash** tour and was immediately signed by MCA Records. The MCA pairing yielded *Miracles* (1994), which was not as successful as expected, as the label mandated that the group adopt a watered-down sound for

Morgan Heritage. © *UrbanImage.tv.*

mass appeal and potential crossover. Regardless of the disappointment, the group toured Africa, where they continued to hone their skills.

They then issued the album *Protect Us Jah* (1997). This album was issued on the VP Records label and marked a departure from the MCA product as the group returned to its core of roots reggae. The album features several singles such as "Let's Make Up," "People Are Fighting," and "Set Yourself Free." By this point the group had shrunk from seven to five members. The remaining members were Memmalatel, Nakamyah, Roy, Peter (vocalist), and Una Morgan. The paired-down group went to Jamaica and recorded with **Bobby "Digital" Dixon** and **King Jammy**. They then released a third album called *One Calling* (1998), which was quickly followed by *Don't Haffi Dread* (1999). In 2000, they issued a live-in-Europe album followed by the *More Teachings* release (2001). In 2003, the group released another solid roots collection, *Three in One*, which appeared on the Heartbeat imprint. Morgan Heritage continues to write and record new material into the new millennium.

MORWELL, BLACKA. *See* WELLINGTON, MAURICE

MORWELLS

The Morwells were a well-respected and long-popular **reggae** band that formed in 1973 in Kingston, Jamaica, comprising **Eric "Bingy Bunny" Lamont** and **Maurice "Blacka Morwell" Wellington**. Before teaming with Wellington, Lamont had recorded with Bongo Herman in 1971 and 1972. Wellington had been in the business as a record salesman and producer for several years. The pair formed the Morwells, a shortening of Maurice and Wellington, and immediately recorded a pair of singles. Eager to escape the tyranny of the existing Jamaican record industry, they released their material on their own Morwell Esquire imprint. The songs "Mafia Boss" and "You Got to Be Holy" were regionally successful.

In 1974, the pair became a trio when Louis Davis joined Wellington and Lamont. Davis was an experienced instrumentalist and tutored Lamont on guitar. Davis was also a skilled arranger and rounded out the group well. In the mid-1970s, the Morwells released a series of successful singles that garnered them attention in the United Kingdom. They arranged an English distribution deal and began releasing their music directly to this new audience. In 1975, their single "Bit by Bit" was a success in both Jamaica and the United Kingdom. Also in 1975, the group released its first two albums, *Presenting the Morwells* and *The Morwells Unlimited Meet King Tubby* (*Dub Me*). In 1976, Wellington took a production job for **Joe Gibbs**, and Lamont joined the **Revolutionaries**. Their unprecedented access to talent made the rest of the 1970s the peak of the Morwells' career. They released singles including "Proverb," "Crab in a Bag," and "We Nah Go Run Away," along with their third album *Crab Race* (1977). The Morwell Esquire label also enjoyed a solid period at the end of the 1970s with recordings from Ranking Trevor, **Nicodemus**, and **Delroy Wilson**.

In 1977, the Morwells added another member when **Errol "Flabba" Holt** joined the group. The year 1979 saw the release of another album, titled *Cool Runnings*, which was followed in rapid succession by *A1 Dub* (1980), *Bingy Bunny and the Morwells* (1981), and *Best of the Morwells* (1981).

However, in the early 1980s the Morwells disbanded. Holt and Lamont formed the **Roots Radics**, and Wellington continued his production work with the Morwell Esquire label. Eric "Bingy Bunny" Lamont died from cancer in 1994, and Maurice "Blacka Morwell" Wellington died in 2000 of adenocarcinoma.

MOWATT, JUDY (1952–)

Born in Kingston, Jamaica, Mowatt emerged during her late teenage years as an active singer and part of the Gaylettes, with Beryl Lawson and Merle Clemonson. The trio backed up a variety of artists around the island, but disbanded in 1970. At this time, Mowatt pursued a solo career and had a series of successful singles. She also launched her own label called Ashandan and professed her faith in **Rastafarianism**. In 1974, she became part of the vocal trio the **I-Threes**. The trio were the backing vocalists for **Bob Marley and the Wailers** and included Mowatt, **Marcia Griffiths**, and **Rita Marley**. The trio remained intact for the next decade and appeared on all subsequent Marley recordings.

Although Mowatt was part of the I-Threes, she continued her solo career. In 1975, she released her debut album *Mellow Mood* on her own label. In 1979, her second album was recorded in Marley's own **Tuff Gong** studios. In the wake of Marley's 1981 death, Mowatt continued her solo efforts and produced seven more albums that spanned the 1980s and 1990s. Examples of her later albums were *Only a Woman* (1982), *Working Wonders* (1985), and *Love Is Overdue* (1986). Mowatt remains active on the **reggae** scene and is in demand as a live performer.

MUNDELL, HUGH "JAH LEVI" (1962–1983)

Born in Kingston, Jamaica, Mundell entered the Jamaican popular music scene as a teenager. Early on he worked with **Joe Gibbs** on the as-yet-unreleased single "Where Is Natty Dread," and then had the good fortune to meet **Augustus Pablo**. Pablo hired Mundell as a **DJ** for his Rockers **sound system**, and Mundell adopted the nickname

Jah Levi. With Pablo, Levi recorded a series of singles such as "Africa Must Be Free," "My Mind," and "Let's All Unite." His debut album was released in 1975 and was titled *Africa Must Be Free by 1983.*

Levi also got into the production side of the music industry and worked on **Junior Reid's** "Speak the Truth" release in 1978. Levi also produced his own material with singles such as "Stop Them Jah" and "Blackman Foundation." His second album was called *Time and Place* and was released on the Muni Music imprint in 1981. The label was Levi's own, and he used it to release a series of singles. He quickly followed this with *Mundell* (1982). Next, Levi split with Pablo and went on to record with producers **Henry "Junjo" Lawes** and **Prince Jammy**.

In 1983, Levi was shot and killed while sitting in a car with Reid. In the wake of his death, there have been several other recordings released under his name, including *Arise* (1987), *Blackman's Foundation* (1988), and *Blessed Youth* (2002).

MUTABARUKA (1952–)

Born Allan Hope in Rae Town, Jamaica, this poet and musician attended Kingston Technical High School, where he gained an education in electronics. Upon leaving school he worked for the Jamaican Telephone Company; it was during this time that he began to learn about **Rastafarianism**. Throughout the latter part of the 1960s and into the 1970s, Hope fashioned himself into an intellectual revolutionary. He deepened his study of Rasta, grew dreadlocks, and left the phone company.

As locks-bearing Kingston residents were regularly harassed by the police, Hope found that it was time to relocate. In 1971, he moved to St. James and began a family. His dedication to Rasta continued to grow, and he spent long hours reasoning about the Jamaican culture and aspects of the religion. In the late 1960s, Hope began writing poetry that was infused with his Rasta beliefs, and by the early 1970s he was ready to begin bringing his written messages to the masses. Hope's early material began to be published in regional magazines, often with the byline Allan Mutabaruka. The name *Mutabaruka* is a contraction of a Rwandan phrase meaning "one who is always victorious." This work continued throughout the 1970s, and the young writer's reputation was further enhanced by live readings of his material.

Through the medium of live performance, Mutabaruka's poetry is fully realized and has resulted in the birth of **dub poetry**. The topics of this type of material are revolutionary and are often scathing in their social commentary. From the early 1970s to the present, Mutabaruka has become an expert in the authorship and delivery of dub poetry (whether or not he rejects the term itself). He began releasing his material in a series of books and has also crossed over into music production. Examples of his published writings are *Outcry, Sun and Moon,* and *The Book: First Poems.*

In 1981, Mutabaruka began releasing his work through recordings with

Mutabaruka. © *UrbanImage.tv.*

his first single, "Every Time a Ear da Soun.'" The delivery of his message in this manner was immediately successful and has led to his appearance in the **Reggae Sunsplash** concert in Jamaica and on tour all over the world. Over the past twenty years, Muta-baruka has released over ten albums on the **RAS**, **Heartbeat**, and **Shanachie** imprints. Over time, his material has moved from direct recitation of his words to full-song versions with some of Jamaica's finest artists as the backing bands. Muta has worked with **reggae** stalwarts such as **Louise Bennett**, **Dennis Brown**, **Bunny Rugs**, **Cocoa Tea**, **Ini Kamoze**, **Freddie McGregor**, **Third World**, and a host of others. Mutabaruka remains active with his blend of music and message.

MYTON, CEDRIC (1947–)

Cedric Myton grew up in St. Catherine, Jamaica, and got his start in the music business singing with the group the Tartans. The group had a series of modestly successful songs with **Duke Reid's Treasure Isle** label in the late 1960s. In the mid-1970s, Myton teamed with **Roydel "Ashanti" Johnson** and formed the **Congos**. The pair had the benefit of working with producer **Lee "Scratch" Perry** in addition to several premier Jamaican instrumentalists, including **Sly Dunbar**, **Ernest Ranglin**, and **Uziah "Sticky" Thompson**. The singing duo released only one album, *The Heart of the Congos* (1977), but the record has gone on to become a seminal **reggae** classic. When the record was released, it received modest attention, but in the wake of the breakup it passed into obscurity. After the split, Myton maintained the Congos name, while Johnson took to calling himself Congo Ashanti Roy.

N

NASH, JOHNNY (1940–)

Born in Houston, Texas, in 1940, Nash got his start singing in church and on a local television show called *Matinee*. Nash continued his early success in the entertainment industry as a soul singer and actor. He scored an early hit with his 1957 single "A Very Special Love" and was poised for success. With Paul Anka and George Hamilton, he had another hit with "The Teen Commandments" in 1958.

While working on the film *Take a Giant Step*, he visited the Caribbean for the first time. In the mid-1960s he returned to Jamaica and worked with **Federal Records** producer **Byron Lee**. With Lee's guidance, Nash turned to **reggae** music and penned the popular single "Hold Me Tight." The song charted in the United States and the United Kingdom and convinced Nash of the value of Caribbean popular music. The song had been issued by Nash's own fledgling label called **JAD**, born out of a partnership with Danny Sims. Nash went on to score another hit with a reggae version of Sam Cooke's "Cupid."

In addition to his singing and acting career, Nash was becoming a music businessman. He recognized **Bob Marley's** talent and was responsible for recording the single "Guava Jelly." Nash himself charted with a version of Marley's "Stir It Up" and had enormous success with his own song "I Can See Clearly Now." When the single was released on an album, it was accompanied by four songs by Marley with the **Wailers** backing him up.

Throughout his career, Nash was more popular in the United Kingdom than the United States, and this resulted in extended stays in Europe. In 1975 he again charted in the United Kingdom, this time with the Little Anthony cover version "Tears on My Pillow." Through the course of his recording career, Nash issued at least fifteen albums in a variety of styles from soul to reggae. More recently, he remains active in the music business. In 2004, Nash penned a deal with Universal Music International to release many of the 211 singles Marley recorded on JAD during 1967–1972.

NICODEMUS (1957–1996)

Born Cecil Willington in Jamaica in 1957, he rose to prominence as a **DJ** and **dancehall toaster** in the late 1970s and eventually ascended to the top ranks of the style. Nicodemus began his career in 1976 with early inspiration from Ranking Trevor. He caught the wave of the new dancehall style at its beginnings and became an influential artist. He first appeared on the Socialist Roots **sound system** in the mid-1970s and moved to the Prince Jammy sound in 1978. In the studio, Nicodemus recorded a series of successful singles at the end of the 1970s, and his reputation was assured. He released the single "Jamaican Rockers Hop" in 1980 with Ranking Trevor and parlayed the single's success into a series of albums in the 1980s.

In 1981, his singles "Gunman Connection" and "Bone Connection" were combined on the album *Gunman Connection*. He released the album *Dancehall Style* (1982) and followed it with the clash record *DJ Clash with Ranking Toyan* (1983). Also in 1983, he released the album *Nice Up the Dance*, which was followed in 1984 by *Nuff Respect*.

By the mid-1980s, Nicodemus's reputation was solid, and he was becoming a veteran of the dancehall. Imitators followed, such as John Taylor, who called himself Nicodemus Junior. Junior went on to call himself **Chaka Demus** and became a hit when he teamed with **Pliers**. The latter half of the 1980s were not as prosperous for Nicodemus. He released periodic singles, but not album-length material. The 1990s saw a rebirth of interest in the DJ. He joined the Apache label and released a series of successful albums including *The Bad, the Ugly, and the Crazy* (1994), *Cabbin Stabbin* (1995), and *Dancehall Greats* (1998). The final release was posthumous, as Nicodemus died of complications from diabetes in 1996.

NIGHTHAWK RECORDS

Founded by Leroy Pierson in the spring of 1976 in St. Louis, Missouri, Nighthawk Records is a label that originally handled American blues reissues, but eventually branched out into Caribbean material. In the 1980s, Nighthawk crossed over into recording **reggae** music and has maintained a commitment to the style for more than twenty years. The label handles all aspects of the recording process and endeavors to create authentic Jamaican music. Over the years, the label has been home to artists such as the **Ethiopians**, the **Gladiators**, the **Itals**, **Justin Hinds** and the Dominos, **Junior Byles**, the **Meditations**, Murder City Players, Idren with Ronnie Davis, the **Tennors**, and Winston Jarrett and the Righteous Flames.

For the recording of this material, Pierson installed himself in a Kingston studio and made authentic Jamaica fare. Pierson also fronted a band called the Leroy Pierson Band, which traveled to Jamaica in 1985. This tour found Pierson on stage with artists such as the **Mighty Diamonds** and **Yellowman**. Additionally, Pierson was employed to work on some of the liner notes for the album *The Complete Wailers: 1967–1972*. Pierson's writing is also found on the **Peter Tosh** box set *Honorary Citizen*, and he is currently co-authoring a biography of **Bunny Wailer** with Roger Steffens.

NINJAMAN (1966–)

Born Desmond Ballentine in Kingston, Jamaica, he began his **toasting** career by appearing on several regional **sound systems**. Ballentine moved into the **dancehall** and his reputation bloomed. He began **DJing** at age twelve with the Black Culture sound system. Next, he appeared with Killimanjaro under the name Double Ugly and cut his first single as Uglyman. His first hit, "Protection," was issued in 1987 with **Courtney Melody**. The single listed Ballentine as Ninja and paved the way for further success. The following year, he released songs with Tinga Stewart and **Flourgon**.

The late 1980s and early 1990s were a period of high productivity and success. He received production assistance from sources as diverse as **King Jammy** and Redman. The early 1990s found Ninja releasing material with the most aggressive tone to date, as the result of an effort to mimic the spirit of the Gulf War. Examples from this time included "Fulfillment," "Reality Yuh Want," and "Murder Weapon." As is common in American hip hop, Ninjaman picked a nemesis, his being **Shabba Ranks**, and he has repeatedly called out the other DJ on recordings. The conflict-breeds-success strategy has worked for many American hip hop artists, the downside of which was illustrated through the slayings of Tupac Shakur and Notorious B.I.G. At this time, Ninjaman christened himself "Original Front Tooth, Gold Tooth, Gun Pon Tooth, Don Gorgon."

By the mid-1990s, Ninjaman's hold on the dancehall had begun to weaken and he lost his record contract. He continued to record for **Henry "Junjo" Lawes** and **Junior Reid** through the mid-1990s. In the late 1990s, Ninjaman cast off the tough and slack image (talk of guns, sex, and drugs) of the dancehall DJ and turned to Christianity, recording as Brother Desmond. This move was made for a variety of reasons. There was substantial backlash to the tough image that he was pushing, and he was battling a drug problem.

Even with a change in image and lyrical content, Ninjaman could not escape negativity. In the late 1990s, he was accused of rape and murder. Ultimately, he was acquitted of the charges but served a year in prison for gun possession. After his release, Ninjaman had a series of other altercations with the law that carried over into the new millennium. Over the course of his twenty-three-album career, Ninjaman earned the pedigree of one of the toughest clash DJs of the past twenty years.

NITTY GRITTY (1957–1991)

Born Glen Augustus Holness in Kingston, Jamaica, Nitty Gritty grew up in a large family and as a youth studied to be an electrician. In his late teenage years, he formed the Soulites and from there landed a 1973 appearance with **Dennis Brown**, the **Mighty Diamonds**, and **George Nooks** on the single "Let the Power Fall on I." Next, Nitty Gritty teamed with **Sugar Minott** for his solo debut single "Every Man Is a Seller," which showcased Gritty's gospel-inflected voice. At **Channel One**, he recorded a series of successful singles, as well as working with the **African Brothers** and **George Phang**.

In 1985, Nitty Gritty moved over to work with **King Jammy**, and together the pair released "Hog Inna Minty." The single was an immediate success and was followed by another series of successful singles. Nitty Gritty released his debut album in 1986, *Turbo Charged*. The same year he issued the album *Nitty Gritty with King Kong: Musical Confrontation*. The following year came *General Penitentiary* on the Black Victory imprint, followed by *Nitty Gritty* (1988) and *Jah in the Family* (1989). This release was followed by *Power House Presents Nitty Gritty with Tenor Saw* (1989).

At the end of the 1980s, Nitty Gritty was a well-established recording artist with a solid reputation. However, his career was cut short when he was shot and killed in Brooklyn, New York, at age thirty-four.

NOOKS, GEORGE (c. 1955–)

George Nooks was born in St. Andrew, Jamaica, and began his professional music career in 1974. Nooks's earliest musical training came as a youth singing in church choirs and was influenced at an early age by American rhythm and blues singers such as Al Green. He was discovered in the early 1970s performing in a local talent show. In 1974, Nooks released his first single, "The Creator," which appeared on a compilation disc issued by **Joe Gibbs**. His first hit was the single "Forty Leg Dread," which he recorded under the name Prince Mohammed.

Throughout his career, Nooks vacillated between his two musical loves, **reggae** and rhythm and blues. He had success with singles such as "I Don't Care" and "A Real Man." He worked with fellow artists Merciless, **Ken Boothe**, and **Dennis Brown**, but his most significant success came from his pairing with Joe Gibbs.

In the early 1990s, Nooks moved away from recording himself and began recording others. He launched his own label, called Total Records, and has spent time producing music as an independent artist. In 1997, Nooks won three Tamika Reggae Music Awards for Best Crossover Artist, Outstanding Male Artist, and Vocalist of the Year. In 2002, he stepped back into the limelight as a performer and won the *Star* newspaper's Singer of the Year Award. Nooks remains active as both a live performer and music businessman.

NOTES, FREDDIE, AND THE RUDIES

A **reggae** group active in the early 1970s and considered one of the most commercially successful UK-based acts of the time, the group formed when the singer Freddie Notes teamed with Sonny Binns, Danny Smith, Earl Dunn, and Ardley White. In 1970, they had a degree of chart success with their cover of the Bobby Bloom song "Montego Bay." They parlayed this success into an album released in 1970 under the same title. The album contained twenty reggae songs including the title track, "Babylon," "Melting Pot," "Let Me Move," and "The Bull."

Soon, Freddie Notes left the band and they changed their name to Greyhound. The group's sound also changed, moving more toward the mainstream. However, they still released periodic reggae-inflected songs at a very early time for the style in the United Kingdom. Greyhound went on to a degree of popularity through the release of several other albums. An interesting aside is that Greyhound played Mick and Bianca Jagger's wedding.

NOW GENERATION

Formed in the early 1970s as a studio band, the group was led by keyboardist **Geoffrey Chung** and included **Mikey Chung** on lead guitar, Val Douglas on bass, Robert Lynn on keyboards, **Earl "Wya" Lindo** on organ, and Mikey "Boo" Richards on drums. Throughout the early 1970s, the group played in the studios of all of the major Jamaican producers including **Clement "Coxsone" Dodd**, **Joe Gibbs**, **Derrick Harriott**, **Ken Khouri**, **Lee "Scratch" Perry**, and **Sonia Pottinger**. An example of their work was their 1971 appearance as the backup band for **Junior Byles's** recording "Beat Down Babylon." The group even recorded its own album. Released in 1974 on the **Trojan** label, *For the Good Times* was the Now Generation's only release. By the mid-1970s, the group had split up, and the members went on to work in a variety of other bands.

NYABINGHI

Nyabinghi is an element of **Rastafarianism** that affects **reggae** music in a variety of ways. In the most literal terms, *nyabinghi* is a Ugandan folk term for "she possesses many things," but is interpreted as Jah's (God's) power to enforce universal justice. Further, through the Rastafarian lens it has come to mean victory over the oppressor. As with Rastafari, nyabinghi contains elements of Pan-Africanism, music, dance, scripture, and reasoning.

Principal aspects of the nyabinghi beliefs are captured in its drumming style. Nyabinghi drumming begins with a heartbeat rhythm in four/four time that is kept on the largest of the three drums. The bass drum is used to keep time and is played with an accent on beat one and dampened on beat three. The other two drums are the **funde** and the **repeater**. Both are pitched higher than the bass, and each has a specific role. The funde rhythm is layered in on top of the bass drum rhythm and plays eight notes on beats one and three. Thus it is supporting what the bass drum is playing and serves as a "heartbeat" to the other drums. The repeater is the highest-pitched drum and is sometimes called the **akete**. The repeater is performed in an improvisational manner and emphasizes the second and fourth beats of the measure. The repeater rhythm is faster than that of the other two drums and has the most fluid line.

In nyabinghi drumming, the three drums are accompanied by the shaka or shekere, shaker types. These shakers are improvisational in role, but do emphasis the first and third beats. In addition to drumming, nyabinghi includes dancing and chanting. The chanting element has also been adopted into Rastafari and has thus found its way into reggae music. Over the course of the existence of Rastafari belief, the nyabinghi drumming tradition has been subsumed into the religious practice. As an extension, some reggae songs exhibit traits of nyabinghi drumming.

OBAN, GEORGE (c. 1950–)

Oban was the original bass player for the UK **reggae** group **Aswad**. When the group formed in 1975, Oban teamed with **Brinsley Forde**, Donald "Benjamin" Griffiths, and **Angus "Drummie Zeb" Gaye**. Oban was replaced in 1981 by Tony Gad after the band's third album. Thus, Oban appears on *Aswad* (1976), *Hulet* (1978), and *Showcase* (1981). Oban stayed in the popular music scene and remains active today. While he was active in Aswad and afterward, Oban played with numerous other musicians such as **Burning Spear**, the Royal Rasses, New Age Steppers, Charlie Couture, **Creation Rebel**, Judy Nylon, **Dub Syndicate**, African Head Charge, **Delroy Washington**, and Singers and Players. Recently, Oban appeared on **Headley Bennett's** album *Thirty Five Years from Alpha* (1999) and Finley Quaye's *Much More Than Much Love* (2004). George Oban remains active as a reggae bassist and percussion player.

O'HARE, BARRY (c. 1960–)

Barry O'Hare began his career in the late 1980s and quickly rose to prominence as a producer, engineer, mixer, composer, arranger, and musician. In the early 1990s, he worked with a variety of **reggae** and mainstream artists such as Link and Chain, **Burning Spear**, **Carlene Davis**, **Tony Rebel**, **Steely and Clevie**, **Third World**, Jigsy King, and Jah Messenger. In most cases, O'Hare does not just produce the recording session, but he also engineers and plays at least one instrument, such as drums or keyboard.

In the latter half of the 1990s, O'Hare worked with **Everton Blender**, **Cocoa Tea**, **Cutty Ranks**, **Beres Hammond**, **Lieutenant Stitchie**, Mikey Spice, Khaled, Stanrick, Tanya Stephens, Glen Washington, **Garnet Silk**, **Steel Pulse**, and others along with a variety of compilation releases. Also during this period, O'Hare launched his own record label called X-Rated. He uses his label to foster the talent of new artists who are turning the **dancehall** tide from slackness (talk of guns, sex, and drugs) to consciousness, such as Mikey Spice and Daweh Congo. In the new millennium, O'Hare's production work has continued with new material from **Beenie Man**, **Burning Spear**, **Macka B**, **Morgan Heritage**, Determine, **Sister Carol**, **Sizzla**, Lieutenant Stitchie, and a wide range of others. Barry O'Hare remains active in the contemporary Jamaican music scene.

ONE BLOOD

A roots reggae band run by Jamaican-born percussionist and lead singer Ira Osbourne, One Blood covered songs by **Gregory Isaacs**, **Bob Marley**, **Third World**, and **Bunny Wailer**, along with original material by Osbourne. The group formed in 1989 in Tucson, Arizona. The lineup included Osbourne, Ozzie Ali on bass, Tony Davies on guitar, Evan Osborne on keyboards, and Owen Rose on drums. The group's style has formed connections between **reggae** music and the music of American Southwest Native Americans.

ONE DROP

In roots reggae music, the one-drop rhythm became quite popular in the mid-1970s. The rhythm was achieved by the drummer and had a distinct sound. In four/four time, one drop was achieved when the drummer was using only the kick drum to accent the third beat of the measure. Whereas European music most often accented the first and third beats and American rock and roll accented the second and fourth beats, reggae's one-drop rhythm was unique. The rhythm was pioneered by the **Wailers'** rhythm section, **Aston "Family Man" Barrett** and his brother **Carlton "Carly" Barrett**. The Wailers used the rhythm extensively throughout the 1970s to the point where they wrote a song about it in 1979. Appearing on the *Survival* album, the song "One Drop" contained lyrics about the rhythm and how it fit into the sound of reggae music at the time.

ONE LOVE PEACE CONCERT

The One Love Peace Concert was a monumental **reggae** concert that took place April 22, 1978, in Kingston, Jamaica. The concert was held at the National Stadium and featured the biggest names in reggae music at the time. The idea of the show came from Bucky Marshall and Jack "Claudie" Massop. The pair, who were political rivals and leaders of the Jamaican Labor Party (JLP) and the People's National Party's (PNP) goon squads, proposed a truce between the two factions. Once the two convinced their respective party affiliates that the truce was solid and that the concert was necessary, the next step was to enlist the talent.

The concert had two purposes: first, to raise money for better sanitary facilities in the west Kingston ghetto (called Trenchtown); and second, to return **Bob Marley** to Jamaica and end his self-imposed exile in the wake of the 1976 attempt on his life. Marley met with Marshall and Massop in London in February 1978 and agreed to the show. The concert was announced and scheduled for April 22 to celebrate the twelfth anniversary of **Haile Selassie's** visit to Jamaica. On the day of the concert, 32,000 reggae fans turned out to see acts such as **Althea and Donna**, **Dennis Brown**, **Culture**, **Dillinger**, the **Meditations**, **Jacob Miller** and **Inner Circle**, **Peter Tosh**, Marley and the **Wailers**, Young Youth, and others.

In attendance were political luminaries such as Edward Seaga and Michael Manley, who would play a role in the Marley set. The two featured performers came on at the end of the concert. Peter Tosh played a militant hourlong set with his **Word, Sound, and Power** band, during which he criticized the police and government for their failure to support the needs of the oppressed black underclass. The climax of the show was Bob Marley's first performance on the island since 1976. Marley took the stage and played a fifty-minute set of songs in the following order: "Lion of Judah," "Natural Mystic," "Trenchtown Rock," "Natty Dread," "War," "Jammin,'" "One Love," and "Jah Live." At the end of "Jammin,'" Marley invited Manley and Seaga on stage to clasp hands with him in a gesture of unity.

ONUORA, OKU (1952–)

Oku Onuora, whose name translates as "Fire in the Desert," was born Orlando Wong in Kingston, Jamaica. As a youth, Onuora became a voice against oppressive government and joined forces with those who sought to unseat the post-colonial government. Onuora was arrested and incarcerated in 1971 for a seven-year sentence and, while in jail, began writing poetry. His crime had been attempted robbery of a post office, but done in the guise of helping fund an alternative school. Thus Onuora did not consider himself a criminal and made this case plainly in his writing. Much of Onuora's writing was spirited out of jail and came to the attention of the Jamaican Literary Festival Commission. The commission was so taken with the young poet's writing that in 1977 it convinced the government to release Onuora.

Upon release, Onuora published a collection of his poems called *Echo*. His next move was into the arena of **dub poetry**. He entered **Tuff Gong** studios and was backed by the rhythm section of the **Wailers**, made of **Aston** and **Carlton Barrett**. Onuora went on to tour around the world and was active at the **One Love Peace Concert**. Over time, his writing has received critical acclaim, and he has amassed a collection of awards. By the early 1980s, he had achieved the status of dub poetry's most visible leader, **Linton Kwesi Johnson**. In addition to continually releasing material, Onuora also launched his own record label, called Kuya. His full-length debut was *Pressure Drop* (1986). This was followed by *New Jerusalem Dub* (1991), *I A Tell Dubwise and Otherwise* (1994), and *Dubbin' Away* (2000). In the 1990s, Onuora teamed with Courtney Panton, who either played or programmed all of the instrumental parts backing up the poetry.

OSBOURNE, JOHNNY (1948–)

Born in Jamaica, Johnny Osbourne rose to prominence as a **reggae** vocalist in the late 1970s and 1980s. He led a vocal group called the Wildcats in his early musical career, and the group recorded for **Winston Riley** in the mid-1960s. By the end of the decade, Osbourne went solo and released the **Clement "Coxsone" Dodd**-produced single "All I Have Is Love." In 1969, he released his debut album, backed by the vocal group the Sensations, called *Come Back Darling*.

After the album's release, Osbourne moved to Canada, where his family had been living. While there he worked with a series of acts and eventually became lead vocalist of the Ishan People. With this group he recorded a pair of modestly successful albums

before the group broke up in 1979. Osbourne returned to Jamaica and for the next year recorded a series of singles for Dodd. The releases led to the album *Truths and Rights* (1979), which became an instant classic. Also in 1979, Osbourne worked for **Prince Jammy**; his output for Jammy resulted in the album *Folly Ranking*. With two successful albums in one year, Osbourne became one of the most highly sought singers on the island. He stayed in this productive phase for several years and released a series of albums including *Never Stop Fighting* (1982), along with a series of albums in 1984. In rapid succession, Osbourne released *Water Pumping* (1983), *Reggae on Broadway* (1983), and *Musical Chopper* (1983). The following year he issued *Bring the Sensi Come* and *Reality*.

Johnny Osbourne. © *UrbanImage.tv.*

Osbourne's productivity remained high throughout the end of the 1980s. He released six more albums before the end of the decade. In the 1990s, Osbourne's output waned and he released only a few albums, including *Nuh Dis, Groovin'* (1992), *Johnny Osbourne* (1994), *Mr. Budy Bye* (1995), and *Nightfall Showcase* (1997). The quality of *Truths and Rights* is absent in the later work, but Osbourne remains capable of regaining his earlier form. In the new millennium, Osbourne issued the album *First Choice* (2000) and continues to write, record, and perform live.

P

PABLO, AUGUSTUS (1953–1999)

Born Horace Swaby in St. Andrew, Jamaica, the future Augustus Pablo grew up in a middle-class family in the Havendale district. While Swaby went on to a successful career in music, he was always a sickly person. He had to drop out of Kingston College due to a persistent illness that would trouble him his entire life. He turned to music and learned to play a variety of different instruments. He studied the clarinet, xylophone, organ, and piano, but took a special interest in the melodica.

In 1969, Swaby teamed with producer Herman Chin-Loy and recorded his first single, "Iggy Iggy." He recorded another single with Chin-Loy before moving on. Before he left, the producer dubbed him Augustus Pablo. Next, Pablo worked with **Clive Chin** and cut the **Randy's Records** release "Java." Chin was also responsible for the instrumental album *This Is Augustus Pablo*.

There followed a period during which the young performer worked for several different producers. He recorded "Lovers Mood" for **Leonard Chin**, then moved over to **Lee "Scratch" Perry** for the production on "Hot and Cold." He also worked with **Gussie Clarke**, **Keith Hudson**, and **Bunny "Striker" Lee**. After working with all of these Jamaican legends, Pablo realized that the only way to control his product and make the money that he deserved was to launch his own label, which he called Rockers. The material released on the album earned a high reputation and included releases such as *King Tubby Meets Rockers Uptown*. The album was a collection of Pablo's most popular songs, in **dub** versions, by **King Tubby**.

In addition to his own material, he also recorded a variety of other artists, and he and his Rockers band played the backing tracks. Pablo enjoyed a long period of success through the late 1960s and the 1970s. However, in the early 1980s, Pablo suffered with the change of style to **dancehall**. Revealing his versatility, he adopted the **dancehall** style and produced material for a variety of artists such as Delroy Williams, **Junior Delgado**, and **Yami Bolo**. This type of success and broad-based approach to the various **reggae** styles kept Pablo in the mainstream through the 1990s. He released an album of new music called *Blowing with the Wind* (1990). The album was his first to

Augustus Pablo. © *UrbanImage.tv.*

incorporate **nyabinghi** drumming and marked another stylistic change for the artist. Augustus Pablo died of a nervous disorder in 1999, ending a fifteen-year reggae odyssey.

PALMA, TRISTON (1962–)

Born Triston Palmer in 1962, Palma has been a fixture in Jamaican popular music for over two decades. Palma made his entry into the music business at a very early age. By age ten, he was singing backup vocals for **Sugar Minott** and **Tony Tuff**. He recorded his first single, "Love Is a Message," for **Bunny Lee's** Justice label while still a teenager. His big break came in 1979 when he was showcased at the Penitentiary Memorial Concert for Jack "Claudie" Massop.

Also at the end of the 1970s, Palma and Ossie Thomas launched their own label called Black Solidarity, thus giving Palma greater control over his output. Palma's voice was sweet and lyrical, and he sang in the roots reggae style with lyrics on consciousness topics. He subsequently released a series of singles on his label including "A-Class Girl," "Susan," and "Spliff Tale." The singles were very successful and led to the Palma and **Jah Thomas** pairing that resulted in the single "Entertainment." The song was an enormous success, and together Thomas and Palma had a string of acclaimed singles.

Palma then went to work with producer **Linval Thompson** and recorded a pair of albums. At this same time, he also worked with **Henry "Junjo" Lawes** on several singles. In the mid-1980s, Palma recorded "Land of Africa" with **Gregory Isaacs**, **Freddie McGregor**, **Mutabaruka**, **Steel Pulse**, and **Third World**. By the late 1980s, the brand of music that Palma was writing was not as popular as it had been the previous decade, having been supplanted by **dancehall**. Thus, he became a producer and limited his songwriting.

In 1995, he released the album *Three against War* with **Dennis Brown** and **Beenie Man**. This release brought Palma back into the mainstream, and he parlayed his success into the 1998 release *Born Naked*. Palma then teamed with the New York-based reggae label **Easy Star Records**. For Easy Star he released 2000's *Two Roads*, which spawned the successful singles "The Struggle" and "Get Up." More recently, Palma released *Showcase* in 2004 and continues to write, record, and perform live.

PALMER, MICHAEL (1964–)

Born in 1964 in Kingston, Jamaica, Palmer began performing as a teenager on an area **sound system** called Echo Tone Hi Fi, which featured the owner **General Echo**. In 1980, General Echo was gunned down, diminishing Palmer's prospects with the loss of the sound system. However, in 1983 he went into the studio with **Jah Thomas** and cut the single "Ghetto Dance." The single was met with a degree of success, and Palmer began the standard Jamaican ritual of moving from studio to studio and recording with a variety of producers. He worked with several of the island's premier studio technicians, including **Joseph "Joe Joe" Hookim**, **King Jammy**, and **Sugar Minott**. With this work, Palmer became better known, and his popularity increased.

In 1984, he achieved a chart-topping hit with the single "Lickshot" and followed this with an album of the same name. He went on to appear at the **Reggae Sunsplash** concert and released a series of albums. The mid-to-late 1980s were the high point of Palmer's career, during which he released *Angella* (1984), *Michael Palmer and Frankie Jones* (1984), *Pull It Up Now* (1985), and *Michael Palmer with Kelly Ranks: Rusty* (1985).

PAMA RECORDS

Pama Records was started by Harry, Jeff, and Carl Palmer in London, England, in the mid-1960s and focused on soul releases. However, they soon realized that Jamaican popular music could be far more profitable in the United Kingdom than American popular music. As a result, Harry Palmer began working distribution deals with studios and artists in Jamaica. In 1967, the Pama label started releasing **rock steady** singles and made their new venture a success. Harry Palmer made arrangements with **Clancy Eccles**, **Alton Ellis**, **Bunny Lee**, and **Lee "Scratch" Perry**, among others.

In addition to working deals with existing Jamaican talent, the Pama brothers set about cultivating local talent. They launched a talent contest, record store, and the Apollo Club to find and distribute material by local acts. This led the label to **Junior English**, the Mowhawks, the Inner Mind, and **Delroy Washington**, in addition to several others. **Derrick Morgan** and his brother-in-law **Bunny Lee** entered the Pama picture when Lee signed on to run Pama operations in Jamaica and Morgan began releasing material on the Pama imprint. In the late 1960s, Morgan was the principal hitmaker on the label, but **Max Romeo** also scored a hit with "Wet Dream." Ultimately, artists such as **Laurel Aitken** and **Pat Kelly** joined the label's roster and helped bring greater acclaim.

In the early 1970s, Pama's success began to dim, as it was increasingly viewed as a copycat label. It was overshadowed by Trojan in the United Kingdom and Atlantic in the United States. In 1974, the Pama Records label dissolved. It did not disappear for long, however, as it was re-formed under the Jet Star Phonographics name and continues to have one of the largest reggae distribution deals in the world. In 1978, Jet Star took over from where Pama had left off. They continued to issue popular singles and recruited top talent from Jamaica. Further, they launched the *Reggae Hits* series in 1984, which has been highly productive and profitable.

Jet Star continues to expand and sits atop the UK **reggae** industry. The label has gotten more diversified along the way and now offers releases in the following styles: reggae, **dancehall**, **lovers rock**, **dub**, soca, and gospel.

PAN HEAD (1966–1993)

Born Anthony Johnson in St. Mary, Jamaica, in the mid-1980s Johnson appeared on the **sound system** scene working for **Black Scorpio** and Exodus. He quickly showed himself to be a strong **DJ** and rose through the ranks. He recorded his first single in 1988 called "Gimme Lickle Loving." In the 1990s, Pan Head's style was in accordance with contemporary **dancehall DJs**, who discussed gun culture and slackness (talk of guns, sex, and drugs). His material from the early 1990s included singles such as "Gunman Tune" and the seminal "Punny Printer." In 1993, Pan Head's lyrical sentiment changed and he began to discuss issues of consciousness and cultural uplift. This new direction was apparent in singles such as "Teaser."

Just as Pan Head was turning the page to the most successful period of his career, he was shot and killed in front of a club in Spanish Town in 1993. The shooting threw the dancehall community into an outrage, and several DJs authored songs decrying the act. In the wake of Pan Head's shooting, **Buju Banton** penned "Murderer," and **Capleton** released "Cold Blooded Murderer."

PAPA SAN (1966–)

Born Tyrone Thompson in Spanish Town, Jamaica, as a young teenager San already wanted to get into the music business. He came from a musical family with a father who played the drums. His older brother also went into the music business and became the popular **dancehall DJ Dirtsman**. San won the Tastee Talent contest in 1981 and later appeared on a variety of **sound systems**, such as **Black Scorpio**, Creation, and Stereosonic. In the mid-1980s, his reputation in the **dancehall** was on the rise. In 1985, he released "Animal Party" on **Triston Palma's** Black Solidarity imprint. This was followed by the successful single "DJ Business" in 1988 on the **Fashion Records** label.

In early 1990, he released *Style and Fashion* based on the success of his single of the same name. He went on to issue *System* in the same year, *Pray for Them* and *Rough Cut* (1992), *In Action* (1993), and *No Place Like Home* (1995). In 1997, San became a born-again Christian, and this change in his spiritual life altered his music. His 1999 album *Victory* reflected his new spirituality. San's music became a mixture of dancehall, hip hop, and gospel. In 2003, San continued down his new path and released *God and I*, which featured the single "Breathe Again." Other featured songs on the album are "I Know" and "Stay Far," all of which continue his stylistic mixture.

PARAGONS, THE

Formed in 1964 in Kingston, Jamaica, and consisting of Leroy Stamp, Garth "Tyrone" Evans, Junior Menz, and **Bob Andy**, the lineup for the Paragons changed drastically during the first year of their existence. Bob Andy went solo in 1964, Leroy Stamp was replaced by **John Holt**, and Junior Menz left and was replaced by Howard Bennett. The group went on to become a classic of the late 1960s. They had a series of hits for **Clement "Coxsone" Dodd** at his legendary **Studio One** facility. In 1966, they worked with producer **Duke Reid** on his **Treasure Isle** imprint and released the **rock steady** hits "Wear You to the Ball," "Love at Last," "Good Luck and Goodbye," "On the Beach," and "The Tide Is High" (which was popularized by the new wave group Blondie about fifteen years later).

The early style in which the Paragons sang was heavily indebted to American rhythm and blues. The close vocal harmonies caught the attention of a wide range of Jamaican listeners and gave the group a high level of success. At the behest of informal group leader Holt, the group members changed their sound to adhere to changing audience expectations in the mid to late 1960s. They took on the **rock steady** sound and scored another series of hits. In 1968 they released *On the Beach* and a variety of other albums in the 1970s and 1980s.

The Paragons disbanded at the end of the decade. They felt that they were not being properly compensated after having issued a significant quantity of number one songs. The group re-formed with Holt, Evans, and Bennett reentering the studio in the second coming of **ska**, called **two tone**, in the late 1970s. The reunion was fruitless, as the three returning members could not get past their standing differences. In the mid-1990s, Evans and Bennett again united, determined to produce new music for Jamaican producer Clive Davidson. They released the *Heaven and Earth* album and began working on an album of new material. However, the group was still missing their third member to round out the harmonies. Davidson solved this problem by adding Winston "Mr. Fix-It" Francis to the existing pair. The resulting album was a collection of Bob Dylan and Beatles songs redone in **reggae** versions.

PARKS, LLOYD (1948–)

Born in Walton Garden, Jamaica, Parks went on to have a long and successful career in Jamaican popular music beginning in the late 1960s. He performed as both a singer and bass player and split his time between work as a bandleader and as a studio musician. His career began in the late 1960s when he joined the Invincibles. He moved from there to the **Termites** when he paired with Wentworth Vernon. From the Termites, Parks went on to the **Techniques**. He soon left to pursue solo work and released the single "Stars." During the end of the 1960s, Parks split his time between solo work and session playing.

In the early 1970s, he worked with producer **Sonia Pottinger** on a series of singles as he continued to move from producer to producer. During this period, Parks's reputation as a session bass player flourished and he joined the Thoroughbreds, the house band at the Tit-for-Tat club. In 1973, Parks diversified his life in music and launched his own record label. It is also in the early 1970s that he recorded a set of his most popular songs, including "Baby Hang Up the Phone," "Officially," and "Girl in the Morning." He was in heavy demand as a session bassist playing with Skin Flesh and Bones, the Professionals, and the **Revolutionaries**. As a member of Skin Flesh and Bones, he ended up in **Joe Gibbs's** studio band, in which he recorded for many of the top artists of the day. The success that he had experienced backing up **Dennis Brown**, **Prince Far I**, and others translated into the formation of his own band.

In 1975, Parks formed the band We the People. The group had immediate success and toured with Dennis Brown. The band was in constant demand and often played the **Reggae Sunsplash** and Sumfest concerts. In addition to Parks, We the People included a horn line with Tony Greene on saxophone, Everol Wray on trumpet, and Everald Gayle on trombone. This lineup was solid from the mid-1980s to the present. The group worked primarily as a backing band and has played behind artists such as **Alton Ellis**, **John Holt**, the **Mighty Diamonds**, and **Leroy Sibbles**. In addition to Parks on bass and the horn line, the We The People band has gone on to include Parks's children. His daughter Tamika played keyboard and his son Craig played drums. The We the People Band has remained in existence for the past twenty-six years and is still in demand in the studio and on the stage.

PATRA (1972–)

Born Dorothy Smith, this singer took the stage name Patra as a shortened form of Cleopatra. Patra was born in Kingston, Jamaica, in the Westmoreland parish, where she began

Patra. © *UrbanImage.tv.*

her musical experiences by singing in the church choir. Her early influences included several American rhythm and blues mainstays such as Tina Turner and Sade. From singing in church, Patra then turned to working the dancehall as a **sound system DJ**. Next, Patra moved to the United States and pursued her recording career in earnest. She guested with **Mad Cobra** and Richie Steven and landed a solo single titled "Hardcore." Her debut album, *Queen of the Pack*, was released in 1993. "Hardcore" was a marquee single, as was "Think about It." The title track of the album was the third single, which was followed by "Worker Man" and "Romantic Call." All of these songs hit in the United States to a varying extent and established Patra's reputation outside of Jamaica. The album was a huge success and stayed on the Billboard **reggae** charts for over four months. Patra parlayed that success into a second album also released on the Sony label.

Scent of Attraction, Patra's second album, was released in 1995. In the same year, she was in high demand from American artists for cameo appearances and sang with Angie Stone, Mary J. Blige, Vanessa Williams, and several others. Her second album featured the single "Pull Up to My Bumper," a samba version of the Grace Jones song. Other notable singles were the duets with Salt-N-Pepa on "Hot Stuff" and Aaron Hall on the title track. More recently, Patra worked on a gospel album, and she continues to write, record, and tour. In 2003, Sony released the album *Take Two*, which compiled Patra's hits with several songs from Lyn Collins and Diana King.

PATRICK, KENDRICK. *See* LORD CREATOR

PATTERSON, ALVIN "SEECO"

Active in the **reggae** music scene since the mid-1970s, his entry into the limelight came when he joined **Bob Marley and the Wailers** as the group's percussionist in 1974. Patterson's work with Marley spanned the rest of his life, and he appeared on the albums *Natty Dread* (1974), *Live* (1975), *Rastaman Vibration* (1976), *Exodus* (1977), *Babylon by Bus* (1978), *Kaya* (1978), *Survival* (1979), *Uprising* (1980), *Confrontation* (1983), *Legend* (1984), *Talk' Blues* (1993), and several posthumous releases. After Marley's death, Patterson continued to perform with a variety of other acts such as John Denver and the Wailers band. In the 1990s, Patterson worked for Gerald LeVert on a series of releases.

PAUL, FRANKIE (1965–)

Born Paul Blake in Kingston, Jamaica, he was blind from birth, but became a highly talented multi-instrumentalist and a versatile singer. At an early age, a portion of his sight was returned through an operation and he was given special glasses that further assisted his vision. As a youth, Paul sang for Stevie Wonder, and the American superstar encouraged the young Jamaican to go into music. In 1980, Paul made his first recording, titled "African Princess."

Paul emerged on the Jamaican popular music scene in 1981 with the single "Worries in the Dance," produced by **Henry "Junjo" Lawes**. The single appeared on a pair of albums from the **Channel One** *Showdown* releases. He was among the original group of **dancehall DJs** and rocketed to notoriety in 1984 with "Pass the Tu-Sheng-Peng." The song was a huge success and would later appear on a variety of versions by artists such as **Dennis Brown**. The song also spawned Paul's debut album, *Pass the Tu-Sheng-Peng* (1985). In the wake of this first success, Paul worked with a variety of producers including **Philip "Fatis" Burrell** and **George Phang** for his next albums. In the late 1980s, his releases included *Warning* (1987), *Casanova* (1988), *Slow Down* (1988), *Dance Hall Duo with Pinchers* (1988), and *Love Line* (1989). With this work, Paul established a strong reputation and showed himself to be a highly prolific recording artist.

In the 1990s, Paul's furious pace continued unabated. He released almost twenty albums in a ten-year period. Much of the material was original, but he also recorded several cover versions along the way. In the new millennium, Paul has continued to record and has released *Remember the Time* in 2001 and *I Be Hold* in the same year. Frankie Paul remains active as a singer, songwriter, and live performer.

PENTHOUSE RECORDS

Penthouse Records was started by CEO Donavan Germaine. It went on to become one of the most active labels in **dancehall** music in the late 1980s and early 1990s. With its own production facilities and with Germaine at the controls, the imprint cultivated a roster of highly skilled **reggae** and dancehall artists. In addition to singles and albums by the artists on its deep roster, Penthouse also offered the *Collectors Series*, which compiled many of the best recordings of the time. Artists on the roster included **Buju Banton**, **Marcia Griffiths**, **Freddie McGregor**, **Morgan Heritage**, Sean Paul, **Daddy Screw**, **Spragga Benz**, **Wayne Wonder**, Jeffrey "Assassin" Campbell, and many others. The label continues to release new material and has entered into a deal with Chris Chin of VP Records to the mutual benefit of both companies.

PERRY, LEE "SCRATCH, JAH LION, PIPE COCK JACKSON, MIGHTY UPSETTER, UPSETTER, SUPER APE" (1936–)

Born Rainford Hugh Perry in St. Mary, Jamaica, Lee began his life in the Jamaican popular music business in the late 1950s when he started selling records for **Clement "Coxsone" Dodd's** Downbeat **sound system**. Perry soon moved from the street to the studio. He began producing and recording for Dodd at the legendary **Studio One**. Soon Perry left Dodd and moved over to **Joe Gibbs's** label Wirl (West Indies Records Limited).

Lee "Scratch" Perry. © *UrbanImage.tv.*

In the late 1960s, Perry again moved on and this time set about building his own studio. During the 1970s, Perry's **Upsetter** imprint was one of the most popular labels on the island. Known for his eccentric personality, Perry is often considered the wild man of **reggae** music, but he has consistently shown himself to be crazy like a fox and remains in the reggae business after forty years. During the 1970s, Perry recorded some of the most important bands of the day, including the **Congos**, the **Wailers**, and an incredible quantity of others.

Perry's production is marked by bass-heavy arrangements and an innovative approach to sound sources. He was on the cutting edge as the **rock steady** sound turned to **reggae**, and he rode the tide into the 1980s. Part of Perry's success should be attributed to his rock-solid studio band that he dubbed the **Upsetters**. The Upsetters' membership was always quite fluid, but the group was anchored by the rhythm section of **Aston "Family Man" Barrett** on bass and his brother **Carlton "Carly" Barrett** on drums. To further control his output, Perry opened his own studio in the early 1970s. He called the studio **Black Ark** and made it the center for his creativity. It was to this situation that the young Wailers came and recorded hits such as "Duppy Conqueror" and several others.

During the late 1970s, Perry worked at a furious pace and branched out from reggae to other types of music. Most notable was his collaboration with the Clash. In the early 1980s, Perry's Black Ark Studios burned to the ground, surrounded by many different stories of the event. This gave Perry the chance that he needed to leave Jamaica and settle in Switzerland. He remains active, though to a lesser extent, in the music business. Perry's influence is palpable both within and outside of the reggae community. He was given a song on the Beastie Boys *Ill Communication* (1994) release and ended up playing live with the New York trio.

During the course of his career, Perry issued his own music in addition to the music of others. In fact, there are over thirty albums by the famous producer, including *Return of Django*, *Super Ape*, *Satan Kicked the Bucket*, *Chicken Scratch*, and *The Wonderman*.

The material that Perry helped create as producer is so vast that it is difficult to catalog; however, an incomplete list of artists includes **Dennis Alcapone**, **Big Youth**, **Alton Ellis**, **Beres Hammond**, **Dillinger**, **Doctor Alimantado**, **I-Roy**, **Junior Byles**, **Pat Kelly**, **Hugh Mundell**, **Augustus Pablo**, **Ras Michael** and the **Sons of Negus**, **Leroy Smart**, **Tappa Zukie**, the **Skatalites**, **U-Roy**, and **Yabby You**. In 2003, Perry won his first Grammy for Best Reggae Album. He continues to be active on the fringe of the music business.

PETERKIN, SHARON. *See* LADY SHABBA

PHANG, GEORGE (1960–)

George Phang emerged on the Jamaican popular music scene in the mid-1980s. Phang's contribution was as a producer at the height of the **dancehall** era. He worked for a variety of dancehall stars throughout the previous twenty years. Phang contributions are felt in the music of **Charlie Chaplin**, **Half Pint**, **Echo Minott**, **Nitty Gritty**, **Michael Palmer**, **Ranking Toyan**, and **Yellowman**. Further, he was a major force behind **Frankie Paul's** seminal "Pass the Tu-Sheng-Peng" and "Tidal Wave" recordings. He was also crucial to the creation of the *20 Super Hits* series. On this collection, Phang paired with artists such as Chaplin, **Barrington Levy**, Half Pint, Yellowman, and **Sugar Minott**. In the early 1990s, Phang worked with **U-Roy** and **Josey Wales** and again teamed with Half Pint and Sugar Minott along with many others.

PINCHERS (c. 1965–)

Jamaican-born singer Delroy Thompson emerged on the **dancehall** scene in 1985 when he recorded a single that brought him local acclaim. As Pinchers, he followed this with success on the 1987 **King Jammy** single "Agony." The success of the early releases resulted in his debut album *Agony*, released on Live and Love in 1987. There was also a series of singles for **Philip "Fatis" Burrell** that included the hit "Mass Out." This single also resulted in a 1987 album on the Exterminator label. Also released in 1987 was a third album, titled *Lift It Up Again*. Pinchers then recorded an album with **Frankie Paul** in 1988 titled *Dancehall Duo*. In the same year, he released material with **Pliers** titled *Pinchers and Pliers*. In 1989, he released *Return of the Don* and *Pinchers Meets Sanchez*.

While he continued to issue new material in the late 1980s, the quality of the early recordings was missing. However, in the early 1990s, Pinchers regained his previous glory and scored an international hit with "Bandolero." There followed a new series of album releases that carried the singer through the 1990s. *Bandolero* was released as a new album in 1991 and was followed by *Dirt Low* in 1993. Pinchers's brand of dance-hall does not involve the typical slack lyrics (talk of guns, sex, and drugs); instead, he works to educate and increase cultural consciousness.

PINE, GARY "NESTA" (1964–)

Active on the **reggae** music scene for fifteen years, Pine has worked in a pair of highly successful bands, City Heat and the **Wailers**. As the lead singer for City Heat, Pine toured internationally and performed with several reggae luminaries including **Cocoa Tea**, **Beres Hammond**, Diane King, **Pinchers**, **Super Cat**, **Bunny Wailer**, **Ziggy Marley and the Melody Makers**, and others. The band began in Jamaica and in 1991 moved to New York. By 1995, they had built a significant new following and had landed a steady gig as a house band.

Pine's problem with City Heat was that it was a cover band and he wanted to sing his own songs. Thus, he struck a deal with **Easy Star Records** to release original music as a solo artist. Also in the late 1990s, Pine joined the Wailers band as the lead singer. In 1998, he assumed the role **Bob Marley** had abdicated through his 1981 death. Parts of the original band are still in place. **Aston "Family Man" Barrett** still plays bass, **Al Anderson** remains on guitar, and **Earl "Wya" Lindo** is still present on keyboards. The rest of the band has been replaced for a variety of reasons. With Pine at the helm, the group performs Marley standards and material from several albums released since Marley's death. Since Marley's death, the Wailers have issued *Mystic Warrior* (1991), *Jah Messenger* (1996), and a series of live shows.

PINKNEY, DWIGHT "BROTHER DEE DEE" (1945–)

Born in Manchester, Jamaica, Pinkney and his family moved to Kingston while he was a youth. As a teenager, Pinkney learned music, and at eighteen he formed the Sharks. The group won the house-band job at a hotel in the Bahamas, and Pinkney's career was off to a strong start. The group made frequent trips to Jamaica to record and often functioned as a backing band in the studio. They worked for **Clement "Coxsone" Dodd** at his legendary **Studio One** where they cut their own singles and backed **reggae** greats such as **Ken Boothe**, the **Gaylads**, and **Bob Marley**.

In the 1980s, Pinkney was involved with a pair of successful bands. He was a leader of the **Zap Pow** group and then moved on to be part of the **Roots Radics**. As part of these bands, Pinkney recorded with a veritable who's who of reggae stars throughout the 1980s and 1990s. He has toured the world and, in addition to his musical achievements, has appeared in three movies. In 1999, he released his debut album, *Jamaican Memories*. The release is a collection of instrumentals that garnered the then-legendary guitarist a pair of awards.

In 2000, he released the followup, *All Occasions*, and in 2002 he released *More Jamaican Memories*. Pinkney remains in constant demand and continues to write, record, and tour. He also makes frequent appearances on U.S. and UK television. Through the course of his thirty-plus-year career, Pinkney has played with artists including **Dennis Brown**, **Alton Ellis**, **Beres Hammond**, **Gregory Isaacs**, **Israel Vibration**, **Luciano**, **Bob Marley**, and many more.

PIONEERS, THE

The Pioneers formed in 1962 when Winston Hewett, **Sydney Crooks**, and Crooks's brother Derrick joined forces. Soon Hewett was replaced by **Glen Adams**, and the group began to experience regional success. By the end of the decade the singing trio had gained a solid reputation and worked with a series of Jamaican producers including **Joe Gibbs** and **Leslie Kong**. In the late 1960s, the lineup dwindled to Sydney Crooks and Jackie Robinson. In 1969, they charted in the United Kingdom with the single "Longshot." The song was produced by Gibbs, and in the wake of its success, the group again grew to a trio with the addition of George Agard. The group changed its name to the Slickers and released the followup to "Longshot," called "Longshot Kicked de Bucket."

In 1969, they released their debut album *Longshot* and followed it in 1970 with *Battle of the Giants*. By this time they had again taken the Pioneers name. In 1970, the group relocated to England, as its material was better received in the United Kingdom than in the Caribbean. The following year the group again had success with a version of **Jimmy Cliff's** song "Let Your Yeah Be Yeah." The group continued to record intermittently throughout the early 1970s. Its productivity waned, and eventually Crooks moved into the production arena.

PLANNO, MORTIMER (1920–)

Born in Kingston, Jamaica, by his late teens Planno was one of the earliest Jamaicans to convert to **Rastafarianism**. He was one of the founding members of one of Kingston's early Rasta encampments, called the Dungle. He eventually ascended to become one of the Rasta elders. His direct significance to **reggae** music was his relationship with **Bob Marley**. Planno met Marley in Trenchtown and the two bonded over Rasta reasoning. Soon, Planno served as Marley's manager and dealt with the business end of the young singer's career. In 1961, Planno was part of a select group who traveled to Africa to examine the feasibility of repatriation. In 1969, Planno was charged with the duty of writing an early text on the Rastafari teaching. The work was titled *The Earth Most Strangest Man: The Rastafarian*. The book is now available in its entirety on the World Wide Web. In addition to his work with Marley and his dedication to Rasta doctrine, Planno served a two-year term (1997–1999) as a Jamaican Folk Fellow at the University of the West Indies.

PLIERS. *See* CHAKA DEMUS AND PLIERS

POTTINGER, SONIA (c. 1940–)

Sonia Pottinger entered the Jamaica popular music scene in the late 1960s and established herself as a talented producer who was soon recruiting talent from around the island. Her career in the industry spanned over twenty-five years, and she has left an indelible mark on the **reggae** music industry. Part of her success was due to her business acumen, which she displayed in launching a series of successful labels, including SEP (her initials), Gayfeet, Highnote, and Gloria. Her success was enormous, which was even more impressive due to the generally sexist attitudes of the reggae industry during the 1970s and 1980s.

Pottinger's artist roster was large and varied, and in the 1970s and 1980s it included **Bob Andy**, **Errol Brown**, **Culture**, **Alton Ellis**, the Hippy Boys, **Marcia Griffiths**, **Justin Hinds**, the **Melodians**, **Toots and the Maytals**, and **U-Roy**. One of her marquee productions was Culture's *Harder Than the Rest* (1978). Pottinger's legacy continued into the new millennium with a vast collection of compilations including *Train to Skaville: Anthology 1966–1975*, *OK Fred: The Best of Errol Dunkley*, and *Peace and Harmony: The Trojan Anthology* of the **Heptones**.

PRATT, GEORGE PHILIP "PHIL" (c. 1950–)

Born in Kingston, Jamaica, Pratt entered the Jamaican popular music scene as a producer and arranger in the mid-1970s and had successful releases with artists such as **Horace Andy**, **Big Youth**, **Ken Boothe**, and **Gregory Isaacs**. Pratt got his start working for legendary Jamaican producer **Clement "Coxsone" Dodd.** This was during the period when a young **Lee "Scratch" Perry** was working for Dodd, so Pratt apprenticed with two of the best. Before going into production, Pratt aspired to be a singer, and he cut a single with Dodd called "Safe Travel." The song was not released, and this led Pratt to move on. He landed at the Carltone imprint and cut a series of singles that had modest success. It was at this point that he turned to production, as he was put in charge of the Carltone subsidiary Sunshot. With Sunshot, Pratt had tremendous success. He worked with several serious talents including **Ken Boothe**, **Dennis Brown**, and **Lynn Taitt**. Pratt scored major hits with **John Holt's** "My Heart Is Gone," Brown's "Let Love In," and **Pat Kelly's** "How Long."

The period 1971–1975 was Pratt's most productive time with Sunshot. He worked with **Dennis Alcapone**, **Dillinger**, **I-Roy**, and **U-Roy** and helped to usher in the first era of **DJs**. With **Big Youth**, Pratt issued a series of successful singles including "Tell It Black" and "Phil Pratt Thing." He then returned to work with Perry at **Black Ark Studios** and cut several new songs including **Linval Thompson's** first single. A strong collection of Pratt's work was issued in 1999, called *The Best of Sunshot*. Another solid collection was 2001's *Phil Pratt Thing*.

PRIEST, MAXI (1962–)

Maxi Priest was born Max Elliot in London, England, to Jamaican immigrant parents. It was from his mother that he got his early love for music; she was the lead singer in their church choir. Early on, Priest worked as a carpenter building speaker boxes for area **sound systems.** This gave him the opportunity to enter the music business as a **dancehall** singer. He quickly ascended through the ranks and caught a break when asked to tour with **Tippa Irie**. He took the surname "Priest" when he converted to **Rastafarianism**. In 1984, he reached a career pinnacle when his single "Mi God Mi King," which was produced by Paul "Barry Boom" Robinson, was the first UK **reggae** single to chart at number one in Jamaica. The following year he released his debut album, *You're Safe*. It featured Priest singing over his band, Caution.

Maxi Priest. © *UrbanImage.tv.*

The latter half of the 1980s was a highly productive period, and he issued the albums *Intentions* (1986) and *Maxi Priest* (1988). The self-titled album was made in collaboration with **Sly and Robbie** and was an international success. In 1988, Priest scored an international hit with a cover version of Cat Stevens's song "Wild World."

The 1990s found Priest in good form. He continued his career in the studio with *Bonafide* (1990), *Fe Real* (1992), *Man with the Fun* (1996), a live album in 1999, and *CombiNation* in the same year. *Man with the Fun* sported the **Shaggy** collaboration "That Girl," which was a success and illustrated Priest's reggae-pop style. In 1990, Priest scored another chart topper with "Close to You."

Over the course of his career, Maxi Priest has been nominated for three Grammy Awards and has had a series of charting singles. Priest continues to write, record, and perform live and is widely considered the most successful UK reggae artist. Priest's musical style is categorized as reggae, but his vocal inflection puts him more in the rhythm and blues camp. As a result, much was made of his pairing with **Shabba Ranks** for the single "Housecall," in which the two styles were combined.

PRINCE ALLAH (1950–)

Born Keith Blake in Kingston, Jamaica, Prince Allah has spent the last thirty years pursuing a career in **reggae** music and through that period has built a strong international reputation. He got his start working with **Joe Gibbs** in the late 1960s in a group called the Leaders. By the end of the decade, the group had disbanded, but Gibbs and Blake continued to work together. Blake then took a hiatus from music as he became heavily involved in the Jamaican **Rastafarian** community. He lived in a commune through most of the 1970s. He re-emerged as Prince Allah and had a series of successful singles. These songs prompted a 1979 album titled *Heaven Is My Roof.* Next, he continued to issue recordings that were met by wide audience approval. In 1988, he issued *Jah Children Gather Round* on the Greensleeves label. Although Allah's recording career contained long breaks, when he was in the studio the product was always of the highest quality.

Allah issued *I Can Hear the Children Sing 1975–1978* as a compilation of his early hits. This was accompanied by two albums on the Blood and Fire label, *Only Love Can Conquer* (1996) and *I Can Hear the Children Singing* (2002). He has recently completed a set of collaborations, one with Jah Warrior and another with the **Disciples**. In 2002, he issued the *More Love* album in the United Kingdom and prompted renewed interest in his music within the European community. This was the result of serious touring throughout Europe. In 2000 he toured Switzerland, in 2001 he played the Montreux Jazz Fest, and in 2002 he gave live shows all over Europe, including Serbia. In 2004, he joined forces with Age of Venus Records and released *More Dub.* The album is a collection of fourteen roots songs redone in **dub** versions. Prince Allah continues to tour in support of this release.

PRINCE BUSTER (1938–)

Cecil Bustamente Campbell was born the son of a railway worker in Kingston, Jamaica. As a young man growing up in working-class Kingston, he spent his early life training to become a professional boxer. Campbell also loved music and made plans to become a singer. However, he had a promising early boxing career that gave him his entrance into the music business. One of his first brushes with music was as a security guard for **Coxsone Dodd's** famous Downbeat **sound system**. During the late 1950s, sound system clashes in Jamaica were notoriously dangerous, and Campbell was a match for anyone looking to disturb Dodd's Downbeat. Next, he went on to start his own sound, dubbed Voice of the People. Campbell also started a record label and record store. Beyond sound system work, Campbell was an aspiring recording artist.

In the early 1960s he went into the studio and recorded the first Jamaican single that used all **Rastafarian** musicians. The title of the single was "Oh Carolina"; it has been a longstanding hit that appears in multiple versions. The recording involved singing by the **Folkes Brothers** and percussion by **Count Ossie**. He also had success selling other singles that he recorded, as well as releases by other artists. He was operating three imprints that included Wild Bells, Voice of the People, and Buster's Record Shack Label. Much of this material was also released in the United Kingdom on the Blue Beat label. Campbell's reputation was increasing, and he began to cultivate a UK following. To cement that reputation, Campbell appeared on the British pop music program *Ready, Steady, Go*, becoming the first Jamaican to score a British Top 20 hit.

His boxing dreams had not yet completely faded, and in 1964 he met famous American boxer Muhammad Ali. This meeting led Campbell to change his own name to Muhammad Yusef Ali. Regardless of his boxing aspirations, Campbell was becoming a successful musician and businessman. His association with Dodd and his early days in boxing had earned him the nickname Prince, while his middle name had been shortened as a youth into Buster. Thus Prince Buster became Campbell's official nickname, used for the rest of his career. The rest of the 1960s was filled with Buster's singles. Additionally, he was saturating the market with over 100 singles by other artists. His success continued growing and was spurred on by touring in the United Kingdom and other European countries.

Buster's exposure influenced other artists; for example, the UK **ska** band Madness took their name from a Prince Buster single. Further, he influenced Alex Hughes, who was a doorman at the time, to adopt the moniker **Judge Dread** and begin doing versions of Buster's hits. Buster's predilection for the music business extended far outside the studio: his Kingston-based record store was wildly successful and still exists, run by his family. He also founded a jukebox company that kept Jamaican singles spinning on the island.

In the 1970s, Buster began to scale back on his recording to devote himself to the business of music. During his recording heyday, he worked in the **rock steady** and ska styles and penned lyrics of Jamaican and African consciousness and Africanism. Many subsequent artists have noted Buster's influence. Additionally, Buster made a brief appearance in the legendary Jamaican film *The Harder They Come*, starring **Jimmy Cliff**.

In the wake of Buster's retirement from music, the tributes continue to mount. Artists ranging from the Specials to the English Beat to the Selectors have covered his work. Buster now lives in Florida in semi-retirement. He no longer works in the studio, but he does maintain ownership of his publishing rights and he makes occasional live performances.

PRINCE FAR I (1944–1983)

Born Michael James Williams in Spanish Town, Jamaica, he learned about the Jamaican popular music scene in the Waterhouse district of Kingston by attending dances and studying the **DJ** and emcees. Soon he entered the scene on the Sir Mike the Magical Dragon **sound system** as King Cry Cry. Far I's style was a chanted approach to delivering lyrics. His words were often delivered in a stream of consciousness approach that kept him firmly rooted in the DJ style.

In the early 1970s, Far I entered the studio with **Bunny Lee** and cut the single "The Great Booga Wooga," a version of Lester Sterling's "Spring Fever." He then began making the studio rounds in the manner in which Jamaican singers were accustomed. He next recorded "Natty Farmyard" with the legendary producer **Clement "Coxsone" Dodd**. From there he moved over to **King Tubby** and recorded "Let Jah Arise." The producer on the track was Enos McLeod, who is also credited with giving the Prince his longstanding name.

In the mid-1970s he released two seminal albums. *Psalms for I* was a collection of chanted biblical passages on top of rhythms created by **Lee "Scratch" Perry** and Bunny Lee. The album contained ten tracks: the Lord's Prayer and nine psalms. The second was *Under Heavy Manners*, a product of Far I and **Joe Gibbs's** 1977 pairing. This second release contained one of Far I's longest-standing hits, "Heavy Manners." In 1976, Far I launched his own Cry Tuff label and entered an extraordinarily productive phase of his career. He released the first of his multi-chapter series, *Cry Tuff Dub Encounter, Chapter 1* in the same year. In England, Far I's material was released on **Adrian Sherwood's** Hit Run imprint, and the first album contained the single "No More War." Far I's deal with Sherwood resulted in his vocals being recorded in Jamaica and the rhythms underlaid in London with Sherwood's band the Arabs (**Roots Radics**) covering the instrumental parts. Next came *Message from the King* in

Prince Far I. © *UrbanImage.tv.*

1978, followed by *Long Life, Free from Sin*, and *Dub Africa* to round out the decade.

In 1979, he recorded *Cry Tuff Dub Encounter, Chapter 2*, which furthered his reputation in both Jamaica and the United Kingdom. In 1980, he issued *Cry Tuff Dub Encounter, Chapter 3*, which appeared in England on the Daddy Kool imprint. There followed *Cry Tuff Dub Encounter, Chapter 4* (1981). The album further solidified Far I's reputation as the "Voice of Thunder." Next, Far I joined with the Songs of Arqa for the single "Wadada Magic." Far I toured off the success of his output and then released *Musical History*. In Jamaica on September 15, 1983, Prince Far I was shot dead during a robbery attempt at his house. His material continued to be issued throughout the 1980s, 1990s, and into the new millennium.

PRINCE JAMMY. *See* KING JAMMY

PRINCE JAZZBO (c. 1950–)

Prince Jazzbo was born Linval Carter in Jamaica. As a young singer coming of age in the dawning of the **dancehall** era, Jazzbo went to work with **Clement "Coxsone" Dodd** on his **Studio One** label and cut a series of singles in the early 1970s. For Dodd, Jazzbo voiced the seminal "Crabwalking" over **Horace Andy's** "Skylarking" rhythm. In the wake of this success, Jazzbo recorded a series of singles with Dodd that included "Pepper Rick," "School," and "Crime Don't Pay." As was the custom, he then moved on, recording for **Bunny Lee**, Glen Brown, and **Lee "Scratch" Perry**. With Perry, Jazzbo cut the single "Penny Reel" that blossomed into the album *Natty Passing Thru* (aka *Ital Corner*). In addition to this work, Jazzbo launched his own label and became a noteworthy producer. His imprint was called Ujima, and Jazzbo recruited talent such as **Frankie Paul** and Zebra. By the end of the 1970s, Jazzbo had turned his attention away from performing dancehall tunes and toward production. However, many of his greatest hits have emerged on collections such as *Choice of Version*, *Head to Head Clash*, and *Mr. Funny.*

PROPHET, MICHAEL (1957–)

Born Michael George Haynes in Greenwich Farm, Kingston, Jamaica, Prophet was discovered by producer **Vivian "Yabby You" Jackson** in the 1970s and released a series of moderately successful singles, the most important of which was "Praise You Jah Jah," recorded at **Channel One**. Other significant singles from the time included "Turn Me Loose," "Warn Them Jah," and "Gates of Zion." His big break came when he issued his debut single on **Island Records** called *Serious Reasoning* (1980). The album was recorded with the **Gladiators** backing up the young singer. With this release he reached a more diverse audience and made an impact in the United Kingdom.

In the 1980s, Prophet made another series of well-respected recordings with **Henry "Junjo" Lawes**, which reflected a rougher **dancehall** style. This partnership with Lawes was crucial for Prophet, as the producer had just signed a deal with Greensleeves. The Lawes and Prophet collective issued a series of singles and the albums *Righteous Are the Conqueror* (1980) and *Michael Prophet* (1981). It is also with Lawes's help that Prophet got on the Volcano **sound system**, which updated his sound from solid roots reggae to the more contemporary **dancehall** fare. In 1988, he moved to London and continued his recording career. At the same time he was releasing **ragga** singles that carried him into the 1990s.

During the 1990s, Prophet released a series of albums such as *Jah Love* (1990), *Bull Talk* (1992), *Cease and Settle* (1994), and *Love Is an Earthly Thing* (1999). In 2001, Prophet teamed with Rootsman at the Third Eye Records studio, and together the pair issued a series of **dub** plates. The pairing resulted in Prophet's 2003 releases "Praises" and "Cry of a Family." Michael Prophet continues to issue solid material.

QUEEN IFRICA (c. 1970–)

Born Ventrice Latora Morgan, Queen Ifrica is one of the children of **reggae** legend **Derrick Morgan**. She was raised in a musical household and early in her life joined the **Rastafarian** faith. She entered the Jamaican popular music scene in her early twenties and has since released solid material. Her duet with **Lady G** on the song "He's Just My Brethren" was a success and brought Ifrica much-deserved attention. Ifrica is aware of the pitfalls female reggae artists must avoid in the male-dominated and sexist market that is reggae music. She got her start in the Magic City Star Search Competition in Montego Bay, Jamaica, where she placed first. This took her to the finals at Club Inferno where she was again a winner. These regional successes led to an appearance on the 1995 installment of Reggae Sumfest. Her debut album *All Woman* appeared in 1996 and garnered her notoriety, if not monetary gain. In 1998, Ifrica teamed with **Tony Rebel** and joined his Flames Crew. Since then, she has released a series of successful singles including "Royal Love" and "Bye Bye." Queen Ifrica is a rising star who has yet to reach the pinnacle of her success.

QUEEN YEMISI (c. 1970–)

Queen Yemisi was born Deborah Owens in South Carolina; however, she relocated to Chicago to pursue a career as a jazz singer. As fortune would have it, Owens was performing in a **reggae** club called Wild Hair when she was heard by Jive Records vice president Wayne Williams. After her performance, Williams encouraged Owens to go to Jamaica and learn more about reggae music. She did and the product was a pairing with DJ Merciless that yielded the number one single "Sexy Lover." Another single soon followed called "Rocking Chair," which was another pairing with Merciless from 1997. The success of these early Jamaican singles brought further recording sessions that produced "I'll Always Come Back to You."

Yemisi's next step was to release the album *Love Fire: The Beryl Dyght-Vacianna Project* in 1997. The record was made with the production company Tressedelle and, while not widely successful, did garner her support in the United Kingdom. Yemisi's style is too eclectic for the Jamaica audience, so she had greater success in other markets. She released a cover version of the Doors' hit "Light My Fire" and returned to the studio for another album. In 2000, she released *I Have Feeling Too*, which was produced by Carl James and has background vocals from **Leeba Hibbert** (one of **Toots Hibberts's** children). The album features the title track and all of the arrangements by Yemisi herself. Queen Yemisi continues to be active in the reggae music scene.

RADICS, SOWELL (c. 1950–)

Born Noel Bailey, Sowell was one of the early members of the legendary studio band the **Roots Radics**. The band emerged in the early 1970s and included the core members **Errol Holt**, **Eric "Bingy Bunny" Lamont**, and **Lincoln Valentine "Style" Scott**. Over time, to this were added various other members, including lead guitarist Sowell Radics. The group's early impact was in the formation of a slowed-down **reggae** sound that was not as hectic as that of the **Revolutionaries**. The group produced long strings of singles as a backing band for producers **Henry "Junjo" Lawes** and **Linval Thompson**. They also toured as a backing band for **Gregory Isaacs** and backed him on the classic album *Night Nurse* (1982). After leaving the Roots Radics, Sowell Radics worked as a studio guitarist with artists such as **Mikey Dread** and **Sugar Minott**.

RAGGA

Ragga was a sub-genre of **reggae** music that emerged in the mid-1980s. It was categorized as a **dancehall toasting** over computer-generated rhythms. Thus, the product is all-digital, except for the vocals. The term itself is short for *raggamuffin*, and the style of music is very closely allied with dancehall. The only real difference is the sound source of the instrumental accompaniment: acoustic is dancehall, and digital is ragga. Ragga became wildly popular with producers, as it was significantly less expensive to make than was traditional dancehall. The use of digital rhythmic elements also enlivened the style, as producers could work with new sound sources instead of continuing to build from rhythms created in the **ska** and **rock steady** eras. Ragga has the same lyrical distinctions as dancehall in that the topics vary widely. Discussion of slack elements, such as womanizing and gun culture, are found alongside discussion of cultural uplift and **Rastafarian** doctrine.

The first ragga single was "Under Me Sleng Teng," recorded by Wayne Smith in 1985. The rhythm for the song was generated with a Casio keyboard that had just been brought into the studio. Examples of ragga artists include **Ini Kamoze**, **Mad Cobra**, **Beenie Man**, **Dennis Brown**, **Shaggy**, and **Pato Banton**, among many others. As a reggae music sub-style, ragga is still being written in the new millennium.

RAGGAMUFFIN. *See* RAGGA

RANDY'S RECORDS

Randy's Records was started by Vincent "Randy" Chin, who entered the record business in the 1950s. Chin began as a record salesman but went on to establish his own business that included a storefront, studio, and label. The business was in Kingston, Jamaica, with a major part of the outfit being Randy's Studio 17 on North Parade Road. The studio opened in the late 1960s, and **reggae** luminaries such as **Black Uhuru**, **Don Carlos**, **Alton Ellis**, **Vin Gordon**, **Gregory Isaacs**, **Bob Marley**, **Tommy McCook**,

Peter Tosh, and many others recorded in the facility. One of the longest-lasting recording artists was **Augustus Pablo**. Pablo recorded the seminal instrumental album *Java* at Randy's in 1971. In the mid-1970s, the Chins moved to the United States and settled in New York. He brought his business interests with him and in 1979 opened VP Records in Jamaica, Queens. On VP, Chin continued the success that he had had with Randy's.

RANGLIN, ERNEST (1932–)

Born in Manchester, Jamaica, Ranglin grew up in the inland rural community of Robin's Hall. While still a youth, he learned to play the guitar from his uncles. His next major influence was American jazz. He learned the style by imitating the guitar playing of jazz music's greatest guitar player, Charlie Christian. At age fourteen, Ranglin moved to Kingston to pursue further schooling, but was really interested in learning more about music. While in the country's capital, Ranglin spent time in the Kingston dance clubs watching and listening to the guitar players who were touring or members of the hotel bands.

Soon Ranglin had acquired the necessary skills to play live, and in 1948 he joined the Val Bennett Orchestra. Bennett's group played the hotel circuit, and Ranglin's talent drew attention to the young guitarist. He was eventually lured away from Bennett and joined the Eric Deans Orchestra. This group was the premier touring band on the island and regularly played all around the Caribbean. The band did not play Jamaican popular music, instead performing standards by American jazz greats such as Duke Ellington.

In 1958, while Ranglin was performing with his own quartet, he met the music business up-and-comer **Christopher Blackwell**. Blackwell offered to record Ranglin, and together they created the first album issued by **Island Records**. By 1959, Ranglin had become part of Cluett Johnson's group Clue J and His Blues Blasters. With Johnson, Ranglin went back to the studio and recorded several singles for **Clement "Coxsone" Dodd** at **Federal Records**. The style that they had taken to playing was heavily influenced by American rhythm and blues, but with an island flavor. One of the songs they recorded was called "Shuffle Bug" and featured a shuffle rhythm played by Ranglin, which was a feature of the New Orleans jump band sound. The song has become widely regarded as the first **ska** recording and marked the dawn of Jamaican popular music.

Throughout the 1960s, Ranglin recorded for a series of the most important producers in Jamaica such as **Clancy**

Ernest Ranglin. © *UrbanImage.tv.*

Eccles, **Lee "Scratch" Perry**, **Duke Reid**, and Dodd. Blackwell again came back into the picture when he invited Ranglin to London to record with a young Jamaican singer named **Millie Small**. Together, they recorded the seminal "My Boy Lollipop" in 1964, and the song became an instant classic. Ranglin went on to record in groups that backed a series of major **reggae** music talents. He also released his own material beginning with 1964's *Wranglin.'*

He continued to release new material for the next thirty years, including *Reflections* (1965), *Ranglin' Roots* (1976), *Below the Bassline* (1996), *E.B. @ Noon* (2000), and several others. The *E.B. @ Noon* album was made with Floyd Lloyd and featured a variety of styles including **rock steady**, reggae, ska, and big band jazz.

In the new millennium, Ranglin released 2000's *Modern Answers to Old Problems*, *Grooving*, and *Gotcha!* Ranglin continues to record and has a busy touring schedule as one of the founders of Jamaican popular music.

RANKING DREAD (c. 1955–)

Ranking Dread was born Winston Brown in Kingston, Jamaica, and rose to prominence as a **dancehall DJ** on **Clement "Coxsone" Dodd's** UK-based **sound system**. He surfaced right at the beginning of the dancehall era and was known for his often-unintelligible lyrics. Through the course of a decade-long career, Dread released four albums. The first was called *Girls Fiesta* (1978), which garnered moderate attention. Next was *Kunte Kinte Roots* (1979), followed by *Lots of Loving* (1980). He recorded the album at **Channel One Studios** in Kingston, Jamaica, and it was produced by Dread and **Sugar Minott**. Featured tracks included the title song, "Loving Devotion," and "Super Star." Of note, Dread was backed on this released by the Black Roots Players featuring **Sly and Robbie**. Dread's fourth album was released in 1982, titled *Ranking Dread in Dub*. It was mixed and engineered by a pair of masters, side A by **King Tubby** and side B by **Scientist**. Featured tracks included "Bom Dub," "No More Waiting," and "Jah Dub." In the mid-1980s, Ranking Dread faded from the Jamaican popular music scene.

RANKING ROGER (1961–)

Born Roger Charlery in Birmingham, England, he entered the **reggae** music scene in 1978 when he joined the band called the Beat. Eventually known as the English Beat, the group consisted of Charlery (nicknamed Ranking Roger), Dave Wakeling, Andy Cox, David Steele, Everett Morton, and Saxa on saxophone. Saxa had come out of the first wave of **ska** and by joining the Beat was paving the way for the second wave. The group played a variety of styles, but focused on the Jamaican ska and reggae.

The band ascended the ranks and soon became the premier UK second-wave band, which is all the more interesting as it had a racially mixed lineup. In the studio, the group started out with their 1979 single "Tears of a Clown," a version of the Smokey Robinson hit. In 1980, they issued a series of successful singles that included "Hands Off . . . She's Mine," "Mirror in the Bathroom," "Best Friend," and "Too Nice to Talk To." There followed a series of three highly popular albums starting with *I Just Can't Stop It* (1980). This was followed by *Wha'ppen?* (1981) and *Special Beat Service* (1982).

After the third album, the band broke up. Next, Ranking Roger entered the band General Public, again alongside Dave Wakeling. While General Public was a direct offshoot of the English Beat, it enjoyed a period of separate successes. Their first album,

All the Rage, was a hit with featured singles such as "Never You Done That." The band included Saxa from the English Beat, Mikey Billingham, Horace Panter, and Mick Jones (of Clash fame) on the guitar. The group went on to release the albums *Hand to Mouth* and *Rub It Better* through the course of the 1990s; it broke up in 1996. While General Public was having its success, the other members of the English Beat were forming Fine Young Cannibals.

In the wake of General Public, Roger went solo and issued a pair of albums titled *Radical Departure* and *Inside My Head*. Next, Roger joined the band Special Beat, which included Neville Staples, Horace Panter, Graeme Hamilton, and others. In 2003 the English Beat reunited and toured the United Kingdom, and Roger remains active on the UK music scene.

RANKING TOYAN (c. 1955–1991)

Ranking Toyan emerged on the scene in 1974 when he began appearing on Kingston, Jamaica, area **sound systems**. Toyan got his big break when he recorded the 1979 single "Disco Pants." There followed a flurry of interest in the young **toaster**, and in the early 1980s he went on to record with **Joseph "Joe Joe" Hookim**, **Jah Thomas**, and **Scientist**. The result of these sessions was a series of hit singles including "Nah Kill Nuh Man," "Just Love," and "Sodom in Jamaica." In 1981, Toyan issued his debut album *How the West Was Won* with the production assistance of **Henry "Junjo" Lawes** and instrumental backing by the **Roots Radics**. He also joined Lawes's sound system Volcano. The year 1982's release, *Spar with Me*, was another Lawes production. This album also made use of Scientist's production skills. The year 1983 saw the release of two albums, *Every Posse Want Me* and *Ghetto Man Skank*. Toyan kept releasing new material for the rest of the decade. In addition, he became a producer in his own right and helped his old friend, Billy Boyo, from the Volcano sound system with a few songs. He ended up making a substantial name for himself as a producer. Toyan's life was cut short when he was murdered in 1991.

RANKS, SHABBA (1965–)

Born Rexton Gordon in St. Ann, Jamaica, Ranks was eight when his parents moved the family to Kingston. He entered the reggae music scene as a **dancehall DJ** and quickly earned a solid reputation. He learned from the best as he listened to **Brigadier Jerry**, **General Echo**, **Josey Wales**, and **Yellowman**. In 1980, Ranks released his debut single at the tender age of fifteen. The song was released under the name Co-Pilot and was titled "Heat under Sufferer's Feet." The single was not successful, and Ranks returned to the dancehall. He again surfaced in 1987 and released a quick series of singles for the producers, such as **Black Scorpio**, **Bobby "Digital" Dixon**, **King Jammy**, and others. He joined Digital's

Shabba Ranks. © *UrbanImage.tv.*

Heatwave **sound system** and began to assert his use of slack lyrics (talk of guns, sex, and drugs). He also recorded a series of singles including "Mama Man," "Peanie Peanie," and the classic "Wicked Inna Bed."

In addition to having prodigious talent, Ranks also had the foresight to know that combination singles doubled his chances for success. Thus he released material on which he was paired with **Dennis Brown**, **Cocoa Tea**, **Gregory Isaacs**, and **Sanchez**. All of this material drove Ranks's stock higher, and by the mid-1990s he was the marquee DJ in the dancehall.

Throughout the decade he released a series of albums that further cemented his solid reputation, including *Rappin' with the Ladies* (1988), *As Raw as Ever* (1991), *Mr. Maximum* (1992), *X-Tra Naked* (1992), *A Mi Shabba* (1995), and *Shine Eye Gal* (1995). An aspect of Shabba's success is his tremendous crossover ability. More than any other dancehall DJ of the 1990s, Ranks moved into the U.S. hip hop scene seamlessly and recorded with a variety of hip hop luminaries such as KRS-ONE. In the new millennium, Ranks's music has been appearing in compilation albums, and the dancehall DJ's productivity has slowed considerably.

RANKS, SLUGGY (c. 1968–)

Born Andrew Gregory in Ray Town, Kingston, Jamaica, he emerged on the Jamaican popular music scene in the mid-1980s. Unlike his **dancehall** contemporaries, Ranks emphasized consciousness lyrics and roots sentiments over the slackness of sex and gun culture. In the late 1980s, he made the rounds of the Jamaican producers and studios before coming to the United States to record. The resulting product was a series of hit singles that included "95% Black, 5% White" and "Ghetto Youth Bust." Ranks's 1994 album *Ghetto Youth Bust* comprises both of these songs and a collection of others. In accord with his reputation for consciousness lyrics, the title track from the album dealt with black-on-black violence. Another marquee single was "No Money Naah Run," which took on the issue of poverty. He also worked a pair of Rasta-themed tracks called "Jah Is Guiding I" and "Badness Na Go Work." Through the rest of the decade he issued two more albums, *Just Call Sluggy* (1997) and *My Time* (1999).

The majority of Ranks's material was issued as singles, resulting in limited crossover potential in the United States. In the new millennium, Ranks has been working with New York-based **reggae** label **Easy Star** and has produced new material. His new singles include "Soddom and Gommorah," "Thunder and Lightning," and "The Coming of the Lord."

RAS MICHAEL (1943–)

Born George Michael Henry in Kingston, Jamaica, Ras Michael grew up in several **Rastafarian** communities in the west Kingston ghetto. As a youth, Michael took up Rasta hand drumming. He would eventually become an international superstar. Michael plays in the **nyabinghi** style and is also renowned for his vocals. His style is pure roots **reggae**, and he infuses it with hand drumming, chanting, and dancing. In the mid-1960s, he formed the band the **Sons of Negus**, a group of singers and drummers. After performing for a variety of Rasta meetings, the group went into the studio and recorded a series of singles including "Lion of Judah" and "Ethiopian National Anthem." **Jackie Mittoo** invited Michael to perform with the **Soul Vendors** in 1966 for **Clement "Coxsone" Dodd**.

In 1974, Michael and the Sons of Negus went back to the studio and recorded their debut album with **Lloyd Charmers** at the **Federal Records** studio. The result was

Dadawah—Peace and Love (1974). The album was popular enough that it came to the attention of **Tommy Cowan**, the longtime emcee for the **Reggae Sunsplash** concert, who brought them back into the studio and recorded *Rastafari* (1975). Unlike the first album, the material on the second was not supplemented with additional studio instrumentalists. The entire release is drumming, chanting, and minimal other instruments (intermittent flute). Since the mid-1970s, Ras Michael and the Sons of Negus have released almost twenty albums. They stand at the pinnacle of nyabinghi and reggae hand drumming and create one of the purest types of Rastafarian music available.

RAS RECORDS

Formed in 1979 by **Gary "Doctor Dread" Himelfarb**, the imprint name stands for "Real Authentic Sound." Dread has spent the last twenty-five years recording authentic Jamaican popular music. Himelfarb got started in the music business through his associations with several Jamaican artists. He set out to bring Jamaican culture, the message of **Rastafari**, and the music of Jamaica to the world. He began the label in his own home, but due to its growth it was soon moved to formal offices in Washington DC. The RAS Records roster grew throughout the 1980s and soon was the home to acts such as **Black Uhuru**, **Don Carlos**, **Inner Circle**, **Freddie McGregor**, **Junior Reid**, and others.

Through Himelfarb's work, the link between Jamaican roots reggae artists and the American market has grown significantly. In pursuit of his goals, Himelfarb has established links to countries as far away as several southern African countries, parts of South America, Holland, and Japan. The current artist roster for RAS includes almost 100 of the finest acts in Jamaican popular music. The roster now lists **Dennis Brown**, **Culture**, **Gregory Isaacs**, **Israel Vibration**, **Barrington Levy**, **Luciano**, **Augustus Pablo**, **Sizzla**, **Sly and Robbie**, **Yami Bolo**, Junior Reid, and many others. Further, Himelfarb is credited as the producer and author of the liner notes for the material released on the label.

In addition to these significant releases, Himelfarb has also launched a series of releases made specifically for children, called *Reggae for Kids*. Another aspect of the label is the release of compilation albums. The RAS catalog currently includes thirty-eight compilation recordings that feature a series of reggae stars. In 2004, RAS released a compilation of songs by American artist Bob Dylan with all songs redone in reggae versions. The album, titled *Is It Rolling Bob: A Reggae Tribute to Bob Dylan*, includes appearances by Apple Gabriel of Israel Vibration, **Angus "Drummie Zeb" Gaye**, **Beres Hammond**, **Toots Hibbert**, **J. C. Lodge**, the **Mighty Diamonds**, Luciano, Michael Rose of Black Uhuru, Sizzla, Gregory Isaacs, and Billy Mystic of the Mystic Revealers. In the past two years, RAS has enjoyed a period of high productivity, which includes new releases by **Horace Andy**, **Dennis Brown**, **Eek-A-Mouse**, **Mad Professor**, **Sly and Robbie**, **Steel Pulse**, Nasio, Gregory Isaacs, Sizzla, Israel Vibration, and Turbulence.

RASTAFARI (RASTAFARIANISM)

Marcus Garvey was a Jamaican-born black nationalist who founded the Universal Negro Improvement Association (UNIA) in the 1920s. Part of what Garvey taught was that all black people were in fact displaced Africans and that they should endeavor to repatriate the African continent. As part of that plan, Garvey traveled through the Caribbean and the eastern United States raising money for the Black Star, a large passenger ship meant to be used for the journey from one hemisphere to the other.

Another of Garvey's teachings was that his followers (Garveyites) should imagine Jesus as a black man. An offshoot of this was the African Orthodox church, which is neither Catholic nor Protestant. The African Orthodox church attempted to be recognized by the Russian Metropolia, but a settlement could not be reached, and instead their bishops were ordained by the American Catholics. The African Orthodox church and the Garveyite church are synonymous, and soon the group had thousands of members on several continents.

In the new millennium, the African Orthodox church has all but disappeared. However, another statement by Garvey had great impact on a longer-lasting religion. It was Garvey himself who said that a king would arise from Africa and deliver the oppressed from tyranny. This king came in the form of the last Ethiopian Emperor Prince Haile Selassie I (Ras Tafari). When Garvey's prophesy and Tafari's lineage and nobility were combined, the Rastafarian movement began. An oddity of the formation of the Rasta belief was that Garvey himself was not a supporter of Tafari and disagreed with some of the ruling class's positions in Ethiopia. Garvey himself had fallen on hard times. His movement had largely collapsed and he was jailed for fraud.

The period from the 1930s to the 1970s are widely considered Rasta's high point. During this period, Rastafari was a major religious movement in Jamaica and throughout the Caribbean. Rasta was a syncretic religion, meaning it combined Christianity with other, non-western religions. It had its own Bible, called the Kebra Nagast, which is also known as the Holy Piby. Within the Jamaican Rasta community there was a collection of elders; however, many of them disagreed, and there was no all-inclusive Rastafarian religion. Due to the lack of agreement in the Rasta elders, there was also no standardized scripture—some used the Holy Piby and some the King James Version of the Bible.

While this all seems counterintuitive to the West, it is just what the elders saw as fit. Without standardization, Rastas were free to follow the will of Jah (God) in the manners that they believed. These ways of following Jah were discerned at sessions called grounations, during which long hours were spent reasoning. These events were filled with discussion of theology, prayer, and music. In trying to interpret Jah's will, Rastas used divine guidance to "overstand" (not understand) the Truth. Another aspect of these sessions was the sacramental smoking of marijuana (ganja) as a means to further enlighten and clarify the discussions.

The Rastas found rural living the most conducive to practicing their religion unadulterated and thus lived in communes in the island's interior. The enclaves were ruled by elders and often segregated by sex, the men living in the communes in the hills and the women and children often living nearer to the coast. In addition to the gender code, the Rasta adhered to a specific mode of cooking. Called "ital," Rastas base their eating on the Pentateuch with some emendations. In general, Rastas do not drink alcohol, they prefer to eat fish, and their diets consist largely of fruits and vegetables. In addition, their grooming is also prescribed. A Rasta does not shave, nor prevent his hair from growing into thin matted braids called "dreadlocks." It is possible for a Rasta to shave or to wear short hair to avoid persecution. Further, not all of the Rastas were accustomed to wearing dreadlocks. Only the most active and devout who had taken the oath of Nazirite were required to wear locks.

One aspect of the Rasta faith that all of the elders agreed on was Selassie's divinity and that part of his plan was to return all blacks to the African continent—further, not just to Africa, but specifically to Ethiopia. The principal problem with repatriation was that the Jamaican government was not about to finance this mass exodus, and the frustration that resulted led to periodic clashes between the Rastas and the police. This came to a head in 1954 when the government destroyed the Rasta enclave called Pinnacle. Pinnacle was the home to many elders and was run by **Leonard Howell**, who disappeared after the enclave was overrun. This was a turning point for the Rastas, as now that their main rural home was destroyed they now needed a new place to live. They moved into the west Kingston ghetto and settled in places called Trenchtown and the Dungle.

Also in the wake of the massacre at Pinnacle, the Rastas were increasingly harassed by the police. This led to the rejection of non-violence by several members of the religion. As a result, there were several armed revolts that were put down by British troops.

When Jamaica achieved independence in 1962, many Rastas hoped that a new day had dawned on the island. While all of the tumult was going on in Jamaica, all was not calm in Ethiopia. Mussolini had exiled Haile Selassie from Ethiopia in 1937, where the head of Rastafarianism remained for the rest of his life. While in exile, Selassie founded the Ethiopian World Federation (EWF), whose purpose was to raise support for black nationalist groups. The EWF came to Jamaica in the late 1930s. They established a chapter that was immediately filled with Rastafarians, including several elders. These events led to Haile Selassie's visit to Jamaica on April 21, 1966, during which he met with a group of Rasta leaders including **Mortimer Planno**. The meeting with the elders culminated with Selassie's insistence that Rastas convert to Ethiopian Orthodoxy and the possibility that Jamaicans could get Ethiopian land grants. In the wake of Selassie's visit, many Rastas were more steadfast in their belief that he was the second coming, while others took his advice and converted.

In the early 1970s, parts of the Rastafari and Orthodoxy movements merged. The EWF leaders built a breed of Rastafarianism that incorporated Garveyism, links to Jamaica, and a respect for Selassie that did not deify him. Interestingly, this is the same period of time during which **reggae** music flourished, and many of its greatest singers wrote lyrics venerating Selassie.

In 1975, it was reported that Haile Selassie had died. The news traveled like a shockwave through the Rasta community, alienating some and steeling the resolve of others. Known Rasta and reggae superstar **Robert Nesta Marley** reacted with the stirring song "Jah Live." Marley himself had been a member of the Rasta sect the Twelve Tribes for most of his adult life. The Twelve Tribes of Israel was the largest and most visible of the Rasta sects. In 1968, Vernon Carrington (Prophet Gad) founded the group with the core belief that Haile Selassie was in fact Jesus Christ returned to Earth. One aspect of the Twelve Tribes is that of all of the Rasta sects, it had the most clearly articulated doctrines.

Since the late 1970s, the believers in Rastafari remain. The movement has gone through periodic ebb and flow. One significant difference between the Rasta of the last millennium and the new millennium is that Rastas are now found all over the world.

RAY, DANNY (c. 1950–)

Born in Kingston, Jamaica, in the early 1950s, Ray entered the Jamaican popular music scene in the mid-1970s through competition in a variety of island talent shows. Next, he relocated to the United Kingdom and formed a band that garnered some success. With his band, the Falcons, he released his debut single "The Scorpion." This was followed by a label change to **Trojan** and a series of successful singles. The most significant of these releases was 1977's "Playboy." At this time he also released "I'm Gonna Get Married," "Sister Big Stuff," and several others. In the late 1970s, Ray launched his own Black Jack label, on which he issued his own material and that of other singers. Dave Barker, Joy White, and Winston Francis all appeared on Ray's new label.

As Ray's production skills bloomed, so did his opportunities. For the past several years, Ray has been working with Jet Star's Charm label at the Cave studio and producing solid UK **reggae**. One of his greatest successes was the **Luciano** record *Great Controversy* (2001). His next project was with the UK band the Rasites, which cemented his reputation as a producer of the highest order. Together the band and the producer made "Jah Love," "High Grade," and "Urban Regeneration." In the new millennium, Ray was heralded as the top reggae producer in the United Kingdom. He continued to work for Jet Star and was responsible for their Reggae Hits series in addition to outstanding new work by **J. C. Lodge**.

RAYVON (c. 1960–)

Born Bruce Brewster, Rayvon rose to prominence in the group of **dancehall DJs** that included **Shaggy**. Unlike his contemporaries, he is known for his smooth rhythm and blues-inflected voice that contrasts well with the gravelly delivery of most others. He entered the music scene as an emcee and DJ in the hip hop style. In the late 1980s, he worked on his dancehall style and in 1988 met Orville "Shaggy" Burrell.

The young DJ became known as part of the Big Yard family that included Shaggy, Rik Rok, Shaun "Sting International" Pizzonia, and Robert Livingston. The Yard family was rounded out by the Hot Shot Band, which backed the artists with solid instrumentals. Rayvon contributed his laid-back vocals to Shaggy's hit single "Mr. Boombastic" in 1996. In the wake of his early success, Rayvon struck out on his own. His early solo material included "No Guns No Murder," produced by hip hop legend Funkmaster Flex. The single was successful and resulted in a Virgin Records recording deal. The next effort was his debut album *Hear My Cry* (1997), which was again successful. The album was a stylistic mixture of dancehall, **reggae**, hip hop, and rhythm and blues.

Next, he released *My Bad* (2002), an album of new material that highlighted the young DJ's lyrical talent. Unlike his previous outings, this material showed a new, harder, and more dancehall style for Rayvon. Featured singles on the album included "Story of My Life," "I'll Die for You," and "2-Way" (featuring Shaggy and Rik Rok). Also on the album was "Playboy Bunny," which was a collaboration with Lady Raw.

REBEL, TONY (c. 1960–)

Born Patrick Barrett in Jamaica, Tony Rebel entered the popular music scene in the late 1980s. His early work was as a singer in local talent competitions. He moved from there to the **sound systems** and became a **DJ**. His brand of lyrical content was different from the standard slackness topics of gun culture and sex; instead Rebel discussed cultural concerns in conscious lyrics. Rebel became a **Rastafarian** during his early musical career and has maintained Rasta themes in his lyrics. As a dancehall performer, Rebel spent ten years honing his skills before going into the studio.

His earliest recordings are combinations with other important recording artists. In 1990, he issued *Tony Rebel with Capleton and Ninjaman: Real Rough*. The following year came volumes one and two of *Tony Rebel with Cutty Ranks: Die Hard*. He then cut a collection of singles including "Fresh Vegetables," "Chatty-Chatty," "Nazerite Vow," and "Sweet Jamaica." His first entry into the studio as a true soloist came with his 1992 album *Rebel with a Cause*. This was quickly followed by 1993's *Vibes of Time*. In 1994, *Tony Rebel Meets Garnett Silk: Dancehall Conference* surfaced. The release with Silk was especially poignant as the two had been longtime friends and Silk died in a fire the same year the album was released. In 1998, Rebel issued *If Jah* on the VP imprint, and RAS released his *Realms of Rebel* album in 2001. The *Realms* album led to a lengthy tour and spawned a series of successful singles such as "Loyal Soul Jah," "Rasta Right Again," and "Judgment." Tony Rebel continues to write and record.

RED DRAGON (c. 1960–)

Born Leroy May, he came onto the **DJ** scene in the early 1980s. He originally took the nickname Redman, but soon changed his name to Red Dragon. Like his **dancehall** contemporaries, he made the rounds of several **sound systems** before entering the studio. His early outings were not successful until he released "Hol a Fresh." The single was a major hit and put Red Dragon on the map. He went on to work with **King Tubby**, **King Jammy**, **Steely and Clevie**, **Bobby "Digital" Dixon**, **Winston Riley**, Danny Browne, **Fashion Records**, and **Sly and Robbie's** Taxi imprint. Through the course of releasing material for these outlets, Dragon's reputation grew and he is now widely revered as a dancehall master. Throughout the 1990s, Dragon released a series of successful albums including *Good Old College* (1992), *Bun Them* (1994), and *Rusty Magnum* (1998). Red Dragon continues to write and record and remains a highly respected dancehall star.

Tony Rebel. © *UrbanImage.tv.*

REGGAE

The term *reggae* came into common use in the late 1960s. The style developed from a combination of island and international influences. Jamaican popular music began in earnest in the early 1960s with the evolution of the **ska** style. This was followed in the mid-1960s by ska's development into **rock steady**. Reggae surfaced in 1968 and adapted elements of ska and rock steady and mixed them with American rhythm and blues and African drumming. Traditional reggae often employed the horns of the ska style, the slowed-down beat of rock steady, the shuffle beat of the New Orleans rhythm and blues, and African **burru** drum rhythms filled with syncopation. The guitar was played on the second and fourth beats of the four-beat measure while the bass guitar emphasized the first and third beats. The role of the drums was absorbed by the percussive playing of the guitar and bass, so the drummer's role was diminished. However, the drum rhythm did take on a very specific character called the **one-drop** rhythm (with only the third beat of a four-beat measure accented).

The term *reggae* went on to encompass a wide variety of styles. It became an umbrella term used to describe the music that preceded it and the styles that came after, such as **dancehall** and **ragga**. This overarching use was mirrored in the American use of the term *rock and roll* to mean a great variety of styles that fit under one general umbrella. As a result, a great many artists described themselves as reggae musicians when they had widely divergent styles. The most internationally renowned style of reggae is the roots variety that was popularized by **Bob Marley and the Wailers** in the 1970s. The roots variety of reggae was marked by the use of a rock band lineup and lyrics that tended to focus on issues related to **Rastafari**. This arrangement was affected by the influences listed above, but it was performed by a band comprising a lead singer, lead guitar, rhythm guitar, bass, drums, percussion, keyboard, and background vocal harmony. This brand of reggae became enormously popular in the late 1970s and the early 1980s and remains so today. The style is featured in the ongoing internationally touring **Reggae Sunsplash** concerts that are staged annually.

An aspect of reggae music that is often overlooked was that not all reggae groups were **Rastafarians**. Many of the most visible singers were, but **Rasta** had its own brand of music called **nyabinghi**, which also affected the development of reggae. An interesting feature of reggae music was that, like American jazz, as new styles emerged the older styles remained popular with their core audiences. Artists who fit under the reggae music umbrella include **Black Uhuru**, **Burning Spear**, **Jimmy Cliff**, **Desmond Dekker**, **Inner Circle**, **Gregory Isaacs**, **Freddie McGregor**, **Augustus Pablo**, **Peter Tosh**, **Bunny Wailer**, and many, many others.

REGGAE SUNSPLASH

Reggae Sunsplash is an annual **reggae** concert that began in Jamaica in 1978. It was the idea of Tony Johnson, the late concert organizer. The first staging came about in the wake of the **One Love Peace Concert**, and **Bob Marley and the Wailers** were meant to be the headline act. However, they ended up being on tour in support of the *Kaya* album and settled for headlining the second year. The Reggae Sunsplash concert went on to be an annual event of the grandest proportions. It drew hordes of people to Jamaica from the United States and Europe, resulting in an annual tour following the kickoff concert in Jamaica. A long-time fixture of the concert was **Tommy Cowan**, the emcee for both the Jamaican and touring shows. The concert is the marquee reggae event of each year, and the auditions to appear in Sunsplash are fierce. Over the past twenty-five years the list of talent that has appeared on the Sunsplash stage has included **Big Youth**, **Dennis Brown**, **Carlene Davis**, **Eek-A-Mouse**, the **Gladiators**, **Israel Vibration**, **Little Lenny**, **Maxi Priest**, the **Mighty Diamonds**, **Mutabaruka**, **Shinehead**, **Garnet Silk**, **Toots and the Maytals**, **Andrew Tosh**, **Yellowman**, and many, many more. The Reggae Sunsplash concert is staged each summer and highlights the best that reggae music has to offer. The concert continues to draw an international crowd and remains an annual touring show.

REID, ARTHUR "DUKE" (1923–1974)

One of the earliest producers of **reggae** music on the island of Jamaica, Duke was born in 1923 with the name Arthur Reid and lived until 1974. Along with **Clement "Coxsone" Dodd**, Reid is generally credited as one of the most important figures in the development of reggae music. Before moving into the music scene, Reid worked on the police force, owned the liquor store *Treasure Isle*, and had a radio show called "Treasure Isle Time." Through his radio show, Reid was well versed in American rhythm and blues and the musical developments coming out of the Mississippi delta area. He entered the music business in the mid-1950s by opening his own **sound system**. The system was called Trojan Sound and directly competed with Dodd's Sir Coxsone

Sound. Many witnesses to the system clashes felt that Reid's sound was the best on the island in the late 1950s.

At the end of the 1950s, Reid launched a small production company called **Treasure Isle Records**. Many of his early recordings were reissues of American rhythm and blues classics, but he soon ventured into island recordings with his backing band the Duke Reid Group. With this arrangement in place, Dodd began recruiting talent such as **Derrick Morgan** and others. Over the Treasure Isle liquor store, Reid built his own studio, and Treasure Isle studios was born. In 1965, the **Skatalites** recorded with Reid, and he cultivated a long relationship with members of the band that led to **Tommy McCook's** Supersonics becoming Reid's session band. The Supersonics had a fluid lineup that at times included McCook, **Gladstone "Gladdy" Anderson**, **Vin Gordon**, **Herman Marquis**, Lennox Brown, Bab Brooks, Jackie Jackson, **Ernest Ranglin**, **Lynn Taitt**, **Winston Wright**, Lloyd Knibb, and Hugh Malcolm. Reid was at the forefront of the musical developments in Jamaica, and it was his recordings with Morgan that heralded the birth of **rock steady** in 1966.

Through the 1970s, Reid released seminal albums by singers such as **Alton Ellis**, the **Ethiopians**, **Justin Hinds**, **John Holt**, **Pat Kelly**, the **Melodians**, the **Paragons**, the **Techniques**, **U-Roy**, and many others. In 1974, Duke Reid died after an extended illness. Material from his Treasure Isle imprint continues to be issued in various forms.

REID, JUNIOR (1965–)

Born Delroy Reid in the Waterhouse district of Kingston, Jamaica, his earliest recordings were with **Hugh Mundell** and included "Know Myself," recorded when he was only fourteen. While still a youth he released a series of successful singles such as "Original Foreign Mind," "Boom Shack-a-Lack," and "Babylon Release the Chain." During this early phase, Reid was also the frontman for the band Voice of Progress, which released the hit single "Mini Bus Driver."

In 1986, he was recruited as the lead singer for **Black Uhuru**, for whom he recorded a pair of albums. The first album was titled *Brutal* (1986) and exhibited the ease with which Reid moved into the place of Michael Rose, the previous singer. Reid showed himself to be a strong singer. However, this was a tumultuous period for the band and Reid departed in 1990.

After leaving Black Uhuru, Reid reestablished his solo career and launched his own production company, called JR Productions and Recording Studio, in Kingston. His solo releases included *Long Road* (1991), *Big Timer* (1993), and *Visa* (1994). Reid's lyrics are of the conscious sort, and he has been an ardent champion of the young and oppressed throughout his career. In the second half of the 1990s, Reid remained productive and issued *Junior Reid and the Bloods*, *Listen to the Voices*, and *Boom Shack-a-Lack*.

In the new millennium, Reid remains productive. He reissued the *Big Timer* album on the Artists Only imprint and re-released *Boom Shack-a-Lack* with new bonus material.

REID, ROY. *See* I-ROY

REVOLUTIONARIES

The Revolutionaries were the house band for legendary producer **Joseph "Joe Joe" Hookim** at his **Channel One Studios**. As was the style of production during the **reggae** era, producers invited singers into the studio to voice their lyrics over instrumental backing supplied by a small and select group of players. These players often moved from one studio to another or worked for a variety of producers at the same time. In the mid-1970s, the Revolutionaries were the group that Hookim used when he needed a backing band in the studio. The group marked the emergence of the powerful rhythm section combination **Sly and Robbie**. Robbie Shakespeare (bass) and Sly Dunbar (drums) were the premier session players since **Aston** and **Carlton Barrett** joined the **Wailers**. In addition to Sly and Robbie, the band consisted of a host of other players including **Tony Chin**, **Ansel Collins**, **Carlton "Santa" Davis**, **Oswald "Ossie" Hibbert**, Errol Nelson, **Bertram "Ranchie" McLean**, **Earl "Chinna" Smith**, Radcliffe "Duggie" Bryan, Robby Lynn, **Leroy "Horsemouth" Wallace**, and horn players such as **Deadly Headley Bennett**, **Vin Gordon**, **Herman Marquis**, and **Tommy McCook**. Other than Sly and Robbie, these members came and went and were not employed unless specifically called for.

The story of Jamaican popular music is muddied by the fact that this same group of players often recorded for other producers. The same general group of players recorded for **Joe Gibbs** as the Professionals, as the **Aggrovators** for **Bunny "Striker" Lee**, and as Black Disciples for Jack Ruby. Although these musicians typically made their living as studio performers, they did go on to record their own material. The Revolutionaries released a series of independent albums including *Revolutionary Sounds* (1976) and *Outlaw Dub* (1979). The core of the band moved on when Sly and Robbie left the studio to tour with **Black Uhuru** and **Peter Tosh** in the early 1980s. With the exit of the powerful rhythm section from the scene, the **Roots Radics** stepped in to fill the gap. During their heyday, the band recorded for **Althea and Donna**, **Dillinger**, **Clint Eastwood**, **Winston "Pipe" Matthews**, the **Mighty Diamonds**, the **Wailing Souls**, and others.

RICHARDS, MIKEY "BOO" (c. 1950–)

Active on the **reggae** music scene since the early 1970s, Richards has worked for a variety of producers and singers and has earned the reputation as one of the most solid drummers on the island. Richards began making a name for himself as a studio player in the early 1970s. He worked for **Lee "Scratch" Perry's Upsetters** and appeared on a wide variety of recordings. Simultaneously, he was playing in the Impact All-Stars, which was the studio band for Vincent "Randy" Chin at his Randy's 17 studios. In addition to the studio band credits, Richard also played on a variety of sessions and recorded with **Culture** on their *Cumbolo* (1979), *International Herb* (1979), *Trob On* (1993), and *One Stone* (1996) albums. As a session player, Richard recorded with the **Abyssinians**, **Jimmy Cliff**, the **Congos**, **Sharon Forrester**, Pablo Moses, the **Heptones**, **J. C. Lodge**, the **Meditations**, **Jacob Miller**, **Junior Byles**, **Lee "Scratch" Perry**, **Prince Far I**, **Junior Reid**, **Max Romeo**, U-Brown, Chevelle Franklyn, and many others. More recently, he recorded with Floyd Lloyd, Perry, Cliff, George Faith, and Philip Michael Thomas. Mikey "Boo" Richards remains an important figure on the reggae music scene.

RILEY, WINSTON (1946–)

Riley began producing Jamaican popular music in the 1960s while still in high school. He was not formally trained in music, but did cultivate a strong sense for popular music. He got his formal start in music when he formed the **Techniques** in 1962. The band also featured Slim Smith, Franklin White, and Frederick White. Over time, the lineup of the band went through many changes and at times included Jackie Parris, Marvin Brooks, **Tyrone Evans**, Ernest Wilson, **Pat Kelly**, Dave Barker, **Lloyd Parks**, and **Bruce Ruffin**.

Next, Riley, whose nickname is Technique, went into production. He launched the Technique label and opened a recording studio. A wide variety of artists benefited from Riley's facilities and expertise, including **Cornell Campbell**, **Chaka Demus and Pliers**, **Ansel Collins**, **Cutty Ranks**, **General Echo**, **Courtney Melody**, **Red Dragon**, and Tyrone Evans. Riley's earliest production efforts stretch back to 1969, and he remains active in the new millennium. Since 2000, Riley has done production for **Anthony B**, **Buju Banton**, Glen Washington, **Alton Ellis**, **King Tubby**, **George Nooks**, Boris Gardiner, and many others.

ROBERTS, LINDON ANDREW. *See* HALF PINT

ROCK STEADY

Rock steady was a sub-style of Jamaican popular music that surfaced in the mid-1960s. It was the evolutionary step after **ska**. The beat of rock steady music is roughly half the speed of the standard ska beat, and the texture of the instrumentation is much less dense. Also, in rock steady the **reggae** accent patterns started to emerge. The guitar was played on the second and fourth beats of the four-beat measure while the bass guitar emphasized the first and third beats. The role of the drums was absorbed by the percussive playing of the guitar and bass, so the drummer's role was diminished. Additionally in rock steady, the ska horn section was largely replaced by the use of a keyboard player.

Many rock steady groups emphasized the lyrics over the instruments, and the lyrical content tended to be delivered in tight vocal harmonies reminiscent of American rhythm and blues. Topics discussed in the lyrics moved more toward cultural awareness and social uplift. Many of the reggae groups that came to prominence in the early 1970s got their start in the rock steady era, among them **Bob Marley and the Wailers**. Examples of rock steady groups and singers included Dave and **Ansel Collins**, **Desmond Dekker**, **Alton Ellis**, the **Ethiopians**, the **Gladiators**, the **Heptones**, the **Melodians**, **Jackie Mittoo**, the **Paragons**, and others. As was the case with ska, when the rock steady era ended in the late 1960s, many artists continued to work in the style and it remained popular.

ROCKERS

Rockers was a sub-style of **reggae** music that was most popular in the mid-1970s. While standard roots reggae emphasized the **one-drop** rhythm (with only the third beat of a four-beat measure accented), the rockers rhythms accented all four beats of the four-beat measure, loosely analogous to American disco. The bass drum was struck on each of the four beats of the measure in rockers songs and propelled the music forward. The style was pioneered by **Sly Dunbar** for **Joseph "Joe Joe" Hookim** at his **Channel One** studio in Kingston, Jamaica, and was most often accompanied by lyrics on socially conscious topics. The double drumming style gave the music a military sound, which caught on with the other producers. From 1975 to 1978, most of the producers in Jamaica ventured into production of rockers material, and the advent of the sound stratified reggae output with roots on one side and rockers on the other.

RODNEY, WINSTON. *See* BURNING SPEAR

RODRIGUEZ, RICO (1934–)

Born Emmanuel Rodriguez in 1934, he attended the legendary **Alpha Boys Catholic School** in Kingston, Jamaica, and there learned to play the trombone under the tutelage of **Donald Drummond**. His school atmosphere was quite conducive to becoming a proficient instrumentalist as his schoolmates ended up filling the studios in the 1960s and 1970s. After leaving school in the early 1950s, Rodriguez worked as a mechanic. From 1954 to 1957, he studied at the Stoney Hill Music School. He apprenticed with a pair of important jazz trombonists, and in 1956 he joined J. J. Johnson's band Clue J and His Blues Blasters. This union was especially significant, as their maiden voyage into the studio was as the backing band for **Clement "Coxsone" Dodd's** first recording session of **Theophilus Beckford** for the single "Easy Snappin.'"

Following this session, Rodriguez played for the most popular dance band on the island, Eric Dean's Orchestra. At the end of the 1950s, Rodriguez became a **Rastafarian** and went to live at the Rasta enclave run by **Oswald "Count Ossie" Williams**. During this period he continued to record and his reputation grew. He played with the Blues Blasters and also appeared with Ossie's group, the Smith All Stars, and Drumbago and His Orchestra. As was the Jamaican custom, he also worked for a series of different producers. In 1961, Rodriguez and producer Vincent Chin recorded his first singles, "Rico Special" and "Rico Farewell." The latter was an indication that he was moving to London.

From 1962 to 1970, Rodriguez played in London, and at the end of the decade he issued the albums *Rico in Reggaeland, Blow Your Horn*, and *Brixton Cat*. For the first half of the 1970s, Rodriguez was part of the Undivided, the premier UK backing band for traveling Jamaican bands. In 1976, Rodriguez secured a solo record deal from **Island Records** and recorded his legendary *Man from Wareika*, the name of Ossie's Rasta commune (1976). In the late 1970s and early 1980s, Rodriguez capitalized on the UK's **ska** revival called the **two-tone** era. During this period, he played with the Specials and moved over to the Two Tone label.

Next, Rodriguez returned to Jamaica and recorded the album *That Man Is Forward* (1981). For the rest of the 1980s, Rodriguez remained in Jamaica and moved back to Ossie's Wareika Hills retreat. During the 1990s, Rodriguez played with a variety of bands in Jamaica. He spent most of the second half of the decade with Jools Holland's Rhythm and Blues Orchestra. In the new millennium, Rodriguez continued to write and record. He released the album *Get Up Your Foot* (2001) and played with Rude Rich and the **Skatalites**. For the past few years, Rodriguez has continued to play live with a variety of groups.

Rico Rodriguez. © *UrbanImage.tv.*

ROMEO, MAX (1947–)

Born Maxwell Smith in Kingston, Jamaica, early on Romeo took a job as a laborer, but caught a break when he won a local talent contest. One of his earliest singles, "Wet Dream," was a massive hit in the United Kingdom until it was banned for its salacious lyrics. Romeo attempted to parlay his success with further rude-boy anthems; however, he was largely unsuccessful.

In the early 1970s, Romeo put away his wicked lyrics and became a devout **Rastafarian**. In the mid-1970s, he joined forces with **Lee "Scratch" Perry** and released a series of roots reggae singles such as "Let the Power Fall" and "Every Man Ought to Know." The success of these singles led to the young singer's debut album *War ina Babylon* (1976). The track was backed by Perry's excellent studio band the **Upsetters** and was a major success for Romeo. Perry and Romeo continued to work together for the rest of the 1970s. Ultimately they split and Romeo moved on to other producers and studios. He was not able to regain the success he had had with Perry, but continues recording to the present. In 1976, Romeo released *Open the Iron Gate* and *Reconstruction*.

There followed a period of relatively low productivity. That same year, Romeo moved to New York and fell in with Keith Richards of the Rolling Stones. With Richard's help he recorded the unsuccessful *I Love My Music*. In 1990, he returned to Jamaica and in 1992 released *Fari I Captain of My Ship* with **Jah Shaka** producing. The following year he issued *Holding Out My Love to You*. Romeo continued to work in the studio and issued *Selassie I Forever*, *Love Message*, and *Something Is Wrong*. In the new millennium Romeo has continued to actively record. He issued *Holy Zion* (2000) and *On the Beach* (2001) and remains a potent force in Jamaican popular music.

ROOTS RADICS

Formed in 1978 with the core of **Errol "Flabba" Holt** and **Eric "Bingy Bunny" Lamont**, the Roots Radics became one of the most highly skilled and prized studio bands in Jamaica. To their core was added a variety of other performers such as **Noel "Sowell Radics" Bailey**, **Eric Clarke**, **Dwight "Brother Dee" Pinkney**, **Style Scott**, and others. The group worked for a variety of producers, but found a home at **Channel One** with producers **Joseph "Joe Joe" Hookim**, **Henry "Junjo" Lawes**, and **Jah Thomas**.

The Radics had their most popular period in the first half of the 1980s in the wake of the **Revolutionaries'** breakup. They recorded with a large number of the most important acts of the day, including **Charlie Chaplin**, **Creation Rebel**, **Earl Sixteen**, **Anthony Graham**, **Gregory Isaacs**, **Israel Vibration**, the **Itals**, **Sugar Minott**, the **Morwells**, **Prince Far I**, **Ranking Toyan**, **Bunny Wailer**, the **Wailing Souls**, and countless others. With Prince Far I, the group toured the United Kingdom as the Arabs. In addition to working with other artists, the Roots Radics were a formidable band in their own right. They recorded a series of albums in the 1980s and were at the forefront of the burgeoning **dub** movement. They released dub-style albums that included *Radical Dub Session* (1982), *Seducer Dubwise* (1982), and *Hot We Hot* (1988). Unfortunately, the 1988 *Hot We Hot* release marked the end for the Radics as they were increasingly replaced by digital sound sources in the **ragga** era in the second half of the decade.

RUDDOCK, OSBOURNE. *See* KING TUBBY

RUFFIN, BRUCE (1952–)

Born Bernardo Constantine Valderama in St. Catherine, Jamaica, he entered the Jamaican popular music scene as a member of the **Techniques**, who went on to become one of the most popular **rock steady** vocal groups in the latter half of the 1960s. The Techniques went through a variety of lineup changes and at times included **Lloyd Parks**, **Slim Smith**, Franklyn White, Frederick Waite, Jackie Paris, Marvin Brooks, and others. Ruffin's greatest successes came in the 1970s as a solo vocalist in the **reggae** style. Before the Techniques, Ruffin sang with **Byron Lee and the Dragonaires**. He entered the Techniques in 1967 and while with the band, sang on hits such as "Love Is Not a Gamble." He was only in the Techniques for a year before going solo.

As was the standard, Ruffin recorded with a series of producers including **Lloyd Charmers**, **Leslie Kong**, and Herman Chin-Loy. During this period he had a series of successful songs, but his biggest hit was a cover version of José Feliciano's tune "Rain." He parlayed this success into another hit in the early 1970s, "Mad about You." For the rest of the 1970s, Ruffin continued to write and release modestly successful pop reggae songs. In the 1980s, Ruffin left the music business and went on to become a lawyer and legal consultant to musicians in the reggae business. A high-quality compilation of Ruffin's best material is *Best of Bruce Ruffin: 1967–71.*

S

SANCHEZ (1967–)

Born Kevin Anthony Jackson in Kingston, Jamaica, he began learning about music at the Rehoboth Apostolic Church, where he sang in the choir and eventually became the lead singer. As a teenager, Jackson was exposed to popular music through **sound systems** such as Small Ax, Rambo, and Crystal. At seventeen, Jackson made his first public performance at the Waterford School and was backed by the Sagittarius Band. Jackson soon began to work for the systems himself and was renamed Sanchez. He was in with the group of **DJs** who included **Flourgon** and **Red Dragon**.

In the mid-1980s, Sanchez started moving into the Kingston area studios. He worked with a variety of producers including **Philip "Fatis" Burrell** and

Sanchez. © *UrbanImage.tv.*

Winston Riley. His first single, "Lady in Red," was issued in 1987. It shot up the charts and gave the young DJ confidence to continue. The following year he had a major hit with the Riley-produced single "Loneliness." On the success of this single, Sanchez was invited to appear at **Reggae Sunsplash**, and he has gone on to record a series of hits. Other important singles included "Fall in Love," "Wild Sanchez," and "One in a Million." With this series of hits, Sanchez was at the top of the dancehall ranks. This popularity carried him through the 1990s and into the new millennium.

In the 1990s, Sanchez changed his style to return closer to his roots, by moving into the gospel reggae arena. In 1999, he penned one of his most popular songs, a gospel version of "Amazing Grace." This was followed by a series of original songs such as "I Can't Wait," "Never Dis the Man," "Leave out a Babylon," and his smash hit "Frenzy." These songs were cut with the help of the Chronic band, Fitz Livermore, Oswald Gordon, Courtney Edwards, and Joslyn McKenzie. In the new millennium, Sanchez's success continued. He was honored for his achievements after twenty years in the Jamaican popular music business and has received recognition in the Caribbean, United States, and United Kingdom. Over the course of his career, Sanchez has issued twenty-eight albums and has toured the world. He continues to be active with a schedule that takes him to the studio and the stage.

SCIENTIST (1960–)

Born Hopeton Brown in Kingston, Jamaica, as a young man Brown hung around the various studios in Kingston. He learned about electronics from his father, who was a television repairman. Still a teenager, Brown visited **Osbourne "King Tubby" Ruddock** to purchase some electronics in order to construct his own **sound system**. Tubby had soon employed the youth to work on various pieces of electronic equipment around his studio, and this led to Brown's entry into the music business. Tubby challenged Brown to remix a record; the product illustrated the young man's potential. There followed a long period during which Brown apprenticed with Tubby and honed his skills. Together, the pair invented the **dub** approach to remixing a record. In dub, a standard band recording is remade, removing (or burying in the mix) the vocals, emphasizing the drum and bass, and adding various effects such as echo, reverb, thunderclaps, and so on.

   With this work, Brown was dubbed Scientist, and his reputation grew. He caught the attention of various other producers and was eventually lured away from Tubby. He landed at **Henry "Junjo" Lawes's Channel One** studio and made a series of highly acclaimed dub records, sometimes under the name Dub Chemist. Just after **Bob Marley's** death in 1981, Scientist was hired by **Tuff Gong Records** as their resident engineer. Scientist immigrated to the United States in 1985 and continued to make dub recordings for the rest of the millennium. His breed of dub music had a spacy feel to it, which became his trademark sound. In addition to recording substantial quantities of material for other artists, Scientist also issued his own recordings. Examples of Scientist's dub releases included *Upset the Upsetter* (1979), *Big Showdown* (1980), *Scientist in the Kingdom* (1981), *Scientist Encounters Pac-Man* (1982), *Crucial Cuts* (1984), *Tribute to King Tubby* (1990), *Respect Due* (1999), and many others. Scientist continues to work as an engineer in the new millennium.

SCOTT, LINCOLN VALENTINE "STYLE" (c. 1955–)

Style got his start in Jamaican popular music when he joined the **Roots Radics**; he was the drummer for the band and worked with them through the majority of their prime. Other members of the band were **Noel "Sowell Radics" Bailey**, **Eric Clarke**, **Errol "Flabba" Holt**, **Eric "Bingy Bunny" Lamont**, and **Dwight "Brother Dee" Pinkney**. The group worked for a variety of producers, but found a home at **Channel One** with producers **Joseph "Joe Joe" Hookim**, **Jah Thomas**, and **Henry "Junjo" Lawes**. The Radics had their most popular period in the first half of the 1980s in the wake of the **Revolutionaries'** breakup. They recorded with a large number of the most important acts of the day, including **Charlie Chaplin**, **Creation Rebel**, **Earl Sixteen**, **Anthony Graham**, **Gregory Isaacs**, **Israel Vibration**, the **Itals**, **Sugar Minott**, the **Morwells**, **Prince Far I**, **Ranking Toyan**, **Bunny Wailer**, the **Wailing Souls**, and others. With Prince Far I, the group toured the United Kingdom as the Arabs. In addition to working with other artists, the Roots Radics were a formidable band in their own right. They recorded a series of albums in the 1980s and were at the forefront of the burgeoning **dub** movement. They released dub style albums that included *Radical Dub Session* (1982), *Seducer Dubwise* (1982), and *Hot We Hot* (1988).

   Unfortunately, the *Hot We Hot* release marked the end for the Radics, as they were increasingly replaced by digital sound sources in the **ragga** era in the second half of the 1980s. Scott was part of the Radics, and after he departed, he played sessions for other artists, such as **Deadly Headley Bennett**, **Al Campbell**, **Clint Eastwood**, **Jah Thomas**, **Sugar Minott**, **Hugh Mundell**, **Johnny Osbourne**, and others.

In the early 1980s, Scott left the Radics and worked with **Adrian Sherwood's** band **Dub Syndicate**. The Syndicate was Sherwood's house band for his label On-U-Sounds. The band consisted of Scott (drums), Bim Sherwood (vocals), **Headley Bennett** (saxophone), and **Doctor Pablo** (melodica). The group was most popular during the late 1970s and early 1980s, during which time they worked with producers such as Sherwood, **Lee "Scratch" Perry**, Skip McDonald, and **U-Roy**.

In 1982, the collective released their debut album *Pounding System*, which was met with a degree of praise. However, they went on to substantial acclaim with subsequent releases such as *One Way System* (1983), *Tunes from the Missing Channel* (1985), and *Strike the Balance* (1990). More recently, Dub Syndicate released two albums in 1996, a disc of new material titled *Ital Breakfast*, and a remix album called *Research and Development*. In 2001, they released *Acres of Space*, which was recorded in Jamaica in collaboration with Adrian Smith. Along the way, the band recorded two albums' worth of material for Lee "Scratch" Perry; however, difficulties with ownership caused a slow release. One such record was *Time Boom X De Devil Dead* (1987). The Dub Syndicate's reputation has grown to the point that their recent guest artists include stars such as **Capleton**, **Gregory Isaacs**, **Luciano**, and **Cedric Myton**.

SELASSIE I, HAILE. *See* RASTAFARI

SHABBA RANKS. *See* RANKS, SHABBA

SHAGGY (1968–)

Born Orville Richard Burrell in Kingston, Jamaica, his nickname was given to him while still a youth; it came from the *Scoobie Doo* character. At eighteen, he moved to New York to join his mother and fell in with the Gibralter **sound system**. His next move was into the American armed forces when at nineteen he joined the U.S. Marines. He went on to serve at Camp Lejeune in North Carolina while continuing to pursue his musical interests. At age twenty, Shaggy entered the studio and cut a pair of singles with Lloyd "Spiderman" Campbell. Next, he met an engineer who would have a major impact on his musical life: Shaun "Sting International" Pizzonia, from whom he got a job making **dub** plates. The versions that Shaggy cut caught on with the New York audience, and his single "Mampie" brought him unprecedented success. He followed this with "Big Up," a duet with the singer **Rayvon**.

Although his reputation in the record industry was growing, Shaggy was still an active duty Marine and was called into service during Operation Desert Storm. After his tour of duty, Shaggy resumed his work in the studio and cut a cover of the Folkes Brothers single "Oh Carolina." The single was a smash hit and led to a duet with **Maxi Priest** on the song "One More Chance." Shaggy's early success earned him a record deal with Virgin, which issued *Pure Pleasure* (1993) and *Original Doberman* (1997). With this new material Shaggy became a star. This success ran counter to the standard **DJ** model. Shaggy's success came without being based in Jamaica and while virtually ignoring the Jamaican **dancehall** scene. In 1995, Shaggy released *Boombastic*, which finally broke through in the United States and earned him a Grammy Award for Best Reggae Album. He toured off of his success and further increased his audience.

In 1997, Shaggy issued *Midnite Lover*, which failed to be as successful as its predecessor. As a result, Virgin dropped Shaggy from its roster, but the singer was not finished with his time in the spotlight. He dueted with Janet Jackson on "Luv Me, Luv Me" and signed a deal with MCA. In 2000, he released *Hot Shot* with the Rik Rok duet single

"It Wasn't Me," and the album became a major hit, going platinum. The duet "Angel of the Morning," with Rayvon, was also a popular single from the release.

His next MCA release was *Lucky Day* (2002), which was not as successful as *Hot Shot*, but did go gold. With these releases, Shaggy has enjoyed higher levels of crossover success in the United States than any other Jamaican dancehall singer. In 2004, Shaggy took his brand of dancehall on the road and toured throughout much of the year. In early March 2005, Shaggy issued the singles "Ready Fi Di Ride" and "Sexy Gyal Whind," in anticipation of another album.

SHAKESPEARE, ROBBIE (1953–)

Shakespeare emerged on the Jamaican popular music scene when he teamed with **Sly Dunbar** in 1975; together the pair, known as the "Riddim Twins," became the most sought-after **reggae** rhythm section after **Aston** and **Carlton Barrett** joined **Bob Marley and the Wailers**. The pair played for a variety of studio bands in the late 1970s and throughout the 1980s. They were members of the **Revolutionaries** and were both experienced studio musicians.

Early in their shared experiences, **Sly and Robbie** launched their own production company and record label called Taxi Records. Their first release was **Chaka Demus and Pliers's** "Murder She Wrote," which was a substantial hit. With their production credits established, the pair went on to produce classics such as **Culture's** *Two Sevens Clash* (1977). Their studio needed a studio band, so Sly and Robbie constructed one from members of the **Roots Radics**. They went on to record **Black Uhuru**, **Junior Delgado**, **General Echo**, **Gregory Isaacs**, **Prince Far I**, **Max Romeo**, **Wailing Souls**, and others. As a duo, Sly and Robbie recorded with **Black Uhuru**, **Dennis Brown**, **Burning Spear**, **Jimmy Cliff**, the **Mighty Diamonds**, **Sugar Minott**, **Peter Tosh**, **U-Roy**, **Bunny Wailer**, Culture, Grace Jones, Joe Cocker, Bob Dylan, Mick Jagger, Herbie Hancock, Robert Palmer, **Yellowman**, and the Rolling Stones, among others.

Over the years, Sly and Robbie have continued to work in the production arena, as well as recording their own and other artists' material. They have over twenty solo albums to their names and innumerable appearances with others. In the new millennium, Sly and Robbie remain active. They have recorded with artists including **Buju Banton**, **Beenie Man**, **Capleton**, **Junior Delgado**, **U-Roy**, No Doubt, and others. Additionally, they continue to issue their own material, such as 2003's *Late Night Tales*. Sly and Robbie remain at the center of Jamaican popular music and have crossed over to the American mainstream. They continue to write, record, produce, and perform.

SHANACHIE

An imprint begun in 1975 as an independent label for the transmission of traditional folk music, the Shanachie label has grown to include branches that deal in jazz, folk, blues, world music, jam bands, Latin music, rock, funk, and **reggae**. The imprint was started by musicologist Richard Nevins and musician Dan Collins. Together, the pair issued several records of Irish folk music from their Bronx, New York, headquarters. One of the most amazing aspects of the label was that it maintained its independence, both in production and distribution. Shanachie branched out into reggae music in the early 1980s and has since become a force in the business. The label drew acts such as **Black Uhuru**, **Culture**, **Rita Marley**, the **Mighty Diamonds**, **Mutabaruka**, **Augustus Pablo**, the **Skatalites**, **Bunny Wailer**, and **Yellowman**. It remained active in the reggae arena through the 1980s and 1990s.

In the new millennium, Shanachie continued to issue music from reggae stars. Their current roster of reggae artists includes **Alpha Blondy**, **Boom Shaka**, **Dennis Brown**,

Lucky Dube, **Eek-A-Mouse**, **Joe Higgs**, **Gregory Isaacs**, **Hugh Mundell**, **Ras Michael**, **Third World**, **Wailing Souls**, and others. Shanachie remains dedicated to releasing high-quality reggae music and attracting the quality artists to their roster.

SHERWOOD, ADRIAN (1958–)
Born in Buckinghamshire, England, Sherwood developed an early love of **reggae** music through artists such as **Judge Dread** and began working with the **Pama** and **Trojan** touring acts. At age seventeen, he launched his first label, Carib Gems. Even though very young, Sherwood made some good moves early on and secured publishing for **Black Uhuru**, recruited **Prince Far I** to his label, and signed a deal to distribute **Sonia Pottinger's** High Note material in England. His label was largely a one-man operation, so he cultivated the skills needed to become a producer. This was illustrated on *Dub from Creation* (1977) by **Creation Rebel**.

In 1978, Sherwood launched the Hitrun imprint, which went on to issue over thirty singles by artists such as Prince Far I, Eastwood, and Doctor Pablo. He also issued the first of the four installments of Far I's *Cry Tuff Dub Encounter* series. In 1979, Sherwood launched another label, On-U-Sound Records. With On-U, Sherwood originally developed live **sound system** concerts, but soon turned to studio work. On this label Sherwood issued dub, **reggae**, funk, and rock. Some of the artists on the early 1980s roster included Creation Rebel, Bim Sherman, African Head Charge, the Mothmen (Simply Red), Johnson, **Roydel "Congo Ashanti Roy" Johnson**, Singers and Players, and **Dub Syndicate**. In addition to reggae acts, Sherwood has produced for Nine Inch Nails, Living Colour, Depeche Mode, Ministry, the Slits, London Underground, the Fall, Public Image Limited, and others. Sherwood has gone on to launch additional labels including Pressure Sounds, Green Tea, and Maximum Pressure. As part of the On-U outfit, Sherwood formed the studio band Tackhead, which included Skip McDonald, Doug Wimbish, and Keith LeBlanc.

While Sherwood's career in music got off to an inauspicious start, by the mid-1980s he was one of the most high-profile producers on the UK popular music scene. In the second half of the 1980s, he produced music for industrial groups such as Skinny Puppy, KMFDM, and Nine Inch Nails. While On-U label continued to issue reggae material, other projects increasingly occupied Sherwood's time and he opted to use Pressure Sounds to release classic reggae and dub material. The On-U roster at its height included African Head Charge, Bim Sherman, Creation Rebel, **Deadly Headley Bennett**, Dub Syndicate, **Junior Delgado**, Tribal Drift, Voice of Authority, and many others. At the end of the 1990s, On-U Sound closed. At that time Sherwood redirected his energy into Pressure Sounds.

SHINEHEAD (c. 1960–)
Born Edmund Carl Aiken in Kent, England, his family moved to Jamaica, but finally settled in New York. In 1980, Shinehead began his career when he entered the New York **sound system** scene. He **toasted** for a variety of sounds including African Love, Papa Moke, Star Wars, and others. After honing his skills, he signed a record deal with Electra, which lasted until 1988.

He began his relationship with Electra having already established his ability, and the young **dancehall DJ** and the record company had a strong partnership, until 1995. During that time, Shinehead released four Electra albums. The first was *Unity* (1988). The release got the young singer off to a good start and established his marketability with the label. Next, he issued *The Real Rock* (1990), featuring the songs "Family

Affair" and "Strive." In 1992 came *Sidewalk University.* The album included "Jamaican in New York," the title track, and a version of Stevie Wonder's "I Just Called to Say I Love You." The final Electra release was *Troddin'* (1994), with songs such as "Troddin' Thru," "Woman like You," and "Buff Bay."

Shinehead's style is an interesting mixture of Jamaican dancehall, **ragga**, and New York hip hop. His vocal delivery is also a mixture of singing, chanting, and **toasting/** rapping. Shinehead continued his recording output with *Praises* (1999). This album featured "Collie Weed," "Pay Me," "Bobo," and "Olivia." In the wake of this release, Shinehead appeared in the movie *Turn It Up*, with Pras from the Fugees and Ja Rule. He continues to write, record, perform, and seek acting roles.

SIBBLES, LEROY (1949–)

Born in Kingston, Jamaica, Sibbles rose to prominence as a singer and bass player when he fronted the legendary group the **Heptones**. The group also included Barry Llewellyn and Earl Morgan. It originally formed in the early 1960s as the Hep Ones. However, over time the name was changed to the current incarnation. All three members of the vocal trio hailed from Kingston and were born in the mid-to-late 1940s. They began working as a unit during the heyday of the **rock steady** style and were categorized as a rock steady vocal trio. They began recording for **Clement "Coxsone" Dodd** at his **Studio One** facility in the late 1960s. Their first hit came in 1966 with the single "Fatty Fatty." Additionally, the Heptones were instrumental in the change of style from **ska** to rock steady. Still with Dodd in the early 1970s, the trio released another hit single, "Pretty Looks Isn't All." For Dodd, the group released their debut album, *On Top* (1970).

Sibbles and Dodd began to have trouble working together and so began the typical Jamaican recording artist activity of moving from one studio to another. The group moved on to work with producer **Joe Gibbs** and then moved again to **Rupie Edwards**. In the mid-1970s, they settled with **Lee "Scratch" Perry** and continued their success. With Perry at the controls, the group was able to update their sound while maintaining their original roots appeal. In 1977, they released the album *Party Time*, which garnered them international notoriety.

However, in 1978, Sibbles went solo and the group replaced him with singer Naggo Morris. Without Sibbles's singing and songwriting skills, the group has not regained its original sound and popularity. However, in 1995, the original trio re-formed and released a new album titled *Pressure*, which was produced by **Tappa Zukie**. The Heptones cultivated a deep catalog of hits in their illustrious career, and their music continues to appear to this day on numerous compilation albums. Of note is the 1997 compilation of Heptones tunes released on Rounders Records, *Sea of Love*, and the most recent Rounders compilation, 2004's *Deep in the Roots.*

SILK, GARNET (1966–1994)

Born Garnet Damion Smith in Manchester, Jamaica, his dream of entering the music business manifested early and, at age twelve, he became a **DJ** under the name Little Bimbo on the Soul Remembrance **sound system**. In his later teenage years, Smith moved to other systems, such as Destiny Outernational, Pepper's Disco, and Stereophonic. Through DJing for these sounds, Smith's vocal prowess evolved, and he began to cultivate his own style.

His recording career began in 1985 when he worked with producer Delroy Collins and cut the single "Problem Everywhere." The single was largely ignored, and he believed that it was because his delivery was in the **toasting** style, instead of being sung. Thus, he changed his style of delivery and cultivated a rich and smoky singing voice. At this point, Smith took the bold step of moving to Kingston in search of a recording studio. He was fortunate enough to link up with **Sugar Minott's** Youth Promotion label and cut the single "No Disrespect." He moved from Minott to **Donovan Germaine**, **King Jammy**, and **King Tubby**.

His big break came with he linked with **Steely and Clevie**, who signed him to a record deal and produced his 1990 album. Further, it was Steely who gave Smith the nickname Silk. Unfortunately, only one single emerged from these sessions, prompting Silk to return to Manchester. At home, he worked on his songwriting. In 1992, Silk met **Tony Rebel** and the **dub poet** Yasus Afari. They were not only responsible for

Garnet Silk. © *UrbanImage.tv.*

introducing Silk to **Rastafari**, but they also introduced him to producer **Courtney Cole**. With Cole, Silk released a series of successful singles including "Nothing Can Divide Us," "Mama," and "Spanish Angels." Through Cole, Silk met **Bobby "Digital" Dixon**, who produced his first album, *It's Growing* (1992). The album was a major success and rode the wave of popularity generated by its single "Hello Africa." With this release, Silk was entering the upper echelon of reggae music.

In 1994, he signed with Kariang Productions, along with Big Beat/Atlantic. With the Atlantic deal in place, Silk entered **Tuff Gong** studios and went to work with producer **Errol Brown**. Before completing the album, he went back to Manchester to visit his mother. At the same time, Steely and Clevie issued *Love Is the Answer*, which featured a series of Silk's songs. With his popularity at its peak, Silk performed at 1994's **Reggae Sunsplash** concert and Reggae Sumfest.

Tragically, Garnet Silk did not live out the year, as he was killed in a 1994 fire. In the wake of his death, his friend Tony Rebel released *Tony Rebel Meets Garnett Silk in a Dancehall Conference* (1994). Additionally, several collections of Silk's music were issued, including *Journey* (1998), *Live at Reggae Sunsplash 1999*, *Garnett Silk Meets the Conquering Lion* (2000), and several others.

SIMPSON, DERRICK "DUCKIE" (c. 1955–)

One of the three foundational members of **Black Uhuru** (*uhuru* is Swahili for "freedom"), when they formed in 1974, Simpson teamed with Euvin "Don Carlos" Spencer and Rudolph "Garth" Dennis to create the group. All three men came from the Waterhouse district of Kingston, Jamaica. After a few years, Spencer and Dennis departed the group, and Simpson was left at the helm of the group. He recruited Michael Rose and Errol Wilson to again make the group a trio. The three went into the studio and recorded the album *Love Crisis* (1977), with **Prince (King) Jammy** at the controls. The standout single from the album was "I Love King Selassie," which has become a classic over the past thirty years.

Next, the group added another new member in the form of female singer **Sandra "Puma" Jones**. Puma's voice rounded out the harmonies and gave the group's vocals a high end that had been lacking. The newly fortified group teamed with **Sly and Robbie** in the early 1980s and released a series of successful albums including *Sinsemilla* (1980), *Black Sounds of Freedom* and *Black Uhuru* (1981), *Guess Who's Coming to Dinner* (1981), *Chill Out* and *Tear It Up—Live* (1983), and *Anthem* (1984). In 1985, the group won the Grammy Award for the Best Reggae Album in the first year of the award's existence. In 1986, Michael Rose departed the group to pursue a solo career and was replaced by **Junior Reid**. In the late 1980s, the albums kept coming. In 1986, *Brutal* was issued, in 1987 *Positive*, and in 1988 there was another live album.

In 1990, Puma died of cancer and at roughly the same time the original three members re-formed. With Spencer and Dennis back in the fold, Simpson and Black Uhuru moved forward into the early 1990s. They stayed together into the mid-1990s, with the addition of Andrew Bees. Albums from the period included *So Dub Now* (1990), *Ice Storm* (1991), *One Love* (1993), *Mystical Truth* (1993), *Strongg* (1994), *Reunification* (1998), and *Black Sounds of Freedom Remix* (1999). Material continued to be issued by the band into the new millennium, including *Dynasty* (2001).

SIR LORD COMIC (c. 1940–)

Sir Lord Comic entered the Jamaican popular music scene in the early 1960s and was originally a dancer with a Kingston-area **sound system**. After watching and learning from several masters, Comic took the microphone and began to **toast**. His style pleased the crowd and led to a recording session, which yielded "Ska-ing West." The single was attributed to Sir Lord Comic and his Cowboys. He went on to record a series of other successful singles including 1967's "The Great Wuga Wuga." He also recorded "Bronco," "Jack of My Trade," and "Doctor Feelgood." Comic's material has gone on to appear on a variety of compilation releases such as *Complete UK Upsetter Singles Collection, Vol. 2*; *Explosive Rock Steady*; *From the Dynamic Treasury, Vol. 1*; *High Explosion*; *Keep on Coming through the Door*; and many others. Sir Lord Comic was active on the cusp between the **ska** and **rock steady** styles.

SISTER CAROL (1959–)

Born Carol East in Kingston, Jamaica, she grew up in the west Kingston ghettos. At age fourteen, she moved to New York with her family. In Brooklyn in the 1970s, Carol became part of the **dancehall** scene and quickly established herself as a world-class **toaster**.

She came from a musical family with a father who worked as a radio station engineer in Jamaica, and who was part of the **reggae** hothouse of **Clement "Coxsone" Dodd's Studio One**. At an early age, Carol fell under the influence of **Brigadier Jerry**, who encouraged her to pursue the toasting, rather than singing, route. Carol asserted her abilities in talent contests in both Jamaica and New York. She came to greater attention when she was granted the opening act spot for the **Meditations**, and this led to opportunity in the studio. Carol entered the studio and recorded her first two albums, the more popular of which was *Black Cinderella* (1984), reissued on Heartbeat in 1995. She also began her acting career, appearing in the movies *Something Wild* and *Married to the Mob*.

In 1981, Carol released the album *Mother Culture* on the **RAS** imprint. There followed a long string of albums including 1989's *Jah Disciple*, *Call Me Sister Carol* (1994), *Lyrically Potent* (1996), *Isis* (1999), and in the new millennium *Direct Hit*

(2001). *Lyrically Potent* garnered the **DJ** a Grammy Award nomination. Her material continued to grow in popularity, and she experienced increasing success and accolades. Her success and staying power were all the more impressive being a woman in a largely sexist business. Her exposure continued to grow with appearances on the David Letterman and Conan O'Brien shows. Sister Carol remains active and continues to star on the dancehall stage.

SISTER NANCY (c. 1960–)

Born Nancy Russell in Kingston, Jamaica, she came from a large group of siblings who included brother **Brigadier Jerry**. Nancy was raised on **dancehall toasting**, and as soon as she could, she took up the microphone herself. Part of Nancy's exposure was through her brother, who was **DJing** on Prince Norman's **sound system** before moving over to the Jahlove Music system. Jerry was older than Nancy, and his career took off while his sister was still a youth. As a teenager, Nancy entered the dancehall working on sound systems herself. She was well received; this led to attention from producer **Winston Riley**, who took her into the studio in 1980. She recorded a successful single and increased her reputation. This led to further recordings and an appearance on the **Reggae Sunsplash** concert. Her singles also began appearing on compilation releases such as *Dee Jay Explosion*, carrying the track "Chalice A Fe Burn."

Her debut album was released in 1982 with production from Riley. Titled *One Two*, the release featured the tracks "Ain't No Stopping Nancy," "Bam Bam," and "Only Woman DJ with Degree." Also on the album was a combination with **Yellowman** called "King and Queen," a version of the classic produced by **Henry "Junjo" Lawes**. Further recording with Yellowman ensued and yielded the album *The Yellow, the Purple, and the Nancy*. The album featured cuts by Nancy, along with material from Yellowman and **Fathead**. On the album was another song with Yellowman called "Jah Mek Us fe a Purpose."

In the 1990s, Nancy took time away from music. However, in the new millennium she has again been appearing live and touring in the United States.

SIZZLA (1976–)

Born Miguel Collins in Kingston, Jamaica, he grew up in the west Kingston ghetto, and this affected the rest of his life and his music. Sizzla infused his music with messages of social consciousness and uplift. Sizzla performed in the **dancehall toasting** style, but unlike his contemporaries his lyrics have gone against gun culture and slackness (talk of guns, sex, and drugs).

Sizzla entered the studio in 1995 and released *Burning Up*, which garnered the young singer a degree of success. *Praise Be Jah* was Sizzla's second album recorded by **Philip "Fatis" Burrell** on the **Exterminator** label. The album was a success and led to further entries into the studio. Next, Sizzla

Sizzla. © *UrbanImage.tv.*

issued a rapid succession of releases that continued to push his reputation. In 1998, he released *Freedom Cry*, *Good Way*, and *Strong*. The following year he issued *Royal Son of Ethiopia*, *Be I Strong*, and a re-release of *Good Way*. By this point Sizzla was one of the leaders of the dancehall scene. His *Royal Son of Ethiopia* album was critically acclaimed and commercially successful.

In the new millennium, Sizzla issued *Bobo Ashanti* and *Words of Truth*, both in 2000. In 2001, he issued *Taking Over*, *Black History*, and *Rastafari Teach I Everything*. This material established Sizzla's amazingly fertile writing output. His prodigious production of albums continued. In 2002, Sizzla issued *Blaze Up Chalwa*, *Ghetto Revolution*, *Up in Fire*, and *Da Real Thing*. The albums *Light of My World* and *Rise to the Occasion* were issued in the following year. In 2004, Sizzla released *Red Alert*, *Speak Of Jah*, *Jah Knows Best*, *Stay Focus*, and *Life*. With this prolific output, Sizzla has stayed on top of the dancehall scene for the past ten years. He remains active and continues to issue new material.

SKA

Ska is a style of Jamaican popular music that surfaced in the early 1960s. It was widely considered to be the first indigenous type of Jamaican popular music. Ska became the most important music in Jamaica in 1961–1962. It replaced the island tendency to remake American rhythm and blues standards and injected Jamaican music with its own spirit. The ska movement coincided with the island's independence and was fostered by an intense interest in asserting Jamaican national identity and pride. The general ska band lineup was a core of singer, guitar, bass, and drums, with the addition of a horn line of varying size. At barest minimum, the horn line included a saxophone, trumpet, and trombone. The style itself was a mixture of influences including Jamaican **mento**, American rhythm and blues, jazz, jump bands, calypso, and others. It took over the island and invaded the radio, dancehalls, and clubs. The ska beat was fast, appropriate for dancing, and emphasized offbeat accents that propelled the music forward.

The style held sway on the island for the next five years before succumbing to the slower **rock steady** beat in 1966–1967. Important ska performers included **Roland Alphonso**, **Desmond Dekker**, **Alton Ellis**, the **Ethiopians**, **Byron Lee**, **Tommy McCook**, **Jackie Mittoo**, **Derrick Morgan**, **Rico Rodriguez**, the **Skatalites**, and others. Although ska was no longer the dominant popular style on the island, it remained active in the background, always ripe for revival. This trend in popular music happened in American jazz and was also the case in Jamaican popular music. In the late 1970s and early 1980s, ska returned to prominence in the United Kingdom with the **two-tone** movement, also called the second wave of ska. More recently, ska revived again with the third wave in the late 1980s and early 1990s. This most recent revival took place mostly in the United States and involved bands such as No Doubt and the Mighty Mighty Bosstones.

SKATALITES, THE

The Skatalites were a **ska** band formed from a group of instrumentalists who studied at the **Alpha Boys Catholic School** in Kingston, Jamaica. The group wrote over 300 songs and had a major presence on the island for an extended period. They formed in June 1964 and lasted until the end of 1965. Although they did not have a lasting physical presence, their musical impact was staggering. They defined the ska sound during its heyday and backed the majority of important ska singers in the middle of the decade.

The band had come together as the result of **Clement "Coxsone" Dodd's** need for an in-house group for his **Studio One** facility. Dodd had hired **Tommy McCook** to form a band and lead it, and in turn McCook recruited his old friends from the Alpha School. He hired **Roland Alphonso, Lloyd Brevett**, Lloyd Knibb, Lester Sterling, **Donald Drummond**, Jerry Haynes, Johnny Moore, Jackie Opel, Donna Schaffer, and **Jackie Mittoo**. For the next fourteen months, the Skatalites worked for all of the major producers in Jamaica and played the backing music for virtually every important ska vocalist.

The band broke up as the result of trombonist **Donald Drummond's** arrest, and McCook went on to form the Supersonics. The Supersonics then became the studio band for **Duke Reid's Treasure Isle** studio. While the Skatalites were instrumental in the birth of ska, the Supersonics helped usher in the **rock steady** era. In the late 1970s and early 1980s, ska was reborn through the UK **two-tone** craze, and McCook reformed the Skatalites. The group reformed and played in Kingston in 1983–1984, and ultimately landed another recording contract. In the late 1980s and early 1990s, ska's third wave was in effect, and the Skatalites launched an international tour. They released a series of new recordings and were nominated for several Grammys.

In the early 1990s, the Skatalites signed a new record deal with the **Island** label and McCook retired from the band. The Skatalites continue on. The lineup has changed significantly since the early days and now includes Lloyd Brevett, Lloyd Knibb, Doreen Shaffer, Lester Sterling, Karl Bryan, **Vin Gordon**, Devon James, Ken Stewart, and Kevin Batchelor.

SKY NOTE RECORDS

An imprint started in London, England, in the mid-1970s, Sky Note Records became an important outlet for Jamaican music for ten years and distributed a variety of Jamaican labels in England during this time. It was originally housed at 169 Hillside Avenue and was moved to 154 Rucklidge Avenue, in London.

The label started in 1977 with the release of material by Jamaican producer **Sonia Pottinger**. Its releases that year were **Marcia Griffiths's** *Naturally*; Sonya Spence's *In the Dark*; a various-artist compilation called *Time to Remember*, which contained tracks by artists such as **Judy Mowatt**; another compilation called *Hits of 77*; and Chalawa's *Exodus Dub*.

In 1978, the label's output broadened to include other producers, and the releases kept coming with material from **Bob Andy**, **Culture**, Marcia Griffiths, and the Melodians. Subsequent releases came from **Jackie Edwards**, **Alton Ellis**, **John Holt**, Marie Brown, the Webber Sisters, Bobby Stringer, Jackie Pioneer, Ossie Scott, **Pat Kelly**, and Tim Chandell. The year 1986 marked the end of activity for the label with the release of **Owen Gray's** *Watch This Sound*. While the Sky Note imprint was a re-release label, it still served an important function as a European distributor of Jamaican popular music.

SLICKERS, THE

A group formed of brothers Derrick and **Sydney Crooks** and Winston Bailey, the Slickers got their start in 1965 as a spinoff from the **Pioneers**. The Pioneers also included the Crooks brothers and various other singers and had formed in 1962. While details of the Slickers's history are murky, it seems that the two bands (Slickers and Pioneers) existed at the same time, through the end of the 1960s and into the early 1970s.

In 1969, the Pioneers had a hit with the single "Long Shot," and at this time the group consisted of Sydney Crooks and Jackie Robinson. The following year, the Slickers had a massive hit with "Johnny Too Bad." The song was performed by the Crooks brothers and a singer named Abraham Green. In 1973, the Slickers's single was used for the classic Jamaica film *The Harder They Come*, featuring **Jimmy Cliff**. The single also appeared on the soundtrack for the film and went on to enjoy a lengthy period of popularity. Further, it has appeared in numerous versions in a litany of styles. The Slickers went on to tour the United States and the United Kingdom and released the songs "You Can't Win" and "Man Beware" in the 1970s. By 1978, the group had disbanded and the Crooks brothers had gone separate ways.

SLUGGY RANKS. *See* **RANKS, SLUGGY**

SLY AND ROBBIE

Called the Riddim Twins, the duo were the rhythm section comprising **Lowell "Sly" Dunbar** (drums) and **Robbie Shakespeare** (bass). The pair appeared on the Jamaican popular music scene in 1975 and soon ascended to the upper echelon of session players. They inherited the marquee position that had been abdicated by **Alton** and **Carlton Barrett** when they joined **Bob Marley and the Wailers**, and were frequently off the island on tour. Sly and Robbie teamed in the studio and were part of the legendary **Revolutionaries**. The pair was extremely active in the studio and ultimately played with the majority of the producers and important artists through the latter half of the 1970s and throughout the 1980s.

Soon after joining forces, Sly and Robbie recognized their shared potential in the studio as recording artists and as producers. They launched their own record label, Taxi Records, and gained greater creative control. The pair marketed themselves as a rhythm section and production team and attracted the attention of stars such as **Burning Spear**, **Jimmy Cliff**, and **Bob Marley**. The duo broke into major stardom when they recorded with **Peter Tosh** on his *Legalized It* album (1976).

With all of the publicity gained from playing with Tosh, Sly and Robbie had instant credibility and were involved in a series of important recordings. Together, Sly and Robbie released *Sly and Robbie Present Taxi* (1981). This touched off a series of releases by the two men that spanned the end of the 1980s and into the 1990s. These albums reflected a shift in their style from roots reggae to the more popular **dub** style. In addition to their own releases, Sly and Robbie continued working for other artists, such as **Black Uhuru**, **Maxi Priest**, Grace Jones, Mick Jagger, Bob Dylan, Cindy Lauper, Herbie Hancock, Carly Simon, and KRS-ONE.

Sly and Robbie. © *UrbanImage.tv.*

At the end of the century, the pair continued to work together, but again altered their style. This time they moved from the dub style into **dancehall**. Sly and Robbie continue to be productive and forward the Riddim Twins name.

SMALL, MILLIE (1946–)

Born Millicent Small in Clarendon, Jamaica, Millie grew up in a rural environment. She went on to become the earliest female singer in the **ska** style and a breakthrough artist in the United Kingdom. Millie got her start recording with **Clement "Coxsone" Dodd** at his **Studio One** facility. Dodd teamed Millie with Roy Panton for the duo Roy and Millie, and the pair had a hit in the early 1960s with "We'll Meet." Millie also teamed with other male singers including **Owen Gray** of Owen and Millie, and **Jackie Edwards** of Jackie and Millie.

Millie's big break came when she met **Christopher Blackwell**, who took her to London to record. Her first Blackwell single was called "Don't You Know" and garnered her minor success. In 1963, Millie and Blackwell recorded "My Boy Lollipop," with backing by a studio band including **Ernest Ranglin** on guitar and a young Rod Stewart on harmonica. The song was an instant hit and charted in the United Kingdom and the United States. Further, it was the first international ska hit with a female lead singer. Millie's career seemed posed for continued success. She had another charting single with "Sweet William" and released her debut album, with additional songs such as "Henry" and the Fats Domino cover "I'm in Love Again." The album was not as popular as the single, and Millie's career did not continue. However, with Millie's success, Blackwell went on to become a major figure in **reggae** music history.

SMART, LEROY (c. 1945–)

Orphaned as a youth, Smart grew up in the **Alpha Boys Catholic School** home in Kingston, Jamaica. At Alpha, Smart received training in music, which he used to overcome his inauspicious early life. In the early 1970s, Smart burst onto the Jamaican popular music scene and worked with producers **Gussie Clarke**, **Joseph "Joe Joe" Hookim**, and **Bunny "Striker" Lee**. Smart sold himself as a Jamaican "Don" and wore flashy clothes and jewelry. His lyrics were a combination of roots sentiments and love songs, and he went on to an extended run in the studio. Smart's popularity was centered in Jamaica, and he did not score any international hits. However, he released solid material for three decades and remains a viable commercial artist.

His debut album was *Superstar* (1976) and marked the beginning of his prolific output. In 1977, he issued four more albums, including *Ballistic Affair* and *Impressions of Leroy Smart*. The following year, four more releases were issued, including *Jah Loves Everyone* and *Propaganda*. In 1979, *Let Every Man Survive*, *Showcase Rub a Dub*, and *Disco Showcase* were released. In the 1980s, Smart continued his hectic schedule in the studio. In 1981, he issued *Too Much Grudgefulness*, which was followed the next year with *She Just a Draw Card*. The year 1983 saw a return to multi-album releases with *On Top*, *She Love It in the Morning*, and *Style and Fashion*.

This productivity continued through the rest of the decade and into the 1990s. Although Smart never had a crossover hit outside of the Caribbean, he was a major recording artist with over twenty albums to his credit.

SMILEY CULTURE (c. 1965–)

Born David Emmanuel in London, England, Culture took a tongue-in-cheek approach to singing about the English working class and made several hit singles from discussions of their circumstances. Culture was born to a Jamaican father and a South American mother and entered the music business through the **sound system** circuit around London. He worked for the Saxon sound system, where he rose to prominence. He became popular through a combination of singing, **toasting**, and appearing on television. In the mid-1980s, he began recording and scored a UK hit with "Cockney Translations." He went on to release an album of the same name in 1984 and followed it with a pair of other releases, *Police Officer* and *Tongue in Cheek*. Culture's fame continued to grow with an appearance on *Top of the Pops* and through his own BBC channel 4 show, *Club Mix*. He continues to be active in the television and movie circles and made an appearance in the movie *Absolute Beginners*. Smiley Culture remains part of the UK **reggae** scene.

SMITH, DENNIS. *See* ALCAPONE, DENNIS

SMITH, DOROTHY. *See* PATRA

SMITH, EARL "CHINNA" (c. 1950–)

Smith has enjoyed a long career in the Jamaican popular music scene. By the early 1970s, he had teamed with **Tony Chin**, **Ansell Collins**, **Carlton "Santa" Davis**, **Bobby Ellis**, **Vin Gordon**, **Bernard "Touter" Harvey**, **Tommy McCook**, **Robbie Shakespeare**, and Lennox Brown as the guitarist in **Bunny "Striker" Lee's** house band the **Aggrovators**. The band played in the **rock steady** and **reggae** styles and backed up artists including **Johnny Clarke** and **Prince Jazzbo** to **Dennis Brown**, **Dillinger**, and **I-Roy**. The Aggrovators worked together under that name from the mid-1970s to the mid-1980s.

Smith's next band was the Riddim Raiders with **Tony Chin** and **George "Fully" Fullwood**. This band quickly turned into the legendary **Soul Syndicate** (also sometimes called the Arabs) from the late 1970s into the 1980s. At largely the same time, Smith was also a member of the Professionals, who were **Joseph "Joe Joe" Hookim's** studio band. In 1976, Smith worked with **Bob Marley and the Wailers** for a period and has subsequently played guitar for Marley's son **Julian**. Over the course of the 1980s, Smith played with artists such as **Junior Delgado**, **Gregory Isaacs**, **Freddie McGregor**, and others.

In the late 1980s, Smith launched his own High Times record label. One of his early finds was **Mutabaruka**. Smith signed the **dub poet** and proceeded to issue his material and play on his release. Smith remains active in the Jamaican popular music scene. His label is still productive and records for a variety of artists, with the backing of the High Times Players. In addition to

Earl "Chinna" Smith. © *UrbanImage.tv.*

playing with Bob and Julian Marley, Smith has also worked extensively with another Marley son, **Ziggy**, and his group the **Melody Makers**.

SMITH, GARNET. *See* SILK, GARNET

SMITH, KEITH. *See* SMITH, SLIM

SMITH, MAXWELL. *See* ROMEO, MAX

SMITH, SLIM (1948–1973)

Born Keith Smith in Kingston, Jamaica, he got an early start in music and joined the group Victor's Youth Band as a singer. In the early 1960s, Smith began recording with **Clement "Coxsone" Dodd** and joined the singing group the **Techniques**. At one time or another, the Techniques included Riley, **Lloyd Parks**, Franklyn White, Frederick Waite, **Bruce Ruffin**, Jackie Paris, **Slim Smith**, Marvin Brooks, and others.

The group formed in 1962 and had a series of successful releases. However, in 1967 Smith left the group to pursue a solo career and was replaced by singer **Pat Kelly**. As a solo artist, he recorded the album *Born to Love* (1979), a smash hit with producer Dodd. In the wake of leaving the Techniques, Smith formed the **Uniques**, with childhood friend Jimmy Riley and a third singer, **Lloyd Charmers**. The Uniques worked with producer **Bunny "Striker" Lee** and scored a series of number one Jamaican hits with songs such as "Let Me Go Girl," "My Conversation," "Watch This Sound," "Beatitudes," and others.

The Uniques lasted for three years before Smith left to again pursue a solo career. His departure from the band was at the behest of Lee, who felt that he would be more marketable as a solo act. He recorded several more fine singles before his death at age twenty-five. The circumstances surrounding Smith's death are still unknown, but the end result was that one of Jamaica's most talented singers was gone in the prime of his career. One version of his death is that Smith committed suicide, and another is that he was injured breaking a window and bled to death.

SMITH, WAYNE (1965–)

Wayne Smith entered the Jamaican popular music scene in the early 1980s. He was a talented singer and pioneer of the **ragga** style that took hold of **reggae** music in the mid-1980s. In the early 1980s, Smith had a relatively successful record called *Youthman Skanking* and went back to the studio. In 1984, Smith was working with **King Jammy** and **Tony Asher**; together with Asher he stumbled upon a new way to create beats for backing reggae vocals. Smith's song "Under Me Sleng Teng" was the first created with digital technology making the background music, instead of live musicians in the studio. The beat for the song was created with the use of Smith's Casio keyboard. It came with a series of pre-made beats installed, and Smith and Asher took one of them and slowed it down, and Smith sang over it.

The idea of using digitally created backing beats was an immediate success and spawned the ragga style. Producers were especially fond of the new technology, as it was much less expensive than studio musicians and allowed for the escape from rehashed **ska** and **rock steady** rhythms. In the wake of this seminal recording, Smith went on to issue a clash album with **Patrick Andy** called *Showdown, Vol. 7* (1984). In 1985 he issued *Super Smoker* and *Wicked Inna Dancehall*. The song "Sleng Teng" was one of the most-versioned songs of the decade and assured Smith's place in the pantheon of reggae music history.

Snagga Puss. © *UrbanImage.tv.*

SNAGGA PUSS (c. 1960–)

Born Norman Suppria in Kingston, Jamaica, he was raised in the west Kingston ghetto and turned to music to rise out of his meager circumstances. His entry into the Jamaican popular music scene came as a **DJ toasting** on the Kingston area **sound systems** in the early 1980s. His first nickname was Dicky Ranks, and under it he built a solid reputation. However, he was disappointed in his level of success and moved to New York. When he returned to Jamaica two years later, he realized that there were still many opportunities for him in the music business. He again changed his name, this time to Snagga Puss, for the Yogi Bear cartoon character Snaggle Puss.

In the early 1990s, Snagga Puss debuted and was picked up by the Shocking Vibes imprint. He went into the studio and recorded a series of successful singles including "Ex-Lover"; "Merl"; and, with **Freddie McGregor**, "Carry Go Bring Come." He parlayed this success into an album called *Whoop Dem Merlene* (1993). Next, he returned to the studio and cut "Tatie," which was also successful and led to such 1995 hits as "Woody Woodpecker," "Popeye," and "Girls Roll Call." In the wake of this success, Snagga Puss toured with the Shocking Vibes Crew. He continued to record and tour in the late 1980s and into the 1990s.

SONS OF JAH

Trevor Bow formed the Sons of Jah in the late 1970s. He was a friend of **reggae** superstar **Bob Marley**, and this connection assisted Bow in his recording endeavors. The Sons of Jah were a singing group; other members included Howard Haughton, Bunny McKensie, or Derrick Donaldson. The group was based in the United Kingdom and worked almost exclusively with producer **Michael Campbell**. In the late 1970s and early 1980s, they released a series of five albums on Bow's Natty Congo imprint, launched in 1978.

Their first album was *Bankrupt Morality.* The release was produced by Campbell, and the backing band was Marley's **Wailers**, namely **Aston** and **Carlton Barrett**. In 1979, the second album, *Burning Black*, was issued. This work was produced by Bow and included songs such as the title track, "Rastaman Tell I So" and "One Son." In 1980, the group followed with *Reggae Hit Showcase* and, in 1982, *Universal Messenger.* The latter featured the songs "Look Mankind," "Might Can't Conquer Right," and "Praises" and was recorded in Jamaica at **Harry J's** and **Tuff Gong** studios, and also in London. In the wake of *Showcase* the group disbanded. However, Bow released *Writing on the Wall* in 1985 under the Sons of Jah name. It contained featured singles such as "Hard Times Love" and "Wise Man Says."

SONS OF NEGUS. *See* RAS MICHAEL

SOUL BROTHERS

Formed at **Studio One** in the wake of the breakup of the **Skatalites**, which had been **Clement "Coxsone" Dodd's** house band, the band formed in 1964 and included **Roland Alphonso, Lloyd Brevett, Donald Drummond, Tommy McCook, Jackie Mittoo**, Johnny Moore, Lloyd Knibbs, **Ernest Ranglin**, and Lester Sterling. The Skatalites did not last for two full years; however, they recorded a vast quantity of songs, and their style became the benchmark of **ska**.

When the Skatalites disbanded in 1965, Alphonso, Mittoo, Moore, and Brevett formed the Soul Brothers. Mittoo and Alphonso led the group, and for two years they were the resident band for Studio One. The band's lineup was flexible, depending on the recording demands. In 1967, the Soul Brothers split and were replaced by the **Soul Vendors**, later becoming Sound Dimension. Mittoo continued to lead the group and remained loyal to Dodd.

During their time together, the Soul Brothers backed a large number of vocalists, but also recorded several albums of their own material. The most significant of these was *Last Train to Skaville* (1967). The record marked the end of the ska era and the dawn of **rock steady**. The album credits include Wallin Cameron on guitar, Bunny Williams on drums, **Dennis Campbell** on saxophone, **Bobby Ellis** on trumpet, Bryan Atkinson on bass, Harry Haughton on guitar, Joe Isaacs on drums, and various other members including Mittoo. In addition to this album, the Soul Brothers released *Carib Soul* and *Hot Shot*.

SOUL SYNDICATE

Formed in the early 1970s as the **reggae** style was being codified, the group formed around the guitar and bass core of **Tony Chin** and **George "Fully" Fullwood**. The pair had worked together as the Riddim Raiders in the late 1960s, during the **rock steady** era. In addition to Chin and Fullwood, the Soul Syndicate included **Carlton "Santa" Davis, Bernard "Touter" Harvey, Earl "Chinna" Smith**, and Keith Sterling. The Syndicate's resume includes support on albums by **Big Youth, Ken Boothe, Dennis Brown, Burning Spear, Johnny Clarke, Don Carlos, Gregory Isaacs, Bob Marley, Freddie McGregor**, the **Mighty Diamonds**, and many others. They also worked for a variety of producers such as **Winston "Niney" Holness, Joseph "Joe Joe" Hookim, Keith Hudson**, and **Bunny "Striker" Lee**. While members of the Soul Syndicate were working for Lee, they became the studio group the **Aggrovators**. As the Soul Syndicate, these musicians released a series of albums such as *Harvest Uptown* (1977), *Famine Downtown*, and *Was Is Always* (1978). A later release from the band was *Friends and Family*, a compilation album released in 1995.

SOUL VENDORS

The Soul Vendors formed in the wake of the **Skatalites'** breakup. The Skatalites had been **Clement "Coxsone" Dodd's** house band at **Studio One**. The band formed in 1967 and included **Roland Alphonso, Lloyd Brevett, Donald Drummond, Tommy McCook, Jackie Mittoo, Ernest Ranglin**, Johnny Moore, Lloyd Knibbs, and Lester Sterling. The Skatalites did not last for two full years; however, they recorded a vast quantity of songs, and their style became the benchmark of **ska**.

When the Skatalites disbanded in 1965, Alphonso, Mittoo, Moore, and Brevett formed the Soul Brothers. Mittoo and Alphonso led the group, and for two years they were the resident band for Studio One. The band's lineup was flexible, depending on the recording demands.

In 1967, the Soul Brothers split and were replaced by the Soul Vendors, who later became Sound Dimension. The Soul Vendors comprised Hector Williams on drums, Lloyd Brevett on upright bass, Roland Alphonso on tenor saxophone, Jackie Mittoo on keyboards, Ernest Ranglin on guitar, Johnny Morris on trumpet, Errol Walters on electric bass, and **Ken Boothe** on vocals. This was the lineup as of 1967 when they backed **Alton Ellis'** *Rock Steady* release. The album was a tutorial on the new sound and a strong statement on the passing of ska. The band went on to back other singers including **Delroy Wilson** and **Prince Jazzbo**. The next incarnation of the group was called Sound Dimension, which was led by Mittoo and worked primarily for producer Dodd.

SOULETTES, THE

The Soulettes were a vocal trio comprising Constantine Anthony "Dream" Walker, **Rita Marley (Anderson)**, and Marlene "Precious" Gifford. Walker and Anderson were cousins and were instrumental in the creation of the trio. The group formed in the early 1960s and was introduced to **Clement "Coxsone" Dodd** in the mid-1960s. Dodd took the young group into his **Studio One** facility, where they met **Bob Marley**, **Peter Tosh**, **Bunny Wailer**, and other important recording artists. Ultimately, the group was assigned Marley as a singing coach and began recording for Dodd. The group occasionally appeared live and backed artists such as Jackie Opel and **Delroy Wilson**. With Wilson, the group had its biggest hit, singing backup on the single "I Love You, Baby." Of note, Walker filled in for Bob Marley when Bob spent time working in an automobile manufacturing plant in the United States in 1966. Walker filled Marley's spot in the Wailers and sang on songs such as "Let Him Go," "Don't Look Back," "The Toughest," "Rock Sweet Rock," "Who Feels It Knows It," "Dancing Shoes," and several others. Upon Marley's return, Walker continued to sing with the Wailers as backup on songs such as "Selassie Is the Chapel."

SOUND SYSTEM

The Jamaican **sound systems** are large, portable amplifier and speaker setups that were used to entertain revelers everywhere from block parties to formal dances. The practice of building these systems began on the island in the early 1950s, and soon a variety of would-be sound engineers were working to create the perfect sound. The first of these system builders to have success was Tom "the Great" Sebastien. The purpose of these sound systems was to provide an opportunity for people to hear the newest records and to dance. Once Sebastien rose to the premier position, a variety of others stepped in to seek the throne. The second generation comprised Lloyd "the Matador" Daley, **Clement "Coxsone" Dodd**, and **Arthur "Duke the Trojan" Reid**. The men each had a name system, with Daley's being Matador, Dodd's Downbeat, and Reid's Trojan. These three came on to the **dancehall** scene and quickly changed the landscape. Dodd, Daley, and Reid were fiercely competitive and would stop at nothing, not even gunplay, to rule the dance. In many cases, one system operator would hire thugs to go and disrupt, or "mash up," another system's dance.

The early music played on the sound systems was American rhythm and blues, and the system operators pursued every opportunity to get the latest recordings. The roots of this music's island popularity were twofold: first, American rhythm and blues could reach the island over shortwave radio and, second, many Jamaicans spent time in the southeastern United States working in the sugar cane industry. The most popular rhythm and blues artists were Fats Domino and Louis Jordan. Clement "Coxsone" Dodd was one such cane worker who became interested in rhythm and blues and helped import the new music when he returned to Jamaica and entered the popular music business.

The exclusivity of any song on a system drove the system's popularity. Thus, when new material came to the island, the sound system operator who possessed it scratched off the label so that others would not even know the name of the song or singer. The Jamaican record industry grew out of the love of rhythm and blues on the sound systems. By the mid-1950s, Dodd and Reid desired making their own recordings to put on their systems. This change coincided with the birth of rock and roll in the United States and the gradual end of Jamaican importation of American rhythm and blues. The Jamaican remedy for the lack of American music was to make new rhythm and blues material on the island. Thus, in the mid-1950s the first Jamaican recording studio was opened: **Federal Records**. Soon each of the sound system operators entered the recording industry to make new songs to fuel their systems. With this the Jamaican record industry began in earnest. The business was geared completely to the sound system owner's/producer's advantage. Session bands were established to back singers, and a wide range of singers was employed to produce single songs at a time, thus starting the Jamaican predisposition to issue new music as singles instead of albums.

The musicians were all paid per song, and the producers owned the material once it was recorded. As the result of this arrangement, a great deal of animosity grew between Jamaican musicians and producers; however, the musicians were all at the mercy of the producers, as they owned the studios. Early on, the sound systems were the proving ground for new material recorded in Jamaica's studios. This has not changed much over the past fifty years.

Of note, the dancehall style actually grew out of the method of delivery of music at dances. The songs were chosen by the selecting person and then introduced by the **DJ**. Over time, the DJ's role increased to the point where special versions of new songs were made (called **dub** plates), which contained the new songs' rhythms without vocals; the DJ **toasted**/rapped new lyrics, often improvising them on the spot. This practice drove the popularity of certain systems based on the DJ's skills. Through the evolution of the **dancehall**, **reggae**, **rock steady**, and **ska** styles, the popularity of new songs is still decided on at dances run by the sound systems.

SPANNER BANNER (c. 1970–)

Spanner Banner was born Joseph Bonner to a musically talented family in Jamaica. Banner's siblings included international reggae star **Pliers** (Everton Bonner) and Ritchie Spice (Richard Bonner). He began his career in the **sound systems** when he joined Bidia studio in St. Andrew. He gained a solid reputation and built his confidence and, in 1989, made his debut in the recording studio with the single "Life Goes On." The song was a smash hit and soared to the top spot on the Jamaican charts. The song was recorded by producer **Winston Riley**, and the pair went back to the studio to complete an album of the same title in 1994.

Banner went on to the typical studio rotations, moving from one producer to another, and worked with a variety of producers. He took each producer's style and used it to his advantage and recognized his strengths. Banner spent time in the studio with **Philip "Fatis" Burrell, Bobby "Digital" Dixon, King Jammy, Sly and Robbie**, and others. Resulting albums were *Chill* (1995) and *Lover's Story* (1998). The *Chill* album was released in 1993 on the Island Jamaica imprint, with which Banner had signed a deal. *Lover's Story* was released on Banner's own Sweet Angel imprint.

In the new millennium, Banner issued *Real Love* in 2001. The year 2000 saw the teaming of all three Bonner brothers on the album *Universal*, which also featured **DJ** Snatcher Dogg. Banner sings in a soulful lovers style, which has been very successful in Jamaica and the United Kingdom. He continues to record, produce, run his label, and perform live.

SPICE, MIKEY (1965–)
Born Michael Theophilus Johnson in 1965 in Kingston, Jamaica, Spice was raised in a musical family; as a youth he learned to play multiple instruments including drums, bass, guitar, trumpet, piano, saxophone, flute, and others. In 1991, Spice entered the Jamaican popular music scene and went into the studio with **Barry O'Hare**. He cut a cover of the Barry White hit "Practice What You Preach," and it set up his debut 1995 album *Happiness*, on the **RAS** label. A **Reggae Sunsplash** concert appearance in 1993 attested to his popularity. He then started the typical studio rounds and worked with a series of producers around the island. Spice released *Born Again* (1996) and followed it with *All about You* in the same year. In 1997, he released *Jah Lift Me Up* and the next year *Spice Rack*.

In the new millennium, Spice continued to issue successful material and scored a major success with *Harder Than Before* (2000). Since then he has released *Toe 2 Toe* (2002), which contained five tracks from **Garnet Silk** and five from Spice (with guest appearances from Prezident Brown and Anthony Malvo). More recently, Spice issued the album *Mikey Spice* (2003). He remains a major figure on the **reggae** music scene.

SPRAGGA BENZ (1969–)
Born Carlton Grant in Kingston, Jamaica, as a skinny youth he was nicknamed "Spaghetti," and this name eventually turned into Spragga. The second half of his name came from his earliest musical experiences. He worked on the L.A. Benz **sound system** as a selector spinning records for **toasters** to sing over, thus resulting in the stage name Spragga Benz.

While working for the sound system, Benz took artists into the studio to record new **dub** plates for use on the sound. Benz happened to record **Buju Banton** and was short one side of music during the recording process. He was convinced to fill the side himself and toasted lyrics for the first time. The experience was a wild success and yielded the "Love Mi Gun" single. With the success of the single, Benz was persuaded to go back into the studio and cut the single "Jack It Up," which again created a frenzy in the **dancehall**. These dub plates were only for use in the dance, and Benz had not made a formal recording yet. This changed in the early 1990s when he went into the studio with producer **Winston Riley** and recorded "Could a Deal" and "Jack It Up." Subsequent recordings included "Girls Hooray," and Benz's success soared. He released a long list of hits such as "Who Next," "No Fun Thing," and "Jump Up and Swear."

In the wake of this success, Benz appeared at Sting in 1993 and was well received. He then cut his debut album, *Jack It Up* (1994). With this, Spragga Benz was among the hottest DJs in the dancehall. With all of this momentum, Benz was offered a recording contract by Capital Records. This partnership resulted in *Uncommonly Smooth* (1995), with singles such as "A-1 Lover" and "Spanish Harlem." The album failed to make major inroads into the United States, and Capital dropped Benz.

For the rest of the 1990s, he worked in Jamaica rebuilding his reputation and cutting new material. He also made increasing impact in the United States through teaming with rappers such as KRS-ONE and Wyclef Jean. At the end of the 1990s, Benz and **Beenie Man** teamed for a clash album called *Two Badd DJs*.

In the new millennium, Benz issued *Fully Loaded* (2000), which was a success, including cameos by dancehall and hip hop luminaries such as **Lady Saw** and Foxy Brown. Also in the new millennium, Benz has branched out and begun to work in the film industry. He appeared in *Brooklyn Babylon* and *Shootas* and, in 2002, issued another album. *Thug Nature* was released on Empire Records and included a series of guest appearances from Benz's Red Square Crew. The crew is a collection of up-and-coming talents whom Benz mentors and helps to break into the business. Artists such as Baby Cham, Black Pearl, and Sugar Slick have emerged as new talents from Benz's crew. Spragga Benz continues to write, release, and tour in addition to working with his Red Square Crew of young artists.

STEEL PULSE

Steel Pulse is a UK-based **reggae** band that formed in 1975 in Birmingham, England. The founding members were David Hinds as the singer and songwriter, **Basil Gabbidon** on guitar, and Ronnie "Stepper" McQueen on bass. The trio took time to hone their skills and learned from playing material by reggae masters such as the **Abyssinians**, **Burning Spear**, **Bob Marley**, and **Peter Tosh**. The group then established a larger lineup by including Steve "Grizzly" Nesbett, **Alphonso "Fonso" Martin**, Michael Riley, and Selwyn Brown.

The group played **Rastafarian**-infused reggae and began working in clubs to estab-

Steel Pulse. © *UrbanImage.tv.*

lish their reputation. They also caught a break when they were adopted by the burgeoning English punk scene in 1976. The group ended up playing live shows with bands such as Generation X (Billy Idol's original group), the Clash, the Police, and others. Their first single was recorded in 1976, called "Kibudu, Mansetta & Abuku." The single was distributed by a company called Dip, and it allowed for the band to move forward.

Through their newfound popularity, the band was able to record subsequent singles, and a song from 1977 topped the UK charts. The band then released a string of singles that were harder than the other UK **reggae** fare, such as "Handsworth Revolution," "Soldier," and "Sound Check." They had gained a substantial reputation and following, which warranted going on tour with **Burning Spear**. This resulted in a record contract with **Chris Blackwell's Island Records** label. In 1978, they released the first Island single, "Ku Klux Klan," which was popular enough to yield an album recording session, the result of which was *Handsworth Revolution* in the same year. The level of fame that Steel Pulse had achieved was attested to by them being named the opening band for **Bob Marley and the Wailers** on the European leg of the *Kaya* tour. In the same year the band backed their UK punk equivalent the Clash on a separate tour. In 1979, they released their second album, *Tribute to the Martyrs*, which was not as successful as the first. It was followed by *Caught You* (1980), which marked their last work for Island. Regardless, they toured the United States twice in the early 1980s and played the **Reggae Sunsplash** concert in 1981. Even though they lacked a record contract, Steel Pulse went back to the studio and cut their most popular album to date, *True Democracy*. Just before going into the studio for this fourth album, Gabbidon quit the band because he felt that Steel Pulse had lost its edge.

Their next release was the Grammy-nominated *Earth Crisis* (1984). It was followed in 1986 by *Babylon the Bandit*, and this release won the Grammy for Best Reggae Album. In 1988, *State of Emergency* was released and continued Steel Pulse's popularity. In the 1990s, the band continued to impact the music scene in the United Kingdom, United States, and Jamaica. They released *Victims* (1991) and earned another Grammy nomination. This was repeated in 1992 with the album *Rastafari Centennial*.

In 1993, the band marked a first, as they were asked to play at Bill Clinton's presidential inauguration ceremony. They were the first reggae group to play this occasion, and it reflected their increasing influence in the United States. Further albums followed, such as 1997's Grammy-nominated *Rage and Fury*. In 1999, the band was the headline act for the Spirit of Unity Tour, which traveled around the world. They also released their *Living Legacy* album on the **Tuff Gong** imprint. In 2004, Steel Pulse released their most recent album, *African Holocaust*. It featured songs such as "Global Warning," "No More Weapons," and "Make Us a Nation." Steel Pulse continues to write, record, and tour and remains a major presence on the international reggae scene.

STEELY AND CLEVIE

Wycliffe "Steely" Johnson (keyboards) and Cleveland "Clevie" Browne surfaced in the **reggae** music scene in the mid-1970s. Clevie had been playing as part of the **In Crowd** and Steely had worked with **Gregory Isaacs, Sugar Minott**, and **Maxi Priest**. The pair came together in the late 1970s at **Lee "Scratch" Perry's Black Ark Studios**, and they immediately knew that they would continue to work together.

Steely and Clevie were a double threat. Not only were they one of the premier rhythm sections in Jamaica, they also worked the production end of the recording process. By the mid-1980s, the pair had established themselves as experts in both areas and had been installed in **King Jammy's** studio as part of the house band and as a production team. In the earlier part of the decade, Steely and Clevie had begun experimenting with new technology, with the drum machine. By the mid-1980s, Jammy was intensely interested in electronic beat making, and this kept the pair involved with all facets of Jammy's musicmaking. With the heyday of **dancehall** and the dawn of the **ragga** style taking place in Jammy's studio, Steely and Clevie maintained an active working schedule for the rest of the decade. They worked for a variety of artists including **Dennis Brown**, **Cocoa Tea**, Tanto Irie, **Ipso Facto**, **David Kelly**, **Lady Shabba**, **Red Dragon**, and **Garnet Silk**.

In 1988, the pair formed their own label to gain greater creative control. On the Steely and Clevie imprint, a host of stars appeared, such as **Aswad**, Foxy Brown, **Dillinger**, **Maxi Priest**, **Shabba Ranks**, and **Tiger**. In addition, they were releasing their own material starting with *Real Rock Style* (1989). This was followed by a host of releases, including *Can't Do the Work*, *Studio One Vintage*, *Ghetto Man Skank*, *Before the Time*, and *High Gear*. As dancehall beatsmiths, the pair was at the top of the list. Their rhythms were used for countless dancehall favorites.

In the new millennium, the duo decided to recapture some of its earlier dancehall fame. They set in motion a plan to create an updated version of dancehall for the modern era. This plan was subverted when Steelie was charged with manslaughter after accidentally killing a pedestrian who crossed the street in front of his sport utility vehicle. In the wake of this occurrence, the pair's plans are gradually coming back on track, and they have tentatively titled their new material the "Sleepy Dog" rhythm, as it is much slower than typical dancehall fare. The acts that will appear on "Sleepy Dog" include Assassin, Elephant Man, Sean Paul, Hawkeye, and others.

STORME, RICHARD. *See* I-KONG

STUDIO ONE

Clement "Coxsone" Dodd began recording Jamaican popular music in 1955, and as his reputation grew he opened his now-legendary Studio One facility. The studio opened in 1960 at 13 Brentford Road, Kingston, Jamaica. Along with Studio One, Dodd also opened the Jamaica Recording and Publishing Company Limited. Through these business endeavors, Dodd was able to stay on the leading edge of Jamaican popular music styles from **ska** to early **dancehall**. His recording and pressing facilities were used by many of the most important artists of the time, including **Roland Alphonso**, **Bob Andy**, **Bob Marley and the Wailers**, **Ken Boothe**, **Burning Spear**, **Donald Drummond**, **Alton Ellis**, the **Ethiopians**, **Marcia Griffiths**, the **Heptones**, **John Holt**, **Lone Ranger**, **Tommy McCook**, **Jackie Mittoo**, **Johnny Osbourne**, **Ernest Ranglin**, the **Skatalites**, **Toots and the Maytals**, and **Wailing Souls**.

In deference to Dodd's impact, Brentford Road was renamed Studio One Boulevard. As one of the first, and at times the most reputable, studios in Jamaica, nearly every important recording artist on the island passed through the Brentford Road doors.

SUNSPLASH. *See* REGGAE SUNSPLASH

SUPER CAT (1961–)

Born William Maragh in Kingston, Jamaica, he got a very early start in the music business when he started **toasting** on **sound systems** at the age of seven. He first appeared on the Soul Imperial sound. His first nickname was Cat-A-Rock, but he soon changed this to Super Cat. He also sometimes appeared under the subsidiary nickname Wild Apache. In 1981, Cat issued his first single, "Mr. Walker," which was produced by **Win-**

ston Riley. The single was successful, but Cat ran afoul of the law and spent time in the General Penitentiary. Upon release, Cat teamed with **Early B** and joined the Killimanjaro sound. There he worked alongside **Lone Ranger** and others.

By the mid-1980s, he was back in the groove and released his first album, *Si Boops Deh*. The record was a hit, and the singles "Boops" and "Cry Fi De Youth" were both successful. On the record, Cat established his style of positive and conscious lyrics delivered in the **dancehall** style. In the wake of this release, Cat started his own label, called Wild Apache Productions. In 1988, he issued *Sweets for My Sweet*, which he produced himself and which was released on the VP imprint. This was followed by 1991's *Cabbin Stabbin* album, which was a first in dancehall, as it featured three **DJs**. Along with Cat, **Junior Demus** and **Nicodemus** appeared on the release. Riding on his Jamaican success, Cat moved to New York and secured a recording contract with Columbia Records. The product of their alliance was the album *Don Dadda* (1992), one of the first major label dancehall albums. The material did well; the followup album, *The Good, the Bad, the Ugly, and the Crazy*, was released a year later by Sony. This record was a four-way collaboration among Nicodemus, Junior Demus, Junior Cat, and Super Cat. Next, Cat issued *The Struggle Continues*, which had enough crossover appeal to lead to his cameo on Sugar Ray's single "Fly."

In the mid-1990s, Cat worked with a variety of other talent such as **Josey Wales** and Kriss Kross and was featured on the soundtrack for the film *Pret a Porter* with the song "My Girl Josephine" (a Fats Domino cover). In 1998, Capital released Cat's next record, called *The Good, the Better, and the Best of Super Cat*. The album was a compilation of many of Cat's hits to that time. Super Cat remains a fixture in Jamaican dancehall. He remains active in the popular music scene both in the United States and Jamaica.

SUTHERLAND, TREVOR. *See* IJAHMAN LEVY

SWABY, HORACE. *See* PABLO, AUGUSTUS

SYMEONN, ROB (c. 1960–)

Rob Symeonn began his career as a **dancehall toaster** for the One Love International **sound system** in Kingston, Jamaica. He then moved to New York in 1978, where he enchanted the immigrant Caribbean music community. While he was toasting for the New York area systems such as Freedom and Macca Bee, he met Ruff Scott. This meeting took place in 1986, and Scott recruited Symeonn for the **Easy Star** label, on which Scott was operating.

After joining the Easy Star roster, Symeonn continued to hone his skills. He came from a diverse background and enjoyed a variety of different types of music. This comes across in his roots reggae stylings. On Easy Star he released the single "Everything for Jah," which promoted a message of universal love. Symeonn's music reflected his distaste of the dancehall themes of slackness (talk of guns, sex, and drugs) and gun culture and his positive and conscious direction. In the wake of the first single, Symeonn released a second offering, "Delilah," which was a combination with Ranking Joe.

Recently, Symeonn performed with internationally known talent such as **Tony Rebel**, **Sister Carol**, and **Yellowman**. Although he grew to focus much of his attention on the education of youth, he kept a hand in the music scene. The artist remains active to the present and continues to have the potential to be a breakout singer, given the right circumstances.

TAFARI, JUDAH ESKENDER

Born Ronald Merrills, he took his stage name for a variety of reasons. *Judah* came from his Twelve Tribes of Israel association and is linked to his birth month, July. *Eskender* is an Ethiopian name suggested to the singer when he was first coming onto the scene. He took *Tafari* from his father in the **Rastafarian** faith.

Tafari got his start in the music business as a guitarist. At first, he did not consider himself a singer, but through singing backup harmonies, he eventually gained confidence in his vocal abilities. In 1978, Tafari entered the studio and worked with producer **Clement "Coxsone" Dodd** at his **Studio One** facility. Tafari met Dodd through one of Dodd's session keyboard and bass players, Bagga Walker. Together, the pair cut a series of cover songs as well as several originals. The first single released was "Jah Light." The song was successful in the Caribbean, the United Kingdom, and Canada. This was followed by "Rastafari Tell You," which was another success. A collection of this work was compiled on the album *African Blood* (1979).

Although Tafari experienced initial success, he opted in 1980 to work as a session bass player as opposed to being a frontman. He became part of the Generation Gap band, which backed a series of singers. Tafari then made several trips to Canada, during which he entered the studio with **Brigadier Jerry** for some session bass work. In 1986, Tafari moved to the United States and settled in New York.

In 1990, he moved to Maryland. He made periodic trips back to Jamaica to record and also traveled to Africa. In 1993, Tafari traveled to England to sing for the Twelve Tribes Organization of African Unity event. He was well received and went to London to work with producer Gussie P at the A-Class studios. Together, the pair produced an album of roots reggae called *Rastafari Tell You*. Tafari remains active on the Jamaican and UK reggae scenes.

TAITT, LYNN (c. 1940–)

Born Nerlynn Taitt in San Fernando, Trinidad, in the early 1940s, his earliest musical influences were the steel drum groups that were abundant on the island. Originally, Taitt planned to join just such a group, but at fourteen he picked up the guitar and never looked back. Soon Taitt was the leader of his own band, which was hired by **Byron "Striker" Lee** to come to Jamaica to play in the celebration of Jamaican independence in 1962. Taitt performed in Jamaica and opted to stay.

There followed a period when he played in a variety of bands that worked the resort and club circuits. These were bands that did not make recordings, but went by the names the Sheiks, the Cavaliers, and the Comets. In 1966, he formed the Jets and went into the studio with **Joe Gibbs**. The group consisted of Taitt on guitar and vocals, **Gladstone "Gladdy" Anderson**, Hux Brown, **Deadly Headley Bennett**, **Hopeton Lewis**, and **Winston Wright**. The band produced the single "Hold Them," which was a successful **rock steady** release. Some believe this single was the first rock steady song; others give that credit to **Derrick Morgan's** "Tougher Than Tough." Taitt credited his rock steady guitar style to trying to imitate the sound of the steel band. Based on the popularity of this song, the group was retained by **Federal Records** as its house band in 1967. With Federal, the Jets supplied a steady stream of hits for the rest of the year. During this period they also played for other producers, such as **Derrick Harriott**, **Bunny Lee**, **Sonia Pottinger**, **Duke Reid**, and others. Although Lynn Taitt was a monument in Jamaican popular music who helped to drive the style forward, he left Jamaica and moved to Canada in 1968.

TAJ MAHAL. *See* MAHAL, TAJ

TAMLINS, THE

A **reggae** group formed in the early 1970s, the Tamlins were a vocal trio consisting of Carlton Smith, Junior Moore, and Derrick Lara. The trio entered the studio in the mid-1970s and recorded a series of singles that had moderate success. Their sound was highly reminiscent of the Gamble and Huff Philadelphia International records material of the 1970s. However, their reputation was made singing backup vocals for artists including **Jimmy Cliff**, **Marcia Griffiths**, **Beres Hammond**, **John Holt**, **Pat Kelly**, and **Delroy Wilson**; and, most importantly, international touring with **Peter Tosh**. The trio's Tosh-support tour was for the *Bush Doctor* album in 1979.

The success of this collaboration led Tosh to recruit the trio for backup vocals on *Mystic Man* (1979) and *Wanted Dead and Alive* (1981). In addition to backing these reggae legends, the group also released a series of solo albums, such as *No Surrender*, *I'll Be Waiting*, and *Love Divine*. Hit singles from these works included "Eighteen with a Bullet," "Stars," "Go Away Dreams," "Ting-a-Ling," and a version of Randy Newman's song "Baltimore." The group continued to perform as a trio, but each member also pursued individual projects, which led to speculation that they had broken up.

In 2004, the group toured the United Kingdom, and their Birmingham show saw **Ken Boothe**, Pat Kelly, and Errol Dunkley join the trio on stage. Further, they continue to work as the background vocal group for **Rita Marley**. Also in 2004, the group went back to the studio to work on a new Tamlins album.

TAPPA ZUKIE (1955–)

Born David Sinclair in Kingston, Jamaica, the singer gained his nickname from the combination of an affectionate term (Tappa) his grandmother had for him and the name of the gang that he ran with (Zukie). Zukie entered the music business working for Kingston-area **sound systems**, such as Discotech and Maccabees, where he exhibited his skills and influences, including **U-Roy** and **Dennis Alcapone**. His sound system work allowed him to hone his **toasting** skills and to gradually get noticed by **Bunny "Striker" Lee**. However, his gang connections were getting him in trouble with the police, so his mother sent him to live in London, with hopes that he would leave his troubled childhood behind. Lee refused to forget about the skills of the rising young star and arranged for him to sing with legendary dancehall performer U-Roy, which resulted in immediate studio time. Zukie went into the Ethnic Records studio and recorded the single "Jump and Twist" in 1973; he had a degree of success.

While in London, Zukie also recorded with producer **Clement Bushay**, and this material surfaced as the album *Man A Warrior* (1973). At the end of that year, Zukie returned to Jamaica and went to work with Lee. The pair recorded "Natty Dread Don't Cry," but had a falling out that led them to part company. Lee gave Zukie a collection of rhythms to work with: Zukie supplemented these with material gained from

Joseph "Joe Joe" Hookim and recorded his second album, *MPLA*, at
King Tubby's studio. The album was
not released until 1976, but marked his
first formal release in Jamaica. In 1975,
Zukie returned to the United Kingdom
and rode the success of *Man A Warrior*
into a UK release of the single "MPLA."
The single was a success and led to
the release of the entire album. With
this early work in place, Zukie was
quickly becoming a popular DJ, both
in Jamaica and England.

Next, Zukie went into the studio
with producer Yabby You and cut a
series of singles including "Natty Dread
on the Mountain Top." His exposure was
further heightened through an appearance with New York punk pioneer Patti
Smith. Smith took Zukie under her wing
and asked him to open for her next
tour. Additionally, she reissued his *Man
A Warrior* album on her own Mer
imprint. In the late 1970s, Zukie had a
burst of activity and released *Man from
Bosrah*, *Tappa Zukie in Dub*, and
Escape from Hell, all in 1977. The following year saw the release of *Peace in
the Ghetto*, *Tappa Roots*, and *Black
Man*. In 1979, he released *Earth Running*, another fine reflection of his skills.

Tappa Zukie. © *UrbanImage.tv.*

During the late 1970s, Zukie also launched his own record label, Stars. He worked as
a producer and quickly accumulated a sizable stable of talent including Errol Dunkley,
Ronnie Davis, **Horace Andy**, and **Prince Allah**. Zukie and Andy worked on the seminal
Natty Dread A Web She Want, with the featured singles "Raggamuffin" and "Run Babylon."

In the 1980s, Zukie returned to Jamaica and released *Raggy Joey Boy* (1982), *People
Are You Ready?* (1983), and *Ragamuffin* (1986). However, he increasingly turned his
attention to production. In the early 1990s, he worked with **Ken Boothe**, **Brigadier
Jerry**, **Dennis Brown**, **Beres Hammond**, the **Mighty Diamonds**, **Sugar Minott**,
Augustus Pablo, **Frankie Paul**, **Max Romeo**, and others. In 1994, Zukie released a
compilation album of the established DJs and the up-and-coming talent called *Old Time
DJ Come Back*.

In the new millennium, Zukie continued his **reggae** legacy. His work is primarily as
a producer on his Tappa label. Featured artists on the label have included **Sly Dunbar**,
Beres Hammond, and **J. C. Lodge**.

TAXI GANG, THE

The Taxi Gang was a studio band for **Sly Dunbar** and **Robbie Shakespeare's** Taxi
Records label. In 1974, Sly and Robbie joined forces and launched the Taxi imprint.

The pair had already had success as the rhythm section for **Black Uhuru** and **Peter Tosh**. Together Sly and Robbie, called the Riddim Twins, were a rhythm section, production team, and label owner who worked with a wide range of artists. The two were the roots of the Taxi Gang, along with guitarist Lloyd "Gitsy" Willis. Other members of the group came and went as demand changed. Another important member of the Taxi Gang was the singer Jimmy Riley. With the Taxi Gang backing him up, Riley had a series of number one hits such as "Love and Devotion" and "Give Me Your Love."

As a backing band, the Taxi Gang worked with a series of artists including **Chaka Demus and Pliers**, **Charlie Chaplin**, **Jackie Edwards**, **Edi Fitzroy**, **Half Pint**, **Sugar Minott**, **Michael Palmer**, the **Paragons**, **Frankie Paul**, **Leroy Smart**, Papa Tullo, Purple Man, Peter Metro, and others. In addition to this material, the group also released its own material on a series of albums through the 1980s and 1990s. Their first was *The Sting* (1986), followed by *Live* in the same year. In 1990, they released *Two Rhythms Clash*, and in 1995 *Hail Up the Taxi*. More recently, the group has recorded with **Beenie Man**, **Ken Boothe**, and **U-Roy**.

TAYLOR, JOHN. *See* CHAKA DEMUS AND PLIERS

TAYLOR, ROD (1957–)

Born in Kingston, Jamaica, Taylor grew up under the musical influence of **Horace Andy**. As a youth, he formed the singing trio the Aliens with Barry Brown and Johnnie Lee. The trio split before going into the studio, and Taylor became a solo singer. He gained notoriety in the early 1970s as a young singer by winning one of the island's many talent competitions. His first single, "Bad Man Comes and Goes," was recorded by **Ossie Hibbert** at **Studio One** and released on the Hound Dog label. This release was followed by a series of hits, and these early recordings were compiled and released on his debut album, *Rod Taylor* (1973). His next foray into the music business came with singing for Bertram Brown's Freedom **sound system** in the late 1970s, under the name Rocker T.

His breakout release was 1978's "Ethiopian Kings," which was an instant classic released by Brown over a scorching **Soul Syndicate** rhythm. His style was straight-ahead roots reggae throughout these early recordings. He followed this hit with "His Imperial Majesty," recorded by **Mikey Dread**. There followed the typical movement from one producer to the next. He worked with **Prince Far I** on the single "No One Can Tell I about Jah" and several others, which yielded a collection of solid singles. These singles were released by Patate Records on a compilation called *Ethiopian Kings 1975–1980*. *Where Is Your Love Mankind* was released in 1980. The production work was done by **Henry "Junjo" Lawes**, and the album was issued on the Greensleeves imprint.

In the early 1980s, Taylor and his wife moved to France, and his recording career gradually abated. He had minor success in the United Kingdom with a pair of albums in the 1990s, but they did not reach the Jamaican audience. In the new millennium, Taylor has rededicated himself to creating roots music. He went into the studio with Jah Warrior and cut a series of singles including a version of "His Imperial Majesty." He also worked at the Third Eye studios on a series of **dub** plates with Rootsman.

TECHNIQUES, THE

The Techniques were a singing group formed in Kingston, Jamaica, in 1962 by **Winston Riley**. At one time or another, the Techniques included Riley, **Lloyd Parks**, Franklyn White, Frederick Waite, **Bruce Ruffin**, Jackie Paris, Marvin Brooks, **Slim**

Smith, and others. They signed a recording deal with **Duke Reid** in 1965 and issued a series of hit singles on his **Treasure Isle** imprint. The singles included "You Don't Care," "Love Is Not a Gamble," "Traveling Man," "Queen Majesty," "It's You I Love," and others. This material was recorded with backing bands such as **Lynn Taitt** and the Jets, **Tommy McCook** and the Supersonics, the Baba Brooks Band, and the Duke Reid All-Stars. In the late 1960s they issued a collection of these hit singles called *Little Did I Know* on the Treasure Isle label.

At the end of the decade, the group broke up as Riley moved into the production arena and formed his own Techniques label. In the early 1980s, the Techniques reformed, with Tyrone Evans singing the lead vocal parts. They re-issued "Love Is Not a Gamble" as a single, and then an album of the same name. Subsequently, the Techniques again disappeared from the Jamaican popular music scene. In 1993, **Heartbeat Records** issued *Run Come Celebrate*, which is the definitive compilation of the Techniques' material from the 1960s.

TENNORS, THE

The Tennors were a **ska** and **rock steady** vocal group formed in the early 1960s by George "Clive" Murphy and Maurice "Professor" Johnson. The original incarnation was called the Tennor Twins, but this changed when Norman Davis joined the group as its third member. Johnson became the lead vocalist, and the trio went into **Clement "Coxsone" Dodd's Studio One** to record. Their first single, "Pressure and Slide," was issued on the Downbeat imprint and was the biggest hit on the island in 1967.

Maurice Johnson's death again made the group a duo, until Milton Wilson joined the group. Murphy was made the lead singer, and the group issued a series of its most popular songs, including "Ride Yu Monkey," "I've Got to Get You off My Mind," "Copy Me Donkey," "You're No Good," "Let Go Yah Donkey," and "Khaki Blue Cat." Soon, Ronnie Davis joined the group and replaced Murphy as the lead singer. With Davis, the Tennors released another series of popular singles such as "Weather Report," "The Stage," and "Another Scorcher." The group membership stabilized, and their consistent hitmaking made them perennial Jamaican favorites. Further, their material began gaining notoriety in the United Kingdom, and their audience base grew.

Throughout the 1970s, the Tennors' popularity continued to grow in the United Kingdom, even as they were losing ground with their local audience in Jamaica. In the mid-1970s, the group broke up; however, in the mid-1980s, Murphy rekindled interest in the band with the album *The Moods of the Tennors*, which he made by digitally remastering the group's original tapes. He also made a series of live appearances in Miami, Florida, area clubs.

TENOR SAW (1966–1988)

Born Clive Bright in Kingston, Jamaica, Saw was one of the most important singers at the dawn of the **ragga** sound in the mid-1980s. He helped to usher in the new digitally backed **dancehall** style of performing with his 1985 hit "Ring the Alarm," which became one of the most-versioned songs in Jamaican history. The song was based on the famous "Stalag 17" rhythm, recreated using digital means.

Next, Saw issued *Fever*, his 1985 debut album. This became a classic, even without the presence of "Ring the Alarm." He went on a three-year run from 1985 to 1988, during which he issued a series of hit singles. In 1988, Tenor Saw was struck and killed by a speeding car while in Houston, Texas, and his death remains shrouded in mystery. On the heels of his death, the album *Wake the Town* was released in 1992.

TERMITES, THE

A vocal duo formed in the mid-1960s, the Termites consisted of **Lloyd Parks** and Wentworth Vernal. The group existed for only a short time, but it did release one full-length album and launched Parks's career. The pair sang in the **rock steady** style, and their lyrical and soulful singing voices helped them stand out from the pack. Their most important single was "Have Mercy Mr. Percy," which was released in the late 1960s and caused enough of a sensation that they recorded the album *Do the Rock Steady*. These releases were produced by **Clement "Coxsone" Dodd** and recorded at his **Studio One** facility. After the release of their album, Vernal left the Jamaican popular music business, and Parks went on to a long and storied music career. He was both a singer and a bass player in a variety of bands and as a solo artist. After the Termites, he joined the **Techniques** and eventually formed his own We the People band.

TERROR FABULOUS

Terror Fabulous was born in the mid-1970s and rose to prominence in the **dancehall** in the wake of artists such as **Buju Banton**. He emerged on the scene in the early 1990s and released several works in the middle of the decade. His style is straight-ahead dancehall **toasting**, with few frills. Fabulous's earliest release came in 1993 with "Gwaney Gwaney," which led to a deal with East West Records for subsequent material. In 1994, the toaster released *Terror Fabulous*, *Yaga Yaga*, *Glamorous*, and in 1996 *Lyrically Rough*. Of the trio of 1994 albums, the most popular was *Yaga Yaga*. This popularity was due in part to its **Dave Kelly** production and guest appearances by several well-known artists. An example is the song "Action," a duet with Nadine Sutherland. The single garnered Fabulous significant attention as it managed a degree of crossover success in the United States. Another favorite from the album was "Miss Goody Goody," a collaboration with **Maxi Priest**. Tony Gold, **Gary Minott**, **Daddy Screw**, **Wayne Wonder**, and others also appear on the album. Fabulous went on to appear on several other artists' records in the wake of his own success. Little has been heard from Terror Fabulous in the new millennium.

THIRD WORLD

Third World formed in 1973 in the wake of a splintering of the original members of **Inner Circle**. The band Inner Circle emerged in the late 1960s with the lineup of brothers Ian and Roger Lewis, with **Michael "Ibo" Cooper**, **Stephen "Cat" Coore**, and **Richard Daley**. Initially, the band played the Jamaican club scene and had modest success. However, in 1973 the band split when Coore, Cooper, and Daley went on to form **Third World**. At this time, the Lewis brothers added **Bernard "Touter" Harvey**, Charles Farquharson, and Rasheed McKenzie to create a reconstituted Inner Circle. The band played its own breed of pop-oriented **reggae** that had crossover appeal. In 1976, **Jacob Miller** joined the group and immediately gave them serious legitimacy. Meanwhile, Third World added drummer Carl Barovier (later replaced by Cornel Marshall), percussionist **Irvine "Carrot" Jarrett**, and lead singer Milton "Prilly" Hamilton to round out the group.

An interesting aspect of Third World was that they were one of the few full bands on the scene at the time. They did not rely on **sound system** notoriety; this caused them trouble getting studio time. Third World got a degree of early exposure when they debuted at the 1973 Jamaican Independence Celebration. In 1974, the group traveled to London and issued their first single, "Railroad Track." Next, the group caught a break when in 1975 **Christopher Blackwell** signed them to a deal with his **Island**

Third World. © *UrbanImage.tv.*

Records imprint and gave them the opening spot on **Bob Marley and the Wailers'** 1975 European tour in support of their album *Burnin'.* There followed success in the recording studio with the release of a self-titled album in 1975 and *96 Degrees in the Shade* in 1977. On the latter album, Willie "Root" Stewart took over the drumming responsibilities and **William "Bunny Rugs" Clarke** became the lead singer. The album and the new members of the band were huge successes.

The group then embarked on an extended period of great creativity that saw the release of twenty albums in eighteen years. Their third album was *Journey to Addis* and was released in 1978. It featured the hit crossover single "Now That We Found Love." The group then released two more albums with Island, *Rise in Harmony* and *Prisoner in the Street,* before changing to the Columbia label.

In the early to mid-1980s, the group released several albums on the new label, including 1982's *You've Got the Power,* 1985's *Sense of Purpose,* and *Hold On to Love* in 1987. *Sense of Purpose* marked a period during which the band worked with Stevie Wonder. With Wonder, the group had the popular crossover hit "Try Jah Love" in the early 1980s. After Columbia, the group recorded for the Mercury imprint. Mercury releases included *Serious Business* in 1989, *It's the Same Old Song* in 1991, and their first **dancehall** style material on 1992's *Committed.* Next, the group released 1995's *Live It Up* on their own Third World imprint.

In the late 1990s the group's lineup changed again. The membership became Stephen "Cat" Coore, Richard Daley, William "Bunny Rugs" Clarke, Leroy "Baarbe" Romans, Lenworth Williams, and Rupert "Gypsy" Bent. Although Irvine "Carrot" Jarrett, Willie Stewart, and Michael "Ibo" Cooper left the group, they remained a vital force and released *Generation Coming* and *Arise in Harmony* in 1999. In the new millennium, the group remained active and issued a live album in 2001, which they followed with *Ain't Giving Up* in 2003, along with a twenty-fifth anniversary collection in the same year. For the material from 2003, Herbert "Herbie" Harris replaced Romans.

The Third World band has been at the top of the reggae/pop scene for almost three decades. They remain a vital recording force and have committed fans on the international scene.

THOMAS, CECIL NICHOLAS "NICKY" (1949–1990)

Born in Portland, Jamaica, Thomas went on to become one of **reggae** music's unsung heroes. He gained early notoriety as a singer with his 1969 **Derrick Harriott**-produced single "Run Nigel Run." In the wake of this single's success, Thomas got the nickname Mr. Nigel. Next, he changed studios to work with **Joe Gibbs** on his seminal release "Love of the Common People." The song was a version of the John Hurley and Ronnie Wilkins original, released in 1970, and sold over 175,000 copies in the United Kingdom. There it charted in the Top 10 and led the young singer to tour the United Kingdom.

While in England, he decided to stay. Thomas released an album titled *Love of the Common People* in 1970, and another in 1971 called *Tell It Like It Is*. Both were issued by the **Trojan Records** company and were regional hits. The 1970s release contained the singer's most famous song, as well as its followup, "God Bless the Children." An interesting side note to Thomas's career is that the band **Misty in Roots** originally formed to back the singer, in 1975.

After continuing to release material sporadically throughout the 1980s, Thomas committed suicide in 1990. There are few details to explain his death.

THOMAS, MKRUMAH MANLEY. *See* JAH THOMAS

THOMAS, PHILIP. *See* CUTTY RANKS

THOMPSON, DELROY. *See* PINCHERS

THOMPSON, ERROL "ERROL T" OR "ET" (1948–2004)

Born in Kingston, Jamaica, Thompson entered the Jamaican popular music scene as the engineer in **Joe Gibbs's** production work. The pair was known as the Mighty Two and worked with many of the most important recording artists through the 1970s and 1980s. Thompson and Gibbs released scores of recordings, and many of them went to the top of the charts. Thompson learned his craft when he worked at **Clement "Coxsone" Dodd's Studio One**, where he engineered **Max Romeo's** 1969 hit "Wet Dream." He also apprenticed with **Winston "Niney" Holness** at **Clive Chin's Randy's** 17 studio before teaming with Gibbs. At Randy's, Thompson engineered several important recordings, including **Augustus Pablo's** 1973 *Rebel Rock Reggae* album and **Big Youth's** *Screaming Target* release in 1974.

In 1974, Thompson left Randy's and went to work with Joe Gibbs in the small studio set up in the back of his record shop. The pair worked on a two-track recorder at first, but gradually built a dedicated studio with a four-track machine (eventually upgraded to a sixteen-track machine). As their expertise grew, the duo became known as the Mighty Two, and Thompson launched a pair of labels called Errol T and Belmont. Next followed a period of high productivity that involved recordings of many of Jamaican popular music's best, including *Rasta Revolution* by **Bob Marley and the Wailers** in 1974. **Hugh Mundell's** *Africa Must Be Free by 1983* and **U-Roy's** *Dread in a Babylon* followed in 1975.

In the late 1970s, they went on to record **Althea and Donna**, **Culture**, and

Prince Far I. This early success ushered even more artists into the studio. In the 1980s, the pair recorded the **Abyssinians**, **Dennis Brown** on several releases, **Burning Spear**, the **Gladiators**, **Ijahman Levy**, **Larry Marshall**, **Mutabaruka**, and **Peter Tosh**. As the **dancehall** era dawned, the Mighty Two got involved with the new style and recorded **Eek-A-Mouse**, **Fathead** and **Yellowman**, **Barrington Levy**, and others. A debilitating legal battle took place when the pair failed to get the proper licensing releases for **J. C. Lodge's** version of "Someone Loves You Honey," and the recording studio was shut down.

In 1993, Gibbs and Thompson re-emerged in a new studio and worked on a variety of compilations including material by Bob Marley and the Wailers, the **Meditations**, **Jacob Miller**, **Ras Michael**, **Junior Reid**, U-Roy, Dennis Brown, and many others. In the new millennium, Thompson remained active on the recording scene. He continued to work as one of the most sought-after engineers on the Jamaican popular music scene until his death from a series of strokes at age fifty-five on November 13, 2004.

THOMPSON, LINVAL (c. 1960–)

Born in Kingston, Jamaica, Thompson entered the Jamaican popular music scene while in his early teenage years, and by the mid-1970s was a known recording artist. He was a teen prodigy who entered the music business as a singer. Thompson began writing when he was twelve and continued through the next several decades. At age fifteen, he moved to Queens, New York, to live with his mother. There he was immersed in the expatriate Caribbean community. He met fellow Jamaican singer **Bunny Rugs** and continued to write and sing. Thompson returned to Kingston in the

mid-1970s and went into the studio. The producer who gave him his first opportunity was **Phil Pratt**, and together the pair recorded "Jah Jah Dreader Than Dread."

The young singer then moved on to work with producer **Lee "Scratch" Perry** and recorded the song "Kung Fu Fighting," which was an original, not a cover, of the Carl Douglas song. Even with this early studio experience, Thompson's music was not being heard. His big break came from his association with neighbor and singer **Johnny Clarke**. Clarke connected Thompson with producers **Bunny "Striker" Lee** and **King Tubby**, and Thompson cut "Don't Cut Off Your Dreadlocks" for Lee. Through continued work with Lee, Thompson issued his debut album of the same name, which was recorded with the **Aggrovators** backing up the young singer. The success of this release spurred Thompson forward, and in 1978 he released his self-produced album *I Love*

Linval Thompson. © *UrbanImage.tv*.

Marijuana. The title track from this release had already been issued in the United Kingdom on Thompson's own Thompson Sound imprint, and it was well received.

There followed a period of split productivity between writing and recording his own music, and producing material for other artists. In 1981, Thompson issued *Look How Me Sexy* and in 1983 *Baby Father.* Much of the material from the early 1980s was the product of a partnership between Thompson and **Henry "Junjo" Lawes**, who worked on both songwriting and producing with Thompson. While issuing this solo material, Thompson was also producing for several others, including Big Joe, **Eek-A-Mouse**, **Barrington Levy**, **Freddie McGregor**, the **Meditations**, Mystic Eyes, **Scientist**, **Trinity**, the **Viceroys**, and the **Wailing Souls**. His preferred studio musicians were the **Roots Radics**, who provided the heavy underpinning for Thompson's production. The work was done at **Clement "Coxsone" Dodd's Studio One** facility. Another aspect of Thompson's production in the 1980s was his association with King Tubby. Thompson would send raw material to Tubby, and the **dub** master added the requisite echo and sound effects, thus creating many great versions of new material. During the late 1980s, Thompson's presence in the studio decreased due to the emergence of the digital **dancehall** and **ragga** sounds. This new style was not to Thompson's liking, as he specialized in live instrument dancehall.

The 1990s saw a marked decrease in Thompson's writing and singing and a steady increase in his production work. During this decade, Thompson produced material for Freddie McGregor, the Meditations, **Admiral Tibet**, **Dennis Brown**, **Johnny Osbourne**, **Tappa Zukie**, **Yellowman**, and others. He issued one album of his own material in this decade, 1995's *Six Babylon.*

In the new millennium, Thompson continued to focus on his production work and made recordings with another long list of stars, worked on compilations for a variety of artists and labels, and re-issued some of his own material from the 1970s. Thompson remains a highly sought-after **reggae** and dancehall producer and is still active in the studio.

THOMPSON, PATRICK. *See* DIRTSMAN

THOMPSON, TYRONE. *See* PAPA SAN

THOMPSON, UZIAH "STICKY" (c. 1955–)

One of the top Jamaican percussionists to surface during the height of the **reggae** era in the mid-1970s, Thompson began playing in the studios of a variety of producers in 1976, and he soon appeared on recordings by artists such as **Big Youth**, **Dennis Brown**, the **Congos**, **Culture**, **Dillinger**, **Sly Dunbar**, **Earth and Stone**, the **Gladiators**, **Jah Woosh**, Prince Hammer, **Mikey Dread**, **Peter Tosh**, the Royals, **U-Roy**, and the **Wailing Souls**. He appeared on the 1976 **Jimmy Cliff** release *In Concert*, as well with his 1977 release *Unlimited.* Furthermore, he played on **Burning Spear's** seminal *Dry and Heavy,* from 1977. During this same period, he appeared on several Peter Tosh releases, including *Bush Doctor* (1978) and *Mystic Man* (1979). In addition, he was a regular session performer for Culture and appeared on *Harder Than the Rest* and *Two Sevens Clash* (both in 1978), and *Cumbolo* (1979).

The latter half of the 1970s was a proving ground for the young percussionist, and his reputation increased with each album. In the 1980s, Thompson went on to play with another illustrious list of heavy hitters on the Jamaican popular music scene: the **Itals**, **Rita Marley**, the **Mighty Diamonds**, the **Paragons**, **Sly and Robbie**, Manu

Dibango, the Royal Rasses, Ranking Joe, Dennis Brown, Grace Jones, Tom Tom Club, **Bunny Wailer**, and the Congos; in addition to repeated appearances with Dillinger, the Wailing Souls, Pablo Moses, and others. Also during the 1980s, Thompson was a regular member of **Black Uhuru** and played on their releases *Sinsemilla* (1980), *Red* (1981), *Chill Out* (1982), and *Dub Factor* (1983). In the second half of the 1980s, Thompson's studio work increased, and he recorded with **Alpha Blondy**, **Gregory Isaacs**, the Wailing Souls, Peter Tosh, Culture, **Ziggy Marley**, **Andrew Tosh**, and Little John, among others. This type of recording schedule persisted through th' 1990s, keeping Thompson at the top of the Jamaican percussionists.

In the new millennium, Thompson continued to make frequent appearances in the studio and began working as a producer on limited projects. He appeared on over twenty compilations of material from the 1970s, featuring artists such as **Eek-A-Mouse** and **Linval Thompson**. Uziah "Sticky" Thompson remains a force on the contemporary Caribbean music scene.

THOMPSON, WINSTON JAMES "DOCTOR ALIMANTADO" (1952–)

Born in Kingston, Jamaica, Thompson was raised in the city's westside ghetto, where he learned about the **Rastafarian** faith. He converted to the Rasta belief, and this shaped much of his adult life and music career. Thompson also realized that the music business was a good way to rise out of the depressed existence that he had in Trenchtown. He began to follow **U-Roy** and quickly learned the craft of **toasting** over a **dub** plate. He found work in the **sound systems** around the Kingston area and honed his vocal skills. The young singer appeared on the Downbeat Studio One sound, Coxsone's Hi Fi sound, and the Lord Tippertone system. Thompson's first break came when he went into the studio with **Lee "Scratch" Perry** and, using the name Winston Price, recorded a series of singles including "Macabee the Third" and "Place Called Africa." Next, Thompson changed his stage name to Winston Cool and/or Ital Winston and continued to record and perform.

Throughout the early 1970s, Thompson issued recordings that were met with limited success; hence, he opted to go into the production end of recording. He launched the Vital Food imprint and began working on his own production, changing his name again, this time to Doctor Alimantado. His material from the mid-1970s was solid roots reggae with lyrical messages of social consciousness. The singles that he released further increased his reputation and even began making an impact in the UK market. In late 1974, Alimantado went to **Black Ark Studios** with producer **Lee "Scratch" Perry** and recorded "Best Dressed Chicken," which was a huge success even though it was quite outside the mainstream. The song spurred enough interest to be packaged with other tracks for the 1978 release *Best Dressed Chicken in Town*.

In 1976, the young singer was struck and nearly killed by a bus, which severely altered his music career. In the wake of his recovery, Alimantado went into the **Channel One** studio and recorded "Born for a Purpose." The song

Doctor Alimantado. © *UrbanImage.tv.*

was about Alimantado's misfortune and, while popular in Jamaica, it was a major hit in the United Kingdom. The song appeared again on the album *Sons of Thunder*, which is also known as *Born with a Purpose*. The UK success was largely due to the burgeoning punk scene catching on to Alimantado's material. In fact, the Sex Pistols and others found a strong kinship with Alimantado. The Clash, who had just formed, also felt an affinity for the singer and mention him in their song "Rudie Can't Fail," from their 1977 debut album. The lyric "Like a doctor who was born for a purpose" comes from the second verse and exemplifies the closeness of late 1970s punk and reggae in the United Kingdom.

In the 1980s, Alimantado continued to release solid material. He issued *In the Mix* (1985); *In the Mix, Part 2* (1986); and *In the Mix, Part 3* (in the same year). Other albums from the 1980s included *Wonderful Life*, *Privileged Few*, and *Love Is*. He then moved to the United Kingdom and launched his own ISDA record label, on which he issued several dub albums.

In the early 1990s, Alimantado disappeared from the music scene. However, in his absence he had been busy re-mastering and re-pressing his entire catalog for Greensleeves records. Recently, he relocated his family to Gambia, in West Africa, and again changed his name, this time to Ras Tado.

TIGER (1960–)

Born Norman Washington Jackson in Kingston, Jamaica, in his teenage years he followed the Kingston-area **sound systems** and soon got a job working as security. He then made the shift to **toasting** on some songs and his confidence grew. Jackson made his first appearance in the studio in 1978 when he recorded a single for Philip Grant. The single was called "Why Can't You Leave Dreadlocks Alone" and was released under the name Ranking Tiger. The musical style was pure **dancehall**, but Tiger offered some variation on the style. The lyrics did not contain the standard slackness and gun talk, dealing instead with issues of consciousness; moreover, the single was delivered in a singing voice rather than being toasted. Tiger went back into the studio for another series of singles to drive up interest and recorded "Knock Three Times" and others. He also went to work on the Black Star sound system to enhance his visibility and garner wider audience acceptance.

In 1986, he issued the single "No Wanga Gut," which was highly successful and led to his debut album *Me Name Tiger*. He then went back into the studio and cut "Bam Bam," which was another major hit and resulted in an album of the same name in 1988. The following year, the rising dancehall talent teamed with **Steely and Clevie** and issued *Ram Dancehall*, which again furthered his reputation. He then entered a period during which he worked with other artists before returning to solo prominence with the single "Cool Me Down," from the soundtrack for *Cool Runnings*. Next, Tiger issued the single "When" and again scored a huge hit. He parlayed that success into several more album releases including *Worries and Problems*, *Claws of the Cat*, *Deadly*, and *New Brand Style*. All of this was issued in the first half of the 1990s and saw the dancehall sensation at the top of his game.

This came to an abrupt halt when Tiger was involved in a serious motorcycle accident in 1994. His ability to sing was altered in the accident, and he required an extended period to regain his early shape. Now recovered from the accident, the future is uncertain for Tiger's musical career.

TIPPA IRIE (1965–)

Born Anthony Henry in London, England, Tippa Irie entered the popular music scene as a **DJ toasting** on the legendary Saxon Sound International **sound system**. The

Saxon sound was the home to DJs such as **Maxi Priest**, Papa Levi, and **Smiley Culture**; Irie was next in line for stardom. He was among the new school of **dancehall** toasters who delivered the words in double time (twice as fast). The style became quite popular; and along with his friend **Pato Banton**, Irie toured extensively, appearing both in the United States and Jamaica.

In the late 1980s, Irie came off of the road and launched his own production company called Shock Out, alongside **Peter Hunnigale**. The duo built a studio in London and set to work increasing Irie's reputation in England. Throughout the 1990s, Irie released solid material, including *New Decade* (1990) with Peter Hunnigale; *Done, Cook* and *Curry, DJ Clash: Tippa Irie Meets Papa San* (1991); *Sapphire and Steel* with Peter Spence (1993); *Rebel on the Roots Corner* (1994); and others. In addition, Irie again teamed with Pato Banton and released "The Good Old Days." Also, Irie worked a great deal with the Long Beach Dub All-Stars (the band Sublime after the death of their lead singer Bradley Nowell), with the product being "Right Back."

More recently, Irie has gone back out on tour with Banton to maintain his visibility. In the new millennium, he issued *Think Twice* and *I Miss* (2000) and *In Combination with Lloyd Brown* (2001). In 2004, he issued *Sign of the Times* and continues to be on top of the UK dancehall scene. Over the course of his career, Irie issued eleven albums and hit number one with "Hello Darling," "Raggamuffin Girl," "Stress," "Superwoman," and "Shouting for the Gunners."

TOASTING

In the 1970s, a series of Jamaican **dancehall** singers emerged to change the musical landscape and style on the island. The first generation of dancehall **DJs** to alter their vocal delivery was **Count Matchuki**, **King Stitt**, and **Sir Lord Comic**. They were quickly followed by a second generation including **Dennis Alcapone**, **U-Roy**, and Scotty, who came on the Jamaican popular music scene and changed both the manner in which the lyrics were delivered and the speed of the delivery. This second generation also had the foresight to take their live products directly to the studio for recording and distribution. The product was called **toasting**, which was essentially the DJ rapping improvised words over an existing beat. Most often the beats were the B-sides of popular singles, which had been made into dub plates or had their original vocals removed, replacing them with sound effects applied to the instrumental lines. The practice of toasting was influenced by black American radio disc jockeys on stations in New Orleans and Miami. These DJs were known for spicing up their shows by talking fast over the introduction to a song or scatting (singing in nonsense syllables) over an instrumental break in a song.

There was a variety of different topics dealt with in the lyrics delivered in this style; early on, DJs such as **Big Youth**, **Doctor Alimantado**, and **Jah Stitch** issued dancehall tunes with consciousness lyrics in what became known as the roots period. However, the style gradually changed. In the mid-1980s, dancehall was altered by the birth of **ragga**, which was dancehall toasting with the backing music created though digital means. Also, many of the up-and-coming DJs preferred to rap about issues referred to as "slackness," which was talk of sex, drugs, crime, and gun culture.

The first major stars of the toasting style made their mark with an excessively fast delivery style. Toasters such as **Charlie Chaplin**, **Josey Wales**, **Yellowman**, and others operated at hyper speeds, but ran the dancehall and were highly marketable. Other significant dancehall DJs included **Beenie Man**, **Bounty Killer**, **Elephant Man**, **Shabba Ranks**, **Sizzla**, and **Yellowman**. The effects that dancehall toasting had on the rest of the world were phenomenal. The Jamaican practice was brought to the

United States by DJ **Kool Herc** and is widely believed to have spawned the New York rap style. This style traveled around the country and in turn generated many other regional styles. Moreover, rap then became hip hop, and an entire subculture has grown up around this style of popular music. In the United Kingdom, the influence has stayed much closer to the Jamaican model, but there were new **sound systems** and DJs toasting across the Atlantic by the 1980s. Further, as the style sped up, it spawned the UK offshoots known as garage and jungle. All of these styles now coexist, and many Jamaican DJs work with American hip hop artists and vice versa.

TONY TUFF (c. 1955–)

Born Winston Morris in Kingston, Jamaica, Tony Tuff entered the Jamaica popular music scene as one third of the singing group the **African Brothers**. The group formed in 1969 with Morris, **Lincoln "Sugar" Minott**, and Derrick "Bubbles" Howard. The three met as teenagers and were influenced by the close harmonies of the **Abyssinians**, the **Gaylads**, and the **Heptones**. The trio took their name from consciousness of their African roots and camaraderie. At first, Morris was the principal songwriter, as he had the most musical experience. However, Minott and Howard learned quickly and began to contribute harmonies.

In 1970, the group began to attract local attention with their roots reggae sound; soon they were in the studio with **Rupie Edwards**. Their first single was "Mystery of Nature." It led to subsequent recordings with **Clement "Coxsone" Dodd**, Winston "Merritone" Blake, and Micron Music. In addition to top producers, the three were also working with the best musicians in Kingston. Session players included **Aston** and **Carlton Barrett**, **Sly and Robbie**, and the **Soul Syndicate**. Hits such as "Party Night" and "Hold Tight" soon followed.

The next step for the three was to produce their own music, which would allow them greater freedom. The results were the 1970s singles "Torturing," "Want Some Freedom," and "Practice What You Preach." By the end of the decade the three decided to move in different directions. Minott and Morris continued as singers, while Howard became a full-time producer, working with acts such as **Cocoa Tea**, **Gregory Isaacs**, and **Sanchez**. The studio **Easy Star Records**, based in New York City, has helped to spur a comeback for the African Brothers. The album *Want Some Freedom*, which contains mid-1970s hits, was released in 2001.

In the wake of the African Brothers' split, Morris engaged in a lively solo career that lasted for several decades. His solo material was issued on a variety of imprints including **Island**, and he worked with producers including **Jah Screw** and **Henry "Junjo" Lawes**. Morris's solo debut came in 1980 with the release of *Presenting Tony Tuff* on the Black Roots imprint. This was followed by *Tuff Selection*, *Tony Tuff*, *Render Your Heart*, *Singers Showcase*, and *Hit and Run*. Each of these releases featured Morris's smooth vocals and his **lovers rock** style.

TOOTS AND THE MAYTALS. *See* HIBBERT, FREDERICK

TOP CAT (c. 1960–)

Born Anthony Codrington in Manchester, London, Top Cat earned his nickname early as an aficionado of the Hanna-Barbera cartoon of that name. Cat's early music experience was as a **DJ** on the London-area **sound systems**. With this experience he went into the studio and cut the single "Love Me Sees" in 1988. He followed this quickly with singles such as "Over Yu Body" and "Request the Style." Cat went on to work with a variety of top producers and studios, including the Saxon and Fashion imprints. Next, he launched his own label called Nine Lives and continued to issue his music with his own production. His style is an interesting blend of **ragga**, **reggae**, and UK jungle.

In the mid-1990s, Cat went into the studio and recorded a series of songs that resulted in three albums. The products were titled *Nine Lives of the Cat* (1995), *Cat O' Nine Tails* (1995), and *King of the Jungle* (1995). The first album was issued on his own label, the second on Jet Star, and the third on the **RAS** imprint. Cat also worked on the Congo Natty imprint and mixed the Jungle style with reggae's militancy and **dancehall toasting**. The result was "Champion DJ," which quickly became a dance-hall anthem in the mid-1990s. The RAS material is a compilation that included his third UK chart-topping single, "Push Up Yu Lighter."

TOSH, ANDREW (1967–)

Born in Kingston, Jamaica, Andrew Tosh is the eldest of **reggae** legend **Peter Tosh's** children. Tosh comes from a strong musical background, as his father's history is well known and his mother was Shirley Livingston, sister to Bunny Wailer. Thus, his uncle is the only living member of the original **Wailers** vocal trio. He entered the music business at age eighteen when he went into the studio and recorded his first single, "Vanity Love."

In the wake of his father's 1987 slaying, Andrew became determined to carry on his father's musical legacy. He performed his father's hit songs "Jah Guide" and "Equal Rights" at the funeral and then went into the studio to record a mixture of his father's material and his own original songs. His debut album was issued in 1988 on the Attack imprint and received a warm response. He followed it in 1989 with another album, *Make Place for the Youth*. This second album garnered the young singer a Grammy nomination and exhibited his ability to step out of the shadow of his famous father. In the wake of these releases, Tosh toured with his father's band, **Word, Sound, and Power**. In 2000, he released *Message from Jah* and quickly followed it with *Andrew Tosh* in 2001.

In 2004, he released a tribute album to his father titled *Andrew Sings Tosh: He Never Died*. Also in the new millennium, Tosh has been busy managing his father's estate, writing new music, and working to set up a Peter Tosh museum in Westmore-land, Jamaica. He performed on the Summerfest tour alongside acts such as **Toots Hibbert**, **Ky-Mani Marley**, and **Maxi Priest**. Tosh currently has a new album in the works, which is tentatively titled *Focus*, and has several new singles, including "Pay Day." Furthermore, he appears on the 2005 *Peter Tosh Tribute* album alongside his brother, **Edi Fitzroy**, **Tippa Irie**, and others.

TOSH, PETER (1944–1987)

Born Winston Hubert McIntosh in Grange Hill, Jamaica, Tosh moved to Belmond with his family while he was still a child. At an early age, Tosh exhibited his love for music. He sang and played instruments that he constructed

Andrew Tosh. © *UrbanImage.tv.*

Peter Tosh. © *UrbanImage.tv.*

himself. At age fifteen, Tosh left the idyllic countryside and moved to the west Kingston ghetto of Trenchtown. There he hung around **Joe Gibbs's** yard and learned about the music business. It was there that he met **Bob Marley** and **Neville "Bunny Wailer" Livingston**. The three formed a singing trio and called themselves the Wailing Wailers.

After long hours of practice, the three felt that they were ready for the studio. They went to **Clement "Coxsone" Dodd's Studio One** facility and recorded several of their early hits, such as "One Love" and "Simmer Down." Tosh took the lead singer role on the single "Hoot Nanny Hoot." The early recordings were all solid successes, but the trio saw very little monetary remuneration from Dodd. As the result of their poor business relationship, the trio moved on to work with producers **Lee "Scratch" Perry** and **Leslie Kong**. Of the three singers, Tosh was the most independent; he wanted more control over their studio products and wanted to be featured as the lead vocalist. Next, the Wailers signed a record deal with **Christopher Blackwell's Island** imprint. The collaboration was a success, and the first product was titled *Catch a Fire.* The album was recorded through the group's **Tuff Gong** production company and released on Island. The album was a major hit and featured the vocal trio with the solid backing of the **Wailers** band. In addition, Blackwell overdubbed some rock guitar and organ lines to give the record more crossover appeal.

Regardless of the success of the release, the vocal trio was coming apart. Peter Tosh wanted more leadership in the group (in the wake of Blackwell targeting Marley as the lead singer), and Bunny Wailer was not happy about working for a white label or leaving the island for extended periods. The group stayed together through the recording of their second album *Burnin',* released in 1973. However, shortly thereafter the three Wailers parted company. Peter and Bunny each embarked on a solo career. Tosh quickly secured a deal with Capital Records in addition to launching his own Intel-Diplo (Intelligent Diplomat) imprint. Before securing his deal, Tosh again worked with Dodd and also cut several solo tracks with the Wailers' old singing teacher Joe Gibbs.

The Capital deal resulted in Tosh's debut album *Legalize It* in 1976. The album showed an increasingly militant Tosh admonishing the police and scolding all who submitted the **Rastafarians** to injustice. The album featured songs such as "Igziabeher," "Why Must I," and "Legalize It." The record was well received, although it was not as successful as Tosh had hoped.

His second album, *Equal Rights*, was issued in 1977 by Columbia. While the Wailers band had played on *Legalize It*, Tosh's own backing band surfaced on this release. The group was called **Word, Sound, and Power** and featured **Sly and Robbie** as the rhythm section. The second album contained many of Tosh's longest-lasting hits, including "Downpressor Man," "Stepping Razor," and "Jah Guide."

Next, Tosh appeared at the **One Love Peace Concert**, where he was noticed by Mick Jagger of the Rolling Stones. Tosh's performance at this concert was later released as a live recording. Jagger signed Tosh to his new Rolling Stones record label. In addition, Tosh was featured as the opening act on Rolling Stones road shows. The *Bush Doctor*, *Mystic Man*, and *Wanted Dread or Alive* releases were made on Jagger's label. Tosh then clashed with the Rolling Stones and moved on to work for EMI.

In 1983, he issued *Mama Africa*, which was well received and featured the Chuck Berry cover "Johnny B. Goode." Tosh's version was no ordinary cover. He altered the words and changed the groove to be uniquely Jamaican. Tosh then toured on the success of the record; his show in Los Angeles was issued as the 1984 *Captured Live* album. There followed a three-year period during which Tosh stayed in Jamaica and spent time with his common-law wife Marlene Brown.

In 1987, he came out of this semi-retirement and issued *No More Nuclear War*. As Tosh was gearing up for a tour to support the album, his house was broken into by three armed men led by Dennis "Leppo" Lobban; the trio had come to rob Tosh. Tosh and his wife had been entertaining guests, and everyone got caught up in the theft attempt. Tragically, after being told that there was no money in the house, the gunmen opened fire, killing Tosh and his guests "Doc" Brown and DJ Jeff "Free I" Dixon.

In the wake of his death, Tosh's musical legacy was entrusted to his eldest son **Andrew**, who continues to oversee the management of his father's vast musical offerings. Recently, an effort was made to issue a commemorative album in Tosh's honor, resulting in the *Peter Tosh Foundation Tribute* album, issued in early 2005. The album is composed of a series of known artists performing Tosh's classic hits. Musicians on the album include J. Mascic (of Dinosaur Jr.), **Edi Fitzroy**, **Tippa Irie**, **Andrew Tosh**, Martha Davis (of the Motels), Jerry Garcia, Daddy Roots, and Mystic Vibrations. An additional feature is the first recording of Jawara "Tosh 1" McIntosh, Peter's youngest son.

TOUSSAINT, ALAN (1938–)

A musician and producer who had an enormous impact on popular music in the United States, Toussaint was a singer, songwriter, pianist, arranger, and producer who worked primarily in the New Orleans area. Over the course of his forty-plus years in the music business, Toussaint was responsible for helping to mold the New Orleans style of rhythm and blues. He was instrumental in fostering the development of artists such as Fats Domino, Huey "Piano" Smith, and Ray Charles. Songs by this trio of vocalists and composers filtered down to Jamaica on the radio and had a direct influence on 1950s music.

Toussaint was active in founding the jump style that was popularized by Louis Jordan, which also affected Jamaica. Toussaint also worked with Chris Kenner, whose music filtered down to the island. Next, Toussaint worked with the Meters and again had impact in Jamaica. Further, he generated arrangements for Paul Simon, who recorded some of his solo material in Jamaica. Through Toussaint's constant evolution of musical style in the southeastern United States, his musical legacy was felt in Jamaica. During the 1950s, Jamaican club bands and those on the island hotel circuit played material coming out of Toussaint's stable of artists. Jamaican **ska** was directly influenced by American rhythm and blues and jump band music in its use of horns. Many early **dancehall** recordings were of Toussaint's artists, and the effects of his influence were felt throughout the island into the 1990s.

TREASURE ISLE RECORDS AND STUDIO

Treasure Isle Records and Studio was an imprint launched by producer **Arthur "Duke" Reid**. He was a **sound system** owner, policeman, and liquor store operator. Reid was born in 1923 in Portland, Jamaica, and in his late teens became a police officer. He retired after ten years to work with his wife in her thriving grocery store. Next, he built a sound system that went on to become one of the three most popular on the island. He maintained his sound system's notoriety by procuring the most recent recordings from New York. In the late 1950s, Reid opened the Treasure Isle liquor store, and by the end of the decade had also opened a small production company. He did his recordings at WIRL, the West Indies Records Limited, but by 1963 had opened his own studio above the liquor store.

Reid was at the forefront of musical developments in Jamaica, and it was his recordings with vocalist **Derrick Morgan** that heralded the birth of **rock steady** in 1966. In the early 1970s, Reid helped launch the **dancehall** style by cutting records together under the **toasting** of **U-Roy**. Reid went on to record myriad talent on his Treasure Isle label. Some of his most successful products were **Donald Drummond**, **Alton Ellis**, the **Paragons**, the **Skatalites**, the **Techniques**, and Derrick Morgan. In the studio, Reid's production was backed by **Tommy McCook's** Supersonics as Reid's session band. The Supersonics had a fluid lineup that at times included McCook, **Gladstone "Gladdy" Anderson**, **Vin Gordon**, **Herman Marquis**, Lennox Brown, Babba Brooks, Jackie Jackson, **Ernest Ranglin**, **Lynn Taitt**, **Winston Wright**, Lloyd Knibb, and Hugh Malcolm. Reid's Treasure Isle Records and Studio closed when he died in 1976 after an extended illness.

Trinity. © *UrbanImage.tv.*

TRINITY (1954–)

Born Wade Everal Brammer in Kingston, Jamaica, he got his start in the recording industry when fellow **DJ Dillinger** took him to the **Channel One Studios**. There he recorded the single "Step Up Yourself," which was a huge success. Trinity parlayed that experience into a series of successful recordings over the second half of the 1970s and throughout the 1980s. In 1977, he released *Dillinger and Trinity Clash*, *Shanty Town Determination*, *Three Piece Suit*, and *Up Town Girl*. Also in this year he released over twenty singles and scored major success with "Three Piece Suit." The single was produced by **Joe Gibbs** and sparked a bit of controversy within the **reggae** community. Later in the same year, **Althea and Donna** released an answer record to "Three Piece Suit" called "Uptown Top Ranking." The following year he released *Three Piece Chicken and Chips* with Ranking Trevor; *At His Toasting Best*, a greatest hits album; *Dreadlocks Satisfaction*; and *Showcase*. In 1979, Trinity issued *African Revolution*, *Rock in the Ghetto*, and *Trinity Meets the Mighty Diamonds*. This collection of late 1970s recordings was Trinity's best work.

In the 1980s, Trinity continued to issue new material; however, the quality gradually waned as the decade wore on. Examples of this material were *Have a Little Faith* (1980), *Bad Card* (1981), and *Teen Jam* (1983) with Little Culture. In the mid-1980s, Trinity changed his stage name to Junior Brammer in an attempt to revitalize his career. He issued *Telephone Line* (1986) and *Hold Your Corner* (1987), but the early magic was no longer in these releases.

TROJAN RECORDS

Trojan Records was a label founded in 1968 as an offshoot of **Arthur "Duke" Reid's Treasure Isle**, a Jamaica-based record company. Trojan took its name from Reid's early nickname from his **sound system** days, when he transported his sound system gear in a massive Leyland "Trojan" truck. The label was conceived in 1967 as a subsidiary of the **Island** imprint, with the early purpose of releasing Treasure Isle's material in the United Kingdom. However, the label soon grew and licensed a variety of material for the UK market. The period of time during which Trojan was most active encompassed the **rock steady** and early **reggae** eras. Early talent to appear on the imprint included **Bob Marley and the Wailers**, **Dennis Brown**, **Desmond Dekker**, **Alton Ellis**, **John Holt**, **Lee "Scratch" Perry**, the **Pioneers**, the **Skatalites**, **Toots and the Maytals**, and others. The earliest incarnation of Trojan did not last long, but the imprint was revived by Lee Goptal as a means of releasing material by more than just Reid's Treasure Isle.

In its late 1960s form, the label issued material from all of the major Jamaican producers in addition to British products. As the company grew, subsidiary imprints were formed to highlight the work of individual producers, such as Clandisc, which featured work by **Clancy Eccles**; Amalgamated for **Joe Gibbs**; Upsetter for **Lee "Scratch" Perry**; and many others. The volume of recordings issued on the label further led to general subsidiaries such as Duke, Big Shot, and Blue Cat. Trojan's impact on the UK market was significant, and the company continued to grow.

From its inception, Trojan focused on re-issuing singles but in the mid-1970s changed its focus to complete albums. From 1969 to 1976, the label issued a series of enormously popular singles onto the UK market. During this time, Trojan products were often in the charts; many of them made it to the number one spot. Also during this time, the label's roster of featured artists increased with the inclusion of **Ken Boothe**, **Jimmy Cliff**, **I-Roy**, **Judge Dread**, **Barrington Levy**, **Mikey Dread**, and many others. Trojan remained active through the changing styles of the 1970s. The early label releases had been in the **ska** and rock steady styles. However, over time it evolved with the current trends in Jamaica and released roots reggae and **dub**.

A major change in the label took place in 1975 when it was purchased by Saga Records. During the second half of the decade, sales waned even though the label continued to issue some of the best reggae music available by artists such as **Sugar Minott**, **Prince Far I**, and **Scientist**. Through the 1980s and 1990s, the label ownership was unstable, moving through a pair of new owners. In 2001 Trojan was bought by the Sanctuary Records Group. Under this new management, the Trojan legacy continued to grow. The imprint has been involved with a wide variety of reissues of its vintage material, and its vaults are increasingly being mined for early gems. Trojan remains a force on the UK music market and has diversified to include **dancehall** and jungle music.

TUFF GONG. *See* MARLEY, ROBERT NESTA

TUFF GONG RECORDS

An imprint created by **reggae** superstar **Robert Nesta Marley** in 1965, the name of the label came from one of Marley's childhood nicknames, "Gong," mixed with the singer's legendary toughness in his dealings with the Jamaican record industry. The imprint was originally created as a venue for Marley to release his own material but eventually grew to become one of the island's most reputable labels. The label was housed at Marley's house at 56 Hope Road in Kingston, where a studio was eventually constructed. Later, it was moved to a location on Marcus Garvey Drive, and a studio and fully functioning record and cassette tape plant were built.

Over the course of Marley's career and in the wake of his 1981 death, the Tuff Gong imprint became one of the most highly respected of the Jamaican labels. Marley released almost one hundred albums on it, in addition to material by Ghetto Youth, the **I-Threes**, **Rita Marley**, **Judy Mowatt**, Cultura Profetica, and others. The label eventually grew into Tuff Gong International, which included one of the largest Caribbean studios with facilities on Jamaica, in Florida, and in New York. Marley's daughter Cedella was appointed chief executive officer of the company in 1993, and through her guidance the imprint has become a proving ground for up-and-coming Jamaican artists. Tuff Gong International has also expanded to include Tuff Gong Pictures, which makes videos for a variety of reggae artists such as Michael Rose, **Bounty Killer**, **Burning Spear**, and **Barrington Levy**. In the new millennium, the Tuff Gong International company has a worldwide presence and continues to advance the careers of Jamaican reggae artists.

TWINKLE BROTHERS, THE

Formed in the early 1960s, the Twinkle Brothers comprised brothers Norman and Ralston Grant. The pair got their start singing in their Sunday school choir and began giving concerts while still very young. In the wake of Jamaica's 1962 independence, the Twinkle Brothers began performing in area talent competitions, which they frequently won. By their third attempt, the pair won the national competition and their popularity continued to grow. For a time in the mid-1960s, the brothers were part of a band called the Cardinals, whose members were all from Falmouth, Jamaica. However, by the end of the decade the pair were on their own again. They sang for all of the major producers and managed to procure a recording session with **Leslie Kong** on his **Beverley's** label. However, this effort featured Norman as a soloist and was unsuccessful. The following year they recorded "Matthew and Mark" as the Twinkle Brothers on **Duke Reid's Treasure Isle** imprint. The song was a success and brought the pair greater popularity.

In the 1970s, the Twinkle Brothers launched their own Twinkle imprint and used it as a vehicle for releasing their own material. They had a strong backing band that included Eric Barnard on piano, Albert Green on percussion, Karl Hyatt on percussion and vocals, Norman Grant on vocals and drums, and Ralston Grant on vocals and guitar. The Twinkle Brothers' music was an interesting mixture of **reggae**, pop, calypso, and soul; and, while not as roots-oriented as much of the island's fare, it did find a respectable audience.

Over the last three decades, the Twinkle Brothers have issued in excess of sixty albums. They have performed on the **Reggae Sunsplash** concert tour and have been active in Jamaica, the United States, Europe, and Africa. In addition to their tremendous musical lives on stage and in the studio, the Twinkle Brothers' Twinkle imprint has become a significant label. Now called Twinkle Music, the label has a strong stable of artists including Sharifa, Errol T., Lorna Asher, Barry Isaacs, Sister Aisha, K. D. Levi, Sista Rebekah, Steve "Santana" Campbell, Sista Allison, Philip Parkson, and Ralston Grant's wife Della.

TWO TONE

As the name for the second wave of Jamaican **ska**, the two-tone ska style surfaced in Jamaica in the early 1960s. It was widely considered to be the first indigenous type of Jamaican popular music. Ska became the most important music in Jamaica in 1961–1962. It replaced the island tendency to remake American rhythm and blues standards and injected Jamaican music with its own spirit. The ska movement coincided with the island's independence and was fostered by an intense interest in asserting Jamaican national identity and pride. The general ska band lineup was a core of singer, guitar, bass, and drums, with the addition of a horn line of varying size. At barest minimum, the horn line included saxophone, trumpet, and trombone. The style itself was a mixture of influences including Jamaican mento, American rhythm and blues, jazz, jump bands, calypso, and others. The style took over the island and invaded the radio, dancehalls, and clubs. The ska beat was fast, appropriate for dancing, and emphasized offbeat accents that propelled the music forward. The ska style held sway on the island for the next five years before succumbing to the slower **rock steady** beat in 1966–1967. Important ska performers included **Roland Alphonso**, **Desmond Dekker**, **Alton Ellis**, the **Ethiopians**, **Byron Lee**, **Tommy McCook**, **Jackie Mittoo**, **Derrick Morgan**, **Rico Rodriguez**, the **Skatalites**, and others. In the wake of the rock steady rise, a ska revival took place.

In the late 1970s and early 1980s, the second wave of ska hit. This new interest in the earlier horn-driven style, called two tone, took hold in the United Kingdom. The most important two-tone band, the Specials, went on to form its 2-Tone label and to help further the careers of other ska revivalists in the movement, including Madness, **UB40**, and the English Beat. Two tone came to the United States through MTV videos of UK bands. The impact of the British two-tone movement was felt in the United States in the late 1980s and early 1990s when several American bands launched a third revival of the ska style. Bands active in this movement were the Mighty Mighty Bosstones, No Doubt, the Hepcats, the Scofflaws, the Slackers, and the Dancehall Crashers.

UB40

Formed in 1978 in England, the band UB40 included brothers Robin and Ali Campbell, Earl Falconer, Mickey Virtue, Brian Travers, Jim Brown, Norman Hassan, and Terence "Astro" Wilson. They entered the British popular music scene through the burgeoning **two-tone** style. The group moved quickly into the mainstream by landing an opening spot on tour with the Pretenders. The first of their charting singles was "Food for Thought," issued on the Graduate label; the single broke the top ten in 1981. This was followed by their ode to Dr. Martin Luther King titled "King." The band's debut album, *Signing Off*, was released in September 1980. The scheme for the album art was based on the band's name, UB40, which was the name of the unemployment form used in England at the time. The title of the album proclaimed the fact that the band members were now off the dole.

Early on, UB40 was thought to be a two-tone band, but their debut album illustrated a style that had more in common with **reggae** than **ska**. In the wake of this album, the band formed its own DEP International label. The second album, *Present Arms*, was issued on this imprint. Featured singles on this release included "Medusa" and "Food for Thought." The second release was as popular as the first and continued UB40's success. The second release was followed by the 1981 album *Present Arms Dub*, which firmly established the band's hardcore reggae roots. In 1982, the band issued *UB40* as their third album and furthered their following with more solid material.

Their 1983 release, *Labour of Love*, was their biggest success yet. This album contained the seminal "Red Red Wine," which became a number one hit in the United States and charted on the international scale. The song was a reggae version of the Neil Diamond original and kept the band at the forefront of the UK music scene through the decade. Through the rest of the 1980s, the band issued a series of over ten albums. As their catalog grew, so did their level of exposure with hits such as a version of the Sonny and Cher tune "I Got You Babe," a collaboration with Chrissie Hynde of the Pretenders. In 1988, Hynde was again with the band for the hit "Breakfast in Bed" from the self-titled album.

In the 1990s, the band continued its success. They issued five more albums, which were well received, along with singles such as a reggae version of Elvis Presley's "I Can't Help Falling in Love with You." Other hit singles followed and UB40 rode this success into the new millennium. In 2003 the band issued *Homegrown* and continued their quest to keep reggae a viable style on the world market.

U-BROWN (1956–)

Born Huford Brown in Kingston, Jamaica, he emerged on the popular music scene at age thirteen when he began **toasting** in the style of the legendary **U-Roy**. He worked the **sound system** circuit and as a **DJ** for the Roots Socialist, Sound of Music, and Tubby's Hi Fi systems, as well as spending time around the **Treasure Isle** studios.

Brown's earliest recordings were a series of well-received singles including "Wet Up Your Pants Foot" and "Jah Jah Whip Team." His first album, *Satta Dread*, was recorded by **Bunny "Striker" Lee** in 1975, and he continued to work with Lee for several more releases, including *London Rock* (1977), *Revelation Time* in the same year, *Starsky and Hutch* and *Mi Brown Something* (1978), and *Can't Keep a Good Man Down* (1979).

In the 1980s, Brown launched his own production company called Hit Sound International and released his own material as well as that of other rising artists. His early 1980s albums included *Jam It Tonight*, *Ravers Party*, and *Tu Sheng Peng* (1983). In the late

U-Brown. © *UrbanImage.tv.*

1980s, Brown moved to the United States and was not as active in the music business. However, in 1991, he returned to Jamaica and worked with producer **Barry O'Hare**. He ultimately settled in London due to his successes with the UK market. There he worked on the Jah Warrior and Patate Records imprints.

UNIQUES, THE

The Uniques consist of **Keith "Slim" Smith**, Roy Shirley, and Franklyn White. The background of the group is confused by its close association with the **Techniques**. In the wake of the Techniques' breakup in the late 1960s, the Uniques formed. However, after their first recordings, the group split up, with Shirley pursuing a solo career in **Clement "Coxsone" Dodd's** studio. At the end of 1967, Smith returned and the Uniques re-formed with Smith, Martin "Jimmy" Riley, and **Lloyd Charmers**. This collective had a series of successful singles in Jamaica over the course of several years. They worked with producer **Bunny "Striker" Lee** and scored a series of number one Jamaican hits with songs such as "Let Me Go Girl," "My Conversation," "Watch This Sound," "Beatitudes," and several others.

The Uniques lasted for three years before Smith left, again to pursue a solo career. His departure from the band was at the behest of Lee, who felt that he would be more marketable as a solo act. He recorded several singles with Lee before his death at age twenty-five. The circumstances surrounding Smith's death are still uncertain; one version of the story is that Smith committed suicide, and another is that he was injured breaking a window and bled to death. Whichever story is true, Jamaica lost one of its most talented vocalists when Slim Smith died. The other two group members disappeared from the music scene.

UPSETTER. *See* PERRY, LEE "SCRATCH, JAH LION, PIPE COCK JACKSON, MIGHTY UPSETTER, UPSETTER, SUPER APE"

UPSETTERS, THE

The Upsetters were **Lee "Scratch" Perry's** studio band that worked with him in the **Black Ark** and other studios. Upsetter was not only the name of Perry's studio band, it was also his own nickname (among others) and the name of his record label. The Upsetters formed out of the ashes of **Max Romeo's** backing band, the Hippy Boys. The Hippy Boys included the rhythm section of **Aston "Family Man" Barrett** and **Carlton "Carly" Barrett** on bass and drums, respectively. The group went on to include a litany of other players, all of whom rallied around Perry. Over the course of time, the Upsetters included Barrett, Jackie Jackson, Boris Gardiner, Radcliffe Bryan, **Robbie Shakespeare**, or Spike on bass; Barrett, Lloyd Adams, Lloyd Knibb, Mikey Richards, **Sly Dunbar**, Benbow Creary, or Hugh Malcolm on drums; **Glen Adams**, **Gladstone "Gladdy" Anderson**, **Theophilus Beckford**, **Ansel Collins**, **Augustus Pablo**, **Winston Wright**, Keith Sterling, Robbie Lyn, Mark Downie, or Russ Cummings on keyboards; Alva Lewis, Hux Brown, **Geoffrey Chung**, **Ernest Ranglin**, **Earl "Chinna" Smith**, Ron Williams, Willie Lindo, Michael Chung, Robert Johnson, Mark Downie, or Tarlok Mann on guitar; **Val Bennett**, **Glen Da Costa**, **Tommy McCook**, Richard "Dirty Harry" Hall, or Lloyd Clarke on saxophone; and **Vin Gordon**, Ron Wilson, Bobby Ellis, David Madden, Egbert Evans, or Trevor Jones on horn.

This influential list of **reggae** instrumentalists helped forge the **rock steady** and **reggae** styles under the eccentric eye of Perry. In addition to backing many of Jamaica's greatest artists, such as **Bob Marley**, the band also issued its own work. The

U-Roy. © *UrbanImage.tv.*

first example was 1969's *Return of Django*, followed by *The Good the Bad and the Upsetters*, *Prisoner*, and *Eastwood Rides Again*, all in 1970. In 1980, the group issued *Blackboard Jungle*, *African's Blood*, and *The Return of the Super Ape*. The last of the Upsetter collection came in 1986 with the release of *Battle of Armagideon*.

U-ROY (1942–)

Born Ewart Beckford in Kingston, Jamaica, he began working in the popular music industry in the early 1960s as a **DJ toasting** on the **sound systems** that were active in the Kingston area, such as Dickies Dynamic, Sir George the Atomic, and King Tubby's Home Town Hi-Fi. It was Beckford's association with Tubby that proved to be the most important in his life. While working for Tubby, the pair discovered the techniques for creating **dub** tracks. By remixing an existing song to remove the vocals and adding sound effects to the remaining rhythm tracks, the dub style began. These records were played at sound system dances, Beckford filling in the vocals with live improvisations that sent the crowd into a frenzy. Beckford recorded a series of dub plates for use on the sound system, and the movement swept Jamaica. These dub plates were not formally produced singles and were not originally commercially released.

At the end of the decade, Beckford (christened U-Roy as a youth, as he could not pronounce *Ewart*) was invited by **Clement "Coxsone" Dodd** to join his Downbeat sound system. U-Roy took this opportunity but was unhappy working as second in command behind **King Stitt**. As a result he returned to Tubby and began a formal recording career in earnest. Early on he worked with **Lee "Scratch" Perry** and **Keith Hudson**. He then paired with **Duke Reid** for the seminal recording "Wake the Town," based on **Alton Ellis's** "Girl I've Got a Date." The song was an instant success and opened the door for U-Roy's further recording.

He followed this success with a pair of singles that cemented his reputation and success, and he parlayed that into a full-length album recorded in the early 1970s. U-Roy continued working with Reid, issuing thirty-two singles and his full-length recordings. The first album was 1972's *Words of Wisdom*, issued on Reid's **Treasure Isle** imprint. It was followed in 1973 by *Version Galore* and a self-titled release in 1974. In 1975, U-Roy worked with producer Tony Robinson, a collaboration that yielded the hugely successful *Dread in a Babylon*. In the second half of the decade, a flurry of albums was issued, including *Original*, *Small Axe*, *Dreadlocks in Jamaica*, *Rasta Ambassador*, *Jah Son of Africa*, and several others. Also in the 1970s, he launched his own Del-Ma and Mego-Ann record labels, as well as his own sound system, Stur-Gav, which featured Ranking Joe as DJ and **Jah Screw** as selector.

In the 1980s, U-Roy's productivity slowed dramatically. He issued a pair of albums titled *Line Up and Come* and *Music Addict*. In the 1990s, U-Roy reasserted himself and again entered a highly productive period. He issued *Version of Wisdom* (1990), *True Born African* (1991), *Rock with I* (1992), *Smile a While* (1993), and five more full-length releases by the end of the decade. His place in history assured, U-Roy moved into the new millennium as one of the most highly respected DJs of all time. He has since issued *Serious Matter* and *The Teacher Meets the Student*.

VERSATILES, THE

A **reggae** vocal trio active in the late 1960s and into the early 1970s, the Versatiles were formed by **Junior Byles** and his friends Ben Davis and Dudley Earl. The trio soon found studio backing with **Joe Gibbs** and recorded with the **Lynn Taitt** band backing them. The work with Gibbs yielded several successful singles including "Trust the Book," "Time Has Come," "Push It In," "Just Can't Win," "Lu Lu Bell," and "Long Long Time." The Gibbs and Versatiles material was issued on the Amalgamated imprint and was greeted with success. Early 1970s material issued on the Crab imprint included the singles "Children Get Ready," "Someone to Love," "I Am King," "I've Been Waiting," "Spread Your Bed," and "Worries a Yard." The group had modest success in Jamaica and the United Kingdom, but disbanded when Byles decided to go solo in the early 1970s. His solo career was spurred on by producer **Lee "Scratch" Perry**, and together the pair had some major successes in the mid-1970s.

VICEROYS, THE

The Viceroys formed in Kingston, Jamaica, in 1966, during the **rock steady** period of Jamaican popular music. The group was composed of Wesley Tinglin, Daniel Bernard, and Bunny Gayle. The trio originally emerged as the Voiceroys and recorded for **Clement "Coxsone" Dodd**. This early incarnation yielded "Fat Fish," "Love and Unity," and "Ya Ho." These recordings were followed by "Lip and Tongue" and "Send Requests." Although they had experienced some success, the group merged with **Winston Riley** and formed the Interns in the early 1970s. This collective had significant success with "Mission Impossible."

The group then adopted the name the Viceroys and included Tinglin, Neville Ingram, and Norris Reid. Reid was already a known soloist and continued his solo career while in the Viceroys. The group had a major success with the 1980 single "Heart Made of Stone," which was followed by subsequent singles. In 1982, they released their debut album, *We Must Unite*. The style of this record was roots reggae with production delivered by **Linval Thompson** and the **Roots Radics** as the backing band. The album was a hit and was followed in 1983 by *Brethren and Sistren*.

Although the Viceroys were enjoying considerable success and were at the height of their productivity, Reid left to continue his solo career and work with **Augustus Pablo**. His spot was filled in 1984 by **Chris Wayne** and the newly constituted group issued *Chancery Lane*. The record was not as successful as the previous recordings had been and marked the beginning of the end for the group. They went into the studio to record their fourth album, but the project was not completed before the group again disbanded.

W

WADE, WAYNE (c. 1960–)

Born in Kingston, Jamaica, Wade entered the popular music scene after having been discovered by producer **Vivian "Yabby You" Jackson**. Wayne's style is a mixture of roots reggae and **lovers rock** songs. With Jackson's help, Wade had early success with the single "Black Is Our Colour." The success of this single was followed by several others, and he subsequently issued *Black Is Our Colour* (1978). He then succumbed to the Jamaican tradition of moving from producer to producer. The second release was *Dancing Time* in 1979, followed by *Evil Woman* in 1980. Wade worked with **Dillinger** in the early 1980s and appeared with him on the "Five Man Army" release. Next came his 1983 effort with Yabby You and **Michael Prophet**, titled *Prophecy*.

After his initial Jamaican success, Wade moved to the Netherlands in 1983. He continued to issue new work through the 1990s and into the new millenium. His most recent recording was the album *Wayne Wade and Friends*, issued on Jetstar in 2000.

WAILER, BUNNY "JAH BUNNY, JAH B" (1947–)

Born Neville O'Riley Livingston in Jamaica, Bunny Wailer is the last surviving original member of the legendary singing trio the **Wailers**, which also included **Bob Marley** and **Peter Tosh**. Livingston began his musical odyssey when he met Marley at Stepney All Age School in Nine Miles, Jamaica. The two were separated when Wailer's father moved his family to Kingston. However, later Marley's mother moved the Marley family, and the pair grew up together, sharing the dream of becoming musicians. Toward that goal they joined with **Peter Tosh** and began studying music with legendary musician **Joe Higgs**.

Also during this time, Bunny was enchanted by the Kingston-area **sound systems**. The boys formed a vocal trio called the Teenagers and in 1963 went into **Studio One** with **Clement "Coxsone" Dodd** to record their first song. The group worked under the name the Wailers and scored some early successes with singles such as "Simmer Down," which went to number one, followed by a string of successful singles that brought the group local notoriety.

In 1966, Marley left for the United States to make enough money to finance a record. During his absence, Bunny penned several successful solo singles such as "Rock Sweet Rock" and "Who Feels It Knows It." His brief run at solo success was abruptly ended

Bunny Wailer. © *UrbanImage.tv*.

when he was incarcerated for marijuana possession the following year. He was released in 1968 in time to rejoin the Wailers for their work on **JAD Records**.

During the early years of the Wailers, Bunny was the shyest of the three vocalists. He began to come into his own in 1970, while the group worked with producer **Lee "Scratch" Perry**; he took center stage for the recording of "Rebel's Hop," "Riding High," and "Brain Washing." In 1972, the Wailers and Perry collaboration yielded a record deal with the **Island** imprint, and Bunny also released material on his own Solomonic label. The following year, the Wailers released the album *Catch a Fire*, which marked the true beginning of their popularity. Next, they released *Burnin*,' which contained a pair of songs showcasing Bunny.

The year 1973 was a turning point for the Wailers, as Bunny refused to tour. Joe Higgs took his place and the rest of the Wailers went on without him. After Tosh and Marley returned to Jamaica, the original three Wailers began to disband. Interestingly, it was at this time that Livingston began to refer to himself as Bunny Wailer. By 1974, neither Tosh nor Wailer was in the group. Wailer continued to work with his own label, in 1976 releasing his first solo album, *Blackheart Man*, which was well received and led to a second album the following year, called *Protest*. In 1979, Wailer released his third album, titled *Struggle*, followed by a Marley tribute album in the wake of the lead Wailer's death in 1981. Bunny remained successful throughout the 1980s, but did not receive well-deserved exposure because he refused to tour outside of Jamaica.

In September 1987, Tosh was murdered in his own house, which left Wailer the last remaining member of the now-legendary trio. In the 1990s, he was active in creating a fifty-song collection of Marley pieces, which was released in 1995 on the album *Hall of Fame*. He has won three Grammys and continues to be active in the Jamaican popular music scene. He currently lives on a farm outside of Kingston.

WAILERS, THE. *See* MARLEY, ROBERT NESTA; TOSH, PETER; WAILER, BUNNY "JAH BUNNY, JAH B"

WAILING SOULS

The Wailing Souls formed in 1968 when the singing duo **Winston "Pipe" Matthews** and Lloyd "Bread" MacDonald came together. The two had been active in a group called the Renegades, with George "Buddy" Haye, since 1965 and had recorded with **Clement "Coxsone" Dodd**. However, in 1968 Haye left the group and Matthews and MacDonald, along with Oswald Downer and Norman Davis among others, became the Wailing Souls.

The group had a degree of success in the late 1960s. They worked with **Clement "Coxsone" Dodd** at the legendary **Studio One** where they recorded a pair of successful singles as Pipe and the Pipers in the early 1970s. Also in the early 1970s, the Wailing Souls moved to **Bob Marley's Tuff Gong** label. This early success kicked off a lengthy career that has included a large quantity of high-quality roots reggae.

In the mid-1970s, the group's lineup again changed, as did its producer. The Wailing Souls moved on to work with **Joseph "Joe Joe" Hookim** and recorded a series of hits for **Channel One**, with the **Revolutionaries** backing them up. To gain greater control of their output, the group then launched their own label called Massive, and their early offerings were well received. The first two singles on the new label were "Bredda Gravalicious" and "Feel the Spirit," both of which were enormously successful. In 1979, the group released its debut album *Wild Suspense* on **Chris Blackwell's Island Records** imprint.

Wailing Souls. © *UrbanImage.tv.*

Next, the Wailing Souls jumped to **Sly and Robbie's** Taxi label and released a pair of albums in the early 1980s. *Fire House Rock* was the next release, produced by **Henry "Junjo" Lawes**, and the group reached the peak of their output. In the 1980s, the Wailing Souls, with MacDonald and Matthews at the helm, continued their success. They even made a brief foray into the newer **dancehall** style with the help of **King Jammy**. In the 1990s, the group continued its steadfast progress, landing a deal on the Sony Records label. In 1992, they released their most adventurous album so far. *All Over the World* saw the enlisting of a new vocalist, Maisha, and a host of guest artists, including **U-Roy**. The album runs the stylistic gamut and earned the group a Grammy nomination.

The Wailing Souls' second and final album for Sony was the live release *Live On.* A few of their more recent releases were their return to roots for *Tension* (1997), the Grammy-nominated *Psychedelic Souls* (1998), and *Equality* (2000). The Sly and Robbie-backed *Equality* album featured the single "Don't Say" and spawned a U.S. tour. In addition, material from the Wailing Souls continues to appear on a variety of compilation albums such as *The Wailing Souls* and *Soul and Power.*

In 2003, the group released *Souvenir from Jamaica*, which featured "Nothing Comes Easy," "Sip and Slide," and "Make That Change." The group now uses Los Angeles as its home base. It remains a powerful musical force and is heavily sought after for live performances.

WALDRON, ANTHONY. *See* LONE RANGER

WALES, JOSEY (c. 1960–)

Born Joseph Winston Sterling in Kingston, Jamaica, Wales burst onto the Jamaican popular music scene as a **DJ**, **toasting** on the Roots Unlimited and **U-Roy's** legendary

Stur-Gav **sound systems**. The young DJ took his nickname from the Clint Eastwood movie *The Outlaw Josey Wales*. He was in good company on the system in the early 1980s, as he worked with fellow DJs **Charlie Chaplin** and **Brigadier Jerry**.

Wales, who was also called the Colonel, was one of the early DJs who helped to bring the **dancehall** style into the limelight. He helped to pioneer the new style's vocal delivery, which was neither sung nor spoken, but was rather a combination of the two. In addition, he was staunchly opposed to dancehall lyrics on slackness topics such as gun culture, sex, and drugs. Instead, Wales was a **Rastafarian** whose lyrics were about issues of social consciousness and uplift. Furthering his connection to the Clint Eastwood nickname, Wales's first album was titled *Outlaw*. It was released in 1983 and featured the single "Let Go Mi Hand," which was a smash hit, as were "In a Fire Bun" and "Beg You Come Home Again." This release rocketed Wales to the top of the dancehall ranks and kept him there through several more recordings.

His next album was 1984's *No Way Better Than Yard*. The album was produced by **Henry "Junjo" Lawes**; Wales' vocals were backed by the **Roots Radics**. Featured singles on the album included "Yu Too Greedy," "Drug Abusing," and "Jah Jah Move." For his 1986 release, *Rules*, Wales moved over to producer **King Jammy**. The album was solid and did well, but came at a time in the decade when dancehall was increasingly ruled by purveyors of the slack culture. Through the 1990s, Wales limited his exposure in the popular music scene. He issued a pair of collaborations, one with his old friend Charlie Chaplin and the other with his original influence U-Roy. His association with the Stur-Gav system remained important as the members reunited at the end of the decade for a reunion tour.

The late 1990s also saw a resurgence in Wales's popularity. In 1997, the DJ was shot during a robbery. He survived and parlayed the news of the incident into a pair of new singles titled "Who Shot the Colonel" and "Bush Wacked." In the new millennium, Josey Wales continues to make periodic live performances and is recognized as one of the early dancehall innovators.

WALKER, CONSTANTINE "DREAM" OR "VISION" (c. 1945–)

Constantine "Dream" or "Vision" Walker was one of **Rita (Anderson) Marley's** cousins and a member of the singing trio the **Soulettes**. The group comprised Walker, Rita Marley, and Marlene "Precious" Gifford, and was initially created by Walker and Marley. The trio formed in the early 1960s and was introduced to **Clement "Coxsone" Dodd** in the mid-1960s. Dodd took the young group into his **Studio One** facility where they met **Bob Marley**, **Peter Tosh**, **Bunny Wailer**, and other important recording artists. Ultimately, the group was assigned Marley as a singing coach and began recording for Dodd.

The group occasionally appeared live and backed artists such as Jackie Opel and **Delroy Wilson**. With Wilson the group had its biggest hit singing backup on the single "I Love You, Baby." Walker filled in for Bob Marley when Marley spent time working in an automobile manufacturing plant in 1966; Walker sang on songs such as "Let Him Go," "Don't Look Back," "The Toughest," "Rock Sweet Rock," "Who Feels It Knows It," "Dancing Shoes," "Can't You See," "Dreamland," "Jerking Time," "Rasta Shook Them Up," "Rock Sweet Rock," "Sinner Man," and several others.

Upon Marley's return, Walker continued to sing with the Wailers as backup on songs such as "Selassie Is the Chapel." In addition to acting as a brief Marley replacement, Walker also worked with other members of the **Wailers**. In 1985, he supplied guitar work for **Bunny Wailer's** *Marketplace* album, and in 1988 he sang harmony

for **Peter Tosh** on the *Toughest* album.
He also worked with **Ziggy Marley** on
the *Jahmekya* album, on which he supplied guitar parts.

WALLACE, LEROY "HORSEMOUTH" (c. 1940–)

Active in the Jamaican popular music
scene since the late 1960s as a session
and live drummer, Horsemouth eventually earned the reputation as one of the
best drummers on the island and rivaled
the standing of **Carlton "Carly" Barrett** and **Sly Dunbar**. Beginning in the
late 1960s, Wallace played with a veritable who's who of Jamaican recording
artists. Part of his career was spent in **Joseph "Joe Joe" Hookim's Channel One** studio band the **Revolutionaries**, which further enhanced his resume. Some of his earliest work was with the **Abyssinians** on their *Forward* and *Declaration of Dub*
albums. He also appeared on their classic *Satta Massagana* release in 1976.

Leroy "Horsemouth" Wallace. © *UrbanImage.tv.*

In the second half of the 1970s, Wallace recorded with **Burning Spear**, **Junior
Delgado**, the **Gladiators**, Pablo Moses, **Justin Hinds**, **I-Roy**, **Mikey Dread**, **Hugh Mundell**, **Prince Far I**, the **Skatalites**, **U-Roy**, and others. He became a master at the **nyabinghi**, **reggae**, **rock steady**, and **ska** drumming styles and was in high demand. In
the 1980s, Wallace recorded with **Gregory Isaacs**, **Mad Professor**, **Rita Marley**, **Jacob
Miller**, **Sugar Minott**, **Judy Mowatt**, **Mutabaruka**, **Augustus Pablo**, and others.

This trend of heavy studio work continued through the 1990s, during which time
his level of activity increased from the previous decade. In the new millennium, Wallace remained active and worked with an ever-increasing collection of reggae stalwarts
including **Dennis Brown**, **Capleton**, **Beres Hammond**, Junior Kelly, and **Trinity**.
Wallace's recent work includes *Roots of Love* with **Ijahman**, *Eek-A-Speeka* with **Eek-
A-Mouse**, and *Reign of Fire* with Capleton. Leroy "Horsemouth" Wallace remains a
highly sought-after reggae legend.

WASHINGTON, DELROY (1952–)

Born in Westmoreland, Jamaica, Delroy Washington, like many of his countrymen, moved
to England while still a youth. He also got involved in the thriving expatriate music
scene and ultimately became a proficient multi-instrumentalist. As such, he worked in
a variety of bands with little success. However, in 1972, he was recruited to sing background vocals for **Bob Marley and the Wailers'** *Catch a Fire* album.

Following his stint with the Wailers, Washington released a number of successful
solo singles. In 1976, he issued his debut full-length album on the Front Line imprint.
The record was titled *I Sus* and contained a series of solid songs including "Jah Wonderful," "Stoney Blows," and "Generation Game." The musicians who were involved in
the album included Bunny McKenzie, Courtney Hemmings, **Al Anderson**, **George
Oban**, **Rico Rodriguez**, and others. The album was a success and Washington followed it a year later with his self-produced *Rasta*. This record featured "Zion," "Chant,"
and "Rasta" and again employed a collection of solid instrumentalists. For the *Rasta*
record, Washington recruited Candy and Bunny McKenzie, **Angus Gaye,** Al Anderson,

Tony Robinson, **Junior Marvin**, Rico Rodriguez, and George Oban. In the wake of these successful releases, Washington took some time off. He did return in the early 1980s but never recaptured his previous success.

WATSON, WINSTON. *See* MIGHTY DREAD

WAYNE, CHRIS (c. 1965–)

Born in Kingston, Jamaica, Wayne established himself early as a solid vocalist. He had success in the Wildcats and the Sensations. However, it was with **Sugar Minott's** Youth Promotion **sound system** that he got his real break. He made it into the studio to record with Minott, but the material was never released. Undeterred, Wayne joined the **Viceroys** when Norris Reid went solo. The group recorded *Chancery Lane*, issued in 1984, for **Winston Riley**. They recorded another album that was not released, and Wayne departed for a solo career.

In 1985, he issued the album *Freedom Street* on the Wackie's imprint. He went on to release *Progress* in 1989 on the **Heartbeat** label and scored some minor success. This was followed by *Talk about Love* (1991), which was a more significant hit. It featured the songs "Ain't That Enough" and "Alms House Business" and brought Wayne greater attention. In 1997, Wayne released *Land Down Under* on the Critique imprint. The album was a series of mixes including "Crossover Mix," "Dance Hall Mix," and "Down Under Mix." Little has been heard from the singer since.

WE THE PEOPLE

Lloyd Parks formed the We the People band in 1975. Parks had already had a successful career in the Jamaican recording industry that dated back into the late 1960s. He was a singer and bass player and worked both as a studio musician and as part of several bands. In the late 1960s he joined the Invincibles, then moved to the **Termites** when he paired with Wentworth Vernon. From the Termites, Parks went on to the **Techniques**. He soon left to pursue solo work and released the single "Stars." During the end of the 1960s, Parks split his time between solo work and session playing. In the early 1970s, he worked with producer **Sonia Pottinger** on a series of singles as he continued to move from producer to producer.

During this period, Parks's reputation as a session bass player flourished and he joined the Thoroughbreds, the house band at the Tit-for-Tat Club. In 1973, Parks diversified his life in music and launched his own record label. It was also in the early 1970s that he recorded a set of his most popular songs, including "Baby Hang Up the Phone," "Officially," and "Girl in the Morning." He was in heavy demand as a session bassist, playing with Skin Flesh and Bones, the Professionals, and the **Revolutionaries**. As a member of Skin Flesh and Bones, he found himself in **Joe Gibbs's** studio band, with whom he recorded for many of the top artists of the day.

The success that he experienced backing up the likes of **Dennis Brown**, **Prince Far I**, and others translated into the formation of his own band. In 1975, Parks formed the band We the People. The group had immediate success; they toured with Dennis Brown, often played the **Reggae Sunsplash** and Sumfest concerts, and were in constant demand. In addition to Parks, We the People included a horn line with Tony Greene on saxophone, Everol Wray on trumpet, and Everald Gayle on trombone. This lineup has been solid from the mid-1980s to the present. The group worked primarily as a backing band and has played behind artists such as **Alton Ellis**, **John Holt**, the **Mighty Diamonds**, and **Leroy Sibbles**. In addition to Parks on bass and the horn line, We the People has gone on to include Parks's children, with his daughter Tamika playing keyboard and his son Craig playing drums. The We the People band has remained in existence for the past twenty-six years and is still in demand in the studio and on the stage.

WELLINGTON, MAURICE "BLACKA MORWELL" (c. 1950–2000)

Wellington was the creative force behind the **Morwells**, a group formed in 1973 in Kingston, Jamaica, that consisted of Wellington and **Eric "Bingy Bunny" Lamont**. Wellington had been in the business as a record salesman and producer for several years before the pair formed the Morwells, a shortening of Maurice and Wellington, and immediately recorded a pair of singles. Eager to escape the tyranny of the existing Jamaican record industry, they released their material on their own Morwell Esquire imprint. The songs "Mafia Boss" and "You Got to Be Holy" were regionally successful.

In 1974, the pair became a trio when Louis Davis joined Wellington and Lamont. Davis was an experienced instrumentalist and tutored Lamont on guitar. Davis was also a skilled arranger, which rounded out the group well. In the mid-1970s, the Morwells released a series of successful singles that garnered them attention in the United Kingdom. They arranged an English distribution deal and began releasing their music directly to this new audience. Their single "Swing and Dub" was a big success in 1974 and helped to establish the **dub** technique of sound effects used with thunderclaps and jet engine takeoff effects.

In 1975, their single "Bit by Bit" was a success in both Jamaica and the United Kingdom. Also in that year the group released its first two albums, *Presenting the Morwells* and *The Morwells Unlimited Meet King Tubby (Dub Me)*. The latter further established the Morwells as pioneers in the dub style as they worked with the master **King Tubby**. In 1976, Wellington took a production job for **Joe Gibbs** and Lamont joined the **Revolutionaries**. This unprecedented access to talent made the rest of the 1970s the peak of the Morwells' career. They released singles including "Proverb," "Crab in a Bag," and "We Nah Go Run Away," along with their third album, *Crab Race*. The Morwell Esquire label also enjoyed a solid period at the end of the 1970s with recordings from Ranking Trevor, **Delroy Wilson**, and **Nicodemus**. In 1977, the Morwells added another member when **Errol "Flabba" Holt** joined the group. The year 1979 saw the release of another album titled *Cool Running*, which was followed in rapid succession by 1980's *A1 Dub* and 1981's *Bingy Bunny and the Morwells* and *Best of the Morwells*.

However, by 1980 the Morwells had come to an end. Holt and Lamont formed the **Roots Radics** and Wellington continued his production work with the Morwell Esquire label. In October 2000, Maurice Wellington died of adenocarcinoma while receiving treatment for the illness in New York.

WILLIAMS, MICHAEL. *See* PRINCE FAR I

WILLIAMS, OSWALD "COUNT OSSIE" (1926–1976)

Born in St. Thomas, Jamaica, in 1926, Williams emerged on the Jamaican popular music scene as one of the most talented **burru** and **nyabinghi** drummers in the **Rastafarian** community. Ossie studied under master burru drummer Brother Job, and when he entered the Rasta mainstream, he brought with him the burru drumming traditions. He participated in grounations (reasoning sessions with music and dancing) and nyabinghi celebrations and began to influence Rasta music.

In the early 1950s, Ossie set up a Rasta commune in the Rennock Lodge Community, on the eastern side of Kingston. This location became a nerve center of early Jamaican popular music. Many of the graduates from the **Alpha Boys Catholic School** descended on Ossie's commune and learned about Rasta. They all engaged in musical performances as well, and Ossie had a cadre of drummers working under him. Ossie and his drummers were under constant demand and in 1959 took on the name Mystic Revelation of Rastafari. The group utilized the standard three-drum setup, including bass drum, **funde**, and **repeater**, along with a periodic horn line. They were called on to back a wide variety of arts, and their influence on the industry increased.

While backing artists such as the **Folkes Brothers** and others, the Mystic Revelation of Rastafari continued to build the music of Rastafarian beliefs. The group became the inspiration of **Bob Marley and the Wailers**, **Ras Michael** and the **Sons of Negus**, and many others. Ossie and his band began going into the studio to record, first appearing on **Prince Tubby** recordings such as the Folkes Brothers' "Oh Carolina." Next, Ossie and his group moved over to work with **Clement "Coxsone" Dodd** at his **Studio One** facility. In the 1970s, Ossie and his group of hand drummers issued a pair of recordings. The first was titled *Grounation: The Indomitable Spirit of Rastafari*, from 1974. The second was issued the following year and was titled *Tales of Mozambique*.

Unfortunately, just as Ossie's recording career was getting started and his legacy was being preserved for future generations, he was killed. Conflicting reports exist concerning the cause of his 1976 death. Some contend that he was trampled by a frightened crowd during a show at Kingston's National Arena; still others claim that he was killed in a car accident following the show. Posthumously, another album of Ossie's material was released in 1996. Titled *Remembering Count Ossie: A Rasta Reggae Legend*, the release was a collection of many of his previously unreleased tracks such as "Babylon Gone," "So Long," and "Sodom and Gomorrah."

WILLINGTON, CECIL. *See* NICODEMUS

WILSON, DELROY (1948–1995)

Born in Kingston, Jamaica, in 1948, Delroy Wilson entered the recording industry while still a youth. He worked for **Clement "Coxsone" Dodd** beginning in 1962 while in his early teenage years and recorded several unmatched soul sides. His first Dodd-produced hit was "If I Had a Beautiful Baby," which was a disappointment. However, Dodd continued to encourage his young singer, and with the help of **Lee "Scratch" Perry**, Wilson soon had a hit.

At the time, Perry was working for Dodd as a ghostwriter and talent scout. He wrote a series of songs that attacked Dodd's principal rival **Prince Buster**, and Wilson did the singing. The first was "Joe Liges" and scored the young singer his first real success. Next came "Prince Pharah," another scathing attack on Buster. The single was another success and is notorious as it is the only extant recorded instance of Dodd's voice in one of his songs. More singles were issued and brought Wilson's vocal prowess an ever-increasing audience. Another significant single, "I Shall Not Remove," resulted in the release of a 1966 album of the same title. Still more popular singles followed and made Wilson the darling of the **ska** era.

Through the end of 1966 and into 1967, Wilson issued a steady stream of popular singles. In addition, his voice began to change and he took part in ushering in the new **rock steady** era. In 1967, he moved over to work with producer **Bunny "Striker" Lee**. Although the pair did not remain linked for long, they did generate a collection of hit singles. Wilson returned to Dodd and released *Good All Over* in 1969.

In 1970 he again split with Dodd and next teamed with **Wilburn "Stranger" Cole** for a series of sides. The material was issued on Wilson's own W&C label; however, the imprint quickly collapsed. In the 1970s, Wilson issued a long series of successful recordings including the 1976 cover of **Bob Marley's** classic "I'm Still Waiting." These records were made with a host of producers that included **Keith Hudson**, **Leslie Kong**, and **Sonia Pottinger**. Also during this period, Wilson released two more albums, *Better Music Come* and *Money.*

In the 1980s, Wilson followed the Jamaican trend of working for a variety of producers in rapid succession, which took him to **Gussie Clarke**, **Winston "Niney" Holness**, **Phil Pratt**, and others. He also worked with **King Jammy**, and the resulting studio product was a **dub** hit for the singer. The single was titled "Don't Put the Blame on Me," which did well for the singer. Wilson died from cirrhosis in 1995 at the age of forty-six. Notwithstanding the singer's relatively early death, his career spanned nearly forty years.

WONDER, WAYNE (1972–)

Born Von Wayne Charles in Portland, Jamaica, Wonder began singing in Sunday school at church and was inspired by his mother, who was in the chorus. Charles was also

exposed to **reggae** and rhythm and blues as he was growing up. In high school he earned his nickname Wonder and also continued to hone his singing skills. He soon progressed to the point where he was encouraged to visit a producer and try to get some session time. He saw and worked with **King Tubby**, with whom he recorded a series of three singles. This work was done during the mid-1980s, which was an era of slackness lyrics (characterized by risqué talk of guns, sex, and drugs) in **dancehall** and the dawn of the **dub** style. Regardless of this external stimulus, Wonder sang in a soulful and refined voice and his lyrics focused on affairs of the heart. His version of Rick Astley's "Never Gonna Give You Up" was his entry into the mainstream.

In the wake of Tubby's death in 1988, Wonder teamed with Lloyd Dennis for the hit "It's Over Now." This early success led to Wonder's first album, titled *No More Chance.* The album was a collection of versions of popular songs and a series of originals. His next important step was to collaborate with **Dave Kelly**, who was working for producer and Penthouse Records owner **Donovan Germaine**.

Wayne Wonder. © *UrbanImage.tv.*

The pairing with Kelly immediately yielded a series of hits and spawned the next album, *Part 2*, in 1991.

The 1990s brought even greater receptiveness to Wonder's music. He worked with Kelly throughout the decade and the pair launched their own Madhouse and Xtra imprints. Examples of major singles from the 1990s include "Joyride," "Bashment Gal," and "Keep Them Coming." In the new millennium Wonder continued his string of hits.

In 2000 he issued the album *Da Vibe*, which marked the beginning of his movement in the hip hop direction. His change in style was exhibited on collaborations with Lisa "Left Eye" Lopez and Foxy Brown. His 2001 album, *Schizophrenic*, was a major success and furthered his crossover into the hip hop arena. He also opened his own record label called Singso, which has recorded Baby Cham, Frankie Sly, and Mr. Easy. In 2003, he issued *No Holding Back*, another fine collection of songs that was well received. Wonder continues to write, produce, and record his brand of soulful crooning over dancehall rhythms.

WORD, SOUND, AND POWER

Peter Tosh formed the Word, Sound, and Power band for the making of his second solo record, after parting company with the **Wailers** in the wake of a dispute with **Christopher Blackwell** and **Bob Marley** over the lead singer role. Tosh's first album, 1976's *Legalize It*, was recorded with the backing of the Wailers band. However, for his second release, *Equal Rights* (1977), he constructed his own band. The group's core was the rhythm section of **Sly and Robbie**, also known as the legendary "Riddim Twins," who worked with Tosh intermittently until his death in 1987. Ultimately, Word, Sound, and Power was anchored by bassist **George "Fully" Fullwood** and percussionist **Carlton "Santa" Davis**. To them were added keyboard player Keith Sterling and Tosh on guitar. Word, Sound, and Power was Tosh's backing band for the rest of his life, appearing on all of his post-Wailers recordings, including *Bush Doctor* (1978), *Mystic Man* (1979), *Wanted Dread or Alive* (1981), *Mama Africa* (1983), and *No More Nuclear War* (1987). In the wake of Tosh's death, the Word, Sound, and Power band mentored his son **Andrew** as he began his own recording career.

WRIGHT, WINSTON (1944–1993)

One of many largely unknown instrumentalists active in the Jamaican music studios from the 1960s to the 1990s, Wright began his career early and was quickly recognized as a talented keyboard player. He became known around the island as a master of the Hammond organ and appeared on recordings for a wide variety of artists in the **ska**, **rock steady**, and **reggae** styles. Wright began his musical odyssey in **Duke Reid's Treasure Isle** studio. He was a member of Reid's session band the Supersonics, led by **Tommy McCook**. In addition, he played for all of the other major producers around the island. In 1969 he began appearing on recordings and put in work for **Clancy Eccles's Dynamites**, **Lee "Scratch" Perry's Upsetters**, and the Supersonics. He maintained a strong business relationship with Eccles and worked in his Dynamites studio group for a large part of his career. In the 1970s, Wright supplied organ parts for artists such as **Dennis Brown**, **Byron Lee and the Dragonaires**, **Jimmy Cliff**, **Gregory Isaacs**, the **Heptones**, **Jackie Mittoo**, **U-Brown**, and others. He was also a member of **Toots Hibbert's Maytals** and appeared on all of their releases from the 1970s and 1980s, in addition to touring with the group.

Although a member of an actively recording and touring band, Wright maintained his presence in the studio and continued working with many of reggae music's luminaries. Wright released his first solo album, *Melody of Love*, in 1977. Recorded at **Channel One** and produced by **Bunny "Striker" Lee**, it featured songs such as "Melody of Love," "Memories of Love," and "Sweet Melody." In the 1980s, Wright played with **Black Uhuru**, **Burning Spear**, **Culture**, **Dillinger**, the **Gladiators**, **Scientist**, **Bunny Wailer**, the **Wailing Souls**, and others.

In the 1990s, Wright's pace in the studio was unmatched. He worked with **Derrick Harriott**, **Gregory Isaacs**, Peter Broggs, and many, many others. Wright's second solo recording, called *Who Done It?* was issued in 1996. The record included the **Harry J's** All-Stars classic "The Liquidator," "Linstead Market," and the title track. This album was issued posthumously, as Wright had died under unknown circumstances in 1993.

XYLON, LIDJ (c. 1975–)

Active on the UK roots reggae and **dub** scene for the past decade, Xylon emerged as a singer and songwriter and quickly became a label owner when he launched Lidj Incorporated. A variety of imprints are released through the corporation, such as Sound Iration, Roots Records, Real Eyes Music, Melak Dimptz, and DredBeat. The corporation also specializes in the creation and release of dub plates for use on the area **sound systems**.

Xylon's music is filled with consciousness themes and roots melodies, and much of his work has been issued on dub plates. His music is further infused with Ethiopian rhythms and musical elements, which reflect Xylon's rootedness in his homeland, Ethiopia. In 2001 at Nagast Music in the United Kingdom, Xylon and Rootshitek formed a collaboration, the result of which was the showcase album *Anbessa Ager-Lion Country*, which featured Xylon's high tenor voice singing songs of empowerment for the African people. The featured single from the album was "Sweet Reggae Rockin'."

Y

YABBY YOU (1950–)

Born Vivian Jackson in Kingston, Jamaica, as a teenager, Jackson was severely malnourished, which led to a period of hospitalization and poor health as an adult. He went on to become the lead singer of the group the Prophets, formed in 1972; the group played in the roots reggae style, and their lyrics were based on traditional **Rastafarian** chants and spirituality. The group entered the Jamaican popular music scene with their debut single "Conquering Lion." It was from this song that Jackson was given his unique nickname.

You went on to form the Prophets label and continued to issue recordings. Much of You's work was done with producer **King Tubby** at the controls; this work resulted in a series of

Yabby You. © *UrbanImage.tv.*

singles with **dub** versions issued simultaneously. In addition, You began working as a producer during the late 1970s and was responsible for the definitive recordings of several popular singers. Examples of You's productions included work with **Jah Stitch**, **Prince Allah**, **Michael Prophet**, **Tony Tuff**, **Trinity**, **Wayne Wonder**, and several others. In 1976, You issued the seminal album *Ram a Dam*, which was followed in the same year by a dub album with Tubby. The next year he issued another classic called *Chant Down Babylon Kingdom* (also called *King Tubby Meets Vivian Jackson*). He also released *Deliver Me from My Enemies* in the same year. In 1978 he issued the album *Beware*, which was followed in 1979 by *Vocal and Dub* with Michael Prophet. In 1980, You released *Jah Jah Way* on the **Island Records** imprint.

The dub tradition continued in 1981 with a collaborative album titled *Yabby You and Michael Prophet Meets Scientist at the Dub Station.* You issued several other albums in the early 1980s, such as *Time to Remember*, *Prophecy*, and *Fleeing from the City.* Yabby You was forced to retire from the music business in the mid-1980s due to poor health. However, in the early 1990s, renewed interest in the talented singer warranted the reissue of several of his more popular albums and he came out of retirement. He issued a new series of singles in 2000 and remains active on the Jamaican popular music scene.

YAMI BOLO (1970–)

Yami Bolo has been producing **Rastafarianism**-infused songs over the past two decades. His focus has been on uplifting lyrics that raise issues of social consciousness, and he has long been an advocate for the underprivileged Jamaican youth. Born Roland Ephraim McLean in Kingston, Jamaica, he began his musical career early, at the age of eleven. He got his start singing in church, but progressively moved into the popular music realm. His early experience was with **Sugar Minott's** Youth Promotion organization; with Minott's help, McLean began honing his vocal skills in the 1980s. He took the stage for the first time during high school and performed his song "When a Man's in Love," which became a hit for the young singer.

At age seventeen, McLean's reputation had already grown to the point that he was offered the opening slot on **Augustus Pablo**'s world tour; it was after the tour that he was known as Yami Bolo. Next, Bolo spent time working in the Jamaican **sound system** scene and **toasted** on the Stur-Mar and Third World systems. In the 1980s, Bolo worked with **Winston Riley's** Techniques label and issued a series of singles. He then began issuing his own solo material as he worked with many of the big-name producers on the island, such as **Clement "Coxsone" Dodd** and **Augustus Pablo**. His catalog of fifteen-plus albums began in the late 1980s with a pair titled *Ransom of a Man's Life* and *Jah Made Them All.* He then released *He Who Knows It Feels It* (1991). This was followed in 1992 with *Up Life Street* and *Yami Bolo Meets Lloyd Hemmings*

Yami Bolo. © *UrbanImage.tv.*

(1994). A second 1994 album was issued, titled *Fighting for Peace.* An offshoot of this album was the single "Brothers Unite," which was voted Best Reggae Single of the year. In addition, *Fighting for Peace* marked the dawning of Bolo's own Yam Euphony production company.

In the latter half of the 1990s, Bolo released *Born Again* (1996), *Star of Love* (1997), *Jah Love* (1998), and *Say a Prayer* (1999). Also in 1999, Bolo teamed with the legendary rhythm section **Sly and Robbie** for the album *Freedom and Liberation.* In the new millennium, Bolo has remained active with a series of well-received albums, including *Love: The Unbreakable Resolve!* (2002) and *Rebelution* (2003). In addition to his own material, Bolo has had major success collaborating with the Ghetto Youths and **Damian** and **Stephen Marley**. Together, the trio earned a number one honor with the single "Still Searchin.'" Further, Bolo was involved with Damian's Grammy Award-winning album *Halfway Tree.* Along with the Ghetto Youths connection, Bolo has worked with **Capleton** and **Josey**

Wales on projects that call attention to the plight of Jamaica's urban youths.

YELLOWMAN (1956–)

Winston Foster was born in Negril, Jamaica, in 1956. He has the distinction of having been born an albino black man, which resulted in ridicule while he was a youth. Relocated to Kingston, he took to music at an early age. His first foray into the music business was as a **DJ** for the Gemini **sound system**. It was at this early stage that he began calling himself Yellowman and wore a yellow suit. It was also at this early stage that he began to develop his own **toasting** personality. Yellowman's lyrics are filled with humor, very often about himself, and stories of his sexual escapades.

In 1979, he won the Tastee Patties talent contest in Kingston; this was the launch pad for his career. It was also at this time that he worked with the Ace sound system, where he was able to enhance his reputation and work on new material. While toasting with Ace, Yellowman often worked with Vernon "Fathead" Rainford, and the two had a

Yellowman. © *UrbanImage.tv.*

strong run that included teaming for a series of albums. The 1980s was the decade of Yellowman's greatest productivity. He released twenty albums during this single decade, often working with several different producers and yielding as many as five records in one year. Early recordings by Yellowman came out on the VP, Greensleeves, **Shanachie**, and **Dynamite** labels and included *Duppy or Gunman*, *Mister Yellowman*, *Bad Boy Skanking*, *Zungguzungguguzunguzeng*, *King Yellowman*, and others arriving in the early 1980s. Early hit singles included the songs "The Good, the Bad, and the Ugly," "Yellowman Getting Married," and "Wreck a Pum Pum."

For the first half of the 1980s, Yellowman made an indelible mark on the Jamaican popular music scene, and his popularity spread to the international level with lyrics that constantly asserted how attractive he was. In 1986, he began to alter his lyrical content and discussed issues of abuse and African freedom. However, just as Yellowman's lyrics were gaining substance, he was diagnosed with cancer. He was treated and recovered quickly. His return to the recording industry was with a Fats Domino cover, "Blueberry Hill." He also moved to the **RAS Records** label and released *Yellow like Cheese*. The album was a success and reasserted Yellowman's talents on the microphone.

There followed another rapid succession of releases in the late 1980s. Examples of this work include *The Negril Chill*, *Sings the Blues*, *Yellowman Rides Again*, and *One in a Million*. The toaster again had health concerns in the early 1990s when he was diagnosed with skin cancer. Yellowman fought through the illness, emerging with a new lyrical perspective. His subsequent song topics have dealt with social consciousness and spiritual uplift. In the wake of his second illness, Yellowman released *Prayer Message to the Work*, *Freedom of Speech*, *Yellow Fever*, and in the new millennium *Murderah Style*. Yellowman's distinctive looks, type of lyrics, and stage show have made him a perennial favorite, and he continues to perform.

YOGIE (c. 1970–)

Born Courtney Morrison in Annotto Bay, St. Mary, Jamaica, Yogie came into a musical family that included his uncle, reggae legend **Beres Hammond**. Morrison's grandmother gave him the nickname Yogie because he wore a Yogi the Bear t-shirt. Yogie was raised on Hammond's music but lists **Bob Marley**, Stevie Wonder, and Lionel Richie as broad influences on his own music writing, begun while in his early teenage years.

In addition to being a talented vocalist, Yogie also works the production side of the music business and has teamed with artists such as **Anthony B**, Determine, Mr. Easy, **Beenie Man**, and **Sizzla**. Along with production, Yogie is also a ghostwriter for artists such as **Culture** and **Marcia Griffiths**. His debut single was issued in 1993 under the title "For Granted." This led to a series of other popular releases such as 1995's "Never Give Up." As a recording artist, Yogie has worked at a variety of studios, and the results are increasingly strong. In the new millennium, he issued a successful collaboration with Anthony B titled "That Was Then," and followed it up with a version of the 1977 Paul Davis classic "I Go Crazy." Yogie's debut album was *Miracle* (2001), with "I Go Crazy" as track two. The album, a collection of cover versions of popular songs and original material, was a success and garnered the singer additional popularity and invitations to perform at several of Jamaica's marquee concert events. More recently, Yogie and DreamWorks released a version of Nelly Furtado's song "Turn Out the Lights," which was produced by Dwight "Duke" Dawes. Yogie is a rising star on the horizon of modern **reggae**.

YVAD (c. 1975–)

Born Kevin Davy in Kingston, Jamaica, Yvad was part of **Bob Marley's** musical legacy. Through **Cedella Marley**, the CEO of **Tuff Gong** International, Yvad has become a presence on the contemporary Jamaican popular music scene. The singer's path crossed with that of the Marley family when he was discovered singing in the yard of the Bob Marley Museum at 56 Hope Road. Cedella picked up the young singer and nurtured his talent until he was ready for the recording studio. Though born in Kingston, Yvad was sent to live in the country at a tender age, and there he grew up. He attended school and church and took to singing in the choir. In addition, he began learning to play the guitar.

As Yvad grew, he began to use music to expose his inner thoughts, eventually becoming an accomplished songwriter through the development of this skill. He also became a member of the **Rastafarian** faith and began to infuse his songs with the Rasta ideology. He returned to the city and began his musical journey with the Marley family. With Cedella's help, Yvad entered Tuff Gong studios in the mid-1990s. He received strong encouragement and backing in the form of the Riddim Twins rhythm section, **Sly and Robbie**. The product was the release *Young, Gifted, and Dread* (1996), issued on **RAS Records**. The album featured songs such as "We Need Love," "No Peace," "Bright Day," and "Music Is the Food of Love." The record was well received, and its popularity resulted in Yvad appearing on MTV Europe and BET.

However, Yvad then seemed to disappear from the popular music scene. In 2004, he re-emerged with the album *Justice* on the Ruff Street imprint. The release featured the songs "Jah Created," "O Mother," and "Living in the Ghetto."

Z

ZAP POW

Guitarist **Dwight "Dee Dee" Pinkney** of **Roots Radics** fame, Max Edwards on drums, David Madden on trumpet, Mike Williams on bass, Joe McCormack on trombone, **Glen Da Costa** on tenor saxophone, and Danny McFarlane formed the legendary **reggae** band Zap Pow in 1970. The group was primarily remembered as the launch pad for **Beres Hammond's** solo career, but it existed for five years before Hammond joined. Other than Hammond, Milton "Prilly" Hamilton and Winston "King" Cole had turns as leaders of the group. Hamilton went on to work as the lead singer of **Third World** and was replaced by Hammond.

Beyond the various singers involved in the group, Zap Pow was essentially an instrumental unit. They began issuing hits in the mid-1970s and had a series of successful albums. Their hit singles included "The System" and "This Is Reggae Music." Their albums from this period included *Revolutionary Zap Pow* (1971), *Now* and *Revolution* (both in 1976), and *Zap Pow* (1978), with much of their material produced by **Harry "Harry J" Johnson**. The horn line from the group was enormously popular and played for a variety of other artists in studios around the island. Zap Pow's influence extended beyond Hammond, and their legendary horn work lives on in many reggae albums.

ZIGGY MARLEY AND THE MELODY MAKERS

David "Ziggy" Marley was born in 1968, the oldest son and second oldest child of **Robert Nesta Marley** and **Rita Marley**. Ziggy was the driving force in the founding of Ziggy Marley and the Melody Makers, which consisted of his sisters Cedella and Sharon and his brother Stephen. The Marley children were not strangers to the business and had already recorded with their father in 1979 for the "Children Playing in the Streets" release. The group made their first musical impact singing at their father's funeral in 1981, and have gone on to critical acclaim since.

In the mid-1980s, Ziggy and the Melody Makers released a pair of albums that sparked interest among the **reggae** community. The releases *Play the Game Right* (1985) and *Hey World* (1986) brought the young group greater notoriety and paved the way for subsequent releases. Ziggy's music picked up the torch that his father carried for two decades. His lyrics contain commentary on social, political, and cultural injustices, which makes them approachable to a wide range of listeners. In 1989, the group released *Conscious Party*, which marked their arrival on the Atlantic Records label. The album was enormously successful and featured the single "Tomorrow People." The group quickly followed this success with the release of *One Bright Day*. This album was also greeted with enthusiasm and cemented Ziggy and the group's reputation as a force to be reckoned with. The album won a 1989 Grammy Award and spent time on the charts.

In 1991, Ziggy and the Melody Makers released *Jahmekya*, another album filled with consciousness lyrics. It was not as commercially successful as the previous two releases had been but did well enough to keep the group's momentum pushing forward. The rest of the 1990s was filled with four more albums that resulted in two more Grammy Awards.

In the new millennium, Ziggy has branched out and formed his own record label, Ghetto Youth United. The label was conceived as an outlet for emerging new Jamaican talent. In 2003, Ziggy went solo and released the album *Dragonfly*; it was a more diverse musical offering but continued forwarding his father's legacy. On this album, Ziggy also departed from his standard recording process. The album was written in Jamaica and recorded in the United States. In more recent releases, Ziggy and the Melody Makers have included diverse influences and styles in their music. The group mixed the sound of roots reggae, American rhythm and blues, hip hop, and blues to create their own musical hybrid. Over the course of the Melody Makers' career they have earned two Grammy Awards and released eight albums. Through this group the legend of Bob Marley lives on.

ZUKIE, TAPPA. *See* **TAPPA ZUKIE**

Bibliography

Austin, Diane. *Urban Life in Kingston, Jamaica*. New York: Gordon and Breach Publishers, 1984.

Backus III, Leroy M. *Stylistic Development of Reggae Music*. M.A. thesis, University of Washington, 1976.

Barrett, Leonard. *The Rastafarians: The Dreadlocks of Jamaica*. Boston: Beacon Press, 1988.

Barrow, Steve, and Peter Dalton. *Reggae: The Rough Guide*. New York: Penguin Books, 1997.

Bennett, Scotty. *Bob Marley*. New York: Virgin Publishing Ltd., 1997.

Booker, Cedella, and Anthony Winker. *Bob Marley: An Intimate Portrait by His Mother*. New York: Viking, 1996.

Boot, Adrian, and Michael Thomas. *Jamaica: Babylon on a Thin Wire*. London: Thames and Hudson, 1976.

Bradley, Lloyd. *Reggae on CD: The Essential Guide*. London: Great Britain, 1996.

———. *This Is Reggae Music: The Story of Jamaica's Music*. New York: Grove Press, 2000.

Bramwell, Osula. *"Redemption Song": Protest Reggae and Jamaica*. Ph.D. dissertation, University of Waterloo (Canada), 1984.

Campbell, Horace. *Rasta and Resistance: From Marcus Garvey to Walter Rodney*. London: Hansib Publishing Limited, 1985.

Chambers, Ian. *Urban Rhythms*. London: Macmillan, 1985.

Chang, Kevin, and Wayne Chen. *Reggae Routes: The Story of Jamaican Music*. Philadelphia: Temple University Press, 1998.

Chevannes, Barry. *Rastafari: Roots and Ideology*. New York: Syracuse University Press, 1994.

Cooper, Carolyn. "Chant Down Babylon: Bob Marley's Songs as Literary Text," *Jamaica Journal* 19 (4) (November 1986): 2–8.

Dalrymple, Henderson. *Bob Marley: Music, Myth, and the Rastas*. Sudbury, UK: Carib-Arawak, 1967.

Davis, Stephen. *Bob Marley*. New York: Doubleday, 1985.

———. *Bob Marley*. Rochester, VT: Schenkman Books, reprint, 1990.

———. *Bob Marley: Conquering Lion of Reggae*. London: Plexus, 1994.

Davis, Stephen, and Peter Simon. *Reggae International*. New York: Alfred A. Knopf, 1983.

Foster, Chuck. *Roots, Rock, Reggae: An Oral History of Reggae Music from Ska to Dancehall*. New York: Billboard Books, 1999.

Goodman, Vivian. *The Black Chord*. New York: Universe Publishing, 1999.

Graham, Ronnie. *Stern's Guide to Contemporary African Music*. London: Zwan Publications, 1988.

Hausman, Gerald, ed. *The Kebra Nagast: The Lost Bible of Rastafarian Wisdom and Faith from Ethiopia and Jamaica*. New York: St. Martin's Press, 1997.

Hebdige, Dick. *Cut 'N' Mix: Culture, Identity, and Caribbean Music*. London: Routledge, 1987.

Horner, Bruce, and Thomas Swiss. *Key Terms in Popular Music and Culture*. London: Blackwell Publishers Limited, 1999.

Jensen, Richard J. "Bob Marley's 'Redemption Song': The Rhetoric of Reggae and Rastafari," *Journal of Popular Culture* 29 (3) (Winter 1995): 17–20.

Johnson, Howard, and Jim Pines. *Reggae: Deep Roots Music*. London: Proteus Books, 1982.

Lacey, Terry. *Violence and Politics in Jamaica, 1960-1970*. Manchester, England: Manchester University Press, 1977.

Larkin, Colin. *The Virgin Encyclopedia of Reggae*. London, Great Britain: Virgin Books, 1998.

Lee, Peter. "Glory to Jah: Remembering Bob Marley," *Guitar Player* 25 (5) (May 1991): 82–87.

Lipsitz, George. *Dangerous Crossroads*. New York: Verso, 1994.

Manuel, Peter. *Caribbean Currents: Caribbean Music from Rumba to Reggae*. Philadelphia: Temple University Press, 1995.

May, Chris. *Bob Marley*. London: Hamish, 1985.

McCann, Ian. *Bob Marley in His Own Words*. New York: Omnibus, Press, 1993.

———. *The Complete Guide to the Music of Bob Marley*. New York: Omnibus Press, 1994.

McKenzie, Clyde. "Bob Marley: For the People," *Reggae Report* 14 (4) (April 1996): 13.

Morris, Dennis. *Bob Marley: A Rebel Life*. London: Plexus Publishing, 1999.

Mulvaney, Rebekah M., and Carlos Nelson. *Rastafari and Reggae: A Dictionary and Source Book*. Westport, CT: Greenwood Publishing, 1990.

Murrell, Nathaniel, William Spencer, and Adrian McFarlane. *The Rastafari Reader: Chanting Down Babylon*. Philadelphia: Temple University Press, 1998.

National Library of Jamaica. *Marley Bibliography*. Kingston, Jamaica, 1985.

Nettleford, Rex. *Caribbean Cultural Identity: Essays in Cultural Dynamics*. Kingston, Jamaica: William Collins and Sangster Ltd., 1970.

———. *Mirror Mirror: Identity, Race, and Protest in Jamaica*. Kingston, Jamaica: William Collins and Sangster Ltd., 1970.

Pollard, Velma. *Dread Talk: The Language of the Rastafari*. Kingston, Jamaica: Canoe Press University of the West Indies, 1995.

Potash, Chris. *Reggae, Rasta Revolution: Jamaican Music from Ska to Dub*. New York: Schirmer Books, 1997.

Rodney, Walter. *The Groundings with My Brothers*. London: Bogle-L'Ouverture Publications, 1969.

Rosen, Craig. "Marley's 'Legend' Lives On." *Billboard* 108 (47) (November 23, 1996): 13–18.

Santoro, Gene. *Stir It Up: Musical Mixes from Rots to Jazz*. New York: Oxford University Press, 1997.

Scott, Derek. *Music, Culture, and Society*. Oxford, UK: Oxford University Press, 2000.

Stephens, Gregory. *On Musical Frontiers: The New Culture of Frederick Douglass, Ralph Ellison, and Bob Marley*. Cambridge, MA: Cambridge University Press, 1999.

Talamon, Bruce W. *Bob Marley: Spirit Dancer*. New York: W.W. Norton, 1994.

Taylor, Don. *Marley and Me: The Real Bob Marley Story*. New York: Barricade Books Inc., 1995.

———. *So Much Things to Say: My Life as Bob Marley's Manager*. New York: Blake Publishers, 1995.

Wagner, Charles. *Jah as Genre: The Interface of Reggae and American Popular Music*. Ph.D. dissertation, Bowling Green University, Bowling Green, OH, 1993.

Warner, Keith. "Calypso, Reggae, and Rastafarianism: Authentic Caribbean Voices." *Popular Music and Society*, 12 (1) (Spring 1988): 53–62.

White, Garth. *The Development of Jamaican Popular Music with Special Reference to the Music of Bob Marley*. Kingston: African-Caribbean Institute of Jamaica, 1982.

White, Timothy. *Catch a Fire: The Life of Bob Marley*. New York: Henry Holt and Company, 1994.

Whitney, Malika, and Dermott Hussey. *Bob Marley: Reggae King of the World*. Kingston, Jamaica: Kingston Publishers, 1984.

Winders, J.A. "Reggae, Rastafarians, and Revolution: Rock Music in the Third World," *Journal of Popular Culture* 17 (1) (January 1983): 62.

WEB SITES

Each of these sites was consulted in the authoring of the encyclopedia. Reference dates are inconsequential, as each site was visited repeatedly over the period of January 2004 to January 2005. All URLs have been verified and only "official" artist and label Web sites were consulted.

Ariwa Sounds. Mad Professor. http://www.ariwa.com/.

Artists Only Records. Reggae Artists. http://www.artistsonly.com/reggae.htm.

BBC Music. http://www.bbc.co.uk/cgi-perl/music/muze/index.

Beenie Man Music. Biography. http://www.beenieman.net/bio.html.

Black Music Collectors. http://www.black-music-collectors.com/labels/uscatalogue.htm.

Bob Marley Music, Inc. Life of Bob Marley. http://www.bobmarley.com/life/.

Boot, Adrian, Ossie Hamilton, Rico D'Rozario, David Katz, Ron Vester, and Tim Barrow. UrbanImage. http://www.urbanimage.tv.

Burning Spear Music. Biography. http://www.burningspear.net/biography.html.

Clarke, Donald. MusicWeb Encyclopaedia of Popular Music. http://www.musicweb.uk.net/encyclopaedia/.

Claydon, Andy. *Gone To Zion: Book of Remembrance.* http://www.hilltop61.freeserve.co.uk/zion.html.

Crazy Baldhead. Artist Index. http://www.geocities.com/SunsetStrip/Disco/6032/main.htm.

Davis, Stephan. Bob Marley Biography. http://www.grovemusic.com/date/articles/music/2/230/23065.xml.

Deeboz Music. Johnny Osborne. http://www.deebozmuzik.com.

Delgado, Junior. Junior Delgado. http://www.juniordelgado.co.uk.

Easy Star Records. Artists Main. http://www.easystar.com/artists.html.

Eek-A-Mouse. www.eeksperience.com.

Freddie McGregor Music. Biography. http://www.freddiemcgregor.com/bio.html.

Gleaner Company Limited. Jamaica Daily Gleaner. http://www.jamaica-gleaner.com.

Hampton Development. ReggaeCD. http://www.reggaecd.com.

Harmony House Music. Beres Hammond. http://www.harmonyhousemusic.net/.

Heartbeat Records. http://www.heartbeatreggae.com/complete_catalog.html.

Himelfarb, Gary. Real Authentic Sound (RAS) Records. http://www.rasrecords.com.

IcebergMedia. The Iceberg. http://www.theiceberg.com/artist.html.

Inner Circle Music. History. http://innercircle-reggae.com/pages/history.html.

IReggae. http://www.ireggae.com/reggae1.htm.

Itations. Emperor Haile Selassie I Ras Tafari. http://www.jahjahchildrencommunity.com/itations.html.

JAD Records. Where the Legend Began. http://www.jadrecords.com/.

Jah Shaka Music. History. http://www.jahshakasoundsystem.com/3024.html.

Jimmy Cliff Music. Biography. http://www.jimmycliffonline.com.

Lee "Scratch" Perry Music. Main. http://www.upsetter.net/scratch/.

Mutabaruka Music. Main. http://www.mutabaruka.com/.

Nighthawk Studios. Artist Main. http://www.nghthwk.com/index.shtml.

On-U Sound. Acts Index. http://www.skysaw.org/onu/artists/acts.html.

Peter Tosh Music. The Man: His Story. http://www.ptosh.com/story.html.

Rank's Reggae Revival. http://www.btinternet.com/~ranksreggaerevival/biographyinfo.htm#E.

Reggae Movement. Players, Singers, Spinners. http://www.reggaemovement.com/rm1/artists.htm.

Reggae Seen. http://www.reggaeseen.com/artists/.

Reggae Train. Artists. http://www.reggaetrain.com/site_artists.asp.

Reggae Women Research. Artist and Reviews Main. http://www.reggaewoman.com/music-reviews.htm.

Roots Archive. http://www.roots-archives.com.

Rootsman. Third Eye Music. http://www.thirdeyemusic.co.uk.

Rounder Records. Label Main. http://www.rounder.com/index.php?id=labels.php.

Shocking Vibes Production. Artists. http://www.shockingvibes.com/artistes.htm.

Skatalites Music. Artist Biographies. http://www.skatalites.com/about/bios_main.htm.

Steel Pulse Music. Biography. http://www.steel-pulse.com.

Studio Won. The Pama Story. http://www.studiowon.com/studiowon/home.htm.

Taj Mahal Music. Biography and Discography. http://www.taj-mo-roots.com/discography/bio.html.

Teacher and Mr. T. Reggae Vibes Productions. http://www.reggae-vibes.com.

Tony Rebel. Tru-Juice Rebel Salute. http://www.tonyrebel.com/rebelsalute/home.html.

Toots and the Maytals Music. Extended Biography. http://www.tootsandthemaytals.net/toots/tootsbiographylong.aspx.

Trojan Records. Main. http://www.trojanrecords.net.

Tuff Gong Studios. Jamaica: Studio, Manufacturing, Distribution, and Record Shop. 1. http://www.tuffgong.com/.

UB40 Music. Band Biography. http://www.ub40-dep.com/biography.php.

Universal Music Group. Artist Index: Bob Marley and the Wailers. 2. http://new.umusic.com/Artists.aspx?Index=1.

Urban Image. Artist Images. http://www.urbanimage.tv/browse.htm?loc1=reggae&.

U-Roy Music. Artist Biography. http://u-roy.20m.com/.

VP Records. Artists Main. http://www.vprecords.com/artistes.php.

Yabby You Music. The Producer, the Singer, the Man, the Legend. http://www.yabbyyou.com/.

Index

Note: Pages for main entries in the encyclopedia are **boldfaced**.

About the Author

DAVID V. MOSKOWITZ is an associate professor of musicology at the University of South Dakota. In addition to teaching at the undergraduate and graduate levels, he is graduate coordinator in music. Further, he coauthored the book chapter "The Limonese Calypso as an Identity Maker" with Dr. Anita Herzfeld for the publication *Creoles, Contact, and Language Change: Linguistic and Social Implications.* His next writing project is *Redemption Songs: Words and Music of Bob Marley* (Praeger), which will present the life of the third world's first superstar through the releases of his seminal albums.